P9-AFZ-413

Living Ideas in America

Living Ideas
IN AMERICA

edited and with commentary by
HENRY STEELE COMMAGER

NEW, ENLARGED EDITION

Harper & Row, Publishers
NEW YORK, EVANSTON, AND LONDON

For permission to include the following selections in this volume, grateful acknowledgment is made to:

APPLETON-CENTURY-CROFTS, INC.: *Forty Years of It* by Brand Whitlock, Copyright, 1914, by D. Appleton & Company.

THE ATLANTIC MONTHLY: "Wanted: American Radicals" by James Bryant Conant, Copyright, 1943, by The Atlantic Monthly Company. "The Indispensable Opposition" by Walter Lippmann. Copyright, 1939, by The Atlantic Monthly Company. "My Creed as an American Catholic" by Alfred E. Smith. Copyright, 1927, by The Atlantic Monthly Company.

BRANDT & BRANDT and RINEHART & COMPANY, INC.: "Western Star" from *Western Star* by Stephen Vincent Benét. Copyright, 1943, by Rosemary Carr Benét.

RALPH COGHLAN: "Boss Pendergast." Copyright 1937.

THE JOHN DAY COMPANY, INC.: *What Is America?* by Frank Ernest Hill. Copyright 1933.

DOUBLEDAY & COMPANY, INC.: *Up From Slavery* by Booker T. Washington. Copyright, 1900, 1901, by Booker T. Washington. *The New Freedom* by Woodrow Wilson. Copyright, 1913, 1933, by Doubleday & Company, Inc.

W. E. B. DU BOIS: *The Souls of Black Folk.* Copyright 1903.

HARCOURT, BRACE & COMPANY: *The Autobiography of Lincoln Steffens.* Copyright, 1931, by Harcourt, Brace & Company, Inc.

HARPER & BROTHERS: *This I Do Believe* by David E. Lilienthal. Copyright, 1949, by David E. Lilienthal. *TVA, Democracy on the March* by David E. Lilienthal. Copyright, 1944, by David E. Lilienthal. *On Active Service in Peace and War* by Henry L. Stimson and McGeorge Bundy. Copyright, 1948, by Henry L. Stimson. *The Adventures of Huckleberry Finn* by Mark Twain.

HARPER'S MAGAZINE: "Due Notice to the F.B.I." by Bernard De Voto. Copyright, 1949, by Harper & Brothers. Reprinted by permission of the author. "Let's Go Back to the Spoils System" by John Fischer. Copyright, 1945, by Harper & Brothers. "Our Worst War Time Mistake" by Eugene V. Rostow. Copyright, 1945, by Harper & Brothers. Reprinted by permission of the author.

HARVARD UNIVERSITY PRESS: *Free Speech in the United States* by Zechariah Chafee, Jr. Copyright 1941. *Education in a Divided World* by James Bryant Conant. Copyright 1948.

HENRY HOLT AND COMPANY, INC.: *The Frontier in American History* by Frederick Jackson Turner. Copyright, 1920, by Frederick Jackson Turner. Copyright, 1948, by Caroline M. S. Turner.

HOUGHTON MIFFLIN COMPANY: *The Promised Land* by Mary Antin. Copyright 1912. "An Ode in Time of Hesitation" from *The Poems and Plays of William Vaughan Moody.* Copyright 1912. *Sin and Society* by Edward A. Ross. Copyright 1907.

ALFRED A. KNOPF, INC.: *The American Language* by H. L. Mencken. Copyright, 1919, 1921, 1923, 1936, by Alfred A. Knopf, Inc. *Notes on Democracy* by H. L. Mencken. Copyright, 1926, by Alfred A. Knopf, Inc.

LITTLE, BROWN & COMPANY: *The Good Society* by Walter Lippmann. Copyright, 1936, 1937, 1943, by Walter Lippmann. *U. S. Foreign Policy* by Walter Lippmann. Copyright, 1943, by Walter Lippmann. *U. S. War Aims* by Walter Lippmann. Copyright, 1944, by Walter Lippmann.

MCGRAW-HILL BOOK COMPANY, INC.: *Rich Land, Poor Land* by Stuart Chase. Copyright, 1939, by Stuart Chase.

(Continued on next page)

To

HARRIET BIRCHOLDT

MARCIA DALPHIN

LYDIA KENDALL FOSTER

Contents

PART TWO: PRINCIPLES, TRADITIONS
AND INSTITUTIONS

PART FOUR: OLD PROBLEMS IN A NEW AGE

Preface

THIS BOOK already has so many introductions, to chapters and to individual items, that further introductory remarks might well be regarded as superfluous. A word about the design and purpose of the book may not, however, be amiss. The book is directed to that growing body of men and women who are concerned about the complex problems that confront our society today and that, so often, seem strange and baffling. It is designed to make clear the historical setting of those problems and our long historical experience with them, in the firm belief that an understanding of the background will illuminate the foreground and that knowledge of the past will guide us in the future.

Because America is a young nation we sometimes assume that our experience is limited, and that we are less prepared than other peoples for the responsibilities which have been thrust upon us. Actually America is in many and in interesting respects very old. Americans have had longer experience with some of the major problems of our time than have any other people—with problems of the reconciliation of liberty and order, for example, or of majority rule and minority rights, or of federalism, or of public education. It is only as a world power that America is relatively young, and even here her experience is longer and deeper than is generally realized.

This book has been prepared out of the conviction that most of the problems that confront Americans today, whatever new and strange forms they may take, are really old and familiar, and that Americans need not look abroad for solutions, or fabricate new ones, but that they can turn, with confidence, to their own historical past. It is, after all, difficult to improve upon what Roger Williams said about freedom of conscience or Madison about the separation of church and state. We have not yet advanced far beyond Jefferson in our concept of democracy, or beyond Madison in our understanding of the nature of federalism, or beyond Marshall in our appreciation of the constitutional basis of nationalism. Horace Mann can still instruct us in the function of education in a democracy, and what Lincoln had to say about the preservation of liberty is as relevant in the crisis of the mid-twentieth as in the crisis of the mid-nineteenth century. So with almost every problem that perplexes us today, even—where principles are concerned—problems of world power and world responsibility. Circumstances change profoundly, but the character of the American people has not changed greatly or the nature of the principles of conduct, public and private, to which they subscribe.

This collection of source material, inevitably inadequate, is drawn from whatever sources seemed relevant and revealing—from historical documents, letters, speeches, memoirs, essays, poetry, and even fiction. The principle of selection is the very simple one that gold is where you find it. As always, in a work of this kind, the chief problem has been that of selection and, alas, of exclusion: ideally each of the chapters here should have been a separate book. Much, then, that should have gone in has been sacrificed to the exigencies of space, and many ideas that may properly be designated "American" have, of necessity, been neglected. Most of the ideas here presented are controversial. I have tried to present opposing points of view, but it would be folly to pretend that I have been wholly objective in my choice of material or to attempt to conceal the fact that my own sympathies are those of a Jeffersonian liberal.

The original suggestion for this book came from officials of the American Library Association. No institution, except the public school, has contributed more to educate Americans in the duties and responsibilities of citizenshp or to preserve the Amercan heritage, than the public library, and I count it a piece of good fortune that this book should be associated with celebration of the seventy-fifth anniversary of the American Library Association. I am particularly happy to be able to dedicate the book to three librarians, each of whom has, in her own way, contributed to the diffusion of American ideas.

For aid in the preparation of this volume, aid which went beyond the call of duty, I am indebted to Dr. Leonard Levy of Brandeis University.

HENRY STEELE COMMAGER

Salzburg, Austria
August 8, 1951

Part I

The American Setting

1

The People

WE BEGIN with the people, and on then to the land that they occupied and subdued. What kind of people were they who first braved the perils of the vast ocean and the "hideous and desolate wilderness" that was America of the seventeenth century—and later? They were, in the beginning, English, and from the first landfall on the shores of Virginia and of Cape Cod down through more than three centuries, the English inheritance and influence were decisive. The English early proved themselves the greatest colonizers the world had known since the days of ancient Greece and Rome. Unlike the Spaniards, the French, and others, they expanded their empire by emigration rather than merely by military conquest, and unlike their competitors, too, they permitted all sorts of people to migrate to their colonies and assured them substantially all the rights and privileges of those who tarried at home. This genius for colonization and this liberal attitude toward colonists the Americans inherited from them. In the nineteenth century it was the Americans who were the greatest of colonizers—a fact we fail to appreciate because they colonized contiguous territory instead of across an ocean—and from the beginning they treated their colonists as equals.

From the beginning America was a haven, a refuge, a land of the second chance. To it came, as Benét has so eloquently reminded us, "the disinherited, the dispossessed"—all those who for one reason or another were discontented with their lot in the Old World. Disinherited and dispossessed of worldly goods they were, for the most part, but they were heirs, nevertheless, of all that England was and meant; they could have said—as Wordsworth was to say later—

> In everything we are sprung
> Of Earth's first blood, have titles manifold.

3

Thus though many of them came empty-handed as far as material goods were concerned, they brought with them those things vital for the making of a nation. There was wealth enough in the New World, after all; what was needed to exploit this wealth and turn it to beneficent purposes was character, and this the seventeenth-century English settlers had—courage, fortitude, industry, dignity, respect for law, devotion to learning, high moral standards, piety and faith. Well might they say with Richard Rush, whose "News from Virginia" is one of the earliest poems about the New World:

> Let England know our willingness, for that our work is good
> We hope to plant a nation, where none before hath stood.

That hope the English had, and it was shared, too, by the others who soon joined and intermingled with them—the Scots and Scots-Irish, the Dutch, the Swedes, the French Huguenots, the Germans, the Negroes who came as slaves, and—in the nineteenth and twentieth centuries—by the Irish, Germans, Scandinavians, Italians, Poles, Russians, Jews and others. All these brought their strength not only of body and heart, but of mind and culture as well; all of them blended eagerly into the American pattern.

Transplanted to the New World, the peoples of the Old threw off their national and racial attachments and became American—American even in physical attributes. And, by some alchemy, out of the blending of inheritance, environment, and historical experience, came a character, too, that could be called American. "The Americans," Walt Whitman was to write, "have the fullest poetical nature." It is not certain that this was an exaggeration; those who think the American character prosaic or materialistic confuse means with ends, or are not sufficiently acquainted with the character of European peoples. In any event Americans built upon their European inheritance something that was clearly part of Western civilization, yet unique. The "American Farmer," Jean de Crèvecoeur, saw this at the very beginning of our national history, and in his famous letters drew the American in lines that are clear even today. A hundred European observers and commentators saw it—magisterial figures like Tocqueville and Lieber, Mackay and Bryce, and many of lesser fame. In time Americans themselves came to appreciate the fact that there had emerged an American mind and character.

The sources presented here tell something of the uprooting from the

Old World and the transplanting to the New. They tell us of the kind of people who came over, the hopes and ideals that inspired them, the hardships that they encountered, and the riches as well, the way they applied their inheritance to the new tasks and responsibilities, and the way that their new environment molded their character and their institutions. They tell us, too, what we need ever to remember, that not Britain alone contributed to the American society, but the whole of Europe, and Africa, and some of Asia as well, and that these contributions were not limited to the colonial era but continued down to our own time. We too readily lose perspective in this matter, too readily ignore the obvious fact that in the twentieth century, for example, America welcomed less than two million emigrants from the British Isles but almost four million from Italy. They attempt to suggest something of the wonderful diversity of the American social scene—the mixture of races and people, cultures and religions, which somehow fused into a unity, vindicating the national motto, *"E pluribus unum."*

That the American type differed in any fundamental way from the English or, let us say, the Norwegian, could not be maintained, but that it did differ was clear, and it was the difference that was interesting. Crèvecoeur was merely the first of a long line of interpreters who addressed himself to the question, What is an American? The question is still being asked—perhaps more insistently now than ever before—and native and foreign students are still trying to answer it. We have given here three or four interpretations of the American character, or of special manifestations of that character.

1. THE INFLUENCE OF THE NEW WORLD ON THE OLD

We begin with an excerpt from one of the most notable of modern books—Sir John Seeley's Expansion of England. *Regius Professor of Modern History at Cambridge University, Seeley was also a member of Parliament and for a short time in one of Gladstone's ministries; he was at all times deeply interested in current politics and especially in imperialism. The* Expansion of England *was an attempt to explain what is certainly one of the most remarkable phenomena in history—how this little island managed to spread its people, its language, its law, its culture, throughout the globe. The pages we present here suggest some-thing of the revolutionary impact that the New World had upon the Old and of the background of English expansion to America.*

THIS was the time when the New World began to exert its in-fluence, and thus the most obvious facts suggest that England owes its modern character and its peculiar greatness from the outset to the New World. It is not the blood of the Vikings that makes us rulers of the sea, nor the industrial genius of the Anglo-Saxon that makes us great in manufactures and commerce, but a much more special cir-cumstance, which did not arise till for many centuries we had been agricultural or pastoral, war-like, and indifferent to the sea. . . .

Till [the discovery of the New World] trade had clung to the Medi-terranean Sea. Till then the Ocean had been a limit, a boundary, not a pathway. There had been indeed a certain amount of intercourse across the narrow seas of the North, which had nourished the trade of the Hanseatic League. But in the main the Mediterranean continued to be the headquarters of industry as of civilisation. . . . France and England had no doubt advanced greatly, but to the Italian in the fifteenth century they still seemed comparatively barbarous, intellec-tually provincial and second-rate. The reason of this was that for prac-tical purposes they were inland, while Italy reaped the benefit of the civilising sea. . . . By the side of the Italian republics, France and England showed like Thessaly and Macedonia in comparison with Athens and Corinth.

Now Columbus and the Portuguese altered all this by substituting the Atlantic Ocean for the Mediterranean Sea as the highway of com-merce. From that moment the reign of Italy is over. . . . The hidden source which fed her energy and glory was dried up by the discovery of the New World. She might be compared to one of those seaports on the coast of Kent from which the sea has receded. Where there had once been life and movement, silence and vacancy must have set in throughout the great city republics of Italy, even if no stranger had crossed the Alps. The Mediterranean Sea had not indeed receded, but it had lost once for all the character which it had had almost from the days of the Odyssey. It had ceased to be the central sea of human intercourse and civilisation, the chief, nay, almost the one sea of history. . . .

The great result was that the centre of movement and intelligence began to pass from the centre of Europe to its Western Coast. Civilisation moves away from Italy and Germany; where it will settle is not yet clear, but certainly farther west. See how strikingly this change stands out from the history of the sixteenth century. At the beginning of that century all the genius in the world seems to live in Italy or Germany. The golden age of modern art is passing in the first country, but if there are any rivals to the Italian painters they are German. . . . Meanwhile the Reformation belongs to Germany. For France and England in those days it seems sufficient glory to have given a welcome to the Renaissance and to the Reformation. But gradually in the latter part of the sixteenth century we become aware that civilisation is shifting its headquarters. Italy and Germany are first rivalled and then eclipsed; gradually we grow accustomed to the thought that great things are rather to be looked for in other countries. In the seventeenth century almost all genius and greatness is to be found in the western or maritime states of Europe.

Now these are the states which were engaged in the struggle for the New World. Spain, Portugal, France, Holland and England have the same sort of position with respect to the Atlantic Ocean that Greece and Italy had in antiquity with respect to the Mediterranean. And they begin to show a similar superiority in intelligence. Vast problems of conquest, colonisation and commerce occupy their minds, which before had vegetated in a rustic monotony. . . .

Such then was the effect of the New World on the Old. It is visible not merely in the wars and alliances of the time, but also in the economic growth and transformation of the Western States of Europe. Civilisation has often been powerfully promoted by some great enterprise in which several generations continuously take part. Such was the war of Europe and Asia to the ancient Greeks; such the Crusades in the Middle Ages. Such then for the Western States of Europe in recent centuries has been the struggle for the New World. It is this more than anything else which has placed these nations, where they never were before, in the van of intellectual progress, and especially it is by her success in this field that our own country has acquired her peculiar greatness.

—JOHN R. SEELEY, *The Expansion of England*

2. "THE DISINHERITED, THE DISPOSSESSED"

"Have you heard the news from Virginia?" the poor of England were asking, in the early years of the seventeenth century—and the adventurers, too. The news as it came from such chroniclers as Captain John Smith was for the most part good, but there was bad news, too—news of poverty and misery, of disease and death. Yet though almost all the early settlers were swept away, more kept coming, for to many of the victims of the economic revolution that was transforming England in these years the New World offered a second chance. Few of the poor of England were able to pay their way across the ocean, but they could earn their passage by binding themselves to service from four to seven years—and many of them did. The myth of Cavalier Virginia still lingers on in some quarters, but it is well to remember what common sense should tell us—that the rich and the noble and the contented did not migrate, and that the vast majority of those who came to Virginia or Maryland or the Carolinas—or later to Pennsylvania—were indeed disinherited and dispossessed.

Gather them up, the bright and drowning stars,
And with them gather, too,
The clay, the iron, and the knotted rope,
The disinherited, the dispossessed,
The hinds of the midland, eaten by the squire's sheep,
The outcast yeoman, driven to tramp the roads,
The sturdy beggars, roving from town to town,
Workless, hopeless, harried by law and State,
The men who lived on nettles in Merry England,
The men of the blackened years
When dog's meat was a dainty in Lincolnshire,
(Have you heard the news from Virginia?)
The poor, the restless, the striving, the broken knights,
The cast-off soldiers, bitter as their own scars,
The younger sons without office or hope of land,

Glover and cooper, mercer and cordwainer,
("Have you heard the news from Virginia? Have you heard?
Wat swears he'll go, for the gold lies heaped on the ground
And Ralph, the hatter, is ready as any man.
I keep my shop but my shop doth not keep me.
Shall I give such chances the go-by and walk the roads?
I am no hind to scratch in the earth for bread.
Nay, a stocking-weaver I, and of good repute
Though lately dogged by mischances. They'll need such men.
Have you heard the news from Virginia?")
Gather the waifs of the London parishes,
The half-starved boys, the sparrows of London streets,
The ones we caught before they could cut a purse,
And bind them out and send them across the sea.
("They will live or die but at least we are rid of them.
We'll pick the likeliest ones. Boy, what's your name?
Good lad. You sail in *The Fortune*. The fool looks mazed.
Well, give him a wash and see he is fitted out.
We'll settle his master later.")
                              Oh, spread the news,
The news of golden Virginia across the sea,
And let it sink in the hearts of the strange, plain men
Already at odds with government and church,
The men who read their Bibles late in the night,
Dissenter and nonconformist and Puritan,
Let it go to Scrooby and stop at the pesthouse there,
Let it go to the little meeting at Austerfield.
(We must worship God as we choose. We must worship God
Though King and law and bishop stand in the way.
It is far, in the North, and they will not touch us here,
Yet I hear they mean to harry the sheep of God
And His elect must be steadfast. I hear a sound
Like the first, faint roll of thunder, but it is far.
It is very far away.
Have you heard the news of Virginia?)

And those who came were resolved to be Englishmen,
Gone to world's end, but English every one,

And they ate the white corn-kernels, parched in the sun,
And they knew it not, but they'd not be English again.

They would try, they would swear they were, they would drink the toast,
They would loyally petition and humbly pray
And over them was another sort of day
And in their veins was another, a different ghost.

For the country is where the life is, not elsewhere.
The country is where the heart and the blood are given.
They could swear to be English by every oath under heaven.
It did not alter the country by a hair.

—STEPHEN VINCENT BENÉT, "Western Star"

3. THE INHABITANTS OF COLONIAL VIRGINIA

One of the earliest, and best, of Virginia historians confirms what Benét tells us—that those who went to Virginia in the colonial era were mostly "Persons of low Circumstances." Beverley himself was anything but that. The son of that Robert Beverley who had helped put down Bacon's Rebellion, he was educated in England, and then returned to Virginia to serve as Clerk of the Assembly and a Burgess from James-town. While in England on business he read Oldmixon's British Empire in America, *and was so exasperated by its inadequacies that as a corrective he wrote* The History and Present State of Virginia, *which was first published in 1705. It remains one of the liveliest of all our early histories.*

I CAN easily imagin with Sir *Josiah Child,* that this, as well as all the rest of the Plantations, was for the most part at first peopled by Persons of low Circumstances, and by such as were willing to seek their Fortunes in a Foreign Country. Nor was it hardly possible it should be otherwise; for 'tis not likely that any Man of a plentiful Estate, should voluntarily abandon a happy Certainty, to roam after imaginary

Advantages, in a New World. Besides which incertainty, he must have propos'd to himself, to encounter the infinite Difficulties and Dangers, that attend a New Settlement. These Discouragements were sufficient to terrifie any Man, that cou'd live easy in *England,* from going to provoke his Fortune in a strange Land.

Those that went over to that Country first, were chiefly single Men, who had not the Incumbrance of Wives and Children in *England;* and if they had, they did not expose them to the fatigue and hazard of so long a Voyage, until they saw how it should fare with themselves. From hence it came to pass, that when they were setled there in a comfortable way of Subsisting a Family, they grew sensible of the Misfortune of wanting Wives, and such as had left Wives in *England,* sent for them; but the single Men were put to their Shifts. They excepted against the *Indian* Women, on account of their being *Pagans,* and for fear they shou'd conspire with those of their own Nation, to destroy their Husbands. Under this Difficulty they had no hopes, but that the Plenty in which they liv'd, might invite Modest Women of small Fortunes, to go over thither from *England.* However, they wou'd not receive any, but such as cou'd carry sufficient Certificate of their Modesty, and good Behaviour. Those if they were but moderately qualified in all other Respects, might depend upon Marrying very well in those Days, without any Fortune. Nay, the first Planters were so far from expecting Money with a Woman, that 'twas a common thing for them to buy a deserving Wife, at the price of 100 Pound, and make themselves believe, they had a hopeful bargain.

But this way of Peopling the Colony was only at first; for after the advantages of the Climate, and the fruitfulness of the Soil were well known, and all the dangers incident to Infant Settlements were over, People of better Condition retir'd thither with their Families, either to increase the Estates they had before, or else to avoid being persecuted for their Principles of Religion, or Government.

Thus in the time of the Rebellion in *England,* several good Cavalier Families went thither with their Effects, to escape the Tyranny of the Usurper. And so again, upon the Restoration, many People of the opposite Party took Refuge there, to shelter themselves from the King's Resentment. But they had not many of these last, because that Country was famous, for holding out the longest for the Royal Family, of any of the *English* Dominions; for which reason, the Roundheads went for the most part to *New-England,* as did most of those, that in the Reign of King *Charles* II. were molested on the account of their Religion, though some of these fell likewise to the share of *Virginia.* As for Malefactors condemn'd to Transportation, they have always receiv'd very few, and for many years last past, their Laws have been severe against them.

—ROBERT BEVERLEY, *The History and Present State of Virginia,* 1705

4. THE COMING OF THE PILGRIMS

It has long been customary to emphasize the contrasts between the early settlers of Virginia and of New England. There were religious differences, to be sure, and some social differences, but on the whole those who went—or were taken—to Virginia and those who sailed for Cape Cod were pretty much the same kind of people. The story of the Pilgrim Fathers is too familiar to rehearse here: how James I threatened to "harry them out of the land," how they went first to Holland, in 1607-8, and a decade later decided to remove to the New World. The reasons for that decision are set forth here in what is surely the noblest of our early histories—William Bradford's own account of the settlement of Plymouth Plantation.

THEIR REMOVAL TO LEYDEN

FOR these and some other reasons they removed to Leyden, a fair and beautiful city, and of a sweet situation, but made more famous by the university wherewith it is adorned, in which of late had been so many learned men. But wanting that traffic by sea which Amsterdam enjoys, it was not so beneficial for their outward means of living and estates. But being now here pitched they fell to such trades and employments as they best could, valuing peace and their spiritual comfort above any other riches whatsoever. And at length they came to raise a competent and comfortable living but with hard and continual labor. . . .

SHOWING THE REASONS AND CAUSES OF THEIR REMOVAL

After they had lived in this city about some eleven or twelve years, and sundry of them were taken away by death and many others began to be well stricken in years, the grave mistress Experience having taught them many things, those prudent governors, with sundry of the sagest members, began both deeply to apprehend their present dangers and wisely to foresee the future and think of timely remedy. In the agitation of their thoughts and much discourse of things hereabout, at length they began to incline to this conclusion, of removal to some other place— not out of any new-fangledness or other such like giddy humor by which men are oftentimes transported to their great hurt and danger, but for sundry weighty and solid reasons, some of the chief of which I will here briefly touch. And first, they saw and found by experience the hardness of the place and country to be such as few in comparison would come to them, and fewer that would bide it out, and continue with them. For many that came to them and many more that desired to be with them could not endure that great labor and hard fare, with other inconveniences which they underwent and were contented with.

Secondly, they saw that though the people generally bore all these difficulties very cheerfully and with a resolute courage, being in the best and strength of their years, yet old age began to steal on many of them (and their great and continual labors, with other crosses and sorrows, hastened it before the time), so as it was not only probably thought, but apparently seen, that within a few years more they would be in danger to scatter, by necessities pressing them, or sink under their burdens, or both.

Thirdly, as necessity was a taskmaster over them, so they were forced to be such, not only to their servants but in a sort to their dearest children; the which as it did not a little wound the tender hearts of many a loving father and mother, so it produced likewise sundry sad and sorrowful effects. But that which was more lamentable, and, of all sorrows, most heavy to be borne, was that many of their children, by these occasions and the great licentiousness of youth in that country, and the manifold temptations of the place, were drawn away by evil examples into extravagant and dangerous courses, getting the reins of their necks and departing from their parents. Some became soldiers, others took upon them far voyages by sea, and others some worse courses, tending to dissoluteness and the danger of their souls, to the great grief of their parents and dishonor of God. So that they saw their posterity would be in danger to degenerate and be corrupted.

Lastly (and which was not least), a great hope and inward zeal they had of laying some good foundation, or at least to make some way thereunto, for the propagating and advancing the gospel of the kingdom of Christ in those remote parts of the world; yea, though they should be but even as stepping-stones unto others for the performing of so great a work.

The place they had thoughts on was some of those vast and unpeopled countries of America, which are fruitful and fit for habitation, being devoid of all civil inhabitants, where there are only savage and brutish men, which range up and down, little otherwise than the wild beasts of the same. This proposition being made public and coming to the scanning of all, it raised many variable opinions amongst men, and caused many fears and doubts amongst themselves. Some, from their reasons and hopes conceived, labored to stir up and encourage the rest to undertake and prosecute the same; others, again, out of their fears, objected against it and sought to divert from it, alleging many things, and those neither unreasonable nor unprobable, as that it was a great design and subject to many unconceivable perils and dangers; as, be-sides the casualties of the seas (which none can be freed from) the length of the voyage was such as the weak bodies of women and other persons worn out with age and travel (as many of them were) could never be able to endure. And yet if they should, the miseries of the land which they should be exposed unto would be too hard to be borne, and likely, some or all of them together, to consume and utterly to ruinate them. For there they should be liable to famine, and nakedness, and the want, in a manner, of all things. The change of air, diet, and drink-ing of water, would infect their bodies with sore sicknesses and grievous diseases. And also those which should escape or overcome these difficulties should yet be in continual danger of the savage people, who are cruel, barbarous, and most treacherous, being most furious in their rage, and merciless where they overcome, not being content only to kill and take away life, but delight to torment men in the most bloody manner that may be, flaying some alive with the shells of fishes, cutting off the members and joints of others by piecemeal, and broiling on the coals, eat the collops of their flesh in their sight whilst they live; with other cruelties horrible to be related. And surely it could not be thought but the very hearing of these things could not but move the very bowels of men to grate within them, and make the weak to quake and tremble.

It was further objected that it would require greater sums of money to furnish such a voyage and to fit them with necessaries than their consumed estates would amount to; and yet they must as well look to be seconded with supplies as presently to be transported. Also many precedents of ill success and lamentable miseries befallen others in the like designs were easy to be found, and not forgotten to be alleged; besides their own experience, in their former troubles and hardships in their removal into Holland, and how hard a thing it was for them to live in that strange place, though it was a neighbor country and a civil and rich commonwealth.

It was answered that all great and honorable actions are accompanied with great difficulties, and must be both enterprised and overcome with answerable courages. It was granted the dangers were great but not desperate; the difficulties were many but not invincible. For though there were many of them likely, yet they were not certain; it might be sundry of the things feared might never befall; others, by provident care and the use of good means, might in a great measure be prevented; and all of them, through the help of God, by fortitude and patience, might either be borne or overcome. True it was that such attempts were not to be made and undertaken without good ground and reason, not rashly or lightly, as many have done for curiosity or hope of gain, etc. But their condition was not ordinary; their ends were good and honorable, their calling lawful and urgent; and therefore they might expect the blessing of God in their proceeding. Yea, though they should lose their lives in this action, yet might they have comfort in the same, and their endeavors would be honorable. . . . After many other particular things answered and alleged on both sides, it was fully concluded by the major part to put this design in execution and to prosecute it by the best means they could.

—WILLIAM BRADFORD, *History of Plimoth Plantation,* 1630

5. "THIS IS THE DOOR THOU HAST OPENED"

Eight years after the Pilgrims landed at Plymouth came the vanguard of the great Puritan migration to Massachusetts Bay. This Puritan exodus —the largest of its kind in the course of the seventeenth century—was animated in large part by religious motives and resulted in the estab-

*lishment of a Puritan theocracy that long exercised a dominant influence
on New England thought and culture.* The Puritans had not one but
several historians—what a historical-minded lot the early settlers were—
and among them Edward Johnson of Canterbury who came over with
Winthrop on the Arabella *and settled in Charlestown.* His Wonder-
Working Providence of Sions Saviour in New England *was written to
encourage the friends and confound the critics of the Bay Colony. Like
Bradford, Johnson strikes a note that was to be heard again and again—
the insistence upon a special Providence for America. Thus he could—
shall we say sing?—*

> *The noble Acts Jehovah wrought, his Israel to redeem,
> Surely this second work of his shall far more glorious seem.*

Of the Voluntary Banishment, Chosen by This People of Christ, and Their Last Farewell Taken of Their Country and Friends

PASSE on and attend with teares, if thou hast any, the following
discourse, while these Men, Women and Children are taking their
last farwell of their Native Country, Kindred, Friends and Acquaintance, while the Ships attend them; Many make choise of some solitary
place to eccho out their bowell-breaking affections in bidding their
Friends farwell, deare friends (sayes one) as neare as my owne soule
doth thy love lodge in my brest, with thought of the heart-burning
Ravishments, that thy Heavenly speeches have wrought: my melting
soule is poured out at present with these words, both of them had their
farther speach strangled from the depth of their inward dolor, with
breast-breaking sobs, till leaning their heads each on others shoulders,
they let fall the salt-dropping dews of vehement affection, striving to
exceede one another, much like the departure of *David* and *Jonathan*:
having a little eased their hearts with the still streames of Teares, they
recovered speech againe. Ah! my much honoured friend, hath Christ
given thee so great a charge as to be Leader of his People into that far
remote, and vast Wildernesse, I, oh, and alas thou must die there and
never shall I see thy Face in the flesh againe, wert thou called to so
great a taske as to passe the pretious Ocean, and hazard thy person in

Battel against thousands of Malignant Enemies there? there were hopes of thy return with triumph, but now after two three, or foure moneths spent with daily expectation of swallowing Waves, and cruell Pirates, you art to be Landed among barbarous *Indians*, famous for nothing but cruelty, where you are like to spend your days in a famishing condition for a long space; Scarce had he uttered this, but presently hee lockes his friend fast in his armes, holding each other thus for some space of time, they weepe againe, But as *Paul* to his beloved flock: the other replies what doe you weeping and breaking my heart? I am now prest for the service of our *Lord Christ*, to re-build the most glorious Edifice of Mount *Sion* in a Wildernesse, and as *John* Baptist, I must cry prepare yee the way of the Lord, make his paths strait, for behold hee is comming againe, hee is comming to destroy *Antichrist*, and give the whore double to drink the very dregs of his wrath. . . .

What dolefull dayes are these, when the best choise our Orthodox Ministers can make is to take up a perpetuall banishment from their native soile, together with their Wives and Children, wee their poore sheepe they may not feede, but by stoledred should they abide here. *Lord Christ*, here they are at thy command, they go, this is the doore thou hast opened upon our earnest request, and we hope it shall never be shut: for *Englands* sake they are going from *England* to pray without ceasing for *England*, O *England*! thou shalt finde *New England* prayers prevailing with their God for thee, but now woe alas, what great hardship must these our indeared Pastors indure for a long season, with these words they lift up their voyces and wept, adding many drops of salt liquor to the ebbing Ocean.

—EDWARD JOHNSON,
Wonder-Working Providence of Sions Saviour in New England, 1655

6. "WHAT IS AN AMERICAN?"

We cannot linger in the colonial period; suffice it to observe that the early English colonists in Virginia and New England were joined in the late seventeenth and in the eighteenth century by colonists from every part of the British Isles and most parts of Western Europe. After the English the most numerous were the Scots-Irish and the Germans, who settled chiefly in the middle colonies, and the Negro slaves. By the end of the colonial period the population of the thirteen colonies was about two and a quarter million, of whom perhaps half a million were slaves. Although many Americans were but recent arrivals from the Old World, something like an American type had already emerged. The first systematic attempt to explain the process of Americanization and to describe the American type came from the pen of a French-born New York farmer—Michel-Guillaume Jean de Crèvecoeur. Crèvecoeur had served with Montcalm in the French and Indian War, explored the Great Lakes and the Ohio country, and in 1765 settled down to farming in Orange County, New York, where he remained until his return to France about 1780. It was during these years that he wrote his Letters from an American Farmer, *as well as the delightful* Sketches of Eighteenth-Century America. *We give here parts of perhaps the most famous of the letters— Letter III, which inquires, "What is an American?"*

I WISH I could be acquainted with the feelings and thoughts which must agitate the heart and present themselves to the mind of an enlightened Englishman, when he first lands on this continent. . . .

He is arrived on a new continent; a modern society offers itself to his contemplation, different from what he had hitherto seen. It is not composed, as in Europe, of great lords who possess every thing, and of a herd of people who have nothing. Here are no aristocratical families, no courts, no kings, no bishops, no ecclesiastical dominion, no invisible power giving to a few a very visible one; no great manufacturers employing thousands, no great refinements of luxury. The rich and the poor are not so far removed from each other as they are in Europe.

Some few towns excepted, we are all tillers of the earth, from Nova Scotia to West Florida. We are a people of cultivators, scattered over an immense territory, communicating with each other by means of good roads and navigable rivers, united by the silken bands of mild government, all respecting the laws without dreading their power, because they are equitable. We are all animated with the spirit of industry, which is unfettered, and unrestrained, because each person works for himself. If he travels through our rural districts, he views not the hostile castle, and the haughty mansion, contrasted with the clay-built hut and miserable cabbin, where cattle and men help to keep each other warm, and dwell in meanness, smoke, and indigence. A pleasing uniformity of decent competence appears throughout our habitations. The meanest of our log-houses is a dry and comfortable habitation. The Lawyer or merchant are the fairest titles our towns afford; that of a farmer is the only appellation of the rural inhabitants of our country. It must take some time ere he can reconcile himself to our dictionary, which is but short in words of dignity, and names of honour. There, on a Sunday, he sees a congregation of respectable farmers and their wives, all clad in neat homespun, well mounted, or riding in their own humble waggons. There is not among them an esquire, saving the unlettered magistrate. There he sees a parson as simple as his flock, a farmer who does not riot on the labour of others. We have no princes, for whom we toil, starve, and bleed: we are the most perfect society now existing in the world. Here man is free as he ought to be; nor is this pleasing equality so transitory as many others are. Many ages will not see the shores of our great lakes replenished with inland nations, nor the unknown bounds of North America entirely peopled. Who can tell how far it extends? Who can tell the millions of men whom it will feed and contain? for no European foot has as yet traveled half the extent of this mighty continent! . . .

In this great American asylum, the poor of Europe have by some means met together, and in consequence of various causes; to what purpose, should they ask one another, what countrymen they are? Alas, two thirds of them had no country. Can a wretch who wanders about, who works and starves, whose life is a continual scene of sore affliction or pinching penury; can that man call England or any other kingdom his country? A country that had no bread for him, whose fields procured him no harvest, who met with nothing but the frowns of the rich, the severity of the laws, with jails and punishments; who owned not a single foot of the extensive surface of this planet? No! urged by a variety of motives, here they came. Every thing has tended to regenerate them: new laws, a new mode of living, a new social system; here they are become men: in Europe they were as so many useless plants, wanting vegetative mould, and refreshing showers; they withered, and were mowed down by want, hunger, and war: but now, by the power of transplantation, like all other plants, they have taken root and flourished! Formerly they were not numbered in any civil list of their country, except in those of the poor; here they rank as citizens. By what invisible power has this surprizing metamorphosis been performed? By that of the laws, and that of their industry. The laws, the indulgent laws, protect them as they arrive, stamping on them the symbol of adoption; they receive ample rewards for their labours; these accumulated rewards procure them lands; those lands confer on them the title of freemen; and to that title every benefit is affixed which men can possibly require. This is the great operation daily performed by our laws. From whence proceed these laws? From our government. Whence that government? It is derived from the original genius and strong desire of the people, ratified and confirmed by government. This is the great chain which links us all, this is the picture which every province exhibits, Nova Scotia excepted. There the crown has done all; either there were no people who had genius, or it was not much attended to: the consequence is, that the province is very thinly inhabited indeed; the power of the crown, in conjunction with the musketos, has prevented men from settling there. Yet some part of it flourished once, and it contained a mild harmless set of people. But for the fault of a few leaders the whole were banished. The greatest political error the crown ever committed in America, was to cut off men from a country which wanted nothing but men!

What attachment can a poor European emigrant have for a country where he had nothing? The knowledge of the language, the love of a few kindred as poor as himself, were the only cords that tied him: his country is now that which gives him land, bread, protection, and consequence: *Ubi panis ibi patria*, is the motto of all emigrants. What then is the American, this new man? He is either an European, or the descendant of an European; hence that strange mixture of blood, which you will find in no other country. I could point out to you a man, whose grandfather was an Englishman, whose wife was Dutch, whose son married a French woman, and whose present four sons have now four wives of different nations. *He* is an American, who, leaving behind him all his ancient prejudices and manners, receives new ones from the new mode of life he has embraced, the new government he obeys, and the new rank he holds. He becomes an American by being received in the broad lap of our great *Alma Mater*.

Here individuals of all nations are melted into a new race of men, whose labours and posterity will one day cause great change in the world. Americans are the western pilgrims, who are carrying along with them that great mass of arts, sciences, vigour, and industry, which began long since in the east; they will finish the great circle. The Americans were once scattered all over Europe; here they are incorporated into one of the finest systems of population which has ever appeared, and which will hereafter become distinct by the power of the different climates they inhabit. The American ought, therefore, to love this country much better than that wherein either he or his forefathers were born. Here the rewards of his industry follow with equal steps the progress of his labour; his labour is founded on the basis of nature, *self-interest;* can it want a stronger allurement? Wives and children, who before in vain demanded of him a morsel of bread, now, fat and frolicsome, gladly help their father to clear those fields whence exuberant crops are to arise to feed and to clothe them all; without any part being claimed, either by a despotic prince, a rich abbot, or a mighty lord. Here religion demands but little of him; a small voluntary salary to the minister, and gratitude to God; can he refuse these? The American is a new man, who acts upon new principles; he must therefore entertain new ideas, and form new opinions. From involuntary idleness, servile dependence, penury, and useless labour, he has passed to toils of a very different nature, rewarded by ample subsistence.—This is an American.

—MICHEL-GUILLAUME-JEAN DE CRÈVECOEUR,
Letters from an American Farmer, 1782

7. THE "DESPISED RACES"

American society was far more heterogeneous than we normally think, and that heterogeneity increased in the years after the Civil War. This and the next two excerpts describe some of the non-English ingredients in that society—the Chinese, the Indians, the Negroes, the so-called "new emigrants" who swarmed into the great cities of the East in the nineties and after. While Americans never subscribed to the kind of racialist doctrine that was later to dishonor Germany, many of them did regard colored peoples as somehow inferior to those from the North and West. The hostility to non-English stock arose in part from an unconscious racism, in part from economic considerations; whatever its origins and motivations, it reflected upon the sincerity of the American dogma of equality. The attitude toward what Stevenson calls the "despised races" involved Americans in what Myrdal, the Swedish sociologist, rightly terms The American Dilemma—*the dilemma of equalitarian profession and intolerant practice.*

The first of our excerpts comes from the skillful pen of Robert Louis Stevenson, who had sailed from Scotland for San Francisco in the fall of 1879. Across the Plains is a record of his trip in an emigrant train, notable alike for its appreciation of the transcontinentals, and for its sympathetic view of the Indians, Chinese, and newly arrived emigrants.

Despised Races

O F ALL stupid ill-feelings, the sentiment of my fellow-Caucasians towards our companions in the Chinese car was the most stupid and the worst. They seemed never to have looked at them, listened to them, or thought of them, but hated them *a priori*. The Mongols were their enemies in that cruel and treacherous battle-field of money. They could work better and cheaper in half a hundred industries, and hence there was no calumny too idle for the Caucasians to repeat, and even to believe. They declared them hideous vermin, and affected a kind of choking in the throat when they beheld them. Now, as a matter of fact, the young Chinese man is so like a large class of European women, that on raising my head and suddenly catching sight of one at a considerable distance, I have for an instant been deceived by the resemblance. I do not say it is the most attractive class of our women, but for all that many a man's wife is less pleasantly favoured. Again, my emigrants declared that the Chinese were dirty. I cannot say they were clean, for that was impossible upon the journey; but in their efforts after cleanliness they put the rest of us to shame. We all pigged and stewed in one infamy, wet our hands and faces for half a minute daily on the platform, and were unashamed. But the Chinese never lost an opportunity, and you would see them washing their feet—an act not dreamed of among ourselves—and going as far as decency permitted to wash their whole bodies. I may remark by the way that the dirtier people are in their persons the more delicate is their sense of modesty. A clean man strips in a crowded boat-house; but he who is unwashed slinks in and out of bed without uncovering an inch of skin. Lastly, these very foul and malodorous Caucasians entertained the surprising illusion that it was the Chinese waggon, and that alone, which stank. I have said already that it was the exception, and notably the freshest of the three.

These judgments are typical of the feeling in all Western America.

The Chinese are considered stupid, because they are imperfectly acquainted with English. They are held to be base, because their dexterity and frugality enable them to underbid the lazy, luxurious Caucasian. They are said to be thieves; I am sure they have no monopoly of that. They are called cruel; the Anglo-Saxon and the cheerful Irishman may each reflect before he bears the accusation. I am told, again, that they are of the race of river pirates, and belong to the most despised and dangerous class in the Celestial Empire. But if this be so, what remarkable pirates have we here! and what must be the virtues, the industry, the education, and the intelligence of their superiors at home!

Awhile ago it was the Irish, now it is the Chinese that must go. Such is the cry. It seems, after all, that no country is bound to submit to immigration any more than to invasion: each is war to the knife, and resistance to either but legitimate defence. Yet we may regret the free tradition of the republic, which loved to depict herself with open arms, welcoming all unfortunates. And certainly, as a man who believes that he loves freedom, I may be excused some bitterness when I find her sacred name misused in the contention. It was but the other day that I heard a vulgar fellow in the Sand-lot, the popular tribune of San Francisco, roaring for arms and butchery. 'At the call of Abreham Lincoln,' said the orator, 'ye rose in the name of freedom to set free the negroes; can ye not rise and liberate yourselves from a few dhirty Mongolians?'

For my own part, I could not look but with wonder and respect on the Chinese. Their forefathers watched the stars before mine had begun to keep pigs. Gunpowder and printing, which the other day we imitated, and a school of manners which we never had the delicacy so much as to desire to imitate, were theirs in a long-past antiquity. They walk the earth with us, but it seems they must be of different clay. They hear the clock strike the same hour, yet surely of a different epoch. They travel by steam conveyance, yet with such a baggage of old Asiatic thoughts and superstitions as might check the locomotive in its course. Whatever is thought within the circuit of the Great Wall; what the wry-eyed, spectacled schoolmaster teaches in the hamlets round Pekin; religions so old that our language looks a halfling boy alongside; philosophy so wise that our best philosophers find things therein to wonder at; all this travelled alongside of me for thousands of miles over plain and mountain. Heaven knows if we had one common thought or fancy all that way, or whether our eyes, which yet were formed upon the same design, beheld the same world out of the railway windows. And when either of us turned his thoughts to home and childhood, what a strange dissimilarity must there not have been in these pictures of the mind—when I beheld that old, gray, castled city, high throned above the firth, with the flag of Britain flying, and the red-coat sentry pacing over all; and the man in the next car to me would conjure up some junks and a pagoda and a fort of porcelain, and call it, with the same affection, home.

Another race shared among my fellow-passengers in the disfavour of the Chinese; and that, it is hardly necessary to say, was the noble red man of old story—he over whose own hereditary continent we had been steaming all these days. I saw no wild or independent Indian; indeed, I hear that such avoid the neighbourhood of the train; but now and again at way stations, a husband and wife and a few children, disgracefully dressed out with the sweepings of civilisation, came forth and stared upon the emigrants. The silent stoicism of their conduct, and the pathetic degradation of their appearance, would have touched any thinking creature, but my fellow-passengers danced and jested round them with a truly Cockney baseness. I was ashamed for the thing we call civilisation. We should carry upon our consciences so much, at least, of our forefathers' misconduct as we continue to profit by ourselves.

If oppression drives a wise man mad, what should be raging in the hearts of these poor tribes, who have been driven back and back, step after step, their promised reservations torn from them one after another as the States extended westward, until at length they are shut up into these hideous mountain deserts of the centre—and even there find themselves invaded, insulted, and hunted out by ruffianly diggers? The eviction of the Cherokees (to name but an instance), the extortion of Indian agents, the outrages of the wicked, the ill-faith of all, nay, down to the ridicule of such poor beings as were here with me upon the train, make up a chapter of injustice and indignity such as a man must be in some ways base if his heart will suffer him to pardon or forget. These old, well-founded, historical hatreds have a savour of nobility for the independent. That the Jew should not love the Christian, nor the Irishman love the English, nor the Indian brave tolerate the thought of the American, is not disgraceful to the nature of man; rather, indeed, honourable, since it depends on wrongs ancient like the race, and not personal to him who cherishes the indignation.

—ROBERT LOUIS STEVENSON, *Across the Plains*

8. "THE SOULS OF BLACK FOLK"

They have made you a shrine and a humorous fable,
But they kept you a slave while they were able,

writes Stephen Benét of the Negro, and it is true that the Negro has been a shrine, a fable, and a slave, as well as a great many other things. From the eighteenth century on, his influence on the American society and economy has been exceeded only by that of the English and perhaps the Irish. For two centuries he has constituted from ten to fifteen per cent of the population, and done more than that percentage of the work; in parts of the South he has actually outnumbered the whites, and his influence in that section has been proportionately stronger. Indeed it is no great exaggeration to say that in one way or another the Negro has largely dominated the social structure, the economy, the politics, and even the culture of that section.

It is difficult to find any one excerpt that adequately expresses what the Negro represents in the American people, but perhaps this highly personal tribute to a Negro preacher, Alexander Crummell, is as good as anything that can be found. It is from the pen of one of the most distinguished leaders of the Negro race during the past half-century, the sociologist and historian, W. E. B. Du Bois.

Of Alexander Crummell

THIS is the history of a human heart,—the tale of a black boy who many long years ago began to struggle with life that he might know the world and know himself. Three temptations he met on those dark dunes that lay gray and dismal before the wonder-eyes of the child: the temptation of Hate, that stood out against the red dawn; the temptation of Despair, that darkened noonday; and the temptation of Doubt, that ever steals along with twilight. Above all, you must hear of the vales he crossed,—the Valley of Humiliation and the Valley of the Shadow of Death. . . .

He was born with the Missouri Compromise and lay a-dying amid the echoes of Manila and El Caney: stirring times for living, times dark

25

to look back upon, darker to look forward to. The black-faced lad that paused over his mud and marbles seventy years ago saw puzzling vistas as he looked down the world. The slave-ship still groaned across the Atlantic, faint cries burdened the Southern breeze, and the great black father whispered mad tales of cruelty into those young ears. From the low doorway the mother silently watched her boy at play, and at nightfall sought him eagerly lest the shadows bear him away to the land of slaves.

So his young mind worked and winced and shaped curiously a vision of Life; and in the midst of that vision ever stood one dark figure alone, —ever with the hard, thick countenance of that bitter father, and a form that fell in vast and shapeless folds. Thus the temptation of Hate grew and shadowed the growing child,—gliding stealthily into his laughter, fading into his play, and seizing his dreams by day and night with rough, rude turbulence. So the black boy asked of sky and sun and flower the never-answered Why? and loved, as he grew, neither the world nor the world's rough ways.

Strange temptation for a child, you may think; and yet in this wide land to-day a thousand thousand dark children brood before this same temptation, and feel its cold and shuddering arms. For them, perhaps, some one will some day lift the Veil,—will come tenderly and cheerily into those sad little lives and brush the brooding hate away, just as Beriah Green strode in upon the life of Alexander Crummell. And before the bluff, kind-hearted man the shadow seemed less dark. Beriah Green had a school in Oneida County, New York, with a score of mischievous boys. "I'm going to bring a black boy here to educate," said Beriah Green, as only a crank and an abolitionist would have dared to say. "Oho!" laughed the boys. "Ye-es," said his wife; and Alexander came. Once before, the black boy had sought a school, had travelled, cold and hungry, four hundred miles up into free New Hampshire, to Canaan. But the godly farmers hitched ninety yoke of oxen to the abolition schoolhouse and dragged it into the middle of the swamp. The black boy trudged away. . . .

In that little Oneida school there came to those schoolboys a revelation of thought and longing beneath one black skin, of which they had not dreamed before. And to the lonely boy came a new dawn of sympathy and inspiration. The shadowy, formless thing—the temptation of Hate, that hovered between him and the world—grew fainter and less sinister. It did not wholly fade away, but diffused itself and lingered thick at the edges. Through it the child now first saw the blue and gold of life,—the sun-swept road that ran 'twixt heaven and earth until in one far-off wan wavering line they met and kissed. A vision of life came to the growing boy,—mystic, wonderful. He raised his head, stretched himself, breathed deep of the fresh new air. Yonder, behind the forests, he heard strange sounds; then glinting through the trees he saw, far, far away, the bronzed hosts of a nation calling,—calling faintly, calling loudly. He heard the hateful clank of their chains, he felt them cringe and grovel, and there rose within him a protest and a prophecy. And he girded himself to walk down the world.

A voice and vision called him to be a priest,—a seer to lead the uncalled out of the house of bondage. He saw the headless host turn toward him like the whirling of mad waters,—he stretched forth his hands eagerly, and then, even as he stretched them, suddenly there swept across the vision the temptation of Despair.

They were not wicked men,—the problem of life is not the problem of the wicked,—they were calm, good men, Bishops of the Apostolic Church of God, and strove toward righteousness. They said slowly, "It is all very natural—it is even commendable; but the General Theological Seminary of the Episcopal Church cannot admit a Negro." And when that thin, half-grotesque figure still haunted their doors, they put their hands kindly, half sorrowfully, on his shoulders, and said, "Now,—of course, we—we know how *you* feel about it; but you see it is impossible, —that is—well—it is premature. Sometime, we trust—sincerely trust— all such distinctions will fade away; but now the world is as it is."

This was the temptation of Despair; and the young man fought it doggedly. Like some grave shadow he flitted by those halls, pleading, arguing, half angrily demanding admittance, until there came the final *No*; until men hustled the disturber away, marked him as foolish, unreasonable, and injudicious, a vain rebel against God's law. And then from that Vision Splendid all the glory faded slowly away, and left an earth gray and stern rolling on beneath a dark despair. Even the kind hands that stretched themselves toward him from out the depths of that dull morning seemed but parts of the purple shadows. He saw them coldly, and asked, "Why should I strive by special grace when the way of the world is closed to me?" All gently yet, the hands urged him on,— the hands of young John Jay, that daring father's daring son; the hands of the good folk of Boston, that free city. And yet, with a way to the priesthood of the Church open at last before him, the cloud lingered there; and even when in old St. Paul's the venerable Bishop raised his white arms above the Negro deacon—even then the burden had not lifted from that heart, for there had passed a glory from the earth.

And yet the fire through which Alexander Crummell went did not burn in vain. Slowly and more soberly he took up again his plan of life. More critically he studied the situation. Deep down below the slavery and servitude of the Negro people he saw their fatal weaknesses, which long years of mistreatment had emphasized. The dearth of strong moral character, of unbending righteousness, he felt, was their great short-coming, and here he would begin. He would gather the best of his people into some little Episcopal chapel and there lead, teach, and inspire them, till the leaven spread, till the children grew, till the world heark-ened, till—till—and then across his dream gleamed some faint after-glow of that first fair vision of youth—only an after-glow, for there had passed a glory from the earth.

One day—it was in 1842, and the springtide was struggling merrily with the May winds of New England—he stood at last in his own chapel in Providence, a priest of the Church. The days sped by, and the dark young clergyman labored; he wrote his sermons carefully; he intoned his prayers with a soft, earnest voice; he haunted the streets and accosted the wayfarers; he visited the sick, and knelt beside the dying. He worked and toiled, week by week, day by day, month by month. And yet month by month the congregation dwindled, week by week the hollow walls echoed more sharply, day by day the calls came fewer and fewer, and day by day the third temptation sat clearer and still more clearly within the Veil; a temptation, as it were, bland and smiling, with just a shade of mockery in its smooth tones. First it came casually, in the cadence of a voice: "Oh, colored folks? Yes." Or perhaps more definitely: "What do you *expect*?" In voice and gesture lay the doubt— the temptation of Doubt. How he hated it, and stormed at it furiously! "Of course they are capable," he cried; "of course they can learn and strive and achieve—" and "Of course," added the temptation softly, "they do nothing of the sort." Of all the three temptations, this one struck the deepest. Hate? He had outgrown so childish a thing. Despair? He had steeled his right arm against it, and fought it with the vigor of determination. But to doubt the worth of his life-work,—to doubt the destiny and capability of the race his soul loved because it was his; to find listless squalor instead of eager endeavor; to hear his own lips whispering, "They do not care; they cannot know; they are dumb driven cattle,—why cast your pearls before swine?"—this, this seemed more than man could bear; and he closed the door, and sank upon the steps of the chancel, and cast his robe upon the floor and writhed.

The evening sunbeams had set the dust to dancing in the gloomy chapel when he arose. He folded his vestments, put away the hymnbooks, and closed the great Bible. He stepped out into the twilight, looked back upon the narrow little pulpit with a weary smile, and locked the door. Then he walked briskly to the Bishop, and told the Bishop what the Bishop already knew. "I have failed," he said simply. And gaining courage by the confession, he added: "What I need is a larger constituency. There are comparatively few Negroes here, and perhaps they are not of the best. I must go where the field is wider, and try again." So the Bishop sent him to Philadelphia, with a letter to Bishop Onderdonk.

Bishop Onderdonk lived at the head of six white steps,—corpulent, red-faced, and the author of several thrilling tracts on Apostolic Succession. It was after dinner, and the Bishop had settled himself for a pleasant season of contemplation, when the bell must needs ring, and there must burst in upon the Bishop a letter and a thin, ungainly Negro. Bishop Onderdonk read the letter hastily and frowned. Fortunately, his mind was already clear on this point; and he cleared his brow and looked at Crummell. Then he said, slowly and impressively: "I will receive you into this diocese on one condition: no Negro priest can sit in my church convention, and no Negro church must ask for representation there." . . .

The Bishop cleared his throat suggestively; then, recollecting that there was really nothing to say, considerately said nothing, only sat tapping his foot impatiently. But Alexander Crummell said, slowly and heavily: "I will never enter your diocese on such terms." And saying this, he turned and passed into the Valley of the Shadow of Death. You might have noted only the physical dying, the shattered frame and hacking cough; but in that soul lay deeper death than that. He found a chapel in New York,—the church of his father; he labored for it in poverty and starvation, scorned by his fellow priests. Half in despair, he wandered across the sea, a beggar with outstretched hands. Englishmen clasped them,—Wilberforce and Stanley, Thirwell and Ingles, and even Froude and Macaulay; Sir Benjamin Brodie bade him rest awhile at Queen's College in Cambridge, and there he lingered, struggling for health of body and mind, until he took his degree in '53. Restless still and unsatisfied, he turned toward Africa, and for long years, amid the spawn of the slave-smugglers, sought a new heaven and a new earth.

So the man groped for light; all this was not Life,—it was the world-wandering of a soul in search of itself, the striving of one who vainly sought his place in the world, ever haunted by the shadow of a death that is more than death,—the passing of a soul that has missed its duty. Twenty years he wandered,—twenty years and more; and yet the hard rasping question kept gnawing within him, "What, in God's name, am I on earth for?" In the narrow New York parish his soul seemed cramped and smothered. In the fine old air of the English University he heard the millions wailing over the sea. In the wild fever-cursed swamps of West Africa he stood helpless and alone. . . .

Out of the temptation of Hate, and burned by the fire of Despair, triumphant over Doubt, and steeled by Sacrifice against Humiliation, he turned at last home across the waters, humble and strong, gentle and determined. He bent to all the gibes and prejudices, to all hatred and discrimination, with that rare courtesy which is the armor of pure souls. He fought among his own, the low, the grasping, and the wicked, with that unbending righteousness which is the sword of the just. He never faltered, he seldom complained; he simply worked, inspiring the young, rebuking the old, helping the weak, guiding the strong.

So he grew, and brought within his wide influence all that was best of those who walk within the Veil.

—W. E. B. Du Bois, *The Souls of Black Folk*

9. A MAP OF NEW YORK

Throughout the first three-quarters of the nineteenth century the vast majority of emigrants came from the British Isles, Germany and Scandinavia, with the Irish contingent leading all the rest. Already by the 1870's there began to appear new types in the stream that was now swelling into a torrent—Austrians, Poles, Serbs, Italians, and Russians. By the 1890's the so-called "new" emigrants from the countries of Southern and Eastern Europe outnumbered the "old," and by the first decade of the new century the ratio of new to old was three to one. Most of these newcomers came to New York, and many of them stayed there, swarm-

ing into the tenements and slums of the great metropolis. Danish-born newspaperman Jacob Riis made it his business to describe these newcomers sympathetically and to dramatize to the rest of America how this "other half" lived. Riis himself became a notable figure in journalism and reform; Theodore Roosevelt later described him as "the best American I ever knew."

NEW YORK'S wage earners have no other place to live, more is the pity. They are truly poor for having no better homes; waxing poorer in purse as the exorbitant rents to which they are tied, as ever was serf to soil, keep rising. The wonder is that they are not all corrupted, and speedily, by their surroundings. If on the contrary there be a steady working up, if not out of the slough, the fact is a powerful argument for the optimist's belief that the world is after all growing better not worse, and would go far toward disarming apprehension were it not for the steadier growth of the sediment of the slums and its constant menace. Such an impulse toward better things there certainly is. The German ragpicker of thirty years ago, quite as low in the scale as his Italian successor, is the thrifty tradesman or prosperous farmer of today.

The Italian scavenger of our time is fast graduating into exclusive control of the corner fruit stands, while his black-eyed boy monopolizes the bootblacking industry in which a few years ago he was an intruder. The Irish hod carrier in the second generation has become a bricklayer, if not the alderman of his ward, while the Chinese coolie is in almost exclusive possession of the laundry business. The reason is obvious. The poorest immigrant comes here with the purpose and ambition to better himself and, given half a chance, might be reasonably expected to make the most of it. To the false plea that he prefers the squalid homes in which his kind are housed there could be no better answer. The truth is his half-chance has too long been wanting, and for the bad result he has been unjustly blamed.

As emigration from east to west follows the latitude, so does the foreign influx in New York distribute itself along certain well-defined lines that waver and break only under the stronger pressure of a more gregarious race or the encroachments of inexorable business. A feeling of dependence upon mutual effort, natural to strangers in a strange land, unacquainted with its language and customs, sufficiently accounts for this.

The Irishman is the true cosmopolitan immigrant. All-pervading, he shares his lodging with perfect impartiality with the Italian, the Greek, and the "Dutchman," yielding only to sheer force of numbers, and objects equally to them all. A map of the city, colored to designate nationalities, would show more stripes than on the skin of a zebra and more colors than any rainbow. The city on such a map would fall into two great halves, green for the Irish prevailing in the West Side tenement districts and blue for the Germans on the East Side. But intermingled with these ground colors would be an odd variety of tints that would give the whole the appearance of an extraordinary crazy quilt. . . .

Were the question raised who makes the most of life thus mortgaged, who resists most stubbornly its leveling tendency—knows how to drag even the barracks upward a part of the way at least toward the ideal plane of the home—the palm must be unhesitatingly awarded the Teuton. The Italian and the poor Jew rise only by compulsion. The Chinaman does not rise at all; here, as at home, he remains stationary. The Irishman's genius runs to public affairs rather than domestic life; wherever he is mustered in force the saloon is the gorgeous center of political activity. The German struggles vainly to learn his trick; his Teutonic wit is too heavy, and the political ladder he raises from his saloon· usually too short or too clumsy to reach the desired goal. The best part of his life is lived at home, and he makes himself a home independent of the surroundings, giving the lie to the saying, unhappily become a maxim of social truth, that pauperism and drunkenness naturally grow in the tenements. He makes the most of his tenement, and it should be added that whenever and as soon as he can save up money enough, he gets out and never crosses the threshold of one again.

—JACOB A. RIIS, *How the Other Half Lives,* 1890

10. "I LIFT MY LAMP BESIDE THE GOLDEN DOOR"

Born in New York City, of a distinguished Sephardic family, Emma Lazarus early revealed those two interests that were to dominate her

brief life: poetry and the Jewish people in America. "The New Colossus,"
surely one of the classics of our literature, was selected as an inscription
on the base of the Statue of Liberty.

Not like the brazen giant of Greek fame,
With conquering limbs astride from land to land;
Here at our sea-washed, sunset gates shall stand
A mighty woman with a torch, whose flame
Is the imprisoned lightning, and her name
Mother of Exiles. From her beacon-hand
Glows world-wide welcome; her mild eyes command
The air-bridged harbor that twin cities frame.
"Keep, ancient lands, your storied pomp!" cries she

With silent lips. "Give me your tired, your poor,
Your huddled masses yearning to breathe free,
The wretched refuse of your teeming shore.
Send these, the homeless, tempest-tost to me,
I lift my lamp beside the golden door!"
—EMMA LAZARUS, "The New Colossus"

11. A TEST OF OPPORTUNITY, NOT OF CHARACTER

During most of the nineteenth century Congress had allowed almost
unrestricted immigration; only criminals or those with dangerous dis-
eases were effectively excluded. In 1882 came the first step toward exclu-
sion—an act excluding Chinese laborers for a period of ten years. The
vast increase in the number of immigrants, and the shift from old to
new immigration, and the hostility of organized labor to competition
from the unskilled laborers of Southern and Eastern Europe combined
to change the Congressional policy from one of selection to restriction,
and then from restriction to exclusion. The favorite selective device was
a literacy test, and a bill incorporating this test had passed one of the two
houses no less than thirty-two times before it was finally adopted. Cleve-

land had vetoed such a bill in 1897; Taft vetoed it in 1913; Wilson in 1915 and again in 1917—when it was finally passed over his veto. We give here Wilson's argument against the principle of the application of the literacy test.

TO THE House of Representatives: It is with unaffected regret that I find myself constrained by clear conviction to return this bill without my signature. . . .

In two particulars of vital consequence this bill embodies a radical departure from the traditional and long established policy of this country, a policy in which our people have conceived the very character of their Government to be expressed, the very mission and spirit of the Nation in respect of its relations to the people of the world outside their borders. It seeks to all but close entirely the gates of asylum which have always been open to those who could find nowhere else the right and opportunity of constitutional agitation for what they conceived to be the natural and inalienable rights of men; and it excludes those to whom the opportunities of elementary education have been denied, without regard to their character, their purposes, or their natural capacity.

Restrictions like these, adopted earlier in our history as a Nation, would very materially have altered the course and cooled the humane ardors of our politics. The right of political asylum has brought to this country many a man of noble character and elevated purpose who was marked as an outlaw in his own less fortunate land, and who has yet become an ornament to our citizenship and to our public councils. The children and compatriots of these illustrious Americans must stand amazed to see the representatives of their Nation now resolved, in the fullness of our national strength and at the maturity of our great institutions, to risk turning such men back from our shores without test of quality or purpose. It is difficult for me to believe that the full effect of this feature of the bill was realized when it was framed and adopted, and it is impossible for me to assent to it in the form in which it is here cast.

The literacy test and the tests and restrictions which accompany it constitute an even more radical change in the policy of the Nation. Hitherto we have generously kept our doors open to all who were not unfitted by reason of disease or incapacity for self-support or such personal records and antecedents as were likely to make them a menace to our peace and order or to the wholesome and essential relationships of life. In this bill it is proposed to turn away from tests of character and of quality and impose tests which exclude and restrict; for the laws here embodied are not tests of quality or of character or of personal fitness, but tests of opportunity. Those who come seeking opportunity are not to be admitted unless they have already had one of the chief of the opportunities they seek, the opportunity of education. The object of such provisions is restriction, not selection.

If the people of this country have made up their minds to limit the number of immigrants by arbitrary tests and so reverse the policy of all the generations of Americans that have gone before them, it is their right to do so. I am their servant and have no license to stand in their way. But I do not believe that they have. I respectfully submit that no one can quote their mandate to that effect. Has any political party ever avowed a policy of restriction in this fundamental matter, gone to the country on it, and been commissioned to control its legislation? Does this bill rest upon the conscious and universal assent and desire of the American people? I doubt it. It is because I doubt it that I make bold to dissent from it. I am willing to bide by the verdict, but not until it has been rendered. Let the platforms of parties speak out upon this policy and the people pronounce their wish. The matter is too fundamental to be settled otherwise.

I have no pride of opinion in this question. I am not foolish enough to profess to know the wishes and ideals of America better than the body of her chosen representatives know them. I only want instruction direct from those whose fortunes with ours, and all men's are involved.

—Woodrow Wilson, Veto of Literacy Test for Immigrants, 1915

12. PUTTING UP THE BARS

Congressional laws make awkward reading. Instead of giving here excerpts from the various Immigration Acts of 1917, 1921, 1924, and 1929, we submit instead a brief summary of immigration policy by the Commissioner-General of Immigration. This summary came in 1923; subsequent legislation changed the situation quantitatively rather than qualitatively. What all this legislation meant can be read in the figures of the Census Bureau: over 4,000,000 immigrants from outside the Western Hemisphere in the decade of the 1920's, about 325,000 in the thirties, and about 150,000 in the forties. Thus it may be said that the immigration legislation of the 1920's marked the end of an era.

PERHAPS it is not very generally realized that the per centum limit law marked the beginning of actual restriction or limitation of immigration to the United States from Europe, Africa, Australia, and a considerable part of Asia. The Chinese exclusion act of 1882, the passport agreement with Japan which became effective in 1908, and the "barred zone" provision in the general immigration law of 1917 had already stopped or greatly reduced the influx of oriental peoples, but so far as others, and particularly Europeans, were concerned, all applicants who met the various tests prescribed in the general law were admitted. This general law, first enacted in 1882 and several times revised and strengthened, was and still is based on the principle of selection rather than of numerical restriction. It is probably true that the provision barring illiterate aliens from admission, which was added to the general law in 1917, was intended as a restrictive measure rather than a quality test, but in its practical effect it was only another addition to the already numerous class of alleged undesirables who were denied admission; and obviously could not be relied upon actually to limit the volume of immigration.

The immigration act of 1882, which, as already indicated, was the first general law upon the subject, provided for the exclusion from the United States of the following classes only: Convicts, lunatics, idiots, and persons likely to become a public charge. This law underwent more or less important revisions in 1891, 1893, 1903, 1907, and 1917, until the last-mentioned act, which is the present general immigration law, denies admission to many classes of aliens, including the following: Idiots, imbeciles, feeble-minded persons, epileptics, insane persons; persons who have had one or more attacks of insanity at any time previously; persons of constitutional psychopathic inferiority; persons with chronic alcoholism; paupers; professional beggars; vagrants; persons afflicted with tuberculosis in any form or with a loathsome or dangerous contagious disease; persons certified by the examining physician as being mentally or physically defective, such physical defect being of a nature which may affect the ability of the alien to earn a living; persons who have been convicted of or admit having committed a felony or other crime or misdemeanor involving moral turpitude; polygamists, or persons who practice polygamy or believe in or advocate the practice of polygamy; anarchists and similar classes; immoral persons and persons coming for an immoral purpose; contract laborers; persons likely to become a public charge; persons seeking admission within one year of date of previous debarment or deportation; persons whose ticket or passage is paid for with the money of another or who are assisted by others to come, unless it is affirmatively shown that such persons do not belong to one of the foregoing excluded classes; persons whose ticket or passage is paid for by any corporation, association, society, municipality, or foreign government, either directly or indirectly; stowaways; children under 16 years of age unless accompanied by one or both of their parents; persons who are natives of certain geographically defined territory; aliens over 16 years of age who are unable to read some language or dialect; certain accompanying aliens, as described in the last proviso of section 18 of the act; and persons who have arrived in Canada or Mexico by certain steamship lines. Persons who fail to meet certain passport requirements were added to the excluded classes in subsequent legislation.

Obviously it would be difficult to find, or even to invent, many other terms denoting individual undesirability which might be added to the foregoing list, but, as already pointed out, the general law is essentially selective in theory, for even its most rigid application with respect to the excludable classes above enumerated could not be depended upon to prevent the coming of unlimited numbers of aliens who were able to meet the tests imposed.

Even a casual survey of congressional discussions of the immigration problem during the past quarter of a century demonstrates very clearly that while the law makers were deeply concerned with the mental, moral, and physical quality of immigrants, there developed as time went on an even greater concern as to the fundamental racial character of the constantly increasing numbers who came. The record of alien arrivals year by year had shown a gradual falling off in the immigration of northwest European peoples, representing racial stocks which were common to America even in colonial days, and a rapid and remarkably large increase in the movement from southern and eastern European countries and Asiatic Turkey. Immigration from the last-named sources reached an annual average of about 750,000 and in some years nearly a million came, and there seems to have been a general belief in Congress that it would increase rather than diminish. At the same time no one seems to have anticipated a revival of the formerly large influx from the "old sources," as the countries of northwest Europe came to be known.

This remarkable change in the sources and racial character of our immigrants led to an almost continuous agitation of the immigration problem both in and out of Congress, and there was a steadily growing demand for restriction, particularly of the newer movement from the south and east of Europe. During the greater part of this period of agitation the so-called literacy test for aliens was the favorite weapon of the restrictionists, and its widespread popularity appears to have been based quite largely on a belief, or at least a hope, that it would reduce to some extent the stream of "new" immigration, about one-third of which was illiterate, without seriously interfering with the coming of the older type, among whom illiteracy was at a minimum.

Presidents Cleveland and Taft vetoed immigration bills because they contained a literacy test provision, and President Wilson vetoed two bills largely for the same reason. In 1917, however, Congress passed a general immigration bill which included the literacy provision over the President's veto, and, with certain exceptions, aliens who are unable to read are no longer admitted to the United States. At that time, however, the World War had already had the effect of reducing immigration from Europe to a low level, and our own entry into the conflict a few days before the law in question went into effect practically stopped it altogether. Consequently, the value of the literacy provision as a means of restricting European immigration was never fairly tested under normal conditions.

The Congress, however, seemingly realized that even the comprehensive immigration law of 1917, including the literacy test, would afford only a frail barrier against the promised rush from the war-stricken countries of Europe, and in December, 1920, the House of Representatives, with little opposition, passed a bill to suspend practically all immigration for the time being. The per centum limit plan was substituted by the Senate, however, and the substitute prevailed in Congress, but it failed to become a law at the time because President Wilson withheld executive approval. Nevertheless, favorable action was not long delayed, for at the special session called at the beginning of the present administration the measure was quickly enacted, and, with President Harding's approval, became a law on May 19, 1921. This law expired by limitation June 30, 1922, but by the act of May 11, 1922, its life was extended to June 30, 1924, and some strengthening amendments were added.

The principal provisions of the per centum limit act, or the "quota law," as it is popularly known, are as follows:

The number of aliens of any nationality who may be admitted to the United States in any fiscal year shall not exceed 3 per cent of the number of persons of such nationality who were resident in the United States according to the census of 1910.

Monthly quotas are limited to 20 per cent of the annual quota.

For the purposes of the act, "nationality" is determined by country of birth.

The law does not apply to the following classes of aliens: Government officials; aliens in transit; aliens visiting the United States as tourists or temporarily for business or pleasure; aliens from countries immigration from which is regulated in accordance with treaties or agreement relating solely to immigration, otherwise China and Japan; aliens from the so-called Asiatic barred zone; aliens who have resided continuously for at least five years in Canada, Newfoundland, Cuba, Mexico, Central or South America, or adjacent islands; aliens under the age of 18 who are children of citizens of the United States.

—*Annual Report of the Commissioner-General of Immigration*, 1923

13. THE AMERICAN LANGUAGE

We turn, finally, to the interpretation of the American character in the twentieth century. That subject is clearly too broad to be dealt with in confines of a few excerpts, and we can do no more than hint at some of its aspects. It is proper to begin with a subject of inexhaustible interest, at home and abroad: the American language. A word of caution is relevant here. While it is true, as H. L. Mencken points out, that American English differs markedly from English English, it is also true that there are fewer differences between American and English than between the French spoken in Canada and that spoken in France, or the Spanish or Portuguese spoken in Latin America and that spoken on the Iberian

Peninsula. Perhaps the most remarkable thing about the American language is that it should have diverged from the mother tongue so little over a period of three centuries.

H. L. Mencken needs no introduction. Long editor of the American Mercury and one of the most vigorous literary critics of his generation, his lasting contribution to American culture has doubtless been his monumental studies in The American Language—the original volume of that title and "Supplements."

THE first Englishman to notice an Americanism sneered at it aloofly, thus setting a fashion that many of his countrymen have been following ever since. He was one Francis Moore, a ruffian who came out to Georgia with Oglethorpe in 1735, and the word that upset him was *bluff*, in the sense of "a cliff or headland with a broad precipitous face." He did not deign to argue against it; he simply dismissed it as "barbarous," apparently assuming that all Englishmen of decent instincts would agree with him. For nearly a century they seem to have done so, and *bluff* lingered sadly below the salt. When it was printed at all in Great Britain it was set off by sanitary quotation marks, or accompanied by other hints of depreciation, as *rubberneck*, *hot spot* and *nerts* are accompanied to-day. But then, in 1830, the eminent Sir Charles Lyell used it shamelessly in the first volume of his monumental "Principles of Geology," and from that day to this it has been a perfectly respectable if somewhat unfamiliar word in England, with a place in every dictionary.

Its history is the history of almost countless other Americanisms. They have been edging their way into English since early colonial times, and, for more than a century past, in constantly increasing volume, but I can't recall one that didn't have to run a gantlet of opposition in the motherland, at times verging upon the frantic. After the Revolution, that opposition took on the proportions of a holy war. Never an American book came out that the English reviewers did not belabor its vocabulary violently. . . .

Three Americanisms borrowed by English to one Briticism come into American! The true score, I suspect, is even more favorable to the Yankee as word-maker. Down to 1820, according to Sir William Craigie, the trans-Atlantic trade in neologisms ran mainly westward, but then it began to shift, and to-day it is very heavily eastward. It would be difficult to recall a dozen British inventions that have entered the common American vocabulary since the World War, but the number of Americanisms taken into English must run to hundreds, and perhaps even to thousands. The American movie and talkie, of course, have been responsible for the introduction of many of them, but there is something beyond that, and something more fundamental. They are adopted in England simply because England has nothing to offer in competition with them—that is, nothing so apt or pungent, nothing so good. His Lordship of Guildford did not apply *speed-cop* to that *mobile policeman* as a voluntary act of subversion, born of a desire to shock and insult the realm; he let it slip for the single reason that it was an irresistibly apposite and satisfying term. And so with all the other Americanisms that challenge and consume their British congeners. They win fairly on palpable points and by every rule of the game. Confronted by the same novelty, whether in object or in situation, the Americans always manage to fetch up a name for it that not only describes it but also illuminates it, whereas the English, since the Elizabethan stimulant oozed out of them, have been content merely to catalogue it. There was a brilliant exemplification of the two approaches in the early days of railways. The English, having to name the wedge-shaped fender that was put in front of the first locomotives, called it a *plough*, which was almost exactly what it was, but the Americans gave it the bold and racy appellation of *cow-catcher*. For the casting which guides the wheels from one rail to another the English coined the depressingly obvious name of *crossing-plate;* the Americans, setting their imaginations free, called it a *frog*. The same sharp contrast appears every time there is a call for a new word to-day. The American *movie* is obviously much better than the English *cinema;* it is even better English. So is *radio* better than *wireless*, though it may be Latin, the *job-holder* better than *public servant,* though it is surely literal enough, and *shock absorber* vastly better than *anti-bounce clip,* and *highball* than *whisky and soda,* and *bouncer* than *chucker-out,* and *chain store* than *multiple shop,* and *string bean* than *French bean,* and *union suit* than *combination.* Confronting the immensely American *rubberneck,* Dr. J. Y. T. Greig of Newcastle could only exclaim "one of the best words ever coined!" And in the face of *lounge lizard,* Horace Annesley Vachell fell silent like Sir Isaac Newton on the seashore, overwhelmed by the solemn grandeur of the linguistic universe.

—HENRY L. MENCKEN, *The American Language*

14. "THE THREE SOUTHWESTERN PEOPLES"

To the student of the national character, one of the most interesting areas of the United States is the Southwest—the one area where the older Indian and Spanish cultures have persisted and where they flourish side by side with what is called, in that region, the "Anglo" civilization. And what is particularly interesting is that in this region the influence of land and climate is particularly powerful—and discernible. Paul Horgan, who here interprets the medley of cultures in the Southwest, is a historian, novelist and poet.

IN THE peoples as they exist today, the marks of inevitable compromise can be read. The country has stamped its character on them in one way or another, and they have so affected one another that to describe them now is to indulge in an essay on survivals. The Indians were changed by the Spaniards, who brought them another God and a different brand of fatalism. Then the life that was made up by the Spaniards and Indians together was altered swiftly and thoroughly by the Americans. While each people lived as ruler of the land, its life and ideas, its belief and tradition had gone for centuries unchanged. But with the American arrival, change came so fast and in so many departments of life that we can only examine the vestiges today and observe how eloquent they are of upheaval.

The Indian: he repeats in ghostly enactment the tragedy of his Eastern cousins, the spectacle of a race of rulers penned off by a benevolent government, and seduced from the integrities of its crafts by the tourist. The Plains tribes of Indians, always more bellicose and restless than the Pueblos, live in reservations where American schools and American clothes unsettle the tribal proprieties in childhood. Through education the Indian's guardian has attempted to give him the benefits of a system of belief and knowledge entirely irrelevant to his kind of life. The spectacle is familiar enough: Indian children are placed in Government Indian schools, where they learn orthodox school subjects, and military drill, and football. When they are old enough to graduate as young men and women, they are turned out, equipped by rote to compete in modern life, but wholly unequipped by temperament, heritage, and desire. One of two courses confronts them: they may either take some menial job in the white man's scheme, a job for which their formal education has provided nothing, or they may return to the pueblo, where the values of a formal education are laughable. But it is the style of the conqueror, and it may take many more years for the birth of the official notion that, instead of remodeling the Indian, it would be wiser to find out what he is, and provide a life for him that is suitable.

Other inevitable corruptions assail the Indian integrity of race and habit. One is his exploitation by and for the tourists that come in thousands to gaze upon his dwellings, his religious dances, his art, and his person. Indians are selling their handiwork rapidly and easily, and as a consequence are now making their handiwork too rapidly and too easily. Things which in the days of his history the Indian made for use, and made beautifully and significantly, are now made for sale. Something of the spirit of their new purpose has come into the work and destroyed the fine meaning of Indian craftsmanship. The Indian, in his native place, is now a show, for viewing which luxuries are provided and a whole industry developed. How long the life of the Pueblo can continue under such organized scrutiny, it is hard to imagine. Indians are sensitive, and they have by gradual association found it necessary in dealing with the Americans to erect a protective shell of irony around their intercourse. Bitterness seems to be one emotion of which the Indian is innocent. Or perhaps his perfect sense of manners covers up a deep concern for the way his meaning in life is going; or perhaps he doesn't care, so long—(the fruits of an American education)—so long as there are plenty of tourists, and the bowls and jars, the necklaces and bracelets, the blankets and drums, are selling rapidly.

The Spaniard: his contribution to posterity was the nomenclature of his discoveries. In the Spanish names of cities, rivers, mountains, and mesas, the Spanish conquest survives. And what liturgical music these names make! What gratified saints find on earth the perpetuation of their glory! The geological piety which seized the explorers on viewing a new range, the confusing zeal with which a newly conquered pueblo would be baptised, these things betray the enthusiasm of the Latin and the natural importance of his religion in his daily acts, an importance so common that the creed may have suffered by a loss of rarity and distinction. Certainly the Spaniard took his agonies of spirit as casually as his descendants today take their daily lives.

The purity of some of the first families still remains intact. In Texas and New Mexico there are establishments where the silver in the dining room has been used every day since the first *conde* or *marqués* and his suite dined at home in his adobe palace; houses where the most profound gallantries are still habitual; where the atavism of an aristocracy is neither surprising nor ridiculous. The pride of name is very strong in such families. It is, it has been for decades, a losing struggle to hold aloft the banners of exclusiveness and pride of race. It will not last long, that attitude. Its perishing will be the end of an occupation. No one will know when the last flicker of the devout procession of the seventeenth century will struggle and expire.

In New Mexico, the twin geniuses of religion and government occupy the men of Mexican blood. In the society of the Penitent Brothers there survives a cruel passionate ritual from the Middle Ages. It is an organization composed of men who celebrate the yearly passion of Holy Week with acts of torture and despair, and of ecstacy and salvation. All the week devotions are held and initiates entered. The badge of the order is three long scars of knife-cuts in the back; the climax of the ritual comes in the procession and crucifixion on Good Friday. On Good Friday the dawn comes melancholy over the yellow-lighted mountains. In the remote villages where the church and the government are without practical authority, it is said that a human being is crucified yearly in imitation of Christ. In any case, a cross is dragged along a Via Dolorosa. Snow is often underfoot and on the foothills, flashing white around the dark green of the roots of the scrub pine, pale against the tufty brown of the winter earth. Out of the town, moaning and whipping, flinging their cords against their bare backs, singing the triumph of death over life and the exaltation of life after death, they toil across the cold rocks, bleeding and weeping with a terrible joy. Their voices and the suck and whip of their flails echo in the bare hills. The tragedy of Christianity is mimed, participation in the sacrificial drama binds men together. And this solidarity is useful in politics.

Mexicans, Spanish-Americans, whatever their title must be, are excellent politicians. They throw a personal passion into the performance of their functions; they shame their American colleagues, for there is nothing perfunctory, nothing cold-blooded, nothing gang-like about the spoils and divisions and urgencies that inform their politics. There is still a power in the Latin heritage, enough to make it necessary to conduct legislation in New Mexico in both Spanish and English. It suggests the duality of Indian religion, and is one of the confusions that must be endured by the conqueror.

The American: a dweller in the strange land of his own mastering, he views the land and its survivals with a certain suspicion, an emotional uncertainty that not only permits him to watch the decay of his predecessors with equanimity, but also permits him to subscribe to the dubious beliefs and impulses which his uncertainty generates. This American is possibly a descendant of the pioneers; he is, just as possibly, a newer immigrant from the East. But in either case, he partakes of a life that is no longer solely of the ground he is on. And the mechanistic regime that establishes the tempo of our national life for us now governs him as thoroughly as the Indian used to be governed by the laws of the weather and the rise and fall of the river.

The cowboy, the cattle king, the cattle rustler, and their retinues of gamblers, deserters from the army, and other frontier characters, crossed and recrossed all of the states in Nueva Granada. They made legend wherever they went. Their songs are still alive. The conversion of loneliness on wide prairies under starred skies into music and gun-play, lynchings and heroic drunks; the experiences of travel across thousands of miles behind a herd of red cattle—these things live for us today in the spirit of that time. As every great business has its antisocial competitors, so the cattle industry had its thieves, who would separate and drive away from the main herd enough cows to make a haul of thousands of dollars. War must follow. Regional civil wars burst into flames, flourished with killings, sensational escapes, heroic jobs of strategy and betrayal and nonchalance.

The conventions of such a society were established as normal for those men who found their lives in the West. It became necessary, in viewing them, to suspend the judgments of older cultures and societies. Life conditions must always be met with compromise. The Westerner who followed the pioneer in possession of the land and its offerings had a different kind of hazard to confront from that of the American trail-maker. It was the necessity of bringing with him some sort of social propriety that would seem natural to the life he was living. But the older patterns of society gradually overtook the frontiersman. He built, at immense trouble and expense, a red brick house with white wooden turrets and scroll-saw embellishments, he uneasily subscribed to the foundation of a church, his cartridge belt was hung up among the skins of the animals he had brought down for food in the old days, and the temper of life in the nineteenth century governed a new territory.

Accelerated commerce and the new communication by telegraph replaced the long wagon-trains and overland mail riders. The slow, the enormous knitting of American national life into a series of related regions got under way. Though local mores still ruled, the localities were no longer independent of the rest of the nation in all particulars. Just as the pioneers conquered the Indian and Spanish civilization they found, so the rest of America conquered the pioneers. What we have from their time is ghostly survivals in legend, in song, and in the persons of a few lingering old men and women whose memories resound dimly with the ancient glories, tragedies and hardships and heroisms of the day when life was tentative and intense. It is well, in watching the present unroll before our eyes, to partake of the wholly human significance of the past; to recognize those qualities of heroism and courage and will that brought earlier peoples to new lands and new lives. And it is desirable to love the land, to study its beauties, and to rely upon its comforts of grandeur and natural resource.

—PAUL HORGAN, "The Three Southwestern Peoples"

15. THE TWENTIETH-CENTURY AMERICAN

The editor has here attempted to explain something of the character of the twentieth-century American.

ALTHOUGH still persuaded that his was the best of all countries, the American of the mid-twentieth century was by no means so sure that his was the best of all times, and after he entered the atomic age he could not rid himself of the fear that his world might end not with a whimper but with a bang. His optimism, which persisted, was instinctive rather than rationalized, and he was no longer prepared to insist that the good fortune which he enjoyed, in a war-stricken world, was the reward of virtue rather than of mere geographical isolation. He knew that if there was indeed any such thing as progress it would continue to be illustrated by America, but he was less confident of the validity of the concept than at any previous time in his history.

As he was less zealous for the future, he became more concerned with the past: small families and the cultivation of genealogy seemed to go together. He seemed more conscious of his own history than at any time since the Civil War and, after a brief interval of cynicism and disillusionment in the decade of the twenties, found more satisfaction in its contemplation. In everything but manners and morals he was more inclined to let the past set his standards than had been customary. While it would be an exaggeration to say that he regarded America as a finished product, it was demonstrable that he did not welcome change with his earlier enthusiasm or regard the future as a romantic adventure.

The tendency to trust the past rather than the future and the familiar rather than the original reflected an instinct for conformity that revealed itself in countless ways. Businessmen were expected to conform in matters of dress as well as in manners of thought, and the business suit became almost a uniform, while women, who yearned to look different, came to seem turned out almost by machine process, each with the same make-up, the same accessories, and the same patter. A thousand books on etiquette, a thousand courses in manners and speech and parlor acquirements, proclaimed the universal fear of being different. Slang, which represented an effort to get away from conventional language, became as conventional as the speech which Victorian novelists ascribed to their characters. As society put a premium on conformity, individualism declined and eccentricity all but disappeared. Standardization, induced by the press, the moving pictures, the radio, schools, business, urban life, and a hundred other agencies and intangibles, permeated American life. From Maine to Florida, from Delaware to California, almost all country clubs were alike, and with the spread of the chain store, the filling station, motion-picture palaces, and beauty parlors, towns and cities all over the country came to take on a standardized appearance. With advertisements dictating styles and manners, conversation and amusements, the habits of eating and drinking, the conventions of friendship and of business, and the techniques of love and marriage, nature conformed to commercial art. . . .

Class consciousness expressed itself in countless ways. The country club supplanted the church as the center of social life in most towns, and neither its standards nor its practices were equalitarian. Old World practices like tipping were acquiesced in by self-respecting workers whose predecessors, a century earlier, would have rejected gratuities as an affront; and so far had Americans strayed from their earlier principles that few realized that the giving and the accepting of gratuities implied class distinctions. The word "society," when used by city newspapers, came to mean not the whole population but that element of it that was prosperous and Nordic, and while every graduate of Vassar could be sure of having her wedding duly reported in the eastern newspapers, the graduate of a mid-western college knew that her wedding was of no public interest. Private schools took on something of the importance of public schools in England and, with the founding of Groton School in 1884, began openly to imitate the English. Finishing schools continued to emphasize the study of French for reasons not primarily literary or scholarly, and hotels innocent of French cooking to print their bills of fare in that language. As Americans became increasingly self-conscious about family, names became longer, and double-barreled names not uncommon: it was perhaps more than fortuitous that between Washington and Lincoln only three presidents boasted more than one Christian name, but five between Taft and Truman.

Religion was fortunately free of that class connection which characterized it in England, but the socially ambitious tended to attach themselves to the Episcopal church and sometimes referred to it as the Anglican, while church architecture departed increasingly from its American antecedents and imitated English and French. The declining prestige of England put an end to that revival of colonialism so marked in New England at the close of the nineteenth century, but presentation at court still meant the Court of St. James's and was still thought desirable. America had not yet produced either a Debrett or a Burke, but in most communities the Social Register was read more assiduously than Who's Who and carried more weight. . . .

Vulgarization proclaimed itself most blatantly in the passing of reticence. Almost every newspaper published advice to the lovelorn, and one omniscient mother-confessor answered three thousand letters a week. Psychoanalysis went on the air, and troubled women told a gaping audience things their mothers would not have confided to their grandmothers. There was a vast palaver about sex, and books that had once been read covertly behind the barn were distributed by reputable book clubs. Buchmanism enjoyed some popularity in prosperous circles and confession magazines in less prosperous, while other magazines devoted to a rehearsal of the most intimate details of the lives of public figures boasted circulations running into the millions, and every schoolboy knew what kind of soap his favorite actress used in her bath. Publicity came to be regarded as good and even bad publicity as better than none, and the socially elect, who had once taken pride in keeping their names out of newspapers, were now avid to put them in. Reporters, ever notorious for their prying ways, were delighted to find that they could count on the cooperation of their victims, and though Woodrow Wilson had smashed the camera of a newspaper photographer bent on invading the privacy of his family, his successors dealt more amiably with the press. Ivy Lee had taught business the value of good public relations, and soon politicians and film stars had their public relations agents, universities that could not afford adequate teachers' salaries found money for public relations offices, and churches arranged that God should have a good press. General Sherman had thrown reporters bodily out of his headquarters, but during World War II the Army and Navy thought it advisable to recommend themselves to a public for whose existence they were fighting.

Nothing, perhaps, was more striking than the change in the character of American humor. Old-fashioned comic books all but disappeared— the *Samantha at Saratoga* and *Peck's Bad Boy* type—and while it is easy to imagine Franklin D. Roosevelt regaling his Cabinet with the latest *New Yorker* story it is difficult to suppose him reading to them from Artemus Ward. The nineteenth-century *Life, Judge,* and *Puck* bore a strong family resemblance to *Punch*: the English weekly persisted, through the decades, along its familiar groove, but *The New Yorker* departed radically from its American predecessors. Nineteenth-century humor had been rural, expansive, exaggerated, amiable, and familiar, its purpose, Constance Rourke wrote, "that of creating fresh bonds, a new unity, the semblance of a society and the rounded completion of an American type." That of the twentieth century was urban, pointed, sophisticated, malicious, and startling, designed to wound rather than to entertain, to divide and destroy rather than to unite and complete. The shift from Artemus Ward and Petroleum V. Nasby and Bill Nye to Ring Lardner and Peter Arno and Damon Runyon was a shift from the verbal and gregarious to the literary and private, from the long story and the tall tale to the anecdote and the epigram, from dialect and slapstick to cleverness and subtlety, and from the robust to the morbid; it was almost a shift from good humor to bad. Mark Twain had been disillusioned, but he was careful to keep his disillusionment to himself or to books designed for posthumous publication, but from O. Henry to Ring Lardner, twentieth-century humor was shot through and through with disillusionment. There were exceptions, of course. Donald Ogden Stewart's *Parody Outline of History* was in the Bill Nye tradition; Robert Benchley often indulged in good-natured farce; James Thurber laughed at rather than indulged in disillusionment; E. B. White, along with much kindliness and charm, displayed that indignation against cruelty and meanness that had distinguished Mark Twain.

Yet American humor between the wars was on the whole barbed and malicious. More, it was often sensational, fantastic, and sadistic, and in its preoccupation with sex it came closer to the French than to its English and American antecedents. The "funnies" of an earlier day had attempted comedy; their successors, the "comics," abandoned themselves to violence and fantasy. Literature, too, was no longer content with the exploitation of the homely situations and familiar characters that had sufficed an earlier generation and continued to suffice such English writers as E. F. Benson and George Birmingham and Humphrey Pakington. Of the major literary figures only Steinbeck continued some of the tradition of frontier humor, while Holmes and Howells and Mark Twain had no successors in prose nor James Russell Lowell or Charles Godfrey Leland in poetry. Politics had always been the natural butt of American humor, and though cartoonists and H. L. Mencken continued to exploit it, Mr. Dooley was the last of the commentators whose observations seemed destined to live.

As the comic story disappeared, the humorous poem withered away, and the funnies turned to fantasies, old-fashioned comedy found a successor in the films, and Harold Lloyd, Charlie Chaplin, and Laurel and Hardy were the true heirs of Bill Nye and Josh Billings. But the films showed the same tendency to evolve from simple slapstick to more sophisticated comedy. Thus Chaplin, greatest of the comedians, made his later films vehicles for social criticism, while the Marx brothers indulged in satire. Radio humor, which nightly convulsed its millions, lingered on in the earlier tradition, as did the joke books which so faithfully revived Joe Miller, but both were more obvious and less innocent than the music-hall or the cracker-box humor of the nineteenth century. . . .

Changes in the habits, practices, and morals of the twentieth-century

American were, on the whole, consistent with those in the realm of ideas. With the growing emphasis on conformity, eccentricity was no longer so amiably indulged: the passion for creating "characters" which the more popular novelists showed was itself evidence of a felt need. It would be misleading to insist that Americans were less self-reliant than formerly, but certainly society as a whole was far more interdependent, and with interdependence went some impatience with independence. The nineteenth-century farmer and craftsman had not needed to rationalize his enterprise into a philosophy, but the practical disappearance of any enterprise really private brought, as so often, a nostalgic rationalization. Americans had always been gregarious, and even with the inevitable associations of urban life and the growth of self-confidence, the habit did not abate. If lodges and clubs attracted them less, business and professional associations claimed them more insistently, and they could scarcely read a book or listen to music or take a walk except in groups. Life became increasingly regimented. Regimentation was not, as political critics would have it, a product of government regulation or of a Communist conspiracy but of a technological economy, and it was, perhaps, inevitable. The necessity of living in the same kind of houses, doing the same kind of work, using the same machinery, reading the same newspapers, was paralleled by the desire to use the same soap, eat the same breakfast food, laugh at the same radio jokes, admire the same movie stars, and digest the same magazine articles as did everybody else. . . .

Prosperity and machinery made possible a degree of self-indulgence unknown in a more exacting age, and it was the opinion of many foreign observers that not only the women and children but the men as well were pampered. Certainly there was no asceticism in American life and little self-denial. The second World War imposed but few restrictions and no austerity upon the American people, yet Americans did not, on the whole, react well to such restrictions as were required, and the rationing of such commodities as meat and gasoline was widely evaded. Americans were generous, but a test such as the admission of a few hundred thousand displaced persons—who might possibly compete in the labor market or demand houses or spread alien doctrines—found them inhospitable and grudging. Children took parental support for granted well into their twenties, and it was far more common for young couples to be supported by their parents or even for young men to be supported by their wives than it had been half a century earlier. Most Americans took for granted, too, comforts unknown to all but the rich in other countries. They overheated their houses, insisted upon a car and a radio, consumed incredible quantities of soft drinks, ice cream, candy, and cigarettes, and spent enough annually on liquor and cosmetics to have supported the whole population of less fortunate countries. Luxury and self-indulgence should, perhaps, have led to debility, and those who still subscribed to the Puritan virtues were constantly recalling the latter days of the Roman Empire, but no one familiar with the conduct of American soldiers in the second World War would argue that American youth was soft or effeminate or that America was suffering from a failure of nerve.

Twentieth-century America, even more than nineteenth, seemed to be a woman's country. The supremacy of woman could be read in the statistics of property ownership, insurance, education, or literature, or in the advertisements of any popular magazine. Women ran the schools and the churches, they determined what would appear in the magazines and the movies and what would be heard over the radio. As many girls as boys attended college, and women made their way successfully into almost every profession. There were a hundred magazines designed especially for their entertainment or edification, and among them some with the largest circulation, while most metropolitan newspapers had a page for women and every radio station a series of programs directed exclusively to their supposed needs. As women spent most of the money, the overwhelming body of advertisements was addressed to them, and advertisers found it advisable to introduce the feminine motive even, or especially, where they hoped to attract men. Traditionally women had ruled the home, but only in America did they design it, build it, furnish it, direct its activities, and fix its standards. Most American children knew more of their mothers' than of their fathers' families, and it was the opinion of many observers of World War II that the silver cord bound American youth more firmly than the youth of any other land. It was appropriate enough that an American, Lester Ward, should have propounded the theory of the natural superiority of the female sex which he called gynecocracy, and American experience appeared to validate the theory.

There was a change, almost imperceptible, in the standards of sportsmanship. The professional spirit largely supplanted the amateur, college athletics were invaded by professionalism, football and basketball became big business. Professional sports themselves were marred by one scandal after another, while evasions of the amateur requirements by those who contended for amateur titles became so commonplace as to cease to be a scandal. As the commercial element entered sports, earning power became more important than the game itself, and the game became primarily a spectacle. Colleges and universities hired coaches who were paid as much as their presidents, spent millions on stadia, bought or seduced players, and retained them, as often as not, without any reference to academic qualifications. President Eliot of Harvard had objected to intercollegiate football because he discovered that the attack was directed against the weakest point in the opposition line: the objection was creditable, and was not voiced by his successors. Where English spectators applauded the play, Americans cheered the team, and where English applause was spontaneous, American cheering was organized, and the "cheer leader" was unique to America. Standards of sportsmanship took on something of a class tinge, vindicating the interpretation which Veblen had advanced in his *Theory of the Leisure Class*. Polo, sailing, riding, skiing, and even hunting and fishing were associated with the upper classes and governed by formal rules, and those who indulged in them were expected to observe both a ritual and a ceremonial habit, while baseball, which became the national pastime, ceased to be a major college sport. Yet the habit of fair play was deeply ingrained, and standards of sportsmanship remained high. The phrase "good sport"—all but untranslatable into other languages—still held connotations flattering to the American character. The tendency to regard both politics and business as a game persisted, and if this suggested immaturity, it implied, too, a wholesome willingness to abide by the rules of the game, acquiesce in decisions, and accept defeat cheerfully.

—Henry Steele Commager, *The American Mind*

2

The Land

AMERICAN ideas and institutions did not grow in a vacuum. They are the product of inheritance, to be sure, but they are the product of environment as well, and of a particular historical experience. The English inheritance, it is relevant to note, did not produce the same results in Canada, or Australia or New Zealand, for instance, as in America, and the differences can be ascribed to the influence of environment and of a history that was itself partly a product of that environment.

The American environment is in many respects unique, unprecedented, and unparalleled. Never before in recorded history had so spacious and rich an area been thrown open to men, nor will anything like this ever happen again in the history of our globe. For the New World discovered by the Old in the fifteenth and sixteenth centuries, and thrown open to settlement in the following three centuries, was not only the largest undeveloped area to which civilized man had ever had access; it was also, as events were to prove, the richest in resources of soil, water, timber, minerals, flora and fauna.

We are apt to miss the significance of some historical facts because of their very obviousness and familiarity. No less important than the spaciousness and richness of the American scene is the fact that the land to which Europeans came was a wilderness, and that white men were over three centuries in conquering that wilderness and converting it to civilization. The spaciousness of the American environment was at once a challenge, an invitation, and a temptation. It operated like a magnet to draw emigrants from the Old World—over thirty-five million of them in the century after 1820—and it operated similarly to draw millions already here from the East to successive Wests. This westward movement from frontier to frontier is a significant factor in American history from the earliest settlements to the present. We think of the westward movement in terms of Daniel Boone and Davy Crockett, the covered wagon

54

and the gold rush, but the problem of shifting population from the Atlantic to the Pacific was a continuous one, and it was the decade of the 1940's that witnessed the largest westward migration in the whole of our history.

In a sense the incomparable richness of the continent, the variety and the accessibility of its resources, went to the collective head of the American people. There was land enough in America, said Jefferson in 1801, for our descendants "to the thousandth and thousandth generation," and this before he acquired Louisiana and sent Lewis and Clark overland to the Pacific! Yet within only three generations the Census Bureau could announce the disappearance of the frontier line, and within another generation the problem of conservation of land itself became acute.

It is no exaggeration to say that the conservation of natural resources is, and has been for half a century, the paramount domestic issue before the American people. To be sure, its significance has not always been appreciated. Public attention has been fastened now on the tariff, now on Civil Service reform, now on the money question, now on the regulation of railways or corporations. Yet all the time the basic issue has been whether in another century or two there would be an America left —or whether it would have washed down the rivers into the oceans. Theodore Roosevelt was the first President fully to appreciate the urgency of the problem of conservation, and to do something about it. His cousin, Franklin D. Roosevelt, was the first to embark upon a comprehensive program designed not only to save but to restore threatened resources. Over the past half-century a little has been accomplished; much remains to be done.

The excerpts we give here tell something of the role of land and resources in the making of modern America, and they attempt to suggest the impact of these not only on the economy but on the imagination as well. They tell us how the richness, the beauty, the spaciousness, the infinite variety of flora and fauna struck the first settlers, and then generations of settlers moving westward. They tell us something of the wonder of the American land—a land continental in dimensions and in variety: the broad sections of East, South, and West, and the complex regions within each of these. They tell us of the role the ever moving frontier has played in our history, and something particularly about that "most American part of America," the West. They tell, too, of the hazards and difficulties with which Nature confronted man as he moved into the interior: the towering mountains, the turbulent streams, the primeval forests, the swamps and marshes and lakes, the vast prairies and the arid plains, the dangers from fire and from insects and animals. And they give us finally the story of the ravaging of the land, of our dawning realization of the imperative necessity for conservation, and of what has been accomplished in that realm.

1. THE SPACIOUSNESS AND DIVERSITY OF THE AMERICAN SCENE

Perhaps the hardest thing for Europeans to remember about America is to think of it in terms of a continent rather than of the average European country. Sometimes Americans themselves have some trouble remembering this. It would be an education for all of us if we were to move about, for a change, on foot or on horseback; then at least we would begin to realize what distances meant to our forebears, and how formidable were the obstacles which Nature presented to them. Then, too, we might realize more than we do the beauty and diversity of the American scene. There is no better appreciation of these things than that in the opening chapter of Frank E. Hill's What Is American?—*a book characterized by the sensitiveness of a poet and the learning of a scholar.*

FROM the first the land convinced the Americans of its size. Even the settlements established along the Atlantic coast covered a great expanse of territory in comparison with John Smith's England or Sieur de la Tonty's France. And the Americans were aware of areas beyond the Allegheny Mountains which were the westward wall to their first homes. There an immense empire stretched to the Mississippi. After they had won their independence in the late eighteenth century, they found this empire theirs. They knew also that the land extended farther still to the west, and in 1803 they bought a large portion of it. They were fully conscious now of the immensity of their domain. . . .

The sheer amount of the land stood forth now, emphatic. There were more than three million square miles of it. It swept across the entire continent of North America, and north and south for twenty-five degrees of latitude. And the broad oceans to east and west and the arm of ocean to the south opened outlets for trade in three directions that seemed to extend the dimensions of the soil. Even on the north a chain of five fresh water lakes, gleaming vast and blue, seemed further to augment size.

And the size of the land worked upon the Americans in a more intimate way. It worked not only as a whole but through the largeness of its various parts. There were for example the mountains. First the settlers had found a long mountain chain following the Atlantic coast. Twice the length of England and Scotland combined it was, and as broad as either. Later they came to know the much higher and broader range running parallel to the Pacific—an area almost as great as all of Europe outside Russia.

The land showed them plains to match the mountains. There was the great plain running for two thousand miles from range to range. And there were many lesser valleys: Shenandoah, Mohawk, Flathead, Columbia River. Most of these were vast in scale compared with smaller valleys of western Europe.

The rivers pouring from the two mountain ranges were enormous too compared with what men called rivers in England or France. This was true, as Captain Smith had noticed, even of the eastern coastal plain. But the rivers falling inland from east or west to drain the great central valley—the Ohio, the Missouri and the Mississippi—were a brood of giant rivers, stirring the Americans with a new sense of vastness. So with the great lakes to the north, and, when they came to know them, the desert lands of the far west.

The land was at work on them with its climate as well as its size.

It was a different climate from western Europe's. We see now the factors which govern it: the land in shape a ragged rectangle, broader at top than base, with the high rims to east and west making the center a basin; the seas sending up vapor as clouds to be drawn inland; the mountain ranges catching much of it in rain or snow, storing it, sending it downward east or west in mighty streams; the clouds often riding on beyond the ranges or rolling northward unimpeded from the Gulf to scatter moisture over the great valley.

All this became known gradually, and with it came the knowledge of variety of climate. In part this was due to rain. Along the southern gulf the rains fell heavily; so also on the northwestern coasts. On the interior snow and rain fell in moderate amounts over the greater part of the land, but on the far western plains and some plateau regions of the western mountains they fell scantily; in a few desert areas almost not at all. . . .

Yet a certain identity ran through all this variety. Extremes, for instance. Almost everywhere the difference between the greatest heat of the year and its greatest cold was marked. . . .

There was another aspect of American climate: changeability. From week to week the weather in America was seen to alter decisively. Heat and cold, wind and rain came in "waves." And these waves, the Americans perceived, were clear cut—whatever the dominant weather element it was intense, and its job once finished, it was quickly gone. A kind of electric briskness of movement prevailed—emphasized often by thunderstorms and strong winds, and even by occasional cyclones and tornadoes in parts of the great valley. This too was different from the suffusing rains and softer sunshine and gentler changes the Americans had known in their Europe.

The Americans found too that it was a bright, clear climate. Even where the rains fell heavily they were intensified and massed, and in general almost half of the fall was at night. So the days in the American land were full of sun and a kind of crisp, almost metallic shine unknown in the European world.

Born of the interaction between great sea areas and a great expanse of land with mountain and valley of varied contour, the weather of the new world had variety; but the power and decision of big earth elements ran through most of its forms. It was almost everywhere a climate of brilliance and decision and energy. . . .

Out of such aspects of the land came a larger and more subtle aspect. This was a certain look of earth. The great dimensions of mountain, lake, river and valley, the masses of unfamiliar trees and shrubs and grasses made an appearance emphatically not the European appearance. Instead of broom or heather or forest of oak and holly or field of daffodil, Americans saw goldenrod, redbud and pecan and redwood, sage and chaparral and yucca flower and orange-flamed poppy. They looked also on sharp accentuations of size and energy set as if for symbols. There were the sculptured domes of Yosemite, and its waterfall plunging more than a sheer half mile from cliff to plain. There were the painted chasm of the Colorado, the eerie sun-drenched blue of the Great Salt Lake, the spume of Yellowstone geysers, the thundering power of Niagara. All this made a world unlike Europe's, as it was also unlike Asia's or Africa's or Australia's. For although Americans, beginning to sense their land, have said that it was more like China or Russia than like France or England, its true character and look are far from any one of them. America differs sharply from China or Russia or Australia or Canada in profoundly important ways: in its relationship to the oceans, or its basic contours, or its rainfall or river distribution, or its position on the earth's surface. So it has the clearest of titles to its own quality. Some Europeans have seen this more clearly than Americans. "Alien, foreign, different," announces Hilaire Belloc. "Not European, not African, not the old world at all."

— FRANK ERNEST HILL, *What Is American?*

2. THE RHYTHM OF FLOWING WATERS

Americans take their rivers for granted, as they take most natural features for granted. Perhaps only those familiar with the streams and rivers of England or France or Germany can appreciate how remarkable are American rivers. But it is not only for their dimensions or their beauty that American rivers are remarkable; it is rather because they so largely determined the course of our history. The rhythm of pioneer life, as Constance Skinner here tells us, was the rhythm of flowing water. Where the rivers flowed into the sea, towns sprang up, and so too at the fall line, where the water came tumbling down from piedmont to coast. Long before there were any roads, pioneers moved into the interior on the bosom of rivers, and one reason that the English stayed close to the Atlantic Coast while the French swarmed into the far interior was that the rivers from Maine to Georgia offered no ingress into the West, while the river-lake system of New France opened up into the Ohio-Mississippi Valley. After the pioneers had conquered the Appalachians and debouched into the forest and prairie region beyond, much of their life was controlled by the intricate network of the Mississippi River system—surely the most remarkable network of rivers anywhere on the globe. But let Miss Skinner herself tell this story. The

essay from which these pages are taken was written by her as an intro-
duction to the Rivers of America *series—a series of some forty or fifty*
volumes designed to tell the story of America in terms of its rivers.

WHEN American folk have troubles which do not end swiftly,
they begin presently to examine their own sources as a nation
and their own story as a people. They forget about these in good times.
But when they are hit they remember that a new story, like no other
in the world, was carried in chapters and cantos across the American
wilderness on a strong rhythm and they catch at phrases to console and
encourage themselves. . . .

The natural rhythm moving the pioneer life of America forward was
the rhythm of flowing water. It is as the story of American rivers that
the folk sagas will be told. . . .

The historical part played by rivers in the folk life is evident but it
may be a new idea to many that geography itself determined that
Americans should first live on and by the rivers.

Here the map of North America unrolls, and comes into the discussion; hinting that Nature foresaw the day when old world folk would
feel the need of a new world, and the new world call for inhabitants,
and therefore set about her topographical modeling of the major part
of the continent, between the Rio Grande and the Arctic sea, with accessibility as her chief aim. She traced large rivers in deep long lines
north and south, such as Mississippi and Mackenzie, and east and west,
as Rio Grande and Missouri. Others she drew with a fanciful touch;
like Ohio and Columbia, which mark the map in large, irregular loops
with an angle or two. There seems to be little logic in their designs yet,
on their careless rambles—Columbia is more erratic than careless—
they make contact with scores of smaller streams and so gather huge
territories about them. The modern map is too crowded to do justice
to the free beauty of the watercourses. They should be studied from
the early pen-and-ink maps of the fur traders, who set down little else;
since beauty wherever found is significant, and nothing is more so, and
these charts show all the land traversed, and its remotest bounds
linked, with rhythm, power, and grace. Philip Turnor's map, the first
ever drawn of the beaver-hunters' canoe trails in the Northwest, is before
me. The slender curving lines of the rivers, with the lakes set in like

jewels, make a design a master goldsmith might choose for an empress's necklace.

In the heyday of the beaver trade, rivers opened most of the territory between the Arctic coast and the Mexican border to the daring, singing voyageurs of the fur fleets. There was the famous Canadian route, traveled yearly from Montreal by the St. Lawrence, Ottawa, Great Lakes, and Lake Winnipeg to the Saskatchewan, which is commonly said to empty into Lake Winnipeg, but which, in reality, flows through its northern end and continues under the name of Nelson to Hudson Bay. From New Orleans the voyageurs went by the Mississippi and the Missouri, the true Upper Mississippi, to Montana: or ascended the Mississippi to its Minnesota headwaters, crossed into Canada by Rainy River, turned west through Lake of the Woods and English and Red rivers into Lake Winnipeg, and out again by either the Nelson, or the Hayes, thus following the whole of the water chain which connects New Orleans, La., with York Factory on Hudson Bay.

Mackenzie opened two new trails whereby traders in canoes could go from Montreal to the Pacific coast, having entered British Columbia by Peace River and to the polar ocean by Slave River, Slave Lake, and the Mackenzie. If they had a mind to go to the mouth of the Mackenzie from the mouth of the Mississippi they could do so, by water and the portages which were a part of all canoe travel.

When the trade was carried west of the Rockies, the favorite route led through the mountains from the headwaters of the Saskatchewan to that bizarre but navigable north angle of the Columbia River thrust up into British Columbia. From this point the voyageurs might choose to follow the river to Astoria at its mouth; or to swing eastward again by the passes, coming out in time on the Missouri at Three Forks and going on from there to St. Louis or New Orleans.

These were the routes of the great journeys, but the singing voyageurs found many other water trails, branching off from Ohio and Mississippi—the Arkansas, Illinois, Red, Canadian (named for them)—and all the smaller rivers lacing the western lands. They had no thought of settlement, their aims were fur and freedom, as they flashed their paddles in every navigable stream and loosed more than a thousand new songs on the air to the rhythms of new waters. Yet little as they thought it (and how much less would they have desired it!) they were opening a continent to the Folk. By the shining, running rivers, which had inspired men to sing in the wilderness, entered "a great number of weake and distressed soules, scattered, poor and persecuted," to grow strong and confident upon their banks. In which connection, let us recall that long before voyageurs caroled of "good wind and swift water," an Indian poet sang prophetically:—

> Bright with flashing light the distant line
> Runs before us, swiftly runs,
> River runs, winding, flowing through the land . . .
> Water brings to us the gift of strength.

. . . .The American nation came to birth upon the rivers. Has the fact colored our temperament? Are we a restless people because motion flowed by us continuously in our youth? Are we optimistic, eager, imaginative, daring, and even recklessly experimental, because of the beckoning of the tides "bright with flashing light" which ran swiftly past our known shores into domains beyond our vision? Are we in any part what we are, because of rivers? Possibly only a poet would answer yes. Poets have written of rivers and men, blending the spiritual overtones of both: Spoon River in our time, Kubla Khan and Sohrab and Rustum of an earlier period. Poets had discerned the power of Nature to influence thought and character long before the geographers of our day—more power to them!—began to contend with the economists for the soul of man.

—CONSTANCE LINDSAY SKINNER, "Rivers and American Folk"

3. "THE EXTREME FRUITFULNESS OF THAT COUNTRY"

We have met Robert Beverley before, describing the people of colonial Virginia. Here we have him at his best, telling of the richness of the soil, the variety of its products, the advantages of husbandry in the New World. "I have seen," he tells us, "more Grapes upon one single Vine than wou'd load a London Cart" and we feel that we are already at the beginning of the Paul Bunyan legends. Everything, it seemed, grew in America, everything thrived; hogs "swarm like Vermine upon the Earth" and even the bees gave more honey than the bees of England.

This note of astonishment, almost of ecstasy, was to recur again and again and again in accounts of America. You can read it in the America letters that newcomers wrote back home; you can read it in William Cobbett's accounts of the groaning tables of the American farmers; you can read it in later writers like Bryce and Brogan, in a hundred journalists, in a thousand travel letters.

Of the Natural Product of Virginia, and the
Advantages of Their Husbandry

THE extream fruitfulness of that Country, has been sufficiently shewn . . . and I think we may justly add, that in that particularly it is not exceeded by any other. No Seed is Sowed there, but it thrives, and most Plants are improved, by being Transplanted thither. And yet there's very little Improvement made among them, nor any thing us'd in Traffique, but Tobacco.

Besides all the natural Productions mention'd in the Second Book, you may take notice, that Apples from the Seed, never degenerate into Crabs, or Wildings there, but produce the same, or better Fruit than the Mother-Tree, (which is not so in *England,*) and are wonderfully improved by Grafting and Managing; yet there are very few Planters that graft at all, and much fewer that take any care to get choice Fruits.

The Fruit-Trees are wonderfully quick of growth, so that in six or seven years time from the Planting, a Man may bring an Orchard to bear in great plenty, from which he may make store of good Cyder, or distill great quantities of Brandy; for the Cyder is very strong, and yields abundance of in Spirit. Yet they have very few, that take any care at all for an Orchard; nay, many that have good Orchards, are so negligent of them, as to let them go to ruine, and expose the Trees to be torn, and barked by the Catle.

Peaches, Nectarines, and Apricocks, as well as Plums and Cherries, grow there upon Standard Trees. They commonly bear in three years from the Stone, and thrive so exceedingly, that they seem to have no need of Grafting or Inoculating, if any Body would be so good a Husband; and truly I never heard of any that did Graft either Plum, Nectarine, Peach or Apricock in that Country.

Peaches and Nectarines I believe to be Spontaneous somewhere or other on that Continent; for the *Indians* have, and ever had greater variety, and finer sorts of them than the *English*. The best sort of these cling to the Stone, and will not come off clear, which they call Plum-Nectarines, and Plum-Peaches, or Cling-Stones. Some of these are 12 or 13 Inches in the Girt. These sorts of Fruits are raised so easily there, that some good Husbands plant great Orchards of them, purposely for their Hogs; and others make a Drink of them, which they call Mobby, and either drink it as Cyder, or Distill it off for Brandy. This makes the best Spirit next to Grapes.

Grape-Vines of the *English* Stock, as well as those of their own Production, bear most abundantly, if they are suffered to run near the Ground, and increase very kindly by Slipping; yet very few have them at all in their Gardens, much less indeavour to improve them by cutting or laying. Indeed my Curiosity the last year, caused me to lay some of the white Muscadine, which came of a Stock removed thither from *England*, and they increased by this method to Admiration: I likewise set several Slips of the cuttings of the same Vine, and the Major part of the Sets bore Grapes in perfection the first year, I remember I had seven full Bunches from one of them.

When a single Tree happens in clearing the Ground, to be left standing with a Vine upon it, open to the Sun and Air; that Vine generally produces as much as 4 or five others, that remain in the Woods. I have seen in this case, more Grapes upon one single Vine, than wou'd load a *London* Cart. And for all this, the People never remove any of them into their Gardens, but content themselves throughout the whole Country, with the Grapes they find thus wild; much less can they be expected to attempt the making of Wine or Brandy from the Grape.

The Almond, Pomgranate and Fig, ripen there very well, and yet there are not ten People in the Country, that have any of them in their Gardens, much less endeavour to preserve any of them for future spending, or to propagate them to make a Trade.

A Garden is no where sooner made than there, either for Fruits, or Flowers. Tulips from the Seed-flower the second year at farthest. All sorts of Herbs have there a perfection in their flavour, beyond what I ever tasted in a more *Northern* Climate. And yet they han't many Gardens in the Country, fit to bear that name.

All sorts of *English* Grain thrive, and increase there, as well as in any other part of the World as for Example, Wheat, Barley, Oats, Rye,

Peas, Rape, &c. And yet they don't make a Trade of any of them. Their Peas indeed, are troubled with Wivels, which eat a Hole in them: But this Hole does neither dammage the Seed, nor make the Peas unfit for Boiling. And such as are sow'd late, and gather'd after *August*, are clear of that Inconvenience.

It is thought too much for the same Man, to make the Wheat, and grind it, bolt it, and bake it himself. And it is too great a charge for every Planter, who is willing to sow Barley, to build a Malt-House, and Brew-House too, or else to have no benefit of his Barley; nor will it answer, if he wou'd be at the Charge. These things can never be expected from a single Family: But if they had cohabitations, it might be thought worth attempting. Neither as they are now settled, can they find any certain Market for their other Grain, which if they had Towns, would be quite otherwise.

Rice has been tried there, and is found to grow as well, as in *Carolina*, or in any other part of the Earth: But it labours under the same inconvenience, the want of a Community, to husk and clean it; and after all, to take it off the Planters Hands.

I have related at large in the first Book, how Flax, Hemp, Cotton, and the Silk-Worms have thriven there, in the several essays made upon them; how formerly there was Incouragement given for making of Linnen, Silk, &c. and how all Persons not performing several things towards produceing of them were put under a Fine: But now all Incouragement of such things is taken away, and People are not only suffer'd to neglect them, but such as do go about them, are discouraged by their Governor, according to the Maxim laid down in the Memorials before recited.

Silk-grass is there spontaneous in many places, and may be cut several times in a Year. I need not mention what Advantage may be made of so useful a Plant, whose Fibres are as fine as Flax, and much stronger than Hemp. Mr. *Purchas* tells us, in his *Fourth Pilgrim*, Page 1786, That in the first Discovery of this part of the World, they presented Q. *Elizabeth* with a Piece of Grogram that had been made of it. And yet to this Day they make no manner of use of this Plant, no, not so much as the *Indians* did, before the *English* came among them, who then made their Baskets, Fishing Nets, and Lines, of it.

The Sheep increase well, and bear good Fleeces, but they generally are suffer'd to be torn off their Backs by Briers, and Bushes, instead of being shorn, or else are left rotting upon the Dunghil with their Skins.

Bees thrive there abundantly, and will very easily yield to the careful Huswife, two Crops of Honey in a Year, and besides lay up a Winter-store sufficient to preserve their Stocks.

The Beeves, when any Care is taken of them in the Winter, come to great Perfection. They have noble Marshes there, which, with the Charge of draining only, would make as fine Pastures as any in the World; and yet there is not an hundred Acres of Marsh drained through-out the whole Country.

Hogs swarm like Vermine upon the Earth, and are often accounted such, insomuch that when an Inventory of any considerable Man's Estate is taken by the Executors, the Hogs are left out, and not listed in the Appraisement. The Hogs run where they list, and find their own Support in the Woods, without any Care of the Owner; and in many Plantations it is well, if the Proprietor can find and catch the Pigs, or any part of a Farrow, when they are young, to mark them; for if there be any markt in a Gang of Hogs, they determine the Property of the rest, because they seldom miss their Gangs; but as they are bred in Company, so they continue to the End.

The Woods produce great Variety of Incense and sweet Gums, which distil from several Trees; as also Trees bearing Honey, and Sugar, as before was mention'd: Yet there's no use made of any of them, either for Profit or Refreshment.

All sorts of Naval Stores may be produced there, as Pitch, Tar, Rosin, Turpentine, Plank, Timber, and all sorts of Masts, and Yards, besides Sails, Cordage, and Iron, and all these may be transported, by an easy Water-Carriage.

These and a Thousand other Advantages that Country naturally affords, which its Inhabitants make no manner of use of. They can see their Naval Stores daily benefit other People, who send thither to build ships; while they, instead of promoting such Undertakings among themselves, and easing such as are willing to go upon them, allow them no manner of Encouragement, but rather the contrary. They receive no Benefit nor Refreshment from the Sweets, and precious things they have growing amongst them, but make use of the Industry of *England* for all such things.

What Advantages do they see the Neighbouring Plantations make of their Grain and Provisions, while they, who can produce them infinitely better, not only neglect the making a Trade thereof, but even a necessary Provision against an accidental Scarcity, contenting themselves with a supply of Food from hand to mouth, so that if it should please God, to send them an unseasonable Year, there wou'd not be found in the Country, Provision sufficient to support the People for three Months extraordinary.

By reason of the unfortunate Method of the Settlement, and want of Cohabitation, they cannot make a beneficial use of their Flax, Hemp, Cotten, Silk, Silkgrass, and Wool, which might otherwise supply their Necessities, and leave the Produce of Tobacco to enrich them, when a gainful Market can be found for it.

Thus they depend altogether upon the Liberality of Nature, without endeavouring to improve its Gifts, by Art or Industry. They spunge upon the Blessings of a warm Sun, and a fruitful Soil, and almost grutch the Pains of gathering in the Bounties of the Earth. I should be asham'd to publish this slothful Indolence of my Countrymen, but that I hope it will rouse them out of their Lethargy, and excite them to make the most of all those happy Advantages which Nature has given them; and if it does this, I am sure they will have the Goodness to forgive me.

—ROBERT BEVERLEY, *The History and Present State of Virginia*, 1705

4. "A HIDEOUS AND DESOLATE WILDERNESS"

Obviously the whole of America was not like Virginia; certainly Cape Cod in the winter looked very different from anything that the Pilgrims had been accustomed to in England or in Holland. It seemed to them, indeed, a "hideous and desolate wilderness," and all the more so because they did not know how to protect themselves against the American winters or how to take advantage of the resources of the American waters and soil. We must keep in mind this side of the story as well as that described by Robert Beverley, for notwithstanding the abounding richness of America, groups of pioneers were to meet hunger and want and cold and disease again and again—to meet them and overcome them.

We have here another passage from Bradford's History of Plimoth Plantation—*one of the most moving and eloquent passages in that noble book.*

BEING thus arrived in a good harbor and brought safe to land, they fell upon their knees and blessed the God of Heaven who had brought them over the vast and furious ocean and delivered them from all the perils and miseries thereof, again to set their feet on the firm and stable earth, their proper element.

But here I cannot but stay and make a pause and stand half amazed at this poor people's present condition; and so I think will the reader too, when he well considers the same. Being thus past the vast ocean and a sea of troubles before in their preparation (as may be remembered by that which went before), they had now no friends to welcome them, nor inns to entertain or refresh their weatherbeaten bodies, no houses or much less towns to repair to, to seek for succor. It is recorded in Scripture as a mercy to the apostle and his shipwrecked company, the barbarians showed them no small kindness in refreshing them, but these savage barbarians, when they met with them (as after will appear) were readier to fill their sides full of arrows than otherwise. And for the season, it was winter, and they that know the winters of that country know them to be sharp and violent and subject to cruel and fierce storms, dangerous to travel to known places, much more to search an unknown coast. Besides, what could they see but a hideous and desolate wilderness full of wild beasts and wild men? And what multitudes there might be of them they knew not. If it be said they had a ship to succor them, it is true; but what heard they daily from the master and company but that with speed they should look out a place with their shallop where they would be at some near distance; for the season was such as he would not stir from thence till a safe harbor was discovered by them where they would be and he might go without danger; and that victuals consumed apace but he must and would keep sufficient for themselves and their return. Yea, it was muttered by some that if they got not a place in time they would turn them and their goods ashore and leave them. Let it also be considered what weak hopes of supply and succor they left behind them that might bear up their minds in this sad condition and trials they were under; and they could not but be very small. It is true, indeed, the affections and love of their brethren at Leyden was cordial and entire towards them, but they had little power to help them or themselves; and how the case stood between them and the merchants at their coming away hath already been declared. What could now sustain them but the spirit of God and His grace? May not and ought not the children of these fathers rightly say: *Our fathers were Englishmen which came over this great ocean, and were ready to perish in this wilderness; but they cried unto the Lord, and he heard their voice and looked on their adversity, etc. Let them therefore praise the Lord, because he is good and his mercies endure forever. Yea, let them which have been redeemed of the Lord show how he hath delivered them from the hand of the oppressor. When they wandered in the desert wilderness out of the way, and found no city to dwell in, both hungry and thirsty, their soul was overwhelmed in them. Let them confess before the Lord his loving kindness, and his wonderful works before the sons of men.*

—WILLIAM BRADFORD, *History of Plimoth Plantation,* 1630

5. "AMERICAN AREAS WITHOUT A TRACE OF EUROPE'S SOIL"

Most of our major writers have been very conscious of the American landscape—Irving, Cooper, Hawthorne, Thoreau, Simms, Mark Twain, to mention but a few; none, it is safe to say, has felt it so deeply or interpreted it so variously and so beautifully as Walt Whitman. Poem after poem comes to mind—"Broad Potomac's Shore," or "By Blue Ontario's Shore," or "O Pioneers!" or "Song of the Redwood-Tree." What is interesting is to find the same fervor and much the same poetic expression in his prose. These passages on the prairies and the plains, the Colorado Mountains and the Mississippi River, were written during or immediately after a trip to Colorado in 1879. They express much the same philosophy that can be read in the "Preface" to Leaves of Grass of 1855 —the notion that "these states are the amplest poem."

THE PRAIRIES AND GREAT PLAINS IN POETRY
(*After traveling Illinois, Missouri, Kansas and Colorado*)

GRAND as the thought that doubtless the child is already born who will see a hundred millions of people, the most prosperous and advanc'd of the world, inhabiting these Prairies, the great Plains, and the valley of the Mississippi, I could not help thinking it would be grander still to see all those inimitable American areas fused in the alembic of a perfect poem, or other esthetic work, entirely western, fresh and limitless—altogether our own, without a trace or taste of Europe's soil, reminiscence, technical letter or spirit. My days and nights, as I travel here —what an exhilaration!—not the air alone, and the sense of vastness, but every local sight and feature. Everywhere something characteristic—the cactuses, pinks, buffalo grass, wild sage—the receding perspective, and the far circle-line of the horizon all times of day, especially forenoon— the clear, pure, cool, rarefied nutriment for the lungs, previously quite unknown—the black patches and streaks left by surface-conflagrations— the deep-plough'd furrow of the "fire-guard"—the slanting snow-racks built all along to shield the railroad from winter drifts—the prairie-dogs and the herds of antelope—the curious "dry rivers"—occasionally a "dugout" or corral—Fort Riley and Fort Wallace—those towns of the northern plains, (like ships on the sea,) Eagle-Tail, Coyoté, Cheyenne, Agate, Monotoyn, Kit Carson—with ever the ant-hill and the buffalo-wallow— ever the herds of cattle and the cow-boys ("cow-punchers") to me a strangely interesting class, bright-eyed as hawks, with their swarthy complexions and their broad-brimm'd hats—apparently always on horseback, with loose arms slightly raised and swinging as they ride.

THE SPANISH PEAKS—EVENING ON THE PLAINS

Between Pueblo and Bent's fort, southward, in a clear afternoon sunspell I catch exceptionally good glimpses of the Spanish peaks. We are in southeastern Colorado—pass immense herds of cattle as our first-class locomotive rushes us along—two or three times crossing the Arkansas, which we follow many miles, and of which river I get fine views, sometimes for quite a distance, its stony, upright, not very high, palisade banks, and then its muddy flats. We pass Fort Lyon—lots of adobe houses —limitless pasturage, appropriately fleck'd with those herds of cattle—in due time the declining sun in the west—a sky of limpid pearl over all—

and so evening on the great plains. A calm, pensive, boundless landscape —the perpendicular rocks of the north Arkansas, hued in twilight—a thin line of violet on the southwestern horizon—the palpable coolness and slight aroma—a belated cow-boy with some unruly member of his herd—an emigrant wagon toiling yet a little further, the horses slow and tired—two men, apparently father and son, jogging along on foot—and around all the indescribable *chiaroscuro* and sentiment, (profounder than anything at sea,) athwart these endless wilds.

America's Characteristic Landscape

Speaking generally as to the capacity and sure future destiny of that plain and prairie area (larger than any European kingdom) it is the inexhaustible land of wheat, maize, wool, flax, coal, iron, beef and pork, butter and cheese, apples and grapes—land of ten million virgin farms— to the eye at present wild and unproductive—yet experts say that upon it when irrigated may easily be grown enough wheat to feed the world. Then as to scenery (giving my own thought and feeling,) while I know the standard claim is that Yosemite, Niagara falls, the upper Yellowstone and the like, afford the greatest natural shows, I am not so sure but the Prairies and Plains, while less stunning at first sight, last longer, fill the esthetic sense fuller, precede all the rest, and make North America's characteristic landscape.

Indeed through the whole of this journey, with all its shows and varieties, what most impress'd me, and will longest remain with me, are these same prairies. Day after day, and night after night, to my eyes, to all my senses—the esthetic one most of all—they silently and broadly unfolded. Even their simplest statistics are sublime.

Earth's Most Important Stream

The valley of the Mississippi river and its tributaries, (this stream and its adjuncts involve a big part of the question,) comprehends more than twelve hundred thousand square miles, the greater part prairies. It is by far the most important stream on the globe, and would seem to have been marked out by design, slow-flowing from north to south, through a dozen climates, all fitted for man's healthy occupancy, its outlet unfrozen all the year, and its line forming a safe, cheap continental avenue for commerce and passage from the north temperate to the torrid zone. Not even the mighty Amazon (though larger in volume) on its line of east and west—not the Nile in Africa, nor the Danube in Europe, nor the three great rivers of China, compare with it. Only the Mediterranean sea has play'd some such part in history, and all through the past, as the Mississippi is destined to play in the future. By its demesnes, water'd and welded by its branches, the Missouri, the Ohio, the Arkansas, the Red, the Yazoo, the St. Francis and others, it already compacts twenty-five millions of people, not merely the most peaceful and money-making, but the most restless and warlike on earth. Its valley, or reach, is rapidly concentrating the political power of the American Union. One almost thinks it *is* the Union—or soon will be. Take it out, with its radiations, and what would be left? From the car windows through Indiana, Illinois, Missouri, or stopping some days along the Topeka and Santa Fe road, in southern Kansas, and indeed wherever I went, hundreds and thousands of miles through this region, my eyes feasted on primitive and rich meadows, some of them partially inhabited, but far, immensely far more untouch'd, unbroken—and much of it more lovely and fertile in its un-plough'd innocence than the fair and valuable fields of New York's, Pennsylvania's, Maryland's or Virginia's richest farms.

Prairie Analogies—The Tree Question

The word Prairie is French, and means literally meadow. The cosmical analogies of our North American plains are the Steppes of Asia, the Pampas and Llanos of South America, and perhaps the Saharas of Africa. Some think the plains have been originally lake-beds; others attribute the absence of forests to the fires that almost annually sweep over them— (the cause, in vulgar estimation, of Indian summer.) The tree question will soon become a grave one. Although the Atlantic slope, the Rocky mountain region, and the southern portion of the Mississippi valley, are well wooded, there are here stretches of hundreds and thousands of miles where either not a tree grows, or often useless destruction has prevail'd; and the matter of the cultivation and spread of forests may well be press'd upon thinkers who look to the coming generations of the prairie States.

—Walt Whitman, *Specimen Days and Collect*

6. THE SIGNIFICANCE OF THE FRONTIER

Other nations have had their frontiers, but for the most part these have been boundaries between different nations or peoples. The American frontier, like the frontiers of Canada, Australia, South Africa, and parts of South America, differed from Old World frontiers in two important respects. It was a moving, not a fixed, line; and it was a line of settlement up against the wilderness.

The first frontiers in America were those on the Atlantic Coast— Jamestown and Plymouth—and in New Mexico; these were frontiers of England and of Spain. Every generation after the first settlements in Virginia and Massachusetts Bay saw the American frontier move into the interior, sometimes northward or southward, but ordinarily westward. It moved up along the rivers, over the piedmont, through the mountain passes and on to the great valley beyond, down the Ohio to the Mississippi and westward to the edge of forest and prairie land. Then, in the 1840's, it made a great leap to the Pacific Coast. The generation after the Civil War saw settlement close in from the East and the West until, by 1890, it was no longer possible to draw a continuous frontier line. Not all the land was gone, but most of the good land had been taken up, and that land which was to afford a haven to Americans "to the thousandth and thousandth generation" was no longer available.

Frederick Jackson Turner was by no means the first student to note the significance of the frontier in our history; Crèvecoeur, it will be remembered, had something to say on this, and so, a century later, had James Bryce. But it was Turner who made the theme central to his interpretation of American history, who elaborated on it, who filled in the essential details, and who founded a school of frontier interpreters. This famous essay was originally a paper read to the American Historical Association at its meeting in 1893, and Turner was, at that time, a young teacher at the University of Wisconsin.

IN A recent bulletin of the Superintendent of the Census for 1890 appear these significant words: "Up to and including 1880 the country had a frontier of settlement, but at present the unsettled area has been so broken into by isolated bodies of settlement that there can hardly be said to be a frontier line. In the discussion of its extent, its westward movement, etc., it can not, therefore, any longer have a place in the census reports." This brief official statement marks the closing of a great historic movement. Up to our own day American history has been in a large degree the history of the colonization of the Great West. The existence of an area of free land, its continuous recession, and the advance of American settlement westward, explain American development.

Behind institutions, behind constitutional forms and modifications, lie the vital forces that call these organs into life and shape them to meet changing conditions. The peculiarity of American institutions is, the fact that they have been compelled to adapt themselves to the changes of an expanding people—to the changes involved in crossing a continent, in winning a wilderness, and in developing at each area of this progress out of the primitive economic and political conditions of the frontier into the complexity of city life. Said Calhoun in 1817, "We are great, and rapidly—I was about to say fearfully—growing!" So saying, he touched the distinguishing feature of American life. All peoples show development; the germ theory of politics has been sufficiently emphasized. In the case of most nations, however, the development has occurred in a limited area; and if the nation has expanded, it has met other growing peoples whom it has conquered. But in the case of the United States we have a different phenomenon. Limiting our attention to the Atlantic coast, we have the familiar phenomenon of the evolution of institutions in a limited area, such as the rise of representative government; the differentiation of simple colonial governments into complex organs; the progress from primitive industrial society, without division of labor, up to manufacturing civilization. But we have in addition to this a recurrence of the process of evolution in each western area reached in the process of expansion. Thus American development has exhibited not merely advance along a single line, but a return to primitive conditions on a continually advancing frontier line, and a new development for that area. American social development has been continually beginning over again on the frontier. This perennial rebirth, this fluidity of American life, this expansion westward with its new opportunities, its continuous touch with the simplicity of primitive society, furnish the forces dominating American character. The true point of view in the history of this nation is not the Atlantic coast, it is the Great West. . . .

In the settlement of America we have to observe how European life entered the continent, and how America modified and developed that life and reacted on Europe. Our early history is the study of European germs developing in an American environment. Too exclusive attention has been paid by institutional students to the Germanic origins, too little to the American factors. The frontier is the line of most rapid and effective Americanization. The wilderness masters the colonist. It finds him a European in dress, industries, tools, modes of travel, and thought. It takes him from the railroad car and puts him in the birch canoe. It strips off the garments of civilization and arrays him in the hunting shirt and the moccasin. It puts him in the log cabin of the Cherokee and Iroquois and runs an Indian palisade around him. Before long he has gone to planting Indian corn and plowing with a sharp stick; he shouts the war cry and takes the scalp in orthodox Indian fashion. In short, at the frontier the environment is at first too strong for the man. He must accept the conditions which it furnishes, or perish, and so he fits himself into the Indian clearings and follows the Indian trails. Little by little he transforms the wilderness, but the outcome is not the old Europe, not simply the development of Germanic germs, any more than the first phenomenon was a case of reversion to the Germanic mark. The fact is, that here is a new product that is American. At first, the frontier was the Atlantic coast. It was the frontier of Europe in a very real sense. Moving westward, the frontier became more and more American. As successive terminal moraines result from successive glaciations, so each frontier leaves its traces behind it, and when it becomes a settled area the region still partakes of the frontier characteristics. Thus the advance of the frontier has meant a steady movement away from the influence of Europe, a steady growth of independence on American lines. And to study this advance, the men who grew up under these conditions, and the political, economic, and social results of it, is to study the really American part of our history. . . .

At the Atlantic frontier one can study the germs ot processes repeated at each successive frontier. We have the complex European life sharply precipitated by the wilderness into the simplicity of primitive conditions. The first frontier had to meet its Indian question, its question of the disposition of the public domain, of the means of intercourse with older settlements, of the extension of political organization, of religious and educational activity. And the settlement of these and similar questions for one frontier served as a guide for the next. The American student needs not to go to the "prim little townships of Sleswick" for illustrations of the law of continuity and development. For example, he may study the origin of our land policies in the colonial land policy; he may see how the system grew by adapting the statutes to the customs of the successive frontiers. He may see how the mining experience in the lead regions of Wisconsin, Illinois, and Iowa was applied to the mining laws of the Sierras, and how our Indian policy has been a series of experimentations on successive frontiers. Each tier of new States has found in the older ones material for its constitutions. Each frontier has made similar contributions to American character, as will be discussed farther on. . . .

The United States lies like a huge page in the history of society. Line by line as we read this continental page from West to East we find the record of social evolution. It begins with the Indian and the hunter; it goes on to tell of the disintegration of savagery by the entrance of the trader, the pathfinder of civilization; we read the annals of the pastoral stage in ranch life; the exploitation of the soil by the raising of unrotated crops of corn and wheat in sparsely settled farming communities; the intensive culture of the denser farm settlement; and finally the manufacturing organization with city and factory system. This page is familiar to the student of census statistics, but how little of it has been used by our historians. Particularly in eastern States this page is a palimpsest. What is now a manufacturing State was in an earlier decade an area of intensive farming. Earlier yet it had been a wheat area, and still earlier the "range" had attracted the cattle-herder. Thus Wisconsin, now developing manufacture, is a State with varied agricultural interests. But earlier it was given over to almost exclusive grain-raising, like North Dakota at the present time.

Each of these areas has had an influence in our economic and political history; the evolution of each into a higher stage has worked political transformations. But what constitutional historian has made any adequate attempt to interpret political facts by the light of these social areas and changes?

The Atlantic frontier was compounded of fisherman, fur-trader, miner, cattle-raiser, and farmer. Excepting the fisherman, each type of industry was on the march toward the West, impelled by an irresistible attraction. Each passed in successive waves across the continent. Stand at Cumberland Gap and watch the procession of civilization, marching single file—the buffalo following the trail to the salt springs, the Indian, the fur-trader and hunter, the cattle-raiser, the pioneer farmer—and the frontier has passed by. Stand at South Pass in the Rockies a century later and see the same procession with wider intervals between. The unequal rate of advance compels us to distinguish the frontier into the trader's frontier, the rancher's frontier, or the miner's frontier, and the farmer's frontier. When the mines and the cow pens were still near the fall line the traders' pack trains were tinkling across the Alleghanies, and the French on the Great Lakes were fortifying their posts, alarmed by the British trader's birch canoe. When the trappers scaled the Rockies, the farmer was still near the mouth of the Missouri. . . .

Having now roughly outlined the various kinds of frontiers, and their modes of advance, chiefly from the point of view of the frontier itself, we may next inquire what were the influences on the East and on the Old World. A rapid enumeration of some of the more noteworthy effects is all that I have time for.

First, we note that the frontier promoted the formation of a composite nationality for the American people. The coast was preponderantly English, but the later tides of continental immigration flowed across to the freelands. This was the case from the early colonial days. The Scotch-Irish and the Palatine Germans, or "Pennsylvania Dutch," furnished the dominant element in the stock of the colonial frontier. With these peoples were also the freed indented servants, or redemptioners, who at the expiration of their time of service passed to the frontier. Governor Spotswood of Virginia writes in 1717, "The inhabitants of our frontiers are composed generally of such as have been transported hither as servants, and, being out of their time, settle themselves where land is to be taken up and that will produce the necessarys of life with little labour." Very generally these redemptioners were of non-English stock. In the crucible of the frontier the immigrants were Americanized, liberated, and fused into a mixed race, English in neither nationality nor characteristics. The process has gone on from the early days to our own. Burke and other writers in the middle of the eighteenth century believed that Pennsylvania was "threatened with the danger of being wholly foreign in language, manners, and perhaps even inclinations." The German and Scotch-Irish elements in the frontier of the South were only less great. In the middle of the present century the German element in Wisconsin was already so considerable that leading publicists looked to the creation of a German state out of the commonwealth by concentrating their colonization. Such examples teach us to beware of misinterpreting the fact that there is a common English speech in America into a belief that the stock is also English.

In another way the advance of the frontier decreased our dependence on England. The coast, particularly of the South, lacked diversified industries, and was dependent on England for the bulk of its supplies.

In the South there was even a dependence on the Northern colonies for articles of food. Governor Glenn, of South Carolina, writes in the middle of the eighteenth century: "Our trade with New York and Philadelphia was of this sort, draining us of all the little money and bills we could gather from other places for their bread, flour, beer, hams, bacon, and other things of their produce, all which, except beer, our new townships begin to supply us with, which are settled with very industrious and thriving Germans. This no doubt diminishes the number of shipping and the appearance of our trade, but it is far from being a detriment to us." Before long the frontier created a de- mand for merchants. As it retreated from the coast it became less and less possible for England to bring her supplies directly to the consumer's wharfs, and carry away staple crops, and staple crops began to give way to diversified agriculture for a time. The effect of this phase of the frontier action upon the northern section is perceived when we realize how the advance of the frontier aroused seaboard cities like Boston, New York, and Baltimore, to engage in rivalry for what Washington called "the extensive and valuable trade of a rising empire."

The legislation which most developed the powers of the national government, and played the largest part in its activity, was conditioned on the frontier. . . .

When we consider the public domain from the point of view of the sale and disposal of the public lands we are again brought face to face with the frontier. The policy of the United States in dealing with its lands is in sharp contrast with the European system of scientific ad- ministration. Efforts to make this domain a source of revenue, and to withhold it from emigrants in order that settlement might be compact, were in vain. The jealousy and fears of the East were powerless in the face of the demands of the frontiersmen. . . .

It was this nationalizing tendency of the West that transformed the democracy of Jefferson into the national republicanism of Monroe and the democracy of Andrew Jackson. The West of the War of 1812, the West of Clay, and Benton and Harrison, and Andrew Jackson, shut off by the Middle States and the mountains from the coast sections, had a solidarity of its own with national tendencies. On the tide of the Father of Waters, North and South met and mingled into a nation. Interstate migration went steadily on—a process of cross-fertilization of ideas and institutions. The fierce struggle of the sections over slavery on the western frontier does not diminish the truth of this statement;

it proves the truth of it. Slavery was a sectional trait that would not down, but in the West it could not remain sectional. It was the greatest of frontiersmen who declared: "I believe this Government can not endure permanently half slave and half free. It will become all of one thing or all of the other." Nothing works for nationalism like inter-course within the nation. Mobility of population is death to localism, and the western frontier worked irresistibly in unsettling population. The effect reached back from the frontier and affected profoundly the Atlantic coast and even the Old World.

But the most important effect of the frontier has been in the pro-motion of democracy here and in Europe. As has been indicated, the frontier is productive of individualism. Complex society is precipitated by the wilderness into a kind of primitive organization based on the family. The tendency is anti-social. It produces antipathy to control, and particularly to any direct control. The tax-gatherer is viewed as a representative of oppression. Prof. Osgood, in an able article, has pointed out that the frontier conditions prevalent in the colonies are important factors in the explanation of the American Revolution, where individual liberty was sometimes confused with absence of all effective government. The same conditions aid in explaining the difficulty of instituting a strong government in the period of the confederacy. The frontier individualism has from the beginning promoted democracy. . . .

From the conditions of frontier life came intellectual traits of pro-found importance. The works of travelers along each frontier from colonial days onward describe certain common traits, and these traits have, while softening down, still persisted as survivals in the place of their origin, even when a higher social organization succeeded. The result is that to the frontier the American intellect owes its striking characteristics. That coarseness and strength combined with acuteness and inquisitiveness; that practical, inventive turn of mind, quick to find expedients; that masterful grasp of material things, lacking in the artistic but powerful to effect great ends; that restless, nervous energy; that dominant individualism, working for good and for evil, and withal that buoyancy and exuberance which comes with freedom—these are traits of the frontier, or traits called out elsewhere because of the existence of the frontier. Since the days when the fleet of Columbus sailed into the waters of the New World, America has been another name for opportunity, and the people of the United States have taken their tone from the incessant expansion which has not only been open but has even been forced upon them. He would be a rash prophet who should assert that the expansive character of American life has now entirely ceased. Movement has been its dominant fact, and, unless this training has no effect upon a people, the American energy will continually demand a wider field for its exercise. But never again will such gifts of free land offer themselves. For a moment, at the frontier, the bonds of custom are broken and unrestraint is triumphant. There is not *tabula rasa*. The stubborn American environment is there with its imperious summons to accept its conditions; the inherited ways of doing things are also there; and yet, in spite of environment, and in spite of custom, each frontier did indeed furnish a new field of opportunity, a gate of escape from the bondage of the past; and freshness, and confidence, and scorn of older society, impatience of its restraints and its ideas, and indifference to its lessons, have accompanied the frontier. What the Mediterranean Sea was to the Greeks, breaking the bond of custom, offering new experiences, calling out new institutions and activities, that, and more, the ever retreating frontier has been to the United States directly, and to the nations of Europe more remotely. And now, four centuries from the discovery of America, at the end of a hundred years of life under the Constitution, the frontier has gone, and with its going has closed the first period of American history.

—Frederick Jackson Turner,
"The Significance of the Frontier in American History," 1893

7. A DEMOCRATIC LAND SYSTEM

We have been concerned, so far in this chapter, with the impact of the land upon Americans. We turn now, in a sense, to the other side of that story—the impact of Americans on the land. Here was a vast continent, surpassingly rich in all those things that could make for an advanced and generous civilization. What did Americans do with it? That they made mistakes is clear: eroded soils, polluted rivers, brush and bramble where forests once stood, and dust bowls are monuments to the abuse of the land by the American people. At the same time it should be remembered that they avoided some mistakes that they might have made—mistakes that would have been very costly indeed. For instance, they avoided the mistake of the Spanish rulers of the land to the south in parceling the land up into great domains of hundreds of thousands of acres. They avoided, too, the mistake made by most European nations of exploiting the land primarily for the benefit of the government or of absentee landlords who stayed home.

The crisis came during the Revolution and the Confederation. With the Revolution each American State reasserted its claims to land in the West. Should this land be kept by the Eastern States—and for the benefit of those who lived in the East? Or should it be disposed of for the common benefit of all the people of the nation? And if it were to be ceded to the United States, how should it be disposed of—by gift, by sale, by grant to great companies? It was not easy to answer these questions. There were those who wanted to keep the Western lands for purposes of revenue; there were those who wanted to give them to great land companies; there were those who, like Gouverneur Morris, felt that "the busy haunts of men, not the remote wilderness, was the proper school of political talents," and that the West should therefore be kept in permanent subordination to the East. Fortunately wise counsels prevailed. Under the leadership of Jefferson, the most West-conscious of the statesmen of that day and the chief architect of our Western land and government policy, the Congress worked out an enlightened land system. Virginia had the largest Western holdings; when she ceded them to the United States other States followed her example. Jefferson then drafted two ordinances, the land Ordinance of 1785 and a report on government in 1784 that laid down the principles followed in the great Northwest Ordinance of 1787. We give here the resolution of Congress on the principle controlling the disposition of public lands, and Jefferson's Ordinance of 1785.

A. "The Common Benefit of the United States"

RESOLVED, that the unappropriated lands that may be ceded or relinquished to the United States, by any particular States, pursuant to the recommendation of Congress on the 6 day of September last, shall be disposed of for the common benefit of the United States, and be settled and formed into distinct republican States, which shall become members of the Federal Union, and shall have the same rights of sov-

ereignty, freedom and independence, as the other States; that each State
which shall be so formed shall contain a suitable extent of territory, not
less than one hundred nor more than one hundred and fifty miles square,
or as near thereto as circumstances will admit;

That the necessary and reasonable expences which any particular State
shall have incurred since the commencement of the present war, in subduing any of the British posts, or in maintaining forts or garrisons within
and for the defence, or in acquiring any part of the territory that may be
ceded or relinquished to the United States, shall be reimbursed;

That the said lands shall be granted and settled at such times and
under such regulations as shall hereafter be agreed on by the United
States in Congress asembled, or any nine or more of them.

—Resolution of Congress on Public Lands, October 10, 1780

B. The Land Ordinance of 1785

*An Ordinance for ascertaining the mode of disposing of Lands in
the Western Territory.*

Be it ordained by the United States in Congress assembled, that the
territory ceded by individual States to the United States, which has been
purchased of the Indian inhabitants, shall be disposed of in the following
manner:

A surveyor from each state shall be appointed by Congress or a Committee of the States, who shall take an oath for the faithful discharge of
his duty, before the Geographer of the United States. . . .

The Surveyors, as they are respectively qualified, shall proceed to
divide the said territory into townships of six miles square, by lines running due north and south, and others crossing these at right angles, as
near as may be, unless where the boundaries of the late Indian purchases
may render the same impracticable, . . .

The first line, running due north and south as aforesaid, shall begin
on the river Ohio, at a point that shall be found to be due north from the
western termination of a line, which has been run as the southern
boundary of the State of Pennsylvania; and the first line, running east
and west, shall begin at the same point, and shall extend throughout the
whole territory. Provided, that nothing herein shall be construed, as
fixing the western boundary of the State of Pennsylvania. The geographer shall designate the townships, or fractional parts of townships, by
numbers progressively from south to north; always beginning each range

with No. 1; and the ranges shall be distinguished by their progressive numbers to the westward. The first range, extending from the Ohio to the lake Erie, being marked No. 1. The Geographer shall personally attend to the running of the first east and west line; and shall take the latitude of the extremes of the first north and south line, and of the mouths of the principal rivers.

The lines shall be measured with a chain; shall be plainly marked by chaps on the trees, and exactly described on a plat; whereon shall be noted by the surveyor, at their proper distances, all mines, salt-springs, salt-licks and mill-seats, that shall come to his knowledge, and all water-courses, mountains and other remarkable and permanent things, over and near which such lines shall pass, and also the quality of the lands.

The plats of the townships respectively, shall be marked by subdivisions into lots of one mile square, or 640 acres, in the same direction as the external lines, and numbered from 1 to 36; always beginning the succeeding range of the lots with the number next to that with which the preceding one concluded. . . .

. . . And the geographer shall make . . . returns, from time to time, of every seven ranges, as they may be surveyed. The Secretary of War shall have recourse thereto, and shall take by lot therefrom, a number of townships . . . as will be equal to one seventh part of the whole of such seven ranges, . . . for the use of the late Continental army. . . .

The board of treasury shall transmit a copy of the original plats, previously noting thereon the townships and fractional parts of townships, which shall have fallen to the several states, by the distribution aforesaid, to the commissioners of the loan-office of the several states, who, after giving notice . . . shall proceed to sell the townships or fractional parts of townships, at public vendue, in the following manner, viz.: The township or fractional part of a township No. 1, in the first range, shall be sold entire; and No. 2, in the same range, by lots; and thus in alternate order through the whole of the first range . . . provided, that none of the lands, within the said territory, be sold under the price of one dollar the acre, to be paid in specie, or loan-office certificates, reduced to specie value, by the scale of depreciation, or certificates of liquidated debts of the United States, including interest, besides the expense of the survey and other charges thereon, which are hereby rated at thirty six dollars the township, . . . on failure of which payment, the said lands shall again be offered for sale.

There shall be reserved for the United States out of every township the four lots, being numbered 8,11,26,29, and out of every fractional part of a township, so many lots of the same numbers as shall be found thereon, for future sale. There shall be reserved the lot No. 16, of every township, for the maintenance of public schools within the said township; also one-third part of all gold, silver, lead and copper mines, to be sold, or otherwise disposed of as Congress shall hereafter direct. . . .

And Whereas Congress . . . stipulated grants of land to certain officers and soldiers of the late Continental army . . . for complying with such engagements, Be it ordained, That the secretary of war . . . determine who are the objects of the above resolutions and engagements . . . and cause the townships, or fractional parts of townships, hereinbefore reserved for the use of the late Continental army, to be drawn for in such manner as he shall deem expedient.

—THOMAS JEFFERSON, Land Ordinance of May 20, 1785

8. A BELT OF TREES FOR THE ARID WEST

We have already noted that the westward-moving frontier came to a halt in the 1840's and then leaped plains and mountains to the Pacific Coast—first to that Oregon country which in its wealth of timber was like the East, then to California, with its abundant rainfall and great forests. For many years the intervening area—what was originally called the Great American Desert and later the Great Plains—presented serious obstacles to colonization. This was the last refuge of the Indian; it was the domain of the cattleman. Not until the pioneer had managed to solve the problem of low rainfall and absence of trees could he successfully farm in this country. There are many theories about the treelessness of the Plains region; the important thing is that the absence of trees meant no timber for fencing or for houses, and an accentuation of the semi-aridity of the area. At a very early day ecologists were concerned about the absence of trees in the Plains area, and recommended a program of planting. Ferdinand Hayden, whose analysis of this problem we give here, was a surgeon who turned after the Civil War to geology. In 1866 he made an expedition to the Far West, under the auspices of the Academy of Natural Sciences of Philadelphia, and the following year a second expedition under the direction of the General Land Office. In subsequent years Hayden explored and surveyed the geology of most of the Far West; his work led directly to the establishment of the United States Geological Survey. It is interesting to note that Hayden's recommendation of a belt of forest was carried out by the Franklin D. Roosevelt administration in the mid-nineteen-thirties.

I WOULD again speak of the great importance of planting trees in this country, and the great ease with which these cultivated forests may be produced. I do not believe that the prairies proper will ever become covered with timber except by artificial means. Since the surface of the country received its present geological configuration no trees have grown there, but, during the tertiary period, when the lignite or "brown coal" beds were deposited, all these treeless plains were covered with a luxuriant growth of forest trees like those of the Gulf States or South America. Here were palm trees, with leaves having a spread of twelve feet; gigantic sycamores—several species; maples, poplars, cedars, hickories, cinnamon, fig, and many varieties now found only in tropical or sub-tropical climates.

Large portions of the Upper Missouri country, especially along the Yellowstone river, are now covered with the silicified trunks of trees, sixty to seventy feet in length and two to four feet in diameter, exhibiting the annual rings of growth as perfectly as in our recent elms or maples. We are daily obtaining more and more evidence that these forests may be restored again to a certain extent, at least, and thus a belt or zone of country about five hundred miles in width east of the base of the mountains be redeemed. It is believed, also, that the planting of ten or fifteen acres of forest trees on each quarter section will have a most important effect on the climate, equalizing and increasing the moisture and adding greatly to the fertility of the soil. The settlement of the country and the increase of the timber has already changed for the better the climate of that portion of Nebraska lying along the Missouri, so that within the last twelve or fourteen years the rain has gradually increased in quantity and is more equally distributed through the year. I am confident this change will continue to extend across the dry belt to the foot of the Rocky mountains as the settlements extend and the forest trees are planted in proper quantities. In the final report I propose to show that these ideas are not purely theoretical, and that the influence of trees on climate and humidity has been investigated by some of the ablest scientific men in this country and in Europe. . . .

The forest presenting a considerable surface for evaporation gives to its own soil and the adjacent ground an abundant and enlivening dew. Forests, in a word, exert in the interior of continents an influence like that of the sea on the climates of islands and of coasts; both water the soil and thereby insure its fertility. . . . Much might also be said in regard to the influence of woods in protecting the soil and promoting the increase in number and the flow of springs, but all I wish is to show the possibility of the power of man to restore to these now treeless and almost rainless prairies the primitive forests and the humidity which accompanies them.

—FERDINAND V. HAYDEN,
Letter to the Commissioner of the General Land Office, 1867

9. THE ARID REGIONS OF THE WEST

Major John Wesley Powell was Director of the Rocky Mountain Survey in the United States Geological Survey, when in 1878 he wrote this report on the "Arid Region" of the United States. The report pointed out that the land system which had obtained from the beginning for the region east of the hundredth meridian, was unsuitable for the arid lands of the West, where access to water was the basic consideration. Although the report had no immediate consequences, its recommendations were eventually incorporated into the national land policy. Powell himself is one of the most striking figures in our history. After a Civil War career which brought him a Majority—and cost him an arm—he had taught natural history at various Illinois colleges and explored widely in the plains and mountains of the then little-known West. In 1869 he conducted a party of eleven men on a perilous exploring expedition down the Colorado River; he was the first white man to make this voyage. In 1875 Powell became Director of the Rocky Mountain Survey and in 1880 succeeded Clarence King as Director of the U. S. Geological Survey. He was a lifelong student of Indian affairs and an ardent advocate of conservation and irrigation.

THE general subject of water rights is one of great importance. In many places in the Arid Region irrigation companies are organized who obtain vested rights in the waters they control, and consequently the rights to such waters do not inhere in any particular tracts of land.

When the area to which it is possible to take the water of any given stream is much greater than the stream is competent to serve, if the land titles and water rights are severed, the owner of any tract of land is at the mercy of the owner of the water right. In general the lands greatly exceed the capacities of the streams. Thus the lands have no value without water. If the water rights fall into the hands of irrigating companies and the lands into the hands of individual farmers, the farmers then will be dependent upon the stock companies, and eventually the monopoly of water rights will be an intolerable burden to the people.

The magnitude of the interests involved must not be overlooked. All the present and future agriculture of more than four-tenths of the area of the United States is dependent upon irrigation, and practically all values for agricultural industries inhere, not in the lands, but in the water. Monopoly of land need not be feared. The question for legislators to solve is to devise some practical means by which water rights may be distributed among individual farmers and water monopolies prevented. . . .

The pioneer is fully engaged in the present with its hopes of immediate remuneration for labor. The present development of the country fully occupies him. For this reason every effort put forth to increase the area of the agricultural land by irrigation is welcomed. Every man who turns his attention to this department of industry is considered a public benefactor. But if in the eagerness for present development a land and water system shall grow up in which the practical control of agriculture shall fall into the hands of water companies, evils will result therefrom that generations may not be able to correct, and the very men who are now lauded as benefactors to the country will, in the ungovernable reaction which is sure to come, be denounced as oppressors of the people.

The right to use water should inhere in the land to be irrigated, and water rights should go with land titles. . . .

Practically, in that country the right to water is acquired by priority of utilization, and this is as it should be from the necessities of the country. But two important qualifications are needed. The *user right* should attach to the *land* where used, not to the individual or company constructing the canals by which it is used; the priority of usage should secure the right. But this needs some slight modification. A farmer settling on a small tract, to be redeemed by irrigation, should be given a reasonable length of time in which to secure his water right by utilization, that he may secure it by his own labor, either directly by constructing the waterways himself, or indirectly by co-operating with his neighbors in constructing systems of waterways. Without this provision there is little inducement for poor men to commence farming operations, and men of ready capital only will engage in such enterprises. . . .

If there be any doubt of the ultimate legality of the practices of the people in the arid country relating to water and land rights, all such doubts should be speedily quieted through the enactment of appropriate laws by the national legislature. Perhaps an amplification by the courts of what has been designated as the *natural right* to the use of water may be made to cover the practices now obtaining; but it hardly seems wise to imperil interests so great by intrusting them to the possibility of some future court made law.

—JOHN W. POWELL, "Report on the Lands of the Arid Region
of the United States," 1879

10. FORESTS, PROSPERITY, AND PROGRESS

Carl Schurz was born in Germany, and learned there what an en-lightened program of conservation and reforestation could accomplish. When in 1877 he became Secretary of the Interior in Hayes's cabinet, he embarked upon an energetic program looking to the preservation of the public domain. As he tells us here, his efforts encountered the most violent opposition from railroads, timber interests, and others who looked upon his notions as "foreign" and therefore somehow "un-American." This excerpt is taken from an address to the Forestry Associations in 1889.

THE more study and thought I have given the matter, the firmer has become my conviction that *the destruction of the forests of this country will be the murder of its future prosperity and progress.* This is no mere figure of speech, no rhetorical exaggeration. It is simply the teaching of the world's history, which no fair-minded man can study without reaching the same conclusion. . . .

Let me say to you that the laws of nature are the same everywhere. Whoever violates them anywhere, must always pay the penalty. No country ever so great and rich, no nation ever so powerful, inventive, and enterprising can violate them with impunity. We most grievously delude ourselves if we think that we can form an exception to the rule. And we have made already a most dangerous beginning, and more than a beginning, in the work of desolation. The destruction of our forests is so fearfully rapid that, if we go on at the same rate, men whose hair is already gray, will see the day when in the United States from Maine to California and from the Mexican Gulf to Puget Sound there will be no forest left worthy of the name.

Who is guilty of that destruction? It is not merely the lumberman cutting timber on his own land for legitimate use in the pursuit of business gain; it is the lumberman who in doing so, destroys and wastes as much more without benefit to anybody. It is not merely the settler or the miner taking logs for his cabin, and fence rails and fire-wood, or timber for building a shaft, but it is the settler and the miner laying waste acres or stripping a mountain slope to get a few sticks. It is all these, serving indeed legitimate wants, but doing it with a wastefulness criminally reckless.

But it is not only these. It is the timber thief—making haste to strip the public domain of what he can lay his hands on, lest another timber thief get ahead of him—and in doing this, destroying sometimes far more than he steals. It is the tourist, the hunter, the mining prospector who, lighting his camp-fire in the woods to boil water for his coffee or to fry his bacon, and leaving that fire unextinguished when he proceeds, sets the woods in flames and delivers countless square miles of forest to destruction.

It is all these, but it is something more, and, let us confess it, something worse. It is a public opinion looking with indifference on this wanton, barbarous, disgraceful vandalism. It is a spendthrift people recklessly wasting its heritage. It is a government careless of the future and unmindful of a pressing duty.

I have had some personal experience of this. The gentleman who introduced me did me the honor of mentioning the attention I devoted to this subject years ago as Secretary of the Interior. When I entered upon that important office, having the public lands in charge, I considered it my first duty to look around me and to study the problems I had to deal with. Doing so I observed all the wanton waste and devastation I have described. I observed the notion, that the public forests were everybody's property, to be taken and used or wasted as anybody pleased, everywhere in full operation. I observed enterprising timber thieves not merely stealing trees, but stealing whole forests. I observed hundreds of saw mills in full blast, devoted exclusively to the sawing up of timber stolen from the public lands.

I observed a most lively export trade going on from Gulf ports as well as Pacific ports, with fleets of vessels employed in carrying timber stolen from the public lands to be sold in foreign countries, immense tracts being devastated that some robbers might fill their pockets.

I thought that this sort of stealing was wrong, in this country no less than elsewhere. Moreover, it was against the spirit and letter of the law. I, therefore, deemed it my duty to arrest that audacious and destructive robbery. Not that I had intended to prevent the settler and the miner from taking from the public lands what they needed for their cabins, their fields, or their mining shafts; but I deemed it my duty to stop at least the commercial depredations upon the property of the people. And to that end I used my best endeavors and the means at my disposal, scanty as they were.

What was the result? No sooner did my attempts in that direction become known, than I was pelted with telegraphic despatches from the regions most concerned, indignantly inquiring what it meant that an officer of the Government dared to interfere with the legitimate business of the country! Members of Congress came down upon me, some with wrath in their eyes, others pleading in a milder way, but all solemnly protesting against my disturbing their constituents in this peculiar pursuit of happiness. I persevered in the performance of my plain duty.

But when I set forth my doings in my annual report and asked Congress for rational forestry legislation, you should have witnessed the sneers at the outlandish notions of this "foreigner" in the Interior Department; notions that, as was said, might do for a picayunish German principality, but were altogether contemptible when applied to this great and free country of ours. By the way, some of the gentlemen who sneered so greatly, might learn some lessons from those picayunish German principalities, which would do them much good. I recently revisited my native land and saw again some of the forests I had known in my younger days—forests which in the meantime had yielded to their owners or to the government large revenues from the timber cut, but were now nevertheless as stately as they had been before, because the cutting had been done upon rational principles and the forests had been steadily improved by scientific cultivation. I passed over a large tract I had known as a barren heath, the heath of Luneburg, which formerly, as the saying was, sustained only the "Heidschnucken," a species of sheep as little esteemed for their wool as their mutton—the same heath now covered with a dense growth of fine forest. Instead of sneering, our supercilious scoffers would do better for themselves as well as for the country, if they devoted their time a little more to studying and learning the valuable lessons with which the experience of other countries abounds.

What the result of my appeals was at the time I am speaking of, you know. We succeeded in limiting somewhat the extent of the depredations upon the public forests, and in bringing some of the guilty parties to justice. A few hundred thousand dollars were recovered for timber stolen, but the recommendations of rational forestry legislation went for nothing. Some laws were indeed passed, but they appeared rather to favor the taking of timber from the public lands than to stop it. Still, I persevered, making appeal after appeal, in public and in private, but I found myself standing almost solitary and alone. Deaf was Congress, and deaf the people seemed to be. Only a few still voices rose up here and there in the press in favor of the policy I pursued.

Thank Heaven, the people appear to be deaf no longer. It is in a great measure owing to your wise and faithful efforts that the people begin to listen, and that in several states practical steps have already been taken in the right direction.

—CARL SCHURZ, "The Need of a Rational Forest Policy in the
United States," 1889

11. "FROM PLYMOUTH ROCK TO DUCKTOWN"

Here Stuart Chase paints, in broad, slashing strokes, a picture of what has happened to the American soil, timber, water, and wild life since white men replaced red. It is a sobering story—a story of ruthless exploitation and selfishness and waste. The Ducktown to which Chase refers here was an eastern Tennessee town laid waste by erosion and industrial pollution. One of our most original economic thinkers, Stuart Chase has written widely on broad questions of public policy and natural resources. The book from which this excerpt is taken was written in the mid-thirties and was not without influence in dramatizing the necessity for an energetic conservation program; it is of some consolation to reflect that conditions are not so bad now as they were when Chase wrote these sober lines.

HOW does the continent look today after three hundred years of occupation? Suppose we climb into a metaphorical airplane and cruise about America, first observing the whole picture, then circling to examine this area and that, finally looking into conditions underground —with the help of whatever scientific instruments may be necessary.

The basic map has changed but little: a slit across the Isthmus of Panama, a few minor shifts in the coast line, small islands thrown up here and there or washed away, some river channels recut. But coming closer we find the cover enormously changed, as well as the denizens thereof. The old forest, the old grasslands have almost completely disappeared. Desert lands have broadened. A dust desert is forming east of the Rockies where firm grass once stood. Woodlands—and a spindly lot they are by comparison—cover only half the area the primeval forest once covered. Grazing areas are still immense but the old types of native grasses have largely gone.

On one-quarter of continental United States are new fields, bare in the winter, green with crops in the summer. Adjacent to these tilled fields are pasture lands, unknown before, of an almost equal area. On some of the old arid grasslands irrigation ditches now run, and between them is the green crops. This is particularly noticeable around Salt Lake in Utah, in regions of the southwest, in the Imperial and Central valleys of California. Scattered about the continent, especially along the rivers and the sea coasts, are the black clusters of cities and the smaller dots of towns and villages. Linking them run a million miles and more of highways, railroads, the tracery of power lines, and pipe lines underground. Comparing the new with the old, in round figures:

THE AMERICA OF 1630

	Millions of Acres
Dense primeval forest	820
Native grass lands—tall and short	600
Open woodlands, arid lands, mountain tops, etc.	430
Desert	50
Total	1,900

THE AMERICA OF 1930

Merchantable forest—not all virgin	150
Cut-over forest—growing	200
Cut-over forest—dying	100
Farm woodlands	150
Grazing lands—open	330
Farm crop lands (irrigated, 25 million)	400
Farm pasture lands, etc.	420
Urban lands	50
Desert and waste	100
Total	1,900

Most of these figures are rough estimates, but they serve to show in a general way the changes which have taken place. Forest and native grasslands have given way to farm lands, both crop and pasture. The total farm land, including farm wood lots, approaches a billion acres, or about half the whole area. In 1630 the only parallel was the stick-furrowed fields of the Indians, which probably did not amount to a million acres all told. . . .

Primeval forest, virgin soil and the waving prairie grasses have given way to open fields, harnessed rivers spanned by steel bridges, tunneled mountains, irrigated arid lands, culm banks, oil fields, canals, drained marshes and roaring, smoky cities. Beauty has been lost, we cry, but progress gained. Wild landscape has been replaced by cultured.

We drop 10,000 feet and look closer still. If this be progress, it is bitter tonic. The continental soil, the center of vitality, is visibly and rapidly declining. The forest cover has been stripped and burned and steadily shrinks. The natural grass cover has been torn to ribbons by steel plows and the hooves of cattle and sheep. The skin of America has been laid open. Streams have lost their measured balance, and, heavy with silt, run wild in flood to the sea at certain seasons, to fall to miserable trickles in the drier months. This land may be bristling with tall chimneys and other evidences of progress, but it has lost its old stability.

The humus is going, and when it is gone natural life goes. Two powerful agents are destroying the soil: erosion and the loss of fertility due to mining the soil for crops. Soils which have been building steadily for 20,000 years since the last ice age now in a single century lose the benefits of several thousand years of accumulation. Corn yields in sections of Iowa have dropped from 50 to 25 bushels per acre within the lifetime of a man not yet old. This, remember, is the richest soil in America. In the northern humid states alone, scientists estimate that one-quarter of the original nitrogen, one-fifth of the phosphorus, one-tenth of the potassium and one-third of the sulphur have gone. The carrying capacity of pasture lands declined seriously between 1919 and 1929, according to the National Resources Board.

The three billion tons of solid material washed out of the fields and pastures of America every year by water erosion contains forty million tons of phosphorus, potassium and nitrogen. This of course is in addition to losses through cropping. To load and haul away this incomprehensible bulk of rich farm soil would require a train of freight cars 475,000 miles long, enough to girdle the planet nineteen times at the equator. Approximately 400 million tons of solid earth is dumped into the Gulf of Mexico by the Mississippi alone—the greater part of it super-soil, richer than that of the Nile. Plant food can be restored to soil that has been worn lean by cropping, but when water takes the soil itself—minerals, humus, microscopic organisms, everything—only nature can restore fertility to that land, and her rate under primeval conditions . . . is one inch in 500 years.

One hundred million acres of formerly cultivated land has been essentially ruined by water erosion—an area equal to Illinois, Ohio, North Carolina and Maryland combined—the equivalent of 1,250,000 eighty-acre farms. In addition, this washing of sloping fields has stripped the greater part of the productive top soil from another 125 million acres now being cultivated. Erosion by wind and water is getting under way on another 100 million acres. More than 300 million acres—one-sixth of the country—is gone, going or beginning to go. This, we note, is on land originally the most fertile.

Kansas farms are blowing through Nebraska at an accelerating rate. In the spring of 1934, the farms of the Dust Bowl—which includes western Oklahoma, western Kansas, eastern Colorado, the panhandle of Texas and parts of Wyoming—blew clear out to the Atlantic Ocean, 2,000 miles away. On a single day 300 million tons of rich top soil was lifted from the Great Plains, never to return, and planted in places where it would spread the maximum of damage and discomfort. Authentic desert sand dunes were laid down. People began to die of dust pneumonia. More than nine million acres of good land has been virtually destroyed by wind erosion, and serious damage is reported on nearly 80 million acres.

Taking the continent as a whole, it is reliably estimated that half of its original fertility has been dissipated by these various agents. The rate of loss tends to follow the laws of compound interest. The stricken areas grow cumulatively larger.

Soil losses due to cropping are the result of foolish marketing procedures, revolving around the one-crop system in cotton, corn, tobacco and wheat. Losses due to erosion are the direct result of stripping the forest and grass cover from the slopes. When the tangle of roots, the sod of the native grasses, gives way to bare plowed fields with cultivated rows running up and down hill, there is nothing to hold the rain. It tears over the contours, taking the soil with it.

Not more than one-tenth of the old virgin forest remains. The Douglas firs of the Pacific northwest are the last great stand of primeval timber. We see them coming down by high-power logging machinery, and, when they have fallen, much of the area is so devastated that trees will not grow again. The soil itself is often burned in the ensuing fires. When new vegetation starts, if at all, it is a different and poorer tree crop. These cut-over, burned-over lands are still called "forest" on the maps, but we see that almost 100 million acres is really dead land—totally unknown in the old America. This is a strange and desolate phenomenon—no farms, no productive forest, no animals, no life. In 1871, 400 square miles were burnt over in Wisconsin and 1,500 people were killed. In 1927, 158,000 forest fires were reported, and they consumed 40 million acres. Meanwhile we note that lumbermen are cutting trees of saw-timber size almost five times as fast as the stands are growing. In 1630 the reserves were 7,000 billion board feet; today the total has shrunk to 1,600 billion. In a generation or less, at this rate of exploitation, there will be no more reserves. Wheat crops ripen every year, sometimes oftener; lumber crops ripen every century on the average.

Some virgin timber still remains; it takes patient search to find virgin grasslands. The primeval sod has been burned, overgrazed, plowed up and destroyed. Where dry farming for wheat has been practised on the Great Plains, the Dust Bowl spreads. Where corn has been planted on the slopes in the tall grass regions, water erosion spreads. The sharp hooves of too many cattle and the close cropping of the grass by too many sheep have torn the cover from the open grazing lands, loosened the ancient sod, and started the gullies and dunes of both water and wind erosion. One hundred and sixty-five million acres of grazing lands has been seriously depleted. As in the case of forests, when new vegetation secures a foothold, the species is inferior to the old climax crop.

From the packed earth of the crop lands, the bare-burned slopes of the devastated forests, the broken sods of the grasslands, rain and melting snow rush to the rivers in a fraction of the time they used to take. In some watersheds runoff which should require three months is carried down to the sea in a month. The rivers run red with mud where once they were clear. Reservoirs are filled, power dams rendered increasingly impotent. Lower a bucket into the Canadian River and allow it to settle. One-quarter of the water turns out to be rich soil which the upstream owner paid for in cash.

The baked earth of the tilled fields prevents the rain from percolating into the artesian basins as it used to percolate through the cover of forest and grass. We see the underground water table falling all over the western half of the continent. In the Dakotas and Iowa the drop is serious; in the Central Valley of California, it is still more serious. Meanwhile pumping for irrigation helps to exhaust the basins. The cool, dark reservoirs which once did so much to equalize flood and drought are sinking. The same is happening with surface reservoirs. Marshes and swamps have been drained in the hope of reclaiming good agricultural land. Sometimes the land is good and sometimes it is bad, unsuited for crops. When it is bad, fires course through the dried underbrush, as in the sterile Wisconsin and Minnesota marshes.

In the lower reaches of the rivers, the old natural side reservoirs have been blocked off by levees. Here is rich farm land, to be sure, but the rivers rise as the silt sinks, and the levees must rise higher still. In New Orleans at flood crests, the Mississippi runs high above the streets of the town. River channels are straightened and further aid the rush to the ocean. Levees break; indeed the whole levee system nears its breaking point as a practicable engineering method for flood control.

Floods under these conditions must grow worse; droughts must grow worse. The safeguards of nature have been stripped away. In times of low water, the pollution of streams becomes an ominous menace. Each community in the watershed area dumps its untreated sewage into the drinking supply of the town below. When the river is low, sewage poisons remain unoxidized.

In uncounted streams, fish lie killed by the wastes of cities and the black refuse of mine and factory. Pollution has destroyed more fish than all the fishermen, and silt has killed more than pollution. When the sun cannot get through because of the mud, the tiny water plants die and fish lose their basic food supply. Oil wastes strangle the fish fry when they come to the surface. Sewage competes with marine life for a limited oxygen supply. Waxy sludge coats the river bottoms and kills plants there. Our streams, according to Sears, have become watery deserts, inimical to life. Simpletons try to restock them. "To release millions of fingerlings into such an enviroment and expect them to live is like driving a flock of yearlings into Death Valley. . . ."

The catch of Pacific halibut and salmon fell steadily to 1930. Now strenuous measures of conservation are reversing the trend. The Atlantic salmon has gone, unless there be a lonely school wandering the Penobscot. The Atlantic shad is greatly reduced and fishing villages are left stranded. The shellfish catch is only a fraction of what it used to be. Oysters are splendid typhoid carriers and city sewage is rank with typhoid bacilli. The extreme low-water stages of the rivers, induced by the failure of the natural reservoirs, have caused salt water to back up into the river mouths, killing rich colonies of shellfish by encouraging enemies which thrive in greater salinity.

The last passenger pigeon died in the Cincinnati Zoo in 1914, the sole survivor on earth of the "most abundant and the most beautiful of all American game birds." Toward the end, a single season's slaughter in Michigan accounted for five million of these creatures. The last heath hen died on Martha's Vineyard in 1932. Recently Mr. William Finley, naturalist and wild-life photographer, exhibited two films of the lower Klamath region in Oregon. The first was taken in 1915 and showed a great watershed swarming with game birds and migratory waterfowl.

The second was taken twenty years later and showed the same area despoiled by promoters, a biological desert devoid of water, food or cover and forsaken by the birds which once lived and nested there. Birds, it must never be forgotten, are the chief enemies of insects. Without their protection plant life and animal life are thrown out of equilibrium, while life for man speedily becomes unendurable.

—Stuart Chase, *Rich Land, Poor Land*

12. A PROGRAM OF CONSERVATION

The official beginnings of a conservation program may be traced back to 1891 when Congress enacted a Forest Reserve Act; under this act Presidents Harrison, Cleveland and McKinley withdrew some forty-five million acres of timber land from public entry. Yet, as Theodore Roosevelt later wrote, "a narrowly legalistic point of view" still controlled the Government Land Office and other government departments that had to do with natural resources. The effective beginnings of conservation date from the Theodore Roosevelt administration. In his first message to Congress he announced that the forest and water problems were the most vital of all those facing the American people, and during his administration he set aside about 150 million acres of timber land and 85 million acres of mineral lands from private entry. He pushed policies of reforestation, irrigation, and flood control, appointed men like Gifford Pinchot to key positions in government service, and by a series of messages and addresses and the calling of a great conservation congress, succeeded in dramatizing the whole problem of conservation to the American people.

To the Senate and House of Representatives:

THE conservation of our natural resources and their proper use constitute the fundamental problem which underlies almost every other problem of our national life. . . . As a nation we not only enjoy a wonderful measure of present prosperity but if this prosperity is used aright it is an earnest of future success such as no other nation will have. The reward of foresight for this nation is great and easily foretold. But there must be the look ahead, there must be a realization of the fact that to waste, to destroy, our natural resources, to skin and exhaust the land instead of using it so as to increase its usefulness, will result in undermining in the days of our children the very prosperity which we ought by right to hand down to them amplified and developed. For the last few years, through several agencies, the government has been endeavoring to get our people to look ahead and to substitute a planned and orderly development of our resources in place of a haphazard striving for immediate profit. Our great river systems should be developed as national water highways, the Mississippi, with its tributaries, standing first in importance, and the Columbia second, although there are many others of importance on the Pacific, the Atlantic, and the Gulf slopes. The National Government should undertake this work, and I hope a beginning will be made in the present Congress; and the greatest of all our rivers, the Mississippi, should receive special attention. From the Great Lakes to the mouth of the Mississippi there should be a deep waterway, with deep waterways leading from it to the East and the West. Such a waterway would practically mean the extension of our coastline into the very heart of our country. It would be of incalculable benefit to our people. If begun at once it can be carried through in time appreciably to relieve the congestion of our great freight-carrying lines of railroads. The work should be systematically and continuously carried forward in accordance with some well-conceived plan. The main streams should be improved to the highest point of efficiency before the improvement of the branches is attempted; and the work should be kept free from every taint of recklessness or jobbery. The inland waterways which lie just back of the whole Eastern and Southern coasts should likewise be developed. Moreover, the development of our waterways involves many other important water problems, all of which should be considered as part of the same general scheme. The government dams should be used to produce hundreds of thousands of horse-power as an incident to improving navigation; for the annual value of the unused water-power of the United States perhaps exceeds the annual value of the products of all our mines. As an incident to creating the deep waterways down the Mississippi, the government should build along its whole lower length levees which, taken together with the control of the head-waters, will at once and forever put a complete stop to all threat of floods in the immensely fertile delta region. The territory lying adjacent to the Mississippi along its lower course will thereby become one of the most prosperous and populous, as it already is one of the most fertile, farming regions in all the world. I have appointed an inland waterways commission to study and outline a comprehensive scheme of development along all the lines indicated. Later I shall lay its report before the Congress.

Irrigation should be far more extensively developed than at present, not only in the States of the great plains and the Rocky Mountains, but in many others, as, for instance, in large portions of the South Atlantic and Gulf States, where it should go hand in hand with the reclamation of swampland. The Federal Government should seriously devote itself to this task, realizing that utilization of waterways and water-power, forestry, irrigation, and the reclamation of lands threatened with overflow, are all interdependent parts of the same problem. The work of the Reclamation Service in developing the larger opportunities of the Western half of our country for irrigation is more important than almost any other movement. The constant purpose of the government in connection with the Reclamation Service has been to use the water resources of the public lands for the ultimate greatest good of the greatest number; in other words, to put upon the land permanent home-makers, to use and develop it for themselves and for their children and children's children. . . .

Legislation . . . is essential in order to preserve the great stretches of public grazing-land which are unfit for cultivation under present methods and are valuable only for the forage which they supply. These stretches amount in all to some 300,000,000 acres, and are open to the free grazing of cattle, sheep, horses, and goats, without restriction. Such a system, or lack of system, means that the range is not so much used as wasted by abuse. As the West settles, the range becomes more and more overgrazed. Much of it cannot be used to advantage unless it is fenced, for fencing is the only way by which to keep in check the owners of nomad flocks which roam hither and thither, utterly destroying the pastures and leaving a waste behind so that their presence is incompatible with the presence of home-makers. The existing fences are all illegal. . . . All these fences, those that are hurtful and those that are beneficial, are alike illegal and must come down. But it is an outrage that the law should necessitate such action on the part of the Administration. The unlawful fencing of public lands for private grazing must be stopped, but the necessity which occasioned it must be provided for. The Federal Government should have control of the range, whether by permit or lease, as local necessities may determine. Such control could secure the great benefit of legitimate fencing, while at the same time securing and promoting the settlement of the country. . . . The government should part with its title only to the actual home-maker, not to the profit-maker who does not care to make a home. Our prime object is to secure the rights and guard the interests of the small ranchman, the man who ploughs and pitches hay for himself. It is this small ranchman, this actual settler and home-maker, who in the long run is most hurt by permitting thefts of the public land in whatever form.

Optimism is a good characteristic, but if carried to an excess it becomes foolishness. We are prone to speak of the resources of this country as inexhaustible; this is not so. The mineral wealth of the country, the coal, iron, oil, gas, and the like, does not reproduce itself, and therefore is certain to be exhausted ultimately; and wastefulness in dealing with it today means that our descendants will feel the exhaustion a generation or two before they otherwise would. But there are certain other forms of waste which could be entirely stopped—the waste of soil by washing, for instance, which is among the most dangerous of all wastes now in progress in the United States, is easily preventable, so that this present enormous loss of fertility is entirely unnecessary. The preservation or replacement of the forests is one of the most important means of preventing this loss. We have made a beginning in forest preservation, but . . . so rapid has been the rate of exhaustion of timber in the United States in the past, and so rapidly is the remainder being exhausted, that the country is unquestionably on the verge of a timber famine which will be felt in every household in the land. . . . The present annual consumption of lumber is certainly three times as great as the annual growth; and if the consumption and growth continue unchanged, practically all our lumber will be exhausted in another generation, while long before the limit to complete exhaustion is reached the growing scarcity will make itself felt in many blighting ways upon our national welfare. About twenty per cent of our forested territory is now reserved in national forests; but these do not include the most valuable timberlands, and in any event the proportion is too small to expect that the reserves can accomplish more than a mitigation of the trouble which is ahead for the nation. . . . We should acquire in the Appalachian and White Mountain regions all the forest-lands that it is possible to acquire for the use of the nation. These lands, because they form a national asset, are as emphatically national as the rivers which they feed, and which flow through so many States before they reach the ocean.

—THEODORE ROOSEVELT, Seventh Annual Message to Congress, 1907

13. THE TVA AND THE SEAMLESS WEB OF NATURE

Theodore Roosevelt's successors showed comparatively little interest in the problem of conservation, and in the quarter-century after he retired from the Presidency, the national domain deteriorated. With the accession of Franklin D. Roosevelt begins a new and happier chapter in the checkered history of conservation. The program he inaugurated constitutes the most far-reaching and the most elaborate effort yet made to preserve and restore the soil, forest, water power and wildlife of the nation. It involved, among other things, the replanting of millions of acres of forest by the Civilian Conservation Corps, the construction of some six million check dams, the enactment of an omnibus flood control bill, a comprehensive program to check erosion on some three hundred million acres of farm land, the elimination of pollution in streams, the creation of numerous game and fish preserves, the closing of grazing lands to homestead entries and—above all—the Tennessee Valley Authority. The story of the TVA is too well known to justify rehearsal here. We have given an excerpt from David Lilienthal's own account of the significance and achievements of this most important of all the New Deal enterprises.

TAMING THE WATERS

BEFORE the men of the Tennessee Valley built these dams, flooding was a yearly threat to every farm and industry, every town and village and railroad on the river's banks, a barrier to progress. Today there is security from that annual danger in the Tennessee Valley. With the erection of local protective works at a few points this region will be completely safe, even against a flood bigger than anything in recorded history. A measure of protection resulting from the Tennessee's control extends even beyond this valley; for no longer will the Tennessee send her torrents at flood crest to add what might be fatal inches to top the levees and spread desolation on the lower Ohio and the Mississippi.

In others of the earth's thousand valleys people live under the shadow of fear that each year their river will bring upon them damage to their property, suffering, and death. Here the people are safe. In the winter of 1942 torrents came raging down this valley's two chief tributaries, in Tennessee and Virginia. Before the river was controlled this would have meant a severe flood; the machinery of vital war industries down the river at Chattanooga would have stopped, under several feet of water, with over a million dollars of direct damage resulting.

But in 1942 it was different. Orders went out from the TVA office of central control to every tributary dam. The message came flashing to the operator in the control room at Hiwassee Dam, deep in the mountains of North Carolina: "Hold back all the water of the Hiwassee River. Keep it out of the Tennessee." The operator pressed a button. Steel gates closed. The water of that tributary was held. To Cherokee Dam on the Holston went the message: "Keep back the flow of the Holston." To Chickamauga Dam just above the industrial danger spot at Chattanooga: "Release water to make room for the waters from above."

Day by day till the crisis was over the men at their control instruments at each dam in the system received their orders. The rate of water release from every tributary river was precisely controlled. The Tennessee was kept in hand. There was no destruction, no panic, no interruption of work. Most of the water, instead of wrecking the valley, actually produced a benefit in power, when later it was released through the turbines. . . .

NEW LIFE FROM THE LAND

The river now is changed. It does its work. But it is on the land that the people live. Millions of acres of the valley's land had lost its vitality. The people had to make it strong again and fruitful if they themselves were to be strong. For here in this valley more people depend for a living upon each acre of farm land than in any other area in America. The farms are usually small, an average of seventy-five acres. Farm families are large, and the birth-rate is the highest in the United States. Many people living on impoverished land—that was the picture ten years ago. If the moral purpose of resource development—the greatest benefit to human beings—was to be achieved, TVA had to see to it that the land changed as well as the river.

THE LAND ON THE MEND

And the land is changing. It is a slow job. Engineering a river with large-scale modern machinery and rebuilding soil that for generations has been losing its vitality are tasks of a different tempo. But even after these few years you can see the difference everywhere. The gullies are being healed. The scars of erosion are on the mend, slowly but steadily. The many wounds yet to be healed are by their contrast eloquent evidence of what a decade's work in restoration has accomplished. The cover of dark green, the pasture and deep meadow and upstanding fields of oats and rye, the marks of fertility and productiveness are on every hand. Matting and sloping, seeding and sodding have given protection to eroded banks on scores of thousands of acres. Ditches to divert the water and little dams to check it, hundreds of thousands of them, help control the course of the water on the land, hold it there till it can soak down and feed the roots of newly planted trees and grasses. A hundred and fifty million seedling trees have been planted on hundreds of thousands of acres of land from TVA nursery stock alone.

The farmers have built terraces on a million acres and more; their graceful design, following the contour, makes a new kind of landscape, one that led Jefferson, observing the effect upon the face of his own Monticello acres, to exclaim that in "point of beauty nothing can exceed" contour plowing with its "waving lines and rows winding along the face of the hills and valleys." . . .

THE SEAMLESS WEB

The TVA Act was nothing inadvertent or impromptu. It was rather the deliberate and well-considered creation of a new national policy. For the first time in the history of the nation, the resources of a river were not only to be "envisioned in their entirety"; they were to be developed *in that unity with which nature herself regards her resources* —the waters, the land, and the forests together, a "seamless web"—just as Maitland saw "the unity of all history," of which one strand cannot be touched without affecting every other strand for good or ill.

Under this new policy, the opportunity of creating wealth for the people from the resources of this valley was to be faced as a single problem. To integrate the many parts of that problem into a unified whole was to be the responsibility of one agency. The Tennessee Valley's resources were not to be dissected into separate bits that would fit into the jurisdictional pigeon-holes into which the instrumentalities of government had by custom become divided. It was not conceded that at the hour of Creation the Lord had divided and classified natural resources to conform to the organization chart of the federal government. The particular and limited concerns of private individuals or agencies in the development of this or that resource were disregarded and rejected in favor of the principle of unity. What God had made one, man was to develop as one.

"Envisioned in its entirety" this river, like every river in the world, had many potential assets. It could yield hydro-electric power for the comfort of the people in their homes, could promote prosperity on their farms and foster the development of industry. But the same river by the very same dams, if they were wisely designed, could be made to provide a channel for navigation. The river could also be made to provide fun for fishermen and fish for food, pleasure from boating and swimming, a water supply for homes and factories. But the river also presented an account of liabilities. It threatened the welfare of the people by its recurrent floods; pollution from industrial wastes and public sewage diminished its value as a source of water supply and for recreation; its current carried to the sea the soil of the hills and fields to be lost there to men forever.

To a single agency, the TVA, these potentialities of the river for good and evil were entrusted. But the river was to be seen as part of the larger pattern of the region, one asset of the many that in nature are interwoven: the land, the minerals, the waters, the forests—and all of these as one—in their relation to the lives of the valley's people. It was the total benefit to all that was to be the common goal and the new agency's responsibility. . . .

Because they sinned against the unity of nature, because they developed some one resource without regard to its relation to every other resource in the life of man, ancient civilizations have fallen into decay and lie buried in oblivion. Everywhere in the world the trail of unbalanced resource development is marked by poverty, where prosperity seemed assured; by ugliness and desolation, with towns now dying that once were thriving; by land that once supported gracious living now eroded and bare, and over wide areas the chill of death to the ambitions of the enterprising young and to the security of the mature.

—DAVID E. LILIENTHAL, *TVA, Democracy on the March,* 1944

Part II

Principles, Traditions, and Institutions

Fundamentals of the American
Political System

AMERICA is the youngest of great nations, but it is in many respects very old. It is, of major countries, the oldest republic, the oldest democracy, the oldest federal system; it has the oldest written constitution and boasts the oldest of genuine political parties. Nor has any people of modern times made more important contributions to political institutions and practices. Americans invented the constitutional convention; they were the first to formulate written constitutions; they set up the first real federal system; they put an end to the colonial problem by the simple device of treating colonies as equals. In short, they worked out great basic principles of government that enabled them to solve some of the most perplexing problems in the realm of government—the problem of liberty and order, of localism and centralization, of church and state, of democracy, of equality, and others scarcely less fundamental.

Time was when we could take these basic principles for granted—who, after all, in the nineteenth century denied the dignity of man, or the precepts of democracy, liberty, and justice? But we have discovered, in the last quarter-century, that we can no longer take any principles for granted—not even the principle of rationality. We have discovered, to our dismay, that those who subscribe to the principles that Jefferson called "self-evident" are in the minority among the peoples of the globe, and that we are now required to vindicate those principles as never before in our past.

More specifically, what are some of these principles? First, the principle of democracy—that government comes from below, not from above, and that it derives its powers from the consent of the governed. Second, the principle of liberty, that all government is limited, that there are some things no government can do, and that among these things are

109

the infringement of the inalienable rights of men. Third, the principle of federalism, that it is both wise and feasible to distribute powers among governments, giving local powers to local governments and general powers to the national government. Fourth, the principle of equality —that men are born equal, that they are equal in the sight of God, equal before the law, and should have equal privileges and opportunities insofar as society can assure these.

Now none of these principles are entirely new; indeed all of them have long historical and philosophical antecedents. What is remarkable is that Americans took these principles and actualized them. They took the principle that men make government and made it into the institu tion of the constitutional convention. They took the principle that government is limited and actualized it by such devices as the written constitution, checks and balances, bills of rights, and judicial review. They took the principle of the distribution of powers and actualized it into a federal system. They took the principle that colonists were not inferior to those who stayed at home and actualized it in the Northwest Ordinance which provided for full equality between colonies and mother country. They took the principle—perhaps we should say the dream—of equality and worked on its social and economic and intellectual implications as well as on its political implications.

The sources and documents we present here are designed to illustrate some of these basic principles and their applications. Thus we have in the Mayflower Compact and Fundamental Orders of Connecticut the beginnings of written constitutions. Thus we have in the essays of John Locke—surely he belongs to American history—and in the remarkable John Wise of Massachusetts, the antecedents to those principles later set forth in the Declaration of Independence. Thus we have in the bill of rights of Virginia the prototype of all subsequent bills of rights, state and federal. The principle of federalism, foreshadowed in the practices of the British Empire, reached its formulation in the Federal Constitution itself —a document too long and too familiar to reproduce here.

With the ratification and establishment of the Constitution, the basic principles were established but by no means vindicated; we are even yet concerned with their vindication. Succeeding chapters of this book will tell something of that story. We have chosen to include in this chapter not only a few of the basic documents of our constitutional system, but some of the more interesting philosophical discussions of the nature of the American political experiment. Thus we have eloquent statements from such diverse people as Washington, Jefferson, Tom Paine, Charles Pinckney, James Wilson, and John Marshall, as well as from latter-day spokesmen like David Lilienthal and Franklin D. Roosevelt. The chapter on democracy will present more specific attacks upon and defenses of democracy.

i. THE MAYFLOWER COMPACT

We have already seen how the Separatists, or Pilgrims as we now call them, set sail from Leyden, Holland, to the New World, and what they found there. It was in November, 1620, that the Mayflower arrived off Cape Cod. Some of the recruits they had picked up at Southampton and London were, as Bradford tells us, "an undesirable lot" and boasted that they were not under the jurisdiction of the Company but "would use their owne libertie." Thus at the very beginning of our history, the settlers were confronted with the problem of liberty versus order. They solved that problem in what was to be a characteristic fashion. Taking for granted that authority was inherent in them, the Pilgrim leaders drew up the Mayflower Compact—an extension to civil conditions of the customary church covenant and of the sea covenant. As the Plymouth settlers were never able to get a charter, the Mayflower Compact remained the only constitution of the colony and has some title to be considered the first written constitution in the New World.

IN THE Name of God, Amen. We, whose names are underwritten, the Loyal Subjects of our dread Sovereign Lord King *James*, by the Grace of God, of *Great Britain, France*, and *Ireland*, King, *Defender of the Faith*, &c. Having undertaken for the Glory of God, and Advancement of the Christian Faith, and the Honour of our King and Country, a Voyage to plant the first colony in the northern Parts of Virginia; Do by these Presents, solemnly and mutually in the Presence of God and one another, convenant and combine ourselves together into a civil Body Politick, for our better Ordering and Preservation, and Furtherance of the Ends aforesaid; And by Virtue hereof do enact, constitute, and frame, such just and equal Laws, Ordinances, Acts, Constitutions, and Offices, from time to time, as shall be thought most meet and convenient for the general Good of the Colony; unto which we promise all due Submission and Obedience. In WITNESS whereof we have hereunto subscribed our names at *Cape Cod* the eleventh of *November*, in the Reign of our Sovereign Lord King *James* of *England, France,* and *Ireland,* the eighteenth and of *Scotland,* the fifty-fourth. *Anno Domini,* 1620

Mr. John Carver	Mr. Stephen Hopkins
Mr. William Bradford	Digery Priest
Mr. Edward Winslow	Thomas Williams
Mr. William Brewster	Gilbert Winslow
Isaac Allerton	Edmund Margesson
Miles Standish	Peter Brown
John Alden	Richard Bitteridge
John Turner	George Soule
Francis Eaton	Edward Tilly
James Chilton	John Tilly
John Craxton	Francis Cooke
John Billington	Thomas Rogers
Joses Fletcher	Thomas Tinker
John Goodman	John Ridgate
Mr. Samuel Fuller	Edward Fuller
Mr. Christopher Martin	Richard Clark
Mr. William Mullins	Richard Gardiner
Mr. William White	Mr. John Allerton
Mr. Richard Warren	Thomas English
John Howland	Edward Doten
	Edward Liester

—The Mayflower Compact, November, 1620

2. THE FUNDAMENTAL ORDERS OF CONNECTICUT

The Fundamental Orders have a better claim than the Mayflower Compact to be considered the first written constitution to establish and sustain a civil government. It was in 1636 that the Reverend Thomas Hooker led his New Town congregation westward from Massachusetts

*Bay to the Connecticut River. By 1638 his followers, now joined by
others, had established the towns of Hartford, Windsor and Wethersfield. In January, 1639, the freemen of these towns gathered at Hartford
and drew up the Fundamental Orders. Thus once again the deep instinct of the earliest settlers for orderly government was asserted and
vindicated.*

FORASMUCH as it hath pleased the Allmighty God by the wise
disposition of his divyne pruvidence so to Order and dispose of
things that we the Inhabitants and Residents of Windsor, Harteford and
Wethersfield are now cohabiting and dwelling in and uppon the River
of Conectecotte and the Lands thereunto adioyneing; And well knowing
where a people are gathered togather the word of God requires that to
mayntayne the peace and union of such a people there should be an
orderly and decent Government established according to God, to order
and dispose of the affayres of the people at all seasons as occation shall
require; doe therefore assotiate and conioyne our selves to be as one
Publike State or Commonwelth; and doe, for our selves and our Successors and such as shall be adioyned to us att any tyme hereafter, enter
into Combination and Confederation togather, to mayntayne and pre-
searve the liberty and purity of the gospell of our Lord Jesus which we
now professe, as also the disciplyne of the Churches, which according to
the truth of the said gospell is now practised amongst us; As also in our
Civell Affaires to be guided and governed according to such Lawes,
Rules, Orders and decrees as shall be made, ordered & decreed, as
followeth:—

1. It is Ordered . . . that there shall be yerely two generall Assemblies
or Courts, . . . one Governour . . . sixe chosen besids the Governour;
which being chosen and sworne according to an Oath recorded for that
purpose shall have power to administer iustice according to the Lawes
here established, and for want thereof according to the rule of the word
of God; which choise shall be made by all that are admitted freemen
and have taken the Oath of Fidellity, and doe cohabitte within this Jurisdiction, (having beene admitted Inhabitants by the major part of the
Towne wherein they live,) or the major parte of such as shall be then
present.

4. It is Ordered . . . that noe person be chosen Governor above once in two yeares, and that the Governor be alwayes a member of some approved congregation, and formerly of the Magestracy within this Jurisdiction; and all the Magestrats Freemen of this Commonwelth: . . .

5. It is Ordered . . . that to the aforesaid Courte of Election the severall Townes shall send their deputyes, and when the Elections are ended they may proceed in any publike searvice as at other Courts. Also the other Generall Courte in September shall be for makeing of lawes, and any other publike occation, which concerns the good of the Commonwelth.

7. It is Ordered . . . that after there are warrants given out for any of the said Generall Courts, the Constable . . . of ech Towne shall forthwith give notice distinctly to the inhabitants of the same, . . . that at a place and tyme by him or them lymited and sett, they meet and assemble them selves togather to elect and chuse certen deputyes to be att the Generall Courte then following to agitate the afayres of the commonwelth; which said Deputyes shall be chosen by all that are admitted Inhabitants in the severall Townes and have taken the oath of fidellity; provided that non be chosen a Deputy for any Generall Courte which is not a Freeman of this Commonwelth. . . .

10. It is Ordered . . . that every Generall Courte . . . shall consist of the Governor, or some one chosen to moderate the Court, and 4 other Magestrats at lest, with the major parte of the deputyes of the severall Townes legally chosen; and in case the Freemen or major parte of them, through neglect or refusall of the Governor and major parte of the magestrats, shall call a Courte, it shall consist of the major parte of Freemen that are present or their deputyes, with a Moderator chosen by them: In which said Generall Courts shall consist the supreme power of the Commonwelth, and they only shall have power to make lawes or repeale them, to graunt levyes, to admitt of Freemen, dispose of lands undisposed of, to severall Townes or persons, and also shall have power to call ether Courte or Magestrate or any other person whatsoever into question for any misdemeanour, and may for just causes displace or deale otherwise according to the nature of the offence; and also may deale in any other matter that concerns the good of this commonwelth, excepte election of Magestrats, which shall be done by the whole boddy of Freemen.

In which Courte the Governour or Moderator shall have power to order the Courte to give liberty of spech, and silence unceasonable and disorderly speakeings, to put all things to voate, and in case the vote be equall to have the casting voice. But non of these Courts shall be adjorned or dissolved without the consent of the major parte of the Court.

11. It is ordered . . . that when any Generall Courte uppon the occasions of the Commonwelth have agreed uppon any summe or sommes of mony to be levyed uppon the severall Townes within this Jurisdiction, that a Committee be chosen to sett out and appoynt what shall be the proportion of every Towne to pay of the said levy, provided the Committees be made up of an equall number out of each Towne.

—Fundamental Orders of Connecticut, January, 1639

3. AN EARLY ASSERTION OF COLONIAL INDEPENDENCE

How early did Americans begin to think of themselves as apart from, and even independent of, the mother country? That is hard to say. All through the colonial period the commercial, religious, and cultural ties between colonies and mother country grew more intricate, yet all through this long period, too, the American colonies were becoming more and more independent. And from almost the beginning many Americans felt that they had all the rights of Englishmen—including the right of self-government. The Massachusetts Bay Charter of 1629 did not specifically provide that the Bay Colony was bound by the laws of Parliament, and on many occasions leaders of the Puritan colony insisted that it was bound only by laws passed by its own representatives. This attitude is implicit, if not explicit, in the famous Massachusetts Body of Liberties of 1641 (see Chapter VIII). This Declaration of Liberties, submitted to the General Court in the summer of 1661, argued that the Bay authorities themselves had "full power and authoritie" in the colony.

CONCERNING our liberties
 1. Wee conceive the pattent (under God) to be the first & maine foundation of our civil politye, by a Gouvernor & Company, according as is therein exprest.

2. The Gouvernor & Company are, by the pattent, a body politicke, in fact & name.

3. This body politicke is vested with power to make freemen. . . .

6. The Gouvernor, Deputy Gouvernor, Asistants, & select representatives or deputies have full power and authoritie, both legislative & executive, for the gouvernment of all the people heere, whither inhabitants or straingers, both concerning eclesiasticks & in civils, without appeale, excepting lawe or lawes repugnant to the lawes of England. . . .

8. Wee conceive any imposition prejudiciall to the country contrary to any just lawe of ours, not repugnant to the lawes of England, to be an infringement of our right.

—Massachusetts' Declaration of Liberties, June, 1661

4. THE ORIGIN AND NATURE OF GOVERNMENT

Although he died in 1704, John Locke has a valid claim to be called the philosopher of the American Revolution. Certainly no other political philosopher, except Jefferson himself, has had so profound an influence on American political thought and practice. Forget that Locke drafted that curious Eternal Constitution for the Carolinas that was designed to provide a feudal framework for a frontier province. What is important is that his Essay on Tolerance *foreshadowed the American attitude toward religions; that his* Essay Concerning Human Understanding *anticipated those empirical arguments that were to be so characteristic of American philosophical thought; and that his* Second Treatise on Government *elaborated the arguments for the origin of government and the relations of man to government which Jefferson summarized so eloquently in the great Declaration. So closely does the preamble of the* Declaration *follow the* Second Treatise *that Jefferson has been accused of plagiarism; in fact Jefferson consulted neither Locke nor any other political theorists; Locke was so much a part of his thinking that he did not need to do so.*

As Locke lay dying in that Essex manorhouse to which he had retired, he wrote to a young friend:

Now, methinks—and these are often old men's dreams—I see openings to truth and direct paths leading to it, wherein a little industry and application would settle one's mind with satisfaction, and leave no darkness or doubt. But this is at the end of my day, when my sun is setting; and though the prospect it has given me be what I would not for anything be without—there is so much irresistible truth, beauty, and consistency in it—yet it is for one of your age . . . to set about it.

In the end it was the Americans of a later age who set about it. If it cannot be said that they left neither darkness nor doubt in the realm of politics, it can be said that they found openings to truth.

87. Man being born, as has been proved, with a title to perfect freedom, and an uncontrolled enjoyment of all the rights and privileges of the law of nature equally with any other man or number of men in the world, hath by nature a power not only to preserve his property—that is, his life, liberty, and estate—against the injuries and attempts of other men, but to judge of and punish the breaches of that law in others as he is persuaded the offense deserves, even with death itself, in crimes where the heinousness of the fact in his opinion requires it. But because no political society can be nor subsist without having in itself the power to preserve the property, and, in order thereunto, punish the offenses of all those of that society, there, and there only, is political society, where every one of the members hath quitted this natural power, resigned it up into the hands of the community in all cases that exclude him not from appealing for protection to the law established by it; and thus all private judgment of every particular member being excluded, the community comes to be umpire; and by understanding indifferent rules and men authorized by the community for their execution, decides all the differences that may happen between any members of that society concerning any matter of right, and punishes those offenses which any member hath committed against the society with such penalties as the law has established; whereby it is easy to discern who are and who are not in political society together. Those who are united into one body, and have a common established law and judicature to appeal to, with authority to decide controversies between them and punish offenders, are in civil society one with another; but those who have no such common appeal—I mean on earth—are still in the state of nature, each being, where there is no other, judge for himself and executioner, which is, as I have before shown it, the perfect state of nature. . . .

95. Men being, as has been said, by nature all free, equal, and independent, no one can be put out of this estate, and subjected to the political power of another, without his own consent, which is done by agreeing with other men to join and unite into a community for their comfortable, safe, and peaceable living one amongst another, in a secure enjoyment of their properties, and a greater security against any that are not of it. This any number of men may do, because it injures not the freedom of the rest; they are left as they were in the liberty of the state of nature. When any number of men have so consented to make one community or government, they are thereby presently incorporated, and make one body politic, wherein the majority have a right to act and conclude the rest.

96. For when any number of men have, by the consent of every individual, made a community, they have thereby made that community one body, with a power to act as one body, which is only by the will and determination of the majority. For that which acts any community being only the consent of the individuals of it, and it being one body must move one way, it is necessary the body should move that way whither the greater force carries it, which is the consent of the majority; or else it is impossible it should act or continue one body, one community, which the consent of every individual that united into it agreed that it should; and so everyone is bound by that consent to be concluded by the majority. And therefore we see that in assemblies empowered to act by positive laws, where no number is set by that positive law which empowers them, the act of the majority passes for the act of the whole, and of course determines, as having by the law of nature and reason the power of the whole.

97. And thus every man, by consenting with others to make one body politic under one government, puts himself under an obligation to every one of that society, to submit to the determination of the majority, and to be concluded by it; or else this original compact, whereby he with others incorporates into one society, would signify nothing, and be no compact, if he be left free and under no other ties than he was in before in the state of nature. For what appearance would there be of any compact? What new engagement if he were no farther tied by any decrees of the society, than he himself thought fit, and did actually consent to? This would be still as great a liberty as he himself had before his compact, or anyone else in the state of nature hath, who may submit himself and consent to any acts of it if he thinks fit. . . .

131. But though men when they enter into society give up the equality, liberty and executive power they had in the state of nature into the hands of the society, to be so far disposed of by the legislative as the good of the society shall require; yet it being only with an intention in everyone the better to preserve himself, his liberty and property (for no rational creature can be supposed to change his condition with an intention to be worse), the power of the society, or legislative constituted by them, can never be supposed to extend farther than the common good, but is obliged to secure everyone's property by providing against those three defects above-mentioned that made the state of nature so unsafe and uneasy. And so whoever has the legislative or supreme power of any commonwealth is bound to govern by established standing laws, promulgated and known to the people, and not by extemporary decrees; by indifferent and upright judges, who are to decide controversies by those laws; and to employ the force of the community at home only in the execution of such laws, or abroad, to prevent or redress foreign injuries, and secure the community from inroads and invasion. And all this to be directed to no other end but the peace, safety, and public good of the people. . . .

135. Though the legislative, whether placed in one or more, whether it be always in being, or only by intervals, though it be the supreme power in every commonwealth, yet,

First, It is not nor can possibly be absolutely arbitrary over the lives and fortunes of the people. For it being but the joint power of every member of the society given up to that person, or assembly, which is legislator; it can be no more than those persons had in a state of nature before they entered into society, and gave it up to the community. For nobody can transfer to another more power than he has in himself; and nobody has an absolute arbitrary power over himself, or over any other to destroy his own life, or take away the life or property of another. A man as has been proved cannot subject himself to the arbitrary power of another; and having in the state of nature no arbitrary power over the life, liberty, or possession of another, but only so much as the law of nature gave him for the preservation of himself, and the rest of mankind; this is all he doth, or can give up to the commonwealth, and by it to the legislative power, so that the legislative can have no more than this. Their power in the utmost bounds of it, is limited to the public good of the society. It is a power that hath no other end but preservation, and therefore can never have a right to destroy, enslave, or designedly to impoverish the subjects. The obligations of the law of nature cease not in society, but only in many cases are drawn closer, and have by human laws known penalties annexed to them to enforce their observation. Thus the law of nature stands as an eternal rule to all men, legislators as well as others. The rules that they make for other men's actions must, as well as their own, and other men's actions be conformable to the law of nature, i.e., to the will of God, of which that is a declaration, and the fundamental law of nature being the preservation of mankind, no human sanction can be good or valid against it.

136. Secondly, The legislative, or supreme authority, cannot assume to itself a power to rule by extemporary arbitrary decrees, but is bound to dispense justice, and decide the rights of the subject by promulgated standing laws, and known authorized judges. . . .

142. These are the bounds which the trust that is put in them by the society, and the law of God and Nature, have set to the legislative power of every commonwealth, in all forms of government.

First, They are to govern by promulgated established laws, not to be varied in particular cases, but to have one rule for rich and poor, for the favorite at court and the countryman at plough.

Secondly, These laws also ought to be designed for no other end ultimately but the good of the people.

Thirdly, They must not raise taxes on the property of the people without the consent of the people, given by themselves or their deputies. And this properly concerns only such governments where the legislative is always in being, or at least where the people have not reserved any part of the legislative to deputies, to be from time to time chosen by themselves.

Fourthly, The legislative neither must nor can transfer the power of making laws to anybody else, or place it anywhere but where the people have.

—John Locke, *Two Treatises on Government,* 1690

5. NATURAL LAW AND DEMOCRACY

We think of democracy as largely a nineteenth-century development, and there are some who ascribe it to the twentieth century, confusing the qualitative principle that men make government with the quantitative principle that the majority of men and women should be involved in the making. The philosophical origin of the qualitative principle is very old; its practical origin, for American purposes, is to be found in Congregational church polity. For it was very easy—especially in a theocratic society—to transfer the principle that men could make a church into the principle that men could make a town or a state. It is no accident that the first elaborate analysis of the relationship between congregationalism and democracy should come out of a theological controversy—the controversy between the Increase Mather party who wanted to enlarge the authority of the ministerial association, and John Wise who argued the independence of the individual congregation. Wise's Vindication of the Government of New England *actually covered broad ground—the democratic origin of civil as well as of church government. The first comprehensive argument for democracy in our literature,* Wise's Vindication *remains one of the most thoughtful and most eloquent.*

THE native liberty of man's nature implies, a faculty of doing or omitting things according to the direction of his judgment. But in a more special meaning, this liberty does not consist in a loose and ungovernable freedom, or in an unbounded licence of acting. . . .

Mans external personal, natural liberty, antecedent to all human parts, or alliances must also be considered. And so every man must be conceived to be perfectly in his own power and disposal, and not to be controuled by the authority of any other. And thus every man, must be acknowledged equal to every man, since all subjection and all command are equally banished on both sides; and considering all men thus at liberty, every man, has a prerogative to judge for himself, *viz.* What shall be most for his behoof, happiness and well-being.

The third capital immunity belonging to mans nature, is an equality amongst men; which is not to be denied by the law of nature, till man has resigned himself with all his rights for the sake of a civil state; and then his personal liberty and equality is to be cherished, and preserved to the highest degree, as will consist with all just distinctions amongst men of honor, and shall be agreable with the public good. For man has a high valuation of himself, and the passion seems to lay its first foundation (not in pride, but) really in the high and admirable frame and constitution of human nature. The word man, says my author, is thought to carry somewhat of dignity in its sound; and we commonly make use of this

as the most proper and prevailing argument against a rude insulter, *viz.*
I am not a beast or a dog. But am a man as well as yourself. Since then
human nature agrees equally with all persons; and since no one can live
a sociable life with another that does not own or respect him as a man;
It follows as a command of the law of nature, that every man esteem
and treat another as one who is naturally his equal, or who is a man as
well as he. . . .

In a word, an aristocracy is a dangerous constitution in the church of
Christ, as it possesses the presbytery of all church power: What has been
observed sufficiently evinces it. And not only so but from the nature of
the constitution, for it has no more barrier to it, against the ambition,
insults, and arbitrary measures of men, then an absolute monarchy. But
to abbreviate; it seems most agreable with the light of nature, that if
there be any of the regular government settled in the church of God it
must needs be,

A democracy. This is a form of government, which the light of nature
does highly value, and often directs to as most agreable to the just and
natural prerogatives of human beings. . . .

That mans original liberty after it is resigned, (yet under due restrictions) ought to be cherished in all wise governments; or otherwise a man in making himself a subject, he alters himself from a freeman, into a slave, which to do is repugnant to the law of nature. Also
the natural equality of men amongst men must be duly favored; in
that government was never established by God or nature, to give one
man a prerogative to insult over another; therefore in a civil, as well
as in a natural state of being, a just equality is to be indulged so far as
that every man, is bound to honor every man, which is agreable both
with nature and religion, . . . The end of all good government is to
cultivate humanity, and promote the happiness of all, and the good
of every man in all his rights, his life, liberty, estate, honor, &c.
without injury or abuse done to any. Then certainly it cannot easily be
thought, that a company of men, that shall enter into a voluntary compact, to hold all power in their own hands, thereby to use and improve
their united force, wisdom, riches and strength for the common and
particular good of every member, as is the nature of a democracy; I say it
cannot be that this sort of constitution, will so readily furnish those in
government with an appetite, or disposition to prey upon each other, or
imbezle the common stock; as some particular persons may be apt to do
when set off, and intrusted with the same power. And moreover this
appears very natural, that when the aforesaid government or power,

settled in all, when they have elected certain capable persons to minister in their affairs, and the said ministers remain accountable to the assembly; these officers must needs be under the influence of many wise cautions from their own thoughts (as well as under confinement by their commission) in their whole administration: And from thence it must needs follow that they will be more apt, and inclined to steer right for the main point, *viz.* The peculiar good, and benefit of the whole, and every particular member fairly and sincerely.

—JOHN WISE, *Vindication of the Government of New England*, 1717

6. GOVERNMENT IS LIMITED

What is significant about the controversy between the colonies and the mother country is not that it revealed the rift between these two branches of the English-speaking peoples, but that it served to crystallize political and constitutional principles of lasting importance. One of these is of particular interest to us today. It is the assertion by Americans that the British Constitution protected Americans in their rights, and that the Constitution itself was fixed and not subject to Parliamentary change or repeal. In other words, government was limited. There were things no government could do—not even Parliament. To this the English could only reply that Parliament was supreme and that the Constitution was what Parliament said it was. But Americans took this principle that government is limited and wrote it into their own constitutional system. We give here two items—first, a brief excerpt from James Otis' "Rights of the British Colonies Asserted and Proved," and next, an extract from a series of letters written in 1768 by Samuel Adams on behalf of the Massachusetts House to friends in England.

A. "PARLIAMENT CANNOT MAKE TWO AND TWO FIVE"

TO SAY the parliament is absolute and arbitrary, is a contradiction. The parliament cannot make 2 and 2, 5; Omnipotency cannot do it. The supreme power in a state, is *jus dicere* only;—*jus dare,* strictly speaking, belongs alone to God. Parliaments are in all cases to *declare* what is for the good of the whole; but it is not the declaration of Parliament that makes it so: There must be in every instance, a higher authority, viz. GOD. Should an act of parliament be against any of *his* natural laws, which are *immutably* true, their declaration would be contrary to eternal truth, equity and justice, and consequently void: and so it would be adjudged by the parliament itself, when convinced of their mistake. Upon this great principle, parliaments repeal such acts, as soon as they find they have been mistaken, in having declared them to be for the public good, when in fact they were not so. When such mistake is evident and palpable . . . the judges of the executive courts have declared the act 'of a whole parliament void.' See here the grandeur of the British constitution! See the wisdom of our ancestors! The supreme *legislative,* and the supreme *executive,* are a perpetual check and balance to each other. If the supreme executive errs, it is informed by the supreme legislative in parliament: If the supreme legislative errs, it is informed by the supreme executive in the King's courts of law—Here, the King appears, as represented by his judges, in the highest lustre and majesty, as supreme executor of the commonwealth; and he never shines brighter, but on his Throne, at the head of the supreme legislative. This is government! This, is a constitution! to preserve which, either from foreign or domestic foes, has cost oceans of blood and treasure in every age; and the blood and the treasure have upon the whole been well spent.

—JAMES OTIS, "Rights of the British Colonies," 1764

B. "IN ALL FREE STATES THE CONSTITUTION IS FIXED"

TO LORD CAMDEN
January 29, 1768

If in all free states, the constitution is fixed, and the supreme legislative power of the nation, from thence derives its authority; can that power overleap the bounds of the constitution, without subverting its own foundation? If the remotest subjects, are bound by the ties of allegiance, which this people and their forefathers have ever acknowledged; are they not by the rules of equity, intitled to all rights of that constitution, which ascertains and limits both sovereignty and allegiance? If it is an essential unalterable right in nature, ingrafted into the British constitution as a fundamental law, and ever held sacred and irrevocable by the subjects within the realm, and that what is a man's

own is absolutely his own; and that no man hath a right to take it from him without his consent; may not the subjects of this province, with a decent firmness, which has always distinguished the happy subjects of Britain, plead and maintain this natural constitutional right?
—Letters of the Massachusetts House, 1768

7. THE DECLARATION OF INDEPENDENCE

This most famous document of American history needs no introduction. We have given here the preamble and the conclusion, leaving out the long list of grievances—the facts that were to be submitted "to a candid world." What is memorable about the Declaration is not only that it proclaimed the birth of a new nation, but that it set forth, with matchless eloquence, the basic philosophy of democracy and liberty. Though the document was technically the product of a Committee of Congress consisting of Jefferson, John Adams, Franklin, Roger Sherman, and R. R. Livingston, it was actually the work of Jefferson. Certainly it is to Jefferson that it owes the felicity and beauty of its phrasing.

W HEN in the Course of human events, it becomes necessary for one people to dissolve the political bands which have connected them with another, and to assume among the Powers of the earth, the separate and equal station to which the Laws of Nature and of Nature's God entitle them, a decent respect to the opinions of mankind requires that they should declare the causes which impel them to the separation.

We hold these truths to be self-evident, that all men are created equal, that they are endowed by their Creator with certain unalienable Rights, that among these are Life, Liberty and the pursuit of Happiness. That to secure these rights, Governments are instituted among Men, deriving their just powers from the consent of the governed. That whenever any Form of Government becomes destructive of these ends, it is the Right of the People to alter or to abolish it, and to institute new Government, laying its foundation on such principles and organizing its powers in such form, as to them shall seem most likely to effect their Safety and

Happiness. Prudence, indeed, will dictate that Governments long established should not be changed for light and transient causes; and accordingly all experience hath shown, that mankind are more disposed to suffer, while evils are sufferable, than to right themselves by abolishing the forms to which they are accustomed. But when a long train of abuses and usurpations, pursuing invariably the same Object evinces a design to reduce them under absolute Despotism, it is their right, it is their duty, to throw off such Government, and to provide new Guards for their future security.—Such has been the patient sufferance of these Colonies; and such is now the necessity which constrains them to alter their former Systems of Government. The history of the present King of Great Britain is a history of repeated injuries and usurpations, all having in direct object the establishment of an absolute Tyranny over these States. To prove this, let Facts be submitted to a candid world. . . .

In every stage of these Oppressions We have Petitioned for Redress in the most humble terms: Our repeated Petitions have been answered only by repeated injury. A Prince, whose character is thus marked by every act which may define a Tyrant, is unfit to be the ruler of a free People.

Nor have We been wanting in attention to our British brethren. We have warned them from time to time of attempts by their legislature to extend an unwarrantable jurisdiction over us. We have reminded them of the circumstances of our emigration and settlement here. We have appealed to their native justice and magnanimity, and we have conjured them by the ties of our common kindred to disavow these usurpations, which would inevitably interrupt our connections and correspondence. They too have been deaf to the voice of justice and of consanguinity. We must, therefore, acquiesce in the necessity, which denounces our Separation, and hold them, as we hold the rest of mankind, Enemies in War, in Peace Friends.

We, therefore, the Representatives of the United States of America, in General Congress, Assembled, appealing to the Supreme Judge of the world for the rectitude of our intentions, do, in the Name, and by the Authority of the good People of these Colonies, solemnly publish and declare, That these United Colonies are, and of Right ought to be Free and Independent States; that they are Absolved from all Allegiance to the British Crown, and that all political connection between them and the State of Great Britain, is and ought to be totally dissolved; and that as Free and Independent States, they have full Power to levy War, con-

clude Peace, contract Alliances, establish Commerce, and to do all other
Acts and Things which Independent States may of right do. And for the
support of this Declaration, with a firm reliance on the Protection of
Divine Providence, we mutually pledge to each other our Lives, our
Fortunes and our sacred Honor.

—THOMAS JEFFERSON, The Declaration of Independence, July 4, 1776

8. REVOLUTION LEGALIZED

*It was all very well to argue that governments derive their powers
from the consent of the governed, and that whenever governments
became destructive of the ends for which they were created people had
the right to alter or abolish them and to institute new governments.
But how was this to be done—above all, how was it to be done without
revolution and violence? Gradually, during the discussion and debate
of these years, Americans were working their way to a solution to this
problem—a solution which was to prove the greatest single contribution
of America to the theory and practice of politics. That was the constitutional convention. John Adams, one of the two or three wisest Americans of his generation, was perhaps the first to see the significance of
this institution and to point out how Americans, by coming together in
conventions and making constitutions, could "realize the theories of the
wisest writers." Here in his* Autobiography *he tells us how he explained
the institution to his fellow Congressmen. Soon the same suggestion
was to come from a number of Massachusetts towns, notably from the
town of Concord, whose town meeting outlined, with wonderful understanding, the steps requisite for transforming a colony into a commonwealth in accordance with the philosophy of democracy.*

A. "How Can the People Institute Governments?"

ALTHOUGH the opposition was still inveterate, many members of
Congress began to hear me with more patience, and some began
to ask me civil questions. "How can the people institute governments?"
My answer was, "By conventions of representatives, freely, fairly, and

proportionably chosen." "When the convention has fabricated a government, or a constitution rather, how do we know the people will submit to it?" "If there is any doubt of that, the convention may send out their project of a constitution, to the people in their several towns, counties, or districts, and the people may make the acceptance of it their own act." "But the people know nothing about constitutions." "I believe you are much mistaken in that supposition; if you are not, they will not oppose a plan prepared by their own chosen friends; but I believe that in every considerable portion of the people, there will be found some men, who will understand the subject as well as their representatives, and these will assist in enlightening the rest." "But what plan of a government would you advise?" "A plan as nearly resembling the government under which we were born, and have lived, as the circumstances of the country will admit. Kings we never had among us. Nobles we never had. Nothing hereditary ever existed in the country; nor will the country require or admit of any such thing. But governors and councils we have always had, as well as representatives. A legislature in three branches ought to be preserved, and independent judges." "Where and how will you get your governors and councils?" "By elections." "How,—who shall elect?" "The representatives of the people in a convention will be the best qualified to contrive a mode."

—John Adams, *Autobiography*, June, 1775

B. Concord Demands a Constitutional Meeting

At a meeting of the Inhabitents of the Town of Concord being free & twenty one years of age and upward, met by adjournment on the twenty first Day of october 1776 to take into Consideration a Resolve of the Honourable house of Representatives of the State on the 17th of September Last the Town Resolved as follows—

Resolve 1st: That this State being at Present destitute of a Properly established form of Government, it is absolutely necessary that one should be emmediatly formed and established.

Resolved 2. That the Supreme Legislative, either in their Proper Capacity or in Joint Committee, are by no means a body proper to form & Establish a Constitution or form of Government; for Reasons following. first Because we Conceive that a Constitution in its Proper Idea intends a System of Principles Established to Secure the Subject in the Possession & enjoyment of their Rights & Privileges, against any Encroachments of the Governing Part. 2—Because the Same Body that forms a Constitution have of Consequence a power to alter it. 3—because a Constitution alterable by the Supreme Legislative is no Security at all to the Subject against any Encroachment of the Governing part on any, or on all of their Rights and priviliges.

Resolved 3d. That it appears to this Town highly necessary & Expedient that a Convention, or Congress be immediately Chosen, to form & establish a Constitution, by the inhabitents of the Respective Towns in this State, being free & of twenty-one years of age and upward, in Proportion as the Representatives of this State formerly were Chosen: the Convention or Congress not to Consist of a greater number than the house of assembly of this State heretofore might Consist of, Except that each Town & District shall have the Liberty to Send one Representative, or otherwise as Shall appear meet to the Inhabitants of this State in General.

Resolve 4th. that when the Convention or Congress have formed a Constitution they adjourn for a Short time and Publish their Proposed Constitution for the Inspection and Remarks of the Inhabitants of this State.

Resolved 5ly. that the honourable house of assembly of this State be Desired to Recommend it to the Inhabitents of the State to Proceed to Chuse a Convention or Congress for the Purpas abovesaid as soon as Possable.

—Resolutions of the Concord Town Meeting, October 22, 1776

9. THE VIRGINIA BILL OF RIGHTS

From the point of view of political philosophy the two great questions of the Revolutionary era were how men make government and how government can be limited. It should never be forgotten that the men who fought the Revolution and wrote the American constitutions feared government. They subscribed, in varying degrees, to the aphorism of Tom Paine that "government, like dress, is the badge of lost innocence" and to Jefferson's comparable aphorism that that government was best that governed least. To them history had taught one grand lesson—that government was never to be trusted, that all governments tended to

be despotic, and that the highest duty of statesmanship was to prevent government from impairing the rights of men.
   But how achieve this much desired end? Bills of rights were the obvi ous answer. After all, Americans had long been familiar with bills of rights—with Magna Charta, with the great Bill of Rights of 1689, and with colonial declarations of rights and liberties. Yet none of these—not even the English—had in the fullest sense the force of paramount law. Those which Americans now inserted in their State Constitutions were designed to have all the force of constitutional law; they were designed, too, to be comprehensive.
   The most famous of American bills of rights was doubtless that of Virginia, drafted originally by George Mason of Gunston Hall and adopted with slight changes by the Virginia Convention of 1776; it was influential not only throughout the American States but throughout Europe as well. The Massachusetts Bill of Rights, drafted almost entirely by John Adams, was even more elaborate than that of Virginia. Both contributed largely to the Bill of Rights that was ultimately added to the Federal Constitution. When we turn to these great documents today we must keep in mind that they were written and adopted by men who believed in "inalienable" rights—rights so sacred that no government could infringe on or impair or deny them. That is a philosophical principle to which we might well return.

A DECLARATION *of rights made by the representatives of the good people of Virginia, assembled in full and free convention; which rights do pertain to them and their posterity, as the basis and foundation of government.*
   1. That all men are by nature equally free and independent, and have certain inherent rights, of which, when they enter into a state of society, they cannot by any compact deprive or divest their posterity; namely, the enjoyment of life and liberty, with the means of acquiring and possessing property, and pursuing and obtaining happiness and safety.
   2. That all power is vested in, and consequently derived from, the people; that magistrates are their trustees and servants, and at all times amenable to them.
   3. That government is, or ought to be instituted for the common benefit, protection, and security of the people, nation, or community;

of all the various modes and forms of government, that is best which is capable of producing the greatest degree of happiness and safety, and is most effectually secured against the danger of maladministration; and that when any government shall be found inadequate or contrary to these purposes, a majority of the community hath an indubitable, unalienable and indefeasible right to reform, alter or abolish it, in such manner as shall be judged most conducive to the public weal.

4. That no man, or set of men, are entitled to exclusive or separate emoluments or privileges from the community, but in consideration of publick services; which, not being descendible, neither ought the offices of magistrate, legislator or judge to be hereditary.

5. That the legislative and executive powers of the state should be separate and distinct from the judiciary; and that the members of the two first may be restrained from oppression, by feeling and participating the burthens of the people, they should, at fixed periods, be reduced to a private station, return into that body from which they were originally taken, and the vacancies be supplied by frequent, certain, and regular elections, in which all, or any part of the former members to be again eligible or ineligible, as the laws shall direct.

6. That elections of members to serve as representatives of the people in assembly, ought to be free; and that all men having sufficient evidence of permanent common interest with, and attachment to the community, have the right of suffrage, and cannot be taxed or deprived of their property for publick uses, without their own consent, or that of their representatives so elected, nor bound by any law to which they have not, in like manner, assented for the public good.

7. That all power of suspending laws, or the execution of laws, by any authority without consent of the representatives of the people, is injurious to their rights, and ought not to be exercised.

8. That in all capital or criminal prosecutions a man hath a right to demand the cause and nature of his accusation, to be confronted with the accusers and witnesses, to call for evidence in his favour, and to a speedy trial by an impartial jury of his vicinage, without whose unanimous consent he cannot be found guilty; nor can he be compelled to give evidence against himself; that no man be deprived of his liberty, except by the law of the land or the judgment of his peers.

9. That excessive bail ought not to be required, nor excessive fines imposed, nor cruel and unusual punishments inflicted.

10. That general warrants, whereby an officer or messenger may be commanded to search suspected places without evidence of a fact com-

mitted, or to seize any person or persons not named, or whose offence is not particularly described and supported by evidence, are grievous and oppressive, and ought not to be granted.

11. That in controversies respecting property, and in suits between man and man, the ancient trial by jury is preferable to any other, and ought to be held sacred.

12. That the freedom of the press is one of the great bulwarks of liberty, and can never be restrained but by despotick governments.

13. That a well-regulated militia, composed of the body of the people trained to arms, is the proper, natural and safe defence of a free state; that standing armies in time of peace should be avoided as dangerous to liberty; and that in all cases the military should be under strict subordination to, and governed by, the civil power.

14. That the people have a right to uniform government; and, therefore, that no government separate from, or independent of the government of Virginia, ought to be erected or established within the limits thereof.

15. That no free government, or the blessings of liberty, can be preserved to any people, but by a firm adherence to justice, moderation, temperance, frugality and virtue, and by frequent recurrence to fundamental principles.

16. That religion, or the duty which we owe to our Creator, and the manner of discharging it, can be directed only by reason and conviction, not by force or violence; and therefore all men are equally entitled to the free exercise of religion, according to the dictates of conscience; and that it is the mutual duty of all to practise Christian forbearance, love, and charity towards each other.

—George Mason, *The Virginia Bill of Rights,* 1776

10. THE CONSTITUTION: PREAMBLE AND BILL OF RIGHTS

The Constitution itself is at once so familiar and so readily available that it seems superfluous to include it here. We have, however, included the noble Preamble, and the so-called Bill of Rights—the first ten Amendments. Familiar as the Preamble is, we have not yet exhausted its meaning or its possibilities; familiar as are the guarantees of the Bill of Rights, we still need to exercise eternal vigilance if we would live up to them. When we come to our chapter on liberty and security we shall explore more fully the meaning of those guarantees, the threats to which they are exposed, and our responsibility for their preservation.

WE THE PEOPLE of the United States, in Order to form a more perfect Union, establish Justice, insure domestic Tranquility, provide for the common defence, promote the general Welfare, and secure the Blessings of Liberty to ourselves and our Posterity, do ordain and establish this Constitution for the United States of America. . . .

Art. I

Congress shall make no law respecting an establishment of religion, or prohibiting the free exercise thereof; or abridging the freedom of speech, or of the press; or the right of the people peaceably to assemble, and to petition the government for a redress of grievances.

Art. II

A well regulated Militia, being necessary to the security of a free State, the right of the people to keep and bear Arms, shall not be infringed.

Art. III

No Soldier shall, in time of peace be quartered in any house, without the consent of the Owner, nor in time of war, but in a manner to be prescribed by law.

Art. IV

The right of the people to be secure in their persons, houses, papers, and effects, against unreasonable searches and seizures, shall not be violated, and no Warrants shall issue, but upon probable cause, supported by Oath or affirmation, and particularly describing the place to be searched, and the persons or things to be seized.

Art. V

No person shall be held to answer for a capital, or otherwise infamous crime, unless on a presentment or indictment of a Grand Jury, except in cases arising in the land or naval forces, or in the Militia, when in actual service in time of War or public danger; nor shall any person be subject for the same offence to be twice put in jeopardy of life or limb; nor shall be compelled in any criminal case to be a witness against himself, nor be deprived of life, liberty, or property, without due process of law; nor shall private property be taken for public use, without just compensation.

Art. VI

In all criminal prosecutions, the accused shall enjoy the right to a speedy and public trial, by an impartial jury of the State and district wherein the crime shall have been committed, which district shall have been previously ascertained by law, and to be informed of the nature and cause of the accusation; to be confronted with the witnesses against him; to have compulsory process for obtaining witnesses in his favor, and to have the Assistance of Counsel for his defence.

Art. VII

In Suits at common law, where the value in controversy shall exceed twenty dollars, the right of trial by jury shall be preserved, and no fact tried by a jury, shall be otherwise re-examined in any Court of the United States, than according to the rules of the common law.

Art. VIII

Excessive bail shall not be required, nor excessive fines imposed, nor cruel and unusual punishments inflicted.

Art. IX

The enumeration in the Constitution, of certain rights, shall not be construed to deny or disparage others retained by the people.

Art. X

The powers not delegated to the United States by the Constitution, nor prohibited by it to the States, are reserved to the States respectively, or to the people.

—The Constitution of the United States

11. THE NORTHWEST ORDINANCE

From the beginning of the modern era every European nation had regarded colonies as existing for the benefit of the mother country and colonists as in some ways inferior to those who remained at home. Of all the European nations England had the most enlightened colonial policies, and of all colonials the English came the closest to having all the rights enjoyed by those in the home country—and perhaps a few that those at home did not enjoy. Yet Franklin was able to say that "every Tom, Dick, and Harry in England jostles himself into the throne of the King and speaks of Our colonies in America." And when the showdown came, Parliament passed in 1766 the Declaratory Act asserting that the colonies were subordinate to King and Parliament in all cases whatsoever. Could any way ever be found of dealing with colonies as equals?

With the Revolution the American States reasserted their claims to Western lands, and the Peace of 1783 acquiesced in those claims. Gradually most of the States ceded their claims to the United States, and thus even during the period of the Confederation the new nation came to have a colonial problem. At least it would have been a colonial problem had Americans permitted it to develop along those lines. Instead they enacted what some European scholars consider the most enlightened law ever passed in America—the Northwest Ordinance. This Ordinance provided for the orderly and speedy organization of Western territories into States, and the admission of these States on a basis of full equality with the original States. It provided, too, that slavery should forever be abolished in the region north of the Ohio. The principle laid down in the Northwest Ordinance was consistently applied to all the territory acquired by the United States west to the Pacific.

AN ORDINANCE FOR THE GOVERNMENT OF THE
TERRITORY OF THE UNITED STATES NORTHWEST
OF THE RIVER OHIO

BE IT ordained . . . So soon as there shall be five thousand free male inhabitants of full age in the district, upon giving proof thereof to the governor, they shall receive authority, with time and place, to elect representatives from their counties or townships to represent them in the

135

general assembly: *Provided,* That, for every five hundred free male inhabitants, there shall be one representative, and so on progressively with the number of free male inhabitants shall the right of representation increase, until the number of representatives shall amount to twenty-five; after which, the number and proportion of representatives shall be regulated by the legislature: . . .

And, for extending the fundamental principles of civil and religious liberty, which form the basis whereon these republics, their laws and constitutions are erected; to fix and establish those principles as the basis of all laws, constitutions, and governments, which forever hereafter shall be formed in the said territory: to provide also for the establishment of States, and permanent government therein, and for their admission to a share in the federal councils on an equal footing with the original States, at as early periods as may be consistent with the general interest:

It is hereby ordained and declared by the authority aforesaid, That the following articles shall be considered as articles of compact between the original States and the people and States in the said territory and forever remain unalterable, unless by common consent, to wit:

ART. 1. No person, demeaning himself in a peaceable and orderly manner, shall ever be molested on account of his mode of worship or religious sentiments, in the said territory.

ART. 2. The inhabitants of the said territory shall always be entitled to the benefits of the writ of *habeas corpus,* and of the trial by jury; of a proportionate representation of the people in the legislature; and of judicial proceedings according to the course of the common law. All persons shall be bailable, unless for capital offences, where the proof shall be evident or the presumption great. All fines shall be moderate; and no cruel or unusual punishments shall be inflicted. No man shall be deprived of his liberty or property, but by the judgment of his peers or the law of the land; and, should the public exigencies make it necessary, for the common preservation, to take any person's property, or to demand his particular services, full compensation shall be made for the same. And, in the just preservation of rights and property, it is understood and declared, that no law ought ever to be made, or have force in the said territory, that shall, in any manner whatever, interfere with or affect private contracts or engagements, *bona fide,* and without fraud, previously formed.

Art. 3. Religion, morality, and knowledge, being necessary to good government and the happiness of mankind, schools and the means of education shall forever be encouraged. The utmost good faith shall always be observed towards the Indians; their lands and property shall never be taken from them without their consent; and, in their property, rights, and liberty, they shall never be invaded or disturbed, unless in just and lawful wars authorized by Congress; but laws founded in justice and humanity, shall from time to time be made for preventing wrongs being done to them, and for preserving peace and friendship with them.

Art. 4. The said territory, and the States which may be formed therein, shall forever remain a part of this Confederacy of the United States of America, subject to the Articles of Confederation, and to such alterations therein as shall be constitutionally made; and to all the acts and ordinances of the United States in Congress assembled, conformable thereto. . . .

Art. 5. There shall be formed in the said territory, not less than three nor more than five States; . . . And, whenever any of the said States shall have sixty thousand free inhabitants therein, such State shall be admitted, by its delegates, into the Congress of the United States, on an equal footing with the original States in all respects whatever, and shall be at liberty to form a permanent constitution and State government: *Provided,* the constitution and government so to be formed, shall be republican, and in conformity to the principles contained in these articles; and, so far as it can be consistent with the general interest of the confederacy, such admission shall be allowed at an earlier period, and when there may be a less number of free inhabitants in the State than sixty thousand.

Art. 6. There shall be neither slavery nor involuntary servitude in the said territory, otherwise than in the punishment of crimes whereof the party shall have been duly convicted: *Provided, always,* That any person escaping into the same, from whom labor or service is lawfully claimed in any one of the original States, such fugitive may be lawfully reclaimed and conveyed to the person claiming his or her labor or service as aforesaid.

—The Northwest Ordinance, July, 1787

12. THE PRINCIPLE OF EQUALITY
IN AMERICAN SOCIETY

In the 1830's Alexis de Tocqueville formulated and elaborated the theory that equality was the central, the pervasive, the dominant fact in American life. Actually Crèvecoeur had already anticipated this interpretation and so too had many others, notably Charles Pinckney of South Carolina. Pinckney was himself a great swell, member of a family long prominent in South Carolina politics and economy, but like many others of that hard-headed generation—Madison, for example, and Wilson and John Adams—he understood well the relation between economy and politics and penetrated to the real character of the American democracy. This extract is from Pinckney's speech in the Federal Convention of June 25, 1787.

THE people of the U. States are perhaps the most singular of any we are acquainted with. Among them there are fewer distinctions of fortune & less of rank, than among the inhabitants of any other nation. Every freeman has a right to the same protection & security; and a very moderate share of property entitles them to the possession of all the honors and privileges the public can bestow: hence arises a greater equality, than is to be found among the people of any other country, and an equality which is more likely to continue—I say this equality is likely to continue, because in a new Country, possessing immense tracts of uncultivated lands, where every temptation is offered to emigration & where industry must be rewarded with competency, there will be few poor, and few dependent—Every member of the Society almost, will enjoy an equal power of arriving at the supreme offices & consequently of directing the strength & sentiments of the whole Community. None will be excluded by birth, & few by fortune, from voting for proper persons to fill the offices of Government—the whole community will enjoy in the fullest sense that kind of political liberty which consists in the power the members of the State reserve to themselves, of arriving at the public offices, or at least, of having votes in the nomination of those who fill them.

If this State of things is true & the prospect of its continuing probable, it is perhaps not politic to endeavour too close an imitation of a Government calculated for a people whose situation is, & whose views ought to be extremely different.

Much has been said of the Constitution of G. Britain. I will confess that I believe it to be the best Constitution in existence; but at the same time I am confident it is one that will not or can not be introduced into this Country, for many centuries. . . . I have remarked that the people of the United States are more equal in their circumstances than the people of any other Country—that they have very few rich men among them,—by rich men I mean those whose riches may have a dangerous influence, or such as are esteemed rich in Europe—perhaps there are not one hundred such on the Continent; that it is not probable this number will be greatly increased: that the genius of the people, their mediocrity of situation & the prospects which are afforded their industry in a Country which must be a new one for centuries are unfavorable to the rapid distinction of ranks. The destruction of the right of primogeniture & the equal division of the property of Intestates will also have an effect to preserve this mediocrity; for laws invariably affect the manners of a people. On the other hand that vast extent of unpeopled territory which opens to the frugal & industrious a sure road to competency & independence will effectually prevent for a considerable time the increase of the poor or discontented, and be the means of preserving that equality of condition which so eminently distinguishes us. . . .

Our true situation appears to me to be this.—a new extensive Country containing within itself the materials for forming a Government capable of extending to its citizens all the blessings of civil & religious liberty—capable of making them happy at home. This is the great end of Republican Establishments. We mistake the object of our Government, if we hope or wish that it is to make us respectable abroad. Conquest or superiority among other powers is not or ought not ever to be the object of republican systems. If they are sufficiently active & energetic to rescue us from contempt & preserve our domestic happiness & security, it is all we can expect from them,—it is more than almost any other Government ensures to its citizens.

I believe this observation will be found generally true:—that no two people are so exactly alike in their situation or circumstances as to admit the exercise of the same Government with equal benefit: that a system must be suited to the habits & genius of the people it is to govern, and must grow out of them. . . .

We must as has been observed suit our Governm^t to the people it is to direct. These are I believe as active, intelligent & susceptible of good Governm^t as any people in the world. The Confusion which has produced the present relaxed State is not owing to them. It is owing to the weakness & [defects] of a Gov^t incapable of combining the various interests it is intended to unite, and destitute of energy.—All that we have to do then is to distribute the powers of Gov^t in such a manner, and for such limited periods, as while it gives a proper degree of permanency to the Magistrate, will reserve to the people, the right of election they will not or ought not frequently to part with.—I am of the opinion that this may be easily done; and that with some amendments the propositions before the Committee will fully answer this end.

—Speech of Charles Pinckney, June 25, 1787

13. WHAT IS A REPUBLIC?

That the United States is a republic is universally conceded, but there is no agreement upon what the term "republic" itself means. The Constitution does not use the term with respect to the United States. It does guarantee a republican form of government to the States, but nowhere does it define the term, nor has the Supreme Court ever submitted a formal definition. In our own day there has developed the very curious notion that a republic is somehow not only different from a democracy but antithetical to a democracy, and that therefore because the United States is a republic it is not a democracy! The evidence is overwhelming that the Framers used the term republic as we now use the term democracy—to describe a state in which the majority governs. We include here two brief discussions of the meaning of the word. The first appears in Number 39 of The Federalist, *and was written by Madison, who probably knew more about the history and philosophy of political institutions than any other man of his generation. The second comes from the gifted pen of Thomas Paine, author of two of the most important and influential tracts of the Revolutionary era,* Common Sense *and* The Crisis. *This excerpt is taken from his book on the* Rights of Man.

A. "A Government Which Derives All Its Power from the People"

THE first question that offers itself is, whether the general form and aspect of the government be strictly republican. It is evident that no other form would be reconcilable with the genius of the people of America; with the fundamental principles of the Revolution; or with that honorable determination which animates every votary of freedom, to rest al' our political experiments on the capacity of mankind for self-government. . . .

If we resort for a criterion to the different principles on which different forms of government are established, we may define a republic to be, or at least may bestow that name on, a government which derives all its powers directly or indirectly from the great body of the people, and is administered by persons holding their offices during pleasure, for a limited period, or during good behavior. It is *essential* to such a government that it be derived from the great body of the society, not from an inconsiderable proportion, or a favored class of it; otherwise a handful of tyrannical nobles, exercising their oppressions by a delegation of their powers, might aspire to the rank of republicans, and claim for their government the honorable title of republic. It is *sufficient* for such a government that the persons administering it be appointed, either directly or indirectly, by the people; and that they hold their appointments by either of the tenures just specified; otherwise every government in the United States, as well as every other popular government that has been or can be well organized, or well executed, would be degraded from the republican character.

—James Madison, The Federalist, No. 39, 1787

B. "It Is Representation Ingrafted upon Democracy"

The only forms of government are the democratical, the aristocratical, the monarchical, and what is now called the representative.

What is called a *republic* is not any *particular form* of government. It is wholly characteristical of the purport, matter, or object for which government ought to be instituted, and on which it is to be employed, *res-publica,* the public affairs, or the public good; or, literally translated, the *public thing.* It is a word of a good original, referring to what ought to be the character and business of government; and in this sense it is naturally opposed to the word *monarchy,* which has a base original signification. It means arbitrary power in an individual person; in the exercise of which, *himself,* and not the *res-publica,* is the object.

Every government that does not act on the principle of a republic, or, in other words, that does not make the *res-publica* its whole and sole object, is not a good government. Republican government is no other than government established and conducted for the interest of the public, as well individually as collectively. It is not necessarily connected with any particular form, but it most naturally associates with the representative form, as being best calculated to secure the end for which a nation is at the expense of supporting it. . . .

Those who have said that a republic is not a *form* of government calculated for countries of great extent mistook, in the first place, the *business* of a government for a *form* of government; for the *res-publica* equally appertains to every extent of territory and population. And in the second place, if they meant anything with respect to *form,* it was the simple democratical form, such as was the mode of government in the ancient democracies, in which there was no representation. The case, therefore, is not that a republic cannot be extensive, but that it cannot be extensive on the simple democratic form; and the question naturally presents itself, *What is the best form of government for conducting the* RES-PUBLICA *or* PUBLIC BUSINESS *of a nation after it becomes too extensive and populous for the simple democratical form?*

It cannot be monarchy, because monarchy is subject to an objection of the same amount to which the democratical form was subject. . . .

As to the aristocratical form, it has the same vices and defects with the monarchical, except that the chance of abilities is better from the proportion of numbers, but there is still no security for the right use and application of them.

Referring, then to the original simple democracy, it affords the true ·data from which government on a large scale can begin. It is incapable of extension, not from its principle, but from the inconvenience of its form; and monarchy and aristocracy from their incapacity. Retaining, then, democracy as the ground, and rejecting the corrupt systems of monarchy and aristocracy, the representative system naturally presents itself; remedying at once the defects of the simple democracy as to form, and the incapacity of the other two with regard to knowledge.

Simple democracy was society governing itself without the use of secondary means. By ingrafting representation upon democracy, we arrive at a system of government capable of embracing and confederating all the various interests and every extent of territory and population; and that also with advantages as much superior to hereditary government as the republic of letters is to hereditary literature.

It is on this system that the American government is founded. It is representation ingrafted upon democracy. It has settled the form by a scale parallel in all cases to the extent of the principle. What Athens was in miniature, America will be in magnitude. The one was the wonder of the ancient world—the other is becoming the admiration and model of the present. It is the easiest of all the forms of government to be understood and the most eligible in practice; and excludes at once the ignorance and insecurity of the hereditary mode and the inconvenience of the simple democracy.

—THOMAS PAINE, *Rights of Man*, 1792

14. WASHINGTON'S FAREWELL ADDRESS

When, in 1796, Washington finally determined to retire from the Presidency and from public life he thought the occasion appropriate for a valedictory and a testament. The "Farewell Address," as it came to be known, influenced American history far more than Washington himself could have anticipated. It emphasized the importance of nationalism and of union, deprecated irresponsible factionalism and partisanship, and warned against "inveterate antipathies against particular nations and passionate attachments for others." Unfortunately this last argument was seized upon and perverted by those who would have the United States evade her responsibilities to other nations and to the international community, while the warnings against particularism, factionalism, and partisanship have been largely ignored. There has been considerable controversy about the authorship of the Address, but it seems clear that notwithstanding suggestions from Madison and verbal and stylistic changes at the hands of Hamilton and Jay, the Address is essentially Washington's.

Friends and Fellow-Citizens:
The period for a new election of a citizen to administer the Executive Government of the United States being not far distant, and the time actually arrived when your thoughts must be employed in designating the person who is to be clothed with that important trust, it appears to me proper, especially as it may conduce to a more distinct expression of the public voice, that I should now apprise you of the resolution I have formed to decline being considered among the number of those out of whom a choice is to be made. . . .

A solicitude for your welfare which can not end with my life, and the apprehension of danger natural to that solicitude, urge me on an occasion like the present to offer to your solemn contemplation and to recommend to your frequent review some sentiments which are the result of much reflection, of no inconsiderable observation, and which appear to me all important to the permanency of your felicity as a people. . . .

Interwoven as is the love of liberty with every ligament of your hearts, no recommendation of mine is necessary to fortify or confirm the attachment.

The unity of government which constitutes you one people is also now dear to you. It is justly so, for it is a main pillar in the edifice of your real independence, the support of your tranquillity at home, your peace abroad, of your safety, of your prosperity, of that very liberty which you so highly prize. But as it is easy to foresee that from different causes and from different quarters much pains will be taken, many artifices employed, to weaken in your minds the conviction of this truth, as this is the point in your political fortress against which the batteries of internal and external enemies will be most constantly and actively (though often covertly and insidiously) directed, it is of infinite moment that you should properly estimate the immense value of your national union to your collective and individual happiness; that you should cherish a cordial, habitual, and immovable attachment to it; accustoming yourselves to think and speak of it as of the palladium of your political safety and prosperity; watching for its preservation with jealous anxiety; discountenancing whatever may suggest even a suspicion that it can in any event be abandoned, and indignantly frowning upon the first dawning of every attempt to alienate any portion of our country from the rest or to enfeeble the sacred ties which now link together the various parts.

For this you have every inducement of sympathy and interest. Citizens by birth or choice of a common country, that country has a right to concentrate your affections. The name of American, which belongs to you in your national capacity, must always exalt the just pride of patriotism more than any appellation derived from local discriminations. With slight shades of difference, you have the same religion, manners, habits, and political principles. You have in a common cause fought and triumphed together. The independence and liberty you possess are the work of joint councils and joint efforts, of common dangers, sufferings, and successes. . . .

While, then, every part of our country thus feels an immediate and particular interest in union, all the parts combined can not fail to find in the united mass of means and efforts greater strength, greater resource, proportionably greater security from external danger, a less frequent interruption of their peace by foreign nations, and what is of inestimable value, they must derive from union an exemption from those broils and wars between themselves which so frequently afflict neighboring countries not tied together by the same governments, which their own rivalships alone would be sufficient to produce, but which opposite foreign alliances, attachments, and intrigues would stimulate and imbitter. Hence, likewise, they will avoid the necessity of those overgrown military establishments which, under any form of government, are inauspicious to liberty, and which are to be regarded as particularly hostile to republican liberty. In this sense it is that your union ought to be considered as a main prop of your liberty, and that the love of the one ought to endear to you the preservation of the other. . . .

Is there a doubt whether a common government can embrace so large a sphere? Let experience solve it. To listen to mere speculation in such a case were criminal. It is well worth a fair and full experiment. With such powerful and obvious motives to union affecting all parts of our country, while experience shall not have demonstrated its impracticability, there will always be reason to distrust the patriotism of those who in any quarter may endeavor to weaken its bands. . . .

Toward the preservation of your Government and the permanency of your present happy state, it is requisite not only that you steadily discountenance irregular oppositions to its acknowledged authority, but also that you resist with care the spirit of innovation upon its principles, however specious the pretexts. One method of assault may be to effect in the forms of the Constitutions alterations which will impair the energy of the system, and thus to undermine what can not be directly overthrown. In all the changes to which you may be invited remember that time and habit are at least as necessary to fix the true character of governments as of other human institutions; that experience is the surest standard by which to test the real tendency of the existing constitution of a country; that facility in changes upon the credit of mere hypothesis and opinion exposes to perpetual change, from the endless variety of hypothesis and opinion; and remember especially that for the efficient management of your common interests in a country so extensive as ours a government of as much vigor as is consistent with the perfect security of liberty is indispensable. Liberty itself will find in such a government, with powers properly distributed and adjusted, its surest guardian. It is, indeed, little else than a name where the government is too feeble to withstand the enterprises of faction, to confine each member of the society within the limits prescribed by the laws, and to maintain all in the secure and tranquil enjoyment of the rights of person and property.

I have already intimated to you the danger of parties in the State, with particular reference to the founding of them on geographical discriminations. Let me now take a more comprehensive view, and warn you in the most solemn manner against the baneful effects of the spirit of party generally.

This spirit, unfortunately, is inseparable from our nature, having its root in the strongest passions of the human mind. It exists under different shapes in all governments, more or less stifled, controlled, or repressed; but in those of the popular form it is seen in its greatest rankness and is truly their worst enemy. . . .

It serves always to distract the public councils and enfeeble the public administration. It agitates the community with ill-founded jealousies and false alarms; kindles the animosity of one part against another; foments occasionally riot and insurrection. It opens the door to foreign influence and corruption, which find a facilitated access to the government itself through the channels of party passion. Thus the policy and the will of one country are subjected to the policy and will of another. . . .

It is substantially true that virtue or morality is a necessary spring of popular government. The rule indeed extends with more or less force to every species of free government. Who that is a sincere friend to it can look with indifference upon attempts to shake the foundation of the fabric? Promote, then, as an object of primary importance, institutions for the general diffusion of knowledge. In proportion as the structure of a government gives force to public opinion, it is essential that public opinion should be enlightened.

—Washington's Farewell Address, September, 1796

15. "WE ARE ALL REPUBLICANS, WE ARE ALL FEDERALISTS"

No less famous than Washington's Farewell Address is Jefferson's First Inaugural Address. It, too, was a declaration of principles; it, too, a testament to the American people. No basic philosophical differences distinguish these two great state papers, but each does reflect the character of its author—the first sober, dignified, judicious, conservative, the second buoyant, enthusiastic, and idealistic. Washington's Farewell Address attaches itself indubitably to the Constitution; Jefferson's First Inaugural harks back to the Declaration of Independence.

Friends and Fellow Citizens:

Called upon to undertake the duties of the first executive office of our country, I avail myself of the presence of that portion of my fellow-citizens which is here assembled to express my grateful thanks for the favor with which they have been pleased to look toward me, to declare a sincere consciousness that the task is above my talents, and that I approach it with those anxious and awful presentiments which the greatness of the charge and the weakness of my powers so justly inspire. A rising nation, spread over a wide and fruitful land, traversing all the seas with the rich productions of their industry, engaged in commerce with nations who feel power and forget right, advancing rapidly to destinies beyond the reach of mortal eye—when I contemplate these transcendent objects, and see the honor, the happiness, and the hopes of this beloved country committed to the issue and the auspices of this day, I shrink from the contemplation, and humble myself before the magnitude of the undertaking. Utterly, indeed, should I despair did not the presence of many whom I here see remind me that in the other high authorities provided by our Constitution I shall find resources of wisdom, of virtue, and of zeal on which to rely under all difficulties. To you, then, gentlemen, who are charged with the sovereign functions of legislation, and to those associated with you, I look with encouragement for that guidance and support which may enable us to steer with safety the vessel in which we are all embarked amidst the conflicting elements of a troubled world.

During the contest of opinion through which we have passed the animation of discussions and of exertions has sometimes worn an aspect which might impose on strangers unused to think freely and to speak and to write what they think; but this being now decided by the voice of the nation, announced according to the rules of the Constitution, all will, of course, arrange themselves under the will of the law, and unite in common efforts for the common good. All, too, will bear in mind this sacred principle, that though the will of the majority is in all cases to prevail, that will to be rightful must be reasonable; that the minority possess their equal rights, which equal law must protect, and to violate would be oppression. Let us, then, fellow-citizens, unite with one heart and one mind. Let us restore to social intercourse that harmony and affection without which liberty and even life itself are but dreary things. And let us reflect that, having banished from our land that religious intolerance under which mankind so long bled and suffered, we have yet gained little if we countenance a political intolerance as despotic, as wicked, and capable of as bitter and bloody persecutions. During the throes and convulsions of the ancient world, during the agonizing spasms of infuriated man, seeking through blood and slaughter his long-lost liberty, it was not wonderful that the agitation of the billows should reach even this distant and peaceful shore; that this should be more felt and feared by some and less by others, and should divide opinions as to measures of safety. But every difference of opinion is not a difference of principle. We have called by different names brethren of the same principle. We are all Republicans, we are all Federalists. If there be any among us who would wish to dissolve this Union or to change its republican form, let them stand undisturbed as monuments of the safety with which error of opinion may be tolerated where reason is left free to combat it. I know, indeed, that some honest men fear that a republican government can not be strong, that this Government is not strong enough; but would the honest patriot, in the full tide of successful experiment, abandon a government which has so far kept us free and firm on the theoretic and visionary fear that this Government, the world's best hope, may by possibility want energy to preserve itself? I trust not. I believe this, on the contrary, the strongest Government on earth. I believe it the only one where every man, at the call of the law, would fly to the standard of the law, and would meet invasions of the public order as his own personal concern. Sometimes it is said that man can not be trusted with the government of himself. Can he, then, be trusted with the government of others? Or have we found angels in the forms of kings to govern him? Let history answer this question.

Let us, then, with courage and confidence pursue our own Federal and Republican principles, our attachment to union and representative government. Kindly separated by nature and a wide ocean from the exterminating havoc of one quarter of the globe; too high-minded to endure the degradations of the others; possessing a chosen country, with room enough for our descendants to the thousandth and thousandth generation; entertaining a due sense of our equal right to the use of our own faculties, to the acquisitions of our own industry, to honor and confidence from our fellow-citizens, resulting not from birth, but from our actions and their sense of them; enlightened by a benign religion, professed, indeed, and practiced in various forms, yet all of them inculcating honesty, truth, temperance, gratitude, and the love of man; acknowledging and adoring an overruling Providence, which by all its dispensations proves that it delights in the happiness of man here and his greater happiness hereafter—with all these blessings, what more is necessary to make us a happy and a prosperous people? Still one thing more, fellow-citizens—a wise and frugal Government, which shall restrain men from injuring one another, shall leave them otherwise free to regulate their own pursuits of industry and improvement, and shall not take from the mouth of labor the bread it has earned. This is the sum of good government, and this is necessary to close the circle of our felicities.

About to enter, fellow-citizens, on the exercise of duties which comprehend everything dear and valuable to you, it is proper you should understand what I deem the essential principles of our Government, and consequently those which ought to shape its Administration. I will compress them within the narrowest compass they will bear, stating the general principle, but not all its limitations. Equal and exact justice to all men, of whatever state or persuasion, religious or political; peace, commerce, and honest friendship with all nations, entangling alliances with none; the support of the State governments in all their rights, as the most competent administrations for our domestic concerns and the surest bulwarks against antirepublican tendencies; the preservation of the General Government in its whole constitutional vigor, as the sheet anchor of our peace at home and safety abroad; a jealous care of the right of election by the people—a mild and safe corrective of abuses which are lopped by the sword of revolution where peaceable remedies are unprovided; absolute acquiescence in the decisions of the majority, the vital principle of republics, from which is no appeal but to force, the vital principle and immediate parent of despotism; a well-disciplined militia, our best reliance in peace and for the first moments of war, till regulars may relieve them; the supremacy of the civil over the military authority; economy in the public expense, that labor may be lightly burthened; the honest payment of our debts and sacred preservation of the public faith; encouragement of agriculture, and of commerce as its handmaid; the diffusion of information and arraignment of all abuses at the bar of the public reason; freedom of religion; freedom of the press, and freedom of person under the protection of the habeas corpus, and trial by juries impartially selected. These principles form the bright constellation which has gone before us and guided our steps through an age of revolution and reformation. The wisdom of our sages and blood of our heroes have been devoted to their attainment. They should be the creed of our political faith, the text of civic instruction, the touchstone by which to try the services of those we trust; and should we wander from them in moments of error or of alarm, let us hasten to retrace our steps and to regain the road which alone leads to peace, liberty, and safety.

—Jefferson's First Inaugural Address, March 4, 1801

16. "A CONSTITUTION FRAMED FOR AGES TO COME"

"If American law were to be represented by a single figure," said Justice Oliver Wendell Holmes in 1901, "skeptic and worshipper alike would agree without dispute that the figure could be one alone, and that one John Marshall." Although Marshall was not a member of the Con-

vention that drafted the Constitution, he is, as surely as Washington, Madison, or Wilson, one of the Founding Fathers. Appointed Chief Justice in 1801 he held that post for thirty-four years, dominating the Court as has no other jurist in our history. To the interpretation of the Constitution Marshall brought Federalist principles, but his Federalism was the broad national Federalism of Washington and Hamilton and John Adams, not the narrow Federalism of Fisher Ames and Timothy Pickering. He established the principle of judicial review; he gave to the ambiguous clauses of the Constitution a broad nationalist interpretation; he narrowed, where he could, the power of the States. From time to time the Court has departed from the Marshall tradition, but it has always returned to it again, and today, it is safe to say, that tradition is as strong as at any time in our history. We give here a brief excerpt from one of the more memorable Marshall opinions concerned with the great issue of national supremacy.

But a constitution is framed for ages to come and is designed to approach immortality as nearly as human institutions can approach it. Its course cannot always be tranquil. It is exposed to storms and tempests, and its framers must be unwise statesmen indeed if they have not provided it, so far as its nature will permit, with the means of self-preservation from the perils it may be destined to encounter. No government ought to be so defective in its organization as not to contain within itself the means of securing the execution of its own laws against other dangers than those which occur every day. . . .

That the United States form, for many and for most important purposes, a single nation, has not yet been denied. In war we are one people. In making peace we are one people. In all commercial regulations we are one and the same people. In many other respects the American people are one, and the Government which is alone capable of controlling and managing their interests in all these respects is the government of the Union. It is their government, and in that character they have no other. America has chosen to be, in many respects, and to many purposes, a nation; and for all these purposes her government is complete; to all these objects it is competent. The people have declared that in the exercise of all the powers given for these objects it is supreme. It can, then, in effecting these objects, legitimately control all individuals or governments within the American territory. The constitution and laws of a

State, so far as they are repugnant to the Constitution and laws of the United States, are absolutely void. These States are constituent parts of the United States. They are members of one great empire—for some purposes sovereign, for some purposes subordinate.

—CHIEF JUSTICE JOHN MARSHALL, Opinion in Cohens *v.* Virginia, 1821

17. THE GETTYSBURG ADDRESS

The battle of Gettysburg was fought the first week of July, 1863, and from the Union victory there dates the beginning of the end of the Confederacy. The battlefield was made a cemetery for the soldiers slain or mortally wounded in that battle, and it was in connection with the consecration of the battleground to this purpose that Lincoln made his immortal address. Here and in the preambles to the Declaration of Independence and the Constitution we find the best succinct summaries of the meaning of America.

FOUR score and seven years ago our fathers brought forth on this continent, a new nation, conceived in Liberty, and dedicated to the proposition that all men are created equal.

Now we are engaged in a great civil war, testing whether that nation or any nation so conceived and so dedicated, can long endure. We are met on a great battle-field of that war. We have come to dedicate a portion of that field, as a final resting place for those who here gave their lives that that nation might live. It is altogether fitting and proper that we should do this.

But, in a larger sense, we can not dedicate—we can not consecrate—we can not hallow—this ground. The brave men, living and dead, who struggled here, have consecrated it, far above our poor power to add or detract. The world will little note, nor long remember what we say here, but it can never forget what they did here. It is for us the living, rather, to be dedicated here to the unfinished work which they who fought here have thus far so nobly advanced. It is rather for us to be here dedicated to the great task remaining before us—that from these honored dead we take increased devotion to that cause for which they gave the last full measure of devotion—that we here highly resolve that these dead shall not have died in vain—that this nation, under God, shall have a new birth of freedom—and that government of the people, by the people, for the people, shall not perish from the earth.

—Lincoln's Gettysburg Address, November 19, 1863

18. LIBERTY, THE NECESSARY CONDITION OF PROGRESS

It was in 1879 that an obscure California printer, Henry George, published Progress and Poverty *in an edition of five hundred copies. Within two years it had sold perhaps one hundred thousand copies; within a quarter of a century, sales in all languages had mounted to over two million copies. Few other American books and certainly no other economic treatise exercised a comparable influence in the world at large.* Progress and Poverty *diagnosed the ills from which modern economy suffered and submitted as a solution for them the Single Tax. It was not however the solution so much as the diagnosis that commanded widest attention in America. Few other books presented so graphically the contrast between an economy of potential abundance and actual scarcity as did this; few others were so suffused by indignation and idealism. We give here an excerpt from the concluding chapter of this great book on the relation of liberty to progress and happiness.*

WE SPEAK of Liberty as one thing, and of virtue, wealth, knowledge, invention, national strength and national independence as other things. But, of all these, Liberty is the source, the mother, the necessary condition. She is to virtue what light is to color; to wealth what sunshine is to grain; to knowledge what eyes are to sight. She is the genius of invention, the brawn of national strength, the spirit of national independence. Where Liberty rises, there virtue grows, wealth increases, knowledge expands, invention multiplies human powers, and in strength and spirit the freer nation rises among her neighbors as

Saul amid his brethren—taller and fairer. Where Liberty sinks, there virtue fades, wealth diminishes, knowledge is forgotten, invention ceases, and empires once mighty in arms and arts become a helpless prey to freer barbarians! . . .

In our time, as in times before, creep on the insidious forces that, producing inequality, destroy Liberty. On the horizon the clouds begin to lower. Liberty calls to us again. We must follow her further; we must trust her fully. Either we must wholly accept her or she will not stay. It is not enough that men should vote; it is not enough that they should be theoretically equal before the law. They must have liberty to avail themselves of the opportunities and means of life; they must stand on equal terms with reference to the bounty of nature. Either this, or Liberty withdraws her light! Either this, or darkness comes on, and the very forces that progress has evolved turn to powers that work destruction. This is the universal law. This is the lesson of the centuries. Unless its foundations be laid in justice the social structure cannot stand.

Our primary social adjustment is a denial of justice. In allowing one man to own the land on which and from which other men must live, we have made them his bondsmen in a degree which increases as material progress goes on. This is the subtle alchemy that in ways they do not realize is extracting from the masses in every civilized country the fruits of their weary toil; that is instituting a harder and more hopeless slavery in place of that which has been destroyed; that is bringing political despotism out of political freedom, and must soon transmute democratic institutions into anarchy.

It is this that turns the blessings of material progress into a curse. It is this that crowds human beings into noisome cellars and squalid tenement houses; that fills prisons and brothels; that goads men with want and consumes them with greed; that robs women of the grace and beauty of perfect womanhood; that takes from little children the joy and innocence of life's morning. . . .

But if, while there is yet time, we turn to Justice and obey her, if we trust Liberty and follow her, the dangers that now threaten must disappear, the forces that now menace will turn to agencies of elevation. Think of the powers now wasted; of the infinite fields of knowledge yet to be explored; of the possibilities of which the wondrous inventions of this century give us but a hint. With want destroyed; with greed changed to noble passions; with the fraternity that is born of equality taking the place of the jealousy and fear that now array men against each other; with mental power loosed by conditions that give to the humblest comfort and leisure; and who shall measure the heights to which our civilization may soar? Words fail the thought! It is the Golden Age of which poets have sung and high-raised seers have told in metaphor! It is the glorious vision which has always haunted man with gleams of fitful splendor. It is what he saw whose eyes at Patmos were closed in a trance. It is the culmination of Christianity—the City of God on earth, with its walls of jasper and its gates of pearl! It is the reign of the Prince of Peace!

—HENRY GEORGE, *Progress and Poverty,* 1879

19. "THERE IS NOTHING MYSTERIOUS ABOUT DEMOCRACY"

No President since Jefferson has had as much to say about the nature and meaning of democracy as Franklin D. Roosevelt. This was not only because Roosevelt was himself passionately committed to democracy as a philosophy and as a way of life, but because it was during his administrations that the basic assumptions of democracy were challenged and required to justify themselves. It is sometimes submitted as a criticism of democracy that it does not lend itself readily to precise definition, or that it appears to change meaning from generation to generation. What this means is that democracy is as much an attitude of mind and inclination of heart as a particular body of beliefs or practices, and that it can adapt itself to historical change. We can read, in the many speeches of Roosevelt—the fireside chats, the messages to Congress, the occasional addresses—how democracy took on new meaning and new significance in the years of depression and of war.

THERE is nothing mysterious about the foundations of a healthy and strong democracy. The basic things expected by our people of their political and economic systems are simple. They are: equality of opportunity for youth and for others; jobs for those who can work; security for those who need it; the ending of special privilege for the few; the preservation of civil liberties for all; the enjoyment of the fruits of scientific progress in a wider and constantly rising standard of living.

These are the simple and basic things that must never be lost sight of in the turmoil and unbelievable complexity of our modern world. The inner and abiding strength of our economic and political systems is dependent upon the degree to which they fulfill these expectations.

—"Four Freedoms" Speech, January 6, 1941

Most of us accept the prosaic fact that the way to make progress is to build on what we have, to take from the lessons of yesterday a little more wisdom and courage to meet the tasks of today. Democracy is not a static thing. It is an everlasting march. When our children grow up, they will still have problems to overcome. It is for us, however, manfully to set ourselves to the task of preparation for them, so that to some degree the difficulties they must overcome may weigh upon them less heavily.

—Address at Los Angeles, California, October 1, 1935

As we have recaptured and rekindled our pioneering spirit, we have insisted that it shall always be a spirit of justice, a spirit of teamwork, a spirit of sacrifice, and, above all, a spirit of neighborliness.

We have sought to adjust the processes of industrial and agricultural life, and in so doing we have sought to view the picture as a whole. Revival of industry, redemption of agriculture, reconstruction of banking, development of public works, the lifting of crushing debt—all these in every part of the Nation call for a willingness to sacrifice individual gains, to work together for the public welfare and for the success of a broad national program of recovery. We have to have courage and discipline and vision to blaze the new trails in life; but underlying all our efforts is the conviction that men cannot live unto themselves alone. A democracy, the right kind of democracy, is bound together by the ties of neighborliness.

—Address before the National Conference of Catholic Charities,
October 4, 1933

In some places in the world the tides are running against democracy. But our faith has not been unsettled. We believe in democracy because of our traditions. But we believe in it even more because of our experience.

Here in the United States we have been a long time at the business of self-government. The longer we are at it the more certain we become that we can continue to govern ourselves; that progress is on the side of majority rule; that if mistakes are to be made we prefer to make them ourselves and to do our own correcting.

—Radio Address, November 2, 1936

Democracy has disappeared in several other great nations—not because the people of those nations disliked democracy, but because they had grown tired of unemployment and insecurity, of seeing their children hungry, while they sat helpless in the face of government confusion and government weakness through lack of leadership in government. Finally, in desperation, they chose to sacrifice liberty in the hope of getting something to eat. We in America know that our own democratic institutions can be preserved and made to work. But in order to preserve them we need to act together, to meet the problems of the Nation boldly, and to prove that the practical operation of democratic government is equal to the task of protecting the security of the people. . . .

History proves that dictatorships do not grow out of strong and successful governments, but out of weak and helpless ones. If by democratic methods people get a government strong enough to protect them from fear and starvation, their democracy succeeds; but if they do not, they grow impatient. Therefore, the only sure bulwark of continuing liberty is a government strong enough to protect the interests of the people, and a people strong enough and well enough informed to maintain its sovereign control over its governments.

—Fireside Chat on Economic Conditions, April 14, 1938

We cannot carelessly assume that a nation is strong and great merely because it has a democratic form of government. We have learned that a democracy weakened by internal dissension, by mutual suspicion born of social injustice, is no match for autocracies which are ruthless enough to repress internal dissension.

Democracy in order to live must become a positive force in the daily lives of its people. It must make men and women, whose devotion it seeks, feel that it really cares for the security of every individual; that it is tolerant enough to inspire an essential unity among its citizens; and that it is militant enough to maintain liberty against social oppression at home and against military aggression abroad.

—Radio Address, November 4, 1938

20. "THIS I DEEPLY BELIEVE"

In the course of hearings on the appointment of David Lilienthal to the Atomic Energy Commission, Senator McKellar of Tennessee implied that the distinguished chairman of the TVA was "leftist" in his sympathies—whatever that meant. It was in response to this charge which, by implication at least, challenged his intellectual integrity, that Lilienthal made this moving and eloquent confession of faith. What McKellar and his fellow critics had to say at that time—or at any other time for that matter—is already forgotten, but it is probable that Lilienthal's statement of his belief will live as long as that other monument to his character and ability, the TVA.

THIS I DO carry in my head, Senator.
"I will do my best to make it clear. My convictions are not so much concerned with what I am against as what I am for; and that excludes a lot of things automatically.

"Traditionally, democracy has been an affirmative doctrine rather than merely a negative one.

"I believe—and I conceive the Constitution of the United States to rest, as does religion, upon the fundamental proposition of the integrity of the individual; and that all government and all private institutions must be designed to promote and protect and defend the integrity and the dignity of the individual; that that is the essential meaning of the Constitution and the Bill of Rights, as it is essentially the meaning of religion.

"Any form of government, therefore, and any other institutions which make men means rather than ends, which exalt the state or any other institutions above the importance of men, which place arbitrary power over men as a fundamental tenet of government are contrary to that conception, and, therefore, I am deeply opposed to them.

"The communistic philosophy as well as the communistic form of government falls within this category, for their fundamental tenet is quite

158

to the contrary. The fundamental tenet of communism is that the state is an end in itself, and that therefore the powers which the state exercises over the individual are without any ethical standard to limit them.

"That I deeply disbelieve.

"It is very easy simply to say that one is not a Communist. And, of course, if despite my record it is necessary for me to state this very affirmatively, then it is a great disappointment to me.

"It is very easy to talk about being against communism. It is equally important to believe those things which provide a satisfying and effective alternative. Democracy is that satisfying, affirmative alternative.

"Its hope in the world is that it is an affirmative belief, rather than being simply a belief against something else and nothing more.

"One of the tenets of democracy that grows out of this central core of a belief that the individual comes first, that all men are the children of God and that their personalities are therefore sacred, is a deep belief in civil liberties and their protection, and a repugnance to anyone who would steal from a human being that which is most precious to him—his good name—either by imputing things to him by innuendo or by insinuation. And it is especially an unhappy circumstance that occasionally that is done in the name of democracy. This, I think, can tear our country apart and destroy it if we carry it further.

"I deeply believe in the capacity of democracy to surmount any trials that may lie ahead, provided only that we practice it in our daily lives.

"And among the things we must practice is this: that while we seek fervently to ferret out the subversive and anti-democratic forces in the country, we do not at the same time, by hysteria, by resort to innuendo, and smears, and other unfortunate tactics, besmirch the very cause that we believe in, and cause a separation among our people—cause one group and one individual to hate another, based on mere attacks, mere unsubstantiated attacks upon their loyalty.

"I want also to add that part of my conviction is based on my training as an Anglo-American common lawyer. It is the very basis and the great heritage of the English people to this country, which we have maintained, that we insist on the strictest rules of credibility of witnesses and on the avoidance of hearsay, and that gossip shall be excluded, in the courts of justice. And that, too, is an essential of our democracy.

"Whether by administrative agencies acting arbitrarily against business organizations, or whether by investigating activities of legislative branches, whenever those principles fail, those principles of the protection of an individual and his good name against besmirchment by gossip, hearsay, and the statements of witnesses who are not subject to cross-examination—then, too, we have failed in carrying forward our ideals in respect to democracy.

"This I deeply believe."

—DAVID E. LILIENTHAL, *This I Do Believe,* 1949

~~ 4 ~~

The Machinery of Government

POLITICAL principles were one thing; political practices another. In the eighteenth century it was the peculiar genius of American leaders to translate principles into practices, and to ground practices firmly upon principles. Thus, as we have already seen, the principle that men make government was realized in the practice of constitutional conventions; thus the principle that government is limited was translated into written constitutions and bills of rights and then strengthened by judicial review.

All this was to the good, but it had one drawback that might become serious. So confident were the Founding Fathers that they had discovered sound principles, and so eager were they to put these principles beyond attack, that they wrote them into constitutions designed to be permanent and difficult to change.

In all free states, they argued, the constitution is fixed, and they assumed that they could achieve "a government of laws and not of men," a government whose basic principles and provisions should be all but unchangeable. So just at a time when expansion and nationalism and the industrial revolution were to introduce profound changes into American life, constitution makers tried to freeze political principles into constitutional formulas. Much of our political history in the last century and a half has been concerned with adapting written constitutions, embodying seventeenth and eighteenth century notions of the nature of government and the relations of men to government, to the changing needs of nineteenth and twentieth century society.

Now it is a very difficult process, as we all know, to change our Federal Constitution, and in only two periods of our history—Reconstruction and the Progressive Era—were any Amendments of basic importance added to that document. But a people as ingenious as the American were not to be frustrated by a written constitution. They developed alongside that written constitution an unwritten constitution.

161

They developed alongside the formal constitutional institutions a whole series of extraconstitutional institutions. They developed alongside the formal government an informal or "invisible" government. Thus the Constitution called for a fairly sharp separation of powers, but the government was a whole, and political parties came along and bridged the separation. Thus the Constitution provided for the election of a President by the complicated machinery of the electoral college; we kept the electoral college but made it a rubber stamp for popular elections. Thus the Constitution attempted to draw pretty clear lines between State and Federal powers, but as State lines began to lose their meaning the constitutional lines too were blurred, and the two sets of powers more and more overlapped.

In the field of practical government one achievement stands preeminent: the political party. There were so-called political parties in eighteenth century England, but Americans created the first modern parties, and the Democratic party is today the oldest genuine political party in the world, and probably the largest. From the beginning, parties took on many of the ordinary functions of government: they nominated candidates, conducted campaigns, managed elections, organized legislative bodies, selected men for public office, and did the hundred and one other things that are part of governmental housekeeping.

Housekeeping is an important and time-consuming task. In an aristocratic society it is assumed that the upper classes, who are also the wealthy and leisure classes, will give their energies and talents to this task. But in a democracy—where the work is far more extensive and time-consuming—some way must be found for keeping and rewarding those who devote their time to the business of politics. This situation led, almost inevitably, to the spoils system and that, in turn, to corruption. There has been a good deal of corruption in American politics, but perhaps we emphasize it overmuch. Certainly it is by no means peculiar to democracy. There was jobbery and corruption enough in eighteenth century English politics; there was corruption of the most blatant character in the Fascist and Nazi states; and from all we hear there is corruption in Communist societies today. It is difficult to make any generalization about American political morals, but it is probably safe to say that over a long period of time political morality has been as high as business morality.

The political party was, from the beginning, a voluntary organization, unknown even to law until the twentieth century. In this it represented the American instinct and the American practice. As one foreign observer after another has pointed out, almost all those things which in the Old World are done by government, in America are done by individuals banding together in associations. All our churches, our parties, our labor unions, our professional societies, our reform organizations, most of our colleges and universities, are examples of voluntary organization. It is, in fact, through voluntary association that American democracy most effectively functions—through homely organizations like the Parent Teachers Association or the League of Women Voters or Hadassah; through formal and powerful organizations like the Republican party or the American Medical Association or the American Legion. The current attack upon the right of association threatens a deeply ingrained principle and practice, and thereby threatens democracy at one of its most vital points.

We have given here something of a miscellany designed to illustrate the workings of our governmental system. We begin with an argument from the perspicacious Madison on the necessity of balancing interests against each other in a republic. We give then descriptions of campaigns, conventions and elections, of bosses and the spoils system, of the way in which the "invisible government" operates. We submit a general interpretation of the political party. We conclude with two interpretations, almost a century apart, of the significance of voluntary associations to American democracy.

1. HOW TO BALANCE CLASSES AND FACTIONS IN A REPUBLIC

We sometimes delude ourselves that ours is the first generation to understand the role of economics in politics. Actually our distinction is rather in misunderstanding than in understanding this role, for we are inclined to suppose that economic considerations control politics instead of knowing that political considerations must control economics. The Framers of the Constitution—a hard-headed and realistic group of statesmen—were fully alive to economic considerations, but they never subordinated political science or philosophy to economics. They had seen the Confederation sink into feebleness because it was not strong enough—or wise enough—to control the conflicting class and interest groups that struggled for preference. They had seen, too, in the writing of State Constitutions and the struggle over legislative programs, the conflict of farmer, planter, speculator and merchant, of debtor and creditor, of low country and back country. In short they knew well that if government is not strong enough to control interests, classes and factions, interests, classes and factions will control government—or destroy it. Madison, particularly, had pondered this problem, and had arrived at a solution, or at as much of a solution as it was possible to achieve. He saw republican institutions as a check upon class and faction, a check upon the danger of the tyranny of the majority or of subversion by minority groups. He first set forth this thesis somewhat tentatively in the course of the debates in the Federal Convention. In Number 10 of The Federalist *papers—probably the best known of all those remarkable papers—he elaborates this thesis in terms that are relevant today. We give here the whole of* Federalist *Number 10.*

To the People of the State of New York:

AMONG the numerous advantages promised by a well-constructed Union, none deserves to be more accurately developed than its tendency to break and control the violence of faction. The friend of popular governments never finds himself so much alarmed for their character and fate as when he contemplates their propensity to this dangerous vice. He will not fail, therefore, to set a due value on any plan which, without violating the principles to which he is attached, provides a proper cure for it. The instability, injustice, and confusion introduced into the public councils, have, in truth, been the mortal diseases under which popular governments have everywhere perished; as they continue to be the favourite and fruitful topics from which the adversaries to liberty derive their most specious declamations. The valuable improvements made by the American constitutions on the popular models, both ancient and modern, cannot certainly be too much admired; but it would be an unwarrantable partiality, to contend that they have as effectually obviated the danger on this side, as was wished and expected. Complaints are everywhere heard from our most considerate and virtuous citizens, equally the friends of public and private faith, and of public and personal liberty, that our governments are too unstable, that the public good is disregarded in the conflicts of rival parties, and that measures are too often decided, not according to the rules of justice and the rights of the minor party, but by the superior force of an interested and overbearing majority. However anxiously we may wish that these complaints had no foundation, the evidence of known facts will not permit us to deny that they are in some degree true. It will be found, indeed, on a candid review of our situation, that some of the distresses under which we labour have been erroneously charged on the operation of our governments; but it will be found, at the same time, that other causes will not alone account for many of our heaviest misfortunes; and, particularly, for that prevailing and increasing distrust of public engagements, and alarm for private rights, which are echoed from one end of the continent to the other. These must be chiefly, if not wholly, effects of the unsteadiness and injustice with which a factious spirit has tainted our public administrations.

By a faction, I understand a number of citizens, whether amounting to a majority or minority of the whole, who are united and actuated by some common impulse of passion, or of interest, adverse to the rights of other citizens, or to the permanent and aggregate interest of the community.

There are two methods of curing the mischiefs of faction: the one, by removing its causes; the other, by controlling its effects.

There are again two methods of removing the causes of faction: the one, by destroying the liberty which is essential to its existence; the other, by giving to every citizen the same opinions, the same passions, and the same interests.

It could never be more truly said than of the first remedy, that it was worse than the disease. Liberty is to faction what air is to fire, an aliment without which it instantly expires. But it could not be less folly to abolish liberty, which is essential to political life, because it nourishes faction, than it would be to wish the annihilation of air, which is essential to animal life, because it imparts to fire its destructive agency.

The second expedient is as impracticable as the first would be unwise. As long as the reason of man continues fallible, and he is at liberty to exercise it, different opinions will be formed. As long as the connection subsists between his reason and his self-love, his opinions and his passions will have a reciprocal influence on each other; and the former will be objects to which the latter will attach themselves. The diversity in the faculties of men, from which the rights of property originate, is not less an insuperable obstacle to a uniformity of interests. The protection of these faculties is the first object of government. From the protection of different and unequal faculties of acquiring property, the possession of different degrees and kinds of property immediately results; and from the influence of these on the sentiments and views of the respective proprietors, ensues a division of the society into different interests and parties.

The latent causes of faction are thus sown in the nature of man; and we see them everywhere brought into different degrees of activity, according to the different circumstances of civil society. A zeal for different opinions concerning religion, concerning government, and many other points, as well of speculation as of practice; an attachment of different leaders ambitiously contending for pre-eminence and power; or to persons of other descriptions whose fortunes have been interesting to the human passions, have, in turn, divided mankind into parties, inflamed them with mutual animosity, and rendered them much more disposed to vex and oppress each other than to co-operate for their common good. So strong is this propensity of mankind to fall into mutual animosities, that where no substantial occasion presents itself, the most frivolous and fanciful distinctions have been sufficient to kindle their unfriendly passions and excite their most violent conflicts. But the most common and durable source of factions has been the various and unequal distribution of property. Those who hold and those who are without property have ever formed distinct interests in society. Those who are creditors, and those who are debtors, fall under a like discrimination. A landed interest, a manufacturing interest, a mercantile interest, a moneyed interest, with many lesser interests, grow up of necessity in civilised nations, and divide them into different classes, actuated by different sentiments and views. The regulation of these various and interfering interests forms the principal task of modern legislation, and involves the spirit of party and faction in the necessary and ordinary operations of the government.

No man is allowed to be a judge in his own cause, because his interest would certainly bias his judgment, and, not improbably, corrupt his integrity. With equal, nay, with greater reason, a body of men are unfit to be both judges and parties at the same time; yet what are many of the most important acts of legislation but so many judicial determinations, not indeed concerning the rights of single persons, but concerning the rights of large bodies of citizens? And what are the different classes of legislators but advocates and parties to the causes which they determine?

Is a law proposed concerning private debts? It is a question to which the creditors are parties on one side and the debtors on the other. Justice ought to hold the balance between them. Yet the parties are, and must be, themselves the judges; and the most numerous party, or, in other words, the most powerful faction must be expected to prevail. Shall domestic manufacturers be encouraged, and in what degree, by restrictions on foreign manufactures? are questions which would be differently decided by the landed and the manufacturing classes, and probably by neither with a sole regard to justice and the public good. The apportionment of taxes on the various descriptions of property is an act which seems to require the most exact impartiality; yet there is, perhaps, no legislative act in which greater opportunity and temptation are given to a predominant party to trample on the rules of justice. Every shilling with which they overburden the inferior number is a shilling saved to their own pockets.

It is in vain to say that enlightened statesmen will be able to adjust these clashing interests, and render them all subservient to the public good. Enlightened statesmen will not always be at the helm. Nor, in many cases, can such an adjustment be made at all without taking into view indirect and remote considerations, which will rarely prevail over the immediate interest which one party may find in disregarding the rights of another or the good of the whole.

The inference to which we are brought is, that the *causes* of faction cannot be removed, and that relief is only to be sought in the means of controlling its *effects*.

If a faction consists of less than a majority, relief is supplied by the republican principle, which enables the majority to defeat its sinister views by regular vote. It may clog the administration, it may convulse the society; but it will be unable to execute and mask its violence under the forms of the Constitution. When a majority is included in a faction, the form of popular government, on the other hand, enables it to sacrifice to its ruling passion or interest both the public good and the rights of other citizens. To secure the public good and private rights against the danger of such a faction, and at the same time to preserve the spirit and the form of popular government, is then the great object to which our inquiries are directed. Let me add that it is the great desideratum by which this form of government can be rescued from the opprobrium under which it has so long laboured, and be recommended to the esteem and adoption of mankind.

By what means is this object obtainable? Evidently by one of two only. Either the existence of the same passion or interest in a majority at the same time must be prevented, or the majority, having such co-existent passion or interest, must be rendered, by their number and local situation, unable to concert and carry into effect schemes of oppression. If the impulse and the opportunity be suffered to coincide, we well know that neither moral nor religious motives can be relied on as an adequate control. They are not found to be such on the injustice and violence of individuals, and lose their efficacy in proportion to the number combined together, that is, in proportion as their efficacy becomes needful.

From this view of the subject it may be concluded that a pure democracy, by which I mean a society consisting of a small number of citizens, who assemble and administer the government in person, can admit of no cure for the mischiefs of faction. A common passion or interest will, in almost every case, be felt by a majority of the whole; a communication and concert result from the form of government itself; and there is nothing to check the inducements to sacrifice the weaker party or an obnoxious individual. Hence it is that such democracies have ever been spectacles of turbulence and contention; have ever been found incompatible with personal security or the rights of property; and have in general been as short in their lives as they have been violent in their death. Theoretic politicians, who have patronised this species of government, have erroneously supposed that by reducing mankind to a perfect equality in their political rights, they would, at the same time, be perfectly equalised and assimilated in their possessions, their opinions, and their passions.

A republic, by which I mean a government in which the scheme of representation takes place, opens a different prospect, and promises the cure for which we are seeking. Let us examine the points in which it varies from pure democracy, and we shall comprehend both the nature of the cure and the efficacy which it must derive from the Union.

The two great points of difference between a democracy and a republic are: first, the delegation of the government, in the latter, to a small number of citizens elected by the rest; secondly, the greater number of citizens, and greater sphere of country, over which the latter may be extended.

The effect of the first difference is, on the one hand, to refine and enlarge the public views, by passing them through the medium of a chosen body of citizens, whose wisdom may best discern the true interest of their country, and whose patriotism and love of justice will be least likely to sacrifice it to temporary or partial considerations. Under such a regulation, it may well happen that the public voice, pronounced by the representatives of the people, will be more consonant to the public good than if pronounced by the people themselves, convened for the purpose. On the other hand, the effect may be inverted. Men of factious tempers, of local prejudices, or of sinister designs, may, by intrigue, by corruption, or by other means, first obtain the suffrages, and then betray the interests, of the people. The question resulting is, whether small or extensive republics are more favourable to the election of proper guardians of the public weal; and it is clearly decided in favour of the latter by two obvious considerations:

In the first place, it is to be remarked that, however small the republic may be, the representatives must be raised to a certain number, in order to guard against the cabals of a few; and that, however large it may be, they must be limited to a certain number, in order to guard against the confusion of a multitude. Hence the number of representatives in the two cases not being in proportion to that of the two constituents, and being proportionally greater in the small republic, it follows that, if the proportion of fit characters be not less in the large than in the small republic, the former will present a greater option, and consequently a greater probability of a fit choice.

In the next place, as each representative will be chosen by a greater number of citizens in the large than in the small republic, it will be more difficult for unworthy candidates to practise with success the vicious arts by which elections are too often carried; and the suffrages of the people being more free, will be more likely to centre in men who possess the most attractive merit and the most diffusive and established character.

It must be confessed that in this, as in most other cases, there is a mean, on both sides of which inconveniences will be found to lie. By enlarging too much the number of electors, you render the representative too little acquainted with all their local circumstances and lesser interests; as by reducing it too much, you render him unduly attached to these, and too little fit to comprehend and pursue great and national objects. The federal constitution forms a happy combination in this respect; the great and aggregate interests being referred to the national, the local and particular to the State legislatures.

The other point of difference is, the greater number of citizens and extent of territory which may be brought within the compass of republican than of democratic government; and it is this circumstance principally which renders factious combinations less to be dreaded in the former than in the latter. The smaller the society, the fewer probably will be the distinct parties and interests composing it; the fewer the distinct parties and interests, the more frequently will a majority be found of the same party; and the smaller the number of individuals composing a majority, and the smaller the compass within which they are placed, the more easily will they concert and execute their plans of oppression. Extend the sphere, and you take in a greater variety of parties and interests; you make it less probable that a majority of the whole will have a common motive to invade the rights of other citizens; or if such a common motive exists, it will be more difficult for all who feel it to discover their own strength, and to act in unison with each other. Besides other impediments, it may be remarked that, where there is a consciousness of unjust or dishonourable purposes, communication is always checked by distrust in proportion to the number whose concurrence is necessary.

Hence, it clearly appears, that the same advantage which a republic has over a democracy, in controlling the effects of faction, is enjoyed by a large over a small republic—is enjoyed by the Union over the States composing it. Does the advantage consist in the substitution of representatives whose enlightened views and virtuous sentiments render them superior to local prejudices and to schemes of injustice? It will not be denied that the representation of the Union will be most likely to possess these requisite endowments. Does it consist in the greater security afforded by a greater variety of parties, against the event of any one party being able to outnumber and oppress the rest? In an equal degree does the increased variety of parties comprised within the Union increase this security? Does it, in fine, consist in the greater obstacles opposed to the concert and accomplishment of the secret wishes of an unjust and interested majority? Here, again, the extent of the Union gives it the most palpable advantage.

The influence of factious leaders may kindle a flame within their particular States, but will be unable to spread a general conflagration through the other States. A religious sect may degenerate into a political faction in a part of the Confederacy; but the variety of sects dispersed over the entire face of it must secure the national councils against any danger from that source. A rage for paper money, for an abolition of

debts, for an equal division of property, or for any other improper or
wicked project, will be less apt to pervade the whole body of the Union
than a particular member of it; in the same proportion as such a malady
is more likely to taint a particular county or district, than an entire
State.

In the extent and proper structure of the Union, therefore, we behold
a republican remedy for the diseases most incident to republican government. And according to the degree of pleasure and pride we feel in
being republicans, ought to be our zeal in cherishing the spirit and supporting the character of Federalists.

PUBLIUS

—JAMES MADISON, *The Federalist*, No. 10, 1787

2. DAVY CROCKETT RUNS FOR LEGISLATURE

*Little things are illuminating: in Britain one stands for office; in the
United States one runs for office. The difference is more than verbal—
or was a century and more ago. From the beginning American politics
were democratic, which meant that almost anyone who could meet
rather simple qualifications could run for office. There were many
offices, and most of them paid salaries. From the beginning, too, political parties came along and systematized the whole business of selecting
candidates, conducting campaigns, and managing elections. This description of how the famous Tennessee Indian-fighter, Davy Crockett, got
himself elected to the state legislature, though written by what we would
now call a ghost writer, reflects faithfully enough frontier politics in the
first quarter of the century.*

I JUST now began to take a rise, as in a little time I was asked to offer
for the Legislature in the counties of Lawrence and Heckman. . . .

I went first into Heckman County to see what I could do among the
people as a candidate. Here they told me that they wanted to move their
town nearer to the center of the county, and I must come out in favor
of it. There's no devil if I knowed what this meant, or how the town

was to be moved; and so I kept dark, going on the identical same plan that I now find is called *noncommittal*. About this time there was a great squirrel hunt on Duck River, which was among my people. They were to hunt two days, then to meet and count the scalps and have a big barbecue, and what might be called a tiptop country frolic. The dinner, and a general treat, was all to be paid for by the party having taken the fewest scalps. I joined one side, taking the place of one of the hunters, and got a gun ready for the hunt. I killed a great many squirrels, and when we counted scalps, my party was victorious.

The party had everything to eat and drink that could be furnished in so new a country, and much fun and good humor prevailed. But before the regular frolic commenced, I mean the dancing, I was called on to make a speech as a candidate, which was a business I was as ignorant of as an outlandish Negro.

A public document I had never seen, nor did I know there were any such things; and how to begin I couldn't tell. I made many apologies and tried to get off, for I knowed I had a man to run against who could speak prime, and I knowed too that I wa'n't able to shuffle and cut with him. He was there, and knowing my ignorance as well as I did myself, he also urged me to make a speech. The truth is, he thought my being a candidate was a mere matter of sport, and didn't think for a moment that he was in any danger from an ignorant backwoods bear hunter. But I found I couldn't get off, and so I determined just to go ahead, and leave it to chance what I should say. I got up and told the people I reckoned they knowed what I come for, but if not, I could tell them. I had come for their votes, and if they didn't watch mighty close, I'd get them too. But the worst of all was, that I couldn't tell them anything about government. I tried to speak about something, and I cared very little what, until I choked up as bad as if my mouth had been jammed and crammed chock-full of dry mush. There the people stood, listening all the while, with their eyes, mouths, and years all open to catch every word I would speak.

At last I told them I was like a fellow I had heard of not long before. He was beating on the head of an empty barrel near the roadside when a traveler who was passing along asked him what he was doing that for. The fellow replied that there was some cider in that barrel a few days before and he was trying to see if there was any then, but if there was, he couldn't get at it. I told them that there had been a little bit of speech in me awhile ago, but I believed I couldn't get it out. They all roared out in a mighty laugh and I told some other anecdotes, equally amusing to them; and believing I had them in a first-rate way, I quit and got down, thanking the people for their attention. But I took care to remark that I was as dry as a powder horn and that I thought it was time for us to wet our whistles a little; and so I put off to the liquor stand and was followed by the greater part of the crowd.

I felt certain this was necessary, for I knowed my competitor could open government matters to them as easy as he pleased. He had, however, mighty few left to hear him as I continued with the crowd, now and then taking a horn and telling good-humored stories till he was done speaking. I found I was good for the votes at the hunt, and when we broke up, I went on to the town of Vernon, which was the same they wanted me to move. Here they pressed me again on the subject, and I found I could get either party by agreeing with them. But I told them I didn't know whether it would be right or not, and so couldn't promise either way.

Their court commenced on the next Monday, as the barbecue was on a Saturday, and the candidates for governor and for Congress as well as my competitor and myself all attended.

The thought of having to make a speech made my knees feel mighty weak and set my heart to fluttering almost as bad as my first love scrape with the Quaker's niece. But as good luck would have it, these big candidates spoke nearly all day, and when they quit, the people were worn out with fatigue, which afforded me a good apology for not discussing the government. But I listened mighty close to them, and was learning pretty fast about political matters. When they were all done, I got up and told some laughable story and quit. I found I was safe in those parts, and so I went home and didn't go back again till after the election was over. But to cut this matter short, I was elected, doubling my competitor and nine votes over. . . .

—A Narrative of the Life of David Crockett

3. ANDREW JACKSON IS INAUGURATED

It was not the intention of the Framers that the people should elect their Presidents. This important duty was to be performed by the electoral college—an assemblage of men who were supposed to exercise judgment—or by the House of Representatives. Within a very short time political parties took over the business of selecting candidates and electing Presidents, and the electoral college became an anachronism. In a sense it could be said that all the early Presidents represented "the people's choice," yet they were selected by processes that seemed remote from the people. Andrew Jackson was actually no more a man of the people than was John Adams or James Monroe, but he seemed to be. He was a popular hero, a military hero, the embodiment of the frontiersman's virtues. He was nominated by State Legislatures rather than by a caucus; he was supported by the small farmers of the West and the working men of the Eastern towns. When he was inaugurated, in 1829, "the backwoods boiled over and spilled into Washington" to celebrate the event. The gentry were reminded of the tumbrels and guillotines of the French Revolution, but the plain people saw nothing improper in taking over the White House. After all it was their White House.

WASHINGTON, March 11, Sunday [1829].—The inauguration was not a thing of detail or a succession of small incidents. No, it was one grand whole, an imposing and majestic spectacle, and to a reflective mind one of moral sublimity. Thousands and thousands of people, without distinction of rank, collected in an immense mass round the Capitol, silent, orderly, and tranquil, with their eyes fixed on the front of that edifice, waiting the appearance of the President in the portico. The door from the rotunda opens; preceded by the marshals, surrounded by the judges of the Supreme Court, the old man with his gray locks, that crown of glory, advances, bows to the people who greet him with a shout that rends the air. The cannons from the heights around, from Alexandria and Fort Warburton, proclaim the oath he has taken, and all the hills reverberate the sound. It was grand—it was sublime! An almost breathless silence succeeded, and the multitude was still, listening to catch the sound of his voice, though it was so low as to be heard only by those nearest to him. After reading his speech the oath was administered to him by the Chief Justice. Then Marshall presented the Bible. The President took it from his hands, pressed his lips to it, laid it reverently down, then bowed again to the people—yes, to the people in all their majesty. And had the spectacle closed here, even Europeans must have acknowledged that a free people, collected in their might, silent and tranquil, restrained solely by a moral power, without a shadow around of military force, was majesty rising to sublimity and far surpassing the majesty of kings and princes surrounded with armies and glittering in gold. . . .

The day was delightful, the scene animating; so we walked backward and forward, at every turn meeting some new acquaintance and stopping to talk and shake hands. Among others we met Zavr. Dickinson with Mr. Frelinghuysen and Doctor Elmendorf, and Mr. Samuel Bradford. We continued promenading here until near three, returned home unable to stand, and threw ourselves on the sofa. Some one came and informed us the crowd before the President's house was so far lessened that they thought we might enter. This time we effected our purpose. But what a scene did we witness! *The majesty of the people* had disappeared, and a rabble, a mob, of boys, Negroes, women, children, scrambling, fighting, romping. What a pity, what a pity! No arrangements had been made, no police officers placed on duty, and the whole house had been inundated by the rabble mob. We came too late. The President, after having been *literally* nearly pressed to death and almost suffocated and torn to pieces by the people in their eagerness to shake hands with Old Hickory, had retreated through the back way or south front and had escaped to his lodgings at Gadsby's. Cut glass and china to the amount of several thousand dollars had been broken in the struggle to get the refreshments. Punch and other articles had been carried out in tubs and buckets, but had it been in hogsheads it would have been insufficient; ice creams and cake and lemonade for twenty thousand people, for it is said that number were there, though I think the estimate exaggerated. Ladies fainted, men were seen with bloody noses, and such a scene of confusion took place as is impossible to describe— those who got in could not get out by the door again but had to scramble out of windows. At one time the President, who had retreated and retreated until he was pressed against the wall, could only be secured by a number of gentlemen forming round him and making a kind of barrier of their own bodies; and the pressure was so great that Colonel Bomford, who was one, said that at one time he was afraid they should have been pushed down or on the President. It was then the windows were thrown open and the torrent found an outlet, which otherwise might have proved fatal.

This concourse had not been anticipated and therefore not provided against. Ladies and gentlemen only had been expected at this levee, not the people en masse. But it was the people's day, and the people's President, and the people would rule. God grant that one day or other the people do not put down all rule and rulers. I fear, enlightened freemen as they are, they will be found, as they have been found in all ages and countries where they get the power in their hands, that of all tyrants, they are the most ferocious, cruel, and despotic. The noisy and disorderly rabble in the President's house brought to my mind descriptions I had read of the mobs in Tuileries and at Versailles. I expect to hear the carpets and furniture are ruined; the streets were muddy, and these guests all went thither on foot.

—Mrs. Samuel Harrison Smith, *The First Forty Years
of Washington Society,* 1829

4. THE SPOILS SYSTEM

The doctrine that to the victors belong the spoils was first blatantly announced by Senator Marcy, but the principle and the practice go back into English history. When Jackson came to the Presidency he found the Federal departments filled with aged functionaries who had been appointed from charitable or political motives; few of these had any sympathy with the frontier democrat from Tennessee. Nor did Jackson have any use for the notion that office-holders were entitled to their offices. "The duties of all public offices," he pointed out, "are plain and simple." Actually Jackson proceeded with circumspection. In eight years in office he removed about one employee in six—the same proportion as Jefferson had removed. We give here an extract from Jackson's first message to Congress and from Senator Marcy's speech.

A. Rotation in Office

THERE are, perhaps, a few men who can for any great length of time enjoy office and power without being more or less under the influence of feeling unfavorable to the faithful discharge of their public duties. Their integrity may be proof against improper considerations immediately addressed to themselves, but they are apt to acquire a habit of looking with indifference upon the public interests and of tolerating conduct from which an unpracticed man would revolt. Office is considered as a species of property, and government rather as a means of promoting individual interests than as an instrument created solely for the service of the people. Corruption in some and in others a perversion of correct feelings and principles divert government from its legitimate ends and make it an engine for the support of the few at the expense of the many. The duties of all public officers are, or at least admit of being made, so plain and simple that men of intelligence may readily qualify themselves for their performance; and I cannot but believe that more is lost by the long continuance of men in office than is generally to be gained by their experience. I submit, therefore, to your consideration whether the efficiency of the Government would not be promoted and official industry and integrity better secured by a general extension of the law which limits appointments to four years.

In a country where offices are created solely for the benefit of the people no one man has any more intrinsic right to official station than another. Offices were not established to give support to particular men at the public expense. No individual wrong is, therefore, done by removal, since neither appointment to nor continuance in office is matter of right. The incumbent became an officer with a view to public benefits, and when these require his removal they are not to be sacrificed to private interests. It is the people, and they alone, who have a right to complain when a bad officer is substituted for a good one. He who is removed has the same means of obtaining a living that are enjoyed by the millions who never held office. The proposed limitation would destroy the idea of property now so generally connected with official station, and although individual distress may be sometimes produced, it would, by promoting that rotation which constitutes a leading principle in the republican creed, give healthful action to the system.

—ANDREW JACKSON, First Annual Message to Congress, 1829

B. The Spoils of Victory

Mr. Marcy, one of the senators of the United States from New York, in the course of the debate on the nomination of Mr. Van Buren said—

"It may be, sir, that the politicians of New York are not so fastidious as some gentlemen are, as to disclosing the principles on which they act. They boldly *preach* what they *practice*. When they are contending for *victory*, they avow their intention of enjoying the fruits of it. If they are successful, they claim, as a matter of right, the advantages of success. They see nothing wrong in the rule that to the VICTOR belongs the spoils of the ENEMY."

—*Niles Register,* September 1, 1832

5. "TROUBLES OF A CANDIDATE"

In the early years of the Republic it was not thought dignified for candidates to campaign actively for themselves, and this tradition lingered on, for Presidential candidates, up to the time of McKinley's "front porch" campaign of 1896. Yet from the very beginning party leaders, campaign managers, editors, office-holders and expectant office-holders conducted campaigns of a vigorous and sometimes of a scurrilous sort. Washington himself complained of the indecency of the attacks upon him, and a later candidate observed that he didn't know whether he was running for the Presidency or the penitentiary. Perhaps the only extenuation of the American habit of indulging in billingsgate during campaigns is that if we have to blow off steam it is better to blow it off verbally than in other ways. We have given here a characteristic Dooley-Hennessy discussion of a Presidential campaign—the campaign of 1900, as it happens—from the inspired pen of Peter Finley Dunne.

I WISHT th' campaign was over," said Mr. Dooley.
"I wisht it'd begin," said Mr. Hennessy. "I niver knew anything so dead. They ain't been so much as a black eye give or took in th' ward an' its less thin two months to th' big day."

" 'Twill liven up," said Mr. Dooley, "I begin to see signs iv th' good times comin' again. 'Twas on'y th' other day me frind Tiddy Rosenfelt opened th' battle mildly be insinuatin' that all dimmycrats was liars, horse thieves an' arnychists. 'Tis true he apologized f'r that be explainin' that he didn't mean all dimmycrats but on'y those that wudden't vote f'r Mack but I think he'll take th' copper off befure manny weeks. A ladin' dimmycratic rayformer has suggested that Mack though a good man f'r an idjiot is surrounded be th' vilest scoundhrels ive seen in public life since th' days iv Joolyus Cæsar. . . .

"In a few short weeks, Hinnissy, 'twill not be safe f'r ayether iv the candydates to come out on th' fr-ront porch till th' waitin' dillygations has been searched be a polisman. 'Tis th' divvle's own time th' la-ads that r-runs f'r th' prisidincy has since that ol' boy Burchard broke loose again' James G. Blaine. Sinitor Jones calls wan iv his thrusty hinchman to his side, an' says he: 'Mike, put on a pig-tail, an' a blue shirt an' take a dillygation iv Chinnymen out to Canton an' congratulate Mack on th' murdher iv mission'ries in China. An',' he says, 'ye might stop off at Cincinnati on th' way over an' arrange f'r a McKinley an' Rosenfelt club to ilict th' British Consul its prisidint an' attack th' office iv th' German newspaper,' he says. Mark Hanna rings f'r his sicrety an', says he: 'Have ye got off th' letther fr'm George Fred Willums advisin' Aggynaldoo to pizen th' wells?' 'Yes sir.' 'An' th' secret communication fr'm Bryan found on an armychist at Pattherson askin' him to blow up th' White House?' 'It's in th' hands iv th' tyepwriter.' 'Thin call up an employmint agency an' have a dillygation iv Jesuites dhrop in at Lincoln, with a message fr'm th' pope proposin' to bur-rn all Protestant churches th' night befure iliction.'

"I tell ye, Hinnissy, th' candydate is kept movin'. Whin he sees a dilly-gation pikin' up th' lawn he must be r-ready. He makes a flyin' leap f'r th' chairman, seizes him by th' throat an' says: 'I thank ye f'r th' kind sintimints ye have conveyed. I am, indeed, as ye have remarked, th' riprisintative iv th' party iv manhood, honor, courage, liberality an' American thraditions. Take that back to Jimmy Jones an' tell him to put it in his pipe an' smoke it.' With which he bounds into th' house an' locks the dure while th' baffled conspirators goes down to a costumer an' changes their disguise. If th' future prisidint hadn't been quick on th' dhraw he'd been committed to a policy iv sthranglin' all the girl babies at birth.

"No, 'tis no aisy job bein' a candydate, an' 'twud be no easy job if th' game iv photygraphs was th' on'y wan th' candydates had to play. Willum Jennings Bryan is photygraphed smilin' back at his smilin' corn fields, in a pair iv blue overalls with a scythe in his hand borrid fr'm th' company that's playin' 'Th' Ol' Homestead,' at th' Lincoln Gran' Opry House. Th' nex' day Mack is seen mendin' a rustic chair with a monkey wrinch. Bryan has a pitcher took in th' act iv puttin' on a shirt marked with th' union label, an' they'se another photygraph iv Mack carryin' a scuttle iv coal up th' cellar stairs. An' did ye iver notice how much th' candydates looks alike, an' how much both iv thim looks like Lydia Pinkham? Thim wondherful boardin' house smiles that our gifted

leaders wears, did ye iver see annythin' so entrancin'? Whin th' las'
photygrapher has packed his ar-rms homeward I can see th' gr-reat
men retirin' to their rooms an' lettin' their faces down f'r a few minyits
befure puttin' thim up again in curl-pa-apers f'r th' nex' day display.
Glory be, what a relief 'twill be f'r wan iv him to raysume permanently
th' savage or fam'ly breakfast face th' mornin' afther iliction! What a
raylief 'twill be to no f'r sure that th' man at th' dure bell is on'y th' gas
collector an' isn't loaded with a speech iv thanks in behalf iv th' Spanish
Gover'mint! What a relief to snarl at wife an' frinds wanst more, to
smoke a seegar with th' thrust magnate that owns th' cider facthry near
th' station, to take ye'er nap in th' afthernoon undisthurbed be th' chirp
iv th' snap-shot! 'Tis th' day afther iliction I'd like f'r to be a candydate,
Hinnissy, no matther how it wint."

"An' what's become iv th' vice-prisidintial candydates?" Mr. Hennessy
asked.

"Well," said Mr. Dooley, "Th' las' I heerd iv Adly, I didn't hear
annythin', an' th' las' I heerd iv Tiddy he'd made application to th'
naytional comity f'r th' use iv Mack as a soundin' board."

—PETER FINLEY DUNNE, "Troubles of a Candidate"

6. "HONEST GRAFT AND DISHONEST GRAFT"

*Senator George Washington Plunkitt, self-appointed Tammany phi-
losopher, seems like a creature of the imagination but was actually a
figure in history. A journalist, William Riordan, had the happy idea of
taking down—doubtless with some exaggeration—some of Plunkitt's
"very plain talks on very practical politics delivered ... from his rostrum,
the New York County Court-House Bootblack stand." From these
"plain talks" we take a discourse on honest and dishonest graft.*

EVERYBODY is talkin' these days about Tammany men growin'
rich on graft, but nobody thinks of drawin' the distinction between honest graft and dishonest graft. There's all the difference in the
world between the two. Yes, many of our men have grown rich in

politics. I have myself. I've made a big fortune out of the game, and I'm gettin' richer every day, but I've not gone in for dishonest graft—blackmailin' gamblers, saloon-keepers, disorderly people, etc.—and neither has any of the men who have made big fortunes in politics.

"There's an honest graft, and I'm an example of how it works. I might sum up the whole thing by sayin': 'I seen my opportunities and I took 'em.'

"Just let me explain by examples. My party's in power in the city, and it's goin' to undertake a lot of public improvements. Well, I'm tipped off, say, that they're going to lay out a new park at a certain place.

"I see my opportunity and I take it. I go to that place and I buy up all the land I can in the neighborhood. Then the board of this or that makes its plan public, and there is a rush to get my land, which nobody cared particular for before.

"Ain't it perfectly honest to charge a good price and make a profit on my investment and foresight? Of course, it is. Well, that's honest graft. . . .

"Somehow, I always guessed about right, and shouldn't I enjoy the profit of my foresight? It was rather amusin' when the condemnation commissioners came along and found piece after piece of the land in the name of George Plunkitt of the Fifteenth Assembly District, New York City. They wondered how I knew just what to buy. The answer is—I seen my opportunity and I took it. I haven't confined myself to land; anything that pays is in my line. . . .

"I've told you how I got rich by honest graft. Now, let me tell you that most politicians who are accused of robbin' the city get rich the same way.

"They didn't steal a dollar from the city treasury. They just seen their opportunities and took them. That is why, when a reform administration comes in and spends a half million dollars in tryin' to find the public robberies they talked about in the campaign, they don't find them.

"The books are always all right. The money in the city treasury is all right. Everything is all right. All they can show is that the Tammany heads of departments looked after their friends, within the law, and gave them what opportunities they could to make honest graft. Now, let me tell you that's never goin' to hurt Tammany with the people. Every good man looks after his friends, and any man who doesn't isn't likely to be popular. If I have a good thing to hand out in private life, I give it to a friend. Why shouldn't I do the same in public life? . . .

"Now, in conclusion, I want to say that I don't own a dishonest dollar. If my worst enemy was given the job of writin' my epitaph when I'm gone, he couldn't do more than write:

"'George W. Plunkitt. He Seen His Opportunities, and He Took 'Em.'"

—WILLIAM L. RIORDAN, *Plunkitt of Tammany Hall*

7. "BOSS PENDERGAST"

The tradition of the "boss" in American politics goes back to Sam Adams and Aaron Burr, to Amos Kendall and Martin Van Buren. These men built up and largely controlled political machines, and to that extent they qualify as bosses. But they differed from the modern boss in that they were not primarily concerned with spoils or graft, they operated in the national arena, and they themselves competed for high political office. When we think of the "boss" today it is rather in terms of men like Tweed and Quay and Cameron and Murphy and Hague— and Pendergast—men who ran State or municipal machines, and who at least countenanced, if they did not encourage, large-scale corruption. Of modern bosses few have been more influential than Pendergast of Kansas City—a boss who, as this account tells us, started Harry S. Truman on his political career. After this account was written—in 1937— Pendergast was sent to the Federal Penitentiary for violation of income tax laws.

THE PENDERGAST machine enjoys all the political patronage in Kansas City and Jackson County, but that is only a small part of the machine's perquisites. It controls State and city contracts. It sells the construction materials which go into public buildings. It can, if it wishes, exercise a virtual monopoly of Kansas City's liquor business and its soft-drink business. The jackals of the machine enjoy the slot-machine, dice, roulette, and prostitution rackets—and a Parisian who recently visited Kansas City described it as the wickedest city he had ever seen. There is hardly a phase of Kansas City's life untouched by this monstrous outfit.

Do the citizens complain? Well, many of the outstanding ones do business with the machine or by its favor. They are mum if, indeed, they are not the machine's apologists. Others cry out, and are intimidated. Their assessments are raised. Their buildings are found defective. . . .

We know that the man we are about to see lifts men to high office with the utmost arrogance and the utmost contempt for all but the form of democratic processes. "I will make you mayor," "I will make you governor," "I will get you a seat in the Senate of the United States," he says.

In the fall of 1932, the Democratic candidate for governor died. There was a meeting of the Democratic State Committee. It was informed that the deceased candidate should be succeeded, by order of the boss, by an obscure Platte County circuit judge, Guy B. Park. The committee affixed the rubber stamp.

In 1934, there was to be an election for the United States Senate. There was also to be an election for Collector of Jackson County. To this latter post, a county judge (an administrative, not a judicial, post), Harry Truman, passionately aspired. It was a job paying a large sum of money, and Truman could use the money. The boss was sorry. He could not endorse Truman for the collectorship but he would put him in the United States Senate. He did. . . . In the senatorial primary, believe it or not, the county judge who wanted to be a collector polled 120,180 votes in Kansas City; and a brilliant and tremendously popular veteran, Mr. Cochrane, got 1,221 votes.

Such is the power of the man we are about to see. . . .

"Mr. Pendergast," we begin, "you are a great power in this State. You were recently called in the *New York Times* . . . the most powerful boss in America and one of the most interesting citizens of America."

"Well!"

"We want to know something about you, about your philosophy, if not of life, of politics. You are a realist, are you not?"

"What do you mean?"

"You take a practical view of things?"

"That's me."

"Why did you go into politics?"

"I went into politics because it appealed to me and it looked like a good business. My brother, Jim, was in politics, and I started helping him. We got along because we made friends and because we gave the people good men. How could we get along in Kansas City for fifty years without giving the people good men?"

"Mr. Pendergast, we notice a long line of people waiting to see you. Do you see so many people every day?"

"I function year in and year out. I don't wait until three weeks before the election. I'm working all the time. I'm kind to people because I like to be. I never give an argument when a man comes in for a dollar and wants help. Maybe he's having an argument with his wife he wants settled—you'd be surprised how many men come in to get things like that fixed up. Maybe he wants a job. I always go out of my way to help."

"So you believe it is the function of the head of a political organization to help people?"

"What's the government for if it isn't to help people? They're interested only in local conditions, not about the tariff or the war debts. They want consideration for their troubles in their own house, across the street, or around the corner. Something like paving, a water main, police protection, consideration for a complaint about taxes. They vote for the fellow who gives it to them. We never ask about their politics. We know pretty well how they'll vote after we help them."

"What are the methods by which you rose to power?"

"I've never bulldozed anybody and never let anybody bulldoze me. Newspapers, churches, reformers, or narrow-minded fellows—they can't bulldoze me. I have never changed my mind when I knew I was right and I have never broken my word. The biggest mistake a man can make is failing to keep his word. Sometimes I've been sorry I made a promise but I've always kept it. I'm just an ordinary fellow that was able to keep his word."

"When you endorse a man for office, Mr. Pendergast—and we understand most of the officeholders in Kansas City and in the State government, besides members of the Senate and House of Representatives, are of your choosing—do you exact any promises in advance?"

"If a candidate hasn't got sense enough to see who helped him win and hasn't sense enough to recognize that man's friends, there is no use asking for favors from that candidate in advance."

"But a little bit more, Mr. Pendergast, about your methods, if you please."

"There are no alibis in politics. The delivery of the votes is what counts. And it is efficient organization in every little ward and precinct that determines national as well as local elections. National elections, national politics are just Kansas City on a big scale. It boils down to the wards and precincts. The whole thing is to have an organization that functions in every ward and precinct. That's where the votes come from. The fundamental secret is to get the vote registered—and then get it out after it's registered. That's all there is to it. All the ballyhoo and showmanship such as they have at the national conventions is all right. It's a great show. It gives folks a run for their money. It makes everybody feel good. But the man who makes the organization possible is the man who delivers the votes, and he doesn't deliver them by oratory. Politics is a business, just like anything else."

"Thank you, Mr. Pendergast."

—RALPH COGHLAN, "Boss Pendergast"

8. INVISIBLE GOVERNMENT

There has never been a national boss in America, but a number of bosses have come pretty close to that position. There was, for example, Thurlow Weed, who sometimes acted as if he were boss of the Whig and then the new Republican party—but found out that he wasn't. There was Mark Hanna, who was chiefly instrumental in putting McKinley into the White House and who probably wanted to go there himself. In our own day there has been James Farley, whose influence, during the early days of the New Deal, was certainly nationwide but who—like earlier bosses—discovered that bossism has its limitations. Boss Platt, who is the subject of these remarks, was one State boss whose influence was nationwide. This analysis of Platt's influence, and of the

*workings of "invisible government" in New York State, is particularly
illuminating because it comes from Elihu Root, a distinguished statesman who served as Secretary of War and Secretary of State, and who
knew as much about the workings of the American government as any
man of his generation.*

FROM the days of Fenton, and Conkling, and Arthur and Cornell, and Platt, from the days of David B. Hill, down to the present time the government of the State has presented two different lines of activity, one of the constitutional and statutory officers of the State, and the other of the party leaders,—they call them party bosses. They call the system—I don't coin the phrase, I adopt it because it carries its own meaning—the system they call "invisible government." For I don't remember how many years, Mr. Conkling was the supreme ruler in this State; the Governor did not count, the legislatures did not count; comptrollers and secretaries of state and what not, did not count. It was what Mr. Conkling said, and in a great outburst of public rage he was pulled down.

Then Mr. Platt ruled the State; for nigh upon twenty years he ruled it. It was not the Governor; it was not the Legislature; it was not any elected officers; it was Mr. Platt. And the capitol was not here; it was at 49 Broadway; Mr. Platt and his lieutenants. It makes no difference what name you give, whether you call it Fenton or Conkling or Cornell or Arthur or Platt, or by the names of men now living. The ruler of the State during the greater part of the forty years of my acquaintance with the State government has not been any man authorized by the Constitution or by the law; and, sir, there is throughout the length and breadth of this State a deep and sullen and long-continued resentment at being governed thus by men not of the people's choosing. The party leader is elected by no one, accountable to no one, bound by no oath of office, removable by no one. . . . It is all wrong that a government not authorized by the people should be continued superior to the government that is authorized by the people.

How is it accomplished? How is it done? Mr. Chairman, it is done by the use of patronage, and the patronage that my friends on the other side of this question have been arguing and pleading for in this

Convention is the power to continue that invisible government against that authorized by the people. Everywhere, sir, that these two systems of government co-exist, there is a conflict day by day, and year by year, between two principles of appointment to office, two radically opposed principles. The elected officer or the appointed officer, the lawful officer who is to be held responsible for the administration of his office, desires to get men into the different positions of his office who will do their work in a way that is creditable to him and his administration. Whether it be a president appointing a judge, or a governor appointing a superintendent of public works, whatever it may be, the officer wants to make a success, and he wants to get the man selected upon the ground of his ability to do the work.

How is it about the boss? What does the boss have to do? He has to urge the appointment of a man whose appointment will consolidate his power and preserve the organization. The invisible government proceeds to build up and maintain its power by a reversal of the fundamental principle of good government, which is that men should be selected to perform the duties of the office; and to substitute the idea that men should be appointed to office for the preservation and enhancement of power of the political leader. The one, the true one, looks upon appointment to office with a view to the service that can be given to the public. The other, the false one, looks upon appointment to office with a view to what can be gotten out of it. . . . I assert that this perversion of democracy, this robbing democracy of its virility, can be changed as truly as the system under which Walpole governed the commons of England, by bribery, as truly as the atmosphere which made the *credit mobilier* scandal possible in the Congress of the United States has been blown away by the force of public opinion. We cannot change it in a moment, but we can do our share. We can take this one step toward, not robbing the people of their part in government, but toward robbing an irresponsible autocracy of its indefensible and unjust and undemocratic control of government, and restoring it to the people to be exercised by the men of their choice and their control.

—Speech of Elihu Root at the New York Convention, 1915

9. "LET'S GO BACK TO THE SPOILS SYSTEM"

Spoils, bosses, and invisible government made for corruption, and for the frustration of responsible government and of democracy. The obvious solution to the problem of corruption in government seemed to be honesty in government, and the way to assure this appeared to be the merit system. Agitation for Civil Service reform began in the 1860's and as early as 1871 a Civil Service Commission was created, with the editor, George William Curtis, as chairman. Grant however scuttled the Commission and in 1875 it was discontinued. The assassination of Garfield by a disappointed office-seeker revived the demand for Civil Service reform, and early in 1883 a none too enthusiastic Congress passed a Civil Service law. Eventually the great majority of regular Federal employees came under the rules of the Civil Service. On the whole this made for improvement in government morale; at the same time it brought some disillusionment. John Fischer here explains the disillusionment and suggests that the time has come to reconsider the whole matter of Civil Service reform.

WHAT'S gone wrong with Civil Service is easy enough to find out. You can get the story, in almost identical terms, from anybody who has ever held an executive job in Washington.

First of all, it's too slow. If you were an administrator in urgent need of a new assistant, you might hope to get somebody on the job—with luck and infinite finagling—in six or eight weeks. (He wouldn't be the man you want, of course.) . . .

When you want to fire a man, the procedure naturally is more tedious. In theory, it is as easy to get rid of an incompetent in the government service as it is in private industry; in practice, the ordeal may drag on for six or eight painful months. If you are an experienced administrator, you will never try to fire anybody—you will foist him off on some unsuspecting colleague in another bureau, or transfer him to the South Dakota field office, or reorganize your section to abolish his position. . . .

Even worse than the Civil Service Commission's leisurely gait is its delight in harassing the operating officials who are responsible for running the government. The typical administrator may spend as much as a third of his time placating the commission and the hordes of minor personnel specialists who infest Washington. He draws organization charts, argues with classification experts, fills out efficiency ratings, justifies the allocation of vacancies, and listens to inspiring lectures on personnel management until he has little energy left for his real job. He may search for hours for those magic words which, properly recited in a job description, will enable him to pay a subordinate $4,600 instead of $3,800. . . .

No bureaucrat can avoid this boondoggling. If he fails to initial a Green Sheet or to attach the duplicate copy of Form 57, the whole machinery of his office grinds to a halt. If he deliberately flouts the established ritual, or neglects to show due respect for the personnel priesthood, his career may be ruined and his program along with it. In a thousand subtle ways the personnel boys can throw sand in the gears. They can freeze appointments and promotions, block transfers, lose papers, and generally bedevil any official who refuses to "cooperate." If they bog down a government project in the process, that is no skin off their backs—nobody can ever hold them responsible.

Nor can the administrator escape the Civil Service investigators, who drop in once or twice a week to question him about the morals, drinking habits, and possibly treasonable opinions of some poor wretch who has applied for a federal job. . . .

These are minor indictments, however. The really serious charge against the Civil Service system is that it violates the most fundamental rule of sound management. That rule is familiar to every businessman: when you hold a man responsible for doing a job, you must give him the authority he needs to carry it out. Above all, he must be free to hire his own staff, assign them to tasks they can do best, and replace them if they don't make good. . . .

Although the defects of Civil Service are plain enough, the reasons for them are not so easy to find.

By no means all the blame rests on the Civil Service Commissioners. They are three earnest, well-meaning people, who grieve sincerely over the flaws in their organization. . . .

Veteran bureaucrats know that their bosses come and go, while they endure forever. They are skilled in the art of passive resistance, and they have no intention of letting any upstart commissioner tamper unduly with their time-hallowed procedures. . . .

They have two guiding principles. The first is Keep the Rascals Out. Civil Service, in their view, is a kind of police force designed to keep political patronage appointees from creeping into federal jobs. This they do well—but they rarely feel any responsibility for positive action to make the government work, or to persuade the best possible men to enter the federal service.

The second aim of the commission bureaucracy is to increase the dignity and power of the personnel profession. To this end, they have developed a special jargon which no outsider can understand, plus an elaborate structure of regulations, red tape, and ritual which can be mastered only after years of study. They demand of the whole government what Dr. Floyd W. Reeves, professor of administration at the University of Chicago, has described as "an almost idolatrous worship" of the commission's "detailed and antiquated rules."

It is hard to blame them for this—after all, they are only doing what the legal and medical professions did centuries ago. The result, however, is a vested interest in complexity and formalism which is largely responsible for the ill-repute of the Civil Service system.

But the greatest share of guilt falls on Congress. Lacking any real enthusiasm for the Civil Service idea, it has never bothered to work out comprehensive legislation for a modern, effective system of personnel administration. Instead, over the course of years it has encrusted the original act of 1883 with scores of piecemeal amendments and special statutes. . . .

Worst of all, Congress has perpetuated the basic flaw in the original Civil Service Act. The commission is still an independent agency, entirely divorced from the normal structure of government. Although it wields great power it is responsible to no one. It serves only as a kind of decrepit watch-dog, which growls at the regular departments, but seldom tries to help them get their job done.

It can be argued, in all seriousness, that Congress would do well to wipe out Civil Service, hide, horns, and tallow, and go back to the old-fashioned spoils system. . . .

Such a forthright return to the patronage system would, however, be a pretty drastic step—probably more drastic than is actually necessary. Before junking Civil Service entirely, maybe Congress should consider replacing the 1883 jalopy with a 1945 model.

The blueprint for a modern and workable Civil Service is already at hand. It was drawn up in 1937, after months of careful study, by a group of experts from outside the government known as the Committee on Administrative Management. The committee's suggestions were warmly endorsed by most of the recognized authorities in this field, and the President urged Congress to put them into effect immediately. As usual, Congress wasn't interested, and nothing happened.

These proposals are still as sensible as they were eight years ago and even more urgently needed. They call for four major reforms:

1. The present commission should be abolished, along with its whole collection of red tape and the senescent bureaucrats who weave it. . . .

2. Each agency should be permitted to hire its own help. They should be chosen strictly on merit, with all political influence ruled out, on the same basis which TVA now is using so successfully. . . .

3. A single Federal Personnel Administrator, responsible directly to the President, would lay down over-all policies for the various agencies, and see to it that they are carried out. . . .

4. A part-time, unpaid, non-political board should be set up to keep a wary eye on the administrator and on the personnel operations of the agencies. From time to time it might suggest general policies or standards. Its main job, however, would be to look out for the public interest, and make sure that the new, decentralized merit system actually worked with a minimum of political interference.

—JOHN FISCHER, "Let's Go Back to the Spoils System"

10. POLITICAL PARTIES IN AMERICA

Political parties originated in America during Washington's adminis-
tration, and have flourished ever since. For over a century and a half
they have performed the day-by-day housekeeping work of politics and
government. On the whole they have done this well. Yet they have re-

ceived more brickbats than bouquets, and this chiefly from people who expect them to conform to some impossible ideal of political philosophy. The editor here explains something of the historical function and sig-nificance of the political party.

THE political party, said Edmund Burke, is "a body of men united for promoting the national interest upon some particular principle upon which they are agreed." However accurate this classical definition of the party may have been for eighteenth century England—and its accuracy even here may be questioned—it is wildly inapplicable to the American political party. In so far as any definition is possible, the American political party may be said to be a body of men (and since the nineteenth Amendment of women) organized to get control of the machinery of government. It is not necessary that they be united upon some principle or even agreed upon some general program. It would be difficult to find any single important policy upon which either of the major political parties have been consistent for any length of time. . . .

If we look to the functions rather than to the chronological history of the American political party, we can see that the party has been, with the possible exception of the Constitution itself, the basic Ameri-can political institution. It has administered the government; broken down the artificial barriers of the federal system and the separation of powers; strengthened national feeling; ameliorated sectional and class conflict; and advanced democracy. Each of these functions deserves some elaboration.

The first job of the American political party has been to run the government. The Fathers of the Constitution drew up an admirable blue print of government—and went off and left it. They made no practical provision for the day by day business of politics or administra-tion. They neither anticipated nor recognized political parties. Parties are not only unknown to the Constitution, they were unknown to law until as late as 1907. But the Constitution was neither a self-starting nor a self-operating mechanism. Political parties came along and ran the government and—with the assistance of a growing permanent civil service—they have been doing it ever since. They have selected men for office, conducted campaigns, managed elections, formulated policies and issues, taken responsibility for legislative programmes. On the whole they have done these things well. As yet no alternative method of running the business of politics and government has been perfected.

Among the most important of the historical functions of the party has been the harmonizing of American political machinery. The Fathers of the Constitution, children of the Age of Reason, fabricated what we may call a Newtonian scheme of government, static rather than dynamic. Not only that, but since experience had taught them that all government was to be feared, they exhausted their ingenuity in devising methods of checking governmental tyranny. They manufactured, to this end, a complicated system of checks and balances—the federal system, the tri-partite division of powers, the bicameral legislature, judicial review, and so forth.

Such a system, if adhered to rigorously, would result very speedily in governmental paralysis. For example, if members of the Electoral College really followed their own independent judgment in voting for a President—as the Framers supposed they would—the elective system would break down completely. Parties came along and took charge of the whole business of electing a President—with the result that only three times has the election gone from the Electoral College to the House of Representatives.

Parties implemented the federal system, a system otherwise perfectly designed to produce deadlock. If states actually followed local interests, the American constitutional fabric would be torn asunder—as it was in 1860. It is the party, again, that harmonizes state and national interests. Parties made possible, too, the effective workings of a tripartite government. Theoretically, executive, legislative and judiciary departments are independent and equal. If the Executive and the Legislature actually maintained their independence, government could not function. Parties normally harmonize these two political branches of the American government. When, as occasionally happens, one party controls the executive branch and another the legislative branch, there is usually a deadlock. Fortunately this happens but seldom, and when it does the good sense of American politicians finds a way out.

The third major function of the party has been—and still is—to strengthen national feeling and ameliorate the otherwise dangerous sectional and class divisions. It should never be forgotten that the United States is comparable to a continent rather than to the average nation, and that it contains within its spacious borders as many geographical, climatic, and economic divisions as are found in Europe or South America. Normally these divisions—roughly sectional in nature—would be disintegrating in effect. Fortunately a variety of forces—historical, political, and economic—have countered the natural particularism of the American scene. Of these forces the three most important have been the Constitution, the frontier, and the political party, and the party is not the least of the three. Occasionally, to be sure, parties have come to represent local or sectional interests, and whenever they have done this they have made for trouble—or disappeared. The Federalists became a purely sectional party—and went under. When, in 1860, the Democratic party split along sectional lines and the Republican party emerged as a strictly Northern party, the Union itself split. The re-creation of the Democratic party as a national institution was perhaps the most effective instrument for the restoration of real Union. It is, in short, the party more than any other political institution that persuades Americans to think nationally rather than locally.

In the same way the party has served to moderate class antagonisms and to reconcile class interests. The party is the great common denominator of American society and economy. This fact is often alleged as a heavy criticism of the American party—especially abroad. Parties do not, it is charged, represent real interests, real groups. They do not adequately represent farmers, labour, business, the middle classes. Nor, it might be added, do they represent whites as such or Negroes as such, Catholics or Protestants or Jews, Baptists or Methodists. They even avoid issues which might give fair expression to the interests of these groups.

The instinct of Americans has always been hostile to the alignment of classes in political parties. For nothing, it is clear, could be more dangerous than such an alignment, and nothing gives greater security than the fact that the two major parties represent all classes and interests of American society.

This does not mean that a particular social or economic interest cannot make itself felt politically. Particular interests, whether economic or political, have two outlets. The first is within the major parties themselves. Thus anyone familiar with the work of platform committees or of conventions, with the compromises and concessions and arrangements that go into the making of party tickets, knows that within the party various interests are represented and can—by eloquence or by political blackmail—get attention to their demands. The second outlet for particular groups or interests is the third or minor party.

The American party system is definitely a two party system. There has never been a successful third party, and minor parties have rarely polled more than a very small percentage of the popular vote. Yet there have been almost innumerable minor parties—Free Soil, Liberty, "Know Nothing," Greenback, Populist, Farmer-Labour, Progressive, Dixiecrat, Socialist, Prohibition, and many others.

The function of the two major parties is to be all things to all men; the function of the minor parties to be something specific to a particular group of men. The business of the major parties is to capture control of the government and run it. The business of the minor parties is not to capture the government—for that is clearly impossible—but to develop so great a nuisance value that one of the major parties will take over their programs.

Finally it may be said that the American party has been an effective instrument for democracy. This is a result not of any inherent quality in the party itself, but rather of the dynamics of American politics. Thus each of the major parties has been forced to look for broad popular support, which means that parties inevitably are advocates of an extension of the suffrage. No party has ever taken the risk of openly opposing such an extension: the consequences to it when the extension of suffrage came—as it always did—would have been disastrous. Thus, too, each of the major parties, not being committed in advance to fundamental principles, has ever been on the look out for popular issues. Whatever issues appear to have wide popular support, these will inevitably be espoused by one or both major parties. Parties know, by experience, that the rewards of election go to the party that has satisfied most popular needs. This does not always mean an aggressive legislative program, for sometimes the public is weary of legislation and wants quiet. But on the whole the natural pressure of American politics is for an aggressive legislative program—such a program as Theodore Roosevelt or Woodrow Wilson or Franklin Roosevelt espoused—and on the whole, therefore, parties tend to champion popular issues.

Nor should it be overlooked, in any analysis of the democratic features of the American party, that the internal structure and organization of the party is, predominantly, democratic. There are exceptions here, to be sure—in the South for example. But those who come to the fore in party politics are the workers, not the aristocrats or the intelligentsia. Almost every political "boss" has worked his way up from ward-leader

or county-leader, and the rewards—spoils or recognition—go to the
workers. Not riches or even a great name, but hard work and faithful-
ness, get results in the political party.

Prophecy is notoriously dangerous, yet it is reasonably safe to make
some broad generalizations about American parties in the foreseeable
future. The United States will continue to maintain a two party system.
There will continue to be third or splinter parties: as long as the Electoral College functions as it does now, these minor parties will have
only local appeal. The two major parties will continue to have a broad
national basis, or will attempt to maintain such a basis. They will differ
relatively little on programs and not at all on principles. Unless some
major crisis arises, both parties will continue along moderately conservative lines. Both will seek as candidates "available" men. It is probable that clashes over particular features of domestic policy will be sharp
but that in the field of foreign relations the two parties will work together with reasonable amity.

—HENRY STEELE COMMAGER, "American Political Parties"

11. PUBLIC AND POLITICAL ASSOCIATIONS
IN THE UNITED STATES

*We come finally to what is the most pervasive and most effective of
all the mechanisms of democracy in America, the voluntary association.
"Wherever," writes Tocqueville, "at the head of some new undertaking,
you see the Government in France, or a man of rank in England, in the
United States you will be sure to find an association." What was true
in the 1830's is equally true more than a century later. This practice
of association, instinctive with Americans, had significant consequences.
First, it proved an invaluable training for politics. Second, it meant
the practical application of the spirit of private initiative and enterprise
in that instead of making government responsible for particular programs, men undertook them themselves. Third, it was the most convenient form for the pluralism and diversity of American interests—
and therefore the best safeguard against the danger of majority tyranny,
against factionalism, and against fanaticism. Thus in a very real sense
voluntary associations served to do what Madison said must be done if*

the Republic were to flourish—they spread, balanced, and canceled out interests and factions in society.

Americans have taken the practice of voluntary association so much for granted that they have not commonly appreciated its significance. But those born or trained to a different tradition have always expressed the liveliest appreciation of this practice, and it is to two of these that we turn for our commentary. Our first interpreter is that magisterial Tocqueville upon whose great Democracy in America *we have already drawn. The excerpts given here are from the separate volumes of that work, and separated by five years.*

IN NO country in the world has the principle of association been more successfully used, or more unsparingly applied to a multitude of different objects, than in America. Besides the permanent associations which are established by law under the names of townships, cities, and counties, a vast number of others are formed and maintained by the agency of private individuals.

The citizen of the United States is taught from his earliest infancy to rely upon his own exertions in order to resist the evils and the difficulties of life; he looks upon social authority with an eye of mistrust and anxiety, and he only claims its assistance when he is quite unable to shift without it. This habit may even be traced in the schools of the rising generation, where the children in their games are wont to submit to rules which they have themselves established, and to punish misdemeanors which they have themselves defined. The same spirit pervades every act of social life. If a stoppage occurs in a thoroughfare, and the circulation of the public is hindered, the neighbors immediately constitute a deliberative body; and this extemporaneous assembly gives rise to an executive power which remedies the inconvenience before anybody has thought of recurring to an authority superior to that of the persons immediately concerned. If the public pleasures are concerned, an association is formed to provide for the splendor and the regularity of the entertainment. Societies are formed to resist enemies which are exclusively of a moral nature, and to diminish the vice of intemperance: in the United States associations are established to promote public order, commerce, industry, morality, and religion; for there is no end which the human will, seconded by the collective exertions of individuals, despairs of attaining.

Hereafter I shall have occasion to show the effects of association upon the course of society, and I must confine myself for the present to the political world. When once the right of association is recognized, the citizens may employ it in several different ways. . . .

It must be acknowledged that the unrestrained liberty of political association has not hitherto produced, in the United States, those fatal consequences which might perhaps be expected from it elsewhere. The right of association was imported from England, and it has always existed in America; so that the exercise of this privilege is now amalgamated with the manners and customs of the people. At the present time the liberty of association is become a necessary guarantee against the tyranny of the majority. In the United States, as soon as a party is become preponderant, all public authority passes under its control; its private supporters occupy all the places, and have all the force of the administration at their disposal. As the most distinguished partisans of the other side of the question are unable to surmount the obstacles which exclude them from power, they require some means of establishing themselves upon their own basis, and of opposing the moral authority of the minority to the physical power which domineers over it. Thus a dangerous expedient is used to obviate a still more formidable danger. . . .

There are no countries in which associations are more needed, to prevent the despotism of faction or the arbitrary power of a prince, than those which are democratically constituted. In aristocratic nations the body of the nobles and the more opulent part of the community are in themselves natural associations, which act as checks upon the abuses of power. In countries in which these associations do not exist, if private individuals are unable to create an artificial and a temporary substitute for them, I can imagine no permanent protection against the most galling tyranny; and a great people may be oppressed by a small faction, or by a single individual, with impunity. . . .

It cannot be denied that the unrestrained liberty of association for political purposes is the privilege which a people is longest in learning how to exercise. If it does not throw the nation into anarchy, it perpetually augments the chances of that calamity. On one point, however, this perilous liberty offers a security against dangers of another kind; in countries where associations are free, secret societies are unknown. In America there are numerous factions, but no conspiracies.

The most natural privilege of man, next to the right of acting for himself, is that of combining his exertions with those of his fellow creatures, and of acting in common with them. I am therefore led to conclude that the right of association is almost as inalienable as the right of personal liberty. No legislator can attack it without impairing the very foundations of society. . . .

The political associations that exist in the United States are only a single feature in the midst of the immense assemblage of associations in that country. Americans of all ages, all conditions, and all dispositions, constantly form associations. They have not only commercial and manufacturing companies, in which all take part, but associations of a thousand other kinds—religious, moral, serious, futile, extensive or restricted, enormous or diminutive. The Americans make associations to give entertainments, to found establishments for education, to build inns, to construct churches, to diffuse books, to send missionaries to the antipodes; and in this manner they found hospitals, prisons, and schools. If it be proposed to advance some truth, or to foster some feeling by the encouragement of a great example, they form a society. Wherever, at the head of some new undertaking, you see the Government in France, or a man of rank in England, in the United States you will be sure to find an association. I met with several kinds of associations in America, of which I confess I had no previous notion; and I have often admired the extreme skill with which the inhabitants of the United States succeed in proposing a common object to the exertions of a great many men, and in getting them voluntarily to pursue it. I have since traveled over England, whence the Americans have taken some of their laws and many of their customs; and it seemed to me that the principle of association was by no means so constantly or so adroitly used in that country. The English often perform great things singly; whereas the Americans form associations for the smallest undertakings. It is evident that the former people consider association as a powerful means of action, but the latter seem to regard it as the only means they have of acting.

Thus the most democratic country on the face of the earth is that in which men have in our time carried to the highest perfection the art of pursuing in common the object of their common desires, and have applied this new science to the greatest number of purposes. Is this the result of accident? or is there in reality any necessary connection between the principle of association and that of equality? Aristocratic communities always contain, among a multitude of persons who by themselves are powerless, a small number of powerful and wealthy citizens, each of whom can achieve great undertakings single-handed. In aristocratic societies men do not need to combine in order to act, because they are strongly held together. Every wealthy and powerful citizen constitutes the head of a permanent and compulsory association, composed of all those who are dependent upon him, or whom he makes subservient to the execution of his designs. Among democratic nations, on the contrary, all the citizens are independent and feeble; they can do hardly anything by themselves, and none of them can oblige his fellow men to lend him their assistance. They all, therefore, fall into a state of incapacity, if they do not learn voluntarily to help each other. If men living in democratic countries had no right and no inclination to associate for political purposes, their independence would be in great jeopardy; but they might long preserve their wealth and their cultivation: whereas if they never acquired the habit of forming associations in ordinary life, civilization itself would be endangered. A people among whom individuals should lose the power of achieving great things single-handed, without acquiring the means of producing them by united exertions, would soon relapse into barbarism. . . .

There is only one country on the face of the earth where the citizens enjoy unlimited freedom of association for political purposes. This same country is the only one in the world where the continual exercise of the right of association has been introduced into civil life, and where all the advantages that civilization can confer are procured by means of it. In all the countries where political associations are prohibited, civil associations are rare. It is hardly probable that this is the result of accident; but the inference should rather be that there is a natural, and perhaps a necessary, connection between these two kinds of associations. . . . Civil associations, therefore, facilitate political association: but, on the other hand, political association singularly strengthens and improves associations for civil purposes. In civil life every man may, strictly speaking, fancy that he can provide for his own wants; in politics, he can fancy no such thing. When a people, then, have any knowledge of public life, the notion of association, and the wish to coalesce, present themselves every day to the minds of the whole community: whatever natural repugnance may restrain men from acting in concert, they will always be ready to combine for the sake of a party. Thus political life makes the love and practice of association more general; it imparts a desire of union, and teaches the means of combination to numbers of men who would have always lived apart. . . .

But even if political association did not directly contribute to the progress of civil association, to destroy the former would be to impair the latter. When citizens can only meet in public for certain purposes, they regard such meetings as a strange proceeding of rare occurrence, and they rarely think at all about it. When they are allowed to meet freely for all purposes, they ultimately look upon public association as the universal, or in a manner the sole means, which men can employ to accomplish the different purposes they may have in view. Every new want instantly revives the notion. The art of association then becomes, as I have said before, the mother of action, studied and applied by all.

When some kinds of associations are prohibited and others allowed, it is difficult to distinguish the former from the latter beforehand. In this state of doubt men abstain from them altogether, and a sort of public opinion passes current, that tends to cause any association whatsoever to be regarded as a bold and almost an illicit enterprise.

It is therefore chimerical to suppose that the spirit of association, when it is repressed on some one point, will nevertheless display the same vigor on all others; and that if men be allowed to prosecute certain undertakings in common, that is quite enough for them eagerly to set about them. When the members of a community are allowed and accustomed to combine for all purposes, they will combine as readily for the lesser as for the more important ones; but if they are only allowed to combine for small affairs, they will be neither inclined nor able to effect it. It is in vain that you will leave them entirely free to prosecute their business on joint-stock account: they will hardly care to avail themselves of the rights you have granted to them; and, after having exhausted your strength in vain efforts to put down prohibited associations, you will be surprised that you cannot persuade men to form the associations you encourage.

—ALEXIS DE TOCQUEVILLE, *Democray in America*, 1835, 1840

12. "IT IS OF THE VERY ESSENCE OF AMERICANISM"

The Spanish-born and Harvard-trained philosopher and poet, George Santayana, wrote almost a century after Tocqueville; what he had to say about the spirit of association was almost the same. Apparently the American trait of co-operation had not changed perceptibly over the years. The twentieth-century American was still a joiner; he still liked to express his individualism in concert with others rather than by himself. Whether this habit, or instinct, of voluntary association can survive the current drive on association and the current doctrine of guilt by association remains to be seen.

THERE is one gift or habit, native to England, that has not only been preserved in America unchanged, but has found there a more favourable atmosphere in which to manifest its true nature—I mean the spirit of free co-operation. . . .

The omnipresence in America of this spirit of co-operation, responsibility, and growth is very remarkable. Far from being neutralised by American dash and bravura, or lost in the opposite instincts of so many alien races, it seems to be adopted at once in the most mixed circles and in the most novel predicaments. In America social servitude is reduced to a minimum; in fact we may almost say that it is reduced to subjecting children to their mothers and to a common public education, agencies that are absolutely indispensable to produce the individual and enable him to exercise his personal initiative effectually; for after all, whatever metaphysical egotism may say, one cannot vote to be created. But once created, weaned, and taught to read and write, the young American can easily shoulder his knapsack and choose his own way in the world. He is as yet very little trammelled by want of opportunity, and he has no roots to speak of in place, class, or religion. Where individuality is so free, co-operation, when it is justified, can be all the more quick and hearty. Everywhere co-operation is taken for granted, as something that no one would be so mean or so short-sighted as to refuse. Together with the will to work and to prosper, it is of the essence of Americanism, and is accepted as such by all the unkempt polyglot peoples that turn to the new world with the pathetic but manly purpose of beginning life on a new principle. Every political body, every public meeting, every club, or college, or athletic team, is full of it. Out it comes whenever there is an accident in the street or a division in a church, or a great unexpected emergency like the late war. The general instinct is to run and help, to assume direction, to pull through somehow by mutual adaptation, and by seizing on the readiest practical measures and working compromises. Each man joins in and gives a helping hand, without a preconceived plan or a prior motive. Even the leader, when he is a natural leader and not a professional, has nothing up his sleeve to force on the rest, in their obvious good-will and mental blankness. All meet in a genuine spirit of consultation, eager to persuade but ready to be persuaded, with a cheery confidence in their average ability, when a point comes up and is clearly put before them, to decide it for the time being, and to move on. It is implicitly agreed, in every case, that disputed questions shall be put to a vote, and that the minority will loyally acquiesce in the decision of the majority and build henceforth upon it, without a thought of ever retracting it.

Such a way of proceeding seems in America a matter of course, because it is bred in the bone, or imposed by that permeating social contagion which is so irresistible in a natural democracy. But if we consider human nature at large and the practice of most nations, we shall see that it is a very rare, wonderful, and unstable convention. It implies a rather unimaginative optimistic assumption that at bottom all men's interests are similar and compatible, and a rather heroic public spirit—such that no special interest, in so far as it has to be overruled, shall rebel and try to maintain itself absolutely.

—GEORGE SANTAYANA, *Character and Opinion in the United States*, 1920

5

Democracy, or Majority Rule and Minority Right

"DEMOCRACY," wrote Governor John Winthrop of the Bay Colony, "is among most Civil nations accounted the meanest and worst of all forms of Government . . . and History does record that it hath been always of least continuance and fullest of trouble." A century and a half later, members of the Convention that wrote the Constitution vied with each other in warning against the "excesses" of democracy and in devising complex mechanisms to prevent unlimited majority rule.

Yet the same Governor Winthrop wrote that "magistracy must be no other, in effect, than a ministerial office, and all authority, both legislative, consultative, and judicial, must be exercised by the people in their body representative." And the Fathers subscribed to the doctrine that all government derives its powers from the consent of the governed, and acknowledged in the very machinery of constitution-making that government came from below, not above, and that men had the power to make it and to unmake it.

Are these views irreconcilable? Some students, especially in our own day, have thought so, and have attempted to distinguish between "republicanism" and "democracy." The distinction is artificial and misleading. Actually the difficulty vanishes if we realize that the term democracy has been used in two different senses, one qualitative, the other quantitative, and that it is only in our own day that these two things have been completely merged. Democracy means the qualitative principle that government derives its authority from people. In this sense it was acknowledged and accepted from the first, in America. It came increasingly to mean that government was controlled by the majority of the people, and that people meant all people. In this sense it triumphed only in the twentieth century, and even then its triumph was a limited one. To suppose, as some overhasty observers do, that there can be no democracy without participation by the majority of all the people is to embrace the curious view that the United States did not become a democracy until August 26, 1920—the date of ratification of the woman suffrage amendment. What is, or should be, clear to everyone is that the concept of the people, for political purposes, is a constantly changing one. The eighteenth century did not think of majority rule in terms of all people, or of all white people, or of all male people, but in terms of those who, presumably, had a stake in the community. The nineteenth century did not think of majority rule in terms of Negroes or of women, but only of adult white men. Even in the twentieth century parts of the nation do not think of democracy in terms of all men and women, but of white men and women. Thus in South Carolina, for example, about five per cent of the inhabitants voted in the Presidential election of 1944, yet South Carolinians would reject the suggestion that theirs was not a democratic State.

Much of our difficulty about the nature of democracy vanishes if we keep clearly in mind two basic principles of our political system: first, that all government derives from the people; second, that all government is limited. Theoretically these principles may be contradictory, for theoretically if people have all the powers of government they have the power to do away with limits on government. But there are two ways of disposing of this theoretical objection to the principles of American constitutionalism. One is a philosophical way, namely, that Americans have always supposed that God Himself, or Nature, if you will, put limits on government, just as God, or Nature, put limits on power. Government, as James Otis said succinctly, cannot make two and two five, and if it tries to do so, its act is void and of no force, for it cannot change natural law. The second way is the pragmatic or the historical one, namely that whatever theory may say, Americans have, in fact, for a century and a half combined these two principles. They have, in fact, subscribed to the principle that government comes from people, and they have maintained a system wherein people acquiesce in self-imposed limitations.

To this task of maintaining limits on majority rule Americans have devoted a great deal of thought, and no little ingenuity. The thought can be read in such philosophical discussions as those by John Adams or John C. Calhoun; the ingenuity can be seen in the complex network of checks and balances which distinguishes our constitutional system. What is interesting here—for our own time—is that while we have left behind us most of the philosophical doubts about democracy, we retain the mechanisms designed to restrain democracy. Few now would subscribe to the observations of an Adams, a Calhoun or a Tocqueville, but for all that we still keep our bicameral legislatures and rejoice in judicial review!

There is no ultimate solution to any of the great problems of politics, but insofar as the problem of majority rule and minority rights can be solved, it will be solved along the lines laid down by Jefferson a century and a half ago. "All," he said, in his First Inaugural Address, "will bear in mind this sacred principle, that though the will of the majority is in all cases to prevail, that will to be rightful must be reasonable; that the minority possess their equal rights, which equal law must protect, and to violate would be oppression." Majority rule to be rightful must be reasonable. This means that a majority must conduct itself like a reasonable man. A reasonable man does not make arbitrary decisions or exercise arbitrary power. A reasonable man considers always the effect of his acts and decisions on those who are dependent upon him or influenced by him—on his wife and children, on his business or professional associates, on his community, on his country.

There are a good many laws to see to it that men conduct themselves reasonably, and we all know that these laws are essential if society is not to come apart at the seams. Even the most ardent individualist does not think that he has a right to drive eighty miles an hour on the road. On the contrary he conforms cheerfully enough to self-imposed limitations that he and his fellow men have written into the law. So a democracy imposes limitations on itself. Certainly the American democracy has done this. Perhaps no other democracy has so many self-imposed limitations: written constitutions, bills of rights, judicial review, the federal system, separation of powers, executive veto, and so forth. These limitations do not repudiate the principle of majority rule any more than the limitations of laws or of social usage repudiate the principle of individual liberty.

We give here some notable documents, and some that are interesting or illuminating rather than notable, in this great debate over majority rule and minority rights. What they reveal is mostly obvious, but none the less important for that. They reveal a persistent faith in the principle of democracy and a steady distrust of its practice. They reveal that Americans have imposed limits on themselves, and have practiced self-restraint. They reveal that articulate distrust of majority rule has come, consistently, from those privileged classes or interests who were primarily concerned about their own privilege or interest, not about the commonwealth. And they reveal, finally, that the concept of democracy is a steadily broadening one—one that broadens both qualitatively and quantitatively, one that takes in social equality and economic security and that broadens out to embrace peoples everywhere on the globe.

1. "CHERISH THE SPIRIT OF THE PEOPLE"

Jefferson's whole life was a monument to his faith in democracy, especially a democracy as enlightened and virtuous as he considered the American. The argument of this letter might be taken as representative of the argument he maintained throughout more than half a century of public life: cherish the people. The letter, written from Paris, took as its point of departure Shays's Rebellion in Massachusetts. This outbreak—an outbreak which should not be dignified by the term rebellion—had furnished the text for many a sermon on the necessity of restraining the mob spirit and strengthening government. Jefferson thought that this reaction had gone much too far. "God forbid," he wrote later in 1787, "we should ever be twenty years without such a rebellion. . . . The tree of liberty must be refreshed from time to time with the blood of patriots and tyrants."

Paris, January 16, 1787

THE tumults in America I expected would have produced in Europe an unfavorable opinion of our political state. But it has not. On the contrary, the small effect of these tumults seems to have given more confidence in the firmness of our governments. The interposition of the people themselves on the side of government has had a great effect on the opinion here. I am persuaded myself that the good sense of the people will always be found to be the best army. They may be led astray for a moment, but will soon correct themselves. The people are the only censors of their governors; and even their errors will tend to keep these to the true principles of their institution. To punish these errors too severely would be to suppress the only safeguard of the public liberty. The way to prevent these irregular interpositions of the people, is to give them full information of their affairs through the channel of the public papers, and to contrive that those papers should penetrate the whole mass of the people. The basis of our governments being the opinion of the people, the very first object should be to keep that right; and were it left to me to decide whether we should have a government without newspapers, or newspapers without a government, I should not hesitate a moment to prefer the latter. But I should mean that every man should receive those papers, and be capable of reading them. I am convinced that those societies (as the Indians) which live without government, enjoy in their general mass an infinitely greater degree of happiness than those who live under the European governments. Among the former, public opinion is in the place of law, and restrains morals as powerfully as laws ever did anywhere. Among the latter, under pretence of governing, they have divided their nations into two classes, wolves and sheep. I do not exaggerate. This is a true picture of Europe. Cherish, therefore, the spirit of our people, and keep alive their intention. Do not be too severe upon their errors, but reclaim them by enlightening them. If once they become inattentive to the public affairs, you and I, and Congress and Assemblies, Judges and Governors, shall all become wolves. It seems to be the law of our general nature, in spite of individual exceptions; and experience declares that man is the only animal which devours his own kind; for I can apply no milder term to the governments of Europe, and to the general prey of the rich on the poor. . . .

—THOMAS JEFFERSON, Letter to Colonel Carrington, January 16, 1787

2. "IT IS ESSENTIAL TO LIBERTY THAT THE RIGHTS OF THE RICH BE SECURED"

Jefferson's confidence in the virtue and intelligence of the people was not shared by most of the Founding Fathers, as witness some of the debates in the Federal Convention of 1787. Jefferson's old friend John Adams was philosophically a democrat insofar as he believed the people

to be the ultimate source of all power, but he was not Jefferson's kind of
Democrat. He would found government not on hope but on fear, not
on confidence but on guarantees. Like Madison, Hamilton, Pinckney,
and others, he was deeply impressed by the extent to which society was
divided into classes, interests, and factions, and like them he was anxious
to devise constitutional methods of balancing these interests against each
other. While Minister to England, in 1787, he devoted a great deal of
thought to this problem. His thinking crystallized around a letter which
the French statesman, Turgot, had written to Dr. Richard Price, criticiz-
ing the Americans for copying European mechanics of government in-
stead of setting up simple democratic governments. The result was
Adams' three-volume Defence of the Constitutions of the United States
against the Attacks of Mr. Turgot. *From this large and impressive work*
we take a brief but characteristic excerpt which reveals at once Adams'
belief in democratic principles and his concern for techniques of limiting
majorities.

THE way to secure liberty is to place it in the people's hands, that is,
to give them a power at all times to defend it in the legislature and
in the courts of justice. But to give the people, uncontrolled, all the
prerogatives and rights of supremacy, meaning the whole executive and
judicial power, or even the whole undivided legislative, is not the way
to preserve liberty. In such a government it is often as great a crime to
oppose or decry a popular demagogue, or any of his principal friends,
as in a simple monarchy to oppose a king, or in a simple aristocracy the
senators. The people will not bear a contemptuous look or disrespectful
word; nay, if the style of your homage, flattery, and adoration, is not
as hyperbolical as the popular enthusiasm dictates, it is construed into
disaffection; the popular cry of envy, jealousy, suspicious temper, vanity,
arrogance, pride, ambition, impatience of a superior, is set up against a
man, and the rage and fury of an ungoverned rabble, stimulated under-
hand by the demagogic despots, breaks out into every kind of insult,
obloquy, and outrage, often ending in murders and massacres, like
those of the De Witts, more horrible than any that the annals of despotism can produce.

It is indeed true, that "the interest of freedom is a virgin that every
one seeks to deflour; and like a virgin it must be kept, or else (so great

is the lust of mankind after dominion) there follows a rape upon the first opportunity." From this it follows, that liberty in the legislature is "more secure in the people's than in any other hands, because they are most concerned in it:" provided you keep the executive power out of their hands entirely, and give the property and liberty of the rich a security in a senate, against the encroachments of the poor in a popular assembly. Without this the rich will never enjoy any liberty, property, reputation, or life, in security. The rich have as clear a right to their liberty and property as the poor. It is essential to liberty that the rights of the rich be secured; if they are not, they will soon be robbed and become poor, and in their turn rob their robbers, and thus neither the liberty or property of any will be regarded. . . .

Is it not an insult to common sense, for a people with the same breath to cry *liberty,* an *abolition of debts,* and *division of goods?* If debts are once abolished, and goods are divided, there will be the same reason for a fresh abolition and division every month and every day. And thus the idle, vicious, and abandoned, will live in constant riot on the spoils of the industrious, virtuous, and deserving. "Powerful and crafty underminers" have nowhere such rare sport as in a simple democracy or single popular assembly. Nowhere, not in the completest despotisms, does human nature show itself so completely depraved, so nearly approaching an equal mixture of brutality and devilism, as in the last stages of such a democracy, and in the beginning of that despotism that always succeeds it.

—JOHN ADAMS, *A Defence of the Constitutions of the United States against the Attacks of Mr. Turgot,* 1787-88

3. "THE COMBINATIONS OF CIVIL SOCIETY ARE NOT LIKE THOSE OF A SET OF MERCHANTS"

The views of Adams, Madison, Pinckney and others of their school prevailed in that the constitutions written during the Revolutionary era incorporated elaborate checks and balances designed to impede majority rule. Of these checks and balances the commonest were the bicameral legislature, the separation of powers, and the executive veto. The Pennsylvania Constitution of 1776, which reflected in a way the views of

Benjamin Franklin, was an exception to the general rule of checks and balances. It provided a unicameral legislature, rotation in office, and a singularly weak executive. These democratic features alarmed many conservatives, and there was a strong demand for constitutional revision. The essay from which we quote here was written by the aged Franklin—he died the following year—in answer to a proposal in the Federal Gazette *that Pennsylvania adopt a bicameral system and limit suffrage for the upper house to freemen with property to the value of a thousand pounds.*

SEVERAL questions may arise upon this proposition. 1st. What is the proportion of freemen possessing lands and houses of one thousand pounds' value compared to that of freemen whose possessions are inferior? Are they as one to ten? Are they even as one to twenty? I should doubt whether they are as one to fifty. If this minority is to choose a body expressly to control that which is to be chosen by the great majority of the freemen, what have this great majority done to forfeit so great a portion of their right in elections? Why is this power of control, contrary to the spirit of all democracies, to be vested in a minority, instead of a majority? Then, is it intended, or is it not, that the rich should have a vote in the choice of members for the lower house, while those of inferior property are deprived of the right of voting for members of the upper house? And why should the upper house, chosen by a minority, have equal power with the lower chosen by a majority? Is it supposed that wisdom is the necessary concomitant of riches and that one man worth a thousand pounds must have as much wisdom as twenty who have each only nine hundred and ninety-nine; and why is property to be represented at all? Suppose one of our Indian nations should now agree to form a civil society; each individual would bring into the stock of the society little more property than his gun and his blanket, for at present he has no other. We know that, when one of them has attempted to keep a few swine, he has not been able to maintain a property in them, his neighbors thinking they have a right to kill and eat them whenever they want provision, it being one of their maxims that hunting is free to all; the accumulation therefore of property in such a society, and its security to individuals in every society, must be an effect of the protection afforded to it by the joint strength of the society in the execution of its laws. Private property therefore is a creature of society and is subject to the calls of that society whenever its necessities shall require it, even to its last farthing; its contributions to the public exigencies are not to be considered as conferring a benefit on the public, entitling the contributors to the distinctions of honor and power, but as the return of an obligation previously received, or the payment of a just debt. The combinations of civil society are not like those of a set of merchants, who club their property in different proportions for building and freighting a ship, and may therefore have some right to vote in the disposition of the voyage in a greater or less degree according to their respective contributions; but the important ends of civil society, and the personal securities of life and liberty there, remain the same in every member of the society; and the poorest continues to have an equal claim to them with the most opulent, whatever difference time, chance or industry may occasion in their circumstances. On these considerations I am sorry to see the signs this paper I have been considering affords, of a disposition among some of our people to commence an aristocracy, by giving the rich a predominancy in government, a choice peculiar to themselves in one-half the legislature to be proudly called the Upper House, and the other branch, chosen by the majority of the people, degraded by the denomination of the Lower; and giving to this Upper House a permanency of four years, and but two to the Lower. I hope, therefore, that our representatives in the convention will not hastily go into these innovations but take the advice of the Prophet: "Stand in the old ways, view the ancient paths, consider them well, and be not among those that are given to change."

—BENJAMIN FRANKLIN, "On the Legislative Branch" 1789

4. "WE ARE DESCENDING INTO A LICENTIOUS DEMOCRACY"

In men like John Adams, Hamilton, and Marshall, Federalism meant sound conservatism. But then, as now, conservatism had its lunatic fringe, and in the first decade of the new century—that is, in the period of the Jeffersonian triumph—this fringe became pretty broad. The leader of what might be called the ultra-Federalists was the eloquent and

*learned Fisher Ames, Senator from Massachusetts and President-elect of
Harvard College (he declined the post). Fisher Ames set the tone which
one generation of successors after another was to echo: the people are
not to be trusted; the people will destroy us; only the good and the wise,
the well-born and the rich, are capable of governing the country. Under
the leadership of men like Ames and his Essex Junto colleagues, Timothy
Pickering, Theophilus Parsons, and others, the Federalist party destroyed
itself.*

THEY are certainly blind who do not see, that we are descending
from a supposed orderly and stable republican government into a
licentious democracy, with a progress that baffles all means to resist, and
scarcely leaves leisure to deplore its celerity. The institutions and the
hopes that Washington raised are nearly prostrate; and his name and
memory would perish, if the rage of his enemies had any power over
history. But they have not—history will give scope to her vengeance,
and posterity will not be defrauded.

But, if our experience had not clearly given warning of our approaching catastrophe, the very nature of democracy would inevitably produce it.

A government by the passions of the multitude, or, no less correctly,
according to the vices and ambition of their leaders, is a democracy. We
have heard so long of the indefeasible sovereignty of the people, and
have admitted so many specious theories of the rights of man, which are
contradicted by his nature and experience, that few will dread at all,
and fewer still will dread as they ought, the evils of an American democracy. They will not believe them near, or they will think them tolerable
or temporary. Fatal delusion!

When it is said, there may be a tyranny of the *many* as well as of the
few, every democrat will yield at least a cold and speculative assent; but
he will at all times act, as if it were a thing incomprehensible, that there
should be any evil to be apprehended in the uncontrolled power of the
people. He will say, arbitrary power may make a tyrant, but how can
it make its possessor a slave? . . .

The people, as a body, cannot deliberate. Nevertheless, they will feel
an irresistible impulse to act, and their resolutions will be dictated to
them by their demagogues. The consciousness, or the opinion, that they

possess the supreme power, will inspire inordinate passions; and the violent men, who are the most forward to gratify those passions, will be their favourites. What is called the government of the people is in fact too often the arbitrary power of such men. Here, then, we have the faithful portrait of democracy. What avails the boasted *power* of individual citizens? or of what value is the will of the majority, if that will is dictated by a committee of demagogues, and law and right are in fact at the mercy of a victorious faction? To make a nation free, the crafty must be kept in awe, and the violent in restraint. The weak and the simple find their liberty arise not from their own individual sovereignty, but from the power of law and justice over all. It is only by the due restraint of others, that I am free.

Popular sovereignty is scarcely less beneficent than awful, when it resides in their courts of justice; there its office, like a sort of human providence, is to warn, enlighten, and protect; when the people are inflamed to seize and exercise it in their assemblies, it is competent only to kill and destroy. Temperate liberty is like the dew, as it falls unseen from its own heaven; constant without excess, it finds vegetation thirsting for its refreshment, and imparts to it the vigour to take more. All nature, moistened with blessings, sparkles in the morning ray. But democracy is a water spout, that bursts from the clouds, and lays the ravaged earth bare to its rocky foundations. The labours of man lie whelmed with his hopes beneath masses of ruin, that bury not only the dead, but their monuments. . . .

The truth is, and let it humble our pride, the most ferocious of all animals, when his passions are roused to fury and are uncontrolled, is man; and of all governments, the worst is that which never fails to excite, but was never found to restrain those passions, that is, democracy. It is an illuminated hell, that in the midst of remorse, horrour, and torture, rings with festivity; for experience shews, that one joy remains to this most malignant description of the damned, the power to make others wretched.

—FISHER AMES, "The Dangers of American Liberty," 1805

5. "DARE WE FLATTER OURSELVES THAT WE ARE A PECULIAR PEOPLE?"

All of the original State Constitutions contained limitations on suffrage; in a general way it was correct to say that in the beginning of our national history voting was limited to free, white, adult, Protestant, propertied males. The property qualifications varied greatly from State to State and varied, too, in the extent to which they were enforced. The triumph of Jeffersonian democracy brought a widespread demand for more liberal suffrage provisions. It was fairly easy to meet this demand in writing constitutions for the new Western States, but somewhat more difficult in the original States of the Atlantic seaboard. Three constitutional conventions—those of New York, Massachusetts, and Virginia— witnessed full-dress debates on the question of suffrage qualifications. Of them all the New York debate was the most illuminating. Here the great Chancellor Kent—in his day one of the most conservative men in America—led the argument for the retention of property qualifications for voting. He was defeated on this issue. After 1821 only a few States retained property qualifications for suffrage and eventually all adopted manhood suffrage—without either society or government coming to an end!

THESE are some of the fruits of our present government; and yet we seem to be dissatisfied with our condition, and we are engaged in the bold and hazardous experiment of remodeling the constitution. . . .

Now, sir, I wish to preserve our senate as the representative of the landed interest. I wish those who have an interest in the soil to retain the exclusive possession of a branch in the legislature as a stronghold in which they may find safety through all the vicissitudes which the state may be destined, in the course of Providence, to experience. I wish them to be always enabled to say that their freeholds cannot be taxed without their consent. The men of no property, together with the crowds of dependents connected with great manufacturing and commercial establishments, and the motley and undefinable population of crowded ports, may, perhaps, at some future day, under skilful management, predom-

215

inate in the assembly, and yet we should be perfectly safe if no laws could pass without the free consent of the owners of the soil. That security we at present enjoy; and it is that security which I wish to retain.

The apprehended danger from the experiment of universal suffrage applied to the whole legislative department is no dream of the imagination. It is too mighty an excitement for the moral constitution of men to endure. The tendency of universal suffrage is to jeopardize the rights of property and the principles of liberty. There is a constant tendency in human society, and the history of every age proves it; there is a tendency in the poor to covet and to share the plunder of the rich; in the debtor to relax or avoid the obligation of contracts; in the majority to tyrannize over the minority and trample down their rights; in the indolent and the profligate to cast the whole burthens of society upon the industrious and the virtuous; and *there is a tendency in ambitious and wicked men to inflame these combustible materials.* It requires a vigilant government, and a firm administration of justice, to counteract that tendency. . . . We are fast becoming a great nation, with great commerce, manufactures, population, wealth, luxuries, and with the vices and miseries that they engender. One-seventh of the population of the city of Paris at this day subsists on charity, and one-third of the inhabitants of that city die in the hospitals; what would become of such a city with universal suffrage? France has upward of four, and England upward of five millions of manufacturing and commercial laborers without property. Could these kingdoms sustain the weight of universal suffrage? The radicals in England, with the force of that mighty engine, would at once sweep away the property, the laws, and the liberties of that island like a deluge.

The growth of the city of New York is enough to startle and awaken those who are pursuing the *ignis fatuus* of universal suffrage.

—Speech of James Kent at the New York Convention, 1821

6. THE TYRANNY OF THE MAJORITY

It is well over a century now since Alexis de Tocqueville, just turned thirty, brought out the first two volumes of his Democracy in America. *That work remains, all in all, the greatest interpretative work ever written on the United States and the classic analysis of the influence of democracy on society, economy ,and government. Tocqueville was not*

concerned exclusively or even primarily with America; he was writing,
actually, for the benefit of his own people, and of the people of the Old
World generally. "I confess," he wrote, "that in America I saw more
than America; I sought the image of democracy itself, with its inclina-
tions, its character, its prejudices, and its passions, in order to learn what
we have to fear or to hope from its progress." Sometimes, as in this fa-
mous chapter on the tyranny of the majority, the fear outstripped the
hope. Tocqueville's fears of majority tyranny were derived in part from
his experience in the Old World, in part from conversations with such
men as Justice Story, Chancellor Kent, and others of that ilk, and in part
from the use of the deductive rather than the inductive method.

THE very essence of democratic government consists in the absolute
sovereignty of the majority; for there is nothing in democratic
States which is capable of resisting it. Most of the American Constitutions have sought to increase this natural strength of the majority by
artificial means.

The legislature is, of all political institutions, the one which is most
easily swayed by the wishes of the majority. The Americans determined
that the members of the legislature should be elected by the people immediately, and for a very brief term, in order to subject them, not only
to the general convictions, but even to the daily passions, of their constituents. The members of both Houses are taken from the same class
in society, and are nominated in the same manner; so that the modifications of the legislative bodies are almost as rapid and quite as irresistible
as those of a single assembly. It is to a legislature thus constituted that
almost all the authority of the government has been entrusted. . . .

Custom, however, has done even more than law. A proceeding which
will in the end set all the guarantees of representative government at
naught is becoming more and more general in the United States; it
frequently happens that the electors, who choose a delegate, point out a
certain line of conduct to him, and impose upon him a number of positive obligations which he is pledged to fulfil. With the exception of the
tumult, this comes to the same thing as if the majority of the populace
held its deliberations in the market place.

Several other circumstances concur in rendering the power of the
majority in America not only preponderant, but irresistible. The moral

authority of the majority is partly based upon the notion that there is more intelligence and more wisdom in a great number of men collected together than in a single individual, and that the number of legislators is more important than their quality. The theory of equality is, in fact, applied to the intellect of man: and human pride is thus assailed in its last retreat by a doctrine which the minority hesitate to admit, and in which they very slowly concur. Like all other powers, and perhaps more than all other powers, the authority of the many requires the sanction of time; at first it enforces obedience by constraint, but its laws are not respected until they have long been maintained. . . .

The moral power of the majority is founded upon yet another principle, which is, that the interests of the many are to be preferred to those of the few. It readily will be perceived that the respect here professed for the rights of the majority must naturally increase or diminish according to the state of parties. When a nation is divided into several irreconcilable factions, the privilege of the majority is often overlooked, because it is intolerable to comply with its demands. . . .

In the United States . . . all parties are willing to recognize the rights of the majority, because they all hope to turn those rights to their own advantage at some future time. The majority therefore in that country exercises a prodigious actual authority, and a moral influence which is scarcely less preponderant; no obstacles exist which can impede or so much as retard its progress, or which can induce it to heed the complaints of those whom it crushes upon its path. This state of things is fatal in itself and dangerous for the future. . . .

The omnipotence of the majority and the rapid as well as absolute manner in which its decisions are executed in the United States has not only the effect of rendering the law unstable, but it exercises the same influence upon the execution of the law and the conduct of the public administration. As the majority is the only power which it is important to court, all its projects are taken up with the greatest ardor, but no sooner is its attention distracted than all this ardor ceases; while in the free States of Europe the administration is at once independent and secure, so that the projects of the legislature are put into execution, although its immediate attention may be directed to other objects. . . .

A majority taken collectively may be regarded as a being whose opinions, and most frequently whose interests, are opposed to those of another being, which is styled a minority. If it be admitted that a man, possessing absolute power, may misuse that power by wronging his adversaries, why should a majority not be liable to the same reproach? Men are not apt to change their characters by agglomeration; nor does their patience in the presence of obstacles increase with the consciousness of their strength. And for these reasons I can never willingly invest any number of my fellow creatures with that unlimited authority which I should refuse to any one of them. . . .

I am of opinion that some one social power must always be made to predominate over the others; but I think that liberty is endangered when this power is checked by no obstacles which may retard its course, and force it to moderate its own vehemence.

Unlimited power is in itself a bad and dangerous thing; human beings are not competent to exercise it with discretion, and God alone can be omnipotent, because his wisdom and his justice are always equal to his power. But no power upon earth is so worthy of honor for itself, or of reverential obedience to the rights which it represents, that I would consent to admit its uncontrolled and all-predominant authority. When I see that the right and the means of absolute command are conferred on a people or upon a king, upon an aristocracy or a democracy, a monarchy or a republic, I recognize the germ of tyranny, and I journey onward to a land of more hopeful institutions.

In my opinion the main evil of the present democratic institutions of the United States does not arise, as is often asserted in Europe, from their weakness, but from their overpowering strength; and I am not so much alarmed at the excessive liberty which reigns in that country as at the very inadequate securities which exist against tyranny.

When an individual or a party is wronged in the United States, to whom can he apply for redress? If to public opinion, public opinion constitutes the majority; if to the legislature, it represents the majority, and implicitly obeys its injunctions; if to the executive power, it is appointed by the majority, and remains a passive tool in its hands; the public troops consists of the majority under arms; the jury is the majority invested with the right of hearing judicial cases; and in certain States even the judges are elected by the majority. However iniquitous or absurd the evil of which you complain may be, you must submit to it as well as you can.

If, on the other hand, a legislative power could be so constituted as to represent the majority without necessarily being the slave of its passions; an executive, so as to retain a certain degree of uncontrolled authority; and a judiciary, so as to remain independent of the two other powers; a government would be formed which would still be democratic without incurring any risk of tyrannical abuse.

I do not say that tyrannical abuses frequently occur in America at the present day, but I maintain that no sure barrier is established against them, and that the causes which mitigate the government are to be found in the circumstances and the manners of the country more than in its laws. . . .

It is in the examination of the display of public opinion in the United States that we clearly perceive how far the power of the majority surpasses all the powers with which we are acquainted in Europe. Intellectual principles exercise an influence which is so invisible, and often so inappreciable, that they baffle the toils of oppression. At the present time the most absolute monarchs in Europe are unable to prevent certain notions, which are opposed to their authority, from circulating in secret throughout their dominions, and even in their courts. Such is not the case in America; as long as the majority is still undecided, discussion is carried on; but as soon as its decision is irrevocably pronounced, a submissive silence is observed, and the friends, as well as the opponents, of the measure unite in assenting to its propriety. The reason of this is perfectly clear: no monarch is so absolute as to combine all the powers of society in his own hands, and to conquer all opposition with the energy of a majority which is invested with the right of making and of executing the laws.

The authority of a king is purely physical, and it controls the actions of the subject without subduing his private will; but the majority possesses a power which is physical and moral at the same time; it acts upon the will as well as upon the actions of men, and it represses not only all contest, but all controversy.

I know of no country in which there is so little true independence of mind and freedom of discussion as in America. In any constitutional state in Europe every sort of religious and political theory may be advocated and propagated abroad; for there is no country in Europe so subdued by any single authority as not to contain citizens who are ready to protect the man who raises his voice in the cause of truth from the consequences of his hardihood. If he is unfortunate enough to live under an absolute government, the people is upon his side; if he inhabits a free country, he may find a shelter behind the authority of the throne, if he require one. The aristocratic part of society supports him in some countries, and the democracy in others. But in a nation where democratic institutions exist, organized like those of the United States, there is but one sole authority, one single element of strength and of success, with nothing beyond it.

In America, the majority raises very formidable barriers to the liberty of opinion: within these barriers an author may write whatever he pleases, but he will repent it if he ever step beyond them. Not that he is exposed to the terrors of an *auto-da-fé,* but he is tormented by the slights and persecutions of daily obloquy. His political career is closed forever, since he has offended the only authority which is able to promote his success. Every sort of compensation, even that of celebrity, is refused to him. Before he published his opinions he imagined that he held them in common with many others; but no sooner has he declared them openly than he is loudly censured by his overbearing opponents, while those who think like him, without having the courage to speak, abandon him in silence. He yields at length, oppressed by the daily efforts he has been making, and he subsides into silence, as if he was tormented by remorse for having spoken the truth.

Fetters and headsmen were the coarse instruments which tyranny formerly employed; but the civilization of our age has refined the arts of despotism, which seemed, however, to have been sufficiently perfected before. The excesses of monarchial power had devised a variety of physical means of oppression: the democratic republics of the present day have rendered it as entirely an affair of the mind as that will which it is intended to coerce. Under the absolute sway of an individual despot the body was attacked in order to subdue the soul, and the soul escaped the blows which were directed against it and rose superior to the attempt; but such is not the course adopted by tyranny in democratic republics; there the body is left free, and the soul is enslaved. The sovereign can no longer say, 'You shall think as I do on pain of death'; but he says: 'You are free to think differently from me, and to retain your life, your property, and all that you possess; but if such be your determination, you are henceforth an alien among your people. You may retain your civil rights, but they will be useless to you, for you will never be chosen by your fellow citizens if you solicit their suffrages, and they will affect to scorn you if you solicit their esteem. You will remain among men, but you will be deprived of the rights of mankind. Your fellow creatures will shun you like an impure being, and those who are most persuaded of your innocence will abandon you too, lest they should be shunned in their turn. Go in peace! I have given you your life, but it is an existence incomparably worse than death.'

Monarchial institutions have thrown an odium upon despotism; let us beware lest democratic republics should restore oppression, and should render it less odious and less degrading in the eyes of the many, by making it still more onerous to the few.

—ALEXIS DE TOCQUEVILLE, *Democracy in America,* 1835

7. THE NUMERICAL AND THE CONCURRENT MAJORITIES

One of the statesmen whose speeches and writings Tocqueville studied was the lordly John C. Calhoun of South Carolina. Calhoun, who had started his political career as an ardent nationalist had by now become the statesman and philosopher of States Rights. But States Rights was not an abstraction. It was designed to protect the peculiar institution and the society and economy built upon it. The majority of the country was by this time committed to freedom—majority either of the people or of the States, and Calhoun realized that majority rule threatened slavery and the interests of the South—just as the principle of equality and of liberty threatened slavery and the South. To meet this threat of the numerical majority Calhoun formulated the doctrine of the concurrent majority. In one sense this doctrine looks back to Federalist *Number 10 and to John Adams' Defense; in another sense it looks ahead to the kind of corporative representation that Mussolini introduced into Italy.*

IT RESULTS, from what has been said, that there are two different modes in which the sense of the community may be taken; one, simply by the right of suffrage, unaided; the other, by the right through a proper organism. Each collects the sense of the majority. But one regards numbers only, and considers the whole community as a unit, having but one common interest throughout; and collects the sense of the greater number of the whole, as that of the community. The other, on the contrary, regards interests as well as numbers;—considering the community as made up of different and conflicting interests, as far as the action of the government is concerned; and takes the sense of each, through its majority or appropriate organ, and the united sense of all, as the sense of the entire community. The former of these I shall call the numerical, or absolute majority; and the latter, the concurrent, or constitutional majority. I call it the constitutional majority, because it is an essential element in every constitutional government,—be its form what it may. So great is the difference, politically speaking, between the two majorities, that they cannot be confounded, without leading to great and fatal errors; and yet the distinction between them has been so entirely overlooked, that when the term *majority* is used in political discussions, it is applied exclusively to designate the numerical,—as if there were no other. Until this distinction is recognized, and better understood, there will continue to be great liability to error in properly constructing constitutional governments, especially of the popular form, and of preserving them when properly constructed. Until then, the latter will have a strong tendency to slide, first, into the government of the numerical majority, and, finally, into absolute government of some other form. To show that such must be the case, and at the same time to mark more strongly the difference between the two, in order to guard against the danger of overlooking it, I propose to consider the subject more at length.

The first and leading error which naturally arises from overlooking the distinction referred to, is, to confound the numerical majority with the people; and this so completely as to regard them as identical. This is a consequence that necessarily results from considering the numerical as the only majority. All admit, that a popular government, or democracy, is the government of the people; for the terms imply this. A perfect government of the kind would be one which would embrace the consent of every citizen or member of the community; but as this is impracticable, in the opinion of those who regard the numerical as the only majority, and who can perceive no other way by which the sense of the people can be taken,—they are compelled to adopt this as the only true basis of popular government, in contradistinction to governments of the aristocratical or monarchical form. Being thus constrained, they are, in the next place, forced to regard the numerical majority, as, in effect, the entire people; that is, the greater part as the whole; and the government of the greater part as the government of the whole. It is thus the two come to be confounded, and a part made identical with the whole. And it is thus, also, that all the rights, powers, and immunities of the whole people come to be attributed to the numerical majority;

and, among others, the supreme, sovereign authority of establishing and abolishing governments at pleasure.

This radical error, the consequence of confounding the two, and of regarding the numerical as the only majority, has contributed more than any other cause, to prevent the formation of popular constitutional governments,—and to destroy them even when they have been formed. It leads to the conclusion that, in their formation and establishment, nothing more is necessary than the right of suffrage,—and the allotment to each division of the community a representation in the government, in proportion to numbers. If the numerical majority were really the people; and if, to take its sense truly, were to take the sense of the people truly, a government so constituted would be a true and perfect model of a popular constitutional government; and every departure from it would detract from its excellence. But, as such is not the case,—as the numerical majority, instead of being the people, is only a portion of them,—such a government, instead of being a true and perfect model of the people's government, that is, a people self-governed, is but the government of a part, over a part,—the major over the minor portion. . . .

Having now explained the reasons why it is so difficult to form and preserve popular constitutional government, so long as the distinction between the two majorities is overlooked. . . .

I shall next proceed to explain, more fully, why the concurrent majority is an indispensable element in forming constitutional governments; and why the numerical majority, of itself, must, in all cases, make governments absolute.

The necessary consequence of taking the sense of the community by the concurrent majority is, as has been explained, to give to each interest or portion of the community a negative on the others. It is this mutual negative among its various conflicting interests, which invests each with the power of protecting itself;—and places the rights and safety of each, where only they can be securely placed, under its own guardianship. Without this there can be no systematic, peaceful, or effective resistance to the natural tendency of each to come into conflict with the others: and without this there can be no constitution. It is this negative power,—the power of preventing or arresting the action of the government,—be it called by what term it may,—veto, interposition, nullification, check, or balance of power,—which, in fact, forms the constitution. They are all but different names for the negative power. In all its forms, and under all its names, it results from the concurrent majority. Without this there can be no negative; and, without a negative, no constitution. The assertion is true in reference to all constitutional governments, be their forms what they may. It is, indeed, the negative power which makes the constitution,—and the positive which makes the government. The one is the power of acting;—and the other the power of preventing or arresting action. The two, combined, make constitutional governments.

But, as there can be no constitution without the negative power, and no negative power without the concurrent majority;—it follows, necessarily, that where the numerical majority has the sole control of the government, there can be no constitution; as constitution implies limitation or restriction,—and, of course, is inconsistent with the idea of sole or exclusive power. And hence, the numerical, unmixed with the concurrent majority, necessarily forms, in all cases, absolute government.
—JOHN C. CALHOUN, *A Disquisition on Government, ca.* 1848-50

8. "DEMOCRACY FURNISHES ITS OWN CHECKS AND BALANCES"

Most of the discussion of the tyranny of the majority goes on in a vacuum. It concerns itself with hypothetical instances of what majorities might do if they were not limited, rather than with actual examples of what majorities have in fact done. The best way to analyze majority rule is not to plunge into metaphysical analyses, but to examine it. It can be examined pretty well in a century or more of our own history. It can be examined even more profitably in English history—more profitably because Britain does not have the written constitution, the checks and balances, and the judicial review which we use to limit majority rule. The editor here calls attention to this aspect of the problem of the "tyranny of the majority."

OUR constitutional system . . . is one of checks and balances. . . . It is sometimes forgotten that our political system is one of checks and balances too. Anyone who has followed the slow and tortuous course of a major public issue—the poll tax, for example, or neutrality—through the arena of public opinion, into the party conventions and caucuses, into the halls of Congress and the rooms of appropriate committees, knows how much of delay, of balance, of compromise, is implicit in our political machinery. A good part of our politics, indeed, seems to be concerned with reconciling majority and minority will, class hostilities, sectional differences, and divergent interests of producer and consumer, of agriculture and labor, of creditor and debtor, of city and country, of tax-payer and tax-beneficiary, of the military and the civilian. In small issues as in great, the result is generally a compromise. Democracy, in short, whether from instinct or from necessity, furnishes its own checks and balances—quite aside from such as may be provided in written constitutions.

Indeed it might plausibly be argued that it is one of the major advantages of democracy over other forms of government that it alone can indulge in the luxury of tolerating minority and dissenting groups because it alone has developed the technique for dealing with them. . . .

There is this to be said of the checks and balances of democratic politics—that they are natural, not artificial; that they are flexible rather than rigid; that they can yield to public opinion and to necessity. They do, sometimes, enable the majority to ride down the minority; they do, far more frequently, enable the minority to delay and defeat the majority. But the responsibility in all this is with the people themselves—where it belongs. Where they indulge their apathy, their carelessness, their blindness, they pay the price, and it is right that they should pay the price. As the fault is theirs, so too the remedy. Where issues appear sufficiently important the majority can have its way even against the recalcitrance of minorities who take refuge in the labyrinths of our party and our legislative systems. But against minorities entrenched in the judiciary there is no effective appeal except through the complicated and slow process of constitutional amendment. Here it is true today, as it was in 1801, that the minority can "retire into the judiciary as a stronghold," and "from that battery" beat down the works of republicanism.

A majority rule system, then, such as ours, is not a system of unlimited government either in theory, in law, or in practice. To the formal limits of the Constitution are added the informal limits of politics. With this in mind we can return to our original question: Is there any reason to suppose that majorities so limited would invade minority rights if it were not for the obstacles interposed by the courts? Or may we advance with equal plausibility the assertion that majorities can be trusted, without judicial assistance, to govern in accordance with the law and to respect minority rights, and that—with full realization of all the risks involved—training in such governance is essential to the maturing of democracy?

Scores of philosophers and historians have attempted to answer these questions, but almost always they have addressed themselves to theory rather than to fact. But answers . . . are to be found in the realm of fact. We are fortunate in having, here in the United States, the most elaborate political laboratory in all history, and one whose findings have been pretty fully recorded. Popular government has been a going concern here, in one form or another, for about three hundred years. We have, for our edification, the history of the experience of the thirteen colonies, of the national government, and of thirteen to forty-eight states, for varying periods of time. What does this record reveal?

It reveals a stability, a respect for law, a zeal for individual and minority rights that cannot be equalled, it is safe to say, by any other type of government in the history of western civilization. In all this period—and in all these governments—there has not been a single example of lawless revolution. In all this period, and for all these governments, there has been but one example of a deliberate and sustained effort by a majority to subvert constitutional rights or oppress a minority, the determination of Southern whites to frustrate the Fourteenth and Fifteenth Amendments, in so far as these attempted to assure political and social rights to Negroes. In all this period and for all these governments there have been comparatively few instances of even temporary aberration.

—HENRY STEELE COMMAGER, "Majority Rule and Minority Rights"

9. "THE PEOPLE IS FIRM AND TRANQUIL"

It was in 1834 that George Bancroft brought out the first volume of his monumental History of the United States—*a history which was permeated with enthusiasm for democracy. That same year Bancroft ran for legislature on the Democratic ticket. It was not surprising that when he came to deliver an address on "The Office of the People in Art, Government, and Religion" he should have voiced an ardent Jef-*

fersonian faith in democracy as well as a Jacksonian faith in the Democracy. Two years later Bancroft was appointed Collector of the Port of Boston; later he went into the Cabinet; and in time he became an elder statesman as well as one of the most distinguished of scholars.

THE best government rests on the people and not on the few, on persons and not on property, on the free development of public opinion and not on authority; because the munificent Author of our being has conferred the gifts of mind upon every member of the human race without distinction of outward circumstances. Whatever of other possessions may be engrossed, mind asserts its own independence. Lands, estates, the produce of mines, the prolific abundance of the seas, may be usurped by a privileged class. Avarice, assuming the form of ambitious power, may grasp realm after realm, subdue continents, compass the earth in its schemes of aggrandizement, and sigh after other worlds; but mind eludes the power of appropriation; it exists only in its own individuality; it is a property which cannot be confiscated and cannot be torn away; it laughs at chains; it bursts from imprisonment; it defies monopoly. A government of equal rights must, therefore, rest upon mind; not wealth, not brute force, the sum of the moral intelligence of the community should rule the State. Prescription can no more assume to be a valid plea for political injustice; society studies to eradicate established abuses, and to bring social institutions and laws into harmony with moral right; not dismayed by the natural and necessary imperfections of all human effort, and not giving way to despair, because every hope does not at once ripen into fruit.

The public happiness is the true object of legislation, and can be secured only by the masses of mankind themselves awakening to the knowledge and the care of their own interests. Our free institutions have reversed the false and ignoble distinctions between men; and refusing to gratify the pride of caste, have acknowledged the common mind to be the true material for a commonwealth. . . .

It is not by vast armies, by immense natural resources, by accumulations of treasure, that the greatest results in modern civilization have been accomplished. The traces of the career of conquest pass away, hardly leaving a scar on the national intelligence. The famous battle grounds of victory are, most of them, comparatively indifferent to the human race; barren fields of blood, the scourges of their times, but affecting the social condition as little as the raging of a pestilence. Not one benevolent institution, not one ameliorating principle in the Roman state, was a voluntary concession of the aristocracy; each useful element was borrowed from the Democracies of Greece, or was a reluctant concession to the demands of the people. The same is true in modern political life. It is the confession of an enemy to Democracy, that "ALL THE GREAT AND NOBLE INSTITUTIONS OF THE WORLD HAVE COME FROM POPULAR EFFORTS."

    —GEORGE BANCROFT, "The Office of the People in Art, Government, and Religion," 1835

10. "EVERY AMERICAN IS AN APOSTLE OF THE DEMOCRATIC CREED"

Of European visitors to the United States before the Civil War, only Tocqueville was more perspicacious than the Scotsman Alexander Mackay, who toured "the Western World" in 1846 and 1847. Unlike most visitors of the forties—Dickens for instance—Mackay was inclined to find mostly good in American democracy. Like Crèvecoeur he was particularly impressed with the speed with which Europeans became Americanized and with the manner in which every American staked out a personal claim to such things as democracy, republicanism, a high standard of living, the size of Niagara Falls or the weather.

INTIMATELY connected with the pride of country which generally distinguishes the Americans is the feeling which they cherish toward their institutions. Indeed, when the national feeling of an American is alluded to, something very different is implied from that which is generally understood by the term. In Europe, and particularly in mountainous countries, the aspect of which is such as to impress itself vividly upon the imagination, the love of country resolves itself into a reverence for locality irrespective of all other considerations. . . . But the American exhibits little or none of the local attachments which distinguish the European. His feelings are more centered upon his institutions than his mere country. He looks upon himself more in the light of a republican than in that of a native of a particular territory. His affections have more to do with the social and political system with which he is connected than with the soil which he inhabits. The national feelings which he and a European cherish being thus different in their origin and their object are also different in their results. The man whose attachments converge upon a particular spot of earth is miserable if removed from it, no matter how greatly his circumstances otherwise may have been improved by his removal; but give the American his institutions and he cares but little where you place him. In some parts of the Union the local feeling may be comparatively strong, such as in New England; but it is astonishing how readily even there an American makes up his mind to try his fortunes elsewhere, particularly if he contemplates removal merely to another part of the Union, no matter how remote or how different in climate and other circumstances from what he has been accustomed to, provided the flag of his country waves over it and republican institutions accompany him in his wanderings.

Strange as it may seem, this peculiarity, which makes an American think less of his country than of the institutions which characterize it, contributes greatly to the pride which he takes in his country. He is proud of it, not so much for itself as because it is the scene in which an experiment is being tried which engages the anxious attention of the world. The American feels himself much more interested in the success of his scheme of government, if not more identified with it, than the European does in regard to his. The Englishman, for instance, does not feel himself particularly committed to the success of monarchy as a political scheme. . . . It is very different, however, with the American. He feels himself to be implicated, not only in the honor and independence of his country, but also in the success of democracy. He has asserted a great principle, and feels that, in attempting to prove it to be practicable, he has assumed an arduous responsibility. He feels himself, therefore, to be directly interested in the success of the political system under which he lives, and all the more so because he is conscious that, in looking to its working, mankind are divided into two great classes—those who are interested in its failure and those who yearn for its success. Every American is thus, in his own estimation, the apostle of a particular political creed, in the final triumph and extension of which he finds both himself and his country deeply involved. This gives him a peculiar interest in the political scheme which he represents; and invests his country with an additional degree of importance in his sight, as in that of many others, from being the scene of an experiment in the success of which not only Americans but mankind are interested. Much, therefore, of the self-importance which the American assumes, particularly abroad, is less traceable to his mere citizenship than to his conscious identification with the success of democracy. Its manifestation may not always be agreeable to others, but the source of his pride is a legitimate and a noble one. It involves not only his own position, but also the hopes and expectations of humanity.

It is this feeling which renders the establishment of monarchy an impossibility in the United States. The American not only believes that his material interests are best subserved by a democratic form of government, but his pride is also mixed up with its maintenance and its permanency. It is a common thing for Europeans to speculate upon the disintegration of the Union, and the consequent establishment, in some part or parts of it, of the monarchical principle. These speculations are generally based upon precedents, but upon precedents which have in reality no application to America. The republics of old are pointed to as affording illustrations of the tendencies of republicanism. But the republics of old afford no criterion by which to judge of republicanism in America. The experiment which is being tried there is one *sui generis*. Not only are the political principles established different from those which have heretofore been practically recognized; but the people are also in a better state of preparation for the successful development of the experiment.

The American Republic, in the first place, differs essentially from all that have preceded it in the principles on which it is founded: it is not a republic in simply not being a monarchy: it is a Democratic Republic, in the broadest sense of the term. If it is not a monarchy, neither is it an oligarchy. It is the people in reality that rule; it is not a mere fraction of them that usurps authority. The success of the American experiment depended, as it still depends, upon the character of the people. As already shown, the stability of the republic is intimately identified with the enlightenment of the public mind—in other words, with the great cause of popular education; it is to the promotion of education that it will in future chiefly owe its success. But its maintenance at first was mainly owing to the political antecedents of the people. It is quite true that they were converted in a day from being the subjects of a monarchy into the citizens of a republic. But let us not overlook the long probation which they underwent for the change. . . .

Many point to the accumulation of wealth as that which will work the change. It is quite true that some of the millionaires of America would have no objection to the establishment of a different order of things. But both in numbers and influence they are insignificant, as compared with the great mass even of the commercial and manufacturing communities, who are staunch democrats at heart. Much more are they so when we take the great agricultural body of America into account. Here, after all, is the stronghold of democracy on the continent. However it may be undermined in the town, its foundations are deeply and securely laid in the township. No one who has mingled much with the American farmers can entertain any serious doubts of the stability of democracy in America. Even were the entire commercial and manufacturing community otherwise disposed, they could make no impression against the strong, sturdy, democratic phalanx engaged in the cultivation of the soil. But the great bulk of the commercial and manufacturing classes are, as already intimated, as devoted to the republican system as any of the farmers can be.

—Alexander Mackay, *The Western World*, 1847

11. THE REAL MEANING OF THE PRINCIPLES
OF THE DECLARATION

Where Jefferson was a democrat by conviction, Lincoln was a democrat by instinct and by experience. And where Jefferson addressed himself especially to the political and philosophical implications of democracy, Lincoln was concerned with its social implications, and particularly with the meaning of the doctrine of equality. Yet there is a profound and even mystical quality about Lincoln's democracy, and it is this quality that gives so much of his writing a religious fervor. We have selected for reproduction here not the familiar Gettysburg Address, or Second Inaugural, or the almost equally familiar appeal for compensated eman-

cipation or the letter to the Manchester Workingmen, *but somewhat lesser known discussions of the meaning of the principles of the great Declaration.*

A. "They Meant to Set Up a Standard for a Free Society"

THERE is a natural disgust in the minds of nearly all white people at the idea of an indiscriminate amalgamation of the white and black races; and Judge Douglas . . . finds the Republicans insisting that the Declaration of Independence includes all men, black as well as white, and forthwith he boldly denies that it includes Negroes at all, and proceeds to argue gravely that all who contend it does, do so only because they want to vote, and eat, and sleep, and marry with Negroes! He will have it that they cannot be consistent else. Now I protest against the counterfeit logic which concludes that, because I do not want a black woman for a slave I must necessarily want her for a wife. I need not have her for either. I can just leave her alone. In some respects she certainly is not my equal; but in her natural right to eat the bread she earns with her own hands without asking leave of any one else, she is my equal, and the equal of all others.

Chief Justice Taney, in his opinion in the Dred Scott case, admits that the language of the Declaration is broad enough to include the whole human family, but he and Judge Douglas argue that the authors of that instrument did not intend to include Negroes, by the fact that they did not at once actually place all white people on an equality with one another. And this is the staple argument of both the chief justice and the senator for doing this obvious violence to the plain, unmistakable language of the Declaration.

I think the authors of that notable instrument intended to include all men, but they did not intend to declare all men equal in all respects. They did not mean to say all were equal in color, size, intellect, moral developments, or social capacity. They defined with tolerable distinctness in what respects they did consider all men created equal—equal with "certain inalienable rights, among which are life, liberty, and the pursuit of happiness." This they said, and this they meant. They did not mean to assert the obvious untruth that all were then actually enjoying that equality, nor yet that they were about to confer it immediately upon them. In fact, they had no power to confer such a boon. They meant simply to declare the right, so that enforcement of it might follow as fast as circumstances should permit.

They meant to set up a standard maxim for free society, which should be familiar to all, and revered by all; constantly looked to, constantly labored for, and even though never perfectly attained, constantly approximated, and thereby constantly spreading and deepening its influence and augmenting the happiness and value of life to all people of all colors everywhere. The assertion that "all men are created equal" was of no practical use in effecting our separation from Great Britain; and it was placed in the Declaration not for that, but for future use. Its authors meant it to be—as, thank God, it is now proving itself— a stumbling-block to all those who in after times might seek to turn a free people back into the hateful paths of despotism. They knew the proneness of prosperity to breed tyrants, and they meant when such should reappear in this fair land and commence their vocation, they should find left for them at least one hard nut to crack.

—ABRAHAM LINCOLN, Speech at Springfield, 1857

B. "To Lift Artificial Weights from All Shoulders"

It may be affirmed without extravagance that the free institutions we enjoy have developed the powers and improved the condition of our whole people beyond any example in the world. . . . Whoever in any section proposes to abandon such a government would do well to consider in deference to what principle it is that he does it—what better he is likely to get in its stead—whether the substitute will give, or be intended to give, so much of good to the people? There are some foreshadowings on this subject. Our adversaries have adopted some declarations of independence in which, unlike the good old one, penned by Jefferson, they omit the words "all men are created equal." Why? They have adopted a temporary national constitution, in the preamble of which, unlike our good old one, signed by Washington, they omit "We the People," and substitute, "We, the deputies of the sovereign and independent States." Why? Why this deliberate pressing out of view the rights of men and the authority of the people?

This is essentially a people's contest. On the side of the Union it is a struggle for maintaining in the world that form and substance of government whose leading object is to elevate the condition of men—to lift artificial weights from all shoulders; to clear the paths of laudable pursuit for all; to afford all an unfettered start, and a fair chance in the race of life. Yielding to partial and temporary departures, from necessity, this is the leading object of the government for whose existence we contend. . . .

Our popular government has often been called an experiment. Two points in it our people have already settled—the successful establishing and the successful administering of it. One still remains—its successful maintenance against a formidable internal attempt to overthrow it. It is now for them to demonstrate to the world that those who can fairly carry an election can also suppress a rebellion; that ballots are the rightful and peaceful successors of bullets; and that when ballots have fairly and constitutionally decided, there can be no successful appeal, except to ballots themselves, at succeeding elections. Such will be a great lesson of peace: teaching men that what they cannot take by an election, neither can they take it by a war; teaching all the folly of being the beginners of a war.

—ABRAHAM LINCOLN, Message to Congress, July 4, 1861

12. "DID YOU SUPPOSE THAT DEMOCRACY WAS ONLY FOR POLITICS?"

Here is Walt Whitman in a sober, even a critical mood. Yet Demo-cratic Vistas, *for all its criticism of the shabbiness and the corruption that threaten democracy, is at the same time a prophecy of a glorious future and a call for cultural independence and cultural democracy. Henry S. Canby has called* Democratic Vistas *"one of the great American pamphlets, to be compared for its ideas . . . with* The Federalist *papers."*

AMERICA, filling the present with greatest deeds and problems, cheerfully accepting the past, including feudalism, (as, indeed, the present is but the legitimate birth of the past, including feudalism,) counts, as I reckon, for her justification and success, (for who, as yet, dare claim success?) almost entirely on the future. Nor is that hope unwarranted. To-day, ahead, though dimly yet, we see, in vistas, a copious, sane, gigantic offspring. For our New World I consider far less important for what it has done, or what it is, than for results to come. Sole among nationalities, these States have assumed the task to put in forms of lasting power and practicality, on areas of amplitude rivaling the operations of the physical kosmos, the moral political speculations of ages, long, long deferr'd, the democratic republican principle, and the theory of development and perfection by voluntary standards, and self-reliance. Who else, indeed, except the United States, in history, so far, have accepted in unwitting faith, and, as we now see, stand, act upon, and go security for, these things? . . .

I will not gloss over the appalling dangers of universal suffrage in the United States. In fact, it is to admit and face these dangers I am writing. To him or her within whose thought rages the battle, advancing, retreating, between democracy's convictions, aspirations, and the people's crudeness, vice, caprices, I mainly write this essay. I shall use the words America and democracy as convertible terms. Not an ordinary one is the issue. The United States are destined either to surmount the gorgeous history of feudalism, or else prove the most tremendous failure of time. Not the least doubtful am I on any prospects of their material success. The triumphant future of their business, geographic and productive departments, on larger scales and in more varieties than ever, is certain. In those respects the republic must soon (if she does not already) outstrip all examples hitherto afforded, and dominate the world. . . .

I say that our New World democracy, however great a success in uplifting the masses out of their sloughs, in materialistic development, products, and in a certain highly-deceptive superficial popular intellectuality, is, so far, an almost complete failure in its social aspects, and in really grand religious, moral, literary, and esthetic results. In vain do we march with unprecedented strides to empire so colossal, outvying the antique, beyond Alexander's, beyond the proudest sway of Rome. In vain have we annex'd Texas, California, Alaska, and reach north for Canada and south for Cuba. It is as if we were somehow being endow'd with a vast and more and more thoroughly-appointed body, and then left with little or no soul. . . .

Did you, too, O friend, suppose democracy was only for elections, for politics, and for a party name? I say democracy is only of use there that it may pass on and come to its flower and fruits in manners, in the highest forms of interaction between men, and their beliefs—in religion, literature, colleges, and schools—democracy in all public and private life, and in the army and navy. I have intimated that, as a paramount scheme, it has yet few or no full realizers and believers. I do not see, either, that it owes any serious thanks to noted propagandists or champions, or has been essentially help'd, though often harm'd, by them. It has been and is carried on by all the moral forces, and by trade, finance, machinery, intercommunications, and, in fact, by all the developments of history, and can no more be stopp'd than the tides, or the earth in its orbit. Doubtless, also, it resides, crude and latent, well down in the hearts of the fair average of the American-born people, mainly in the agricultural regions. But it is not yet, there or anywhere, the fully-receiv'd, the fervid, the absolute faith. . . .

Assuming Democracy to be at present in its embryo condition, and that the only large and satisfactory justification of it resides in the future, mainly through the copious production of perfect characters among the people, and through the advent of a sane and pervading religiousness, it is with regard to the atmosphere and spaciousness fit for such characters, and of certain nutriment and cartoon-draftings proper for them, and indicating them for New World purposes, that I continue the present statement—an exploration, as of new ground, wherein, like other primitive surveyors, I must do the best I can, leaving it to those who come after me to do much better. (The service, in fact, if any, must be to break a sort of first path or track, no matter how rude and ungeometrical.)

—WALT WHITMAN, *Democratic Vistas*, 1871

13. "THE ETERNAL MOB"

Most of those who wrote on democracy after Whitman repeated the familiar arguments of the older writers—Jefferson, Franklin, Lincoln, or Adams, Tocqueville, Calhoun. Sometimes there was a return to the rhetoric of Bancroft or to the stridency of Fisher Ames. An example of the latter can be found in Henry L. Mencken's Notes on Democracy. *Yet there are important differences. Where Ames was querulous, Mencken is good-humored. Where Ames fell back on theory and dogma,*

Mencken makes a pretense, at least, of finding support in history and experience. In any event, Mencken performed, for thirty years, a valuable service to the American people. He made it his special business to expose the vulgarity, the complacency, the fatuousness of much of American society, and he did this on the whole good-naturedly.

THE fact is that liberty, in any true sense, is a concept that lies quite beyond the reach of the inferior man's mind. He can imagine and even esteem, in his way, certain false forms of liberty—for example, the right to choose between two political mountebanks, and to yell for the more obviously dishonest—but the reality is incomprehensible to him. And no wonder, for genuine liberty demands of its votaries a quality he lacks completely, and that is courage. The man who loves it must be willing to fight for it; blood, said Jefferson, is its natural manure. More, he must be able to *endure* it—an even more arduous business. Liberty means self-reliance, it means resolution, it means enterprise, it means the capacity for doing without. The free man is one who has won a small and precarious territory from the great mob of his inferiors, and is prepared and ready to defend it and make it support him. All around him are enemies, and where he stands there is no friend. He can hope for little help from other men of his own kind, for they have battles of their own to fight. He has made of himself a sort of god in his little world, and he must face the responsibilities of a god, and the dreadful loneliness. Has *Homo boobiens* any talent for this magnificent self-reliance? He has the same talent for it that he has for writing symphonies in the manner of Ludwig van Beethoven, no less and no more. That is to say, he has no talent whatsoever, nor even any understanding that such a talent exists. Liberty is unfathomable to him. He can no more comprehend it than he can comprehend honour. What he mistakes for it, nine times out of ten, is simply the banal right to empty hallelujahs upon his oppressors. He is an ox whose last proud, defiant gesture is to lick the butcher behind the ear. . . .

Again I summon the historians, some of whom begin to grow honest. America was settled largely by slaves, some escaped but others transported in bondage. The Revolution was imposed upon them by their betters, chiefly, in New England, commercial gents in search of greater profits, and in the South, country gentlemen ambitious to found a nobility in the wilderness. Universal manhood suffrage, the corner-stone of modern free states, was only dreamed of until 1867, and economic freedom was little more than a name until years later.

Thus the lower orders of men, however grandiloquently they may talk of liberty to-day, have actually had but a short and highly deceptive experience of it. It is not in their blood. The grandfathers of at least half of them were slaves, and the great-grandfathers of three-fourths, and the great-great-grandfathers of seven-eighths, and the great-great-great-grandfathers of practically all. The heritage of freedom belongs to a small minority of men, descended, whether legitimately or by adultery, from the old lords of the soil or from the patricians of the free towns. It is my contention that such a heritage is necessary in order that the concept of liberty, with all its disturbing and unnatural implications, may be so much as grasped—that such ideas cannot be implanted in the mind of man at will, but must be bred in as all other basic ideas are bred in. The proletarian may mouth the phrases, as he did in Jefferson's day, but he cannot take in the underlying realities, as was also demonstrated in Jefferson's day. What his great-great-grandchildren may be capable of I am not concerned with here; my business is with the man himself as he now walks the world. Viewed thus, it must be obvious that he is still incapable of bearing the pangs of liberty. They make him uncomfortable; they alarm him; they fill him with a great loneliness. There is no high adventurousness in him, but only fear. He not only doesn't long for liberty; he is quite unable to stand it. What he longs for is something wholly different, to wit, security. He needs protection. He is afraid of getting hurt. All else is affectation, delusion, empty words. . . .

It follows that the inferior man, being a natural slave himself, is quite unable to understand the desire for liberty in his superiors. If he apprehends that desire at all it is only as an appetite for a good of which he is himself incapable. He thus envies those who harbour it, and is eager to put them down. Justice, in fact, is always unpopular and in difficulties under democracy, save perhaps that false form of so-called social justice which is designed solely to get the laborer more than his fair hire. The wars of extermination that are waged against heretical minorities never meet with any opposition on the lower levels. The proletarian is always ready to help destroy the rights of his fellow proletarian, as was revealed brilliantly by the heroic services of the American Legion in the pogrom against Reds, just after the late war, and even more brilliantly by the aid that the American Federation of Labour gave to the same gallant crusade. The city workman, oppressed by Prohibition, mourns the loss of his beer, not the loss of his liberty. He is ever willing to support similar raids upon the liberty of the other fellow, and he is not outraged when they are carried on in gross violation of the most elemental principles of justice and common decency. When, in a democratic state, any protest against such obscenities is heard at all, it comes from the higher levels. There a few genuine believers in liberty and justice survive, huddled upon a burning deck. It is to be marvelled at that most of them, on inspection, turn out to be the grandsons of similar heretics of earlier times? I think not. It takes quite as long to breed a libertarian as it takes to breed a race-horse. Neither may be expected to issue from a farm mare.

The whole progress of the world, even in the direction of ameliorating the lot of the masses, is always opposed by the masses. The notion that their clamour brought about all the governmental and social reforms of the last century, and that those reforms were delayed by the superior minority, is sheer nonsense; even Liberals begin to reject it as absurd. . . .

Such is man on the nether levels. Such is the pet and glory of democratic states. Human progress passes him by. Its aims are unintelligible to him and its finest fruits are beyond his reach: what reaches him is what falls from the tree, and is shared with his four-footed brothers. He has changed but little since the earliest recorded time, and that change is for the worse quite as often as it is for the better. He still believes in ghosts, and has only shifted his belief in witches to the political sphere. He is still a slave to priests, and trembles before their preposterous magic. He is lazy, improvident and unclean. All the durable values of the world, though his labour has entered into them, have been created against his opposition. He can imagine nothing beautiful and he can grasp nothing true. Whenever he is confronted by a choice between two ideas, the one sound and the other not, he chooses almost infallibly, and by a sort of pathological compulsion, the one that is not. Behind all the great tyrants and butchers of history he has marched with loud hosannas, but his hand is eternally against those who seek to liberate the spirit of the race.

HENRY L. MENCKEN, *Notes on Demcracy*, 1926

14. "DEMOCRACY IS NOT DYING"

No President since Jefferson has seen himself more consciously as the champion of democracy and none, it is safe to say, has done more to defend democracy from her enemies, than Franklin D. Roosevelt. As with Jefferson, our choice of material is embarrassingly wide. The First Inaugural, for example, would fit naturally here—but we have used it elsewhere. Some of the war messages, too, like those of Lincoln and of Wilson, are suffused with an almost mystical faith in democracy. There is perhaps nothing better than the Third Inaugural Address—an address which looked backward to the democratic achievements in the domestic arena and forward to the challenge to democracy then looming up so alarmingly on the world horizon.

O N EACH national day of Inauguration since 1789, the people have renewed their sense of dedication to the United States.

In Washington's day the task of the people was to create and weld together a Nation.

In Lincoln's day the task of the people was to preserve that Nation from disruption from within.

In this day the task of the people is to save that Nation and its institutions from disruption from without.

To us there has come a time, in the midst of swift happenings, to pause for a moment and take stock—to recall what our place in history has been, and to rediscover what we are and what we may be. If we do not, we risk the real peril of isolation, the real peril of inaction.

Lives of Nations are determined not by the count of years, but by the lifetime of the human spirit. The life of a man is threescore years and ten: a little more, a little less. The life of a Nation is the fullness of the measure of its will to live.

There are men who doubt this. There are men who believe that democracy, as a form of government and a frame of life, is limited or measured by a kind of mystical and artificial fate—that, for some unexplained reason, tyranny and slavery have become the surging wave of the future—and that freedom is an ebbing tide.

But we Americans know that this is not true.

Eight years ago, when the life of this Republic seemed frozen by a fatalistic terror, we proved that this is not true. We were in the midst of shock—but we acted. We acted quickly, boldly, decisively.

These later years have been living years—fruitful years for the people of this democracy. For they have brought to us greater security and, I hope, a better understanding that life's ideals are to be measured in other than material things.

Most vital to our present and to our future is this experience of a democracy which successfully survived crisis at home; put away many evil things; built new structures on enduring lines; and, through it all, maintained the fact of its democracy.

For action has been taken within the three-way framework of the Constitution of the United States. The coordinate branches of the Government continue freely to function. The Bill of Rights remains inviolate. The freedom of elections is wholly maintained. Prophets of the downfall of American democracy have seen their dire predictions come to naught.

No, democracy is not dying.

We know it because we have seen it revive—and grow.

We know it cannot die—because it is built on the unhampered initiative of individual men and women joined together in a common enterprise—an enterprise undertaken and carried through by the free expression of a free majority.

We know it because democracy alone, of all forms of government, enlists the full force of men's enlightened will.

We know it because democracy alone has constructed an unlimited civilization capable of infinite progress in the improvement of human life.

We know it because, if we look below the surface, we sense it still spreading on every continent—for it is the most humane, the most advanced, and in the end the most unconquerable of all forms of human society.

A Nation, like a person, has a body—a body that must be fed and clothed and housed, invigorated and rested, in a manner that measures up to the standards of our time.

A Nation, like a person, has a mind—a mind that must be kept informed and alert, that must know itself, that understands the hopes and the needs of its neighbors—all the other Nations that live within the narrowing circle of the world.

A Nation, like a person, has something deeper, something more permanent, something larger than the sum of all its parts. It is that something which matters most to its future—which calls forth the most sacred guarding of its present.

It is a thing for which we find it difficult—even impossible—to hit upon a single, simple word.

And yet, we all understand what it is—the spirit—the faith of America. It is the product of centuries. It was born in the multitudes of those who came from many lands—some of high degree, but mostly plain people—who sought here, early and late, to find freedom more freely.

The democratic aspiration is no mere recent phase in human history. It is human history. It permeated the ancient life of early peoples. It blazed anew in the Middle Ages. It was written in Magna Charta.

In the Americas its impact has been irresistible. America has been the New World in all tongues, and to all peoples, not because this continent was a new-found land, but because all those who came here believed they could create upon this continent a new life—a life that should be new in freedom.

Its vitality was written into our own Mayflower Compact, into the Declaration of Independence, into the Constitution of the United States, into the Gettysburg Address.

Those who first came here to carry out the longings of their spirit, and the millions who followed, and the stock that sprang from them— all have moved forward constantly and consistently toward an ideal which in itself has gained stature and clarity with each generation.

The hopes of the Republic cannot forever tolerate either undeserved poverty or self-serving wealth.

We know that we still have far to go; that we must more greatly build the security and the opportunity and the knowledge of every citizen, in the measure justified by the resources and the capacity of the land.

But it is not enough to achieve these purposes alone. It is not enough to clothe and feed the body of this Nation, to instruct, and inform its mind. For there is also the spirit. And of the three, the greatest is the spirit.

Without the body and the mind, as all men know, the Nation could not live.

But if the spirit of America were killed, even though the Nation's body and mind, constricted in an alien world, lived on, the America we know would have perished.

That spirit—that faith—speaks to us in our daily lives in ways often unnoticed, because they seem so obvious. It speaks to us here in the Capital of the Nation. It speaks to us through the processes of governing in the sovereignties of 48 States. It speaks to us in our counties, in our cities, in our towns, and in our villages. It speaks to us from the other Nations of the hemisphere, and from those across the seas— the enslaved, as well as the free. Sometimes we fail to hear or heed these voices of freedom because to us the privilege of our freedom is such an old, old story.

The destiny of America was proclaimed in words of prophecy spoken by our first President in his first Inaugural in 1789—words almost directed, it would seem, to this year of 1941: "The preservation of the sacred fire of liberty and the destiny of the republican model of government are justly considered . . . deeply, . . . finally, staked on the experiment intrusted to the hands of the American people."

If you and I in this later day lose that sacred fire—if we let it be smothered with doubt and fear—then we shall reject the destiny which Washington strove so valiantly and so triumphantly to establish. The preservation of the spirit and faith of the Nation does, and will, furnish the highest justification for every sacrifice that we may make in the cause of national defense.

In the face of great perils never before encountered, our strong purpose is to protect and to perpetuate the integrity of democracy.

For this we muster the spirit of America, and the faith of America.

We do not retreat. We are not content to stand still. As Americans, we go forward, in the service of our country, by the will of God.

—Franklin D. Roosevelt, Third Inaugural Address, January 20, 1941

15. THE FAULTS AND STRENGTH OF AMERICAN DEMOCRACY

We conclude our chapter on democracy with some observations from two generations ago. It would be easy to find philosophical interpretations of democracy from the 1940's and 1950's, but it would not be easy to find anything as astute, as penetrating, and as sagacious as these pages from the pen of James Bryce. It is a tribute to the interest that America has always excited in the rest of the world that her best interpreters have been foreigners—men like Tocqueville or Mackay, or, in our day, Denis Brogan and George Santayana. It is to this company that Bryce belongs; of all the books written about the United States only Tocqueville's Democracy *can hold its own with* The American Commonwealth. *All his life Bryce was interested in the nature of democracy and in its national manifestations, and the last of his important books was a two-volume study of* Modern Democracies.

A. The True Faults of American Democracy

W E MAY properly begin by asking, What are the evils to which we may expect such a form of government to be exposed? and may then go on to see whether any others are discoverable in the United States, which, though traceable to democracy, are not of its essence, but due to the particular form which it has there taken. . . .

What are the consequences which we may expect to follow from these characteristics of democracy and these conditions under which it is forced to work?

Firstly, a certain commonness of mind and tone, a want of dignity and elevation in and about the conduct of public affairs, an insensibility to the nobler aspects and finer responsibilities of national life.

Secondly, a certain apathy among the luxurious classes and fastidious minds, who find themselves of no more account than the ordinary voter, and are disgusted by the superficial vulgarities of public life.

Thirdly, a want of knowledge, tact, and judgment in the details of legislation, as well as in administration, with an inadequate recognition of the difficulty of these kinds of work, and of the worth of special experience and skill in dealing with them. Because it is incompetent, the multitude will not feel its incompetence, and will not seek or defer to the counsels of those who possess the requisite capacity.

Fourthly, laxity in the management of public business. The persons entrusted with such business being only average men, thinking themselves and thought of by others as average men, with a deficient sense of their high responsibilities, may succumb to the temptations which the control of legislation and the public funds present, in cases where persons of a more enlarged view and with more of a social reputation to support would remain incorruptible. To repress such derelictions of duty is every citizen's duty, but for that reason it is in large communities apt to be neglected. Thus the very causes which implant the mischief favour its growth.

The above-mentioned tendencies are all more or less observable in the United States. . . .

The tone of public life is lower than one expects to find it in so great a nation. Just as we assume that an individual man will at any supreme moment in his own life rise to a higher level than that on which he usually moves, so we look to find those who conduct the affairs of a great state inspired by a sense of the magnitude of the interests entrusted to them. Their horizon ought to be expanded, their feeling of duty quickened, their dignity of attitude enhanced. Human nature with all its weaknesses does show itself capable of being thus roused on its imaginative side; and in Europe, where the traditions of aristocracy survive, everybody condemns as mean or unworthy acts done or language held by a great official which would pass unnoticed in a private citizen. It is the principle of *noblesse oblige* with the sense of duty and trust substituted for that of mere heredity rank.

Such a sentiment is comparatively weak in America. . . . There is no want of an appreciation of the collective majesty of the nation, for this is the theme of incessant speeches, nor even of the past and future glories of each particular State in the Union. But these sentiments do not bear their appropriate fruit in raising the conception of public office, of its worth and its dignity. The newspapers assume public men to be selfish and cynical. Disinterested virtue is not looked for, is perhaps turned into ridicule where it exists. The hard commercial spirit which pervades the meetings of a joint-stock company is the spirit in which most politicians speak of public business, and are not blamed for speaking. Something, especially in the case of newspapers, must be allowed for the humorous tendencies of the American mind, which likes to put forward the absurd and even vulgar side of things for the sake of getting fun out of them. But after making such allowances, the fact remains that, although no people is more emotional, and even in a sense more poetical, in no country is the ideal side of public life, what one may venture to call the heroic element in a public career, so ignored by the mass and repudiated by the leaders. This affects not only the elevation but the independence and courage of public men; and the country suffers from the want of what we call distinction in its conspicuous figures. . . .

The growth of intelligence and independence among the people, as well as the introduction of severe penalties for bribery, and the extinction of small constituencies, have now almost extinguished electoral corruption. So in America it may be expected that the more active conscience of the people and the reform of the civil service will cut down, if they do not wholly eradicate, such corruption as now infests the legislative bodies, while better ballot and election laws may do the same for the constituencies. . . .

Perhaps no form of government needs great leaders so much as democracy. The fatalistic habit of mind perceptible among the Americans needs to be corrected by the spectacle of courage and independence taking their own path, and not looking to see whither the mass are moving. Those whose material prosperity tends to lap them in self-complacency and dull the edge of aspiration, need to be thrilled by the emotions which great men can excite, stimulated by the ideals they present, stirred to a loftier sense of what national life may attain. In some countries men of brilliant gifts may be dangerous to freedom; but the ambition of American statesmen has been schooled to flow in constitutional channels, and the Republic is strong enough to stand any strain to which the rise of heroes may expose her.

B. The Strength of American Democracy

Those merits of American government which belong to its Federal Constitution have been already discussed: we have now to consider such as flow from the rule of public opinion, from the temper, habits, and ideas of the people.

I. The first is that of Stability.—As one test of a human body's soundness is its capacity for reaching a great age, so it is high praise for a political system that it has stood no more changed than any institution must change in a changing world, and that it now gives every promise of durability. The people are profoundly attached to the form which their national life has taken. The Federal Constitution is, to their eyes, an almost sacred thing, an Ark of the Covenant, whereon no man may lay rash hands. Everywhere in Europe one hears schemes of radical change freely discussed. . . . But in the United States the discussion of political problems busies itself with details and assumes that the main lines must remain as they are for ever. This conservative spirit, jealously watchful even in small matters, sometimes prevents reforms, but it assures to the people an easy mind, and a trust in their future which they feel to be not only a present satisfaction but a reservoir of strength. . . .

II. Feeling the law to be its own work, the people is disposed to obey the law. . . . It is the best result that can be ascribed to the direct participation of the people in their government that they have the love of the maker for his work, that every citizen looks upon a statute as a regulation made by himself for his own guidance no less than for that of others, every official as a person he has himself chosen, and whom it is therefore his interest, with no disparagement to his personal independence, to obey. . . . The habit of living under a rigid constitution superior to ordinary statutes—indeed two rigid constitutions, since the State Constitution is a fundamental law within its own sphere no less than is the Federal—intensifies this legality of view, since it may turn all sorts of questions which have not been determined by a direct vote of the people into questions of legal construction. It even accustoms people to submit to see their direct vote given in the enactment of a State Constitution nullified by the decision of a court holding that the Federal Constitution has been contravened. . . .

III. There is a broad simplicity about the political ideas of the people, and a courageous consistency in carrying them out in practice. When they have accepted a principle, they do not shrink from applying it "right through," however disagreeable in particular cases some of the results may be. I am far from meaning that they are logical in the French sense of the word. They have little taste either for assuming abstract propositions or for syllogistically deducing practical conclusions therefrom. But when they have adopted a general maxim of policy or rule of action they show more faith in it than the English for instance would do, they adhere to it where the English would make exceptions, they prefer certainty and uniformity to the advantages which might occasionally be gained by deviation. If this tendency is partly the result of obedience to a rigid constitution, it is no less due to the democratic dislike of exceptions and complexities, which the multitude finds not only difficult of comprehension but disquieting to the individual who may not know how they will affect him. Take for instance the boundless freedom of the press. There are abuses obviously incident to such freedom, and these abuses have not failed to appear. But the Americans deliberately hold that in view of the benefits which such freedom on the whole promises, abuses must be borne with and left to the sentiment of the people and the private law of libel to deal with. . . .

IV. It is a great merit of American government that it relies very little on officials, and arms them with little power of arbitrary interference.... It is natural to fancy that a government of the people and by the people will be led to undertake many and various functions for the people, and in the confidence of its strength will constitute itself a general philanthropic agency for their social and economic benefit. There has doubtless been of late years a tendency in this direction. . . . But it has taken the direction of acting through the law rather than through the officials. That is to say, when it prescribes to the citizen a particular course of action it has relied upon the ordinary legal sanctions, instead of investing the administrative officers with inquisitorial duties or powers that might prove oppressive, and when it has devolved active functions upon officials, they have been functions serving to aid the individual and the community rather than to interfere with or supersede the action of private enterprise. . . .

V. There are no struggles between privileged and unprivileged orders, not even that perpetual strife of rich and poor which is the oldest disease of civilized states. One must not pronounce broadly that there are no classes, for in parts of the country social distinctions have begun to grow up. But for political purposes classes scarcely exist. . . .

A European censor may make two reflections on the way in which I have presented this part of the case. He will observe that, after all, it is no more than saying that when you have got to the bottom you can fall no farther. You may be wounded and bleeding for all that. And he will ask whether, if property is safe and contentment reigns, these advantages are not due to the economical conditions of a new and resourceful country, with an abundance of unoccupied land and mineral wealth, rather than to the democratic structure of the government. The answer to the first objection is, that the descent towards equality and democracy has involved no injury to the richer or better educated classes: to the second, that although much must doubtless be ascribed to the bounty of nature, her favours have been so used by the people as to bring about a prosperity, a general diffusion of property, an abundance of freedom, of equality, and of good feeling which furnish the best security against the recurrence in America of chronic Old World evils, even when her economic state shall have become less auspicious than it now is. Wealthy and powerful such a country must have been under any form of government, but the speed with which she has advanced, and the employment of the sources of wealth to diffuse comfort among millions of families, may be placed to the credit of stimulative freedom. Wholesome habits have been established among the people whose value will be found when the times of pressure approach, and though the troubles that have arisen between labour and capital may not soon pass away, the sense of human equality, the absence of offensive privileges distinguishing class from class, will make those troubles less severe than in Europe, where they are complicated by the recollection of old wrongs, by arrogance on the one side and envy on the other.

VI. The government of the Republic, limited and languid in ordinary times, is capable of developing immense vigour. It can pull itself together at moments of danger, can put forth unexpected efforts, can venture on stretches of authority transcending not only ordinary practice but even ordinary law. This is the result of the unity of the nation. . . . That faith in the popular voice whereof I have already spoken strengthens every feeling which has once become strong, and makes it rush like a wave over the country, sweeping everything before it. I do not mean that the people become wild with excitement, for beneath their noisy demonstrations they retain their composure and shrewd view of facts. I mean only that the pervading sympathy stirs them to unwonted efforts. . . .

VII. Democracy has not only taught the Americans how to use liberty without abusing it, and how to secure equality: it has also taught them fraternity. That word has gone out of fashion in the Old World, and no wonder, considering what was done in its name in 1793, considering also that it still figures in the programme of assassins. Nevertheless there is in the United States a sort of kindliness, a sense of human fellowship, a recognition of the duty of mutual help owed by man to man, stronger than anywhere in the Old World, and certainly stronger than in the upper or middle classes of England, France, or Germany. The natural impulse of every citizen in America is to respect every other citizen, and to feel that citizenship constitutes a certain ground of respect. The idea of each man's equal rights is so fully realized that the rich or powerful man feels it no indignity to take his turn among the crowd, and does not expect any deference from the poorest. . . .

It may seem strange to those who know how difficult European states have generally found it to conduct negotiations with the government of the United States, and who are accustomed to read in European newspapers, the defiant utterances which American politicians address from Congress to the effete monarchies of the Old World, to be told that this spirit of fraternity has its influence on international relations also. Nevertheless if we look not at the irresponsible orators, who play to the lower feelings of a section of the people, but the the general sentiment of the whole people, we shall recognize that democracy makes both for peace and for justice between nations. Despite the admiration for military exploits which the Americans have sometimes shown, no country is at bottom more pervaded by a hatred of war, and a sense that national honour stands rooted in national fair dealing. The nation is often misrepresented by its statesmen, but although it allows them to say irritating things and advance unreasonable claims it has not for more than forty years permitted them to abuse its enormous strength, as most European nations possessed of similar strength have in time past abused theirs.

The characteristics of the nation which I have passed in review are not due solely to democratic government, but they have been strengthened by it, and they contribute to its solidity and to the smoothness of its working. As one sometimes sees an individual man who fails in life because the different parts of his nature seem unfitted to each other, so that his action, swayed by contending influences, results in nothing definite or effective, so one sees nations whose political institutions are either in advance of or lag behind their social conditions, so that the unity of the body politic suffers, and the harmony of its movements is disturbed. America is not such a nation. It is made all of a piece; its institutions are the product of its economic and social conditions and the expression of its character. The new wine has been poured into new bottles: or to adopt a metaphor more appropriate to the country, the vehicle has been built with a lightness, strength, and elasticity which fit it for the roads it has to traverse.

—JAMES BRYCE, *The American Commonwealth,* 1888

State and Nation

PROBABLY the most persistent grand issue in American politics, and in American constitutionalism, has been the relation between States and Nation. Basic to the problem is the question of the nature of the Union and the location of sovereignty in the American political system. Was sovereignty in the United States, or in the States? Obviously in neither, as such, for it is a basic principle of American political theory that sovereignty is in the people. But what people? The people of the States or the people of the United States? Is there such a political entity as the people of a State? Is there such a thing as the people of the United States? Anyone acquainted with the heterogeneous population of such a State as New York may well doubt the first. And as late as 1881 Jefferson Davis categorically denied the second.

If, as one school of thought persistently maintained, the States made the Union, could they unmake it? If they made the Constitution, could they dissolve it? If they acceded to the Union as States, could they secede, as States? Fortunately these questions need no longer trouble us; they were settled at Appomattox. Yet the problems of State-Federal relations are still very real. For if we no longer trouble ourselves over theoretical questions of sovereignty, we take a very lively interest in practical questions of power. We are, all of us, deeply concerned with questions of the nature and extent of Federal authority. Those questions cannot be answered by reference to the Constitution. For while the Constitution is a document of enumerated powers, it employs, of necessity, words that are vague and ambiguous. What, after all, is the commerce power? what is the power to tax? what is the war power? what is the executive power? Where is the line to be drawn between interstate commerce and intrastate commerce, or between the regulatory power of the Federal Government and the police power of the States? Or—to look to specific issues—does the Federal Government have the constitutional authority to impose a program of civil rights on the States; or to forbid

252

the exaction of poll taxes for voting? Does it have authority to legislate on education, or on public health? How far can it go in the regulation of the hours and wages of labor; how far may it go in the area of what we call social security? Where are the limits of the commerce power, the tax power, the war powers?

These are not mere theoretical questions. Nor, for that matter, were earlier issues theoretical merely, though debates over them often took the form of discussion of constitutional theory. Actually the issues of these early years were as concrete and as real as the issues that agitate us to-day. Could the national government go into the States and establish branches of a national bank? Could States grant monopolies to individuals or corporations engaged in interstate commerce? Could the national government embark upon a program of internal improvements, and if so what was embraced in that all-inclusive term? Were there any limits on State authority over slavery, or on national authority in the Territories?

In one form or another, then, the question of State and Federal authority, of localism and centralization, has been a constant in our history. And no one who reads that history can doubt that there has been a steady and almost uninterrupted tendency toward expanding the scope of the national power. This expansion has not always been at the expense of the States—State authority has been enlarged as well as national —but often the Federal Government appears to be crowding the States out of ground traditionally theirs.

Pressure for the expansion of Federal authority has come not from theorists who were zealous to aggrandize power. It has come from the circumstances of the case. In every instance of the extension of Federal regulation into economic areas, for example, economic centralization has preceded political centralization. Thus corporations engaged in interstate business long before Congress regulated that business: thus industry and labor took on national characteristics long before Congress legislated on either industry or labor. Federal centralization is the product of many forces: of the nationalization of our economy; of the growth of a technology that makes State boundary lines artificial; of immigration and internal migration that drains reality from State loyalty and dissipates State attachments; from depressions and relief and reform movements which States are not competent to solve; from war and the implacable demands that war puts upon the national government.

All these things have operated so persistently and effectively that some observers have concluded that we are confronted here with a law of history. They have concluded that Federalism has served its historical function, that it has had its day, that the time has come to recognize that it is an anachronism, and to embrace the reality of centralized power.

But the instinct of most Americans is against any such counsel. The opposition to Federal centralization is varied in character and motivation. It comes from those who are stubbornly opposed to political reforms, such as the abolition of poll taxes, or to social reforms, like the abolition of segregation in housing or in education, and who find "States Rights" the most effective bulwark against these policies. It comes from those who genuinely believe that Federal regulation of activities heretofore considered local is unwise and immoral. It comes from those who are genuinely convinced that Big Government is worse than the evils it is designed to cure.

The excerpts we give here touch on all of these factors, historical and political. We begin with the constitutional argument as elaborated by Jefferson and Hamilton and Madison, the great debate over the first Bank of the United States, and the even greater debate over the Alien and Sedition Acts. We give next something of the controversy over nullification and secession, with the views of Davis, Jackson, Webster, and Lincoln, on the nature of the Union. The Civil War settled the constitutional issue, but it could not settle the issue of propriety or of wisdom, and this remained to trouble later generations. By the Wilson administration the principle of Federal supervision over the economy was pretty well established, but it remained for the New Deal to push that principle to its logical conclusions. Meantime the debate over State versus Nation had merged and blended with a parallel debate over rugged individualism versus the welfare state—a debate which we can follow in our next chapter.

1. "WITH OUR FATE WILL THE DESTINY OF UNBORN MILLIONS BE INVOLVED"

Here, in a sense, is the first of Washington's Farewell Addresses. He had assumed command of the Continental forces at a time when the prospects for ultimate success were dim and distant; by the force of his character, by his fortitude and courage and devotion, by the influence

he commanded, he had been in large part responsible for that ultimate
victory which crowned American efforts. Now he sent to the States—
who had so often failed to fulfill their obligations either to the Army or
to the government of the Confederation—a final plea for justice for his
soldiers, and a series of admonitions for the future. Particularly interest-
ing here is the strong sense of nationalism that flows through and ani-
mates the whole of this memorable Circular.

Head Quarters, Newburgh, June 8, 1783

SIR: The great object for which I had the honor to hold an appointment in the Service of my Country, being accomplished, I am now
preparing to resign it into the hands of Congress, and to return to that
domestic retirement, which, it is well known, I left with the greatest
reluctance, a Retirement, for which I have never ceased to sigh through
a long and painful absence, and in which (remote from the noise and
trouble of the World) I meditate to pass the remainder of life in a state of
undisturbed repose; But before I carry this resolution into effect, I think
it a duty incumbent on me, to make this my last official communication,
to congratulate you on the glorious events which Heaven has been
pleased to produce in our favor, to offer my sentiments respecting some
important subjects, which appear to me, to be intimately connected with
the tranquility of the United States, to take my leave of your Excellency
as a public Character, and to give my final blessing to that Country, in
whose service I have spent the prime of my life, for whose sake I have
consumed so many anxious days and watchfull nights, and whose happiness being extremely dear to me, will always constitute no inconsiderable part of my own. . . .

The Citizens of America, placed in the most enviable condition, as the
sole Lords and Proprietors of a vast Tract of Continent, comprehending
all the various soils and climates of the World, and abounding with all
the necessaries and conveniencies of life, are now by the late satisfactory
pacification, acknowledged to be possessed of absolute freedom and Independency; They are, from this period, to be considered as the Actors
on a most conspicuous Theatre, which seems to be peculiarly designated
by Providence for the display of human greatness and felicity; Here,
they are not only surrounded with every thing which can contribute to
the completion of private and domestic enjoyment, but Heaven has

crowned all its other blessings, by giving a fairer oppertunity for political happiness, than any other Nation has even been favored with. Nothing can illustrate these observations more forcibly, than a recollection of the happy conjuncture of times and circumstances, under which our Republic assumed its rank among the Nations; The foundation of our Empire was not laid in the gloomy age of Ignorance and Superstition, but at an Epocha when the rights of mankind were better understood and more clearly defined, than at any former period, the researches of the human mind, after social happiness, have been carried to a great extent, the Treasures of knowledge, acquired by the labours of Philosophers, Sages and Legislatures, through a long succession of years, are laid open for our use, and their collected wisdom may be happily applied in the Establishment of our forms of Government; the free cultivation of Letters, the unbounded extension of Commerce, the progressive refinement of Manners, the growing liberalty of sentiment, and above all, the pure and benign light of Revelation, have had a meliorating influence on mankind and increased the blessings of Society. At this auspicious period, the United States came into existence as a Nation, and if their Citizens should not be completely free and happy, the fault will be intirely their own.

Such is our situation, and such are our prospects: but notwithstanding the cup of blessing is thus reached out to us, notwithstanding happiness is ours, if we have a disposition to seize the occasion and make it our own; yet, it appears to me there is an option still left to the United States of America, that it is in their choice, and depends upon their conduct, whether they will be respectable and prosperous, or contemptable and miserable as a Nation; This is the time of their political probation, this is the moment when the eyes of the whole World are turned upon them, this is the moment to establish or ruin their national Character forever, this is the favorable moment to give such a tone to our Federal Government, as will enable it to answer the ends of its institution, or this may be the ill-fated moment for relaxing the powers of the Union, annihilating the cement of the Confederation, and exposing us to become the sport of European politics, which may play one State against another to prevent their growing importance, and to serve their own interested purposes. For, according to the system of Policy the States shall adopt at this moment, they will stand or fall, and by their confirmation or lapse, it is yet to be decided, whether the Revolution must ultimately be considered as a blessing or a curse: a blessing or a curse, not to the present age alone, for with our fate will the destiny of unborn Millions be involved. . . .

There are four things, which I humbly conceive, are essential to the well being, I may even venture to say, to the existence of the United States as an Independent Power:

1st. An indissoluble Union of the States under one Federal Head.

2dly. A sacred regard to Public Justice.

3dly. The adoption of a proper Peace Establishment, and

4thly. The prevalence of that pacific and friendly Disposition, among the People of the United States, which will induce them to forget their local prejudices and policies, to make those mutual concessions which are requisite to the general prosperity, and in some instances, to sacrifice their individual advantages to the interest of the Community.

These are the Pillars on which the glorious Fabrick of our Independency and National Character must be supported; Liberty is the Basis, and whoever would dare to sap the foundation, or overturn the Structure, under whatever specious pretexts he may attempt it, will merit the bitterest execration, and the severest punishment which can be inflicted by his injured Country.

—George Washington, Circular to the States, 1783

2. THE CONSTITUTION PARTLY FEDERAL, PARTLY NATIONAL

The central problem of the Constitutional Convention—as of Federalism generally—was this: how make the central government strong enough for its duties without impairing the rights of States; how preserve the integrity of the States without weakening the central government. The cardinal fault of the Articles of Confederation was a lack of authority in the central government, and this lack the Framers of the Constitution supplied in the new document. They were faced with one of the most delicate problems in the whole realm of politics—the problem of balancing the claims of the central and the local authorities. This problem they solved by creating a government which had ample powers in the national field, but whose powers were limited to that field. In Number 39 of The Federalist, *Madison tries to explain what the Con-*

vention did. If his explanation seems a bit confusing, two things should be remembered. First, he was leaning over backward to reassure all those who feared centralization, and therefore overemphasized the extent to which the new Constitution was what he called "federal" in character. Second, Americans had done something new under the political sun, and they were not yet themselves wholly clear as to just what kind of government they had created. For that matter the questions that Madison discusses are still subjects of controversy today.

I N ORDER to ascertain the real character of the government, it may be considered in relation to the foundation on which it is to be established; to the sources from which its ordinary powers are to be drawn; to the operation of those powers; to the extent of them; and to the authority by which future changes in the government are to be introduced.

On examining the first relation, it appears, on one hand, that the Constitution is to be founded on the assent and ratification of the people of America, given by deputies elected for the special purpose; but, on the other, that this assent and ratification is to be given by the people, not as individuals composing one entire nation, but as composing the distinct and independent States to which they respectively belong. It is to be the assent and ratification of the several States, derived from the supreme authority in each State,—the authority of the people themselves. The act, therefore, establishing the Constitution, will not be a *national*, but a *federal* act.

That it will be a federal and not a national act, as these terms are understood by the objectors; the act of the people, as forming so many independent States, not as forming one aggregate nation, is obvious from this single consideration, that it is to result neither from the decision of a *majority* of the people of the Union, nor from that of a *majority* of the States. It must result from the *unanimous* assent of the several States that are parties to it, differing no otherwise from their ordinary assent than in its being expressed, not by the legislative authority, but by that of the people themselves. Were the people regarded in this transaction as forming one nation, the will of the majority of the whole people of the United States would bind the minority, in the same manner as the majority in each State must bind the minority; and the will of the majority must be determined either by a comparison of the individual votes, or by considering the will of the majority of the States as evidence of the will of a majority of the people of the United States. Neither of these rules has been adopted. Each State, in ratifying the Constitution, is considered as a sovereign body, independent of all others, and only to be bound by its own voluntary act. In this relation, then, the new Constitution will, if established, be a *federal*, and not a *national* constitution.

The next relation is, to the sources from which the ordinary powers of government are to be derived. The House of Representatives will derive its powers from the people of America; and the people will be represented in the same proportion, and on the same principle, as they are in the legislature of a particular State. So far the government is *national*, not *federal*. The Senate, on the other hand, will derive its powers from the States, as political and coequal societies; and these will be represented on the principle of equality in the Senate, as they now are in the existing Congress. So far the government is *federal*, not *national*. The executive power will be derived from a very compound source. The immediate election of the President is to be made by the States in their political characters. The votes allotted to them are in a compound ratio, which considers them partly as distinct and coequal societies, partly as unequal members of the same society. The eventual election, again, is to be made by that branch of the legislature which consists of the national representatives; but in this particular act they are to be thrown into the form of individual delegations, from so many distinct and co-equal bodies politic. From this aspect of the government, it appears to be of a mixed character, presenting at least as many *federal* as *national* features.

The difference between a federal and national government, as it relates to the *operation of the government*, is supposed to consist in this, that in the former the powers operate on the political bodies composing the Confederacy, in their political capacities; in the latter, on the individual citizens composing the nation, in their individual capacities. On trying the Constitution by this criterion, it falls under the *national*, not the *federal* character; though perhaps not so completely as has been understood. In several cases, and particularly in the trial of controversies to which States may be parties, they must be viewed and proceeded against in their collective and political capacities only. So far the national countenance of the government on this side seems to be disfigured by a few federal features. But this blemish is perhaps unavoidable in any plan; and the operation of the government on the people, in their individual capacities, in its ordinary and most essential proceedings, may, on the whole, designate it, in this relation, a *national* government.

But if the government be national with regard to the *operation* of its powers, it changes its aspect again when we contemplate it in relation to the extent of its powers. The idea of a national government involves in it, not only an authority over the individual citizens, but an indefinite supremacy over all persons and things, so far as they are objects of lawful government. Among a people consolidated into one nation, this supremacy is completely vested in the national legislature. Among communities united for particular purposes, it is vested partly in the general and partly in the municipal legislatures. In the former case, all local authorities are subordinate to the supreme; and may be controlled, directed, or abolished by it at pleasure. In the latter, the local or municipal authorities form distinct and independent portions of the supremacy, no more subject, within their respective spheres, to the general authority, than the general authority is subject to them, within its own sphere. In this relation, then, the proposed government cannot be deemed a *national* one; since its jurisdiction extends to certain enumerated objects only, and leaves to the several States a residuary and inviolable sovereignty over all other objects. It is true that in controversies relating to the boundary between the two jurisdictions, the tribunal which is ultimately to decide, is to be established under the general government. But this does not change the principle of the case. The decision is to be impartially made, according to the rules of the Constitution; and all the usual and most effectual precautions are taken to secure this impartiality. Some such tribunal is clearly essential to prevent an appeal to the sword and a dissolution of the compact; and that it ought to be established under the general rather than under the local governments, or, to speak more properly, that it could be safely established under the first alone, is a position not likely to be combated.

If we try the Constitution by its last relation to the authority by which amendments are to be made, we find it neither wholly *national* nor wholly *federal*. Were it wholly national, the supreme and ultimate authority would reside in the *majority* of the people of the Union; and this authority would be competent at all times, like that of a majority of every national society, to alter or abolish its established government. Were it wholly federal, on the other hand, the concurrence of each State in the Union would be essential to every alteration that would be binding on all. The mode provided by the plan of the convention is not founded on either of these principles. In requiring more than a majority, and particularly in computing the proportion by *States*, not by *citizens*, it departs from the *national* and advances towards the *federal* character; in rendering the concurrence of less than the whole number of States sufficient, it loses again the *federal* and partakes of the *national* character.

The proposed Constitution, therefore, is, in strictness, neither a national nor a federal Constitution, but a composition of both. In its foundation it is federal, not national; in the sources from which the ordinary powers of the government are drawn, it is partly federal and partly national; in the operation of these powers, it is national, not federal; in the extent of them, again, it is federal, not national; and, finally in the authoritative mode of introducing amendments, it is neither wholly federal nor wholly national.

PUBLIUS

—JAMES MADISON, *The Federalist*, No. 39, 1788

3. "A RISING, NOT A SETTING SUN"

The familiar episode of Franklin's final speech in the Constitutional Convention needs no introduction. Franklin himself was far from satisfied with the Constitution as it came from the hands of the Framers, but he realized that no constitution would satisfy everyone and that this was the best that could be agreed upon. Franklin himself contributed as much as any other American to the solution of the problem of Federalism written into the Constitution. He was the author of the Albany Plan of Union of 1754; he was on the committee that framed the Articles of Confederation; he gave sagacious counsel on the Constitution.

THE engrossed Constitution being read [September 17, 1787], Dr. Franklin rose with a speech in his hand, which he had reduced to writing for his own convenience, and which Mr. Wilson read in the words following:

"Mr. President: I confess that there are several parts of this Constitution which I do not at present approve, but I am not sure I shall never approve them. For, having lived long, I have experienced many instances of being obliged, by better information or fuller consideration, to change opinions, even on important subjects, which I once thought right, but found to be otherwise. It is therefore that, the older I grow, the more apt I am to doubt my own judgment, and to pay more respect to the judgment of others. Most men, indeed, as well as most sects in religion, think themselves in possession of all truth, and that wherever others differ from them, it is so far error. Steele, a Protestant, in a dedication, tells the Pope, that the only difference between our churches, in their opinions of the certainty of their doctrines, is, 'the Church of Rome is infallible, and the Church of England is never in the wrong.' But though many private persons think almost as highly of their own infallibility as of that of their sect, few express it so naturally as a certain French lady, who, in a dispute with her sister, said, 'I don't know how it happens, sister, but I meet with nobody but myself that is always in the right— *il n'y a que moi qui a toujours raison.*'

"In these sentiments, sir, I agree to this Constitution, with all its faults, if they are such; because I think a general government necessary for us, and there is no form of government, but what may be a blessing to the people if well administered; and believe further, that this is likely to be well administered for a course of years, and can only end in despotism, as other forms have done before it, when the people shall become so corrupted as to need despotic government, being incapable of any other. I doubt, too, whether any other convention we can obtain may be able to make a better constitution. For, when you assemble a number of men to have the advantage of their joint wisdom, you inevitably assemble with those men all their prejudices, their passions, their errors of opinion, their local interests, and their selfish views. From such an assembly can a perfect production be expected? It therefore astonishes me, sir, to find this system approaching so near to perfection as it does; and I think it will astonish our enemies, who are waiting with confidence to hear that our councils are confounded, like those of the builders of Babel, and that our States are on the point of separation, only to meet hereafter for the purpose of cutting one another's throats. Thus I consent, sir, to this Constitution, because I expect no better, and because I am not sure that it is not the best. The opinions I have had of its errors I sacrifice to the public good. I have never whispered a syllable of them abroad. Within these walls they were born, and here they shall die. If every one of us, in returning to our constituents, were to report the objections he has had to it, and endeavor to gain partisans in support of them, we might prevent its being generally received, and thereby lose all the salutary effects and great advantages resulting naturally in our favor among foreign nations, as well as among ourselves, from our real or apparent unanimity. Much of the strength and efficiency of any government, in procuring and securing happiness to the people, depends on opinion— on the general opinion of the goodness of the government, as well as of the wisdom and integrity of its governors. I hope, therefore, that for our own sakes, as a part of the people, and for the sake of posterity, we shall act heartily and unanimously in recommending this Constitution (if approved by Congress and confirmed by the conventions) wherever our influence may extend, and turn our future thoughts and endeavors to the means of having it well administered.

"On the whole, sir, I cannot help expressing a wish that every member of the Convention, who may still have objections to it, would with me, on this occasion, doubt a little of his own infallibility, and, to make manifest our unanimity, put his name to this instrument." He then moved that the Constitution be signed by the members, and offered the following as a convenient form, viz.: "Done in Convention by the unanimous consent of *the States* present, the 17th of September, etc. In witness whereof, we have hereunto subscribed our names." . . .

Whilst the last members were signing, Dr. Franklin, looking towards the president's chair, at the back of which a rising sun happened to be painted, observed to a few members near him, that painters had found it difficult to distinguish, in their art, a rising from a setting sun. "I have," said he, "often and often, in the course of the session, and the vicissitudes of my hopes and fears as to its issue, looked at that behind the president, without being able to tell whether it was rising or setting; but now, at length, I have the happiness to know that it is a rising, and not a setting sun."

—BENJAMIN FRANKLIN, Speech before Federal Convention,
September 17, 1787

4. STRICT OR BROAD CONSTRUCTION?

Ratification of the Federal Constitution was carried out against a powerful opposition—an opposition which may well have represented a majority of the potential voters of the nation. Once the Constitution was ratified, however, those who formerly had opposed it became its most zealous champions. The hostility of this element toward a powerful centralized government now took the form of insisting upon a strict or narrow construction of the Constitution. It is well to get clearly in mind, however, why influential elements in American politics wanted the Constitution construed narrowly. It was not either in the 1790's or at any time thereafter for doctrinaire reasons; Americans are not doctrinaire. It was rather because they feared what the central government was doing, or was going to do, and put their faith in the States. Actually there is no consistent States Rights party in the United States; indeed it is no great exaggeration to say that there has never been a genuine States Rights party in the nation. Those who have championed a narrow construction, or States Rights, have almost always been out of office; once in office they have generally forgotten their misgivings about national powers.

This is not to say that strict construction is merely a shibboleth for those who happen to be out of office. But it is to say that States Rights has never flourished in a vacuum, but has always been about something. Thus Jefferson wanted a narrow construction because he was opposed to a national bank, because he was opposed to tariffs and manufactures, and all the things that he thought threatened agrarian democracy, and because he believed the States the best guardians of the liberties of men. But Jefferson in office was ready enough to construe the Constitution broadly, and to exercise broad general powers. Thus Calhoun championed States Rights because he believed the States the safest guardians of the institution of slavery. Thus those who fought Federal child labor legislation were not so much disturbed over the exercise of Federal power as they were by the specter of national labor legislation. Thus the Dixiecrats of our own day believe in States Rights because they oppose Federal enforcement of the guarantees of the Fourteenth and Fifteenth Amendments; they are ready enough to forget States Rights when it comes to farm subsidies or other Federal hand-outs.

The first great debate over the construction of the Constitution remains perhaps the best, for it was a debate between giants. When Hamilton's bill establishing a national bank passed Congress Washington, doubtful about its constitutionality, asked Hamilton and Jefferson to submit written opinions on this question. Here are the opinions. Washington accepted Hamilton's reasoning and signed the bill; in the great case of M'Culloch versus Maryland, in 1819, the Supreme Court endorsed Hamilton's reasoning. It is suggestive that the argument between Hamilton and Jefferson concerned the interpretation of phrases whose meaning still tantalizes us: "regulate," "necessary and proper," and "general welfare."

A. "Lace Them Up Straitly Within the Enumerated Powers"

THE bill for establishing a national bank, in 1791, undertakes, among other things,—

1. To form the subscribers into a corporation.
2. To enable them, in their corporate capacities, to receive grants of lands; and, so far, is against the laws of *mortmain*.
3. To make *alien* subscribers capable of holding lands; and so far is against the laws of *alienage*.
4. To transmit these lands, on the death of a proprietor, to a certain line of successors; and so far, changes the course of *descents*.
5. To put the lands out of the reach of forfeiture, or escheat; and so far, is against the laws of *forfeiture* and *escheat*.
6. To transmit personal chattels to successors, in a certain line; and so far, is against the laws of *distribution*.
7. To give them the sole and exclusive right of banking, under the national authority; and, so far, is against the laws of *monopoly*.
8. To communicate to them a power to make laws, paramount to the laws of the states; for so they must be construed, to protect the institution from the control of the state legislatures; and so probably they will be construed.

I consider the foundation of the Constitution as laid on this ground—that *all powers not delegated to the United States, by the Constitution, nor prohibited by it to the states, are reserved to the states, or to the people* (12th amend.). To take a single step beyond the boundaries thus specially drawn around the powers of Congress, is to take possession of a boundless field of power, no longer susceptible of any definition.

The incorporation of a bank, and the powers assumed by this bill, have not, in my opinion, been delegated to the United States by the Constitution.

I. *They are not among the powers specially enumerated. For these are,—*
1. A power to *lay taxes* for the purpose of paying the debts of the United States. But no debt is paid by this bill, nor any tax laid. Were it a bill to raise money, its organization in the Senate would condemn it by the Constitution.

2. To "borrow money." But this bill neither borrows money nor insures the borrowing of it. The proprietors of the bank will be just as free as any other money-holders to lend, or not to lend, their money to the public. The operation proposed in the bill, first to lend them two millions, and then borrow them back again, cannot change the nature of the latter act, which will still be a payment, and not a loan, call it by what name you please.

3. "To regulate commerce with foreign nations, and among the states, and with the Indian tribes." To erect a bank, and to regulate commerce, are very different acts. He who erects a bank creates a subject of commerce in its bills; so does he who makes a bushel of wheat, or digs a dollar out of the mines; yet neither of these persons regulates commerce thereby. To make a thing which may be bought and sold, is not to prescribe regulations for buying and selling. Besides, if this were an exercise of the power of regulating commerce, it would be void, as extending as much to the internal commerce of every state, as it is external. For the power given to Congress by the Constitution does not extend to the internal regulation of the commerce of a state . . . which remains exclusively with its own legislature; but to its external commerce only, that is to say, its commerce with another state, or with foreign nations, or with the Indian tribes. Accordingly, the bill does not propose the measure as a "regulation of trade," but as "productive of considerable advantage to trade."

Still less are these powers covered by any other of the special enumerations.

II. Nor are they within either of the general phrases, which are the two following:—

1. "To lay taxes to provide for the general welfare of the United States";

that is to say, "to lay taxes *for the purpose* of providing for the general welfare"; for the laying of taxes is the *power,* and the general welfare the *purpose* for which the power is to be exercised. Congress are not to lay taxes *ad libitum, for any purpose they please;* but only to *pay the debts, or provide for the welfare, of the Union.* In like manner, they are not *to do anything they please*, to provide for the general welfare, but only *to lay taxes* for that purpose. To consider the latter phrase, not as describing the purpose of the first, but as giving a distinct and independent power to do any act they please which might be for the good of the Union, would render all the preceding and subsequent enumerations of power completely useless. It would reduce the whole instrument to a single phrase—that of instituting a Congress with power to do whatever would be for the good of the United States; and, as they would be the sole judges of the good or evil, it would be also a power to do whatever evil they pleased. It is an established rule of construction, where a phrase will bear either of two meanings, to give it that which will allow some meaning to the other parts of the instrument, and not that which will render all the others useless. Certainly no such universal power was meant to be given them. It was intended to lace them up straitly within the enumerated powers, and those without which, as means, these powers could not be carried into effect. It is known that the very power now proposed *as a means,* was rejected *as an end by the Convention which formed the Constitution.* A proposition was made to them, to authorize Congress to open canals, and an amendatory one to empower them to incorporate. But the whole was rejected; and one of the reasons of objection urged in debate was, that they then would have a power to erect a bank, which would render great cities, where there were prejudices and jealousies on that subject, adverse to the reception of the Constitution.

2. The second general phrase is, "to make all laws *necessary* and proper for carrying into execution the enumerated powers." But they can all be carried into execution without a bank. A bank, therefore, is not *necessary,* and consequently not authorized by this phrase.

It has been much urged that a bank will give great facility or convenience in the collection of taxes. Suppose this were true; yet the Constitution allows only the means which are "necessary," not those which are merely "convenient," for effecting the enumerated powers. If such a latitude of construction be allowed to this phrase as to give any non-enumerated power, it will go to every one; for there is no one which ingenuity may not torture into a *convenience, in some way or other, to some one* of so long a list of enumerated powers. It would swallow up all the delegated powers, and reduce the whole to one phrase, as before observed. Therefore it was that the Constitution restrained them to the *necessary* means; that is to say, to those means without which the grant of the power would be nugatory. . . .

Perhaps bank bills may be a more *convenient* vehicle than treasury orders. But a little *difference* in the degree of convenience cannot constitute the necessity which the Constitution makes the ground for assuming any non-enumerated power. . . .

Can it be thought that the Constitution intended that, for a shade or two of *convenience*, more or less, Congress should be authorized to break down the most ancient and fundamental laws of the several states such as those against mortmain, the laws of alienage, the rules of descent, the acts of distribution, the laws of escheat and forfeiture, and the laws of monopoly.

Nothing but a necessity invincible by other means, can justify such a prostration of laws, which constitute the pillars of our whole system of jurisprudence. Will Congress be too strait-laced to carry the Constitution into honest effect, unless they may pass over the foundation laws of the state governments, for the slightest convenience to theirs?

The negative of the President is the shield provided by the Constitution to protect, against the invasions of the legislature, 1. *The rights of the executive;* 2. *Of the judiciary;* 3. *Of the states and state legislatures.* The present is the case of a right remaining exclusively with the states, and is, consequently, one of those intended by the Constitution to be placed under his protection.

It must be added, however, that, unless the President's mind, on a view of everything which is urged for and against this bill, is tolerably clear that it is unauthorized by the Constitution, if the *pro* and the *con* hang so evenly as to balance his judgment, a just respect for the wisdom of the legislature would naturally decide the balance in favor of their opinion. It is chiefly for cases where they are clearly misled by error, ambition, or interest, that the Constitution has placed a check in the negative of the President.

—THOMAS JEFFERSON,
Opinion on the Constitutionality of the Bank, February 15, 1791

B. "There Are Implied as Well as Express Powers"

In entering upon the argument it ought to be premised that the objections of the Secretary of State and the Attorney-General are founded on a general denial of the authority of the United States to erect corporations. The latter, indeed, expressly admits, that if there be anything in the bill which is not warranted by the Constitution, it is the clause of incorporation.

Now it appears to the Secretary of the Treasury that this *general principle* is *inherent* in the very *definition* of government, and *essential* to every step of the progress to be made by that of the United States, namely: That every power vested in a government is in its nature *sovereign,* and includes, by *force* of the *term* a right to employ all the *means* requisite and fairly applicable to the attainment of the ends of such power, and which are not precluded by restrictions and exceptions specified in the Constitution, or not immoral, or not contrary to the *essential ends* of political society. . . .

If it would be necessary to bring proof to a proposition so clear, as that which affirms that the powers of the federal government, as to *its objects,* were sovereign, there is a clause of the Constitution which would be decisive. It is that which declares that the Constitution, and the laws of the United States made in pursuance of it, . . . shall be the *supreme law of the land.* The power which can create a *supreme law of the land,* in any case, is doubtless *sovereign* as to such case.

This general and indisputable principle puts at once an end to the *abstract* question, whether the United States have power to erect a corporation; that is to say, to give a *legal* or *artificial capacity* to one or more persons, distinct from the *natural.* For it is unquestionably incident to *sovereign power* to erect corporations, and consequently to *that* of the United States, in *relation* to the *objects* intrusted to the management of the government. The difference is this: where the authority of the government is general, it can create corporations in *all cases;* where it is confined to certain branches of legislation, it can create corporations *only* in those cases. . . .

It is not denied that there are *implied* as well as *express powers,* and that the *former* are as effectually delegated as the *latter.* And for the sake of accuracy it shall be mentioned, that there is another class of powers, which may be properly denominated *resulting powers.* It will not be doubted, that if the United States should make a conquest of any of the territories of its neighbours, they would possess sovereign jurisdiction over the conquered territory. This would be rather a result, from the whole mass of the powers of the government, and from the nature of political society, than a consequence of either of the powers specially enumerated. . . .

It is conceded that *implied powers* are to be considered as delegated equally with *express ones*. Then it follows, that as a power of erecting a corporation may as well be *implied* as any other thing, it may as well be employed as an *instrument* or *mean* of carrying into execution any of the specified powers, as any other *instrument* or *mean* whatever. The only question must be, in this, as in every other case, whether the mean to be employed, or in this instance, the corporation to be erected, has a natural relation to any of the acknowledged objects or lawful ends of the government. Thus a corporation may not be erected by Congress for superintending the police of the city of Philadelphia, because they are not authorized to *regulate* the *police* of that city. But one may be erected in relation to the collection of taxes, or to the trade with foreign countries, or to the trade between the States, or with the Indian tribes; because it is the province of the federal government to *regulate* those objects and because it is incident to a general *sovereign* or *legislative* power to *regulate* a thing, to employ all the means which relate to its regulation to the best and greatest advantage. . . .

Through this mode of reasoning respecting the right of employing all the means requisite to the execution of the specified powers of the government, it is objected, that none but necessary and proper means are to be employed; and the Secretary of State maintains, that no means are to be considered as *necessary* but those without which the grant of the power would be *nugatory*. . . .

It is essential to the being of the national government, that so erroneous a conception of the meaning of the word *necessary* should be exploded.

It is certain, that neither the grammatical nor popular sense of the term requires that construction. According to both, *necessary* often means no more than *needful, requisite, incidental, useful,* or *conducive to.* . . . And it is the true one in which it is to be understood as used in the Constitution. The whole turn of the clause containing it indicates, that it was the intent of the Convention, by that clause, to give a liberal latitude to the exercise of the specified powers. The expressions have peculiar comprehensiveness. They are "to make all *laws* necessary and proper for *carrying into execution* the *foregoing powers,* and *all other powers,* vested by the Constitution in the *government* of the United States, or in any *department* or *officer* thereof.

To understand the word as the Secretary of State does, would be to depart from its obvious and popular sense, and to give it a restrictive operation, an idea never before entertained. It would be to give it the same force as if the word *absolutely* or *indispensably* had been prefixed to it. . . .

The *degree* in which a measure is necessary, can never be a *test* of the legal right to adopt it; that must be a matter of opinion, and can only be a *test* of expediency. The *relation* between the *measure* and the *end*; between the *nature* of the *mean* employed towards the execution of a power, and the object of that power, must be the criterion of constitutionality, not the more or less of *necessity* or *utility*. . . .

This restrictive interpretation of the word *necessary* is also contrary to this sound maxim of construction; namely, that the powers contained in a constitution of government, especially those which concern the general administration of the affairs of a country, its finances, trade, defence &c., ought to be construed liberally in advancement of the public good. . . . The means by which national exigencies are to be provided for, national inconveniences obviated, national prosperity promoted, are of such infinite variety, extent, and complexity, that there must of necessity be great latitude of discretion in the selection and application of those means. Hence, consequently, the necessity and propriety of exercising the authorities intrusted to a government on principles of liberal construction. . . .

But the doctrine which is contended for is not chargeable with the consequences imputed to it. It does not affirm that the national government is sovereign in all respects, but that it is sovereign to a certain extent; that is is, to the extent of the objects of its specified powers.

It leaves, therefore, a criterion of what is constitutional and of what is not so. This criterion is the *end*, to which the measure relates as a *mean*. If the *end* be clearly comprehended within any of the specified powers, and if the measure have an obvious relation to that *end*, and is not forbidden by any particular provision of the Constitution, it may safely be deemed to come within the compass of the national authority. There is also this further criterion, which may materially assist the decision; Does the proposed measure abridge a pre-existing right of any State or of any individual? If it does not, there is a strong presumption in favor of its constitutionality, and slighter relations to any declared object of the Constitution may be permitted to turn the scale. . . .

It is presumed to have been satisfactorily shown in the course of the preceding observations:

1. That the power of the government, *as* to the objects intrusted to its management, is, in its nature, sovereign.

2. That the right of erecting corporations is one inherent in, and inseparable from, the idea of sovereign power.

3. That the position, that the government of the United States can exercise no power but such as is delegated to it by its Constitution, does not militate against this principle.

4. That the word *necessary*, in the general clause, can have no *restrictive* operation derogating from the force of this principle; indeed, that the degree in which a measure is or is not *necessary*, cannot be a *test* of *constitutional right*, but of *expediency only*.

5. That the power to erect corporations is not to be considered as an *independent* or *substantive* power, but as an *incidental* and *auxiliary* one, and was therefore more properly left to implication than expressly granted.

6. That the principle in question does not extend the power of the government beyond the prescribed limits, because it only affirms a power to *incorporate* for purposes *within the sphere* of the *specified powers*.

And lastly, that the right to exercise such a power in certain cases is unequivocally granted in the most *positive* and *comprehensive* terms. . . .

A hope is entertained that it has, by this time, been made to appear, to the satisfaction of the President, that a bank has a natural relation to the power of collecting taxes—to that of regulating trade—to that of providing for the common defence—and that, as the bill under consideration contemplates the government in the light of a joint proprietor of the stock of the bank, it brings the case within the provision of the clause of the Constitution which immediately respects the property of the United States.

Under a conviction that such a relation subsists, the Secretary of the Treasury, with all deference, conceives, that it will result as a necessary consequence from the position, that all the specified powers of government are sovereign, as to the proper objects; that the incorporation of a bank is a constitutional measure; and that the objections taken to the bill, in this respect, are ill-founded.

—Alexander Hamilton,
Opinion on the Constitutionality of the Bank, February 23, 1791

5. THE CONSTITUTION A COMPACT

Within less than a decade the controversy over the nature and extent of national powers flared up anew, and once again Thomas Jefferson was spokesman for those who challenged the authority or the pretended authority of the Federal Government. This time the issue was more important than the question of the chartering of a bank; it involved the great issue of freedom. Alarmed and frightened by the "Jacobin" menace, and by the vehemence of criticisms directed against the administration, the Federalists in Congress pushed through, and John Adams signed, a series of Alien and Sedition Acts—acts which appeared to many to violate the First Amendment of the Constitution. Among other things the Sedition Act made it a penal offense to "publish any false, scandalous and malicious writings against the government of the United States, or either house of the Congress, or the President . . . or to bring them into contempt or disrepute." This was going pretty far. Aroused at this assault upon freedom of speech and of the press and by what appeared to be a gross betrayal of the principles of the Revolution, Jefferson led Virginia and Kentucky in a series of protests. He had "sworn upon the altar of God eternal hostility against every form of tyranny over the mind of man," and he was prepared to make an exception least of all for his own country. What he did was to get together with his friend and disciple Madison to draft resolutions for the States of Kentucky and Virginia to pass. These resolutions, it must be remembered, were not primarily concerned with presenting a philosophy of States Rights, or a compact theory of government, but rather with restating the fundamental principles of the Revolutionary struggle—the principle that government is limited, that there are certain things no government can do, and that among these is depriving men of liberty. It was liberty that Jefferson and Madison were concerned with here, not constitutional doctrine.

A. Kentucky Resolutions

I. *Resolved*, that the several States composing the United States of America, are not united on the principle of unlimited submission to their general government; but that by compact under the style and title of a Constitution for the United States and of amendments thereto, they constituted a general government for special purposes, delegated to that government certain definite powers, reserving each State to itself, the residuary mass of right to their own self-government; and that whensoever the general government assumes undelegated powers, its acts are unauthoritative, void, and of no force: That to this compact each State acceded as a State, and is an integral party, its co-States forming, as to itself, the other party: That the government created by this compact was not made the exclusive or final judge of the extent of the powers delegated to itself; since that would have made its discretion, and not the Constitution, the measure of its powers; but that as in all other cases of compact among parties having no common Judge, *each party has an equal right to judge for itself, as well of infractions as of the mode and measure of redress.* . . .

III. *Resolved*, that it is true as a general principle, and is also expressly declared by one of the amendments to the Constitution that "the powers not delegated to the United States by the Constitution, nor prohibited by it to the States, are reserved to the States respectively or to the people"; and that no power over the freedom of religion, freedom of speech, or freedom of the press being delegated to the United States by the Constitution, nor prohibited by it to the States, all lawful powers respecting the same did of right remain, and were reserved to the States, or to the people: That thus was manifested their determination to retain to themselves the right of judging how far the licentiousness of speech and of the press may be abridged without lessening their useful freedom, and how far those abuses which cannot be separated from their use should be tolerated rather than the use be destroyed; and thus also they guarded against all abridgment by the United States of the freedom of religious opinions and exercises, and retained to themselves the right of protecting the same, as this State, by a law passed on the general demand of its citizens, had already protected them from all human restraint or interference: And that in addition to this general principle and express declaration, another and more special provision has been made by one of the amendments to the Constitution which expressly declares, that "Congress shall make no law respecting an establishment of religion, or prohibiting the free exercise thereof, or abridging the freedom of speech, or of the press," thereby guarding in the same sentence, and under the same words, the freedom of religion, of speech, and of the press, insomuch, that whatever violates either, throws down the sanctuary which covers the others, and that libels, falsehoods, defamation equally with heresy and false religion, are withheld from the cognizance of Federal tribunals. That therefore [the Sedition Act], which does abridge the freedom of the press, is not law, but is altogether void and of no effect.

—THOMAS JEFFERSON, Kentucky Resolutions, 1798

B. VIRGINIA RESOLUTIONS

Resolved, That the General Assembly of Virginia doth unequivocally express a firm resolution to maintain and defend the Constitution of the United States, and the Constitution of this state, against every aggression either foreign or domestic; and that they will support the Government of the United States in all measures warranted by the former.

That this Assembly most solemnly declares a warm attachment to the union of the states, to maintain which it pledges all its powers; and that, for this end, it is their duty to watch over and oppose every infraction of those principles which constitute the only basis of that Union, because a faithful observance of them can alone secure its existence and the public happiness.

That this Assembly doth explicitly and peremptorily declare that it views the powers of the Federal Government as resulting from the compact to which the states are parties, as limited by the plain sense and intention of the instrument constituting that compact; as no further valid than they are authorized by the grants enumerated in that compact; and that, in case of a deliberate, palpable, and dangerous exercise of other powers not granted by the said compact, the states, who are parties thereto, have the right and are in duty bound to interpose for arresting the progress of the evil, and for maintaining within their respective limits the authorities, rights, and liberties appertaining to them. . . .

That the General Assembly doth particularly PROTEST against the palpable and alarming infractions of the Constitution in the two late cases of the "Alien and Sedition Acts," passed at the last session of Congress; the first of which exercises a power nowhere delegated to the Federal Government, and which, by uniting legislative and judicial powers to those of [the] executive, subverts the general principles of free government, as well as the particular organization and positive provisions of the Federal Constitution: and the other of which acts exercises, in like manner, a power not delegated by the Constitution, but, on the contrary, expressly and positively forbidden by one of the amendments thereto,—a power which, more than any other, ought to produce universal alarm, because it is levelled against the right of freely examining public characters and measures, and of free communication among the people thereon, which has ever been justly deemed the only effectual guardian of every other right.

—James Madison, Virginia Resolutions, 1798

6. "THE ORIGIN OF THIS GOVERNMENT AND THE SOURCE OF ITS POWER"

Toward the end of the 1820's, sectional feeling between the North and the South, already inflamed by differences over slavery and over the admission of Western States, was further exacerbated by the enactment of the so-called Tariff of Abominations. Calhoun, who had already abandoned his earlier nationalism, now turned to sharpening his doctrines of States Rights and nullification, doctrines soon to appear in his famous "Exposition." Meantime sectional differences found expression in a controversy over public land policy. Late in December, 1829, Senator Foot of Connecticut introduced a resolution looking to a restriction on the sale of public lands. This led to a general free-for-all in the Senate, with Senator Hayne of South Carolina accusing the New Englanders of being narrowly sectional in their interests. It was in the course of his second reply to Hayne—one of the greatest speeches ever delivered in the Senate—that Webster made the following philosophical observations on the nature of the Union.

THIS leads us to inquire into the origin of this government and the source of its power. Whose agent is it? Is it the creature of the State Legislatures, or the creature of the people? If the Government of the United States be the agent of the State governments, then they may control it, provided they can agree in the manner of controlling it; if it be the agent of the people, then the people alone can control it, restrain it, modify it, or reform it. It is observable enough, that the doctrine for which the honorable gentleman contends leads him to the necessity of maintaining, not only that this General Government is the creature of the States, but that it is the creature of each of the States, severally, so that each may assert the power for itself of determining whether it acts within the limits of its authority. It is the servant of four-and-twenty masters, of different wills and different purposes, and yet bound to obey all. This absurdity (for it seems no less) arises from a misconception as to the origin of this government and its true character. It is, sir, the people's Constitution, the people's government, made for the people, made by the people, and answerable to the people. The people of the United States have declared that this Constitution shall be supreme law. We must either admit the proposition, or deny their authority. The States are, unquestionably, sovereign, so far as their sovereignty is not affected by this supreme law. But the State Legislatures, as political bodies, however sovereign, are yet not sovereign over the people. So far as the people have given power to the General Government, so far the grant is unquestionably good, and the Government holds of the people, and not of the State governments. We are all agents of the same supreme power, the people. The General Government and the State governments derive their authority from the same source. Neither can, in relation to the other, be called primary, though one is definite and restricted, and the other general and residuary. The National Government possesses those powers which it can be shown the people have conferred on it, and no more. All the rest belongs to the State Governments, or to the people themselves. So far as the people have restrained State sovereignty by the expression of their will, in the Constitution of the United States, so far, it must be admitted, State sovereignty is effectually controlled. I do not contend that it is, or ought to be, controlled farther. The sentiment to which I have referred propounds that State sovereignty is only to be controlled by its own "feeling of justice"—that is to say, it is not to be controlled at all, for one who is to follow his own feelings is under no legal control. Now, however men may think this ought to be, the fact is that the people of the United States have chosen to impose control on State sovereignties. There are those, doubtless, who wish they had been left without restraint; but the Constitution has ordered the matter differently. To make war, for instance, is an exercise of sovereignty; but the Constitution declares that no State shall make war. To coin money is another exercise of sovereign power; but no State is at liberty to coin money. Again, the Constitution says that no sovereign State shall be so sovereign as to make a treaty. These prohibitions, it must be confessed, are a control on the State sovereignty of South Carolina, as well as of the other States, which does not arise "from her own feelings of honorable justice." The opinion referred to, therefore, is in defiance of the plainest provisions of the Constitution. . . .

But, sir, the people have wisely provided, in the Constitution itself, a proper, suitable mode and tribunal for settling questions of constitutional law. There are in the Constitution grants of powers to Congress, and restrictions on these powers. There are also prohibitions on the States. Some authority must, therefore, necessarily exist, having the ultimate jurisdiction to fix and ascertain the interpretation of these grants, restrictions, and prohibitions. The Constitution has itself pointed out, ordained, and established that authority. How has it accomplished this great and essential end? By declaring, sir, that "*the Constitution and the laws of the United States made in pursuance thereof, shall be the supreme law of the land, any thing in the Constitution or laws of any State to the contrary notwithstanding.*" . . .

I have thus stated the reasons of my dissent to the doctrines which have been advanced and maintained. I am conscious, sir, of having detained you and the Senate much too long. I was drawn into the debate with no previous deliberation such as is suited to the discussion of so grave and important a subject. But it is a subject of which my heart is full, and I have not been willing to suppress the utterance of its spontaneous sentiments. I cannot even now persuade myself to relinquish it without expressing once more my deep conviction that, since it respects nothing less than the Union of the states, it is of most vital and essential importance to the public happiness. I profess, sir, in my career hitherto, to have kept steadily in view the prosperity and honor of the whole country and the preservation of our federal Union. It is to that Union we owe our safety at home and our consideration and dignity abroad. It is to that Union that we are chiefly indebted for whatever makes us most proud of our country. That Union we reached only by the discipline of our virtues in the severe school of adversity. It had its origin in the necessities of disordered finance, prostrate commerce, and ruined credit. Under its benign influence, these great interests immediately awoke as from the dead and sprang forth with newness of life. Every year of its duration has teemed with fresh proofs of its utility and its blessings, and although our territory has stretched out wider and wider and our population spread farther and farther, they have not outrun its protection or its benefits. It has been to us all a copious fountain of national, social, and personal happiness. I have not allowed myself, sir, to look beyond the Union, to see what might lie hidden in the dark recess behind. I have not coolly weighed the chances of preserving liberty when the bonds that unite us together shall be broken asunder. I have not accustomed myself to hang over the precipice of disunion, to see whether, with my short sight, I can fathom the depth of the abyss below; nor could I regard him as a safe counselor, in the affairs of this government, whose thoughts should be mainly bent on considering, not how the Union should be best preserved, but how tolerable might be the condition of the people when it shall be broken up and destroyed. While the Union lasts, we have high, exciting, gratifying prospects spread out before us, for us and our children. Beyond that, I seek not to penetrate the veil. God grant that in my day, at least, that curtain may not rise. God grant that, on my vision, never may be opened what lies behind. When my eyes shall be turned to behold for the last times the sun in heaven, may I not see him shining on the broken and dishonored fragments of a once glorious Union; on states dissevered, discordant, belligerent; on a land rent with civil feuds, or drenched, it may be, in fraternal blood! Let their last feeble and lingering glance rather behold the gorgeous ensign of the republic, now known and honored throughout the earth, still full high advanced, its arms and trophies streaming in their original luster, not a stripe erased or polluted, nor a single star obscured, bearing for its motto no such miserable interrogatory as, What is all this worth? nor those other words of delusion and folly, Liberty first, and Union afterward; but everywhere, spread all over in characters of living light, blazing on all its ample folds, as they float over the sea and over the land, and in every wind under the whole heavens, that other sentiment, dear to every true American heart— Liberty *and* Union, now and forever, one and inseparable!

—Daniel Webster, Second Reply to Hayne, January 26, 1830

7. "A COMPACT IS A BINDING OBLIGATION"

Outraged by the tariff of July, 1832, the Legislature of South Carolina met in special session and called a convention to consider what should be done. The Convention met in November of that year and adopted an Ordinance of Nullification—an ordinance declaring the tariff law null and void as far as it concerned South Carolina, requiring all State officers to take an oath of loyalty to the State—and the Ordinance —and forbidding any judge to take cognizance of any case challenging the Ordinance. Against this unconstitutional act President Jackson launched his memorable proclamation. The proclamation contains a general review of the whole question of States Rights. The danger of a showdown between State and Nation was averted by the enactment of a compromise tariff in 1833, but the doctrines of nullification and secession persisted to plague the nation at a later date.

THE ordinance is founded, not on the indefeasible right of resisting acts which are plainly unconstitutional and too oppressive to be endured, but on the strange position that any one State may not only declare an act of Congress void, but prohibit its execution; that they may do this consistently with the Constitution; that the true construction of that instrument permits a State to retain its place in the Union and yet be bound by no other of its laws than those it may choose to consider as constitutional. It is true, they add, that to justify this abrogation of a law it must be palpably contrary to the Constitution; but it is evident that to give the right of resisting laws of that description, coupled with the uncontrolled right to decide what laws deserve that character, is to give the power of resisting all laws; for as by the theory there is no appeal, the reasons alleged by the State, good or bad, must prevail. If it should be said that public opinion is a sufficient check against the abuse of this power, it may be asked why it is not deemed a sufficient guard against the passage of an unconstitutional act by Congress? There is, however, a restraint in this last case which makes the assumed power of a State more indefensible, and which does not exist in the other. There are two appeals from an unconstitutional act passed by Congress—one to the judiciary, the other to the people and the States. There is no appeal from the State decision in theory, and the practical illustration shows that the courts are closed against an application to review it, both judges and jurors being sworn to decide in its favor. But reasoning on this subject is superfluous when our social compact, in express terms, declares that the laws of the United States, its Constitution, and treaties made under it are the supreme law of the land, and, for greater caution, adds "that the judges in every State shall be bound thereby, anything in the constitution or laws of any State to the contrary notwithstanding." And it may be asserted without fear of refutation that no federative government could exist without a similar provision. . . .

I consider, then, the power to annul a law of the United States, assumed by one State, *incompatible with the existence of the Union, contradicted expressly by the letter of the Constitution, unauthorized by its spirit, inconsistent with every principle on which it was founded, and destructive of the great object for which it was formed.* . . .

Here is a law of the United States, not even pretended to be unconstitutional, repealed by the authority of a small majority of the voters of a single State. Here is a provision of the Constitution which is solemnly abrogated by the same authority.

On such expositions and reasonings the ordinance grounds not only an assertion of the right to annul the laws of which it complains, but to enforce it by a threat of seceding from the Union if any attempt is made to execute them.

This right to secede is deduced from the nature of the Constitution, which, they say, is a compact between sovereign States who have preserved their whole sovereignty and therefore are subject to no superior; that because they made the compact they can break it when in their opinion it has been departed from by the other States. Fallacious as this course of reasoning is, it enlists State pride and finds advocates in the honest prejudices of those who have not studied the nature of our Government sufficiently to see the radical error on which it rests. . . .

The Constitution of the United States, then, forms a *government*, not a league; and whether it be formed by compact between the States or in any other manner, its character is the same. It is a Government in which all the people are represented, which operates directly on the people individually, not upon the States; they retained all the power they did not grant. But each State, having expressly parted with so many powers as to constitute, jointly with the other States, a single nation, can not, from that period, possess any right to secede, because such secession does not break a league, but destroys the unity of a nation; and any injury to that unity is not only a breach which would result from the contravention of a compact, but it is an offense against the whole Union. To say that any State may at pleasure secede from the Union is to say that the United States are not a nation, because it would be a solecism to contend that any part of a nation might dissolve its connection with the other parts, to their injury or ruin, without committing any offense. Secession, like any other revolutionary act, may be morally justified by the extremity of oppression; but to call it a constitutional right is confounding the meaning of terms, and can only be done through gross error or to deceive those who are willing to assert a right, but would pause before they made a revolution or incur the penalties consequent on a failure.

Because the Union was formed by a compact, it is said the parties to that compact may, when they feel themselves aggrieved, depart from it; but it is precisely because it is a compact that they can not. A compact is an agreement or binding obligation. It may by its terms have a sanction or penalty for its breach, or it may not. If it contains no sanction, it may be broken with no other consequence than moral guilt; if it have a sanction, then the breach incurs the designated or implied penalty. A league between independent nations generally has no sanction other than a moral one; or if it should contain a penalty, as there is no common superior it can not be enforced. A government, on the contrary, always has a sanction, express or implied; and in our case it is both necessarily implied and expressly given. An attempt, by force of arms, to destroy a government is an offense, by whatever means the constitutional compact may have been formed; and such government has the right by the law of self-defense to pass acts for punishing the offender, unless that right is modified, restrained, or resumed by the constitutional act. In our system, although it is modified in the case of treason, yet authority is expressly given to pass all laws necessary to carry its powers into effect, and under this grant provision has been made for punishing acts which obstruct the due administration of the laws. . . .

How, then, with all these proofs that under all changes of our position we had, for designated purposes and with defined powers, created national governments, how is it that the most perfect of those several modes of union should now be considered as a mere league that may be dissolved at pleasure? It is from an abuse of terms. Compact is used as synonymous with league, although the true term is not employed, because it would at once show the fallacy of the reasoning. It would not do to say that our Constitution was only a league, but it is labored to prove it a compact (which in one sense it is) and then to argue that as a league is a compact every compact between nations must of course be a league, and that from such an engagement every sovereign power has a right to recede. But it has been shown that in this sense the States are not sovereign, and that even if they were, and the national Constitution had been formed by compact, there would be no right in any one State to exonerate itself from its obligations.

—ANDREW JACKSON, Proclamation to the People of South Carolina,
December 10, 1832

8. "A SEPARATION OF THESE STATES IS A MORAL IMPOSSIBILITY"

Once again, in 1850, the Union seemed on the verge of disruption. This time the controversy was over a whole series of issues, but most important were those having to do with the organization of Western Territories on a free or a slave basis, and the rendition of fugitive slaves. In the course of the debate Calhoun and other Southerners had threatened secession. On March 7, toward the conclusion of the long debate, Webster rose to make a plea for compromise and for union. He rebuked alike the extremists of the North and the South—those who would rather destroy the Union than enforce the odious Fugitive Slave Act, and those who would rather secede than compromise on the question of the West. The Seventh of March speech was not only Webster's greatest effort; it has some claim to the title of the greatest speech ever delivered in the Senate.

MR. PRESIDENT,—I wish to speak to-day, not as a Massachusetts man, nor as a northern man, but as an American, and a member of the Senate of the United States. It is fortunate that there is a Senate of the United States; a body not yet moved from propriety, not lost to a just sense of its own dignity and its own high responsibilities, and a body to which the country looks, with confidence, for wise, moderate, patriotic, and healing counsels. It is not to be denied that we live in the midst of strong agitations, and are surrounded by very considerable dangers to our institutions and government. The imprisoned winds are let loose. The East, the West, the North, and the stormy South, all combine to throw the whole sea into commotion, to toss its billows to the skies, and disclose its profoundest depths. I do not affect to regard myself, Mr. President, as holding, or as fit to hold, the helm in this combat with the political elements; but I have a duty to perform, and I mean to perform it with fidelity—not without a sense of existing dangers, but not without hope. I have a part to act, not for my own security or safety, for I am looking out for no fragment upon which to float away from the wreck, if wreck there must be, but for the good of the whole, and the preservation of the whole; and there is that which will keep me to my duty during this struggle, whether the sun and the stars shall appear, or shall not appear for many days. I speak to-day for the preservation of the Union. "Hear me for my cause." I speak to-day, out of a solicitous and anxious heart, for the restoration to the country of that quiet and that harmony which make the blessings of this union so rich and so dear to us all. These are the topics that I propose to myself to discuss; these are the motives, and the sole motives, that influence me in the wish to communicate my opinions to the Senate and the country; and if I can do anything, however little, for the promotion of these ends, I shall have accomplished all that I desire. . . .

Mr. President, I should much prefer to have heard, from every member on this floor, declarations of opinion that this Union could never be dissolved, than the declaration of opinion that in any case, under the pressure of circumstances, such a dissolution was possible. I hear with pain, and anguish, and distress, the word secession, especially when it falls from the lips of those who are eminently patriotic, and known to the country, and known all over the world, for their political services. Secession! Peaceable secession! Sir, your eyes and mine are never destined to see that miracle. The dismemberment of this vast country without convulsion! The breaking up of the fountains of the great deep without ruffling the surface! Who is so foolish—I beg every body's pardon—as to expect to see any such thing? Sir, he who sees these States, now revolving in harmony around a common centre, and expects to see them quit their places and fly off without convulsion, may look the next hour to see the heavenly bodies rush from their spheres, and jostle against each other in the realms of space, without producing the crush of the universe. There can be no such thing as a peaceable secession. Peaceable secession is an utter impossibility. Is the great Constitution under which we live—covering this whole country—is it to be thawed and melted away by secession, as the snows on the mountain melt under the influence of a vernal sun—disappear almost unobserved, and die off? No, sir! No, sir! I will not state what might produce the disruption of the states; but, sir, I see it as plainly as I see the sun in heaven—I see that disruption must produce such a war as I will not describe, in its twofold characters. . . .

Sir, I may express myself too strongly, perhaps—but some things, some moral things, are almost as impossible, as other natural or physical things; and I hold the idea of a separation of these States—those that are free to form one government, and those that are slaveholding to form another—as a moral impossibility. We could not separate the States by any such line, if we were to draw it. We could not sit down here to-day and draw a line of separation, that would satisfy any five men in the country. There are natural causes that would keep and tie us together, and there are social and domestic relations which we could not break if we would, and which we should not, if we could. Sir, nobody can look over the face of this country at the present moment—nobody can see where its population is the most dense and growing—without being ready to admit, and compelled to admit, that ere long, America will be in the valley of the Mississippi. . . .

And now, Mr. President, instead of speaking of the possibility or utility of secession, instead of dwelling in these caverns of darkness, instead of groping with those ideas so full of all that is horrid and horrible, let us come out into the light of day; let us enjoy the fresh air of liberty and union; let us cherish those hopes which belong to us; let us devote ourselves to those great objects that are fit for our consideration and our action; let us raise our conceptions to the magnitude and the importance of the duties that devolve upon us; let our comprehension be as broad as the country for which we act, our aspirations as high as its certain destiny; let us not be pigmies in a case that calls for men. Never did there devolve, on any generation of men, higher trusts than now devolve upon us for the preservation of this Constitution and the harmony and peace of all who are destined to live under it. Let us make our generation one of the strongest and brightest links in that golden chain which is destined, I fully believe, to grapple the people of all the States to this Constitution, for ages to come. It is a great popular constitutional Government, guarded by legislation, law, and by judicature, and defended by the affections of the whole people. No monarchical throne presses the States together; no iron chain of military power encircles them; they live and stand upon a Government popular in its form, representative in its character, founded upon principles of equality, and calculated, we hope, as to last forever. In all its history, it has been beneficent; it has trodden down no man's liberty; it has crushed no State. Its daily respiration is liberty and patriotism; its yet youthful veins are full of enterprise, courage, and honorable love of glory and renown. Large before, the country has now, by recent events, become vastly larger. This republic now extends, with a vast breadth, across the whole continent. The two great seas of the world wash the one and the other shore. We realize on a mighty scale, the beautiful description of the ornamental border of the buckler of Achilles—

> Now the broad shield complete the artist crowned,
> With his last band, and poured the ocean round;
> In living silver seemed the waves to roll,
> And beat the buckler's verge, and bound the whole.

—DANIEL WEBSTER, "Seventh of March Speech," 1850

9. "THE FICTITIOUS IDEA OF ONE PEOPLE OF THE UNITED STATES"

The doctrines of nullification and secession were shelved, rather than abandoned, after the compromise of 1833. With the controversy over slavery in the territory acquired from Mexico, they were revived and elaborated, first by Calhoun himself, then by his disciples like Robert Barnwell Rhett, Judah P. Benjamin, and Jefferson Davis. We give here not an extract from Calhoun's various analyses of the nature of the Union, for these are overlong for reproduction, but rather a summary statement of the whole doctrine from the man upon whom Calhoun's

mantle was to fall—Jefferson Davis of Mississippi, President of the Con-
federate States of America. Those who formulated the doctrine of States
Rights found support in logic rather than in history, and in the notion
of a fixed and unalterable constitutional system. Perhaps the most in-
teresting thing about this statement from Jefferson Davis is that it was
written some fifteen years after Appomattox!

LOOKING back for a moment at the ground over which we have
gone, I think it may be fairly asserted that the following propositions have been clearly and fully established:

1. That the states of which the American union was formed, from
the moment when they emerged from their colonial or provincial condition, became severally sovereign, free, and independent States—not
one State, or nation.

2. That the union formed under the Articles of Confederation was
a compact between the States, in which these attributes of "sovereignty,
freedom, and independence," were expressly asserted and guaranteed.

3. That, in forming the "more perfect union" of the Constitution,
afterward adopted, the same contracting powers formed an *amended
compact*, without any surrender of these attributes of sovereignty, freedom, and independence, either expressed or implied: on the contrary,
that, by the tenth amendment to the Constitution, limiting the power
of the Government to its express grants, they distinctly guarded against
the presumption of a surrender of anything by implication.

4. That political sovereignty resides, neither in individual citizens,
nor in unorganized masses, nor in fractional subdivisions of a community, but in the people of an organized political body.

5. That no "republican form of government," in the sense in which
that expression is used in the Constitution, and was generally understood by the founders of the Union—whether it be the government of
a State or of a confederation of States—is possessed of any sovereignty
whatever, but merely exercises certain powers delegated by the sovereign
authority of the people, and subject to recall and reassumption by the
same authority that conferred them.

6. That the "people" who organized the first confederation, the people who dissolved it, the people who ordained and established the Constitution which succeeded it, the only people, in fine, known or referred

to in the phraseology of that period—whether the term was used collectively or distributively—were the people of the respective States, each acting separately and with absolute independence of the others.

7. That, in forming and adopting the Constitution, the States, or the people of the States—terms which, when used with reference to acts performed in a sovereign capacity, are precisely equivalent to each other—forming a new *Government,* but no new *people;* and that, consequently, no new sovereignty was created—for sovereignty in an American republic can belong only to a people, never to a government—and that the Federal Government is entitled to exercise only the powers delegated to it by the people of the respective States.

8. That the term "people," in the preamble to the Constitution and in the tenth amendment, is used distributively; that the only "people of the United States" known to the Constitution are the people of each State in the Union; that no such political community or corporate unit as one people of the United States then existed, has ever been organized, or yet exists; that no political action by the people of the United States in the aggregate has ever taken place, or ever can take place, under the Constitution.

The fictitious idea of *one* people of the United States, contradicted in the last paragraph, has been so impressed upon the popular mind by false teaching, by careless and vicious phraseology, and by the ever-present spectacle of a great Government, with its army and navy, its custom-houses and post-offices, its multitude of office-holders, and the splendid prizes which it offers to political ambition, that the tearing away of these illusions and presentation of the original fabric, which they have overgrown and hidden from view, have no doubt been unwelcome, distasteful, and even repellent to some of my readers. The artificial splendor which makes the deception attractive is even employed as an argument to prove its reality.

—JEFFERSON DAVIS,
"The Rise and Fall of the Confederate Government," 1881

10. "THE UNION IS OLDER THAN THE CONSTITUTION"

The slavery controversy, and the election of Lincoln, brought secession, and the organization of the Confederate States of America. When Lincoln took the oath of office, on March 4, 1861, he was faced with a Union already shattered. His inaugural address was at once a skillful argument against the validity and the constitutionality of secession and a noble and eloquent plea for union.

FELLOW-CITIZENS OF THE UNITED STATES:

A DISRUPTION of the Federal Union, heretofore only menaced, is now formidably attempted.

I hold that, in contemplation of universal law and of the Constitution, the Union of these States is perpetual. Perpetuity is implied, if not expressed, in the fundamental law of all national governments. It is safe to assert that no government proper ever had a provision in its organic law for its own termination. Continue to execute all the express provisions of our national Constitution, and the Union will endure forever—it being impossible to destroy it except by some action not provided for in the instrument itself.

Again, if the United States be not a government proper, but an association of States in the nature of contract merely, can it as a contract be peaceably unmade by less than all the parties who made it? One party to a contract may violate it—break it, so to speak; but does it not require all to lawfully rescind it?

Descending from these general principles, we find the proposition that in legal contemplation the Union is perpetual confirmed by the history of the Union itself. The Union is much older than the Constitution. It was formed, in fact, by the Articles of Association in 1774. It was matured and continued by the Declaration of Independence in 1776. It was further matured, and the faith of all the then thirteen States expressly plighted and engaged that it should be perpetual, by the Articles of Confederation in 1778. And, finally, in 1787 one of the declared objects for ordaining and establishing the Constitution was "to form a more perfect Union."

But if the destruction of the Union by one or by a part only of the States be lawfully possible, the Union is less perfect than before the Constitution, having lost the vital element of perpetuity.

It follows from these views that no State upon its own mere motion can lawfully get out of the Union; that resolves and ordinances to that effect are legally void; and that acts of violence, within any State or States, against the authority of the United States, are insurrectionary or revolutionary, according to circumstances.

I therefore consider that, in view of the Constitution and the laws, the Union is unbroken; and to the extent of my ability I shall take care, as the Constitution itself expressly enjoins upon me, that the laws of the Union be faithfully executed in all the States. Doing this I deem to be only a simple duty on my part; and I shall perform it so far as practicable, unless my righful masters, the American people, shall withhold the requisite means, or in some authoritative manner direct the contrary. I trust this will not be regarded as a menace, but only as the declared purpose of the Union that it will constitutionally defend and maintain itself. . . .

Plainly, the central idea of secession is the essence of anarchy. A majority held in restraint by constitutional checks and limitations, and always changing easily with deliberate changes of popular opinions and sentiments, is the only true sovereign of a free people. Whoever rejects it does, of necessity, fly to anarchy or to despotism. Unanimity is impossible; the rule of a minority, as a permanent arrangement, is wholly inadmissible; so that, rejecting the majority principle, anarchy or despotism in some form is all that is left. . . .

Physically speaking, we cannot separate. We cannot remove our respective sections from each other, nor build an impassable wall between them. A husband and wife may be divorced and go out of the presence and beyond the reach of each other; but the different parts of our country cannot do this. They cannot but remain face to face, and intercourse, either amicable or hostile, must continue between them. Is it possible, then, to make that intercourse more advantageous or more satisfactory after separation than before? Can aliens make treaties easier than friends can make laws? Can treaties be more faithfully enforced between aliens than laws can among friends? Suppose you go to war, you cannot fight always; and when, after much loss on both sides, and no gain on either, you cease fighting, the identical old questions as to terms of intercourse are again upon you.

This country, with its institutions, belongs to the people who inhabit it. . . .

Why should there not be a patient confidence in the ultimate justice of the people? Is there any better or equal hope in the world? In our present differences is either party without faith of being in the right? If the Almighty Ruler of nations, with his eternal truth and justice, be on your side of the North, or on yours of the South, that truth and that justice will surely prevail by the judgment of this great tribunal of the American people.

By the frame of the government under which we live, this same people have wisely given their public servants but little power for mischief; and have, with equal wisdom, provided for the return of that little to their own hands at very short intervals. While the people retain their virtue and vigilance, no administration, by any extreme of wickedness or folly, can very seriously injure the government in the short space of four years.

My countrymen, one and all, think calmly and well upon this whole subject. Nothing valuable can be lost by taking time. If there be an object to hurry any of you in hot haste to a step which you would never take deliberately, that object will be frustrated by taking time; but no good object can be frustrated by it. Such of you as are now dissatisfied still have the old Constitution unimpaired, and, on the sensitive point, the laws of your own framing under it; while the new administration will have no immediate power, if it would, to change either. If it were admitted that you who are dissatisfied hold the right side in the dispute, there still is no single good reason for precipitate action. Intelligence, patriotism, Christianity, and a firm reliance on Him who has never yet forsaken this favored land, are still competent to adjust in the best way all our present difficulty.

In your hands, my dissatisfied fellow-countrymen, and not in mine, is the momentous issue of civil war. The government will not assail you. You can have no conflict without being yourselves the aggressors. You have no oath registered in heaven to destroy the government, while I shall have the most solemn one to "preserve, protect, and defend" it.

I am loath to close. We are not enemies, but friends. We must not be enemies. Though passion may have strained, it must not break, our bonds of affection. The mystic chords of memory, stretching from every battle-field and patriot grave to every living heart and hearthstone all over this broad land, will yet swell the chorus of the Union when again touched, as surely they will be, by the better angels of our nature.

—ABRAHAM LINCOLN, First Inaugural Address, March 4, 1861

11. THE FOURTEENTH AMENDMENT

The Civil War settled forever the question of the right of a State to secede. It brought in its train a constitutional revolution—a transfer of authority from State to Federal Government. This constitutional revolution was at once dramatized and accelerated by the Fourteenth Amendment, the first section of which reversed the traditional relationship of citizen to his government by throwing the protection of the Federal Government around rights that might be invaded by States. Only in the last quarter-century have Congress and the Courts begun to exploit the full potentialities of this first section of the Fourteenth Amendment.

SEC. 1. All persons born or naturalized in the United States, and subject to the jurisdiction thereof, are citizens of the United States and of the State where in they reside. No State shall make or enforce any law which shall abridge the privileges or immunities of citizens of the United States; nor shall any State deprive any person of life, liberty, or property, without due process of law; nor deny to any person within its jurisdiction the equal protection of the laws. . . .

—The Fourteenth Amendment, July 28, 1868

12. "GOVERNMENT AT THE SERVICE OF HUMANITY"

The Fourteenth Amendment made the Federal Government the protector of the rights of persons against impairment by States. Not until the twentieth century, however, was it effectively invoked for this purpose. For a long time its significance was a very different one;

it served as a barrier against State laws regulating hours of labor, or railroad rates, or economic conditions generally. What happened—as we shall see in our next chapter—was that those who controlled the Congress saw to it that the Federal Government did not enter the field of social reform, while the Courts pretty well saw to it that the States did not—or could not. The decade of the eighties and nineties saw such legislation as the Interstate Commerce Act and the Sherman Anti-Trust Act, to be sure, but these were not very effective. Not until Theodore Roosevelt came to the Presidency was there any genuine expansion of Federal authority, and then chiefly in familiar areas such as conservation or the regulation of railroads. It was Woodrow Wilson—a Southerner and a Democrat—who most clearly saw the necessity of expanding the scope of Federal legislation and who pushed through a series of reforms that are known, collectively, as the New Freedom. We give here Wilson's Inaugural Address, one of the most profound statements of its kind in our literature.

My Fellow Citizens:

THERE has been a change of government. It began two years ago, when the House of Representatives became Democratic by a decisive majority. It has now been completed. The Senate about to assemble will also be Democratic. The offices of President and Vice-President have been put into the hands of Democrats. What does the change mean? That is the question that is uppermost in our minds to-day. That is the question I am going to try to answer, in order, if I may, to interpret the occasion.

It means much more than the mere success of a party. The success of a party means little except when the Nation is using that party for a large and definite purpose. No one can mistake the purpose for which the Nation now seeks to use the Democratic Party. It seeks to use it to interpret a change in its own plans and point of view. Some old things with which we had grown familiar, and which had begun to creep into the very habit of our thought and of our lives, have altered their aspect as we have latterly looked critically upon them, with fresh, awakened eyes; have dropped their disguises and shown themselves alien and sinister. Some new things, as we look frankly upon them, willing to comprehend their real character, have come to assume the aspect of things long believed in and familiar, stuff of our own convictions. We have been refreshed by a new insight into our own life.

We see that in many things that life is very great. It is incomparably great in its material aspects, in its body of wealth, in the diversity and sweep of its energy, in the industries which have been conceived and built up by the genius of individual men and the limitless enterprise of groups of men. It is great, also, very great, in its moral force.

Nowhere else in the world have noble men and women exhibited in more striking forms the beauty and the energy of sympathy and helpfulness and counsel in their efforts to rectify wrong, alleviate suffering, and set the weak in the way of strength and hope. We have built up, moreover, a great system of government, which has stood through a long age as in many respects a model for those who seek to set liberty upon foundations that will endure against fortuitous change, against storm and accident. Our life contains every great thing, and contains it in rich abundance.

But the evil has come with the good, and much fine gold has been corroded. With riches has come inexcusable waste. We have squandered a great part of what we might have used, and have not stopped to conserve the exceeding bounty of nature, without which our genius for enterprise would have been worthless and impotent, scorning to be careful, shamefully prodigal as well as admirably efficient. We have been proud of our industrial achievements, but we have not hitherto stopped thoughtfully enough to count the human cost, the cost of lives snuffed out, of energies overtaxed and broken, the fearful physical and spiritual cost to the men and women and children upon whom the dead weight and burden of it all has fallen pitilessly the years through. The groans and agony of it all had not yet reached our ears, the solemn, moving undertone of our life, coming up out of the mines and factories and out of every home where the struggle had its intimate and familiar seat. With the great Government went many deep secret things which we too long delayed to look into and scrutinize with candid, fearless eyes. The great Government we loved has too often been made use of for private and selfish purposes, and those who used it had forgotten the people.

At last a vision has been vouchsafed us of our life as a whole. We see the bad with the good, the debased and decadent with the sound and vital. With this vision we approach new affairs. Our duty is to cleanse, to reconsider, to restore, to correct the evil without impairing the good, to purify and humanize every process of our common life without weakening or sentimentalizing it. There has been something crude and heartless and unfeeling in our haste to succeed and be great. Our thought has been "Let every man look out for himself, let every generation look out for itself," while we reared giant machinery which made it impossible that any but those who stood at the levers of control should have a chance to look out for themselves. We had not forgotten our morals. We remembered well enough that we had set up a policy which was meant to serve the humblest as well as the most powerful, with an eye single to the standards of justice and fair play, and remembered it with pride. But we were very heedless and in a hurry to be great.

We have come now to the sober second thought. The scales of heedlessness have fallen from our eyes. We have made up our minds to square every process of our national life again with the standards we so proudly set up at the beginning and have always carried at our hearts. Our work is a work of restoration.

We have itemized with some degree of particularity the things that ought to be altered and here are some of the chief items: A tariff which cuts us off from our proper part in the commerce of the world, violates the just principles of taxation, and makes the Government a facile instrument in the hands of private interests; a banking and currency system based upon the necessity of the Government to sell its bonds fifty years ago and perfectly adapted to concentrating cash and restricting credits; an industrial system which, take it on all its sides, financial as well as administrative, holds capital in leading strings, restricts the liberties and limits the opportunities of labor, and exploits without renewing or conserving the natural resources of the country; a body of agricultural activities never yet given the efficiency of great business undertakings or served as it should be through the instrumentality of science taken directly to the farm, or afforded the facilities of credit best suited to its practical needs; water-courses undeveloped, waste places unreclaimed, forests untended, fast disappearing without plan or prospect of renewal, unregarded waste heaps at every mine. We have studied as perhaps no other nation has the most effective means of production, but we have not studied cost or economy as we should either as organizers of industry, as statesmen, or as individuals.

Nor have we studied and perfected the means by which government may be put at the service of humanity, in safeguarding the health of the Nation, the health of its men and its women and its children, as well as their rights in the struggle for existence. This is no sentimental duty. The firm basis of government is justice, not pity. These are matters of justice. There can be no equality or opportunity, the first essential of justice in the body politic, if men and women and children be not shielded in their lives, their very vitality, from the consequences of great industrial and social processes which they can not alter, control, or singly cope with. Society must see to it that it does not itself crush or weaken or damage its own constituent parts. The first duty of law is to keep sound the society it serves. Sanitary laws, pure food laws, and laws determining conditions of labor which individuals are powerless to determine for themselves are intimate parts of the very business of justice and legal efficiency.

These are some of the things we ought to do, and not leave the others undone, the old-fashioned, never-to-be-neglected, fundamental safeguarding of property and of individal right. This is the high enterprise of the new day: To lift everything that concerns our life as a Nation to the light that shines from the hearthfire of every man's conscience and vision of the right. It is inconceivable that we should do this as partisans; it is inconceivable we should do it in ignorance of the facts as they are or in blind haste. We shall restore, not destroy. We shall deal with our economic system as it is and as it may be modified, not as it might be if we had a clean sheet of paper to write upon; and step by step we shall make it what it should be, in the spirit of those who question their own wisdom and seek counsel and knowledge, not shallow self-satisfaction or the excitement of excursions whither they can not tell. Justice, and only justice, shall always be our motto.

And yet it will be no cool process of mere science. The Nation has been deeply stirred, stirred by a solemn passion, stirred by the knowledge of wrong, of ideals lost, of government too often debauched and made an instrument of evil. The feelings with which we face this new age of right and opportunity sweep across our heartstrings like some air out of God's own presence, where justice and mercy are reconciled and the judge and the brother are one. We know our task to be no mere task of politics but a task which shall search us through and through, whether we be able to understand our time and the need of our people, whether we be indeed their spokesmen and interpreters, whether we have the pure heart to comprehend and the rectified will to choose our high course of action.

This is not a day of triumph; it is a day of dedication. Here muster, not the forces of party, but the forces of humanity. Men's hearts wait upon us; men's lives hang in the balance; men's hopes call upon us to say what we will do. Who shall live up to the great trust? Who dares fail to try? I summon all honest men, all patriotic, all forward-looking men, to my side. God helping me, I will not fail them, if they will but counsel and sustain me!

—WOODROW WILSON, First Inaugural Address, March 4, 1913

13. BROADENING THE COMMERCE POWER

The great depression of the early thirties brought an insistent demand that the Federal Government step in with a program of relief and recovery; we shall see something of the nature of that program when we come to our chapter on the welfare state. Confident that the con-stitutional powers of the Federal Government were adequate to deal with the emergency, President Roosevelt pushed through Congress a whole series of far-reaching acts designed to strengthen the national economy. Some of these appeared to invade fields heretofore thought sacred to the States, and thus raised interesting constitutional questions. A series of Supreme Court decisions—the Schechter case, the Carter case, the Railroad Retirement Board case, and the Butler case—denied the authority of the Federal Government over broad fields of labor, transportation, the coal industry, and agriculture. These decisions were based on what Justice Stone called "a tortured construction" of the Constitution. Under the impact of Roosevelt's judiciary reform bill, and of public opinion, the strict constructionists on the Court resigned, and thus permitted the Court to return to the great Marshall-Story tradition of constitutionalism. Perhaps the most dramatic evidence of that return was the Court opinion in the Jones and Laughlin case—an opinion sustaining the constitutionality of the National Labor Relations Act.

HUGHES, C. J. In a proceeding under the National Labor Rela-tions Act of 1935, the National Labor Relations Board found that the petitioner, Jones & Laughlin Steel Corporation, had violated the Act by engaging in unfair labor practices affecting commerce. . . .

The National Labor Relations Board, sustaining the charge, ordered the corporation to cease and desist from such discrimination and coercion. . . .

Contesting the ruling of the Board, the respondent argues (1) that the Act is in reality a regulation of labor relations and not of interstate commerce; (2) that the Act can have no application to the respondent's relations with its production employees because they are not subject to regulation by the federal government; and (3) that the provisions of the Act violate Section 2 of Article III and the Fifth and Seventh Amendments of the Constitution of the United States.

The facts as to the nature and scope of the business of the Jones & Laughlin Steel Corporation have been found by the Labor Board and, so far as they are essential to the determination of this controversy, they are not in dispute. The Labor Board has found: The corporation is organized under the laws of Pennsylvania and has its principal office at Pittsburgh. It is engaged in the business of manufacturing iron and steel in plants situated in Pittsburgh and nearby Aliquippa, Pennsylvania. It manufactures and distributes a widely diversified line of steel and pig iron, being the fourth largest producer of steel in the United States. With its subsidiaries—nineteen in number—it is a completely integrated enterprise, owning and operating ore, coal and limestone properties, lake and river transportation facilities and terminal railroads located at its manufacturing plants. It owns or controls mines in Michigan and Minnesota. It operates four ore steamships on the Great Lakes, used in the transportation of ore to its factories. It owns coal mines in Pennsylvania. It operates tow-boats and steam barges used in carrying coal to its factories. It owns limestone properties in various places in Pennsylvania and West Virginia: It owns the Monongahela connecting railroad which connects the plants of the Pittsburgh works and forms an interconnection with the Pennsylvania, New York Central and Baltimore and Ohio Railroad systems. It owns the Aliquippa and Southern Railroad Company which connects the Aliquippa works with the Pittsburgh and Lake Erie, part of the New York Central system. Much of its product is shipped to its warehouses in Chicago, Detroit, Cincinnati and Memphis,—to the last two places by means of its own barges and transportation equipment. In Long Island City, New York, and in New Orleans it operates structural steel fabricating shops in connection with the warehousing of semi-finished materials sent from its works. Through one of its wholly-owned subsidiaries it owns, leases and operates stores, warehouses and yards for the distribution of equipment and supplies for drilling and operating oil and gas mills and for pipe lines, refineries and pumping stations. It has sales offices in twenty cities in the United States and a wholly-owned subsidiary which is devoted exclusively to distributing its product in Canada. Approximately 75 per cent. of its product is shipped out of Pennsylvania.

Summarizing these operations, the Labor Board concluded that the works in Pittsburgh and Aliquippa "might be likened to the heart of a self-contained, highly integrated body. They draw in the raw materials from Michigan, Minnesota, West Virginia, Pennsylvania in part through arteries and by means controlled by the respondent; they transform the materials and then pump them out to all parts of the nation through the vast mechanism which the respondent has elaborated."

To carry on the activities of the entire steel industry, 33,000 men mine ore, 44,000 men mine coal, 4,000 men quarry limestone, 16,000 men manufacture coke, 343,000 men manufacture steel, and 83,000 men transport its product. Respondent has about 10,000 employees in its Aliquippa plant, which is located in a community of about 30,000 persons. . . .

First. The scope of the Act.—The Act is challenged in its entirety as an attempt to regulate all industry, thus invading the reserved powers of the States over their local concerns. It is asserted that the references in the Act to interstate and foreign commerce are colorable at best; that the Act is not a true regulation of such commerce or of matters which directly affect it but on the contrary has the fundamental object of placing under the compulsory supervision of the federal government all industrial labor relations within the nation. The argument seeks support in the broad words of the preamble and in the sweep of the provisions of the Act, and it is further insisted that its legislative history shows an essential universal purpose in the light of which its scope cannot be limited by either construction or by the application of the separability clause.

If this conception of terms, intent and consequent inseparability were sound, the Act would necessarily fall by reason of the limitation upon the federal power which inheres in the constitutional grant. . . . The authority of the federal government may not be pushed to such an extreme as to destroy the distinction, which the commerce clause itself establishes, between commerce "among the several States" and the internal concerns of a State. That distinction between what is national and what is local in the activities of commerce is vital to the maintenance of our federal system.

But we are not at liberty to deny effect to specific provisions, which

Congress has constitutional power to enact, by superimposing upon them inferences from general legislative declarations of an ambiguous character, even if found in the same statute. . . .

The grant of authority to the Board does not purport to extend to the relationship between all industrial employees and employers. Its terms do not impose collective bargaining upon all industry regardless of effects upon interstate or foreign commerce. It purports to reach only what may be deemed to burden or obstruct that commerce and, thus qualified, it must be construed as contemplating the exercise of control within constitutional bounds. It is the effect upon commerce, not the source of the injury, which is the criterion. Whether or not particular action does affect commerce in such a close and intimate fashion as to be subject to federal control, and hence to lie within the authority conferred upon the Board, is left by the statute to be determined as individual cases arise. We are thus to inquire whether in the instant case the constitutional boundary has been passed. . . .

Third. The application of the Act to employees engaged in production.—The principle involved.—Respondent says that whatever may be said of employees engaged in interstate commerce, the industrial relations and activities in the manufacturing department of respondent's enterprise are not subject to federal regulation. The argument rests upon the proposition that manufacturing in itself is not commerce.

The Government distinguishes these cases. The various parts of respondent's enterprise are described as interdependent and as thus involving "a great movement of iron ore, coal and limestone along well-defined paths to the steel mills, thence through them, and thence in the form of steel products into the consuming centers of the country—a definite and well-understood course of business." It is urged that these activities constitute a "stream" or "flow" of commerce, of which the Aliquippa manufacturing plant is the focal point, and that industrial strife at that point would cripple the entire movement. Reference is made to our decision sustaining the Packers and Stockyards Act. The Court found that the stockyards were but a "throat" through which the current of commerce flowed and the transactions which there occurred could not be separated from that movement.

Respondent contends that the instant case presents material distinctions.

We do not find it necessary to determine whether these features of defendant's business dispose of the asserted analogy to the "stream of commerce" cases. The congressional authority to protect interstate commerce from burdens and obstructions is not limited to transactions which can be deemed to be an essential part of a "flow" of interstate or foreign commerce. Burdens and obstructions may be due to injurious action springing from other sources. The fundamental principle is that the power to regulate commerce is the power to enact "all appropriate legislation" for "its protection and advancement"; to adopt measures "to promote its growth and insure its safety"; "to foster, protect, control and restrain." That power is plenary and may be exerted to protect interstate commerce "no matter what the source of the dangers which threaten it." Although activities may be intrastate in character when separately considered, if they have such a close and substantial relation to interstate commerce that their control is essential or appropriate to protect that commerce from burdens and obstructions, Congress cannot be denied the power to exercise that control. Undoubtedly the scope of this power must be considered in the light of our dual system of government and may not be extended so as to embrace effects upon interstate commerce so indirect and remote that to embrace them, in view of our complex society, would effectually obliterate the distinction between what is national and what is local and create a completely centralized government. The question is necessarily one of degree.

That intrastate activities, by reason of close and intimate relation to interstate commerce, may fall within federal control is demonstrated in the case of carriers who are engaged in both interstate and intrastate transportation. There federal control has been found essential to secure the freedom of interstate traffic from interference or unjust discrimination and to promote the efficiency of the interstate service. . . .

The close and intimate effect which brings the subject within the reach of federal power may be due to activities in relation to productive industry although the industry when separately viewed is local. This has been abundantly illustrated in the application of the federal Anti-Trust Act.

Upon the same principle, the Anti-Trust Act has been applied to the conduct of employees engaged in production.

It is thus apparent that the fact that the employees here concerned were engaged in production is not determinative. The question remains as to the effect upon interstate commerce of the labor practice involved.
—CHIEF JUSTICE CHARLES EVANS HUGHES, Opinion in N.L.R.B.
v. Jones & Laughlin Steel Corporation, 1937.

14. "THE OBSOLESCENCE OF FEDERALISM"

Federalism developed in an age when economy was essentially local and when, therefore, local authorities were best fitted to deal with most problems of government. Thus, in the eighteenth century, it seemed entirely proper to leave to the local authorities such matters as agriculture, labor, education, health and sanitation, roads, the conservation of forest and of soil, and so forth. But with the Industrial Revolution and the growth of a national economy, all this changed. Localities and States were no longer competent to cope with problems that were national in character, or to deal with corporations richer and more powerful than many individual States. Thus it was impossible to argue, in the mid-twentieth century, that such things as child labor, or coal mining, or soil conservation, or farm prices, or water-power development, were purely local, and it was becoming increasingly difficult to maintain that such matters as education and public health were of local concern only. Viewing the implacable growth of a centralized economy, with a handful of billion-dollar corporations controlling a major part of industry, finance, transportation and utilities, and noting, too, the increasing importance of national defense, many students concluded that Federalism had had its day, and that the time had come to give the national government broad authority over the whole field of economy and society. One of the most persuasive arguments for this came from the Englishman, Harold Laski, a political philosopher who had long made the United States the object of his particular attention.

NO ONE can travel the length and breadth of the United States without the conviction of its inexpugnable variety. East and West, South and North, its regions are real and different, and each has problems real and different too. The temptation is profound to insist that here, if ever, is the classic place for a federal experiment. Union without unity—except in the Soviet Union and China, has variety ever so fully invited the implications of the famous definition? Geography, climate, culture, all of them seem to have joined their forces to insist

302

that, wherever centralization is appropriate, here, at least, it has no meaning. Tradition demands its absence; history has prohibited its coming. The large unit, as in Lamennais' phrase, would result in apoplexy at the center and anemia at the extremities. Imposed solutions from a distant Washington, blind, as it must be blind, to the subtle minutiae of local realities, cannot solve the ultimate problems that are in dispute. A creative America must be a federal America. The wider the powers exercised from Washington, the more ineffective will be the capacity for creative administration. Regional wisdom is the clue to the American future. The power to govern must go where that regional wisdom resides. So restrained, men learn by the exercise of responsibility the art of progress. They convince themselves by experiment from below. To fasten a uniformity that is not in nature upon an America destined to variety is to destroy the prospect of an ultimate salvation.

This kind of argument is familiar in a hundred forms. I believe that, more than any other philosophic pattern, it is responsible for the malaise of American democracy. My plea here is for the recognition that the federal form of state is unsuitable to the stage of economic and social development that America has reached. I infer from this postulate two conclusions: first, that the present division of powers, however liberal be the Supreme Court in its technique of interpretation, is inadequate to the needs America confronts; and, second, that any revision of those powers is one which must place in Washington, and Washington only, the power to amend that revision as circumstances change. I infer, in a word, that the epoch of federalism is over, and that only a centralized system can effectively confront the problems of a new time.

To continue with the old pattern, in the age of giant capitalism, is to strike into impotence that volume of governmental power which is necessary to deal with the issues giant capitalism has raised. Federalism, I suggest, is the appropriate governmental technique for an expanding capitalism, in which the price of local habit—which means, also, local delay—admits of compensation in the total outcome. But a contracting capitalism cannot afford the luxury of federalism. It is insufficiently positive in character; it does not provide for sufficient rapidity of action; it inhibits the emergence of necessary standards of uniformity; it relies upon compacts and compromises which take insufficient account of the urgent category of time; it leaves the backward areas a restraint, at once parasitic and poisonous, on those which seek to move forward; not least, its psychological results, especially in an age of crisis, are depressing to a democracy that needs the drama of positive achievement to retain its faith. . . .

Giant capitalism has, in effect, concentrated the control of economic power in a small proportion of the American people. It has built a growing contrast between the distribution of that economic power and the capacity of the political democracy effectively to control the results of its exercise. It has transcended the political boundaries of the units in the American federation so as to make them largely ineffective as areas of independent government. Whether we take the conditions of labor, the level of taxation, the standards of education, public health, or the supply of amenities like housing and recreation, it has become clear that the true source of decision is no longer at the circumference, but at the center, of the state. For forty-eight separate units to seek to compete with the integrated power of giant capitalism is to invite defeat in every element of social life where approximate uniformity of condition is the test of the good life.

The poor state is parasitic on the body politic. It offers privileges to giant capitalism to obtain its taxable capacity, offers escape from the impositions of rich states, in order to wrest from the wealthy some poor meed of compensation for its backwardness. It dare not risk offending the great industrial empires—cotton, coal, iron and steel, tobacco—lest it lose the benefits of their patronage. Their vested interests thus begin to define the limits within which the units of the federation may venture to move. And since the division of powers limits, in its turn, the authority of the federal government to intervene—the latter being a government of limited powers—it follows that the great industrial empires can, in fact, prevent the legislation necessary to implement the purposes of a democratic society. The situation may, briefly, be summarized by saying that the Constitution inhibits the federal government from exercising the authority inherent in the idea of a democracy; while the risk to a state government of attack upon the conditions exacted by those industrial empires for their patronage is too great to permit the states to jeopardize what they have by issuing challenge. Whether, therefore, it be the hours of labor, the standards of health and housing, the effective organization of the trade unions, at every point the formal powers of the states are rarely commensurate with the actual authority they may venture to exercise. And it is the common citizen of the United States who pays the price of that margin between formal and effective power.

Political systems live by the results they can obtain for the great mass of their citizens. A democracy is not likely to survive on formal grounds merely; it will survive as it is able to convince its citizens that it adequately protects their powers to satisfy the expectations they deem their experience to warrant. In the present phase of American capitalist democracy, the central government largely lacks the power to implement the ends it is essential it should serve if its democratic context is to be maintained. It cannot obtain adequate standards of government in many of the major fields it seeks to enter. It is hamstrung, partly by the division of powers from which it derives its authority; partly because the Constitution has not enabled it to develop the instrumentalities essential to the purposes it must seek to fulfill. Its effort to obtain the proper recognition of collective bargaining may be stricken into impotence by a state law against picketing. Its effort to produce proper control of public utilities may be rendered vain by local franchises granted in a period when the recognition of the need for uniformity in this field had not dawned upon the public consciousness. So, also, with conservation; with the provision of adequate educational opportunity; with the effective prohibition (a commonplace of any well-ordered state) of child labor; with the coördination of relief for unemployment; with public works, especially in the utilization of the possible sources of electric power; with public-health legislation, not least in the field of maternity and child hygiene; with a proper policy of public roads—witness the breakdown of federal-state cooperation in Arkansas in 1923, in Kansas in 1926 and Maine in 1929; with a proper policy in housing. I take examples only. The central point of my argument is the simple one that in every major field of social regulation, the authority of which the federal government can dispose is utterly inadequate to the issues it is expected to solve.

I do not think this argument is invalidated by the rise of cooperation between the federal government and the states, or between groups of states. . . .

My argument is the very different one: that (a) there are certain objects of administrative control now left to the states for which they are no longer suitable units of regulation. Economic centralization makes necessary at least minimum standards of uniform performance in these objects, e.g., health, education, unemployment relief; and in others, e.g., labor conditions, railroad rates, electric power, complete federal control without interference by the states; and (b) that the proper objects of federal supervision cannot any longer be dependent upon state consent. Where this dependency exists, state consent will be, in its turn, largely controlled by giant capitalism. That is why Delaware is merely a pseudonym of the du Ponts, and Montana little more than a symbol of the Anaconda Copper Corporation. That is why the people of the state of Washington, who ought long ago to have been permitted to have the advantage of the municipal electric-power plant of Seattle, still suffer from the division of its potential benefits through the survival of the Puget Sound Light and Power Company.

Nor would the problem be met if, instead of the states, America were divided, as writers like Professor Howard Odum suggest, into regions more correspondent with the economic realities of the situation. If America were to consist of seven or nine regions, instead of forty-eight states, that would still leave unsolved the main issues if they operated upon the basis of the present division of powers, and if their consent were necessary to any fundamental change in that division. Once again, it must be emphasized that the unity which giant capitalism postulates in the economic sphere postulates a corresponding unity in the conference of political powers upon the federal government. There is no other way, up to a required minimum, in which the questions of taxation, labor relations and conditions, conservation, public utilities (in the widest sense), to take examples only, can be met. . . .

The view here urged, of course, looks toward a fundamental reconstruction of traditional American institutions. It is not impressed by the view, associated with the great name of Mr. Justice Brandeis, that the "curse of bigness" will descend upon any serious departure from the historic contours of federalism. The small unit of government is impotent against the big unit of giant capitalism. It may be that the very power of giant capitalism is no longer of itself compatible with the maintenance of a democratic political structure in society; there is much evidence to support this view. What, at least, is certain is this: that a government the powers of which are not commensurate with its problems will not be able to cope with them. Either, therefore, it must obtain those powers, or it must yield to a form of state more able to satisfy the demands that it encounters. That is the supreme issue before the United States today; and the more closely it is scrutinized the more obviously does its resolution seem to be bound up with the obsolescence of the federal system.

For that system presents the spectacle of forty-nine governments seeking to deal with issues for many of which they are inappropriate as instrumentalities whether in the area they cover or in the authority they may invoke. They are checked and balanced upon a theory of the state completely outmoded in the traditional ends upon which its postulates are based. Giant industry requires a positive state; federalism, in its American form, is geared to vital negations which contradict the implications of positivism. Giant industry requires uniformities in the field of its major influence; American federalism is the inherent foe, both in time and space, of those necessary uniformities. Giant industry, not least, requires the opposition of a unified public will to counteract its tendency to undemocratic procedure through the abuse of power; a federal system of the American kind dissipates the unity of public opinion in those fields where it is most urgently required. And, above all, it is urgent to note that giant industry, in an age of economic contraction, is able to exploit the diversities of a federal scheme, through the delays they permit in the attainment of uniformity, to reactionary ends. Thereby, they discredit the democratic process at a time when it is least able to afford that discredit. For, thereby, the confidence of the citizen body in its power to work out democratic solutions of its problems is gravely undermined.

Men who are deprived of faith by inability to attain results they greatly desire do not long remain content with the institutions under which they live. The price of democracy is the power to satisfy living demands. American federalism, in its traditional form, cannot keep pace with the tempo of the life giant capitalism has evolved. To judge it in terms of its historic success is to misconceive the criteria by which it becomes valid for the present and the future. No political system has the privilege of immortality; and there is no moment so fitting for the consideration of its remaking as that which permits of reconstruction with the prospect of a new era of creative achievement.

—Harold J. Laski, "The Obsolescence of Federalism," 1939

15. CENTRAL POLICY AND LOCAL ADMINISTRATION

Federal centralization dates from the 1880's—from the beginnings of immigration legislation, the Civil Service Commission, the Interstate Commerce Commission and, in 1890, the first anti-trust law. But it is in the last quarter-century that the Federal Government has been called upon to exercise more and more authority, that the Civil Service has grown by the hundred thousand, and that Federal appropriations—even nonmilitary appropriations—have mounted to over ten billions of dollars. Is it possible to have Big Government without developing a rigid bureaucracy, without losing the advantages of initiative and diversity, without drying up democracy at the grass roots? Opinion here is sharply divided. There are some who feel, rather inconsistently, that Federal centralization is bad per se, and that no good can come out of Washington. There are others who feel that Federal centralization is bound to increase in order to keep pace with an increasingly centralized economy, and that discussion of the pros and cons is therefore merely academic. In between stand those who, like the distinguished Chairman of the TVA and the Atomic Energy Commission, argue for centralized control of policy with local administration. After all, they feel, the TVA experiment has proved that a Federal enterprise locally administered can actually strengthen State and local governments and communities.

DEMOCRACY, to be truly responsive to our aspirations for individual freedom, must increasingly develop and nourish and strengthen local institutions of government. Few precepts of American life are more deeply felt than this.

In actual practice, however, this policy has given way to a tendency that is its very opposite; an unbroken, and to me disquieting, increase in centralization of administration in Washington.

Here is a direct contradiction between the way we want our institutions of government to function, and the way in fact they do function. Some of those who bear responsibility for this weakening of democracy are unaware of the effect of what they are doing. Others, however, defenders or apologists for the trend, assert that centralized control by Congress and by the administrators in Washington cannot be avoided. Some public administrators and experts in government appear to be now in the process of seeking to persuade the American people that Big Government is inevitable.

I deny that Big Government is inevitable. I assert that there is a workable alternative, and that we should pursue that alternative to ever bigger Big Government. There is no wave of the future before which the American people and their great heritage of localized democracy are powerless.

To judge by what people say on this subject there is hardly anyone in private or public life who is in favor of what is taking place. And yet it goes right on, and at an accelerated pace. Surely this is a curious situation. Some of the most outspoken opponents of centralization I know (judging by their speeches) propose or support legislative controls or appropriation "riders" that make Washington control ever tighter. As a consequence one more prospect for genuine decentralization of Federal administration is dimmed or killed. By the same act they turn their back on still another opportunity to delegate to local, state, or Federal regional agencies functions that need not be and should not be administered by Washington bureaus nor controlled by the Federal Congress.

Federal aid to education provides an important illustration. There is almost universal *verbal* assent to the proposition that Federal financial support to education should avoid any trace of control from the Congress and the Federal departments in Washington.

But what has actually happened? The evidence is unmistakable that during the past twenty years (with support from both political parties), the trend has been in the other direction, and continues in that direction today.

The land grant college system, with its origin back in Lincoln's administration, provided the country a tested pattern whereby local and state institutions concerned with education could appropriately and productively receive Federal funds without the Congress and the Washington executive agencies sticking their fingers into education. Under one guise or another, however, the land grant college principle and practice has been steadily weakened. An opportunity for further decentralization in education has been lost. The new policy of Federal financial aid to the school systems of the states makes this recent history all the more a matter of practical and immediate concern. . . .

Just what is the basis of the argument that Big Government is inevitable, and ever greater Washington control inescapable?

The stream of dialectics begins with a full agreement that "of course" everyone desires strong, dynamic local government in the communities and in the states of the United States. The Big Government apologists never question that proposition. We are told that these are "fine ideals" —the ideal of home rule, the ideal of a flourishing community and state government. Following close upon this disarming prelude, however, it is said that the complexities of modern living make this older ideal merely nostalgic. Our technical society, so they say, has made it obsolete and unworkable. The airplane, the telegraph, the telephone, swift transportation both within the United States and throughout the world make it regrettably necessary that the older ideal give way to the facts of modern life. Over and over again the story is repeated of the complex interrelation, the intricacies, the interdependence of American life. The nation has be⁻ me a most complex fabric quite beyond the comprehension of the ordinary citizen, a fabric no longer separable, and hence national in its every aspect. What happens in Sacramento, California, affects a transaction in Portland, Maine, and so on. The thesis is too familiar to require repetition.

Generally speaking this is all true enough. But the conclusion that is drawn from this familiar picture is that since virtually every governmental problem has become a national problem, therefore every phase of government action must inevitably be administered nationally from Washington. Since—so the argument runs—local administration or state administration is obviously impossible where national interrelation is so complete, therefore Big Government is inevitable. We are told, in short, that Big Government is the price that must be paid for the wonderful technical development of this nation.

Those who have resigned themselves to this idea rarely defend centralization; they deplore it. They admit that remote administration from Washington is not desirable. They will even agree that the withdrawal of more and more decisions out of local communities and out of the state into Congress and into bureaus in Washington is unfortunate and corrodes our democratic institutions. They say however, that we must bow our heads before the inevitable trend toward centralization, because the nation has developed technically to such a point that centralized administration is the only means whereby a complex modern national economy can be governed. It is that or chaos. They assert that we must trust our legislators and administrators in Washington with more and more power of decision and control, with better and better tools of government. Why? Is it so that those in Washington may reverse this unwholesome trend, so they may decentralize and delegate to the agencies of the states and the communities? Not at all. It is so that these central government administrators may make centralization of administration more effective and efficient—more nearly uniform in its nationwide applications.

In any such discussion as this an important distinction has to be made. It is not new, but it is one that is often overlooked. It is the distinction between a national policy and central administration of that policy.

It is obvious that many problems that once could be dealt with as a matter of local or state policy now definitely require a national policy, determined through Congressional action. Problems once predominantly local in their scope and effect now have repercussions on other parts of the country—and the whole world for that matter—that did not exist in an earlier stage in our development. These often require the enunciation of a national policy and expenditure of Federal funds.

But because the central government through the Congress must and should determine upon a national policy in a particular field, it does not by any means follow that *the administration of that policy* must necessarily also be on a nationwide basis. This distinction between a centralized or national policy and the decentralized or localized administration of that national policy, is a distinction of fundamental importance. It is, moreover, a distinction the apologists of Big Government so frequently and persistently overlook. It is a distinction which unless observed and respected by corrective action in the way of decentralized administration of national policies can lead to the progressive atrophy of most local and state governmental functions.

The distinction between authority and its administration is a vital one. For a long time all of us—administrators, citizens, and legislators—have been none too clear on this point. We have assumed that, as new powers were granted to the government with its seat at Washington, these powers therefore must also be administered from Washington. We have taken it for granted that the price of Federal action was a top-heavy, cumbersome administration. Clearly this is not true. The problem is to divorce the two ideas of authority and administration of authority.

Effective techniques of decentralization—not better ways to centralize—should claim our first attention. The very first question we should ask ourselves is: "Why cannot these Federal activities be decentralized; if not in whole, why not in part?" The problem of first concern we must ever keep in mind is: Does this or that Federal program really have to be centralized and to what extent? Here is the real job to which our students and experts in public administration and our members of Congress should address themselves. It is a continuing, day-by-day task requiring the focus of administrative and legislative attention upon every opportunity for decentralization as it comes along.

The TVA is a concrete demonstration that ways and means can be devised to decentralize the administration of many of the functions of the central government. Indeed, one of the public's chief interests in TVA these days is as practical, living proof that despite the interrelation of our vast country, despite the need for national policy on many matters heretofore local, the actual carrying out of those national policies can effectively be placed in the hands of local community and state agencies and instrumentalities. TVA's methods of decentralized administration may well prove to be the most important single product of the experiment in the Tennessee Valley.

The TVA, a public development corporation, is an agency of the central government. It was created by Congress. Its charter is a national charter. Its responsibilities and its powers derive from national powers defined in the Constitution of the United States. The responsibility of TVA, as defined by Congress, is to develop or aid the people of the Valley to develop and to utilize their natural resources in a region of substantial size, embracing parts of seven states of the Southeast. These functions and these responsibilities for natural resources and their development are in general, and taken one by one, familiar and long-time responsibilities and functions of the Federal government. They deal with navigation, flood control, electric power, the problems of our soils and forests, and research.

These are characteristic Federal functions. Nevertheless in virtually every aspect of the TVA's activities, TVA's management has found it possible to carry out such clearly Federal functions and policies through the medium of local community or state agencies and instrumentalities.

TVA is decentralized in more than one sense. First, it is a Federal corporation directed not from Washington but from the Tennessee Valley. It is not incorporated within any Washington bureau or department. This is the first step of its decentralization.

But there are other steps, made possible by the first, but of even greater importance. The TVA has by persistent effort delegated and thereby decentralized its functions so that most of them are carried out *not by Federal employees at all*, but by local and state personnel. . . .

It seems to me however that as against the folly of centralized administration the risks involved in delegations and agreements with state and local agencies seem clearly preferable. Indeed, are not these risks implicit in our democratic faith?

Nor should we overlook the deeper question of how we can help our state and local government gain in competence and in capacity. Surely we should not encourage state and local governments to escape from their duties or abdicate their responsibilities to Big Government, for this is a process that perpetuates whatever are the local weaknesses.

To turn administration of localized problems over to Washington on the ground that thus we escape the inefficiencies and political shenanigans of state and local communities, is nonsense. It merely transfers the political pressures from local into Federal political channels. Moreover, centralization to avoid unsavory local influences surely deprives the people of the chance to draw their issues locally and to clean up their own local inadequacies. The fundamental solution is to crowd more, not less responsibility into the community. Only as the consequences of administrational errors become more localized, can we expect citizens to know which rabbit to shoot.

Overcentralized administration is not something simply to be made more palatable, more efficient, and better managed. It is a hazard to democracy. It is a hazard to freedom. Centralization at the national capital or in a business undertaking always glorifies the importance of pieces of paper. This dims the sense of reality. As men and organizations acquire a preoccupation with papers, they become less understanding, less perceptive of the reality of those matters with which they should be dealing: particular human problems, particular human beings, actual things in a real America—highways, wheat, barges, drought, floods, backyards, blast furnaces. The facts with which a highly centralized institution deals tend to be the men and women of that institution itself, and their ideas and ambitions. To maintain perspective and human understanding in the atmosphere of centralization is a task that many able and conscientious people have found well-nigh impossible.

Many administrators recognize this simple truth. But we are so prone to accept Big Government, to improve and refine it at the center to the sad neglect of the periphery where the people live and work, that the Federal administrator who tries to reverse the trend is hailed as the exception to the rule. I cite one noteworthy illustration—there are many more. The Secretary of the Interior, Hon. J. A. Krug, has urged the creation of a decentralized regional agency, to aid in the unified development of the Columbia River Valley. In explaining the decentralizing consequences of this proposal Secretary Krug has said: "Final decisions would be made here in the Northwest instead of in my Department in Washington. I would like to give up some of my power and authority exercised at Washington and see it exercised here." In such a spirit of self-imposed restraint among administrators and in Congress lies the road to a workable alternative to Big Government.

Big Government will get bigger and more highly centralized unless there is a conscious, continuous, creative administrative and legislative effort to reverse the trend. The community's impulse to hand its local problems over piecemeal to one remote agency after another, feeds this hazardous push toward Big Government. The surrender of local responsibility for a part of the community's function generates further local weaknesses which furnish the reason for yet another surrender. Local communities and state governments can help by resisting these temptations to take the easy way out. They can help the administrators of Federal programs to work out the methods of decentralization case by case.

Those who believe devoutly in the democratic process should be the first to urge the use of methods that will keep the administration of national functions from becoming so concentrated at the national capital, so distant from the everyday life of ordinary people as to wither and deaden the average citizen's sense of participation and partnership in government affairs. For it is this citizen participation that nourishes the strength of a democracy.

—David E. Lilienthal, *This I Do Believe,* 1949

⋙ 7 ⋘

The Welfare State
and Rugged Individualism

In his First Inaugural Address Jefferson summed up good government. What was it? "A wise and frugal government which shall restrain men from injuring one another, shall leave them otherwise free to regulate their own pursuits of industry and improvement, and shall not take from the mouth of labor the bread it has earned." A little more than a century later, those who counted themselves disciples and followers of Jefferson were championing farm subsidies, minimum wages, government operation of hydroelectric power, social security, and similar programs that, collectively, go by the term "welfare state." If this is a paradox, how is it to be explained?

Let us look first at the basis for the Jeffersonian faith in the ability of the individual to fend for himself and the Jeffersonian fear of government. Both were based upon realities, both upon historical experience. In the America of 1800, men were, for the most part, able to take care of themselves. The country was surpassingly rich, and land was to be had almost for the taking. There was little poverty and no unemployment. The new nation was wonderfully fortunate. There was no standing army to support, no established church to maintain, no idle aristocracy to subsidize. There was little for government to do, and much that men individually and collectively could do for themselves, especially men as virtuous and enlightened as the Americans of that generation appeared to be.

History re-enforced the lessons that Nature inculcated. Americans themselves had never known governmental tyranny in any direct sense, but they had had—so at least they thought—a horrid warning of what it might mean under George III, and they had fought a revolution to be free from tyrannical government. As the Fathers of the Revolution read

315

history, it taught one grand and solemn lesson: that all government tends to tyranny, that no government is to be trusted, and that government is best that governs least.

The lessons of Nature and of history were translated into constitutional doctrines. So determined were Americans to safeguard against tyranny that they created governments checked and balanced and limited in every conceivable way. There were the limits of written constitutions, of a federal system, of separation of powers, of bicameral legislatures, of executive vetoes, and others as well; we will see something of the significance of all this in our chapter on liberty and order.

In a sense, much of this was misleading or irrelevant. Fear of government, for example, was misleading, for in a democracy men did not need to fear government. After all they were the government. A complex system of checks and balances was in a sense misleading. It assumed that the business of government was purely negative whereas in fact the business of government was positive. It assumed that government was a compartmentalized thing, whereas in fact government was a unit. Even the abounding richness of Nature was in a sense misleading—certainly the sense of infinity was. Jefferson said there would be land enough forever, but the best land was gone in a hundred years, and more and more the natural resources of the nation fell into the hands of small privileged groups or corporations.

As an agrarian order was transformed into an industrial one, as cities grew at the expense of the country, as millions of immigrants poured into the nation, as the control over industry, banking, railroads, mines, oil fields, communications became more and more concentrated in the hands of a few corporate directors, the old generalizations about government leaving men to regulate their own pursuits became meaningless. "Of what purpose to intone the old litanies?" said Henry Demarest Lloyd as he contemplated the Standard Oil Company.

Yet the old litanies were still intoned. And soon new voices were added to the chorus—voices from overseas. For just as the shibboleths of private enterprise were wearing thin, they were re-enforced by the teachings of those whom, for want of a better name, we call the Social Darwinists. These applied to the realm of politics and economy the doctrine of the survival of the fittest. Leave Nature alone, they said, and in the long run she will produce the ideal adaptation to environment. Just as Nature produced an ideal in the biological field, so she will produce an ideal in the field of politics or of economy or of society.

A curious amalgam, then, of Jeffersonian liberalism, pioneer individualism, and Social Darwinism, hardened into a philosophy of *laissez faire*. And this philosophy, in turn, was taken over by leading statesmen like Grover Cleveland and Herbert Hoover, by businessmen like Carnegie and Rockefeller, by jurists like Justice Field and Justice Sutherland.

At the same time a very different tradition and a very different philosophy persisted and this, too, traced back to Jefferson. For while it is true that Jefferson feared government, it is equally true that he feared concentrations of financial or commercial interest, and feared, above all, a combination of government and special economic interests. While it is true that he had great confidence in the ability of the individual to fend for himself, it is equally true that he had confidence in the individual only if the individual was free and equal—free from restraint, free from fear, free from oppression, free in mind as in body.

So good Jeffersonians found it entirely possible and even logical to demand that government intervene to protect men and women against giant corporations, against conditions over which they had no control whatsoever. Good Jeffersonians did not hesitate to support programs of government intervention—even of government welfare. Jefferson himself had advocated a liberal land grant policy—certainly a manifestation of the welfare state—and government support to education. The fundamental principle of Jeffersonianism was not, after all, a doctrinaire fear of government, but a passion for democracy and for freedom and thus for all of those things which make for effective democracy and effective freedom.

By the close of the nineteenth century the *laissez faire* principles were too palpably the servants of privileged interests to go unchallenged. They were challenged philosophically by men like Henry George and Edward Bellamy and Lester Ward. They were challenged in politics by leaders like Weaver and Altgeld, Bryan and Theodore Roosevelt, and eventually by Woodrow Wilson. They were challenged in the arena of law by jurists like Oliver Wendell Holmes and Louis Brandeis.

The debate persisted and raged, all through the first half of the twentieth century, but in somewhat changed form. By the time of Woodrow Wilson the principle of the welfare state had been all but universally accepted; the actual issue was on the matter of degree rather than of principle. How far should the welfare state go? How far could it go without drying up private initiative or injuring local enterprise? A grand climacteric in the struggle came in 1928-32, and ended with the triumph of the New Deal. That triumph was re-enacted in successive elections. Yet the full nature of the triumph is not to be read in the election returns, but rather in two other factors: first, the fact that after 1936 Republican platforms adopted the New Deal program almost in toto, and second, the fact that after 1936 the Supreme Court abandoned its Spencerian position and accepted the principle of governmental authority in the economic realm.

We give here a series of sources and documents designed to illustrate the centuries-long debate over these principles of government abstinence and government action. Some are Presidential statements; some are judicial opinions; some are campaign documents; some are philosophical essays. Yet they all fall into a common pattern, and it is a pattern that we will do well to study today.

1. TRUE AND FALSE PRINCIPLES OF ECONOMY IN THE BAY COLONY

The English economy in the sixteenth and seventeenth centuries, as Justice Waite pointed out in his famous opinion in Munn *versus* Illinois, *was one in many respects closely controlled by the state. The principle that the state should regulate wages, prices, services, and other aspects of economy was inherited by the Puritans and re-enforced by the teachings of religion. The New World environment, however, was not favorable to the maintenance of rigid controls, and there were many who, like the hapless Robert Keaine of this account, revolted against them. Perhaps the most interesting passage in this account of the censure passed on Keaine is the argument on his behalf "because all men through the country, in sale of cattle, corn, labor, etc., were guilty of the like excess in prices." Keaine was not only fined one hundred pounds—a fine the equivalent of at least a thousand dollars today—but admonished by the church.*

NOVEMBER 9, 1639. At a general court holden at Boston, great complaint was made of the oppression used in the country in sale of foreign commodities; and Mr. Robert Keaine, who kept a shop in Boston, was notoriously above others observed and complained of; and, being convented, he was charged with many particulars; in some, for taking above six-pence in the shilling profit; in some above eight-pence; and in some small things, above two for one. . . . The cry of the country was so great against oppression, and some of the elders and magistrates had declared such detestation of the corrupt practice of this man (which was the more observable, because he was wealthy . . .). After the court had censured him, the church of Boston called him also in question, where (as before he had done in court) he did, with tears, acknowledge and bewail his covetous and corrupt heart, yet making some excuse for many of the particulars, which were charged upon him, as partly by pretence of ignorance of the true price of some wares, and chiefly by being misled by some false principles, as, 1. That, if a man lost in one commodity, he might help himself in the price of another. 2. That if, through want of skill or other occasion, his commodity cost him more than the price of the market in England, he might then sell it for more than the price of the market in New England, &c. These things gave occasion to Mr. Cotton, in his publick exercise the next lecture day, to lay open the errour of such false principles, and to give some rules of direction in the case.

Some false principles were these:

1. That a man might sell as dear as he can, and buy as cheap as he can.

2. If a man lose by casualty of sea, &c. in some of his commodities, he may raise the price of the rest.

3. That he may sell as he bought, though he paid too dear, &c. and though the commodity be fallen, &c.

4. That, as a man may take the advantage of his own skill or ability, so he may of another's ignorance or necessity.

5. Where one gives time for payment, he is to take like recompense of one as of another.

The rules for trading were these:

1. A man may not sell above the current price, i. e. such a price as is usual in the time and place, and as another (who knows the worth of the commodity) would give for it, if he had occasion to use it; as that is called current money, which every man will take, &c.

2. When a man loseth in his commodity for want of skill, &c. he must look at it as his own fault or cross, and therefore must not lay it upon another.

3. Where a man loseth by casualty of sea, or, &c., it is a loss cast upon

himself by providence, and he may not ease himself of it by casting it upon another; for so a man should seem to provide against all providences, &c. that he should never lose; but where there is a scarcity of the commodity, there men may raise their price; for now it is a hand of God upon the commodity, and not the person.

5. A man may not ask any more for his commodity than his selling price, as Ephron to Abraham, the land is worth thus much.

The causes being debated by the church, some were earnest to have him excommunicated; but the most thought an admonition would be sufficient. Mr. Cotton opened the causes, which required excommunication, out of that in 1 Cor. 5. 11. The point now in question was, whether these actions did declare him to be such a covetous person, &c. Upon which he showed, that it is neither the habit of covetousness, (which is in every man in some degree,) nor simply the act, that declares a man to be such but when it appears, that a man sins against his conscience, or the very light of nature, and when it appears in a man's whole conversation. But Mr. Keaine did not appear to be such, but rather upon an errour in his judgment, being led by false principles; and, beside, he is otherwise liberal, as in his hospitality, and in church communion, &c. So, in the end, the church consented to an admonition.

—JOHN WINTHROP, *The History of New England from 1630 to 1649*

2. AN EARLY PROGRAM OF SOCIAL SECURITY

We think of Tom Paine as the pamphleteer of the American Revolution, author of Common Sense *and* The Crisis, *coiner of one gleaming phrase after another: "These are the times that try men's souls," "the summer soldier and the sunshine patriot," "government like dress the badge of lost innocence," and so forth. Or we think of him, perhaps, as the author of the* Age of Reason, *long considered a leading tract on infidelity. Paine was a superb propagandist, a political theorist of some talent, and a Deist; he was also one of the most original and far-sighted of economic thinkers. His economic ideas can be traced best in* Agrarian Justice *and in part two of the* Rights of Man—*Paine's reply to Burke's* Reflections on the French Revolution. *We give here some fragmentary extracts embracing Paine's plan for what we should now call a social security program. It is concerned, of course, with Britain, not America, and it is based on the assumption that a wise reallocation of appropriations would make available some four million pounds a year to be spent for the benefit of society. In order to finance further plans for social improvement, Paine proposed both a graduated income tax and a very steep inheritance tax.*

HAVING thus ascertained the greatest number that can be supposed to need support on account of young families, I proceed to the mode of relief or distribution, which is,

To pay as a remission of taxes, to every poor family, out of the surplus taxes and in room of poor-rates, four pounds a year for every child under fourteen years of age; enjoining the parents of such children to send them to school, to learn reading, writing, and common arithmetic; the ministers of every parish, of every denomination, to certify jointly to an office, for this purpose, that the duty is performed. The amount of this expense will be: For six hundred and thirty thousand children at four pounds each per annum . . . £2,520,000.

By adopting this method, not only the poverty of the parents will be relieved, but ignorance will be banished from the rising generation, and the number of poor will hereafter become less, because their abilities by the aid of education, will be greater. Many a youth, with good natural genius, who is apprenticed to a mechanical trade, such as a carpenter . . . is prevented getting forward the whole of his life, from the want of a little common education when a boy.

I now proceed to the case of the aged.

I divide the aged into two classes. First the approach of old age, beginning at fifty. Secondly, old age commencing at sixty.

At fifty . . . the bodily powers are on the decline. He begins to earn less, and is less capable of enduring the wind and weather; and in those retired employments where much sight is required, he fails apace, and feels himself like an old horse, beginning to be turned adrift.

At sixty, his labor ought to be over, at least from direct necessity. It is painful to see old age working itself to death, in what are called civilized countries, for its daily bread. . . .

Pay to every such person of the age of fifty years, and until he shall arrive at the age of sixty, the sum of six pounds per annum out of the surplus taxes; and ten pounds per annum during life, after the age of sixty. The expense of which will be . . . £1,120,000. . . .

I have extended the probable claims to one-third of the number of aged persons in the nation. Is it then better that the lives of one hundred and forty thousand aged persons be rendered comfortable, or that a million a year of public money be expended on any one individual, and he often of the most worthless and insignificant character? Let reason and justice, let honor and humanity, let even hypocrisy, sycophancy . . . answer the question. . . .

After all the above cases are provided for, there will still be a number of families who, though not properly of the class of poor, yet find it difficult to give education to their children, and such children, under such a case, would be in a worse condition than if their parents were actually poor. A nation under a well regulated government should permit none to remain uninstructed. It is monarchical and aristocratical governments only, that require ignorance for their support. . . .

Allow for each of those children ten shillings a year for the expense of schooling, for six years each, which will give them six months schooling each year, and a half a crown a year for paper and spelling books. . . .

Notwithstanding the great modes of relief which the best instituted and best principled government may devise, there will still be a number of smaller cases, which it is good policy as well as beneficence in a nation to consider.

Were twenty shillings to be given to every woman immediately on the birth of a child, who should make the demand, . . . it might relieve a great deal of instant distress.

There are about two hundred thousand births yearly in England; and if claimed by one-fourth, the amount would be . . . £500,000.

Also twenty thousand pounds to be appropriated to defray the funeral expenses of persons, who, traveling for work, may die at a distance from their friends. By relieving parishes from this charge, the sick stranger will be better treated.

—THOMAS PAINE, *Rights of Man*, 1792.

3. "ALL COMMUNITIES ARE APT TO LOOK TO GOVERNMENT FOR TOO MUCH"

Jacksonian democracy was unalterably opposed to the kind of "private enterprise" represented by Nicholas Biddle and the Bank of the United States, or to such monopolies as those represented by the Charles River Bridge Company, but it was champion of that private enterprise which rejected governmental interference. The Panic of 1837, brought on by reckless speculation in land and overdevelopment of internal improvements, was the most severe depression that the country had yet known. Many of those who were hardest hit looked to the government for aid. President Van Buren, however, rejected the suggestion that the government had any responsibility in the matter. The evil, he felt, would have to run its course. This excerpt comes from his message to Congress of September, 1837.

THOSE who look to the action of this Government for specific aid to the citizen to relieve embarrassments arising from losses by revulsions in commerce and credit lose sight of the ends for which it was created and the powers with which it is clothed. It was established to give security to us all in our lawful and honorable pursuits under the lasting safeguard of republican institutions. It was not intended to confer special favors on individuals or on any classes of them, to create systems of agriculture, manufactures, or trade, or to engage in them either separately or in connection with individual citizens or organized associations. If its operations were to be directed for the benefit of any one class, equivalent favors must in justice be extended to the rest, and the attempt to bestow such favors with an equal hand, or even to select those who should most deserve them, would never be successful.

All communities are apt to look to government for too much. Even in our own country, where its powers and duties are so strictly limited, we are prone to do so, especially at periods of sudden embarrassment and distress. But this ought not to be. The framers of our excellent Constitution and the people who approved it with calm and sagacious deliberation acted at the time on a sounder principle. They wisely judged that the less government interferes with private pursuits the better for the general prosperity. It is not its legitimate object to make men rich or to repair by direct grants of money or legislation in favor of particular pursuits, losses not incurred in the public service. This would be substantially to use the property of some for the benefit of others. But its real duty—that duty the performance of which makes a good government the most precious of human blessings—is to enact and enforce a system of general laws commensurate with, but not exceeding, the objects of its establishment, and to leave every citizen and every interest to reap under its benign protection the rewards of virtue, industry, and prudence.

I cannot doubt that on this as on all similar occasions the Federal Government will find its agency most conducive to the security and happiness of the people when limited to the exercise of its conceded powers. In never assuming, even for a well-meant object, such powers as were not designed to be conferred upon it, we shall in reality do most for the general welfare. To avoid every unnecessary interference with the pursuits of the citizen will result in more benefit than to adopt measures which could only assist limited interests, and are eagerly, but perhaps naturally, sought for under the pressure of temporary circumstances. If, therefore, I refrain from suggesting to Congress any specific plan for regulating the exchanges of the country, relieving mercantile embarrassments, or interfering with the ordinary operations of foreign or domestic commerce, it is from a conviction that such measures are not within the constitutional province of the General Government, and that their adoption would not promote the real and permanent welfare of those they might be designed to aid.

—Martin Van Buren, Message to Congress, September 4, 1837

4. AFFECTATION WITH A PUBLIC INTEREST

That it was the responsibility of government to protect the health, welfare, safety and morals of its citizens had long been acknowledged; the authority here was called the "police power." But how far did the police power go? Where were its bounds? Who was to decide when government had gone beyond the vague and general terms of police power? Did regulation of business—of such things as public utilities charges—come under the police power? If so, what was a public utility, and who was to decide? And how far might government regulate public utilities? Could regulation go all the way to confiscation—or to "deprivation of property"?

These were some of the vexatious questions which came to the fore in the post-Civil War years with the growth of the corporation, of giant industries, of railroads. Exorbitant rates charged by railroads or by railroad-owned warehouses led to the enactment in many States of so-called Granger legislation fixing the rates that might be charged. The railroads promptly challenged this legislation on constitutional grounds. It was, they argued, a "deprivation of property" without "due process of law," and therefore a violation of the Fourteenth Amendment. In the great case of Munn versus Illinois Justice Waite disposed of this objection. What gives this opinion its historic significance is that it formulates the basic principle upon which all governmental regulation of economic activities is based—the principle of affectation with a public interest.

WAITE, C. J. The question to be determined in this case is whether the general assembly of Illinois can, under the limitations upon the legislative powers of the States imposed by the Constitution of the United States, fix by law the maximum of charges for the storage of grain in warehouses at Chicago and other places in the State having not less than one hundred thousand inhabitants, "in which grain is stored in bulk, and in which the grain of different owners is mixed together, or in which grain is stored in such a manner that the identity of different lots or parcels cannot be accurately preserved." . . .

The Constitution contains no definition of the word "deprive," as used in the Fourteenth Amendment. To determine its signification, therefore, it is necessary to ascertain the effect which usage has given it, when employed in the same as a like connection.

While this provision of the amendment is new in the Constitution of the United States, as a limitation upon the powers of the States, it is old as a principle of civilized government. It is found in Magna Charta, and, in substance if not in form, in nearly or quite all the constitutions that have been from time to time adopted by the several States of the

Union. By the Fifth Amendment, it was introduced into the Constitution of the United States as a limitation upon the powers of the national government, and by the Fourteenth, as a guarantee against any encroachment upon an acknowledged right of citizenship by the legislatures of the States. . . .

When one becomes a member of society, he necessarily parts with some rights or privileges which, as an individual not affected by his relations to others, he might retain. "A body politic," as aptly defined in the preamble of the constitution of Massachusetts, "is a social compact by which the whole people covenants with each citizen, and each citizen with the whole people, that all shall be governed by certain laws for the common good." This does not confer power upon the whole people to control rights which are purely and exclusively private; but it does authorize the establishment of laws requiring each citizen to so conduct himself, and so use his own property, as not unnecessarily to injure another. This is the very essence of government. . . . Under these powers the government regulates the conduct of its citizens one towards another, and the manner in which each shall use his own property, when such regulation becomes necessary for the public good. In their exercise it has been customary in England from time immemorial, and in this country from its first colonization, to regulate ferries, common carriers, hackmen, bakers, millers, wharfingers, innkeepers, &c., and in so doing to fix a maximum of charge to be made for services rendered, accommodations furnished, and articles sold. To this day, statutes are to be found in many of the States upon some or all these subjects; and we think it has never yet been successfully contended that such legislation came within any of the constitutional prohibitions against interference with private property. . . .

From this it is apparent that, down to the time of the adoption of the Fourteenth Amendment, it was not supposed that statutes regulating the use, or even the price of the use, of private property necessarily deprived an owner of his property without due process of law. Under some circumstances they may, but not under all. The amendment does not change the law in this particular: it simply prevents the States from doing that which will operate as such a deprivation.

This brings us to inquire as to the principles upon which this power of regulation rests, in order that we may determine what is within and what without its operative effect. Looking, then, to the common law, from whence came the right which the Constitution protects, we find that when private property is "affected with a public interest, it ceases to be *juris privati* only." This was said by Lord Chief Justice Hale more than two hundred years ago, in his treatise *De Portibus Maris*, 1 Harg. Law Tracts, 78, and has been accepted without objection as an essential element in the law of property ever since. Property does become clothed with a public interest when used in a manner to make it of public consequence, and affect the community at large. When, therefore, one devotes his property to a use in which the public has an interest, he, in effect, grants to the public an interest in that use, and must submit to be controlled by the public for the common good, to the extent of the interest he has thus created. He may withdraw his grant by discontinuing the use; but, so long as he maintains the use, he must submit to the control.

—CHIEF JUSTICE WAITE, Opinion in Munn *v.* Illinois, 1876

5. "LIBERTY, INEQUALITY, SURVIVAL OF THE FITTEST"

We are now fairly into what is surely one of the three or four great debates of modern American history—the debate between the champions of rugged individualism and those of the welfare state. The beginnings of this debate, as we have seen, go back to the earliest colonial period. But it was not until the rise of modern corporations so powerful that they threatened not only the working man, the small businessman, and the consumer, but even the state, that the problem of the role of the government became acute. At one extreme were those who subscribed to complete laissez-faire *and argued that all government intervention was bad, even intervention in such elementary matters as education or sanitation. These found their inspiration in the teachings of the great English sociologist, Herbert Spencer, and their ablest spokesman here in the Yale economist, William Graham Sumner. At the other extreme were those who argued the necessity and inevitability of government regulation in every important part of the national economy, and government responsibility for the welfare and prosperity of all its citizens. These held that only the government was strong enough to curb great aggregations of private power and give every man an equal and fair chance, and they thought of themselves as good Jeffersonians. Their ablest spokesman was the neglected sociologist, Lester Ward. In between these extremes were the great mass of Americans who accepted the necessity of some governmental controls but cherished free enterprise, and were puzzled to know just how the two could be balanced. We give here first a characteristic outburst from William Graham Sumner, written about 1880 and called, with characteristic self-confidence, "The Challenge of Facts."*

THE condition for the complete and regular action of the force of competition is liberty. Liberty means the security given to each man that, if he employs his energies to sustain the struggle on behalf of himself and those he cares for, he shall dispose of the product exclusively as he chooses. It is impossible to know whence any definition or criterion of justice can be derived, if it is not deduced from this view of things; or if it is not the definition of justice that each shall enjoy the fruit of his own labor and self-denial, and of injustice that the idle and the industrious, the self-indulgent and the self-denying, shall share equally in the product. Aside from the *a priori* speculations of philosophers who have tried to make equality an essential element in justice, the human race has recognized, from the earliest times, the above conception of justice as the true one, and has founded upon it the right of property. . . .

Private property, also, which we have seen to be a feature of society organized in accordance with the natural conditions of the struggle for existence produces inequalities between men. The struggle for existence is aimed against nature. It is from her niggardly hand that we have to wrest the satisfactions for our needs, but our fellow-men are our competitors for the meager supply. Competition, therefore, is a law of nature. Nature is entirely neutral; she submits to him who most energetically and resolutely assails her. She grants her rewards to the fittest, therefore, without regard to other considerations of any kind. If, then, there be liberty, men get from her just in proportion to their works, and their having and enjoying are just in proportion to their being and their doing. Such is the system of nature. If we do not like it, and if we try to amend it, there is only one way in which we can do it. We can take from the better and give to the worse. We can deflect the penalties of those who have done ill and throw them on those who have done better. We can take the rewards from those who have done better and give them to those who have done worse. We shall thus lessen the inequalities. We shall favor the survival of the unfittest, and we shall accomplish this by destroying liberty. Let it be understood that we cannot go outside of this alternative: liberty, inequality, survival of the fittest; not-liberty, equality, survival of the unfittest. The former carries society forward and favors all its best members; the latter carries society downwards and favors all its worst members. . . .

What we mean by liberty is civil liberty, or liberty under law; and this means the guarantees of law that a man shall not be interfered with while using his own powers for his own welfare. It is, therefore, a civil and political status; and that nation has the freest institutions in which the guarantees of peace for the laborer and security for the capitalist are the highest. Liberty, therefore, does not by any means do away with the struggle for existence. We might as well try to do away with the need of eating, for that would, in effect, be the same thing. What civil liberty does is to turn the competition of man with man from violence and brute force into an industrial competition under which men vie with one another for the acquisition of material goods by industry, energy, skill, frugality, prudence, temperance, and other industrial virtues. Under this changed order of things the inequalities are not done away with. Nature still grants her rewards of having and enjoying, according to our being and doing, but it is now the man of the highest training and not the man of the heaviest fist who gains the highest reward. It is impossible that the man with capital and the man without capital should be equal. To affirm that they are equal would be to say that a man who has no tool can get as much food out of the ground as the man who has a spade or a plough; or that the man who has no weapon can defend himself as well against hostile beasts or hostile men as the man who has a weapon. If that were so, none of us would work any more. We work and deny ourselves to get capital just because, other things being equal, the man who has it is superior, for attaining all the the ends of life, to the man who has it not. Considering the eagerness with which we all seek capital and the estimate we put upon it, either in cherishing it if we have it, or envying others who have it while we have it not, it is very strange what platitudes pass current about it in our society so soon as we begin to generalize about it. If our young people really believed some of the teachings they hear, it would not be amiss to preach them a sermon once in a while to reassure them setting forth that it is not wicked to be rich, nay even, that it is not wicked to be richer than your neighbor.

It follows from what we have observed that it is the utmost folly to denounce capital. To do so is to undermine civilization, for capital is the first requisite of every social gain, educational, ecclesiastical, political, aesthetic, or other. . . .

The man who has capital possesses immeasurable advantages for the struggle of life over him who has none. The more we break down privileges of class, or industry, and establish liberty, the greater will be the inequalities and the more exclusively will the vicious bear the penalties. Poverty and misery will exist in society just so long as vice exists in human nature.

—WILLIAM GRAHAM SUMNER, "The Challenge of Facts," ca. 1880

6. THE COURTS AS GUARDIANS OF THE STATUS QUO

Every industrialized society faced the problem of adjusting the conflicting claims of society and economy, of state regulation and private enterprise. In America, however, the problem took peculiar form. Here it was not just a question of what seemed wise or expedient; to these considerations was added the question of constitutionality. Suppose that the people, through their legislatures, did want to regulate the charges of railroads or the hours of labor of women or the conditions of work in tenements or any one of a hundred similar things. Could they do these things constitutionally? After all, the Fifth Amendment said that Congress might not deprive any person of property without due process of law, and the Fourteenth Amendment applied the same prohibition to the States. Was legislation regulating hours, let us say, depriving a worker of his liberty of contract? Was legislation regulating rates depriving a corporation of its property? It was for the Courts to say. And the Courts took, for the most part, a very conservative view. Indeed from the 1880's down to the 1930's, the Courts were the chief citadel of the laissez-faire philosophy. We cannot trace this in detail, but we give here two characteristic decisions, separated by approximately forty years from each other. The first concerns a New York State law of 1882 forbidding cigar-making in tenement houses. The Court said here that this was taking the worker away from the hallowed associations of his home, and voided the law. Our second case is from the Supreme Court and involves the interpretation of an Act of Congress fixing minimum wages for women in the District of Columbia. Justice Sutherland said here that there was no basis for any such legislation and that it deprived women of liberty of contract and might discourage business, and was therefore void. Needless to say, the court opinions have been subsequently reversed by the Courts themselves, but for a long time, bench and bar co-operated to delay the necessary reform legislation in the United States.

A. "Such Governmental Interferences Disturb the . . . Social Fabric"

EARL, J. These facts showed a violation of the provision of the act which took effect immediately upon its passage and the material portions of which are as follows: "Section 1. The manufacture of cigars or preparation of tobacco in any form on any floor, or in any part of any floor, in any tenement-house is hereby prohibited, if such floor or any part of such floor is by any person, occupied as a home or residence for the purpose of living, sleeping, cooking or doing any household work therein. . . ."

To justify this law it would not be sufficient that the use of tobacco may be injurious to some persons, or that its manipulation may be injurious to those who are engaged in its preparation and manufacture; but it would have to be injurious to the public health. This law was not intended to protect the health of those engaged in cigar-making, as they are allowed to manufacture cigars everywhere except in the forbidden tenement-houses. It cannot be perceived how the cigar maker is to be improved in his health or his morals by forcing him from his home and its hallowed associations and beneficent influences, to ply his trade elsewhere. It was not intended to protect the health of that portion of the public not residing in the forbidden tenement-houses, as cigars are allowed to be manufactured in private houses, in large factories and shops in the too crowded cities, and in all other parts of the State. What possible relation can cigarmaking in any building have on the health of the general public? Nor was it intended to improve or protect the health of the occupants of tenement-houses. If there are but three families in the tenement-house, however numerous and gregarious their members may be, manufacture is not forbidden; and it matters not how large the number of the occupants may be if they are not divided into more than three families living and cooking independently. If a store is kept for the sale of cigars on the first floor of one of these houses, and thus more tobacco is kept there than otherwise would be, and the baneful influence of tobacco, if any, is thus increased, that floor, however numerous its occupants, or the occupants of the house, is exempt from the operation of the act. What possible relation to the health of the occupants of a large tenement-house could cigarmaking in one of its remote rooms have? If the legislature had in mind the protection of the occupants of the tenement-houses, why was the act confined in its operation to the two cities only? Is it plain that this is not a health law, and that it has no relation whatever to the public health. . . . Such legislation may invade one class of rights to-day and another to-morrow, and if it can be sanctioned under the Constitution, while far removed in time we will not be far away in practical statesmanship from those ages when governmental prefects supervised the building of houses, the rearing of cattle, the sowing of seed and the reaping of grain, and governmental ordinances regulated the movements and labor of artisans, the rate of wages, the price of food, the diet and clothing of the people, and a large range of other affairs long since in all civilized lands regarded as outside of governmental functions. Such governmental interferences disturb the normal adjustments of the social fabric, and usually derange the delicate and complicated machinery of industry and cause a score of ills while attempting the removal of one.

When a health law is challenged in the courts as unconstitutional on the ground that it arbitrarily interferes with personal liberty and private property without due process of law, the courts must be able to see that it has at least in fact some relation to the public health, that the public health is the end aimed at, and that it is appropriate and adapted to that end. This we have not been able to see in this law, and we must, therefore, pronounce it unconstitutional and void.

—JUSTICE EARL, Opinion in *In Re* Jacobs, 1885

B. "THE POLICE POWER WILL HAVE BEEN WIDENED TO A GREAT AND DANGEROUS DEGREE"

SUTHERLAND, J. The question presented for determination by these appeals is the constitutionality of the Act of September 19, 1918, providing for the fixing of minimum wages for women and children in the District of Columbia. . . .

It is declared that the purposes of the act are "to protect the women and minors of the District from conditions detrimental to their health and morals, resulting from wages which are inadequate to maintain decent standards of living; and the act in each of its provisions and in its entirety, shall be interpreted to effectuate these purposes." . . .

The statute now under consideration is attacked upon the ground that it authorizes an unconstitutional interference with the freedom of contract included within the guaranties of the due process clause of the 5th Amendment. That the right to contract about one's affairs is a part of the liberty of the individual protected by this clause is settled by the decisions of this Court and is no longer open to question. Within this liberty are contracts of employment of labor. In making such contracts, generally speaking, the parties have an equal right to obtain from each other the best terms they can as the result of private bargaining. . . .

There is, of course, no such thing as absolute freedom of contract. It it subject to a great variety of restraints. But freedom of contract is, nevertheless, the general rule and restraint the exception; and the exercise of legislative authority to abridge it can be justified only by the existence of exceptional circumstances. Whether these circumstances exist in the present case constitutes the question to be answered. . . .

The standard furnished by the statute for the guidance of the board is so vague as to be impossible of practical application with any reasonable degree of accuracy. What is sufficient to supply the necessary cost of living for a woman worker and maintain her in good health and protect her morals is obviously not a precise or unvarying sum—not even approximately so. The amount will depend upon a variety of circumstances: the individual temperament, habits of thrift, care, ability to buy necessaries intelligently, and whether the woman live alone or with her family. To those who practice economy, a given sum will afford comfort, while to those of a contrary habit the same sum will be wholly inadequate. The coöperative economies of the family group are not taken into account though they constitute an important consideration in estimating the cost of living, for it is obvious that the individual expense will be less in the case of a member of a family than in the case of one living alone. The relation between earnings and morals is not capable of standardization. It cannot be shown that well paid women safeguard their morals more carefully than those who are poorly paid. Morality rests upon other considerations than wages; and there is, certainly, no such prevalent connection between the two as to justify a broad attempt to adjust the latter with reference to the former. As a means of safeguarding morals the attempted classification in our opinion, is without reasonable basis. No distinction can be made between women who work for others and those who do not; nor is there ground for distinction between women and men, for, certainly, if women require a minimum wage to preserve their morals men require it to preserve their honesty. For these reasons, and others which might be stated, the inquiry in respect of the necessary cost of living and of the income necessary to preserve health and morals, presents an individual and not a composite question, and must be answered for each individual considered by herself and not by a general formula prescribed by a statutory bureau. . . .

Finally, it may be said that if, in the interest of the public welfare, the police power may be invoked to justify the fixing of a minimum wage, it may, when the public welfare is thought to require it, be invoked to justify a maximum wage. The power to fix high wages connotes, by like reasoning, the power to fix low wages. If, in the face of the guaranties of the 5th Amendment, this form of legislation shall be legally justified, the field for the operation of the police power will have been widened to a great and dangerous degree. If, for example, in the opinion of future lawmakers, wages in the building trades shall become so high as to preclude people of ordinary means from building and owning homes, an authority which sustains the minimum wage will be invoked to support a maximum wage for building laborers and artisans, and the same argument which has been here urged to strip the employer of his constitutional liberty of contract in one direction will be utilized to strip the employee of his constitutional liberty of contract in the opposite direction. A wrong decision does not end with itself; it is a precedent, and, with the swing of sentiment, its bad influence may run from one extremity of the arc to the other.

It has been said that legislation of the kind now under review is required in the interest of social justice, for whose ends freedom of contract may lawfully be subjected to restraint. The liberty of the individual to do as he pleases, even in innocent matters, is not absolute. It must frequently yield to the common good, and the line beyond which the power of interference may not be pressed is neither definite nor unalterable but may be made to move, within limits not well defined, with changing need and circumstance. Any attempt to fix a rigid boundary would be unwise and futile. But, nevertheless, there are limits to the power, and when these have been passed, it becomes the plain duty of the courts in the proper exercise of their authority to so declare. To sustain the individual freedom of action contemplated by the Constitution, is not to strike down the common good but to exalt it; for surely the good of society as a whole cannot be better served than by the preservation against arbitrary restraint of the liberties of its constituent members.

It follows from what has been said that the act in question passes the limit prescribed by the Constitution, and, accordingly, the decrees of the court below are affirmed.

—JUSTICE SUTHERLAND, Opinion in Adkins *v.* Children's Hospital, 1923

7. "THE DOCTRINE OF *LAISSEZ-FAIRE* IS UNSAFE IN POLITICS AND UNSOUND IN MORALS"

We turn now to the other side of the argument—the argument against uninhibited private enterprise and for governmental regulation. We do well to begin with a statement drafted by the young economist, Richard T. Ely, to explain the resolutions adopted by the newly organized American Economic Association. These resolutions, which had the approval of such various men as the University of Pennsylvania economist, Simon Patten, the famous Christian Socialist, Washington Gladden, and the young historian, Woodrow Wilson, were a veritable declaration of independence from the tyranny of the laissez-faire *philosophy.*

ONE aim of our association should be the education of public opinion in regard to economic questions and economic literature. In no other science is there so much quackery and it must be our province to expose it and bring it into merited contempt. A review at each of our meetings of the economic works of the past year, if published in our proceedings, might help in the formation of enlightened judgment.

Coming to the platform, a position is first of all taken in regard to the state, because it is thought necessary precisely at this time to emphasize its proper province. No one invited to join this association, certainly no one who has been active in calling this meeting, contemplates a form of pure socialism. "We recognize the necessity of individual initiative." We would do nothing to weaken individual activity, but we hold that there are certain spheres of activity which do not belong to the individual, certain functions which the great cooperative society, called the state—must perform to keep the avenues open for those who would gain a livelihood by their own exertions. The avenues to wealth and preferment are continually blocked by the greed of combinations of men and by monopolists, and individual effort and initiative are thus discouraged. Two examples will suffice— You know that in the Western grazing regions water is often scarce, and those who control the streams virtually own the country. Now it is a notorious fact that unlawful combinations seize upon these streams and, keeping others from them, retain exclusive privileges which shut off effectually individual exertions on the part of those not in the ring. A second example is found in unjust discriminations in freight charges which have built up the fortunes of the favored, and ruined competitors. In looking over the field of economic life, it is evident that there is a wide feeling of discouragement, repressing the activities of the individual, because the avenues to material well-being are so often blocked. Then there are things which individuals ought not to perform because the functions concerned are public; and in certain places the wastes of private competition are too enormous. There are, likewise, important things which individual effort is powerless to effect, e.g., the education of the masses.

We hold that the doctrine of *laissez-faire* is unsafe in politics and unsound in morals, and that it suggests an inadequate explanation of the relations between the state and the citizens. In other words we believe in the existence of a system of social ethics; we do not believe that any man lives for himself alone, nor yet do we believe social classes are devoid of mutual obligations corresponding to their infinitely varied inter-relations. All have duties as well as rights, and, as Emerson said several years ago, it is time we heard more about duties and less about rights. We who have resolved to form an American Economic Association hope to do something towards the development of a system of social ethics.

It is asked: what is meant by *laissez-faire?* It is difficult to define *laissez-faire* categorically, because it is so absurd that its defenders can never be induced to say precisely what they mean. Yet it stands for a well-known, though rather vague set of ideas, to which appeal is made every day in the year by the bench, the bar, the newspapers and our legislative bodies. It means that government, the state, the people in their collective capacity, ought not to interfere in industrial life; that, on the contrary, free contract should regulate all the economic relations of life and public authority should simply enforce this, punish crime and preserve peace. It means that the laws of economic life are natural laws like those of physics and chemistry, and that this life must be left to the free play of natural forces. One adherent uses these words: "This industrial world is governed by natural laws. These laws are superior to man. Respect this providential order—let alone the work of God."

The platform then emphasizes the mission of the State and the mission of the individual in that State. *To distinguish between the proper functions of the two must be one of the purposes of our association.*

—Statement by Richard T. Ely, 1886

8. GOVERNMENT IS BUT ONE OF THE TOOLS OF MAN

Lester Ward was the first major scholar to attack the inadequate science, the dubious logic, and the specious rhetoric of the Spencer-Sumner school, and he remains the ablest. To the study of sociology he brought immense resources of scientific and philosophical learning and a firm grasp of the meaning of evolution to social development. What he stressed, above all, was that man transformed environment just as environment transformed man; that civilization was a product of art and of interference with the processes of nature; and that government was but one of the tools which man used in conquering nature. Throughout his voluminous writings there runs, as Franklin Giddings has said, "one dominating and organizing thought. Human society . . . is not the passive product of unconscious forces. It lies within the domain of cosmic law, but so does the mind of man, and this mind of man has knowingly, artfully, adapted and readapted its social environment." We give here extracts from Ward's most valuable book, The Psychic Factors of Civilization.

THE prevailing idea is wholly false which claims that it is the fittest possible that survive in this struggle. The effect of competition is to prevent any form from attaining its maximum development, and to maintain a certain comparatively low level of development for all forms that succeed in surviving. This is a normal result of the rhythmic character of all purely natural, i.e., not rational or teleological, phenomena, as explained a few pages back. The greater part of what is gained in the flood tide is lost in the ebb. Wherever competition is wholly removed, as through the agency of man in the interest of any one form, great strides are immediately made by the form thus protected, and it soon outstrips all those that depend upon competition for their motive to advancement. Such has been the case with the cereals and fruit trees, and with domestic animals, in fact, with all the forms of life that man has excepted from the biologic law and subjected to the law of mind. The supposed tendency of such forms to revert to their original wild state, about which so much has been said, is simply their inability when remanded to their pristine competitive struggle to maintain the high position which they had acquired during their halcyon days of exemption from that struggle, which they can no more do than they can attain that position while subjected to it. Competition, therefore, not only involves the enormous waste which has been described, but it prevents the maximum development, since the best that can be attained under its influence is far inferior to that which is easily attained by the artificial, i.e., the rational and intelligent, removal of that influence.

Hard as it seems to be for modern philosophers to understand this, it was one of the first truths that dawned upon the human intellect. Consciously or unconsciously it was felt from the very outset that the mission of mind was to grapple with the law of competition and as far as possible to resist and defeat it. This iron law of nature, as it may be appropriately called . . . was everywhere found to lie athwart the path of human progress, and the whole upward struggle of rational man, whether physical, social or moral, has been with this tyrant of nature—

the law of competition. And in so far as he has progressed at all beyond the purely animal stage he has done so through triumphing little by little over this law and gaining somewhat the mastery in this struggle. In the physical world he has accomplished this so far as he has been able through invention, from which have resulted the arts and material civilization. Every implement or utensil, every mechanical device, every object of design, skill, and labor, every artificial thing that serves a human purpose, is a triumph of mind over the physical forces of nature in ceaseless and aimless competition. The cultivation and improvement of economic plants and the domestication of useful animals involve the direct control of biologic forces and the exemption of these forms of life from the operation of the great organic law which dwarfs their native powers of development. All human institutions—religion, government, law, marriage, custom—together with innumerable other modes of regulating social, industrial, and commercial life, are, broadly viewed, only so many ways of meeting and checkmating the principle of competition as it manifests itself in society. And finally, the ethical code and the moral law of enlightened man are nothing else than the means adopted by reason, intelligence, and refined sensibility for suppressing and crushing out the animal nature of man—for chaining the competitive egoism that all men have inherited from their animal ancestors. . . .

The competition which we see in the social and industrial world, competition aided and modified by reason and intelligence, while it does not differ in either its principle or its purpose from the competition among animals and plants, differs widely in its methods and its effects. We see in it the same soulless struggle, the same intense egoism, the same rhythm by which existing inequalities are increased, the same sacrifice of the weaker to the stronger, and the same frenzy of the latter to possess and monopolize the earth. But along with this the antagonistic principle is also in active operation. This is the law of mind making for a true economy of energy. It is mind alone that perceives that competition is wasteful of energy, and therefore in the interest of the very success that competition seeks, it proceeds to antagonize competition and to substitute for it art, science, and coöperation. By the aid of these the success of those who use them is increased many hundred fold. In society, therefore, competition tends to defeat itself by inciting against it the power of thought. It cannot endure. It is at best only a temporary condition or transition state. On the one hand the competition between men resolves itself into a competition between machines, and instead of the fittest organism it is the fittest mechanism that survives. On the other hand the competition between individuals becomes a competition between associations of individuals. Such associations are the result of coöperation which is the opposite of competition. Economists talk of free competition, but in society this is scarcely possible. Only the simplest operations, those conducted with the least intelligence, can continue for any length of time to compete. The least skilled forms of labor approach this condition most closely, but freedom is here limited by the relations that labor sustains to capital. The chief difference between employers and employed until recently has been that the former have used the rational method while the latter have used the natural method. Capital has always combined and coöperated while labor has only competed. But such is the power of the former method and its superiority over the latter that competing labor has had no chance in the struggle with combining capital. Latterly, however, labor has begun in a small way to call to its aid the psychological economy of coöperation. So strange and unexpected did this seem that it was at first looked upon as a crime against society, and many still so regard it. Indeed, all the laws of modern nations are framed on the assumption that capital naturally combines while labor naturally competes, and attempts on the part of labor to combine against capital are usually suppressed by the armed force of the state, while capitalists are protected by the civil and military authority of the state against such assumed unlawful attempts. This enormous odds against which labor struggles in its effort to adopt and apply the economics of mind will greatly retard the progress of industrial reform which aims to place labor on an equal footing with capital in this respect. . . .

A new and revised political economy will doubtless be largely devoted to showing, not so much the glories of competition, which society does not enjoy, as how society may conduct itself in order to secure whatever benefits competition can offer, and also how the competition that cannot be prevented can be shorn of its wasteful and aggressive features. . . .

The existing governments of the world are not the very best they can be or can ever be made. Other governments at least stand a chance of being brought up to the standard of our philosopher's present government, and as that is admitted to be very bad, there may, at least if his teachings are heeded, be some hope of improving even that. But how does the improvement of an existing government differ in this respect from the origination of a government where none existed? At what point in the progress of governments did it become preposterous to attempt to reform them? If that point is the one at which our philosopher happened to live and write, how is it that it might not have fallen at some other time? It would probably be urged that all real reform in government has consisted in restricting its action. This carried to its logical results would take us back to anarchy, and this we may assume would not be advised. Then there must be such a thing as governmental reform somewhat short of the complete abolition of government. What such reform would consist in need not now be considered; the fact of its possibility is all that is contended for.

No one will deny that government is a part of evolution, a product of human intelligence operating in a normal manner, but it is only one of the many human institutions that have been developed in the same way. The attempts to reform or in any way change it belong to the same class as the attempts to establish it, and are also normal. Intelligence has operated on government in the same way that it operates on all other things. Why then should government be singled out as the only product of intelligence that furnishes illustrations of the failure of all attempts to counteract the law of evolution? Civilization consists of something else besides government. That institution has indeed played an important rôle, but this has been thus far chiefly that of enabling the more direct civilizing influences to operate. Its function has been principally that of protection, that of affording security to other normal processes. It has done this with a certain degree of efficiency, a very variable and imperfect degree, it is allowed, but it has done it. Few will probably insist that it has wholly failed, and nearly all believe that without it there could have been very little or no social progress. Let any one reflect how jealously vested rights are guarded by law, how commerce and industry are permitted to go on unmolested, how personal liberty is guaranteed and crimes against person and property are punished, and figure to himself what the state of things would be in the total absence of governmental supervision.

—LESTER WARD, *The Psychic Factors of Civilization*, 1883

9. THE COURTS ACCEPT GOVERNMENTAL
REGULATION

From the beginning there were jurists who protested against the conscription of the Constitution and the Courts to the service of the doctrine of laissez-faire. The Constitution, they held, was not a barrier but an instrument, and it was designed to encourage experimentation. As for the judges, it was not their business to write their personal likes or dislikes into constitutional law, but to accept the laws of the political branches of the government unless these laws were obviously and palpably contrary to the Constitution. The most eloquent and persuasive spokesman for this view was Oliver Wendell Holmes, for twenty years on the Massachusetts Supreme Court and for thirty on the Supreme Court of the United States. In his day Holmes was known as the "great dissenter"; what is impressive is that every one of his major dissents was subsequently accepted by the Court as law. Holmes himself did not live to witness the complete triumph of his juridical philosophy, but Brandeis, Cardozo, and Frankfurter did. We give here Holmes's famous dissent in the New York bakeshop case—Lochner versus New York— and part of the opinion of Chief Justice Hughes in the Washington Minimum Wage case—a decision reversing Adkins versus Children's Hospital and accepting Holmes's dissent in that case.

A. "The Fourteenth Amendment Does Not Enact Herbert Spencer's Social Statics"

HOLMES, J., dissenting. The case is decided upon an economic theory which a large part of the country does not entertain. If it were a question whether I agreed with that theory, I should desire to study it further and long before making up my mind. But I do not conceive that to be my duty, because I strongly believe that my agreement or disagreement has nothing to do with the right of a majority to embody their opinions in law. It is settled by various decisions of this court that state constitutions and state laws may regulate life in many ways which we as legislators might think as injudicious, or if you like as tyrannical, as this, and which, equally with this, interfere with the liberty to contract. Sunday laws and usury laws are ancient examples. A more modern one is the prohibition of lotteries. The liberty of the citizen to do as he likes so long as he does not interfere with the liberty of others to do the same, which has been a shibboleth for some well-known writers, is interfered with by school laws, by the post-office, by every state or municipal institution which takes his money for purposes thought desirable, whether he likes it or not. The Fourteenth Amendment does not enact Mr. Herbert Spencer's Social Statics. . . . United States and state statutes and decisions cutting down the liberty to contract by way of combination are familiar to this court. . . . Some of these laws embody convictions or prejudices which judges are likely to share. Some may not. But a constitution is not intended to embody a particular economic theory, whether of paternalism and the organic relation of the citizen to the state or of *laissez faire*. It is made for people of fundamentally differing views, and the accident of our finding certain opinions natural and familiar, or novel, and even shocking, ought not to conclude our judgement upon the question whether statutes embodying them conflict with the Constitution of the United States.

General propositions do not decide concrete cases. The decision will depend on a judgement or intuition more subtle than any articulate major premise. But I think that the proposition just stated, if it is accepted, will carry us far toward the end. Every opinion tends to become a law. I think that the word "liberty," in the Fourteenth Amendment, is perverted when it is held to prevent the natural outcome of a dominant opinion, unless it can be said that a rational and fair man necessarily would admit that the statute proposed would infringe fundamental principles as they have been understood by the traditions of our people and our law. It does not need research to show that no such sweeping condemnation can be passed upon the statute before us. A reasonable man might think it a proper measure on the score of health. Men whom I certainly could not pronounce unreasonable would uphold it as a first instalment of a general regulation of the hours of work. Whether in the latter aspect it would be open to the charge of inequality I think it unnecessary to discuss.

—Justice Holmes,
Dissenting Opinion in Lochner *v.* New York, 1905

B. "The Liberty Safeguarded Is Liberty in a Social
Organization Which Requires Protection"

Hughes, C. J. The Supreme Court of Washington has upheld the
minimum wage statute of that State. It has decided that the statute
is a reasonable exercise of the police power of the State. In reaching
that conclusion the state court has invoked principles long established
by this Court in the application of the Fourteenth Amendment. The
state court has refused to regard the decision in the *Adkins* case as
determinative and has pointed to our decisions both before and since
that case as justifying its position. We are of the opinion that this ruling
of the state court demands on our part a reexamination of the *Adkins*
case. The importance of the question, in which many States having
similar laws are concerned, the close division by which the decision
in the *Adkins* case was reached, and the economic conditions which
have supervened, and in the light of which the reasonableness of the
exercise of the protective power of the State must be considered, make
it not only appropriate, but we think imperative, that in deciding the
present case the subject should receive fresh consideration. . . .

The principle which must control our decision is not in doubt. The
constitutional provision invoked is the due process clause of the Fourteenth Amendment governing the States, as the due process clause
invoked in the *Adkins* case governed Congress. In each case the
violation alleged by those attacking minimum wage regulation for
women is deprivation of freedom of contract. What is this freedom?
The Constitution does not speak of freedom of contract. It speaks of
liberty and prohibits the deprivation of liberty without due process of
law. In prohibiting that deprivation the Constitution does not recognize an absolute and uncontrollable liberty. Liberty in each of its phases
has its history and connotation. But the liberty safeguarded is liberty
in a social organization which requires the protection of law against
the evils which menace the health, safety, morals and welfare of the
people. Liberty under the Constitution is thus necessarily subject to the
restraints of due process, and regulation which is reasonable in relation
to its subject and is adopted in the interests of the community is due
process. . . .

With full recognition of the earnestness and vigor which characterize
the prevailing opinion in the *Adkins* case, we find it impossible to
reconcile that ruling with these well-considered declarations. What

can be closer to the public interest than the health of women and their protection from unscrupulous and overreaching employers? And if the protection of women is a legitimate end of the exercise of state power, how can it be said that the requirement of the payment of a minimum wage fairly fixed in order to meet the very necessities of existence is not an admissible means to that end? The legislature of the State was clearly entitled to consider the situation of women in employment, the fact that they are in the class receiving the least pay, that their bargaining power is relatively weak, and that they are the ready victims of those who would take advantage of their necessitous circumstances. The legislature was entitled to adopt measures to reduce the evils of the "sweating system," the exploiting of workers at wages so low as to be insufficient to meet the bare cost of living thus making their very helplessness the occasion of a most injurious competition. The legislature had the right to consider that its minimum wage requirements would be an important aid in carrying out its policy of protection. The adoption of similar requirements by many States evidences a deep-seated conviction both as to the presence of the evil and as to the means adapted to check it. Legislative response to that conviction cannot be regarded as arbitrary or capricious and that is all we have to decide. Even if the wisdom of the policy be regarded as debatable and its effects uncertain, still the legislature is entitled to its judgment.

There is an additional and compelling consideration which recent economic experience has brought into a strong light. The exploitation of a class of workers who are in an unequal position with respect to bargaining power and are thus relatively defenceless against the denial of a living wage is not only detrimental to their health and well being but casts a direct burden for their support upon the community. What these workers lose in wages the taxpayers are called upon to pay. The bare cost of living must be met. We may take judicial notice of the unparalleled demands for relief which arose during the recent period of depression and still continue to an alarming extent despite the degree of economic recovery which has been achieved. It is unnecessary to cite official statistics to establish what is of common knowledge through the length and breadth of the land. While in the instant case no factual brief has been presented, there is no reason to doubt that the State of Washington has encountered the same social problem that is present elsewhere. The community is not bound to provide what is in effect a subsidy for unconscionable employers. The community may direct its law-making power to correct the abuse which springs from their selfish disregard of the public interest. The argument that the legislation in question constitutes an arbitrary discrimination, because it does not extend to men, is unavailing. This Court has frequently held that the legislative authority, acting within its proper field, is not bound to extend its regulation to all cases which it might possibly reach. The legislature "is free to recognize degrees of harm and it may confine its restrictions to those classes of cases where the need is deemed to be clearest." If "the law presumably hits the evil where it is most felt, it is not to be overthrown because there are other instances to which it might have been applied." There is no "doctrinaire requirement" that the legislation should be couched in all embracing terms. This familiar principle has repeatedly been applied to legislation which singles out women, and particular classes of women, in the exercise of the State's protective power. Their relative need in the presence of the evil, no less than the existence of the evil itself, is a matter for the legislative judgment.

Our conclusion is that the case of *Adkins* v. *Children's Hospital, supra*, should be, and it is, overruled. The judgment of the Supreme Court of the State of Washington is affirmed.

—CHIEF JUSTICE HUGHES,
Opinion in Washington Minimum Wage Case, 1937

10. "THE OLD ORDER CHANGETH"

Theodore Roosevelt was the first President to understand the changes that the Industrial Revolution and the rise of corporations had brought to politics. Fundamentally conservative, he saw the necessity of eliminating some of the grosser abuses of corporate privilege in order to save business from radical attack. Actually, little was done during the Roosevelt administration in the way of effective regulation of business, industry, finance, or labor. A historian of the welfare state, then, would put Theodore Roosevelt in an introductory chapter, and begin his story proper with Woodrow Wilson. A Manchester liberal, Wilson had experienced a change of heart in the last years of his Presidency of Princeton University, and as Governor of New Jersey had pushed through a remarkable program of reform. Nominated to the Presidency with the help and the blessing of the old crusader, William Jennings Bryan, Wilson waged an aggressive campaign calling for a "new freedom"—freedom from control by powerful organizations that threatened both the liberties of men and the authority of government. This extract is taken from his book, The New Freedom, which in turn was made up of his campaign addresses.

AMERICAN industry is not free, as once it was free; American enterprise is not free; the man with only a little capital is finding it harder to get into the field, more and more impossible to compete with the big fellow. Why? Because the laws of this country do not prevent the strong from crushing the weak. That is the reason, and because the strong have crushed the weak the strong dominate the industry and the economic life of this country. No man can deny that the lines of endeavor have more and more narrowed and stiffened; no man who knows anything about the development of industry in this country can have failed to observe that the larger kinds of credit are more and more difficult to obtain, unless you obtain them upon the terms of uniting your efforts with those who already control the industries of the country; and nobody can fail to observe that any man who tries to set himself up in competition with any process of manufacture which has been taken under the control of large combinations of capital will presently find himself either squeezed out or obliged to sell and allow himself to be absorbed.

There is a great deal that needs reconstruction in the United States. I should like to take a census of the business men,—I mean the rank and file of the business men,—as to whether they think that conditions in this country, or rather whether the organization of business in this country, is satisfactory or not. I know what they would say if they dared. If they could vote secretly they would vote overwhelmingly that the present organization of business was meant for the big fellows and was not meant for the little fellows; that it was meant for those who are at the top and was meant to exclude those who were at the bottom; that it was meant to shut out beginners, to prevent new entries in the race, to prevent the building up of competitive enterprises that would interfere with the monopolies which the great trusts have built up.

What this country needs above everything else is a body of laws which will look after the men who are on the make rather than the men who are already made. Because the men who are already made are not going to live indefinitely, and they are not always kind enough to leave sons as able and as honest as they are.

The originative part of America, the part of America that makes new enterprises, the part into which the ambitious and gifted workingman makes his way up, the class that saves, that plans, that organizes, that presently spreads its enterprises until they have a national scope and character,—that middle class is being more and more squeezed out by the processes which we have been taught to call processes of prosperity. Its members are sharing prosperity, no doubt; but what alarms me is that they are not *originating* prosperity. No country can afford to have its prosperity originated by a small controlling class. The treasury of America does not lie in the brains of the small body of men now in control of the great enterprises that have been concentrated under the direction of a very small number of persons. The treasury of America lies in those ambitions, those energies, that cannot be restricted to a special favored class. It depends upon the inventions of unknown men, upon the originations of unknown men, upon the ambitions of unknown men. Every country is renewed out of the ranks of the unknown, not out of the ranks of those already famous and powerful and in control.

There has come over the land that unAmerican set of conditions which enables a small number of men who control the government to get favors from the government; by those favors to exclude their fellows from equal business opportunity; by those favors to extend a network of control that will presently dominate every industry in the country, and so make men forget the ancient time when America lay in every hamlet, when America was to be seen in every fair valley, when America displayed her great forces on the broad prairies, ran her fine fires of enterprise up over the mountainsides and down into the bowels of the earth, and eager men were everywhere captains of industry, not employees; not looking to a distant city to find out what they might do, but looking about among their neighbors, finding credit according to their character, not according to their connections, finding credit in proportion to what was known to be in them and behind them, not in proportion to the securities they held that were approved where they were not known. In order to start an enterprise now, you have to be authenticated, in a perfectly impersonal way, not according to your-self, but according to what you own that somebody else approves of your owning. You cannot begin such an enterprise as those that have made America until you are so authenticated, until you have succeeded in ob-taining the good-will of large allied capitalists. Is that freedom? That is dependence, not freedom.

We used to think in the old-fashioned days when life was very simple that all government had to do was to put on a policeman's uniform, and say, "Now don't anybody hurt anybody else." We used to say that the ideal of government was for every man to be left alone and not interfered with, except when he interfered with somebody else; and that the best government was the government that did as little govern-ing as possible. That was the idea that obtained in Jefferson's time. But we are coming now to realize that life is so complicated that we are not dealing with the old conditions, and that the law has to step in and create new conditions under which we may live, the conditions which will make it tolerable for us to live.

—WOODROW WILSON, *The New Freedom*, 1913

11. THE PHILOSOPHY OF RUGGED INDIVIDUALISM

The conflict between laissez-faire and the welfare state came to a head in the campaigns of 1928 and 1932. The Wilsonian New Freedom had, apparently, been repudiated, and the Republicans who were in con-trol of the government all through the twenties gave enthusiastic support to private enterprise. These policies, instinctive rather than reasoned with men like Harding and Coolidge, became articulate with Herbert Hoover. It was Hoover who coined—or at least popularized— the apt phrase "rugged individualism." We give here a characteristic presentation of the Hoover philosophy: his veto of the Muscle Shoals Bill—a bill calling for government operation of the Tennessee Valley dams that were later to be an essential part of the TVA. It would be difficult to find a neater or more dramatic illustration of the difference in political philosophy between the rugged individualists and the welfare-staters than Hoover's veto of the Muscle Shoals Bill and Roosevelt's successful advocacy of the TVA.

To the Senate:

I RETURN herewith, without my approval, Senate Joint Resolution 49, "To provide for the national defense by the creation of a corporation for the operation of the Government properties at and near Muscle Shoals in the State of Alabama; to authorize the letting of the Muscle Shoals properties under certain conditions; and for other purposes."

This bill proposes the transformation of the war plant at Muscle Shoals, together with important expansions, into a permanently operated Government institution for the production and distribution of power and the manufacture of fertilizers. . . .

I am firmly opposed to the Government entering into any business the major purpose of which is competition with our citizens. There are national emergencies which require that the Government should temporarily enter the field of business, but they must be emergency actions and in matters where the cost of the project is secondary to much higher considerations. There are many localities where the Federal Government is justified in the construction of great dams and reservoirs, where navigation, flood control, reclamation or stream regulation are of dominant importance, and where they are beyond the capacity or purpose of private or local government capital to construct. In these cases power is often a by-product and should be disposed of by contract or lease. But for the Federal Government deliberately to go out to build up and expand an occasion to the major purpose of a power and manufacturing business is to break down the initiative and enterprise of the American people; it is destruction of equality of opportunity of our people; it is the negation of the ideals upon which our civilization has been based.

This bill raises one of the important issues confronting our people. That is squarely the issue of Federal Government ownership and operation of power and manufacturing business not as a minor by-product but as a major purpose. Involved in this question is the agitation against the conduct of the power industry. The power problem is not to be solved by the project in this bill. The remedy for abuses in the conduct of that industry lies in regulation and not by the Federal Government entering upon the business itself. I have recommended to the Congress on various occasions that action should be taken to establish Federal regulation of interstate power in cooperation with State authorities. This bill would launch the Federal Government upon a policy of ownership and operation of power utilities upon a basis of competition instead of by the proper Government function of regulation for the protection of all the people. I hesitate to contemplate the future of our institutions, of our country if the preoccupation of its officials is to be no longer the promotion of justice and equal opportunity but is to be devoted to barter in the markets. That is not liberalism, it is degeneration.

—HERBERT HOOVER, Veto of the Muscle Shoals Bill, 1931

12. "WHETHER MEN SERVE GOVERNMENT OR WHETHER GOVERNMENT EXISTS TO SERVE MEN"

The calamitous depression of 1929 and the failure of the Hoover administration to take effective action either for relief or for reconstruction, brought home to millions of Americans the shortcomings of the philosophy of laissez-faire. Franklin D. Roosevelt, the Democratic nominee for the Presidency, submitted a program of positive governmental action on many fronts. This program had grown out of his study of American economic and political history and of his experience as Governor of New York State. The campaign address at the Commonwealth Club in San Francisco contains Roosevelt's most elaborate analysis of the historic issue of laissez-faire and the welfare state. The election was a mandate to reverse the Hoover policies and use the full resources of government to restore prosperity and conserve human and natural resources. Here, then, is the beginning of that final chapter which we are, in a sense, still reading.

I WANT to speak not of politics but of Government. I want to speak not of parties, but of universal principles. They are not political, except in that larger sense in which a great American once expressed a definition of politics, that nothing in all of human life is foreign to the science of politics. . . .

I want to invite you, to consider with me in the large, some of the relationships of Government and economic life that go deeply into our daily lives, our happiness, our future and our security.

The issue of Government has always been whether individual men and women will have to serve some system of Government or economics, or whether a system of Government and economics exists to serve individual men and women. This question has persistently dominated the discussion of Government for many generations. On questions relating to these things men have differed, and for time immemorial it is probable that honest men will continue to differ. . . .

It was in the middle of the nineteenth century that a new force was released and a new dream created. The force was what is called the industrial revolution, the advance of steam and machinery and the rise of the forerunners of the modern industrial plant. The dream was the dream of an economic machine, able to raise the standard of living for everyone; to bring luxury within the reach of the humblest; to annihilate distance by steam power and later by electricity, and to release everyone from the drudgery of the heaviest manual toil. It was to be expected that this would necessarily affect Government. Heretofore, Government had merely been called upon to produce conditions within which people could live happily, labor peacefully, and rest secure. Now it was called upon to aid in the consummation of this new dream. There was, however, a shadow over the dream. To be made real, it required use of the talents of men of tremendous will and tremendous ambition, since by no other force could the problems of financing and engineering and new developments be brought to a consummation.

So manifest were the advantages of the machine age, however, that the United States fearlessly, cheerfully, and, I think, rightly, accepted the bitter with the sweet. It was thought that no price was too high to pay for the advantages which we could draw from a finished industrial system. The history of the last half century is accordingly in large measure a history of a group of financial Titans, whose methods were not scrutinized with too much care, and who were honored in proportion as they produced the results, irrespective of the means they used. The financiers who pushed the railroads to the Pacific were always ruthless, often wasteful, and frequently corrupt; but they did build railroads, and we have them today. It has been estimated that the American investor paid for the American railway system more than three times over in the process; but despite this fact the net advantage was to the United States. As long as we had free land; as long as population was growing by leaps and bounds; as long as our industrial plants were insufficient to supply our own needs, society chose to give the ambitious man free play and unlimited reward provided only that he produced the economic plant so much desired.

During this period of expansion, there was equal opportunity for all and the business of Government was not to interfere but to assist in the development of industry. This was done at the request of business men themselves. The tariff was originally imposed for the purpose of "fostering our infant industry," a phrase I think the older among you will remember as a political issue not so long ago. The railroads were subsidized, sometimes by grants of money, oftener by grants of land; some of the most valuable oil lands in the United States were granted to assist the financing of the railroad which pushed through the Southwest. A nascent merchant marine was assisted by grants of money, or by mail subsidies, so that our steam shipping might ply the seven seas. Some of my friends tell me that they do not want the Government in business. With this I agree; but I wonder whether they realize the implications of the past. For while it has been American doctrine that the Government must not go into business in competition with private enterprises, still it has been traditional, particularly in Republican administrations, for business to ask the Government to put at private disposal all kinds of Government assistance. The same man who tells you that he does not want to see the Government interfere in business—and he means it, and has plenty of good reasons for saying so—is the first to go to Washington and ask the Government for a prohibitory tariff on his product. When things get just bad enough, as they did two years ago, he will go with equal speed to the United States Government and ask for a loan; and the Reconstruction Finance Corporation is the outcome of it. Each group has sought protection from the Government for its own special interests, without realizing that the function of Government must be to favor no small group at the expense of its duty to protect the rights of personal freedom and of private property of all its citizens.

In retrospect we can now see that the turn of the tide came with the turn of the century. We were reaching our last frontier; there was no more free land and our industrial combinations had become great uncontrolled and irresponsible units of power within the State. Clear-sighted men saw with fear the danger that opportunity would no longer be equal; that the growing corporation, like the feudal baron of old, might threaten the economic freedom of individuals to earn a living. In that hour, our anti-trust laws were born. The cry was raised against the great corporations. Theodore Roosevelt, the first great Republican Progressive, fought a Presidential campaign on the issue of "trust busting" and talked freely about malefactors of great wealth. If the Government had a policy it was rather to turn the clock back, to destroy the large combinations and to return to the time when every man owned his individual small business. . . .

Just as freedom to farm has ceased, so also the opportunity in business has narrowed. It still is true that men can start small enterprises, trusting to native shrewdness and ability to keep abreast of competitors; but area after area has been preempted altogether by the great corporations, and even in the fields which still have no great concerns, the small man starts under a handicap. The unfeeling statistics of the past three decades show that the independent business man is running a losing race. Perhaps he is forced to the wall; perhaps he cannot command credit; perhaps he is "squeezed out," in Mr. Wilson's words, by highly organized corporate competitors, as your corner grocery man can tell you. Recently a careful study was made of the concentration of business in the United States. It showed that our economic life was dominated by some six hundred odd corporations who controlled two-thirds of American industry. Ten million small business men divided the other third. More striking still, it appeared that if the process of concentration goes on at the same rate, at the end of another century we shall have all American industry controlled by a dozen corporations, and run by perhaps a hundred men. But plainly, we are steering a steady course toward economic oligarchy, if we are not there already.

Clearly, all this calls for a reappraisal of values. A mere builder of more industrial plants, a creator of more railroad systems, an organizer of more corporations, is as likely to be a danger as a help. The day of the great promoter or the financial Titan, to whom we granted anything if only he would build, or develop, is over. Our task now is not discovery or exploitation of natural resources, or necessarily producing more goods. It is the soberer, less dramatic business of administering resources and plants already in hand, of seeking to reestablish foreign markets for our surplus production, of meeting the problem of under-consumption, of adjusting production to consumption, of distributing wealth and products more equitably, of adapting existing economic organizations to the service of the people. The day of enlightened administration has come.

Just as in older times the central Government was first a haven of refuge, and then a threat, so now in a closer economic system the central and ambitious financial unit is no longer a servant of national desire, but a danger. I would draw the parallel one step farther. We did not think because national Government had become a threat in the 18th century that therefore we should abandon the principle of national Government. Nor today should we abandon the principle of strong economic units called corporations, merely because their power is susceptible of easy abuse. In other times we dealt with the problem of an unduly ambitious central Government by modifying it gradually into a constitutional democratic Government. So today we are modifying and controlling our economic units.

As I see it, the task of Government in its relation to business is to assist the development of an economic declaration of rights, an economic constitutional order. This is the common task of statesman and business man. It is the minimum requirement of a more permanently safe order of things. . . .

I feel that we are coming to a view through the drift of our legislation and our public thinking in the past quarter century that private economic power is, to enlarge an old phrase, a public trust as well. I hold that continued enjoyment of that power by any individual or group must depend upon the fulfillment of that trust. The men who have reached the summit of American business life know this best; happily, many of these urge the binding quality of this greater social contract.

The terms of that contract are as old as the Republic, and as new as the new economic order.

Every man has a right to life; and this means that he has also the right to make a comfortable living. He may by sloth or crime decline to exercise that right; but it may not be denied him. We have no actual famine or dearth; our industrial and agricultural mechanism can produce enough and to spare. Our Government formal and informal, political and economic, owes to everyone an avenue to possess himself of a portion of that plenty sufficient for his needs, through his own work.

Every man has a right to his own property; which means a right to be assured, to the fullest extent attainable, in the safety of his savings. By no other means can men carry the burdens of those parts of life which, in the nature of things, afford no chance of labor; childhood, sickness, old age. In all thought of property, this right is paramount; all other property rights must yield to it. If, in accord with this principle, we must restrict the operations of the speculator, the manipulator, even the financier, I believe we must accept the restriction as needful, not to hamper individualism but to protect it.

These two requirements must be satisfied, in the main, by individuals who claim and hold control of the great industrial and financial combinations which dominate so large a part of our industrial life. They have undertaken to be, not business men, but princes of property. I am not prepared to say that the system which produces them is wrong. I am very clear that they must fearlessly and competently assume the responsibility which goes with the power. So many enlightened business men know this that the statement would be little more than a platitude, were it not for an added implication.

This implication is, briefly, that the responsible heads of finance and industry instead of acting each for himself, must work together to achieve the common end. They must, where necessary, sacrifice this or that private advantage; and in reciprocal self-denial must seek a general advantage. It is here that formal Government—political Government, if you choose—comes in. Whenever in the pursuit of this objective the lone wolf, the unethical competitor, the reckless promoter, the Ishmael or Insull whose hand is against every man's, declines to join in achieving an end recognized as being for the public welfare, and threatens to drag the industry back to a state of anarchy, the Government may properly be asked to apply restraint. Likewise, should the group ever use its collective power contrary to the public welfare, the Government must be swift to enter and protect the public interest.

The Government should assume the function of economic regulation only as a last resort, to be tried only when private initiative, inspired by high responsibility, with such assistance and balance as Government can give, has finally failed. As yet there has been no final failure, because there has been no attempt; and I decline to assume that this nation is unable to meet the situation.

The final term of the high contract was for liberty and the pursuit of happiness. We have learned a great deal of both in the past century. We know that individual liberty and individual happiness mean nothing unless both are ordered in the sense that one man's meat is not another man's poison. We know that the old "rights of personal competency," the right to read, to think, to speak, to choose and live a mode of life, must be respected at all hazards. We know that liberty to do anything which deprives others of those elemental rights is outside the protection of any compact; and that Government in this regard is the maintenance of a balance, within which every individual may have a place if he will take it; in which every individual may find safety if he wishes it; in which every individual may attain such power as his ability permits, consistent with his assuming the accompanying responsibility.

—FRANKLIN D. ROOSEVELT,

Commonwealth Club Address, September 23, 1932

13. THE FAIR DEAL SUCCEEDS THE NEW DEAL

President Truman fell heir not only to Roosevelt's office but to his program. By no means an old-line progressive like Senator George Norris, nor yet one of Roosevelt's disciples like Harry Hopkins, Truman proved himself nevertheless a faithful champion of the Rooseveltian tradition. Effective opposition from a coalition of Republicans and Southern Democrats prevented him from carrying through any substantial reforms in the first three years of his administration. But his 1948 campaign was waged largely on domestic issues, and when he won the election he returned to the unfinished business of the domestic reform program. To all this he gave the name Fair Deal to distinguish it from the New Deal; actually the one was merely an extension of the other.

D URING the last 16 years the American people have been creating a society which offers new opportunities for every man to enjoy his share of the good things of life.

In this society we are conservative about the values and principles which we cherish; but we are forward-looking in protecting those values and principles and in extending their benefits. We have rejected the discredited theory that the fortunes of the Nation should be in the hands of a privileged few. We have abandoned the "trickle down" concept of national prosperity. Instead, we believe that our economic system should rest on a democratic foundation and that wealth should be created for the benefit of all.

The recent election shows that the American people are in favor of this kind of society and want to go on improving it.

The American people have decided that poverty is just as wasteful and just as unnecessary as preventable disease. We have pledged our common resources to help one another in the hazards and struggles of individual life. We believe that no unfair prejudice or artificial distinction should bar any citizen of the United States from an education, or from good health, or from a job that he is capable of performing.

Reinforced by these policies, our private enterprise system has reached new heights of production. Since the boom year of 1929, while our population has increased by only 20 percent, our agricultural production has increased by 45 percent, and our industrial production has increased by 75 percent. We are turning out far more goods and more wealth per worker than we have ever done before.

But, great as our progress has been, we still have a long way to go.

As we look around the country, many of our shortcomings stand out in bold relief.

We are suffering from excessively high prices.

Our production is still not large enough to satisfy our demands.

Our minimum wages are far too low.

Small business is losing ground to growing monopoly.

Our farmers still face an uncertain future. And too many of them lack the benefits of our modern civilization.

Some of our natural resources are still being wasted.

We are acutely short of electric power, although the means for developing such power are abundant.

Five million families are still living in slums and firetraps. Three million families share their homes with others.

Our health is far behind the progress of medical science. Proper medical care is so expensive that it is out of reach of the great majority of our citizens.

Our schools, in many localities, are utterly inadequate.

Our democratic ideals are often thwarted by prejudice and intolerance.

Each of these shortcomings is also an opportunity—an opportunity for the Congress and the President to work for the good of the people.

Our first great opportunity is to protect our economy against the evils of "boom and bust." . . .

The Employment Act of 1946 pledges the Government to use all its resources to promote maximum employment, production, and purchasing power. This means that the Government is firmly committed to protect business and the people against the dangers of recession and against the evils of inflation. This means that the Government must adapt its plans and policies to meet changing circumstances. . . .

We should strengthen our anti-trust laws by closing those loopholes that permit monopolistic mergers and consolidations.

Our national farm program should be improved—not only in the interest of the farmers but for the lasting prosperity of the whole Nation. Our goals should be abundant farm production and parity of income for agriculture. Standards of living on the farm should be just as good as anywhere else in the country.

Farm price supports are an essential part of our program to achieve these ends. Price supports should be used to prevent farm price declines which are out of line with general price levels, to facilitate adjustments in production to consumer demands and to promote good land use. . . .

We must push forward with the development of our rivers for power, irrigation, navigation, and flood control. We should apply the lessons of our Tennessee Valley experience to our other great river basins.

I again recommend that action be taken by the Congress to approve the St. Lawrence seaway and power project.

This is about the fifth time I have recommended it. . . .

The present coverage of the social-security laws is altogether inadequate, and benefit payments are too low. One-third of our workers are not covered. Those who receive old age and survivors insurance benefits receive an average payment of only $25 a month. Many others who cannot work because they are physically disabled are left to the mercy of charity. We should expand our social-security program, both as to size of benefits and extent of coverage, against the economic hazards due to unemployment, old age, sickness, and disability.

We must spare no effort to raise the general level of health in this country. In a nation as rich as ours, it is a shocking fact that tens of millions lack adequate medical care. We are short of doctors, hospitals, and nurses. We must remedy these shortages. Moreover, we need—and we must have without further delay—a system of prepaid medical insurance which will enable every American to afford good medical care.

The housing shortage continues to be acute. As an immediate step, the Congress should enact the provisions for low-rent public housing, slum clearance, farm housing, and housing research which I have repeatedly recommended. The number of low-rent public housing units provided for in the legislation should be increased to 1,000,000 units in the next 7 years. Even this number of units will not begin to meet our need for new housing.

Most of the houses we need will have to be built by private enterprise, without public subsidy. By producing too few rental units and too large a proportion of high-priced houses, the building industry is rapidly pricing itself out of the market. Building costs must be lowered.

The driving force behind our progress is our faith in our democratic institutions. That faith is embodied in the promise of equal rights and equal opportunities which the founders of our Republic proclaimed to their countrymen and to the whole world.

The fulfillment of this promise is among the highest purposes of government. The civil rights proposals I made to the Eightieth Congress, I now repeat to the Eighty-first Congress. They should be enacted in order that the Federal Government may assume the leadership and discharge the obligations clearly placed upon it by the Constitution.

—HARRY S. TRUMAN, "State of the Union" Message, January, 1949.

14. "THE AGENDA OF LIBERALISM"

The heated controversy between the supporters of rugged individualism and of the welfare state tended to confuse rather than to clarify the real issues before the American people. Rugged individualists were not, in fact, anarchists; welfare-staters were not, in reality, socialists. What was needed was a reconsideration of the true nature of liberalism. What was needed was to rescue liberalism from the creeping paralysis that had set in with Ricardo and Mill and Spencer. To this task the most sagacious of contemporary American publicists turned his talents, and the result was a classic of political economy: The Good Society. *Confronted by the conflicting claims of liberty and of governmental intervention, Lippmann went far toward resolving the conflict.* The Good Society *did for its generation what the writings of Lester Ward had done for an earlier one. We can conclude our consideration of the*

welfare state and rugged individualism with these pages in the con-
fident assurance that they will help to explain one of the most difficult
of all contemporary problems and to suggest a solution for it.

A FREE choice between a liberal and a collectivist order does not
exist in fact. That is to say, it does not exist for ordinary men who
wish to maintain and to improve their standard of life.

There is no choice because men are committed to the division of
labor, and it is as impossible for them to live by any other means as
it was for their ancestors in the villages clustered around regional
market towns to exist without a high degree of self-sufficiency. The
apparent choice between a liberal and a collectivist order exists only
in the mind, only *until* collectivism is put fully into practice, only in
the realm of hopes and projects where men discuss what they think
they would like to do. The choice does not exist when they come to find
out what they can do. For there is no way of practising the division of
labor, and of harvesting the fruits of it, except in a social order which
preserves and strives to perfect the freedom of the market. This is the
inexorable law of the industrial revolution, and while men may disobey
that law, the price of their disobedience is the frustration of all their
hopes.

For that reason the débacle of nineteenth-century liberalism may
confidently be ascribed to intellectual error rather than to historical fate.
The renascence of liberalism may be regarded as assured. Behind the
liberal philosophy is the whole force of man's commitment to the
economy of the division of labor, and that necessity must compel the
invention of an appropriate social order. The name "liberal" may be
forgotten, those who call themselves liberals may relapse into humiliated
silence, but still the necessities of the mode of production will compel
men to rediscover and to reëstablish the essential principles of a liberal
society. That is the lesson of the Russian experiment where we see a
nation which has no liberal tradition, which has been indoctrinated with
contempt for liberalism, and is nevertheless compelled by sheer economic
necessity to rediscover by trial and error the rudiments of liberalism.

We may ascribe the eclipse of liberalism to errors that inhibited
necessary reforms. The latter-day liberals became mired in statu quo by
the political dogma of laissez-faire which held them to the idea that

nothing should be done, by the confusion of the classical economics which held them to the idea that nothing needed to be done. In the time of Adam Smith and Jeremy Bentham,—from, say, 1776 to 1832,—liberalism was a philosophy which led the way in adapting the social order to the needs of the new industrial economy; by the middle of the nineteenth century, liberalism had become a philosophy of neglect and refusal to proceed with social adaptation. The impasse to which liberalism had come may be studied in the later teachings of Herbert Spencer and in a line of decisions of the United States Supreme Court under the "due process" clause. But this need not have happened. The classical economics, properly understood, was not an apologetic description of the status quo; it was a normative science which criticized the status quo, disclosing the points at which reform was necessary, and indicating the kind of reform that was desirable. . . .

The real problems of modern societies arise where the social order is not consistent with the requirements of the division of labor. A survey of all the current problems would be a catalogue of these inconsistencies. The catalogue would begin with the pre-natal endowment of the human stock, would traverse all customs, laws, institutions, and policies, and would not be complete until it had included man's conception of his destiny on earth and his valuation of his soul and of the souls of all other men. For where there is conflict between the social heritage and the manner in which men must earn their living, there will be disorder in their affairs and division in their spirits. When the social heritage and the economy do not form a seamless web, there must be rebellion against the world or renunciation of the world. That is why in epochs like our own, when society is at odds with the conditions of its existence, discontent drives some to active violence and some to asceticism and other-worldliness. When the times are out of joint some storm the barricades and others retire into a monastery. Thus it is that the greater part of the literature of our time is in one mood a literature of revolution and in another, often completely fused with it, a literature of escape.

This malaise of the spirit reflects, like the discomfort of a badly fitted shoe, the maladjustment of men to the way they must obtain a living. There are those who are born handicapped; by the deterioration of the stock from which they spring they are without the capacity to make their way. Others grow up handicapped by disease in childhood, by malnutrition and neglect. Others are the casualties of a vicious or stupid family life, carrying with them forever the scars of inferiority and perversion. They do not adapt themselves easily. Then there are those who have been broken by the poverty and squalor of their youth, and who never do obtain an equal opportunity to develop their faculties. There is the whole unresolved task of educating great populations, of equipping men for a life in which they must specialize, yet be capable of changing their specialty. The economy of the division of labor requires, and the classical economics assumes, a population in which these eugenic and educational problems are effectively dealt with. But they are not yet dealt with. Nor do they settle themselves, as the dogma of laissez-faire supposes. And so they must take their place upon the agenda of liberal policy.

The economy requires not only that the quality of the human stock, the equipment of men for life, shall be maintained at some minimum of efficiency, but that the quality should be progressively improved. To live successfully in a world of the increasing interdependence of specialized work requires a continual increase of adaptability, intelligence, and of enlightened understanding of the reciprocal rights and duties, benefits and opportunities, of such a way of life. . . .

There is nothing whatever in the necessities of the new economy which compels society to be indifferent to the human costs. There is no reason whatever why some part of the wealth produced should not be taken by taxation and used to insure and indemnify human beings against their personal losses in the progress of industry. If technological improvement increases wealth,—and, of course, it does,—if society as a whole is richer when an industry moves from a place where costs are high to one where they are lower, then some part of that increased wealth can be used to relieve the victims of progress. It can be used to tide them over while they are changing their occupations, to reëducate them for new occupations, to settle them in new places if they have to move.

Not only is there no reason why a liberal state should not insure and indemnify against its own progressive development, but there is every reason why it should. For if it is properly devised, such a system of social insurance would facilitate the necessary technological changes, and reduce the very human resistance which comes from those who now see themselves the appointed victims of progress. No one can blame a man for hating a machine that will place him in the bread line and unfit him for the only job he has learned to do. . . .

If, now, we consider the agenda as a whole, we shall see, I think, that they imply a different distribution of incomes from that which now obtains in most organized societies. For one thing the effect of these reforms would be drastically to reduce the opportunities for making money by necessitous bargains and by levying tolls through the exercise of legal privileges. These reforms strike at the source of the big incomes which arise from the various kinds of monopoly, from exclusive rights in land and natural resources, from bad markets in which the ignorant and the helpless are at a disadvantage. Income arising from these inequalities of opportunity and legal status are unearned by the criterion of the exchange economy. They are parasitical upon it, not integral with it, and if the actual world corresponded with the theory of the classical economists, these unearned incomes would not be obtained. They are not the wages of labor or management, the interest on capital, or the profits of enterprise, as determined in free and efficient markets, but tolls levied upon wages, interest, and profits by the subversion or the manipulation of the market price for goods and services.

The reformers of liberalism must aim, therefore, at correcting the conditions under which such unearned incomes arise, and in so far as the reforms are thoroughgoing and effective the unearned incomes will not arise. Now the correction of the conditions involves, as we have seen, large social expenditure on eugenics and on education; the conservation of the people's patrimony in the land and natural resources; the development of the people's estate through public works which reclaim land, control floods and droughts, improve rivers and harbors and highways, develop water power, and establish the necessary facilities for transporting and exchanging goods and services; providing the organization of markets by information, inspections, and other services; insurance and indemnification against the risks and losses of technological and economic change; and many other things, such as providing the opportunities for recreation which would not otherwise exist in specialized and congested communities. . . .

I realize that since the existing rights of property and contract are greatly affected by the liberal agenda, many will regard such a disturbance of the status quo as socialism. But that is sheer obfuscation of the mind. It is true that liberalism recognizes the same social problems as does gradual collectivism, and that its reforms cut deep. How could it fail to recognize the problems and still pretend to guide human action? It is true, also, that the liberal remedies require the liquidation of some, and the modification of many, vested rights. How can social maladjustment be cured except by altering vested rights? The status quo cannot be reformed and yet preserved as it is. But, except to the prejudiced, it will be clear that liberal reforms differ radically from collectivist reforms. The difference is that liberalism seeks to improve the exchange economy whereas collectivism would abolish it. Liberalism is radical in relation to the social order but conservative in relation to the division of labor in a market economy. In the liberal philosophy the ideal regulator of the labor of mankind is the perfect market; in the collectivist philosophy it is the perfect plan imposed by an omnipotent sovereign.

Thus, while liberalism must seek to change laws and greatly to modify property and contract as they are now recognized by the laws, the object of liberal reforms is to preserve and facilitate the division of labor in the existing exchange economy. It is in order to fit men for their new way of life that the liberal would spend large sums of public money on education. This does not mean only the training of versatile specialists, though that is necessary. It means also that the whole population must be provided with the cultural equipment that men must have if they are to live effectively, and at ease with themselves, in an interdependent Great Society. The liberal reforms lay great emphasis on the conservation of natural resources and their development: the purpose of these reforms is to maintain the physical foundations of the division of labor. The liberal attack on monopoly, unfair competition, and necessitous bargaining has as its guiding purpose the maintenance of that equal opportunity which the exchange economy presupposes and a high degree of divided labor requires; the method by which liberalism controls the economy is to police the markets, to provide in the broadest sense weights and measures, to make the bargains represent the exchange of true equivalents rather than the victory of superior strength, inside information, legal privileges, conspiracies, secret combinations, corruption, and legalized sharp practices. . . .

If, as in the second half of the nineteenth century, the need for progressive readjustment is misunderstood, neglected, and resisted, the accumulated maladjustments must lead to illiberal reaction. In our time the liberal philosophy is engaged in a struggle to survive and to be reborn, and in this struggle its own failings are the chief strength of its opponents. Liberalism is the normal philosophy of men who live in a Great Society.

—WALTER LIPPMANN, *The Good Society*, 1937

8

Liberty and Order

PERHAPS the most difficult of all the great problems that confront a democratic people is that of reconciling the conflicting claims of liberty and order, freedom and security, conscience and law. It is a very old problem, to be sure. Sophocles addressed himself to it in *Antigone*:

> Nor did I deem thine edicts of such force
> That they, a mortal's bidding, should o'erride
> Unwritten laws, eternal in the heavens.
> Not of today or yesterday are these,
> But live from everlasting. . . .

So did Roman statesmen and philosophers, so too medieval churchmen. It is an ever new problem, one that commands the attention of every Congress and every Court.

There are, however, certain basic considerations we would do well to keep in mind. First, we should remember the absolutely fundamental principle that liberties are inalienable. They are not something conferred on men by a gracious government, and thus subject to being withheld or withdrawn or modified at the pleasure of government; they are something inherent in men as men. There cannot be a question how much liberty government may permit, but only and always how far society may impose limits on the exercise of its own liberties for the common good. A second principle to keep in mind is that order is not an end in itself, but a means to an end. We do not have liberty or, let us say, free enterprise, in order to achieve order; we have order in order to allow liberty and free enterprise to flourish. And orderly society is not a conclusion; it is a point of departure. In any scale of values to which democratic peoples subscribe order takes a place well below that of liberty.

Third, we cannot and must not push either of these concepts to a

366

logical or even to a verbal extreme. Liberty does not mean anarchy, order does not mean totalitarian authority. Or, to put it another way, there is no absolute liberty, and there is no absolute order. Liberty flourishes only in society and in conformity to the requirements of the social order. Absolute order would be a motionless equilibrium, and can be attained only in the graveyard—a lesson the Germans were on their way to learning and that the Communists have yet to learn.

This discovery, that we cannot push either liberty or order to a logical extreme, should neither disconcert us nor disturb us. There are, after all, few absolutes in life. Nor must we hastily conclude that unless we enjoy absolute liberty we have no liberty at all, or that unless we can be sure of complete order we are threatened by anarchy. In every society there must be room for the joints to work, and in a society as big, as varied, and as dynamic as ours this is particularly true. We must apply to these concepts the same common sense standards that we apply to other concepts and practices of society. We do not give up our schools because they cannot guarantee some absolute educational product. We do not abandon the institution of marriage because love is sometimes less than perfect and a high proportion of marriages end in divorce. We do not repudiate the jury system because it cannot achieve absolute justice. We do not reject organized religion because after a good many years with it sin somehow still flourishes. When we deal with such complex and delicate things as the nature of liberty and the nature of authority we must retain our perspective and our balance.

Actually the problem never, or very rarely, confronts us in the abstract but almost always in the concrete. It comes to us in the form of a fugitive slave act and its enforcement in free communities, or of sedition acts in time of war, or of allowing the doctrines of Democracy and Communism to compete in the market place of ideas, or of requiring school children to salute the flag. What this means is that questions involving the conflicting claims of liberty and order cannot be decided in a vacuum or by some abstract and absolute standard, but on their merits, and in the context of the particular problem.

But it is impossible to decide questions on their merits unless we have some prior standard of what is meritorious. If men and women have radically different standards of the meritorious, if they have profoundly different values, there is bound to be trouble. Fortunately the American people are fairly well agreed on their standards, even though they often seem confused about the application of these standards.

And one thing we are agreed upon is that in any scale of values liberty takes precedence over order. Why is this? It is not only because liberty is traditionally, one of those inalienable rights with which all men were born. It is not only because it is guaranteed in the most sacred fashion in State and Federal Constitutions. It is not only because liberty is an essential part of the great tradition of our people and our race, all of us cherishing those great lines of Wordsworth:

> It is not to be thought that the Flood
> Of British freedom, which, to the open sea
> Of the world's praise, from dark antiquity
> Hath flowed . . .
> That this most famous Stream in bogs and sands
> Should perish; and to evil and to good
> Be lost forever. In our halls is hung
> Armoury of the invincible Knights of old:
> We must be free or die, who speaks the tongue
> That Shakespeare spake; the faith and morals hold
> Which Milton held.—In everything we are sprung
> Of Earth's first blood, have titles manifold.

All these considerations assure liberty a favored place in any scale of values that Americans maintain. But an equally strong consideration is that liberty is a necessity. Certainly it is a necessity for our kind of democracy, for our kind of society, for our kind of economy. We do not maintain liberty in order to indulge error; we maintain liberty in order to discover truth. We do not protect science in order to indulge scientists; we protect science in order to make sure of scientific progress. We do not protect academic freedom in order to indulge teachers; we protect academic freedom in order that our colleges and universities may flourish. We cherish liberty, in other words, because we know from experience that we cannot get along without it.

While this problem of liberty and authority is a constant in our history, it has its own fever chart, as it were, and its own climacterics. Four of these command our attention. The first developed out of the conflict between the claims of freedom of conscience and of religion, on the one hand, and of the established church order, on the other. The second came during the early years of the Republic, and grew out of the claims of a rising democracy in challenging the established political order. The third came in connection with slavery and the attempt to enforce fugitive slave laws in the North. The fourth is with us even now. It has come from the reaction to the Communist threat—a reaction which has tempted many of us to attempt to insure loyalty by compulsion and to stamp out nonconformity and dissent.

Every major threat to constituted authority in the past has seemed—to those in authority—to be peculiarly dangerous, so dangerous that it was proper to depart from the principle of toleration and liberty and suppress the particular threat. The first effort, to put down religious dissent, failed because America was too big, the frontier too near, the people too heterogeneous, to make a program of conformity or of compulsion work. The second effort, to put down democracy, failed because the vast majority of the people wanted democracy. The third effort, to maintain the institution of slavery and enforce the fugitive slave laws, failed because, confronted with a conflict between the law of slavery and the ideal of freedom, men chose freedom. It remains to be seen whether the fourth attempt, that of achieving loyalty through compulsion will succeed.

1. THE MASSACHUSETTS BODY OF LIBERTIES

The Puritan founders of the Bay Colony brought with them the Charter of the Massachusetts Bay Company which they transformed into the constitution of the colony. This charter authorized the Governor and assistants to "make Lawes and Ordinances for the Good and Welfare of the saide Company." In accordance with this mandate, and in response to pressure from the freemen, they appointed the Reverend Nathaniel Ward of Ipswich—the "Simple Cobler of Agawam"—to draw up a body of laws or, as it is known, a body of liberties. This was no "libertarian" document. Among other things it provided capital punishment for those who refused to profess faith in God—a provision not, to be sure, enforced. Some aspects of religious intolerance in the colonial period will be examined in our chapter on church and state. But it reasserted fundamental rights that went back to Magna Carta and embraced, as well, many of the guarantees of the recent Petition of Right. Francis Gray, who rediscovered these laws in 1810, calls them "a code of fundamental principles which, taken as a whole, for wisdom, equity, and adaptation to the wants of their community challenge a comparison with any similar production."

THE free fruition of such liberties, immunities, and privileges as humanity, civility, and Christianity call for as due to every man in his place and proportion without impeachment and infringement hath ever been and ever will be the tranquillity and stability of churches and commonwealths. And the denial or deprival thereof, the disturbance if not the ruin of both.

We hold it, therefore, our duty and safety whilst we are about the further establishing of this government to collect and express all such freedoms as for present we foresee may concern us, and our posterity after us, and to ratify them with our solemn consent.

We do, therefore, this day religiously and unanimously decree and confirm these following rights, liberties, and privileges concerning our churches and civil state to be respectively, impartially, and inviolably enjoyed and observed throughout our jurisdiction forever.

1. No man's life shall be taken way, no man's honor or good name shall be stained, no man's person shall be arrested, restrained, banished, dismembered, nor any ways punished, no man shall be deprived of his wife or children, no man's goods or estate shall be taken away from him, nor any way indamaged under color of law or countenance of authority, unless it be by virtue or equity of some express law of the country warranting the same, established by a general court and sufficiently published, or in case of the defect of a law in any particular case by the word of God. And in capital cases, or in cases concerning dismembring or banishment, according to that word to be judged by the General Court.

2. Every person within this jurisdiction, whether inhabitant or foreigner, shall enjoy the same justice and law that is general for the plantation, which we constitute and execute one toward another without partiality or delay. . . .

8. No man's cattle or goods of what kind soever shall be pressed or taken for any public use or service, unless it be by warrant grounded upon some act of the General Court, nor without such reasonable prices and hire as the ordinary rates of the country do afford. And if his

cattle or goods shall perish or suffer damage in such service, the owner shall be sufficiently recompensed.

9. No monopolies shall be granted or allowed amongst us, but of such new inventions that are profitable to the country, and that for a short time. . . .

17. Every man of, or within, this jurisdiction shall have free liberty, notwithstanding any civil power to remove both himself and his family at their pleasure out of the same, provided there be no legal impediment to the contrary. . . .

89. If any people of other nations professing the true Christian religion shall flee to us from the tyranny or oppression of their persecutors, or from famine, wars, or the like necessary and compulsory cause, they shall be entertained and succored amongst us, according to that power and prudence God shall give us.

90. If any ships or other vessels, be it friend or enemy, shall suffer shipwreck upon our coast, there shall be no violence or wrong offered to their persons or goods. But their persons shall be harbored, and relieved, and their goods preserved in safety till authority may be certified thereof, and shall take further order therein.

91. There shall never be any bond slavery, villeinage, or captivity amongst us unless it be lawful captives taken in just wars, and such strangers as willingly sell themselves or are sold to us. And these shall have all the liberties and Christian usages which the law of God established in Israel concerning such persons doth morally require. This exempts none from servitude who shall be judged thereto by authority.

—Massachusetts Body of Liberties, 1641

2. "A TRUE PICTURE OF A COMMONWEALTH"

Roger Williams is familiar to all of us as the earliest and most eloquent champion of religious freedom. He was that; he was also the earliest champion of democracy—of the principle that the "soveraigne, originall and foundation of civill power lies in the People." He was, as Vernon Parrington has said in one of the most splendid of his biographical sketches, "primarily a political philosopher rather than a theologian— one of the acutest and most searching of his generation of Englishmen, the teacher of Vane and Cromwell and Milton, a forerunner of Locke and the natural rights school, one of the most notable democratic thinkers that the English race has produced." We give here a brief letter which is addressed to the same problem that Winthrop discussed —the old but ever new problem of reconciling liberty and order in society.

THAT ever I should speak or write a tittle, that tend to such an infinite liberty of conscience, is a mistake, and which I have ever disclaimed and abhorred. To prevent such mistakes, I shall at present only propose this case: There goes many a ship to sea, with many hundred souls in one ship, whose weal or woe is common, and is a true picture of a commonwealth, or a human combination or society. It hath fallen out sometimes, that both papists and protestants, Jews and Turks, may be embarked in one ship; upon which supposal I affirm, that all the liberty of conscience, that ever I pleaded for, turns upon these two hinges—that none of the papists, protestants, Jews, or Turks, be forced to come to the ship's prayers or worships, nor compelled from their own particular prayers or worship, if they practice any. I further add, that I never denied, that notwithstanding this liberty, the commander of this ship ought to command the ship's course, yea, and also command that justice, peace and sobriety, be kept and practiced, both among the seamen and all the passengers. If any of the seamen refuse to perform their services, or passengers to pay their freight; if any refuse to help, in person or purse, toward the common charges or defence; if any refuse to obey the common laws and orders of the ship, concerning their common peace or preservation; if any shall mutiny and rise up against their commanders and officer; if any should preach or write that there ought to be no commanders or officers, because all are equal in Christ, therefore no masters nor officers, no laws nor orders, nor corrections nor punishments;—I say, I never denied, but in such cases, whatever is pretended, the commander or commanders may judge, resist, compel and punish such transgressors, according to their deserts and merits. This if seriously and honestly minded, may, if it so please the Father of lights, let in some light to such as willingly shut not their eyes.

I remain studious of your common peace and liberty.

—Roger Williams, "On the Limits of Freedom," 1655

3. "THE PUBLIC JUDGMENT WILL CORRECT FALSE REASONING"

No American, perhaps no figure in modern history, contributed more to freedom or to the philosophy of freedom than Thomas Jefferson. We have drawn upon the inexhaustible source of his writings before, and shall draw upon it again. Almost all of his major public papers are permeated with enthusiasm for liberty, boundless confidence in the ability of men—especially men in America—to justify liberty, and an understanding of the nature of the problems that the exercise of liberty was to create. We have given elsewhere the First Inaugural Address, the Kentucky Resolutions, and other public papers that touch on various aspects of the great question of liberty; we must content ourselves here with an extract from the less-known Second Inaugural Address. Here Jefferson addresses himself to a problem that was to become increasingly—and painfully—familiar with the passing of time, the problem of the excesses of the press. The Federalists, as we have seen, were so alarmed by these excesses that they attempted to stop them by the Sedition Act. Since then those who fear the people, and who fear criticism, have resorted again and again to some form of censorship or intimidation. No President was more abused by his contemporaries than Jefferson, but he bore this abuse with equanimity, willing—as he says—that "an experiment should be . . . made whether freedom of discussion, unaided by power, is not sufficient for the . . . protection of truth."

URING the course of this administration, and in order to disturb it, the artillery of the press has been levelled against us, charged with whatsoever its licentiousness could devise or dare. These abuses of an institution so important to freedom and science, are deeply to be regretted, inasmuch as they tend to lessen its usefulness, and to sap its safety; they might, indeed, have been corrected by the wholesome punishments reserved and provided by the laws of the several States against falsehood and defamation; but public duties more urgent press on the time of public servants, and the offenders have therefore been left to find their punishment in the public indignation.

Nor was it uninteresting to the world, that an experiment should be fairly and fully made, whether freedom of discussion, unaided by power, is not sufficient for the propagation and protection of truth—whether a government, conducting itself in the true spirit of its constitution, with zeal and purity, and doing no act which it would be unwilling the whole world to witness, can be written down by falsehood and defamation. The experiment has been tried; you have witnessed the scene; our fellow citizens have looked on, cool and collected, they saw the latent source from which these outrages proceeded; they gathered around these public functionaries, and when the constitution called them to the decision by the suffrage, they pronounced their verdict, honorable to those who had served them, and consolatory to the friend of man, who believes he may be intrusted with his own affairs.

No inference is here intended, that the laws, provided by the State against false and defamatory publications, should not be enforced. He who has time, renders a service to public morals and public tranquillity, in reforming these abuses by the salutary coercions of the law, but the experiment is noted, to prove that, since truth and reason have maintained their ground against false opinions in league with false facts, the press, confined to truth, needs no other legal restraint; the public judgment will correct false reasonings and opinions, on a full hearing of all parties; and no other definite line can be drawn between the inestimable liberty of the press and its demoralizing licentiousness. If there be still improprieties which this rule would not restrain, its supplement must be sought in the censorship of public opinion.

—THOMAS JEFFERSON, Second Inaugural Address, March 4, 1805

4. ON THE MURDER OF ELIJAH LOVEJOY

"I tremble for my country when I reflect that God is just," wrote Jefferson in his Notes on Virginia, *and he was thinking of slavery. It was slavery that challenged, and mocked, the claims of liberty in America for, as Lincoln pointed out in his great Peoria speech of 1854, "it deprives our republican example of its just influence in the world; enables the enemies of free institutions with plausibility to taunt us as hypocrites; causes the real friends of freedom to doubt our sincerity;*

and . . . forces so many good men among ourselves into an open war with the very fundamental principles of civil liberty." In defense of the institution of slavery Southerners formulated not only a pro-slavery argument and a States Rights argument, but an anti-equalitarian and anti-libertarian argument as well. And slavery was a catalytic agent to Northern political thought as well as to Southern. For the Constitution and the law enjoined the rendition of slaves who fled to the North. Was this law to be enforced? More to the point, was it to be obeyed? Or was there a higher law than the Constitution—a law of conscience that might even require civil disobedience?

Our next three documents all deal with one or another aspect of this tremendous problem—a problem which goes straight to the heart of the question of liberty. Was it possible to maintain slavery without fatally harming liberty? Were slavery and liberty compatible; could they exist side by side? Could those who supported slavery tolerate liberty in the long run—liberty even for white men? Or would they illustrate the principle that those who would enslave others must first enslave themselves? Could those who believed in liberty have any part in maintaining slavery? Or would they react as Emerson did, when he heard of the passage of the Fugitive Slave Law of 1850: "This filthy enactment was made in the nineteenth century, by men who could read and write. I will not obey it, by God." Would they say with Thoreau that there was a duty of civil disobedience? More, would they act with the Reverend Theodore Parker to batter down jail doors and rescue fugitive slaves? Would they act with John Brown at Harper's Ferry?

The slavery question has been settled, now, but the issues of political philosophy and conduct which it raised are not of antiquarian interest merely. Every generation has to settle them anew for itself, and perhaps every individual for himself, the great question of man-made law and God-made law or, if that phrasing is too old-fashioned, of law versus conscience. The doctrine of the higher law is in disrepute right now, but a nation which forgets or ignores or suppresses the principle of the higher law is in danger of losing its soul.

But let us turn to Wendell Phillips' eloquent discussion of one aspect of this problem. On November 7, 1837, an abolitionist editor, the Reverend Elijah Lovejoy, was murdered by a mob in Alton, Illinois, while trying to protect his printing press from destruction. The next month a meeting was held in historic Faneuil Hall, Boston, to protest this outrage. At this meeting the pro-slavery Attorney-General of

*Massachusetts, one James T. Austin, came to the defense of the mob
that had murdered Lovejoy and declared that Lovejoy himself had
"died as the fool dieth." It was this extraordinary speech which inspired
young Wendell Phillips—he was then but twenty-six years old—to make
this address. This was the first public appearance of the man who was to
become the greatest orator of his generation and who for the rest of his
life devoted his oratorical and intellectual gifts to the service of the poor
and the oppressed.*

MR. CHAIRMAN:—We have met for the freest discussion of these
resolutions, and the events which gave rise to them. [Cries of
"Question," "Hear him," "Go on," "No gagging," etc.] I hope I shall be
permitted to express my surprise at the sentiments of the last speaker,—
surprise not only at such sentiments from such a man, but at the
applause they have received within these walls. A comparison has been
drawn between the events of the Revolution and the tragedy at Alton.
We have heard it asserted here, in Faneuil Hall, that Great Britain had
a right to tax the Colonies, and we have heard the mob at Alton, the
drunken murderers of Lovejoy, compared to those patriot fathers who
threw the tea overboard! [Great applause.] Fellow-citizens, is this
Faneuil Hall doctrine? ["No, no."] The mob at Alton were met to
wrest from a citizen his just rights,—met to resist the laws. We have
been told that our fathers did the same; and the glorious mantle of
Revolutionary precedent has been thrown over the mobs of our day. . . .
To draw the conduct of our ancestors into a precedent for mobs, for a
right to resist laws we ourselves have enacted, is an insult to their
memory. The difference between the excitements of those days and our
own, which the gentleman in kindness to the latter has overlooked, is
simply this: the men of that day went for the right, as secured by the
laws. They were the people rising to sustain the laws and constitution of
the Province. The rioters of our day go for their own wills, right or
wrong. Sir, when I heard the gentleman lay down principles which
place the murderers of Alton side by side with Otis and Hancock, with
Quincy and Adams, I thought those pictured lips [pointing to the portraits in the Hall] would have broken into voice to rebuke the recreant
American,—the slanderer of the dead. [Great applause and counter
applause.] The gentleman said that he should sink into insignificance if
he dared to gainsay the principles of these resolutions. Sir, for the sentiments he has uttered, on soil consecrated by the prayers of Puritans and

the blood of patriots, the earth should have yawned and swallowed him up. . . .

Throughout that terrible night I find nothing to regret but this, that within the limits of our country, civil authority should have been so prostrated as to oblige a citizen to arm in his own defence, and to arm in vain. The gentleman says Lovejoy was presumptuous and imprudent, —he "died as the fool dieth." And a reverend clergyman of the city tells us that no citizen has a right to publish opinions disagreeable to the community! If any mob follows such publication, on *him* rests its guilt! He must wait, forsooth, till the people come up to it and agree with him! This libel on liberty goes on to say that the want of right to speak as we think is an evil inseparable from republican institutions! If this be so, what are they worth? Welcome the despotism of the Sultan, where one knows what he may publish and what he may not, rather than the tyranny of this many-headed monster, the mob, where we know not what we may do or say, till some fellow-citizen has tried it, and paid for the lesson with his life. This clerical absurdity chooses as a check for the abuses of the press, not the *law*, but the dread of a mob. By so doing, it deprives not only the individual and the minority of their rights, but the majority also, since the expression of *their* opinion may sometimes provoke disturbance from the minority. A few men may make a mob as well as many. The majority, then, have no right, as Christian men, to utter their sentiments, if by any possibility it may lead to a mob! Shades of Hugh Peters and John Cotton, save us from such pulpits!

Imprudent to defend the liberty of the press! Why? Because the defence was unsuccessful? Does success gild crime into patriotism, and the want of it change heroic self-devotion to imprudence? Was Hampden imprudent when he drew the sword and threw away the scabbard? Yet he, judged by that single hour, was unsuccessful. After a short exile, the race he hated sat again upon the throne.

Imagine yourself present when the first news of Bunker Hill battle reached a New England town. The tale would have run thus: "The patriots are routed,—the redcoats victorious,—Warren lies dead upon the field." With what scorn would that *Tory* have been received who should have charged Warren with *imprudence*! who should have said that, bred a physician, he was "out of place" in that battle, and "died as the *fool dieth*"! [Great applause.] How would the intimation have been received that Warren and his associates should have waited a better time? But if success be indeed the only criterion of prudence, *Respice finem*,—wait till the end.

Presumptuous to assert the freedom of the press on American ground! Is the assertion of such freedom before the age? So much before the age as to leave one no right to make it because it displeases the community? Who invents this libel on his country? It is this very thing which entitles Lovejoy to greater praise. The disputed right which provoked the Revolution—taxation without representation—is far beneath that for which he died. [Here there was a strong and general expression of disapprobation.] One word, gentlemen. As much as *thought* is better than money, so much is the cause in which Lovejoy died nobler than a mere question of taxes. James Otis thundered in this Hall when the King did but touch his *pocket*. Imagine, if you can, his indignant eloquence, had England offered to put a gag upon his lips. [Great applause.]

The question that stirred the Revolution touched our civil interests. *This* concerns us not only as citizens, but as immortal beings. Wrapped up in its fate, saved or lost with it, are not only the voice of the statesman, but the instructions of the pulpit, and the progress of our faith.

The clergy "marvellously out of place" where free speech is battled for,—liberty of speech on national sins? Does the gentleman remember that freedom to preach was first gained, dragging in its train freedom to print? I thank the clergy here present, as I reverence their predecessors, who did not so far forget their country in their immediate profession as to deem it duty to separate themselves from the struggle of '76,—the Mayhews and Coopers, who remembered they were citizens before they were clergymen.

Mr. Chairman, from the bottom of my heart I thank that brave little band at Alton for resisting. We must remember that Lovejoy had fled from city to city,—suffered the destruction of three presses patiently. At length he took counsel with friends, men of character, of tried integrity, of wide views, of Christian principle. They thought the crisis had come: it was full time to assert the laws. They saw around them, not a community like our own, of fixed habits, of character moulded and settled, but one "in the gristle, not yet hardened into the bone of manhood." The people there, children of our older States, seem to have forgotten the blood-tried principles of their fathers the moment they lost sight of our New England hills. Something was to be done to show them the priceless value of the freedom of the press, to bring back and set right their wandering and confused ideas. He and his advisers looked out on a community staggering like a drunken man, indifferent to their rights and confused in their feelings. Deaf to argument, haply they might be stunned into sobriety. They saw that of which we cannot judge, the *necessity* of resistance. Insulted law called for it. Public opinion, fast hastening on the downward course, must be arrested.

Does not the event show they judged rightly? Absorbed in a thousand trifles, how has the nation all at once come to a stand? Men begin, as in 1776 and 1640, to discuss principles, to weigh characters, to find out where they are. Haply we may awake before we are borne over the precipice.

I am glad, Sir, to see this crowded house. It is good for us to be here. When Liberty is in danger, Faneuil Hall has the right, it is her duty, to strike the key-note for these United States. I am glad, for one reason, that remarks such as those to which I have alluded have been uttered here. The passage of these resolutions, in spite of this opposition, led by the Attorney-General of the Commonwealth, will show more clearly, more decisively, the deep indignation with which Boston regards this outrage.

—WENDELL PHILLIPS, Speech on the Murder of Lovejoy, 1837

5. THE DUTY OF CIVIL DISOBEDIENCE

This famous essay needs no introduction and little explanation. It grew out of Thoreau's own experience. Bitterly opposed to slavery and disturbed by the coming of war with Mexico—a war which he thought was fought for the expansion of slave territory—Thoreau decided to disassociate himself from his government by refusing to pay taxes. In the summer of 1845 he was arrested and jailed, but was released the next day when a relative paid the disputed taxes. Nothing that Thoreau ever wrote, not even Walden, *has been more widely read or more influential than this essay which first appeared in 1849 under the title, "Resistance to Civil Government."*

THE practical reason why, when the power is once in the hands of the people, a majority are permitted, and for a long period continue, to rule is not because they are most likely to be in the right, nor because this seems fairest to the minority, but because they are physically the strongest. But a government in which the majority rule in all cases cannot be based on justice, even as far as men understand it. Can there not be a government in which majorities do not virtually decide right and wrong, but conscience?—in which majorities decide only those questions to which the rule of expediency is applicable? Must the citizen ever for a moment, or in the least degree, resign his conscience to the legislator? Why has every man a conscience, then? I think that we should be men first, and subjects afterward. It is not desirable to cultivate a respect for the law, so much as for the right. The only obligation which I have a right to assume is to do at any time what I think right. It is truly enough said, that a corporation has no conscience; but a corporation of conscientious men is a corporation *with* a conscience. Law never made men a whit more just; and, by means of their respect for it, even the well-disposed are daily made the agents of injustice. . . .

The mass of men serve the state thus, not as men mainly, but as machines, with their bodies. They are the standing army, and the militia, jailors, constables, posse comitatus, etc. In most cases there is no free exercise whatever of the judgment or of the moral sense; but they put themselves on a level with wood and earth and stones; and wooden men can perhaps be manufactured that will serve the purpose as well. Such command no more respect than men of straw or a lump of dirt. They have the same sort of worth only as horses and dogs. Yet such as these even are commonly esteemed good citizens. Others—as most legislators, politicians, lawyers, ministers, and office-holders—serve the state chiefly with their heads; and, as they rarely make any moral distinctions, they are as likely to serve the Devil, without *intending* it, as God. A very few, as heroes, patriots, martyrs, reformers in the great sense, and *men*, serve the state with their consciences also, and so necessarily resist it for the most part; and they are commonly treated as enemies by it. . . .

How does it become a man to behave toward this American government to-day? I answer, that he cannot without disgrace be associated with it. I cannot for an instant recognize that political organization as *my* government which is the *slave's* government also.

All men recognize the right of revolution; that is, the right to refuse allegiance to, and to resist, the government, when its tyranny or its inefficiency are great and unendurable. But almost all say that such is not the case now. But such was the case, they think, in the Revolution of '75. If one were to tell me that this was a bad government because it taxed certain foreign commodities brought to its ports, it is most probable that I should not make an ado about it, for I can do without them. All machines have their friction; . . . But when the friction comes to have its machine, and oppression and robbery are organized, I say, let us not have such a machine any longer. In other words, when a sixth of the population of a nation which has undertaken to be the refuge of liberty are slaves, and a whole country is unjustly overrun and conquered by a foreign army, and subjected to military law, I think that it is not too soon for honest men to rebel and revolutionize. What makes this duty the more urgent is the fact that the country so overrun is not our own, but ours is the invading army. . . .

Practically speaking, the opponents to a reform in Massachusetts are not a hundred thousand politicians at the South, but a hundred thousand merchants and farmers here, who are more interested in commerce and agriculture than they are in humanity, and are not prepared to do justice to the slave and to Mexico, *cost what it may*. I quarrel not with far-off foes, but with those who, near at home, coöperate with, and do the bidding of, those far away, and without whom the latter would be harmless. We are accustomed to say, that the mass of men are unprepared; but improvement is slow, because the few are not materially wiser or better than the many. It is not so important that many should be as good as you, as that there be some absolute goodness somewhere; for that will leaven the whole lump. There are thousands who are *in opinion* opposed to slavery and to the war, who yet in effect do nothing to put an end to them; who, esteeming themselves children of Washington and Franklin, sit down with their hands in their pockets, and say that they know not what to do, and do nothing; who even postpone the question of freedom to the question of free-trade, and quietly read the prices-current along with the latest advices from Mexico, after dinner, and, it may be, fall asleep over them both. What is the price-current of an honest man and patriot to-day? They hesitate, and they regret, and sometimes they petition; but they do nothing in earnest and with effect. They will wait, well disposed, for others to remedy the evil, that they may no longer have it to regret. At most, they give only a cheap vote, and a feeble countenance and God-speed, to the right, as it goes by them. There are nine hundred and ninety-nine patrons of virtue to one virtuous man. But it is easier to deal with the real possessor of a thing than with the temporary guardian of it. . . .

Unjust laws exist: shall we be content to obey them, or shall we endeavor to amend them, and obey them until we have succeeded, or shall we transgress them at once? Men generally, under such a government as this, think that they ought to wait until they have persuaded the majority to alter them. They think that, if they should resist, the remedy would be worse than the evil. But it is the fault of the government itself that the remedy *is* worse than the evil. *It* makes it worse. Why is it not more apt to anticipate and provide for reform? Why does it not cherish its wise minority? Why does it cry and resist before it is hurt? Why does it not encourage its citizens to be on the alert to point out its faults, and *do* better than it would have them? Why does it always crucify Christ, and excommunicate Copernicus and Luther, and pronounce Washington and Franklin rebels? . . .

I do not hesitate to say, that those who call themselves Abolitionists should at once effectually withdraw their support, both in person and property, from the government of Massachusetts and not wait till they constitute a majority of one, before they suffer the right to prevail through them. I think that it is enough if they have God on their side, without waiting for that other one. Moreover, any man more right than his neighbors constitutes a majority of one already.

I meet this American government, or its representative, the state government, directly, and face to face, once a year—no more—in the person of its tax-gatherer; this is the only mode in which a man situated as I am necessarily meets it; and it then says distinctly, Recognize me; and the simplest, most effectual, and, in the present posture of affairs, the indispensablest mode of treating with it on this head, of expressing your little satisfaction with and love for it, is to deny it then. My civil neighbor, the tax-gatherer, is the very man I have to deal with,—for it is, after all, with men and not with parchment that I quarrel,—and he has voluntarily chosen to be an agent of the government. How shall he ever know well what he is and does as an officer of the government, or as a man, until he is obliged to consider whether he shall treat me, his neighbor, for whom he has respect, as a neighbor and well-disposed man, or as a maniac and disturber of the peace, and see if he can get over this obstruction to his neighborliness without a ruder and more impetuous thought or speech corresponding with his action. I know this well, and if one thousand, if one hundred, if ten men whom I could name,—if ten *honest* men only,—ay if *one* HONEST man, in this State of Massachusetts, *ceasing to hold slaves*, were actually to withdraw from this copartnership, and be locked up in the county jail therefor, it would be the abolition of slavery in America. For it matters not how small the beginning may seem to be: what is once well done is done forever. . . .

Under a government which imprisons any unjustly, the true place for a just man is also a prison. The proper place to-day, the only place which Massachusetts has provided for her freer and less desponding spirits, is in her prisons, to be put out and locked out of the State by her own act, as they have already put themselves out by their principles. It is there that the fugitive slave, and the Mexican prisoner on parole, and the Indian come to plead the wrongs of his race should find them; on that separate, but more free and honorable ground, where the State places those who are not *with* her, but *against* her,—the only house in a slave State in which a free man can abide with honor. If any think that their influence would be lost there, and their voices no longer afflict the ear of the State, that they would not be as an enemy within its walls, they do not know by how much truth is stronger than error, nor how much more eloquently and effectively he can combat injustice who has experienced a little in his own person. Cast your whole vote, not a strip of paper merely, but your whole influence. A minority is powerless while it conforms to the majority; it is not even a minority then; but it is irresistible when it clogs by its whole weight. If the alternative is to keep all just men in prison, or give up war and slavery, the State will not hesitate which to choose. If a thousand men were not to pay their tax-bills this year, that would not be a violent and bloody measure, as it would be to pay them, and enable the State to commit violence and shed innocent blood. This is, in fact, the definition of a peaceable revolution, if any such is possible. If the tax-gatherer, or any other public officer, asks me, as one has done, "But what shall I do?" my answer is, "If you really wish to do anything, resign your office." When the subject has refused allegiance, and the officer has resigned his office, then the revolution is accomplished. But even suppose blood should flow. Is there not a sort of blood shed when the conscience is wounded? Through this wound a man's real manhood and immortality flow out, and he bleeds to an everlasting death. I see this blood flowing now. . . .

The authority of government, even such as I am willing to submit to, —for I will cheerfully obey those who know and can do better than I, and in many things even those who neither know nor can do so well,— is still an impure one: to be strictly just, it must have the sanction and consent of the governed. It can have no pure right over my person and property but what I concede to it. The progress from an absolute to a limited monarchy, from a limited monarchy to a democracy, is a progress toward a true respect for the individual. Even the Chinese philosopher was wise enough to regard the individual as the basis of the empire. Is a democracy, such as we know it, the last improvement possible in government? Is it not possible to take a step further towards recognizing and organizing the rights of man? There will never be a really free and enlightened State until the State comes to recognize the individual as a higher and independent power, from which all its own power and authority are derived, and treats him accordingly. I please myself with imagining a State at last which can afford to be just to all men, and to treat the individual with respect as a neighbor; which even would not think it inconsistent with its own repose if a few were to live aloof from it, not meddling with it, nor embraced by it, who fulfilled all the duties of neighbors and fellow-men. A State which bore this kind of fruit, and suffered it to drop off as fast as it ripened, would prepare the way for a still more perfect and glorious State, which also I have imagined, but not yet anywhere seen.

—HENRY DAVID THOREAU, "Civil Disobedience," 1849

6. HUCK AND JIM ON THE RAFT

If there is a "great American novel," it is, by all but common consent, Huckleberry Finn. *This wonderful chapter goes far to explain why. For here is not only an enthralling story; here is a sermon as well. What Thoreau said in "Civil Disobedience," Mark Twain here says in unforgettable narrative. The vast majority of Americans who came up against the problem of the conflict between law and conscience were not saints like Whittier or geniuses like Thoreau; they were simple people like Huck. And most of those who solved the problem in favor of conscience did so pretty much as Huck did when he saved his friend Jim.* Huckleberry Finn *was written in the 1870's and published in 1885, but describes life along the Mississippi in the fifties.*

WE SLEPT most all day, and started out at night, a little ways behind a monstrous long raft that was as long going by as a procession. She had four long sweeps at each end, so we judged she carried as many as thirty men, likely. She had five big wigwams aboard, wide apart, and an open campfire in the middle, and a tall flag-pole at each end. There was a power of style about her. It *amounted* to something being a raftsman on such a craft as that.

We went drifting down into a big bend, and the night clouded up and got hot. The river was very wide, and was walled with solid timber on both sides; you couldn't see a break in it hardly ever, or a light. We talked about Cairo, and wondered whether we would know it when we got to it. I said likely we wouldn't, because I had heard say there warn't but about a dozen houses there, and if they didn't happen to have them lit up, how was we going to know we was passing a town? Jim said if the two big rivers joined together there, that would show. But I said maybe we might think we was passing the foot of an island and coming into the same old river again. That disturbed Jim—and me too. So the question was, what to do? I said, paddle ashore the first time a light showed, and tell them pap was behind, coming along with a trading-scow, and was a green hand at the business, and wanted to know how far it was to Cairo. Jim thought it was a good idea, so we took a smoke on it and waited.

There warn't nothing to do now but to look out sharp for the town, and not pass it without seeing it. He said he'd be mighty sure to see it, because he'd be a free man the minute he seen it, but if he missed it he'd be in a slave country again and no more show for freedom. Every little while he jumps up and says:

"Dah she is?"

But it warn't. It was Jack-o'-lanterns, or lightning-bugs; so he set down again, and went to watching, same as before. Jim said it made him all over trembly and feverish to be so close to freedom. Well, I can tell you it made me all over trembly and feverish, too, to hear him, because I begun to get it through my head that he *was* most free—and who was to blame for it? Why, *me*. I couldn't get that out of my conscience, no how nor no way. It got to troubling me so I couldn't rest; I couldn't stay still in one place. It hadn't ever come home to me before, what this thing was that I was doing. But now it did; and it stayed with me, and scorched me more and more. I tried to make out to myself that *I* warn't to blame, because *I* didn't run Jim off from his rightful owner; but it warn't no use, conscience up and says, every time, "But you knowed he was running for his freedom, and you could 'a' paddled ashore and told somebody." That was so—I couldn't get around that no way. That was where it pinched. Conscience say to me, "What had poor Miss Watson done to you that you could see her nigger go off right under your eyes and never say one single word? What did that poor old woman do to you that you could treat her so mean? Why, she tried to learn you your book, she tried to learn you your manners, she tried to be good to you every way she knowed how. *That's* what she done."

I got to feeling so mean and so miserable I most wished I was dead. I fidgeted up and down the raft, abusing myself to myself, and Jim was fidgeting up and down past me. We neither of us could keep still. Every time he danced around and says, "Dah's Cairo!" it went through me like a shot, and I thought if it *was* Cairo I reckoned I would die of miserableness.

Jim talked out loud all the time while I was talking to myself. He was saying how the first thing he would do when he got to a free state he would go to saving up money and never spend a single cent, and when he got enough he would buy his wife, which was owned on a farm close to where Miss Watson lived; and then they would both work to buy the two children, and if their master wouldn't sell them, they'd get an Ab'litionist to go and steal them.

It most froze me to hear such talk. He wouldn't ever dared to talk such talk in his life before. Just see what a difference it made in him the minute he judged he was about free. It was according to the old saying, "Give a nigger an inch and he'll take an ell." Thinks I, this is what comes of my not thinking. Here was this nigger, which I had as good as helped to run away, coming right out flat-footed and saying he would steal his children—children that belonged to a man I didn't even know; a man that hadn't ever done me no harm.

I was sorry to hear Jim say that, it was such a lowering of him. My conscience got to stirring me up hotter than ever, until at last I says to it, "Let up on me—it ain't too late yet—I'll paddle ashore at the first light and tell." I felt easy and happy and light as a feather right off. All my troubles was gone. I went to looking out sharp for a light, and sort of singing to myself. By and by one showed. Jim sings out:

"We's safe, Huck, we's safe! Jump up and crack yo' heels! Dat's de good ole Cairo at las', I jis knows it!"

I says:

"I'll take the canoe and go and see, Jim. It mightn't be, you know."

He jumped and got the canoe ready, and put his old coat in the bottom for me to set on, and give me the paddle; and as I shoved off, he says:

"Pooty soon I'll be a-shoutin' for joy, en I'll say, it's all on accounts o' Huck; I's a free man, en I couldn't ever ben free ef it hadn't ben for Huck; Huck done it. Jim won't ever forgit you, Huck; you's de bes' fren' Jim's ever had, en you's de *only* fren' ole Jim's got now."

I was paddling off, all in a sweat to tell on him; but when he says this, it seemed to kind of take the tuck all out of me. I went along slow then, and I warn't right down certain whether I was glad I started or whether I warn't. When I was fifty yards off, Jim says:

"Dah you goes, de ole true Huck; de on'y white genlman dat ever kep' his promise to ole Jim."

Well, I just felt sick. But I says, I *got* to do it—I can't get *out* of it. Right then along comes a skiff with two men in it with guns, and they stopped and I stopped. One of them says:

"What's that yonder?"

"A piece of raft," I says.

"Do you belong on it?"

"Yes, sir."

"Any men on it?"

"Only one, sir."

"Well, there's five niggers run off to-night up yonder, above the head of the bend. Is your man white or black?"

I didn't answer up promptly. I tried to, but the words wouldn't come. I tried for a second or two to brace up and out with it, but I warn't man enough—hadn't the spunk of a rabbit. I see I was weakening; so I just give up trying, and up and says:

"He's white."

"I reckon we'll go and see for ourselves."

"I wish you would," says I, "because it's pap that's there, and maybe you'd help me tow the raft ashore where the light is. He's sick—and so is mam and Mary Ann."

"Oh, the devil! we're in a hurry, boy. But I s'pose we've got to. Come, buckle to your paddle, and let's get along."

I buckled to my paddle and they laid to their oars. When we had made a stroke or two, I says:

"Pap'll be mighty much obleeged to you, I can tell you. Everybody goes away when I want them to help me tow the raft ashore, and I can't do it by myself."

"Well, that's infernal mean. Odd, too. Say, boy, what's the matter with your father?"

"It's the—a—the—well, it ain't anything much."

They stopped pulling. It warn't but a mighty little ways to the raft now. One says:

"Boy, that's a lie. What *is* the matter with your pap? Answer up square now, and it'll be the better for you."

"I will, sir, I will, honest—but don't leave us, please. It's the—the— Gentlemen, if you'll only pull ahead, and let me heave you the head-line, you won't have to come a-near the raft—please do."

"Set her back, John, set her back!" says one. They backed water. "Keep away, boy—keep to looard. Confound it, I just expect the wind has blowed it to us. Your pap's got the smallpox, and you know it precious well. Why didn't you come out and say so? Do you want to spread it all over?"

"Well," says I, a-blubbering, "I've told everybody before, and they just went away and left us."

"Poor devil, there's something in that. We are right down sorry for you, but we—well, hang it, we don't want the smallpox, you see. Look here, I'll tell you what to do. Don't you try to land by yourself, or you'll smash everything to pieces. You float along down about twenty miles, and you'll come to a town on the left-hand side of the river. It will be long after sun-up then, and when you ask for help you tell them your folks are all down with chills and fever. Don't be a fool again, and let people guess what is the matter. Now we're trying to do you a kindness; so you just put twenty miles between us, that's a good boy. It wouldn't do any good to land yonder where the light is—it's only a wood-yard. Say, I reckon your father's poor, and I'm bound to say he's in pretty hard luck. Here, I'll put a twenty-dollar gold piece on this board, and you get it when it floats by. I feel mighty mean to leave you; but my kingdom! it won't do to fool with smallpox, don't you see?"

"Hold on, Parker," says the man, "here's a twenty to put on the board for me. Good-by, boy; you do as Mr. Parker told you, and you'll be all right."

"That's so, my boy—good-by, good-by. If you see any runaway niggers you get help and nab them, and you can make some money by it."

"Good-by, sir," says I; "I won't let no runaway niggers get by me if I can help it."

They went off and I got aboard the raft, feeling bad and low, because I knowed very well I had done wrong, and I see it warn't no use for me to try to learn to do right; a body that don't get *started* right when he's little ain't got no show—when the pinch comes there ain't nothing to back him up and keep him to his work, and so he gets beat. Then I thought a minute, and says to myself, hold on; s'pose you'd 'a' done right and give Jim up, would you felt better than what you do now? No, says I, I'd feel bad—I'd feel just the same way I do now. Well, then, says I, what's the use you learning to do right when it's troublesome to do right and ain't no trouble to do wrong, and the wages is just the same? I was stuck. I couldn't answer that. So I reckoned I wouldn't bother no more about it, but after this always do whichever come handiest at the time.

I went into the wigwam; Jim warn't there. I looked all around; he warn't anywhere. I says:

"Jim!"

"Here I is, Huck. Is dey out o' sight yit? Don't talk loud."

He was in the river under the stern oar, with just his nose out. I told him they were out of sight, so he come aboard. He says:

"I was a-listenin' to all de talk, en I slips into de river en was gwyne to shove for sho' if dey come aboard. Den I was gwyne to swim to de raf' agin when dey was gone. But lawsy, how you did fool 'em, Huck! Dat *wuz* de smartes' dodge! I tell you, chile, I 'spec it save' ole Jim—ole Jim ain't going to forgit you for dat, honey."

Then we talked about the money. It was a pretty good raise—twenty dollars apiece. Jim said we could take deck passage on a steamboat now, and the money would last us as far as we wanted to go in the free states. He said twenty mile more warn't far for the raft to go, but he wished we was already there.

—MARK TWAIN, *The Adventures of Huckleberry Finn*

7. THE CONSTITUTIONAL LIMITS OF FREE SPEECH

The problem that perplexed Lincoln—how far it was right for government to restrain liberty in order to preserve the nation—came up again in the First and Second World Wars. The answer could not be a doctrinaire one, nor could any answer wholly satisfy either those who thought first in terms of order or those who thought first in terms of freedom. As so often in our history, it was the Supreme Court which worked out a compromise solution—if any compromise can ever be a solution. This came chiefly in a series of notable opinions by Justice Oliver Wendell Holmes. The first of these, involving the constitutionality of the Espionage Act of 1917, furnished the occasion for the formulation of the "clear and present danger" test—the test which has now been all but officially adopted by the courts. The second was a dissenting opinion, but as with most of Holmes's dissents, the principles pronounced were later accepted by the Court as sound law. This, Abrams versus the United States, like the first, involved the interpretation of the First Amendment. This is possibly the most famous of all Holmes's dissents.

A. "A Clear and Present Danger"

HOLMES, J. This is an indictment in three counts. The first charges a conspiracy to violate the Espionage Act of June 15, 1917 . . . by causing and attempting to cause insubordination, &c., in the military and naval forces of the United States, and to obstruct the recruiting and enlistment service of the United States, when the United States was at war with the German Empire, to wit, that the defendants wilfully conspired to have printed and circulated to men who had been called and accepted for military service under the Act of May 18, 1917, a document set forth and alleged to be calculated to cause such insubordination and obstruction. The count alleges overt acts in pursuance of the conspiracy, ending in the distribution of the document set forth. . . . They set up the First Amendment to the Constitution forbidding Congress to make any law abridging the freedom of speech, or of the press, and bringing the case here on that ground have argued some other points also of which we must dispose.

It is argued that the evidence, if admissible, was not sufficient to prove that the defendant Schenck was concerned in sending the documents. According to the testimony Schenck said he was general secretary of the Socialist party and had charge of the Socialist headquarters from which the documents were sent. He identified a book found there as the minutes of the Executive Committee of the party. The book showed a resolution of August 13, 1917, that 15,000 leaflets should be printed on the other side of one of them in use, to be mailed to men who had passed exemption boards, and for distribution. Schenck personally attended to the printing. On August 20 the general secretary's report said, "Obtained new leaflets from printer and started work addressing envelopes" &c.; and there was a resolve that Comrade Schenck be allowed $125 for sending leaflets through the mail. He said that he had about fifteen or sixteen thousand printed. There were files of the circular in question in the inner office which he said were printed on the other side of the one sided circular and were there for distribution. Other copies were proved to have been sent through the mails to drafted men. Without going into confirmatory details that were proved, no reasonable man could doubt that the defendant Schenck was largely instrumental in sending the circulars about. . . .

The document in question upon its first printed side recited the first section of the Thirteenth Amendment, said that the idea embodied in it was violated by the Conscription Act and that a conscript is little better than a convict. In impassionated language it intimated that conscription was despotism in its worse form and a monstrous wrong against humanity in the interest of Wall Street's chosen few. It said, "Do not submit to intimidation," but in form at least confined itself to peaceful measures such as a petition for the repeal of the act. The other and later printed side of the sheet was headed "Assert Your Rights." It stated reasons for alleging that any one violated the Constitution when he refused to recognize "your right to assert your opposition to the draft," and went on "If you do not assert and support your rights, you are helping to deny or disparage rights which it is the solemn duty of all citizens and residents of the United States to retain." It described the arguments on the other side as coming from cunning politicians and a mercenary capitalist press, and even silent consent to the conscription law as helping to support an infamous conspiracy. It denied the power to send our citizens away to foreign shores to shoot up the people of other lands, and added that words could not express the condemnation such cold-blooded ruthlessness deserves, &c., &c., winding up "You must do your share to maintain, support and uphold the rights of the people of this country." Of course the document would not have been sent unless it had been intended to have some effect, and we do not see what effect it could be expected to have upon persons subject to the draft except to influence them to obstruct the carrying of it out. The defendants do not deny that the jury might find against them on this point.

But it is said, suppose that that was the tendency of this circular, it is protected by the First Amendment to the Constitution. . . . We admit that in many places and in ordinary times the defendants in saying all that was said in the circular would have been within their constitutional rights. But the character of every act depends upon the circumstances in which it is done. The most stringent protection of free speech would not protect a man in falsely shouting fire in a theatre and causing a panic. It does not even protect a man from an injunction against uttering words that may have all the effect of force. The question in every case is whether the words used are used in such circumstances and are of such a nature as to create a clear and present danger that they will bring about the substantive evils that Congress has a right to prevent. It is a question of proximity and degree. When a nation is at war many things that might be said in time of peace are such a hindrance to its effort that their utterance will not be endured so long as men fight and that no Court could regard them as protected by any constitutional right. It seems to be admitted that if an actual obstruction of the recruiting service were proved, liability for words that produced that effect might be enforced. The statute of 1917 in sec. 4 punishes conspiracies to obstruct as well as actual obstruction. If the act, (speaking, or circulating a paper,) its tendency and the intent with which it is done are the same, we perceive no ground for saying that success alone warrants making the act a crime. . . .
Judgements affirmed.

—JUSTICE OLIVER WENDELL HOLMES,
Opinion in Schenck *v.* United States, 1919

B. "FREE TRADE IN IDEAS"

HOLMES, J.   In this case sentences of twenty years imprisonment have been imposed for the publishing of two leaflets that I believe the defendants had as much right to publish as the Government has to publish the Constitution of the United States now vainly invoked by them. Even if I am technically wrong and enough can be squeezed from these poor and puny anonymities to turn the color of legal litmus paper; I will add, even if what I think the necessary intent were shown; the most nominal punishment seems to me all that possibly could be inflicted, unless the defendants are to be made to suffer not for what the indictment alleges but for the creed that they avow—a creed that I believe to be the creed of ignorance and immaturity when honestly held, as I see no reason to doubt that it was held here, but which, although made the subject of examination at the trial, no one has a right even to consider in dealing with the charges before the Court.

Persecution for the expression of opinions seems to me perfectly logical. If you have no doubt of your premises or your power and want a certain result with all your heart you naturally express your wishes in law and sweep away all opposition. To allow opposition by speech seems to indicate that you think the speech impotent, as when a man says that he has squared the circle, or that you do not care whole-heartedly for the result, or that you doubt either your power or your premises. But when men have realized that time has upset many fighting faiths, they may come to believe even more than they believe the very foundations of their own conduct that the ultimate good desired is better reached by free trade in ideas—that the best test of truth is the power of the thought to get itself accepted in the competition of the market, and that truth is the only ground upon which their wishes safely can be carried out. That at any rate is the theory of our Constitution. It is an experiment, as all life is an experiment. Every year if not every day we have to wager our salvation upon some prophecy based upon imperfect knowledge. While that experiment is part of our system I think that we should be eternally vigilant against attempts to check the expression of opinions that we loathe and believe to be fraught with death, unless they so imminently threaten immediate interference with the lawful and pressing purposes of the law that an immediate check is required to save the country. I wholly disagree with the argument of the Government that the First Amendment left the common law as to seditious libel in force. History seems to me against the notion. I had conceived that the United States through many years had shown its repentence for the Sedition Act of 1798, by repaying fines that it imposed. Only the emergency that makes it immediately dangerous to leave the correction of evil counsels to time warrants making any exception to the sweeping command, "Congress shall make no law . . . abridging the freedom of speech." Of course I am speaking only of expressions of opinion and exhortations, which were all that were uttered here, but I regret that I cannot put into more impressive words my belief that in their conviction upon this indictment the defendants were deprived of their rights under the Constitution of the United States.

Mr. Justice Brandeis concurs with the foregoing opinion.

—Justice Oliver Wendell Holmes,
Dissenting Opinion in Abrams *v.* United States, 1919

8. "IT IS THE FUNCTION OF SPEECH TO FREE MEN FROM THE BONDAGE OF IRRATIONAL FEAR"

The "clear and present danger" rule was early accepted by the Court, but two vexatious questions remained. First, where was the line to be drawn between a remote and a present danger and second, who was to draw the line? These questions were to come up again and again, most dramatically, perhaps, in the decision on the trial of Communist leaders for conspiracy in 1951, Dennis versus the United States. We give here the eloquent and sagacious observations of Justice Louis Brandeis, with Holmes the most distinguished figure on the Supreme Court in the first half of the twentieth century.

FEAR OF serious injury cannot alone justify suppression of free speech and assembly. Men feared witches and burnt women. It is the function of speech to free men from the bondage of irrational fears. To justify suppression of free speech there must be reasonable ground to fear that serious evil will result if free speech is practiced. There must be a reasonable ground to believe that the danger apprehended is imminent. There must be reasonable ground to believe that the evil to be prevented is a serious one. Every denunciation of existing law tends in some measure to increase the probability that there will be violation of it. Condonation of a breach enhances the probability. Propagation of the criminal state of mind by teaching syndicalism increases it. Advocacy of law-breaking heightens it still further. But even advocacy of violation, however reprehensible morally, is not a justification for denying free speech where the advocacy falls short of incitement and there is nothing to indicate that advocacy would be immediately acted on. The wide difference between advocacy and incitement, between preparation and attempt, between assembling and conspiracy, must be borne in mind. In order to support a finding of a clear and present danger it must be shown either that immediate serious violence was to be expected or was advocated, or that the past conduct furnished reason to believe that such advocacy was then contemplated.

Those who won our independence by revolution were not cowards. They did not fear political change. They did not exalt order at the cost of liberty. To courageous, self-reliant men, with confidence in the power of free and fearless reasoning applied through the processes of popular government, no danger flowing from speech can be deemed clear and present, unless the incidence of the evil apprehended is so imminent that it may befall before there is an opportunity for full discussion. If there be time to expose through discussion the falsehood and fallacies to avert the evil by processes of education, the remedy to be applied is more speech, not enforced silence.

—JUSTICE LOUIS BRANDEIS, Opinion in Whitney *v*. California, 1927

9. "TO THE END THAT CHANGES MAY BE OBTAINED BY PEACEFUL MEANS"

Here is still another contribution from the Supreme Court to the reconciliation of liberty and order. This decision concerned the extent to which the States might limit those freedoms of speech and of assembly guaranteed in the First and Fourteenth Amendments. More specifically it concerned the constitutionality of an Oregon criminal syndicalism law which made it a criminal offense even to attend a meeting of any organization whose doctrines embraced the overthrow of government by force. Here Chief Justice Hughes carried on the tradition of Holmes.

HUGHES, C. J. Appellant, Dirk De Jonge, was indicted in Multnomah County, Oregon, for violation of the Criminal Syndicalism Law of that State. . . . The charge is that appellant assisted in the conduct of a meeting which was called under the auspices of the Communist party, an organization advocating criminal syndicalism. The defense was that the meeting was public and orderly and was held for a lawful purpose; that while it was held under the auspices of the Communist party, neither criminal syndicalism nor any unlawful conduct was taught or advocated at the meeting either by appellant or by others. . . .

The stipulation, after setting forth the charging part of the indictment, recites in substance the following: . . .

That the defendant De Jonge, the second speaker, was a member of the Communist party and went to the meeting to speak in its name; that in his talk he protested against conditions in the county jail, the action of city police in relation to the maritime strike then in progress in Portland and numerous other matters; that he discussed the reason for the raids on the Communist headquarters and workers' halls and offices; that he told the workers that these attacks were due to efforts on the part of the steamship companies and stevedoring companies to break the maritime longshoremen's and seamen's strike; that they hoped to break the strike by pitting the longshoremen and seamen against the Communist movement; that there was also testimony to the effect that defendant asked those present to do more work in obtaining members for the Communist party and requested all to be at the meeting of the party to be held in Portland on the following evening and to bring their friends to show their defiance to local police authority and to assist them in their revolutionary tactics. . . .

Having limited the charge to defendant's participation in a meeting called by the Communist party, the State Court sustained the conviction upon that basis regardless of what was said or done at the meeting.

We must take the indictment as thus construed. Conviction upon a charge not made would be sheer denial of due process. It thus appears that, while defendant was a member of the Communist party, he was not indicted for participating in its organization, or for joining it, or for soliciting members or for distributing its literature. He was not charged with teaching or advocating criminal syndicalism or sabotage or any unlawful acts, either at the meeting or elsewhere.

He was accordingly deprived of the benefit of evidence as to the orderly and lawful conduct of the meeting and that it was not called or used for the advocacy of criminal syndicalism or sabotage or any unlawful action. His sole offense as charged, and for which he was convicted and sentenced to imprisonment for seven years, was that he had assisted in the conduct of a public meeting, albeit otherwise lawful, which was held under the auspices of the Communist party.

The broad reach of the statute as thus applied is plain. While defendant was a member of the Communist party, that membership was not necessary to conviction on such a charge. A like fate might have attended any speaker, although not a member who "assisted in the conduct" of the meeting. However innocuous the object of the meeting, however lawful the subjects and tenor of the addresses, however reasonable and timely the discussion, all those assisting in the conduct of the meeting would be subject to imprisonment as felons if the meeting were held by the Communist party.

This manifest result was brought out sharply at this bar by the concessions which the Attorney General made, and could not avoid, in the light of the decision of the State court. Thus if the Communist party had called a public meeting in Portland to discuss the tariff, or the for‧ eign policy of the government, or taxation, or relief, or candidacies for the offices of President, members of Congress, Governor or State legislators, every speaker who assisted in the conduct of the meeting would be equally guilty with the defendant in this case, upon the charge as here defined and sustained. . . .

While the States are entitled to protect themselves from the abuse of the privileges of our institutions through an attempted substitution of force and violence in the place of peaceful political action in order to effect revolutionary changes in government, none of our decisions go to the length of sustaining such a curtailment of the right of free speech and assembly as the Oregon statute demands in its present application.

Freedom of speech and of the press are fundamental rights which are safeguarded by the due process clause of the Fourteenth Amendment of the Federal Constitution. The right of peaceable assembly is a right cognate to those of free speech and free press and is equally fundamental.

As this court said in *United States* v. *Cruikshank*, "The very idea of a government, republican in form, implies a right on the part of its citizens to met peaceably for consultation in respect to public affairs and to petition for a redress of grievances."

The First Amendment of the Federal Constitution expressly guarantees that right against abridgment by Congress. But explicit mention there does not argue exclusion elsewhere. For the right is one that cannot be denied without violating those fundamental principles of liberty and justice which lie at the base of all civil and political institutions, principles which the Fourteenth Amendment embodies in the general terms of its due process clause.

These rights may be abused by using speech or press or assembly in order to incite to violence and crime. The people, through their Legislatures, may protect themselves against that abuse. But the legislative intervention can find constitutional justification only by dealing with the abuse. The rights themselves must not be curtailed.

The greater the importance of safeguarding the community from incitements to the overthrow of our institutions by force and violence, the more imperative is the need to preserve inviolate the constitutional rights of free speech, free press and free assembly in order to maintain the opportunity for free political discussion, to the end that government may be responsive to the will of the people and that changes, if desired, may be obtained by peaceful means. Therein lies the security of the republic, the very foundation of constitutional government.

It follows from these considerations that, consistently with the Federal Constitution, peaceable assembly for lawful discussion cannot be made a crime. The holding of meetings for peaceable political action can not be proscribed. Those who assist in the conduct of such meetings cannot be branded as criminals on that score. The question, if the rights of free speech and peaceable assembly are to be preserved, is not as to the auspices under which the meeting is held, but as to its purpose; not as to the relations of the speakers, but whether their utterances transcend the bounds of the freedom of speech which the Constitution protects. . . .

We hold that the Oregon statute as applied to the particular charge as defined by the State court is repugnant to the due process clause of the Fourteenth Amendment. The judgment of conviction is reversed and the cause is remanded for further proceedings not inconsistent with this opinion. It is so ordered.

—Chief Justice Hughes, Opinion in De Jonge *v.* Oregon, 1937

10. "TO AN ANXIOUS FRIEND"

The decade of the twenties saw not only "Red-baiting" but labor-baiting as well. Federal and State governments united to break the great railroad strike of 1922. One method was a sweeping Federal injunction which prohibited the strikers from even discussing the issues of the strike. Out in Kansas, Governor Henry J. Allen issued an order forbidding the strikers to picket. As a result the strikers printed posters presenting their case, but the Attorney-General ruled that this was just another form of picketing and ordered all posters taken down. The famous editor of the Emporia Gazette, William Allen White, thought the strikers had a right to picket and believed this order "an infamous infraction of the right of free press and free speech"—which it was. He defied it by putting the offending posters in the windows of his newspaper office. For this he was arrested, but never brought to trial. White's defiance of the Governor and the Attorney-General brought anguished protests from friends, and it was in reply to one of these that he wrote this famous editorial.

YOU tell me that law is above freedom of utterance. And I reply that you can have no wise laws nor free enforcement of wise laws until there is free expression of the wisdom of the people—and, alas, their folly with it. But if there is freedom, folly will die of its own poison, and the wisdom will survive. That is the history of the race. It is the proof of Man's kinship with God. You say that freedom of utterance is not for time of stress, and I reply with the sad truth that only in time of stress is freedom of utterance in danger. No one questions it in calm days, because it is not needed. And the reverse is true also; only when free utterance is suppressed is it needed and when it is needed, it is most vital to justice. Peace is good. But if you are interested in peace through force and without discussion, that is to say, free utterance decently and in order—your interest in justice is slight. And peace without justice is tyranny, no matter how you may sugar coat it with expediency. This state today is in more danger from suppression than from violence, because, in the end, suppression leads to violence. Violence, indeed, is the child of suppression. Whoever pleads for justice helps to keep the peace; and whoever tramples upon the plea for justice, temperately made in the name of peace, only outrages peace and kills something fine in the heart of man which God put there when we got our manhood. When that is killed, brute meets brute on each side of the line.

So, dear friend, put fear out of your heart. This nation will survive, this state will prosper, the orderly business of life will go forward if only men can speak in whatever way given them to utter what their hearts hold—by voice, by posted card, by letter or by press. Reason never has failed men. Only force and repression have made the wrecks in the world.

—WILLIAM ALLEN WHITE, "To an Anxious Friend," July 27, 1922

11. "THE INDISPENSABLE OPPOSITION"

Freedom of speech and of the press, freedom of investigation, and of criticism, academic freedom and scientific freedom—all these things trace back to those "inalienable rights" which were celebrated in the Declaration and guaranteed in the Constitution. But they have practical as well as philosophical justification, and it is of the necessity of freedom rather than of the right to freedom that Walter Lippmann here writes.

WERE they pressed hard enough, most men would probably confess that political freedom—that is to say, the right to speak freely and to act in opposition—is a noble ideal rather than a practical necessity. As the case for freedom is generally put today, the argument lends itself to this feeling. It is made to appear that, whereas each man claims his freedom as a matter of right, the freedom he accords to other men is a matter of toleration. Thus, the defense of freedom of opinion tends to rest not on its substantial, beneficial, and indispensable consequences, but on a somewhat eccentric, a rather vaguely benevolent, attachment to an abstraction.

It is all very well to say with Voltaire, "I wholly disapprove of what you say, but will defend to the death your right to say it," but as a matter of fact most men will not defend to the death the rights of other men: if they disapprove sufficiently what other men say, they will somehow suppress those men if they can.

So, if this is the best that can be said for liberty of opinion, that a man must tolerate his opponents because every one has a "right" to say what he pleases, then we shall find that liberty of opinion is a luxury, safe only in pleasant times when men can be tolerant because they are not deeply and vitally concerned.

Yet actually, as a matter of historic fact, there is a much stronger foundation for the great constitutional right of freedom of speech, and as a matter of practical human experience there is a much more compelling reason for cultivating the habits of free men. We take, it seems to me, a naïvely self-righteous view when we argue as if the right of our opponents to speak were something that we protect because we are magnanimous, noble, and unselfish. The compelling reason why, if liberty of opinion did not exist, we should have to invent it, why it will eventually have to be restored in all civilized countries where it is now suppressed, is that we must protect the right of our opponents to speak because we must hear what they have to say.

We miss the whole point when we imagine that we tolerate the freedom of our political opponents as we tolerate a howling baby next door, as we put up with the blasts from our neighbor's radio because we are too peaceable to heave a brick through the window. If this were all there is to freedom of opinion, that we are too good-natured or too timid to do anything about our opponents and our critics except to let them talk, it would be difficult to say whether we are tolerant because we are magnanimous or because we are lazy, because we have strong principles or because we lack serious convictions, whether we have the hospitality of an inquiring mind or the indifference of an empty mind. And so, if we truly wish to understand why freedom is necessary in a civilized society, we must begin by realizing that, because freedom of discussion improves our own opinions, the liberties of other men are our own vital necessity.

We are much closer to the essence of the matter, not when we quote Voltaire, but when we go to the doctor and pay him to ask us the most embarrassing questions and to prescribe the most disagreeable diet. When we pay the doctor to exercise complete freedom of speech about the cause and cure of our stomachache, we do not look upon ourselves as tolerant and magnanimous, and worthy to be admired by ourselves. We have enough common sense to know that if we threaten to put the doctor in jail because we do not like the diagnosis and the prescription it will be unpleasant for the doctor, to be sure, but equally unpleasant for our own stomachache. That is why even the most ferocious dictator would rather be treated by a doctor who was free to think and speak the truth than by his own Minister of Propaganda. For there is a point, the point at which things really matter, where the freedom of others is no longer a question of their right but of our own need.

The point at which we recognize this need is much higher in some men than in others. The totalitarian rulers think they do not need the freedom of an opposition: they exile, imprison, or shoot their opponents. We have concluded on the basis of practical experience, which goes back to Magna Carta and beyond, that we need the opposition. We pay the opposition salaries out of the public treasury.

In so far as the usual apology for freedom of speech ignores this experience, it becomes abstract and eccentric rather than concrete and human. The emphasis is generally put on the right to speak, as if all that mattered were that the doctor should be free to go out into the park and explain to the vacant air why I have a stomachache. Surely that is a miserable caricature of the great civic right which men have bled and died for. What really matters is that the doctor should tell *me* what ails me, that I should listen to him; that if I do not like what he says I should be free to call in another doctor; and that then the first doctor should have to listen to the second doctor; and that out of all the speaking and listening, the give-and-take of opinions, the truth should be arrived at.

This is the creative principle of freedom of speech, not that it is a system for the tolerating of error, but that it is a system for finding the truth. It may not produce the truth, or the whole truth all the time, or often, or in some cases ever. But if the truth can be found, there is no other system which will normally and habitually find so much truth. Until we have thoroughly understood this principle, we shall not know why we must value our liberty, or how we can protect and develop it. . . .

The only reason for dwelling on all this is that if we are to preserve democracy we must understand its principles. And the principle which distinguishes it from all other forms of government is that in a democracy the opposition not only is tolerated as constitutional but must be maintained because it is in fact indispensable.

The democratic system cannot be operated without effective opposition. For, in making the great experiment of governing people by consent rather than by coercion, it is not sufficient that the party in power should have a majority. It is just as necessary that the party in power should never outrage the minority. That means that it must listen to the minority and be moved by the criticisms of the minority. That means that its measures must take account of the minority's objections, and that in administering measures it must remember that the minority may become the majority.

The opposition is indispensable. A good statesman, like any other sensible human being, always learns more from his opponents than from his fervent supporters. For his supporters will push him to disaster unless his opponents show him where the dangers are. So if he is wise he will often pray to be delivered from his friends, because they will ruin him. But, though it hurts, he ought also to pray never to be left without opponents; for they keep him on the path of reason and good sense.

The national unity of a free people depends upon a sufficiently even balance of political power to make it impracticable for the administration to be arbitrary and for the opposition to be revolutionary and irreconcilable. Where that balance no longer exists, democracy perishes. For unless all the citizens of a state are forced by circumstances to compromise, unless they feel that they can affect policy but that no one can wholly dominate it, unless by habit and necessity they have to give and take, freedom cannot be maintained.

—WALTER LIPPMANN, "The Indispensable Opposition"

12. "YOU CANNOT CREATE LOYALTY BY COMPULSION"

No scholar has contributed more to an understanding of the nature of the problem of freedom than Zechariah Chafee, Professor at the Harvard Law School and author of one of the classics of our time, Free Speech in the United States, *from which this excerpt is taken.*

SPEECH should be fruitful as well as free. Our experience introduces this qualification into the classical argument of Milton and John Stuart Mill, that only through open discussion is truth discovered and spread. In their simpler times, they thought it enough to remove legal obstacles like the censorship and sedition prosecutions. Mill assumed that if men were only left alone, their reasoning powers would eventually impel them to choose the best ideas and the wisest course of action. To us this policy is too exclusively negative. For example, what is the use of telling an unpopular speaker that he will incur no criminal penalties by his proposed address, so long as every hall owner in the city declines to rent him space for his meeting and there are no vacant lots available? There should be municipal auditoriums, schoolhouses out of school hours, church forums, parks in summer, all open to thresh out every question of public importance, with just as few restrictions as possible; for otherwise the subjects that most need to be discussed will be the very subjects that will be ruled out as unsuitable for discussion.

We must do more than remove the discouragements to open discussion. We must exert ourselves to supply active encouragements.

Physical space and lack of interference alone will not make discussion fruitful. We must take affirmative steps to improve the methods by which discussion is carried on. Of late years the argument of Milton and Mill has been questioned, because truth does not seem to emerge from a controversy in the automatic way their logic would lead us to expect. For one thing, reason is less praised nowadays than a century ago; instead, emotions conscious and unconscious are commonly said to dominate the conduct of men. Is it any longer possible to discover truth amid the clashing blares of advertisements, loud speakers, gigantic billboards, party programs, propaganda of a hundred kinds? To sift the truth from all these half-truths seems to demand a statistical investigation beyond the limits of anybody's time and money. So some modern thinkers despairingly conclude that the great mass of voters cannot be trusted to detect the fallacies in emotional arguments by Communists and so on, and hence must be prevented from hearing them. Even the intellectuals do not seem to do much better in reaching Truth by conflicting arguments. For example, take controveries between professors. They talk and talk, and at the end each sticks to his initial position. On which side does Truth stand? We still do not know. Then, too, the emergencies seem greater and more pressing than of yore. We are less willing to await the outcome of prolonged verbal contests. Perhaps Truth will win in the long run; but in the long run, as Walter Lippmann says, we shall all be dead—and perhaps not peacefully in our beds either. Debating is only fiddling while Rome burns. Away with all this talk; let's have action—now.

Nevertheless, the main argument of Milton and Mill still holds good. All that this disappointment means is that friction is a much bigger drag on the progress of Truth than they supposed. Efforts to lessen that friction are essential to the success of freedom of speech. It is a problem, not for law, but for education in the wide sense that includes more than schools and youngsters. The conflict of oral evidence and arguments can be made increasingly profitable by wise improvements in technique. Anybody who has attended a forum knows how much depends on an able chairman and on sensible rules enforced by him. Journalists and other writers value accuracy of facts far more than formerly—we can expect even more from them in future. None of us can get rid of our emotions, but we can learn to drive them in harness. As for blazing propaganda on both sides, young Americans can be trained to keep alive the gumption which comes down to us from Colonial farmers; this will make them distrust all men who conceal greed or a lust for power behind any flag, whether red or red-white-and-blue.

Reason is more imperfect than we used to believe. Yet it still remains the best guide we have, better than our emotions, better even than patriotism, better than any single human guide, however exalted his position.

A second point deserves renewed emphasis. The effect of suppression extends far beyond the agitators actually put in jail, far beyond the pamphlets physically destroyed. A favorite argument against free speech is that the men who are thus conspicuously silenced had little to say that was worth hearing. Concede for the moment that the public would suffer no serious loss if every communist leaflet were burned or if some prominent pacifist were imprisoned, as perhaps he might be . . . for discouraging drafted men by talk about plowing every fourth boy under. Even so, my contention is that the pertinacious orators and writers who get hauled up are merely extremist spokesmen for a mass of more thoughtful and more retiring men and women, who share in varying degrees the same critical attitude toward prevailing policies and institutions. When you put the hotheads in jail, these cooler people do not get arrested—they just keep quiet. And so we lose things they could tell us, which would be very advantageous for the future course of the nation. Once the prosecutions begin, then the hush-hush begins too. Discussion becomes one-sided and artificial. Questions that need to be threshed out do not get threshed out.

The evils of such a policy of suppression are especially acute during a national emergency like the World War or the present rapid development of national defense. . . .

The Supreme Court, though much more anxious to support liberty of speech than it was twenty years ago, can do nothing to keep discussion open during an emergency. Cases of suppression will get to Washington long after the emergency is over. What counts is what the local United States judges do. Still more important is the attitude of the prosecutors and police, because they can stifle free speech by breaking up meetings by arrests and confiscating pamphlets, and then not bothering to bring many persons to trial. Above all, the maintenance of open discussion depends on all the great body of unofficial citizens. If a community does not respect liberty for unpopular ideas, it can easily drive such ideas underground by persistent discouragement and sneers, by social ostracism, by boycotts of newspapers and magazines, by refusal to rent halls, by objections to the use of municipal auditoriums and schoolhouses, by discharging teachers and professors and journalists, by mobs and threats of lynching. On the other hand, an atmosphere of open and unimpeded controversy may be made as fully a part of the life of a community as any other American tradition. The law plays only a small part in either suppression or freedom. In the long run the public gets just as much freedom of speech as it really wants.

This brings me to my final argument for freedom of speech. It creates the happiest kind of country. It is the best way to make men and women love their country. Mill says:

> A State which dwarfs its men, in order that they may be more docile instruments in its hands even for beneficial purposes, will find that with small men no great thing can really be accomplished.

And Arthur Garfield Hays tells the story of a liberated slave who met his former master on the street. The master asked, "Are you as well off as before you were free?" The Negro admitted that his clothes were frayed, his house leaked, and his meals were nothing like the food on the old plantation. "Well, wouldn't you rather be a slave again?" "No, massa. There's a sort of looseness about this here freedom that I likes." . . .

Behind the dozens of sedition bills in Congress last session, behind teachers' oaths and compulsory flag salutes, is a desire to make our citizens loyal to their government. Loyalty is a beautiful idea, but you cannot create it by compulsion and force. A government is at bottom the officials who carry it on: legislators and prosecutors, school superintendents and police. If it is composed of legislators who pass shortsighted sedition laws by overwhelming majorities, of narrow-minded school superintendents who oust thoughtful teachers of American history and eight-year-old children whose rooted religious convictions prevent them from sharing in a brief ceremony—a government of snoopers and spies and secret police—how can you expect love and loyalty? You make men love their government and their country by giving them the kind of government and the kind of country that inspire respect and love: a country that is free and unafraid, that lets the discontented talk in order to learn the causes for their discontent and end those causes, that refuses to impel men to spy on their neighbors, that protects its citizens vigorously from harmful acts while it leaves the remedies for objectionable ideas to counter-argument and time.

Plutarch's Lives were the favorite reading of the men who framed and ratified our Constitution. There they found the story of Timoleon who saved his native city of Syracuse from the Carthaginian tyrants. In later years young hotheads used to get up in the public assembly and abuse Timoleon as an old fossil. His friends urged him just to say the word, and they would soon silence his detractors. But Timoleon insisted on letting the vituperative youngsters have their say. "He had taken all the extreme pains and labor he had done, and had passed so many dangers, in order that every citizen and inhabitant of Syracuse might frankly use the liberty of their laws. He thanked the gods that they had granted him the thing he had so oft requested of them in his prayers, which was, that he might some day see the Syracusans have full power and liberty to say what they pleased."

—ZECHARIAH CHAFEE, JR., *Free Speech in the United States*

13. THE LOYALTY PROGRAM

The rise of Communism and of totalitarianism created a new kind of danger in the conflict of loyalties which it produced and in its techniques of infiltration and subversion. Unfamiliar with these things which were commonplaces of Eastern European history, Americans reacted with perhaps immoderate alarm, and soon the air was heavy with charges of "subversion," "disloyalty" and "un-American activities." In 1938 the House of Representatives created a Committee on Un-American activities and this Committee at once embarked upon a prolonged and increasingly sensational hunt for Communists, Fascists, radicals, and nonconformists. The charge of widespread disloyalty in the Civil Service persuaded President Truman to set up machinery for loyalty investigations. This machinery was originally designed as much to safeguard civil servants against harassment and intimidation as to track down those who might be disloyal. Under this program almost three million civil servants or applicants for government positions were screened, and less than three hundred dismissed as "security risks." The original standard of "reasonable grounds for belief that the person involved is disloyal" was modified, in 1951, to "reasonable doubts" as to loyalty. The loyalty investigation raised interesting and important constitutional issues. Must investigations be conducted in accordance with "due process"— or might the loyalty boards disregard procedural safeguards? Was the Attorney-General authorized to draw up a list of "subversive" organizations and to make membership in these a test of loyalty, or was this an exercise of arbitrary power and an invasion of private rights?

WHEREAS each employe of the Government of the United States is endowed with a measure of trusteeship over the democratic processes which are the heart and sinew of the United States; and

Whereas, it is of vital importance that persons employed in the Federal service be of complete and unswerving loyalty to the United States; and

Whereas, although the loyalty of by far the overwhelming majority of all Government employes is beyond question, the presence within the Government service of any disloyal or subversive person constitutes a threat to our democratic processes; and

Whereas maximum protection must be afforded the United States against infiltration of disloyal persons into the ranks of its employes, and equal protection from unfounded accusations of disloyalty must be afforded the loyal employes of the Government:

Now, therefore . . . it is hereby, in the interest of the internal management of the Government, ordered as follows:

Part I. Investigation of Applicants

1. There shall be a loyalty investigation of every person entering the civilian employment of any department or agency of the Executive Branch of the Federal Government. . . .

Part V. Standards

1. The standard for the refusal of employment or the removal from employment in an executive department or agency on grounds relating

to loyalty shall be that, on all the evidence, reasonable grounds exist for belief that the person involved is disloyal to the Government of the United States.

2. Activities and associations of an applicant or employe which may be considered in connection with the determination of disloyalty may include one or more of the following:

A. Sabotage, espionage, or attempts or preparations therefor, knowingly associating with spies or saboteurs;

B. Treason or sedition or advocacy thereof;

C. Advocacy of revolution of force or violence to alter the constitutional form of Government of the United States;

D. Intentional, unauthorized disclosure to any person, under circumstances which may indicate disloyalty to the United States, of documents or information of a confidential or non-public character obtained by the person making the disclosure as a result of his employment by the Government of the United States;

E. Performing or attempting to perform his duties, or *otherwise acting, so as to serve the interests of another government in preference to the interests of the United States.*

F. Membership in, affiliation with or *sympathetic association* with any foreign or *domestic* organization, association, movement, *group or combination* of persons, designated by the Attorney General as totalitarian, Fascist, Communist, or *subversive,* or as having adopted a policy of advocating or approving the commission of acts of force or violence to deny other persons their rights under the Constitution of the United States, or as seeking to alter the form of Government of the United States by unconstitutional means.

—PRESIDENT TRUMAN, Loyalty Order, March 22, 1947

14. "WHO IS LOYAL TO AMERICA?"

The editor here raises some fundamental questions about the whole concept of loyalty and about the loyalty program of State and Federal governments.

I

WHAT is the new loyalty? It is, above all, conformity. It is the uncritical and unquestioning acceptance of America as it is—the political institutions, the social relationships, the economic practices. It rejects inquiry into the race question or socialized medicine, or public housing, or into the wisdom or validity of our foreign policy. It regards as particularly heinous any challenge to what is called "the system of private enterprise," identifying that system with Americanism. It abandons evolution, repudiates the once popular concept of progress, and regards America as a finished product, perfect and complete.

It is, it must be added, easily satisfied. For it wants not intellectual conviction nor spiritual conquests, but mere outward conformity. In matters of loyalty it takes the word for the deed, the gesture for the principle. It is content with the flag salute, and does not pause to consider the warning of our Supreme Court that "a person gets from a symbol the meaning he puts into it, and what is one man's comfort and inspiration is another's jest and scorn." It is satisfied with membership in respectable organizations and, as it assumes that every member of a liberal organization is a Communist, concludes that every member of a conservative one is a true American. It has not yet learned that not everyone who saith Lord, Lord, shall enter into the kingdom of Heaven. It is designed neither to discover real disloyalty nor to foster true loyalty.

II

What is wrong with this new concept of loyalty? What, fundamentally, is wrong with the pusillanimous retreat of the Washington educators, the barbarous antics of Washington legislators, the hysterical outbursts of the D.A.R., the gross and vulgar appeals of business cor-

410

porations? It is not merely that these things are offensive. It is rather that they are wrong—morally, socially, and politically.

The concept of loyalty as conformity is a false one. It is narrow and restrictive, denies freedom of thought and of conscience, and is irremediably stained by private and selfish considerations. "Enlightened loyalty," wrote Josiah Royce, who made loyalty the very core of his philosophy,

> *means harm to no man's loyalty. It is at war only with disloyalty, and its warfare, unless necessity constrains, is only a spiritual warfare. It does not foster class hatreds; it knows of nothing reasonable about race prejudices; and it regards all races of men as one in their need of loyalty. It ignores mutual misunderstandings. It loves its own wherever upon earth its own, namely loyalty itself, is to be found.*

Justice, charity, wisdom, spirituality, he added, were all definable in terms of loyalty, and we may properly ask which of these qualities our contemporary champions of loyalty display.

Above all, loyalty must be to something larger than oneself, untainted by private purposes or selfish ends. But what are we to say of the attempts by the NAM and by individual corporations to identify loyalty with the system of private enterprise? Is it not as if officeholders should attempt to identify loyalty with their own party, their own political careers? Do not those corporations which pay for full-page advertisements associating Americanism with the competitive system expect, ultimately, to profit from that association? Do not those organizations that deplore, in the name of patriotism, the extension of government operation of hydro-electric power expect to profit from their campaign?

Certainly it is a gross perversion not only of the concept of loyalty but of the concept of Americanism to identify it with a particular economic system. This precise question, interestingly enough, came before the Supreme Court in the Schneiderman case not so long ago—and it was Wendell Willkie who was counsel for Schneiderman. Said the Court:

> *Throughout our history many sincere people whose attachment to the general Constitutional scheme cannot be doubted have, for various and even divergent reasons, urged differing degrees of governmental ownership and control of natural resources, basic means of pro-*

duction, and banks and the media of exchange, either with or without
compensation. And something once regarded as a species of private
property was abolished without compensating the owners when the
institution of slavery was forbidden. Can it be said that the author of
the Emancipation Proclamation and the supporters of the Thirteenth
Amendment were not attached to the Constitution?

There is, it should be added, a further danger in the willful identification of Americanism with a particular body of economic practices.
Many learned economists predict for the near future an economic crash
similar to that of 1929. If Americanism is equated with competitive
capitalism, what happens to it if competitive capitalism comes a cropper?
If loyalty and private enterprise are inextricably associated, what is to
preserve loyalty if private enterprise fails? Those who associate
Americanism with a particular program of economic practices have a
grave responsibility, for if their program should fail, they expose
Americanism itself to disrepute.

The effort to equate loyalty with conformity is misguided because it
assumes that there is a fixed content to loyalty and that this can be
determined and defined. But loyalty is a principle, and eludes definition
except in its own terms. It is devotion to the best interests of the commonwealth, and may require hostility to the particular policies which
the government pursues, the particular practices which the economy
undertakes, the particular institutions which society maintains. "If
there is any fixed star in our Constitutional constellation," said the
Supreme Court in the Barnette case, "it is that no official, high or petty,
can prescribe what shall be orthodox in politics, nationalism, religion,
or other matters of opinion, or force citizens to confess by word or act
their faith therein. If there are any circumstances which permit an exception they do not now occur to us."

True loyalty may require, in fact, what appears to the naïve to be disloyalty. It may require hostility to certain provisions of the Constitution
itself, and historians have not concluded that those who subscribed to
the "Higher Law" were lacking in patriotism. We should not forget that
our tradition is one of protest and revolt, and it is stultifying to celebrate the rebels of the past—Jefferson and Paine, Emerson and Thoreau
—while we silence the rebels of the present. "We are a rebellious
nation," said Theodore Parker, known in his day as the Great American
Preacher, and went on:

Our whole history is treason; our blood was attainted before we were born; our creeds are infidelity to the mother church; our constitution, treason to our fatherland. What of that? Though all the governors in the world bid us commit treason against man, and set the example, let us never submit.

Those who would impose upon us a new concept of loyalty not only assume that this is possible, but have the presumption to believe that they are competent to write the definition. We are reminded of Whitman's defiance of the "never-ending audacity of elected persons." Who are those who would set the standards of loyalty? They are Rankins and Bilbos, officials of the D.A.R. and the Legion and the NAM, Hearsts and McCormicks. May we not say of Rankin's harangues on loyalty what Emerson said of Webster at the time of the Seventh of March speech: "The word honor in the mouth of Mr. Webster is like the word love in the mouth of a whore."

What do men know of loyalty who make a mockery of the Declaration of Independence and the Bill of Rights, whose energies are dedicated to stirring up race and class hatreds, who would straitjacket the American spirit? What indeed do they know of America—the America of Sam Adams and Tom Paine, of Jackson's defiance of the Court and Lincoln's celebration of labor, of Thoreau's essay on Civil Disobedience and Emerson's championship of John Brown, of the America of the Fourierists and the Come-Outers, of cranks and fanatics, of socialists and anarchists? Who among American heroes could meet their tests, who would be cleared by their committees? Not Washington, who was a rebel. Not Jefferson, who wrote that all men are created equal and whose motto was "rebellion to tyrants is obedience to God." Not Garrison, who publicly burned the Constitution; or Wendell Phillips, who spoke for the underprivileged everywhere and counted himself a philosophical anarchist; not Seward of the Higher Law or Sumner of racial equality. Not Lincoln, who admonished us to have malice toward none, charity for all; or Wilson, who warned that our flag was "a flag of liberty of opinion as well as of political liberty"; or Justice Holmes, who said that our Constitution is an experiment and that while that experiment is being made "we should be eternally vigilant against attempts to check the expression of opinions that we loath and believe to be fraught with death."

III

There are further and more practical objections against the imposition of fixed concepts of loyalty or tests of disloyalty. The effort is itself a confession of fear, a declaration of insolvency. Those who are sure of themselves do not need reassurance, and those who have confidence in the strength and the virtue of America do not need to fear either criticism or competition. The effort is bound to miscarry. It will not apprehend those who are really disloyal, it will not even frighten them; it will affect only those who can be labeled "radical." It is sobering to recall that through the Japanese relocation program, carried through at such incalculable cost in misery and tragedy, was justified to us on the ground that the Japanese were potentially disloyal, the record does not disclose a single case of Japanese disloyalty or sabotage during the whole war. The warning sounded by the Supreme Court in the Barnett flag-salute case is a timely one:

> *Ultimate futility of such attempts to compel obedience is the lesson of every such effort from the Roman drive to stamp out Christianity as a disturber of pagan unity, the Inquisition as a means to religious and dynastic unity, the Siberian exiles as a means to Russian unity, down to the fast-failing efforts of our present totalitarian enemies. Those who begin coercive elimination of dissent soon find themselves exterminating dissenters. Compulsory unification of opinion achieves only the unanimity of the graveyard.*

Nor are we left to idle conjecture in this matter; we have had experience enough. Let us limit ourselves to a single example, one that is wonderfully relevant. Back in 1943 the House un-American Activities Committee deeply disturbed by alleged disloyalty among government employees wrote a definition of subversive activities and proceeded to apply it. The definition was admirable, and no one could challenge its logic or its symmetry.

> *Subversive activity derives from conduct intentionally destructive or inimical to the Government of the United States—that which seeks to undermine its institutions, or to distort its functions, or to impede its projects, or to lessen its efforts, the ultimate end being to overturn it all.*

Surely anyone guilty of activities so defined deserved not only dismissal but punishment. But how was the test applied? It was applied to two distinguished scholars, Robert Morss Lovett and Goodwin Watson, and to one able young historian, William E. Dodd, Jr., son of our former Ambassador to Germany. Of almost three million persons employed by the government, these were the three whose subversive activities were deemed the most pernicious, and the House cut them off the payroll. The sequel is familiar. The Senate concurred only to save a wartime appropriation; the President signed the bill under protest for the same reason. The Supreme Court declared the whole business a "bill of attainder" and therefore unconstitutional. Who was it, in the end, who engaged in "subversive activities"—Lovett, Dodd, and Watson, or the Congress which flagrantly violated Article One of the Constitution?

Finally, disloyalty tests are not only futile in application, they are pernicious in their consequences. They distract attention from activities that are really disloyal, and silence criticism inspired by true loyalty. That there are disloyal elements in America will not be denied, but there is no reason to suppose that any of the tests now formulated will ever be applied to them. It is relevant to remember that when Rankin was asked why his Committee did not investigate the Ku Klux Klan he replied that the Klan was not un-American, it was American!

Who are those who are really disloyal? Those who inflame racial hatreds, who sow religious and class dissensions. Those who subvert the Constitution by violating the freedom of the ballot box. Those who make a mockery of majority rule by the use of the filibuster. Those who impair democracy by denying equal educational facilities. Those who frustrate justice by lynch law or by making a farce of jury trials. Those who deny freedom of speech and of the press and of assembly. Those who press for special favors against the interest of the commonwealth. Those who regard public office as a source of private gain. Those who would exalt the military over the civil. Those who for selfish and private purposes stir up national antagonisms and expose the world to the ruin of war.

Will the House Committee on un-American Activities interfere with the activities of these? Will Mr. Truman's disloyalty proclamation reach these? Will the current campaigns for Americanism convert these? If past experience is any guide, they will not. What they will do, if they are successful, is to silence criticism, stamp out dissent—or drive it underground. But if our democracy is to flourish it must have criticism, if our government is to function it must have dissent. Only totalitarian governments insist upon conformity and they

—as we know—do so at their peril. Without criticism abuses will go un-rebuked; without dissent our dynamic system will become static. The American people have a stake in the maintenance of the most thorough-going inquisition into American institutions. They have a stake in nonconformity, for they know that the American genius is nonconformist. They have a stake in experimentation of the most radical character, for they know that only those who prove all things can hold fast that which is good.

IV

It is easier to say what loyalty is not than to say what it is. It is not conformity. It is not passive acquiescence in the status quo. It is not preference for everything American over everything foreign. It is not an ostrich-like ignorance of other countries and other institutions. It is not the indulgence in ceremony—a flag salute, an oath of allegiance, a fervid verbal declaration. It is not a particular creed, a particular version of history, a particular body of economic practices, a particular philosophy.

It is a tradition, an ideal, and a principle. It is a willingness to subordinate every private advantage for the larger good. It is an appreciation of the rich and diverse contributions that can come from the most varied sources. It is allegiance to the traditions that have guided our greatest statesmen and inspired our most eloquent poets—the traditions of freedom, equality, democracy, tolerance, the tradition of the higher law, of experimentation, co-operation, and pluralism. It is a realization that America was born of revolt, flourished on dissent, became great through experimentation.

Independence was an act of revolution; republicanism was something new under the sun; the federal system was a vast experimental laboratory. Physically Americans were pioneers; in the realm of social and economic institutions, too, their tradition has been one of pioneering. From the beginning, intellectual and spiritual diversity have been as characteristic of America as racial and linguistic. The most distinctively American philosophies have been transcendentalism—which is the philosophy of the Higher Law—and pragmatism—which is the philosophy of experimentation and pluralism. These two principles are the very core of Americanism: the principle of the Higher Law, or of obedience to the dictates of conscience rather than of statutes, and the principle of pragmatism, or the rejection of a single good and of the notion of a finished universe. From the beginning Americans have known that there were new worlds to conquer, new truths to be discovered. Every effort to confine Americanism to a single pattern, to constrain it to a single formula, is disloyalty to everything that is valid in Americanism.

—HENRY STEELE COMMAGER, "Who Is Loyal to America?" 1947

15. "DUE NOTICE TO THE FBI"

During the war the Federal Bureau of Investigation began security checks on all government employees, and with the elaboration of the loyalty program this activity was continued and enlarged. The methods and techniques used by FBI agents aroused widespread criticism and brought charges that the United States was becoming a "police state." Bernard De Voto, whose memorable criticism of the FBI is reproduced here, is the editor of Harper's *"Easy Chair," a novelist and historian of distinction, and one of the most useful private citizens in the nation.*

THE quietly dressed man at your door shows you credentials that identify him as Mr. Charles Craig of the Bureau of Internal Revenue. He says he would like to ask you a few questions about one of your neighbors. The Harry S. Deweys are friends of yours, aren't they? Yes, you tell him. How long have you known them? Ever since they moved to Garden Acres eight or nine years ago—or was it seven?—no, thirteen. Mr. Craig says the Deweys moved into their house June 1, 1935, which makes it fourteen years. By the way, have they got a mortgage on it? Sure, you say, we all have. Harry didn't buy till about eight years ago. He is paying it off on a monthly basis; must be down to a couple of thousand by now.

Mr. Dewey's older son graduated from Yale this spring? Mr. Craig asks. Yes, you say. The daughter—she's at Vassar? Yes, she's a sophomore. And the other boy?—Exeter? Yes, first form. Mr. Dewey bought a new car last year, a Buick? Yes, he'd driven that Chevrolet for nine years. Who is his tailor? Gummidge? Pretty high-priced firm. Does Mrs. Dewey spend a lot on clothes? The trash barrels were on the curb when Mr. Craig came by and he noticed several empty Black and White bottles—do the Deweys drink a lot? Didn't they have Zimmerman, the caterer, for that big party last April?—Zimmerman comes high. Have you noticed their garbage—pretty rich stuff? What labels have you seen? Bellows & Co., maybe, or Charles & Co., Inc.? Do you happen to know what Mr. Dewey's income is?

By this time you are, I hope, plenty mad. You say, for God's sake, it's none of my business. Mr. Craig explains. Investigation by the Bureau of Internal Revenue does not necessarily mean that the person being investigated is under suspicion. These checks are routine in certain kinds of cases. Orders to make them come from above; the local echelons do not initiate inquiries, they simply find out what they can. Then back in Washington the information thus gathered is evaluated. No improper use is made of anything and of course the evaluators know that most of the stuff sent in is mixed, idle, or untrue—they simply go through the vast chaff in order to find an occasional grain of wheat. The Bureau, Mr. Craig points out, is part of the United States government. It conducts its inquiries with entire legality and under rigid safeguards. The duty of a citizen is to assist his government when he is asked to.

So you say, look, Harry is district manager of the Interstate Gas Furnace Corporation and everybody knows that IGF pays district managers fifteen thousand a year. Yes, Mr. Craig says, IGF pays him fifteen thousand but one wonders whether he hasn't got other sources of income. How can he send three children to prep school and college, buy a house and a new Buick, and patronize Gummidge and Zimmerman on fifteen thousand? And he belongs to the City Club and the Garden Acres Country Club. He took Mrs. Dewey to Bermuda last winter. He has heavy insurance premiums to pay. He had a new roof put on the house last fall and this spring Mrs. Dewey had the whole second floor repainted and repapered. How come? Does it make sense? Where's he getting it from?

Does Harry S. Dewey belong to the Wine and Food Society? The Friends of Escoffier? Has he ever attended a meeting of either group? Does he associate with members of either? Has he ever been present at a meeting of any kind, or at a party, at which a member of either was also present? Has he ever read Brillat-Savarin's *The Physiology of*

Taste? Does he associate with people who have read it? Has he ever been present at a meeting or a party at which anyone who has read it was also present? Does he subscribe to or read *Daily Racing Forms?* Has he ever made a bet on a horse race? A dog race? A football game? Does he play poker or shoot craps? Has he ever been present at a meeting or a party at which anyone who makes bets or plays poker was also present? Does he play the market? Do you know whether Harry puts any cash into diamonds? Does he associate with people who own diamonds? Does he know any millionaires, or people who own cabin cruisers, or people who have accounts in more than one bank? Has he ever attended meetings of such persons? Has he ever been present at a meeting or a party at which such persons were also present? Does he read the *Wall Street Journal?* Has he ever been present at a cocktail party at which anyone who does read it was present? Is it true that Harry gave his secretary half a dozen pairs of nylon stockings for Christmas? Could she be fronting or dummying for business deals that are really his? What kind of girl is she? Does she always leave the office at five o'clock? Whom does she associate with?

Where does Harry stand on the Bureau of Internal Revenue and the income tax laws? Have you ever heard him say that the income tax laws ought to be changed or the Bureau reorganized or abolished? Have you ever heard him damn the income tax? Does he associate with people who damn it? Has he ever been present at a meeting or a party where people who want to abolish the Bureau or revise the tax laws were also present?

Let us assume that you remember nothing which indicates that Harry S. Dewey is a tax-dodger or a crook. But Mr. Craig goes a few doors down the street and interviews Frances Perkins Green, who is a prohibitionist and has suffered from nervous indigestion for many years. She has seen truffles and artichokes and caviar in the Dewey garbage. The Deweys' maid has told Mrs. Green that they have porterhouses much oftener than frankforts, that they always have cocktails and frequently have wine, that sometimes cherries and peaches come all the way from Oregon by mail. Mrs. Green has seen many suspicious-looking characters come to the Dewey house. She doesn't know who they are but it's striking that mostly they don't come till after dark, seven o'clock or later. Some of them, she says, are staggering when they leave at midnight. So Mr. Craig tries the next house and finds Henry Cabot White at home. Cabot is doing all right now but he had tough going for a couple of years after Harry Dewey fired him. Everyone in Garden Acres is familiar with the neighborhood feud and would tend to discount Cabot's revelation to Mr. Craig that Harry's secretary used to work as a cashier at a race track. He confirms the nylons but says there were a dozen pairs. Sure Harry is sleeping with her—Cabot has seen them lunching together several times. Matter of fact Harry only took Mrs. Dewey to Bermuda because she blew up about the girl. Yes, and do you know who was on that boat? Gooks McGonigle—you remember, he runs the numbers racket and they almost got him for wire-tapping. Cabot wouldn't like to say anything either way, but Harry took the same boat and Harry manages to lay his hands on money when he needs it.

I have *hung this fantasy on the Bureau of Internal Revenue precisely because it does* NOT *operate in this way*. When it suspects that someone is making false tax returns its investigators go to the suspect's books, his bank, the regular channels of his business, and similar focal points where factual evidence can be uncovered and made good. If Harry S. Dewey reads Brillat-Savarin or serves Stilton with the cocktails, the Bureau is not interested. It does not ask his friends or enemies to report on his wife's visits to the hairdresser as a patriotic duty.

But if it did, would you be surprised? In fact, would you be surprised if any government bureau sent round its Mr. Craig to ask you if Harry Dewey reads the *New Republic* or has ever gone swimming in the nude at Bay View? I think you wouldn't be surprised. What is worse, I think that for a moment Mr. Craig and his questions would seem quite natural to you. And this feeling that the interrogation of private citizens about other citizens is natural and justified is something new to American life. As little as ten years ago we would have considered it about on a par with prohibition snooping, night-riding, and blackmail. A single decade has come close to making us a nation of common informers.

It began with the war. Candidates for commission in the services or for jobs in non-military agencies had to be investigated. If enormous asininities resulted, if enormous injustice was done, they were inevitable, part of the cost of war. They are not inevitable now. But several branches of the government are acting as if they were. Several branches of the government and far too many of us private citizens are acting as if they didn't matter.

True, we have occasional qualms. The Committee on Un-American

Activities blasts several score reputations by releasing a new batch of gossip. Or a senator emits some hearsay and officially unaccused persons lose their jobs without recourse. Or another senator blackens the name of a dead man and then rejoices in his good deed, though the people he claimed to be quoting announce that they didn't say what he said they did. Or some atrocious indignity inflicted on a government employee by a loyalty board comes to light. Or we find out that the FBI has put at the disposal of this or that body a hash of gossip, rumor, slander, backbiting, malice, and drunken invention which, when it makes the headlines, shatters the reputations of innocent and harmless people and of people who our laws say are innocent until someone proves them guilty in court. We are shocked. Sometimes we are scared. Sometimes we are sickened. We know that the thing stinks to heaven, that it is an avalanching danger to our society. But we don't do anything about it.

Do you think the questions I have put in Mr. Craig's mouth are absurd? They are exactly like the questions that are asked of every government employee about whom a casual derogatory remark has been unearthed, even if that remark was made twenty years ago, even if a fool or an aspirant to the employee's job made it. They are exactly like the questions asked of anyone who is presumed to know anything about him, whether casual acquaintance, grudgeholder, or habitual enemy. They are exactly like the questions asked about anyone outside the government of whom anyone else has reported that he has radical sympathies. Have you (has he) ever studied Karl Marx? Have you (has he) ever been present at a meeting or a party where anyone sympathetic to Communism was also present? Did you (did he) belong to the Liberal Club in college? Did you (did he) escort to a dance a girl who has read Lenin or is interested in abstract painting? Have you (has he) recommended the *Progressive* to a friend? Those questions and scores like them, or worse, have been asked of and about millions of American citizens.

The FBI—to name only one agency that asks such questions—tells us that everything is properly safeguarded. The investigators gather up what they can and send it in, but trained specialists evaluate it, and whatever is idle, untrue, false, malicious, or vicious is winnowed out. So the FBI says. But we are never told who does the evaluating and we have seen little evidence that anyone does it. Along comes the Coplon case, for instance, and we find out that a sack has simply been emptied on the table. The contents are obviously in great part idle and false, in great part gossip and rumor, in great part unverifiable—and unverified. Investigator K-7 reports that Witness S-17 (for we have to cover up for our agents and our spies) said that Harry S. Dewey is a member of the Party, or wants to make the revolution, or knows some fellow-travelers, or once advised someone to read Marx, or spent a weekend at a summer resort where there were members of an organization on the Attorney-General's list. If K-7 is only two degrees better than half-witted, if S-17 is a psychopath or a pathological liar or Harry's divorced wife, no matter. And also, no one can be held accountable. If the same sack has previously emptied for the loyalty board of any government department nobody can be held responsible for that act, either, and Harry Dewey has no recourse. He will never know and neither will you and I. We will never learn who K-7 or S-17 is, in what circumstance the information was given, whether or not it is true or deliberate falsehood, how far it has been spread or by whom.

In the Coplon trial the government did its utmost to keep from the public view certain information which it was using and which had been gathered by the FBI. That was a sagacious effort. For when the judge ruled that it must be made public some of it turned out to be as irresponsible as the chatter of somewhat retarded children: it would have been farcical if it had not been vicious. For instance, some S-17 had given some K-7 a list of people whom he considered Communists or Communist-sympathizers. One of them was the president of a large university. In all candor, he is not continentally celebrated for intelligence but his economic and political ideas are a hundred miles to the right of Chester A. Arthur. He is a man of unquestionable patriotism, loyalty, integrity, and probity, incapable of any kind of behavior with which the FBI is authorized to concern itself. But it was the privilege of someone—perhaps a fool, a personal enemy, a boy who had flunked out, a maniac—to lodge in the FBI's files a declaration that he is a Red.

Well, the university president will not suffer in public esteem. But his university may be damaged in many ways, now, next week, ten years hence. And Senator Mundt or Congressman Dondero or any public official with the gleam of a headline in his eye can denounce the university, its students, and all who have acquired their guilt by contagion—on the basis of a remark which may have been made by an imbecile and for which no one can be held to account. And that remark remains permanently indexed in the FBI files. And what about humbler names on that list? How many people have been fired? How many are having their reading, their recreation, and their personal associations secretly investigated? Against how many of them are neighbors with grudges or senile dementia testifying to some Mr. Craig, hereafter and alias K-7? What redress have they got? What redress has anyone got whom anyone at all has named to the FBI or any other corps of investigators as a Communist, a Communist-sympathizer, a fellow-traveler, a bemused dupe, or just a person who happened to be in the bar at the New Willard when a subscriber to the *Nation* was buying a drink?

I say it has gone too far. We are dividing into the hunted and the hunters. There is loose in the United States today the same evil that once split Salem Village between the bewitched and the accused and stole men's reason quite away. We are informers to the secret police. Honest men are spying on their neighbors for patriotism's sake. We may be sure that for every honest man two dishonest ones are spying for personal advancement today and ten will be spying for pay next year.

None of us can know how much of this inquiry into the private lives of American citizens and government employees is necessary. Some of it is necessary—but we have no way of knowing which, when, or where. We have seen enough to know for sure that a great deal of it is altogether irresponsible. Well, there is a way making it all responsible, of fixing responsibility. As one citizen of the United States, I intend to take that way, myself, from now on.

Representatives of the FBI and of other official investigating bodies have questioned me, in the past, about a number of people and I have answered their questions. That's over. From now on any representative of the government, properly identified, can count on a drink and perhaps informed talk about the Red (but non-Communist) Sox at my house. But if he wants information from me about anyone whomsoever, no soap. If it is my duty as citizen to tell what I know about someone, I will perform that duty under subpoena, in open court, before that person and his attorney. This notice is posted in the courthouse square: I will not discuss anyone in private with any government investigator.

I like a country where it's nobody's damned business what magazines anyone reads, what he thinks, whom he has cocktails with. I like a country where we do not have to stuff the chimney against listening ears and where what we say does not go into the FBI files along with a note from S-17 that I may have another wife in California. I like a country where no college-trained flatfeet collect memoranda about us and ask judicial protection for them, a country where when someone makes statements about us to officials he can be held to account. We had that kind of country only a little while ago and I'm for getting it back. It was a lot less scared than the one we've got now. It slept sound no matter how many people joined Communist reading circles and it put common scolds to the ducking stool. Let's rip off the gingerbread and restore the original paneling.

—BERNARD DE VOTO, "Due Notice to the FBI," 1949

16. CIVIL RIGHTS IN THE NATION'S CAPITAL

Deeply concerned for the maintenance and enlargement of civil liberties, President Truman in 1946 set up a Committee on Civil Rights. This Committee issued the following year what may be a historic document—a survey of civil rights in the United States and an analysis of what still remained to be achieved if the guarantees of the Constitution were to be made real. From this report—readily available to all from the Government Printing Office—we take this sobering picture of civil rights in Washington. The report itself was drafted by Robert Carr of Dartmouth College.

THROUGHOUT the country, our practice lags behind the American tradition of freedom and equality. A single community—the nation's capital—illustrates dramatically the shortcomings in our record and the need for change. The District of Columbia should symbolize to our own citizens and to the people of all countries our great tradition of civil liberty. Instead, it is a graphic illustration of a failure of democracy. As the seat of our federal government under the authority of Congress, the failure of the District is a failure of all of the people.

For Negro Americans, Washington is not just the nation's capital. It is the point at which all public transportation into the South becomes "Jim Crow." If he stops in Washington, a Negro may dine like other men in the Union Station, but as soon as he steps out into the capital, he leaves such democratic practices behind. With very few exceptions, he is refused service at downtown restaurants, he may not attend a downtown movie or play, and he has to go into the poorer section of the city to find a night's lodging. The Negro who decides to settle in the District must often find a home in an overcrowded, substandard area. He must often take a job below the level of his ability. He must send his children to the inferior public schools set aside for Negroes and entrust his family's health to medical agencies which give inferior service. In addition, he must endure the countless daily humiliations that the system of segregation imposes upon the one-third of Washington that is Negro.

The origin of the pattern of discrimination in Washington is partly explained by its location in a border area where many southern customs prevail. Certain political and local pressure groups, and the administrative decisions of municipal officials contribute to its persistence. Attempts to guarantee equal rights on a segregated basis have failed. In recent years the "separate and unequal" pattern has been extended to areas where it had not previously existed. Except where the federal government has made a few independent advances, as in federal employment and the use of federal recreational facilities, racial segregation is rigid. It extends to ludicrous extremes. Inconsistencies are evident: Constitution Hall, owned by the Daughters of the American Revolution, seats concert audiences without distinctions of color, but allows no Negroes on its stage to give regular commercial concerts. On the other hand, the commercial legitimate theater has had Negro actors on its stage, but stubbornly refuses to admit Negro patrons.

Discrimination in education.—The core of Washington's segregated society is its dual system of public education. It operates under congressional legislation which assumes the fact of segregation but nowhere makes it mandatory. The Board of Education and a white Superintendent of Schools administer two wholly separate school systems. The desire of Congress to insure equal facilities is implemented by a requirement that appropriations be allocated to white and Negro education in proportion to the numbers of children of school age. But this has not been successful. Negro schools are inferior to white schools in almost every respect. The white school buildings have a capacity which is 27 percent greater than actual enrollment. In the colored schools, enrollment exceeds building capacity by eight percent. Classes in the Negro schools are considerably larger and the teaching load of the Negro teachers considerably heavier. Less than one percent of all white school children, but over 15 percent of colored children, receive only part-time instruction. Similar inequalities exist in school buildings, equipment, textbook supplies, kindergarten classes, athletic, and recreational facilities.

The District Superintendent of Schools recently answered charges of inequality in school facilities with the statement that "Absolute equality of educational opportunity is impossible. Reasonable equality . . . is the goal." The conditions described above eloquently document the extent to which even "reasonable equality" is impossible in a segregated school system.

Official freezing of the segregated school system is complete. The Board of Education frowns on visits by whites to Negro schools and by Negroes to white schools. Intercultural education programs are stillborn because they are considered a threat to the prevailing pattern. Interracial athletic and forensic competition is forbidden. Two cases illustrate the lengths to which the District's officialdom goes to prevent interracial contact. During the war, the Office of Price Administration asked permission to use a school building at night for in-service training of its clerks. The request was denied solely because the class would have included both white and colored employees. In the other case a white girl was ordered to withdraw from a Negro vocational school where she had enrolled for a course not offered by any other public school in Washington.

Private universities in the District have followed the lead of the public schools. Two of the large universities and most of the smaller schools admit no colored students. American University admits them to its School of Social Science and Public Affairs, but not to the College of Arts and Sciences. Catholic University, on the other hand, presents an outstanding example of successful interracial education. In the last few years, Negroes have been admitted, and there is no color distinction in classes. Last year a Negro was elected a class officer. The presence of Howard University in Washington alleviates somewhat the problem of higher education for the District's Negroes. While Howard University is primarily a Negro institution, it also admits white students.

Discrimination in housing.—In the past, many of Washington's Negroes and whites have lived close together in many parts of the city, and where mixed neighborhoods still exist, incidents of racial friction are rare. Now, however, Negroes are increasingly being forced into a few overcrowded slums.

Programs for the development of highways, parks, and public buildings have often played an unfortunate role in rooting out Negro neighborhoods. There has been a commendable desire to beautify the city of Washington. But there has been little concern for the fate of persons displaced by beautification projects.

The superior economic position of whites also contributes to the shrinkage of Negro neighborhoods. In areas like Georgetown and the old fort sites, white residents and realtors have been buying up Negro properties and converting them to choice residential use. Only occasionally does this process work in reverse: in deteriorating areas, white owners can sometimes get higher prices from Negroes, who have little from which to choose, than they can from white buyers.

The chief weapon in the effort to keep Negroes from moving out of overcrowded quarters into white neighborhoods is the restrictive covenant. New building sites and many older areas are now covenanted. Some covenants exclude all nonmembers of the Caucasian race; others bar only Negroes, or Negroes and members of "Semitic races." Even where covenants do not prevail, the powerful local real estate fraternity protects white areas from "invasion." The all-white Washington Real Estate Board has a "code of ethics" which prohibits its members from selling land in predominantly white areas to Negroes, and the realtors are supported in this practice by nonmember dealers, banks, and loan companies. Two of the city's newspapers will not accept ads offering property in white areas for sale to Negroes. Because the policy of the National Capital Housing Authority is to follow the "community pattern," all public housing projects are completely segregated and housing for Negroes is built only in established Negro neighborhoods. The Authority has spent most of its funds for permanent housing to build homes for Negroes, but its appropriations have been limited.

Housing conditions are poor for Washington residents in general, but largely because of the pressures just described, they are much worse for Negroes. According to a recent Board of Trade report on city planning, 70 percent of the inhabitants of the city's three worst slum areas are Negroes. The largest single slum in the District houses about seven percent of the white and 30 percent of the Negro population. In 1940, one-eighth of the white dwellings in Washington and 40 percent of those occupied by Negroes were substandard; 15 percent of white-occupied and 38 percent of Negro-occupied dwellings had more than one person per room.

Discrimination in employment.—More than one-third of the jobs in Washington are with the federal government. Therefore, discriminatory practices of government agencies, which have already been discussed, are important to District Negroes. The District government itself has only a small proportion of Negro employees, and most of these are confined to unskilled and menial jobs. Partial exceptions to this are the Metropolitan Police, the segregated Fire Service, and the school system with its segregated staff. A ranking District official during the war told an interviewer: "Negroes in the District of Columbia have no right to ask for jobs on the basis of merit," the rationalization being that whites own most of the property and pay the bulk of municipal taxes.

Negroes are confined to the lowest paid and least skilled jobs in private employment. In 1940, three-fourths of all Negro workers in Washington were domestics, service workers or laborers, while only one-eighth of the white workers held jobs of that type. At the other end of the scale, only one-eighth of all Negro workers were clerks, salesmen, managers, proprietors or professionals, while two-thirds of the white workers were in jobs of this kind. There are similar striking racial differences in average income and length of workweek. . . .

Discrimination in health services.—The greatest inequalities are evident in Washington's concern for the health of its residents. Freedmen's Hospital, federally supported and affiliated with Howard University, is for Negroes only, and three-fourths of the beds in the municipal Gallinger Hospital are usually occupied by Negroes in segregated wards. Four of the twelve private hospitals in the city do not admit Negro in-patients, and the rest accept only a few in segregated wards. It is peculiarly shocking to find church hospitals practicing discrimination. Far fewer hospital beds in proportion to population are available to Negroes than to whites. Sickness rates are higher among Negroes than whites, which aggravates this situation. All but the smallest clinics are segregated. Group Health Association, however, does not discriminate either in membership or services.

No Negro physician is allowed to practice in Gallinger Hospital, although it is publicly supported and the majority of its patients are colored. Nor are they allowed in St. Elizabeth's, a federal institution, or any of the private hospitals. Only Freedmen's is open to them, and then only for the care of assigned ward patients. Thus the Negro physician cannot follow his own patients into the hospital. Negro medical students are similarly discriminated against in the provision of training facilities.

Public and private agency welfare services are available to both colored and white residents, but institutional care is provided only on a segregated basis and the institutions for Negroes are far inferior in both number and quality to those for whites. Here again, the lower economic position of Negroes and their consequent need for care aggravates the problem.

Discrimination in recreational services.—In the field of public recreation, compulsory segregation has increased over the past 25 years. Various public authorities have closed to one race or the other numerous facilities where whites and Negroes once played together harmoniously. In 1942, the District of Columbia Board of Recreation was set up to centralize the control of public recreation facilities. Congress eliminated from the locally sponsored bill a provision that would have required the new Board to continue segregation. But it took no positive stand on the issue, and the Board has adopted regulations which enforce segregation in all the parks and playgrounds under its control.

Under this policy, facilities in seven out of 26 "natural areas" in the District have been turned over to Negroes. Because the Negro areas are disproportionately concentrated in the older, crowded parts of the city, white facilities are generally superior to those allotted to Negroes. Furthermore, whites and Negroes alike who live far from facilities open to their race have easy access to none. White residents who had shared with Negroes the use of the Rose Park Tennis Courts protested in vain against being barred from them.

On the other hand, recreation facilities under the jurisdiction of the Department of the Interior are open to all races, and serious friction is nonexistent. District officials have tried repeatedly to have these facilities turned over to the Recreation Board. The transfer has not been made because the Board will not agree to refrain from imposing segregation in their use.

Most private recreational groups follow the official policy of segregation, although occasional interracial competitions have been held successfully by some. The Washington Branch of the Amateur Athletic Union allows no interracial contests under its auspices. For example, no Negro may enter the local Golden Gloves Tournament, although they compete in the national tournament.

Discrimination in places of public accommodation.—Public transportation is provided without separation of the races, and the spectators at most professional sporting events are unsegregated. But other public accommodations are a focal point of Negro resentment, because rigorous segregation in practice means exclusion. No downtown theater except the burlesque house admits Negroes. They may see movies only in their neighborhood houses. Some department stores and many downtown shops exclude Negro patrons by ignoring them or refusing to show the stock they request or making them wait until all white customers have been served. A Negro is seldom accepted at the downtown hotels unless special arrangements are made. Although they may dine at the Union Station, the YWCA, and the cafeterias in government office buildings, the overwhelming majority of downtown restaurants are closed to them.

The shamefulness and absurdity of Washington's treatment of Negro Americans is highlighted by the presence of many dark-skinned foreign visitors. Capital custom not only humiliates colored citizens, but is a source of considerable embarrassment to these visitors. White residents, because they are the dominant group, share in both the humiliation and the embarrassment. Foreign officials are often mistaken for American Negroes and refused food, lodging and entertainment. However, once it is established that they are not Americans, they are accommodated.

This is the situation that exists in the District of Columbia. The Committee feels most deeply that it is intolerable.

—"To Secure These Rights," 1947

17. A UNIVERSAL DECLARATION OF HUMAN RIGHTS

"My country is the world; my countrymen are mankind" is the motto that William Lloyd Garrison used in his Liberator. *It took a long time for Americans to realize that if liberty were denied in one part of the country it was in danger everywhere. It took an even longer time for people to realize that this axiom holds good for the entire world. Yet*

the events of the thirties and the forties dramatized this principle in an unforgettable way. The persecution of the Jews in Germany, the suppression of minorities in Italy, the judicial murder of dissenters in Russia, all made clear that an attack upon liberty could not be isolated but affected mankind everywhere. It was a realization of this that persuaded the General Assembly of the United Nations to adopt this Universal Declaration of Human Rights, which is here given in full.

THE GENERAL ASSEMBLY

PROCLAIMS this Universal Declaration of Human Rights as a common standard of achievement for all peoples and all nations, to the end that every individual and every organ of society, keeping this declaration constantly in mind, shall strive by teaching and education to promote respect for these rights and freedoms and by progressive measures, national and international, to secure their universal and effective recognition and observance, both among the peoples of Member States themselves and among the peoples of territories under their jurisdiction.

Art. 1. All human beings are born free and equal in dignity and rights. They are endowed with reason and conscience and should act towards one another in a spirit of brotherhood.

Art. 2. Everyone is entitled to all the rights and freedoms set forth in this Declaration, without distinction of any kind, such as race, colour, sex, language, religion, political or other opinion, national or social origin, property, birth, or other status.

Furthermore, no distinction shall be made on the basis of the political, jurisdictional, or international status of the country or territory to which a person belongs, whether it be an independent, trust, or non-self-governing territory or under any limitation of sovereignty.

Art 3. Everyone has the right to life, liberty, and security of person.

Art. 4. No one shall be held in slavery or servitude; slavery and the slave trade shall be prohibited in all their forms.

Art. 5. No one shall be subjected to torture or to cruel, inhuman, or degrading treatment or punishment.

Art. 6. Everyone has the right to recognition everywhere as a person before the law.

Art. 7. All are equal before the law and are entitled without any discrimination to equal protection of the law. All are entitled to equal protection against any discrimination in violation of this Declaration and against any incitement to such discrimination.

Art. 8. Everyone has the right to an effective remedy by the competent national tribunals for acts violating the fundamental rights granted him by the Constitution or by law.

Art. 9. No one shall be subjected to arbitrary arrest, detention, or exile.

Art. 10. Everyone is entitled in full equality to a fair and public hearing by an independent and impartial tribunal, in the determination of his rights and obligations and of any criminal charge against him.

Art. 11. 1. Everyone charged with a penal offence has the right to be presumed innocent until proved guilty according to law in a public trial at which he has had all the guarantees necessary for his defence.

2. No one shall be held guilty of any penal offence on account of any act or omission which did not constitute a penal offence, under national or international law, at the time when it was committed. Nor shall a heavier penalty be imposed than the one that was applicable at the time the penal offence was committed.

Art. 12. No one shall be subjected to arbitrary interference with his privacy, family, home, or correspondence, nor to attacks upon his honour and reputation. Everyone has the right to the protection of the law against such interference or attacks.

Art. 13. 1. Everyone has the right to freedom of movement and residence within the borders of each State.

2. Everyone has the right to leave any country, including his own, and to return to his country.

Art. 14. 1. Everyone has the right to seek and to enjoy in other countries asylum from persecution.

2. This right may not be invoked in the case of prosecutions genuinely arising from non-political crimes or from acts contrary to the purposes and principles of the United Nations.

Art. 15. 1. Everyone has the right to a nationality.

2. No one shall be arbitrarily deprived of his nationality nor denied the right to change his nationality.

Art. 16. 1. Men and women of full age, without any limitation due to race, nationality, or religion, have the right to marry and to found a family. They are entitled to equal rights as to marriage, during marriage, and at its dissolution.

2. Marriage shall be entered into only with the free and full consent of the intending spouses.

3. The family is the natural and fundamental group unit of society and is entitled to protection by society and the State.

Art. 17. 1. Everyone has the right to own property alone as well as in association with others.

2. No one shall be arbitrarily deprived of his property.

Art. 18. Everyone has the right to freedom of thought, conscience, and religion; this right includes freedom to change his religion or belief, and freedom either alone or in community with others and in public or private, to manifest his religion or belief in teaching, practice, worship, and observance.

Art. 19. Everyone has the right to freedom of opinion and expression, this right includes freedom to hold opinions without interference and to seek, receive, and impart information and ideas through any media and regardless of frontiers.

Art. 20. 1. Everyone has the right to freedom of peaceful assembly and association.

2. No one may be compelled to belong to an association.

Art. 21. 1. Everyone has the right to take part in the Government of his country, directly or through freely chosen representatives.

2. Everyone has the right of equal access to public service in his country.

3. The will of the people shall be the basis of the authority of Government; this will shall be expressed in periodic and genuine elections which shall be by universal and equal suffrage and shall be held by secret vote or by equivalent free voting procedures.

Art. 22. Everyone as a member of society, has the right to social security and is entitled to the realisation, through national effort and international co-operation and in accordance with the organisation and resources of each State, of the economic, social, and cultural rights indispensable for his dignity and the free development of his personality.

Art. 23. 1. Everyone has the right to work, to free choice of employment, to just and favourable conditions of work, and to protection against unemployment.

2. Everyone, without any discrimination, has the right to equal pay for equal work.

3. Everyone who works has the right to just and favourable remuneration, insuring for himself and his family an existence worthy of human dignity, and supplemented, if necessary by other means of social protection.

4. Everyone has the right to form and to join trade unions for the protection of his interests.

Art. 24. Everyone has the right to rest and leisure, including reasonable limitation of working hours and periodic holidays with pay.

Art. 25. 1. Everyone has the right to a standard of living adequate for the health and wellbeing of himself and of his family, including food, clothing, housing, and medical care and necessary social services, and the right to security in the event of unemployment, sickness disability, widowhood, old age, or other lack of livelihood in circumstances beyond his control.

2. Motherhood and childhood are entitled to special care and assistance. All children, whether born in or out of wedlock, shall enjoy the same social protection.

Art. 26. 1. Everyone has the right to education. Education shall be free, at least in the elementary and fundamental stages. Elementary education shall be compulsory. Technical and professional education shall be made generally available, and higher education shall be equally accessible to all on the basis of merit.

2. Education shall be directed to the full development of the human personality and to the strengthening of respect for human rights and fundamental freedoms, it shall promote understanding, tolerance, and friendship among all nations, racial or religious groups, and shall further the activities of the United Nations for the maintenance of peace.

3. Parents have a prior right to choose the kind of education that shall be given to their children.

Art. 27. 1. Everyone has the right freely to participate in the cultural life of the community, to enjoy the arts, and to share in scientific advancement and its benefits.

2. Everyone has the right to the protection of the moral and material interests resulting from any scientific, literary, or artistic production of which he is the author.

Art. 28. Everyone is entitled to a social and international order in which the rights and freedoms set forth in this declaration can be fully realised.

Art. 29. 1. Everyone has duties to the community in which alone the free and full development of his personality is possible.

2. In the exercise of his rights and freedoms, everyone shall be subject only to such limitations as are determined by law solely for the purpose of securing due recognition and respect for the rights and freedoms of others and of meeting the just requirements of morality, public order, and the general welfare in a democratic society.

3. These rights and freedoms may in no case be exercised contrary to the purposes and principles of the United Nations.

Art. 30. Nothing in this Declaration may be interpreted as implying for any State, group, or person any right to engage in any activity or to perform any act aimed at the destruction of any of the rights and freedoms set forth herein.

—United Nations, Universal Declaration of Human Rights, 1948

9

The Tradition of
Change and Reform

AMERICANS themselves fail to realize how deeply engrained is their habit of change and of reform, but foreign observers have not failed to note this from the very beginning. Few Americans suppose their station in life fixed by the accident of birth or of education or training. They shift cheerfully from job to job, from profession to profession, from country to city or from State to State. Sons of farmers go into business; businessmen try their hand at farming; lawyers become company directors; teachers turn to law; doctors try teaching. Nothing seems fixed, nothing but the habit of experiment and of change.

The sources of this habit lie in the American environment and historical experience. The settlement of America, as Lewis Mumford sagely observes, was the unsettlement of Europe. Everyone who came from the Old World to the New had made so great a change that thereafter all lesser changes seemed unimportant, and the shift from the Old World to the New was a continuous one for three hundred years. So, too, the successive waves of the westward movement, the endless migrations that carried the American people from the Atlantic to the Pacific and that, even in the decade of the 1940's, took almost five million persons to the Pacific Coast. Democracy, too—as Tocqueville pointed out—made for change, for in a democracy no one took his place in society or economy as unalterably fixed, but everyone felt that he could change to any work in any place at any time he pleased. In a democracy every road was clear, every door was open, and there was nothing to prevent anyone from trying them all.

This habit of change could not but affect the American attitude toward institutions—institutions of church, school, the professions, politics, and so forth. The ease with which Americans—at least those of Protestant backgrounds—change from church to church, from denomination to denomination is familiar enough, So, too, the readiness with which the American young shop around from college to college and curriculum to curriculum; the elective system is a product not only of democracy but of the American democracy. Few Americans regard the age of an institution or of a practice as in itself a virtue. Where in England, for example, the fact that something has always been done a certain way is sufficient reason why it should continue to be done that way, such a consideration is in America rather a challenge than a conclusion.

Americans have not, then, in the past been afraid of change, and they have customarily regarded reform as part of the natural, almost of the cosmic, order. Certainly they have customarily regarded with equanimity changes that enlarged the scope of democracy, either in the political or in the social and economic realms. To be sure—as we saw in our chapter on majority rule and minority right—there have always been some who were alarmed or startled or outraged or grieved when upstarts pushed their way into areas heretofore reserved for gentlemen, but these have never been numerous enough or powerful enough to stem for any length of time the tide of change and reform.

What is perhaps most remarkable is that the American passion for change has affected so little basic institutions of politics or law. In these areas we seem radical but are, in fact, conservative. Thus during only three periods of our history have we inserted important changes in our constitutional fabric, and only one of these—the Fourteenth Amendment—can be regarded as truly revolutionary. Thus though the Constitution permits endless experimentation in the laboratories of the States, almost all of our State Constitutions are as alike as the proverbial peas in pods. Since Pennsylvania abandoned its unicameral legislature in the eighteenth century, there has been only one other such experiment in our State history. Thus though the Constitution does not limit the number of judges who may be appointed to the Supreme Court or require inferior courts, any suggestion for significant changes in the Supreme Court or for the abolition of the inferior courts would be regarded as heresy.

On the whole, too, Americans have been conservative in the realm of economy. There has been boldness, experimentation, ingenuity, in what might be called technical fields—in physical pioneering, in the adaptation of tools to environment, in the exploitation of natural resources.

Almost instinctively the American figures out a better and quicker and cheaper way of doing whatever has to be done. It is to all this that we refer when we speak—as we do rather frequently—of free enterprise. But fundamental experiments in the economic realm have not been popular. Both American business and American labor have been suspicious of fundamental experiments, and suspicious, too, of ideas and philosophies. The TVA, perhaps the most original and certainly the most interesting of all social-economic experiments in America, is still suspect in some respectable quarters. And though it has been the most spectacularly successful of all the New Deal undertakings, the pattern it established has not been adopted for any other river valley region in the country. It is as if the Ford car having proved successful, should have no imitators and no rivals.

The New Deal ushered in reforms comparable to those of any previous reform period. It was not followed by reaction, but it was followed by quiescence. Thus where the New Deal was realized, the Fair Deal bogged down. The difference here is not only the difference between Roosevelt and Truman. It is the difference between a program announced and carried through during a period of depression, and a program announced—and not carried through—during a period of prosperity. It is perhaps inevitable that prosperity should make for satisfaction with the status quo, and even for complacency. This would account sufficiently for the failure to carry through the implications of the New Deal. It does not explain, in itself, the suspicion of the very concept of reform. That is to be explained by the growth of Communism in Eastern Europe and of Socialism in Western Europe, the confusion of the two, and the association of change and reform with either or both of them. In any event, by mid-twentieth century change had become suspect and reform had taken on a vaguely subversive tinge.

At a time when the whole world is experiencing far-reaching and even cataclysmic changes, it is of utmost importance that Americans recapture their traditional sympathy for change, even for revolutionary change. In the past European liberals looked to America for leadership and for encouragement; it would be tragic if liberals of other countries should come to regard the United States as the chief bulwark of the status quo, the chief opponent of change. It would be tragic, too, if Americans themselves abandoned their traditional habit of change and reform, or confined it to the narrow channels of technology and science.

After all, the great tradition of America is the tradition of reform. And, after all, the arena in which free enterprise has the greatest scope is not in business or industry, but in the realm of ideas.

1. EVERY GENERATION HAS A RIGHT TO MAKE ITS OWN CONSTITUTION

Jefferson was the most logical, the most consistent, and the most thoroughgoing democrat ever to occupy high office in the United States, and we have not yet exhausted his concept of democracy. He believed not only in majority rule, but in the rule of the living majority; he believed not only that men make government, but that each generation has the right to make government anew. His conviction that each generation should write its own fundamental law has sometimes been regarded as merely a conceit, but there can be no doubt that Jefferson himself was entirely serious about it.

These two letters illuminate the question of majority rule and minority rights. They also illuminate the question of change and reform. For what Jefferson is saying here—among other things—is that not only laws but the very frame of government must be adapted to changing conditions. What he is saying is that the earth belongs to the living, not the dead; that each generation has a right to make constitutions anew; that one generation is to another as one independent nation to another; that the Revolution did not exhaust democracy or liberty but left new worlds of democracy and of liberty to be conquered by future generations. This is pretty strong doctrine.

A. "Some Men Look at Constitutions with Sanctimonious Reverence"

SOME men look at constitutions with sanctimonious reverence, and deem them like the ark of the covenant, too sacred to be touched. They ascribe to the men of the preceding age a wisdom more than human, and suppose what they did to be beyond amendment. I knew that age well; I belonged to it, and labored with it. It deserved well of its country. It was very like the present, but without the experience of the present; and forty years of experience in government is worth a century of bookreading; and this they would say themselves, were they to rise from the dead. I am certainly not an advocate for frequent and untried changes in laws and constitutions. I think moderate imperfections had better be borne with; because, when once known, we accommodate ourselves to them, and find practical means of correcting their ill effects. But I know also, that laws and institutions must go hand in hand with the progress of the human mind. As that becomes more developed, more enlightened, as new discoveries are made, new truths disclosed, and manners and opinions change with the change of circumstances, institutions must advance also, and keep pace with the times. We might as well require a man to wear still the coat which fitted him when a boy, as civilized society to remain ever under the regimen of their barbarous ancestors. It is this preposterous idea which has lately deluged Europe in blood. Their monarchs, instead of wisely yielding to the gradual change of circumstances, of favoring progressive accommodation to progressive improvement, have clung to old abuses, entrenched themselves behind steady habits, and obliged their subjects to seek through blood and violence rash and ruinous innovations, which, had they been referred to the peaceful deliberations and collected wisdom of the nation, would have been put into acceptable and salutary forms. Let us follow no such examples, nor weakly believe that one generation is not as capable as another of taking care of itself, and of ordering its own affairs. Let us, as our sister States have done, avail ourselves of our reason and experience, to correct the crude essays of our first and unexperienced, although wise, virtuous, and well-meaning councils. And lastly, let us provide in our constitution for its revision at stated periods. What these periods should be, nature herself indicates. By the European tables of mortality, of the adults living at any one moment of time, a majority will be dead in about nineteen years. At the end of that period, then, a new majority is come into place; or, in other words, a new generation. Each generation is as independent as the one preceding, as that was of all which had gone before. It has then, like them, a right to choose for itself the form of government it believes most promotive of its own happiness; consequently, to accommodate to the circumstances in which it finds itself, that received from its predecessors; and it is for the peace and good of mankind, that a solemn opportunity of doing this every nineteen or twenty years, should be provided by the constitution; so that it may be handed on, with periodical repairs, from generation to generation, to the end of time, if anything human can so long endure. It is now forty years since the constitution of Virginia was formed. The same tables inform us, that, within that period, two-thirds of the adults then living are now dead. Have then the remaining third, even if they had the wish, the right to hold in obedience to their will, and to laws heretofore made by them, the other two-thirds, who, with themselves, compose the present mass of adults? If they have not, who has? The dead? But the dead have no rights. They are nothing; and nothing cannot own something. Where there is no substance, there can be no accident. This corporeal globe, and everything upon it, belong to its present corporeal inhabitants, during their generation. They alone have a right to direct what is the concern of themselves alone, and to declare the law of that direction; and this declaration can only be made by their majority. That majority, then, has a right to depute representatives to a convention, and to make the constitution what they think will be the best for themselves. But how collect their voice? This is the real difficulty. If invited by private authority, or county or district meetings, these divisions are so large that few will attend; and their voice will be imperfectly, or falsely pronounced. Here, then, would be one of the advantages of the ward divisions I have proposed. The mayor of every ward, on a question like the present, would call his ward together, take the simple yea or nay of its members, convey these to the county court, who would hand on those of all its wards to the proper general authority; and the voice of the whole people would be thus fairly, fully, and peaceably expressed, discussed, and decided by the common reason of the society. If this avenue be shut to the call of sufferance, it will make itself heard through that of force, and we shall go on, as other nations are doing, in the endless circle of oppression, rebellion, reformation; and oppression, rebellion, reformation, again; and so on forever.

These, Sir, are my opinions of the governments we see among men, and of the principles by which alone we may prevent our own from falling into the same dreadful track.

—THOMAS JEFFERSON, Letter to Samuel Kercheval, July 12, 1816

B. "ALL EYES ARE OPEN TO THE RIGHTS OF MAN"

RESPECTED SIR,—The kind invitation I receive from you, on the part of the citizens of the city of Washington, to be present with them at their celebration on the fiftieth anniversary of American Independence, as one of the surviving signers of an instrument pregnant with our own, and the fate of the world, is most flattering to myself, and heightened by the honorable accompaniment proposed for the comfort of such a journey. It adds sensibly to the sufferings of sickness, to be deprived by it of a personal participation in the rejoicings of that day. But acquiescence is a duty, under circumstances not placed among those we are permitted to control. I should, indeed, with peculiar delight, have met and exchanged there congratulations personally with the small band, the remnant of that host of worthies, who joined with us on that day, in the bold and doubtful election we were to make for our country, between submission or the sword; and to have enjoyed with them the consolatory fact, that our fellow citizens, after half a century of experience and prosperity, continue to approve the choice we made. May it be to the world, what I believe it will be, (to some parts sooner, to others later, but finally to all,) the signal of arousing men to burst the chains under which monkish ignorance and superstition had persuaded them to bind themselves, and to assume the blessings and security of self-government. That form which we have substituted, restores the free right to the unbounded exercise of reason and freedom of opinion. All eyes are opened, or opening, to the rights of man. The general spread of the light of science has already laid open to every view the palpable truth, that the mass of mankind has not been born with saddles on their backs, nor a favored few booted and spurred, ready to ride them legitimately, by the grace of God. These are grounds of hope for others. For ourselves, let the annual return of this day forever refresh our recollections of these rights, and an undiminished devotion to them.

I will ask permission here to express the pleasure with which I should have met my ancient neighbors of the city of Washington and its vicinities, with whom I passed so many years of a pleasing social intercourse; an intercourse which so much relieved the anxieties of the public cares, and left impressions so deeply engraved in my affections, as never to be forgotten. With my regret that ill health forbids me the gratification of an acceptance, be pleased to receive for yourself, and those for whom you write, the assurance of my highest respect and friendly attachments.

    --THOMAS JEFFERSON, Letter to Roger C. Weightman, June 24, 1826

2. THE DECLARATION OF INDEPENDENCE AND THE SPIRIT OF REFORM

Speaking in 1857 of the generation that adopted the Declaration of Independence, Lincoln said, "They meant to set up a standard maxim for free society, which should be . . . constantly looked to, constantly labored for, and even though never perfectly attained, constantly approximated, and thereby constantly spreading and deepening its influence and augmenting the happiness and value of life to all people of all colors everywhere." This, in any event, was the history of the Declaration—that it became a standard for free society. And for the future, the most important phrase in the Declaration was the phrase, "all men are created equal." Obviously not a description of conditions as they actually existed in America in 1776, this phrase became a slogan for what ought to exist. That ought became, during the great reform period of 1830-60, one of the most important of concepts. Wherever men and women found conditions that contrasted too flagrantly with the assumed promise of equality, they set about changing the conditions in order to achieve equality. Two examples of this familiar process are given here. The first has to do with the abolition of slavery; the second with woman's rights. Each of these is an important chapter in our history and merits far more elaborate examination than we can give it here. Our immediate interest in these great reforms is in the way that they were inspired by, appealed to, and depended on the Declaration of Independence—that is the way in which they linked themselves to the American tradition and became in turn part of that tradition. We give first William Lloyd Garrison's Number I of The Liberator, *and then excerpts from the Woman's Declaration of Independence at Seneca Falls, New York, in 1848.*

A. "THE STANDARD OF EMANCIPATION IS NOW UNFURLED"
TO THE PUBLIC

IN THE month of August, I issued proposals for publishing *"The Liberator"* in Washington City; but the enterprise, though hailed in different sections of the country, was palsied by public indifference. Since that time, the removal of the *Genius of Universal Emancipation* to the Seat of Government has rendered less imperious the establishment of a similar periodical in that quarter.

During my recent tour for the purpose of exciting the minds of the people by a series of discourses on the subject of slavery, every place that I visited gave fresh evidence of the fact, that a greater revolution in public sentiment was to be effected in the free states—*and particularly in New England*—than at the south. I found contempt more bitter, opposition more active, detraction more relentless, prejudice more stubborn, and apathy more frozen, than among slave owners themselves. Of course, there were individual exceptions to the contrary. This state of things afflicted, but did not dishearten me. I determined, at every hazard, to lift up the standard of emancipation in the eyes of the nation, *within sight of Bunker Hill and in the birth place of liberty.* That standard is now unfurled; and long may it float, unhurt by the spoliations of time or the missiles of a desperate foe—yea, till every chain be broken, and every bondman set free! Let Southern oppressors tremble —let their secret abettors tremble—let their Northern apologists tremble —let all the enemies of the persecuted blacks tremble.

I deem the publication of my original Prospectus unnecessary, as it has obtained a wide circulation. The principles therein inculcated will be steadily pursued in this paper, excepting that I shall not array myself as the political partisan of any man. In defending the great cause of human rights, I wish to derive the assistance of all religions and of all parties.

Assenting to the "self evident truth" maintained in the American Declaration of Independence, "that all men are created equal, and endowed by their Creator with certain inalienable rights—among which are life, liberty and the pursuit of happiness," I shall strenuously contend for the immediate enfranchisement of our slave population. In Park-Street Church, on the Fourth of July, 1829, in an address on slavery, I unreflectingly assented to the popular but pernicious doctrine of *gradual* abolition. I seize this opportunity to make a full and unequivocal recantation, and thus publicly to ask pardon of my God, of my country, and of my brethren the poor slaves, for having uttered a sentiment so full of timidity, injustice and absurdity. A similar recantation, from my pen, was published in the *Genius of Universal Emancipation* at Baltimore, in September, 1829. My conscience is now satisfied.

I am aware, that many object to the severity of my language; but is there not cause for severity? I *will be* as harsh as truth, and as uncompromising as justice. On this subject, I do not wish to think, or speak, or write, with moderation. No! No! Tell a man whose house is on fire, to give a moderate alarm; tell him to moderately rescue his wife from the hands of the ravisher; tell the mother to gradually extricate her babe from the fire into which it has fallen;—but urge me not to use moderation in a cause like the present. I am in earnest—I will not equivocate—I will not excuse—I will not retreat a single inch—*AND I WILL BE HEARD*. The apathy of the people is enough to make every statue leap from its pedestal, and to hasten the resurrection of the dead.

It is pretended, that I am retarding the cause of emancipation by the coarseness of my invective, and the precipitancy of my measures. *The charge is not true.* On this question my influence,—humble as it is,—is felt at this moment to a considerable extent, and shall be felt in coming years—not perniciously, but beneficially—not as a curse, but as a blessing; and posterity will bear testimony that I was right. I desire to thank God, that he enables me to disregard "the fear of man which bringeth a snare," and to speak his truth in its simplicity and power.

—WILLIAM LLOYD GARRISON,
First Number of *The Liberator*, January 1, 1831

B. "ALL MEN AND WOMEN ARE CREATED EQUAL"

1. DECLARATION OF SENTIMENTS

The history of mankind is a history of repeated injuries and usurpations on the part of man toward woman, having in direct object the establishment of an absolute tyranny over her. To prove this, let facts be submitted to a candid world.

He has never permitted her to exercise her inalienable right to the elective franchise.

He has compelled her to submit to laws, in the formation of which she had no voice.

He has withheld from her rights which are given to the most ignorant and degraded men—both natives and foreigners.

Having deprived her of this first right of a citizen, the elective franchise, thereby leaving her without representation in the halls of legislation, he has oppressed her on all sides.

He has made her, if married, in the eye of the law, civilly dead.

He has taken from her all right in property, even to the wages she earns.

He has made her, morally, an irresponsible being, as she can commit many crimes with impunity, provided they be done in the presence of her husband. In the covenant of marriage, she is compelled to promise obedience to her husband, he becoming, to all intents and purposes, her master—the law giving him power to deprive her of her liberty, and to administer chastisement.

He has so framed the laws of divorce, as to what shall be the proper causes, and in case of separation, to whom the guardianship of the children shall be given, as to be wholly regardless of the happiness of women—the law, in all cases, going upon a false supposition of the supremacy of man, and giving all power into his hands.

After depriving her of all rights as a married woman, if single, and the owner of property, he has taxed her to support a government which recognizes her only when her property can be made profitable to it.

He has monopolized nearly all the profitable employments, and from those she is permitted to follow, she receives but a scanty remuneration. He closes against her all the avenues to wealth and distinction which he considers most honorable to himself. As a teacher of theology, medicine, or law, she is not known.

He has denied her the facilities for obtaining a thorough education, all colleges being closed against her.

He allows her in Church, as well as State, but a subordinate position, claiming Apostolic authority for her exclusion from the ministry, and, with some exceptions, from any public participations in the affairs of the Church.

He has created a false public sentiment by giving to the world a different code of morals for men and women, by which moral delinquencies which exclude women from society, are not only tolerated, but deemed of little account in man.

He has usurped the prerogative of Jehovah himself, claiming it as his right to assign for her a sphere of action, when that belongs to her conscience and to her God.

He has endeavored, in every way that he could, to destroy her confidence in her own powers, to lessen her self-respect and to make her willing to lead a dependent and abject life.

Now, in view of this entire disfranchisement of one-half the people of this country, their social and religious degradation—in view of the unjust laws above mentioned, and because women do feel themselves aggrieved, oppressed, and fraudulently deprived of their most sacred rights, we insist that they have immediate admission to all the rights and privileges which belong to them as citizens of the United States.

In entering upon the great work before us, we anticipate no small amount of misconception, misrepresentation, and ridicule; but we shall use every instrumentality within our power to effect our object. We shall employ agents, circulate tracts, petition the State and National legislatures, and endeavor to enlist the pulpit and the press in our behalf. We hope this Convention will be followed by a series of Conventions embracing every part of the country.

—The Seneca Falls Declaration of Sentiments, 1848

3. THE FERMENT OF REFORM

The period from 1830 to the Civil War was the great reform generation of American history. In these decades every institution was called before the bar of Religion and of Reason, and made to justify itself. It was the era of woman's rights, prison and penal reform, religious liberalism, educational progress, humanitarian crusades, and anti-slavery. The philosophical basis for this remarkable reform movement was the conviction that there was divinity in all men, and that anything that interfered with or prevented the fullest spiritual, moral, intellectual, or social development of men was wrong. Much of the reform activity was concentrated in New England, and especially in and around Boston. Here a wonderful group of reformers and crusaders included Horace Mann, Wendell Phillips, William Lloyd Garrison, William Ellery Channing, Dorothea Dix, Samuel Gridley Howe, Charles Sumner, Thomas Wentworth Higginson, Bronson Alcott, Ralph Waldo Emerson, and—not least—Theodore Parker. He was, wrote Emerson, "our Savonarola, an excellent scholar, in frank and affectionate communication with the best minds of the day, yet the tribune of the people, and the stout Reformer to urge and defend every cause of humanity with and for the humblest of mankind." From the time he moved in to be Minister of the Twenty-Eighth Congregational Society of Boston, in 1845, Parker

*was in the center of the reform movement of his time. We give here
an extract from his memorable "Experience as a Minister"—the best
account of the reform movement in our literature.*

MR. GARRISON, with his friends, inheriting what was best in
the Puritan founders of New-England, fired with the zeal of
the Hebrew prophets and Christian martyrs, while they were animated
with a spirit of humanity rarely found in any of the three, was beginning his noble work, but in a style so humble that, after much
search, the police of Boston discovered there was nothing dangerous
in it, for "his only visible auxiliary was a Negro boy." Dr Channing
was in the full maturity of his powers, and after long preaching the
dignity of man as an abstraction, and piety as a purely inward life,
with rare and winsome eloquence, and ever progressive humanity,
began to apply his sublime doctrines to actual life in the individual, the
state, and the church. In the name of Christianity, the great American
Unitarian called for the reform of the drunkard, the elevation of the
poor, the instruction of the ignorant, and, above all, for the liberation of the American slave. A remarkable man, his instinct of progress
grew stronger the more he travelled and the further he went, for he
surrounded himself with young life. Horace Mann, with his coad-
jutors, began a great movement, to improve the public education of
the people. Pierpont, single-handed, was fighting a grand and two-fold
battle—against drunkenness in the street, and for righteousness in the
pulpit—against fearful ecclesiastic odds, maintaining a minister's right
and duty to oppose actual wickedness, however popular and destructive.
The brilliant genius of Emerson rose in the winter nights, and hung
over Boston, drawing the eyes of ingenuous young people to look
up to that great, new star, a beauty and a mystery, which charmed
for the moment, while it gave also perennial inspiration, as it led them
forward along new paths, and toward new hopes. America had seen
no such sight before; it is not less a blessed wonder now.

Besides, the Phrenologists, so ably represented by Spurzheim and
Combe, were weakening the power of the old supernaturalism, leading men to study the constitution of man more wisely than before,
and laying the foundation on which many a beneficent structure was
soon to rise. The writings of Wordsworth were becoming familiar

to the thoughtful lovers of nature and of man, and drawing men to natural piety. Carlyle's works got reprinted at Boston, diffusing a strong, and then, also, a healthy influence on old and young. The writings of Coleridge were reprinted in America, all of them "aids to reflection," and brilliant with the scattered sparks of genius; they incited many to think, more especially young Trinitarian ministers; and, spite of the lack of both historic and philosophic accuracy, and the utter absence of all proportion in his writings; spite of his haste, his vanity, prejudice, sophistry, confusion, and opium—he yet did great service in New-England, helping to emancipate enthralled minds. The works of Cousin, more systematic, and more profound as a whole, and far more catholic and comprehensive, continental, not insular, in his range, also became familiar to the Americans—reviews and translations going where the eloquent original was not heard—and helped to free the young mind from the gross sensationalism of the academic philosophy on one side, and the grosser supernaturalism of the ecclesiastic theology on the other.

The German language, hitherto the priceless treasure of a few, was becoming well known, and many were thereby made acquainted with the most original, deep, bold, comprehensive, and wealthy literature in the world, full of theologic and philosophic thought. Thus, a great storehouse was opened to such as were earnestly in quest of truth. . . .

The rights of labor were discussed with deep philanthropic feeling, and sometimes with profound thought, metaphysic and economic both. The works of Charles Fourier—a strange, fantastic, visionary man, no doubt, but gifted also with amazing insight of the truths of social science—shed some light in these dark places of speculation. Mr Ripley, a born Democrat, in the high sense of that abused word, and one of the best cultured and most enlightened men in America, made an attempt at Brookfarm in West Roxbury, so to organize society that the results of labour should remain in the workman's hand, and not slip thence to the trader's till; that there should be "no exploitation of man by man," but toil and thought, hard work and high culture, should be united in the same person.

The natural rights of women began to be inquired into, and publicly discussed; while in private, great pains were taken in the chief towns of New-England, to furnish a thorough and comprehensive education to such young maidens as were born with two talents, mind and money.

Of course, a strong reaction followed. At the Cambridge Divinity school, Professor Henry Ware, jun., told the young men, if there appeared to them any contradiction between the reason of man and the letter of the Bible, they "must follow the written word," "for you can never be so certain of the correctness of what takes place in your own mind, as of what is written in the Bible." In an ordination sermon, he told the young minister not to preach himself, but Christ; and not to appeal to human nature for proof of doctrines, but to the authority of revelation. Other Unitarian ministers declared, "There are limits to free inquiry:" and preached, "Reason must be put down, or she will soon ask terrible questions;" protested against the union of philosophy and religion, and assumed to "prohibit the banns" of marriage between the two. Mr Norton—then a great name at Cambridge, a scholar of rare but contracted merit, a careful and exact writer, born for controversy, really learned and able in his special department, the interpretations of the New Testament—opened his mouth and spoke: the mass of men must accept the doctrines of religion solely on the authority of the learned, as they do the doctrines of mathematical astronomy; the miracles of Jesus—he made merry at those of the Old Testament—are the only evidence of the truth of Christianity; in the popular religion of the Greeks and Romans, there was no conception of God; the new philosophic attempts to explain the facts of religious consciousness were "the latest form of infidelity;" the great philosophical and theological thinkers of Germany were "all atheists;" "Schleiermacher was an atheist," as was also Spinoza, his master, before him; and Cousin, who was only "that Frenchman," was no better; the study of philosophy, and the neglect of "Biblical criticism," were leading mankind to ruin—everywhere was instability and insecurity!

Of course, this reaction was supported by the ministers in the great churches of commerce, and by the old literary periodicals, which never knew a star was risen till men wondered at it in the zenith; the Unitarian journals gradually went over to the opponents of freedom and progress, with lofty scorn rejecting their former principles, and repeating the conduct they had once complained of; Cambridge and Princeton seemed to be interchanging cards. . . .

I count it a piece of good fortune that I was a young man when these things were taking place, when great questions were discussed, and the public had not yet taken sides.

—Theodore Parker, "Experience As a Minister," 1859

4. MAN THE REFORMER

It was Emerson who was the philosopher of the New England reform movement. He himself stood aloof—or did so when his friends let him—but he inspired the whole phalanx of reformers. "What is a man born for but to be a reformer?" he asked, and a hundred zealots took him at his word. He made clear the philosophical basis of the reform movement; he connected the individual reform with Universal Reform. We give here excerpts from one of his essays on reform: "Man the Reformer."

THE idea which now begins to agitate society has a wider scope than our daily employments, our households, and the institutions of property. We are to revise the whole of our social structure, the state, the school, religion, marriage, trade, science, and explore their foundations in our own nature; we are to see that the world not only fitted the former men but fits us, and to clear ourselves of every usage which has not its roots in our own mind. What is a man born for but to be a reformer, a remaker of what man has made; a renouncer of lies; a restorer of truth and good, imitating that great Nature which embosoms us all, and which sleeps no moment on an old past, but every hour repairs herself, yielding us every morning a new day, and with every pulsation a new life? Let him renounce everything which is not true to him, and put all his practices back on their first thoughts, and do nothing for which he has not the whole world for his reason. If there are inconveniences and what is called ruin in the way, because we have so enervated and maimed ourselves, yet it would be like dying of perfumes to sink in the effort to reattach the deeds of every day to the holy and mysterious recesses of life.

The power which is at once spring and regulator in all efforts of reform is the conviction that there is an infinite worthiness in man, which will appear at the call of worth, and that all particular reforms are the removing of some impediment. Is it not the highest duty that man should be honored in us? I ought not to allow any man, because he has broad lands, to feel that he is rich in my presence. I ought

451

to make him feel that I can do without his riches, that I cannot be bought—neither by comfort, neither by pride—and though I be utterly penniless, and receiving bread from him, that he is the poor man beside me. And if, at the same time, a woman or a child discovers a sentiment of piety, or a juster way of thinking than mine, I ought to confess it by my respect and obedience, though it go to alter my whole way of life.

The Americans have many virtues, but they have not faith and hope. I know no two words whose meaning is more lost sight of. We use these words as if they were as obsolete as Selah and Amen. And yet they have the broadest meaning and the most cogent application to Boston in this year. The Americans have little faith. They rely on the power of a dollar; they are deaf to a sentiment. They think you may talk the north wind down as easily as raise society; and no class is more faithless than the scholars or intellectual men. Now if I talk with a sincere wise man, and my friend, with a poet, with a conscientious youth who is still under the dominion of his own wild thoughts, and not yet harnessed in the team of society to drag with us all in the ruts of custom, I see at once how paltry is all this generation of unbelievers and what a house of cards their institutions are, and I see what one brave man, what one great thought executed, might effect. I see that the reason of the distrust of the practical man in all theory is his inability to perceive the means whereby we work. Look, he says, at the tools with which this world of yours is to be built. As we cannot make a planet, with atmosphere, rivers, and forests, by means of the best carpenters' or engineers' tools, with chemist's laboratory and smith's forge to boot—so neither can we ever construct that heavenly society you prate of out of foolish, sick, selfish men and women, such as we know them to be. But the believer not only beholds his heaven to be possible but already to begin to exist—not by the men or materials the statesman uses but by men transfigured and raised above themselves by the power of principles. To principles something else is possible that transcends all the power of expedients. . . .

But there will dawn ere long on our politics, on our modes of living, a nobler morning than that Arabian faith, in the sentiment of love. This is the one remedy for all ills, the panacea of nature. We must be lovers, and at once the impossible becomes possible. Our age and history, for these thousand years, has not been the history of kindness, but of selfishness. Our distrust is very expensive. The money we spend for courts and prison is very ill laid out. We make, by distrust, the thief, and burglar, and incendiary, and by our court and jail we keep him so. An acceptance of the sentiment of love throughout Christendom for a season would bring the felon and the outcast to our side in tears, with the devotion of his faculties to our service. See this wide society of laboring men and women. We allow ourselves to be served by them, we live apart from them, and meet them without a salute in the streets. We do not greet their talents, nor rejoice in their good fortune, nor foster their hopes, nor in the assembly of the people vote for what is dear to them. Thus we enact the part of the selfish noble and king from the foundation of the world. . . . Let our affection flow out to our fellows; it would operate in a day the greatest of all revolutions. It is better to work on institutions by the sun than by the wind. The state must consider the poor man, and all voices must speak for him. Every child that is born must have a just chance for his bread. Let the amelioration in our laws of property proceed from the concession of the rich, not from the grasping of the poor. Let us begin by habitual imparting. Let us understand that the equitable rule is that no one should take more than his share, let him be ever so rich. . . .

—RALPH WALDO EMERSON, "Man the Reformer," 1841

5. THE SEARCH FOR UTOPIA

In a sense America was itself Utopia, and continued to be, for millions of emigrants from the Old World, down into the twentieth century. But again and again those who supposed that the principle of the perfectibility of man would be realized in America, were disappointed. For the vast majority of people, life in the New World was better than life in the Old, but it still failed to come up to the expectations of some idealists. The Industrial Revolution, the growth of cities with their dangerous and perishing classes, the ever increasing disparity between the rich and the poor, the persistence of slavery, corruption in politics and in business—all these things persuaded some high-flying souls to escape from a society they found disappointing, and create their own Utopias. The result was a movement which, in the decades of the forties and the fifties, created some half a hundred Utopian communities. Emerson wrote Carlyle that anyone you met in the street might produce a new community project from his waistcoat pocket. Some com-

munities were primarily religious; some—like Owen's New Harmony— were communistic; some, like Noyes's Oneida Community, went in for experiments in sex and family relations. Many of them had their inspiration in the writings of the French theorist, Charles Fourier. The most famous of these was Brook Farm, outside Boston, which during its brief existence attracted such persons as Nathaniel Hawthorne, Margaret Fuller, Isaac Hecker, and Charles Dana. Hawthorne's novel, The Blithedale Romance, *is based in large part on his Brook Farm experience. We give here the Constitution of Brook Farm and an excerpt from the Hawthorne novel.*

A. The Constitution of the Brook Farm Association

Constitution

IN ORDER more effectually to promote the great purposes of human culture; to establish the external relations of life on a basis of wisdom and purity; to apply the principles of justice and love to our social organization in accordance with the laws of Divine Providence; to substitute a system of brotherly coöperation for one of selfish competition; to secure to our children and those who may be entrusted to our care, the benefits of the highest physical, intellectual and moral education, which in the progress of knowledge the resources at our command will permit; to institute an attractive, efficient, and productive system of industry; to prevent the exercise of worldly anxiety, by the competent supply of our necessary wants; to diminish the desire of excessive accumulation, by making the acquisition of individual property subservient to upright and disinterested uses; to guarantee to each other forever the means of physical support, and of spiritual progress; and thus to impart a greater freedom, simplicity, truthfulness, refinement, and moral dignity, to our mode of life;—we the undersigned do unite in a voluntary Association, and adopt and ordain the following articles of agreement, to wit:

Article I

Sec. 1. The name of this Association shall be "THE BROOK-FARM ASSOCIATION FOR INDUSTRY AND EDUCATION." All persons who shall hold one or more shares in its stock, or whose labor and skill shall be considered an equivalent for capital, may be admitted by the vote of two-thirds of the Association, as members thereof.

Sec. 2. No member of the Association shall ever be subjected to any religious test; nor shall any authority be assumed over individual freedom of opinion by the Association, nor by any one member over another; nor shall any one be held accountable to the Association, except for such overt acts, omissions of duty, as violate the principles of justice, purity, and love, on which it is founded; and in such cases the relation of any member may be suspended, or discontinued, at the pleasure of the Association.

ARTICLE II

Sec. 1. The members of this Association shall own and manage such real and personal estate in joint stock proprietorship, divided into shares of one hundred dollars, each, as may from time to time be agreed on. . . .

Sec. 4. The shareholders on their part, for themselves, their heirs and assigns, do renounce all claim on any profits accruing to the Association for the use of their capital invested in the stock of the Association, except five per cent, interest on the amount of stock held by them, payable in the manner described in the preceding section.

ARTICLE III

Sec. 1. The Association shall provide such employment for all its members as shall be adapted to their capacities, habits, and tastes; and each member shall select and perform such operations of labor, whether corporal or mental, as shall be deemed best suited to his own endowments, and the benefit of the Association.

Sec. 2. The Association guarantees to all its members, their children, and family dependents, house-rent, fuel, food, and clothing, and the other necessaries of life, without charge, not exceeding a certain fixed amount to be decided annually by the Association; no charge shall ever be made for support during inability to labor from sickness or old age, or for medical or nursing attendance, except in case of shareholders, who shall be charged therefor . . . but no charge shall be made to any members for education or the use of library and public rooms. . . .

ARTICLE V

Sec. 5. The departments of Education and Finance shall be under the control each of its own Direction, which shall select, and in concurrence with the General Direction, shall appoint such teachers, officers, and agents, as shall be necessary to the complete and systematic organization of the department. No Directors or other officers shall be deemed to possess any rank superior to the other members of the Association, nor shall they receive any extra remuneration for their official services. Sec. 6. The department of Industry shall be arranged in groups and series, as far as practicable, and shall consist of three primary series; to wit, Agricultural, Mechanical, and Domestic Industry. The chief of each series shall be elected every two months by the members thereof.

—The Constitution of the Brook Farm Association, 1841

B. BLITHEDALE

Emerging into the genial sunshine, I half fancied that the labors of the brotherhood had already realized some of Fourier's predictions. Their enlightened culture of the soil, and the virtues with which they sanctified their life, had begun to produce an effect upon the material world and its climate. In my new enthusiasm, man looked strong and stately,— and woman, oh how beautiful!—and the earth a green garden, blossoming with many-colored delights. Thus Nature, whose laws I had broken in various artificial ways, comported herself towards me as a strict but loving mother, who uses the rod upon her little boy for his naughtiness, and then gives him a smile, a kiss, and some pretty playthings to console the urchin for her severity. . . .

On the whole, it was a society such as has seldom met together; nor, perhaps, could it reasonably be expected to hold together long. Persons of marked individuality—crooked sticks, as some of us might be called— are not exactly the easiest to bind up into a fagot. But, so long as our union should subsist, a man of intellect and feeling, with a free nature in him, might have sought far and near without finding so many points of attraction as would allure him hitherward. We were of all creeds and opinions, and generally tolerant of all, on every imaginable subject. Our bond, it seems to me, was not affirmative, but negative. We had individually found one thing or another to quarrel with in our past life, and were pretty well agreed as to the inexpediency of lumbering along with the old system any further. As to what should be substituted, there was much less unanimity. We did not greatly care—at least, I never did—for the written constitution under which our millennium had commenced. My hope was, that, between theory and practice, a true and available mode of life might be struck out; and that, even should we ultimately fail, the months or years spent in the trial would not have been wasted, either as regarded passing enjoyment, or the experience which makes men wise. . . .

After a reasonable training, the yeoman life throve well with us. Our faces took the sunburn kindly; our chests gained in compass, and our shoulders in breadth and squareness; our great brown fists looked as if they had never been capable of kid gloves. The plough, the hoe, the scythe, and the hay-fork grew familiar to our grasp. The oxen responded to our voices. We could do almost as fair a day's work as Silas Foster himself, sleep dreamlessly after it, and awake at daybreak with only a little stiffness of the joints, which was usually quite gone by breakfast-time.

To be sure, our next neighbors pretended to be incredulous as to our real proficiency in the business which we had taken in hand. They told slanderous fables about our ability to yoke our own oxen, or to drive them afield when yoked, or to release the poor brutes from their con-jugal bond at nightfall. They had the face to say, too, that the cows laughed at our awkwardness at milking-time, and invariably kicked over the pails; partly in consequence of our putting the stool on the wrong side, and partly because, taking offence at the whisking of their tails, we were in the habit of holding these natural fly-flappers with one hand and milking with the other. They further averred that we hoed up whole acres of Indian corn and other crops, and drew the earth care-fully about the weeds; and that we raised five hundred tufts of burdock, mistaking them for cabbages; and that, by dint of unskilful planting few of our seeds ever came up at all, or, if they did come up it was stern-foremost; and that we spent the better part of the month of June in reversing a field of beans, which had thrust themselves out of the ground in this unseemly way. They quoted it as nothing more than an ordinary occurrence for one or other of us to crop off two or three fingers, of a morning, by our clumsy use of the hay-cutter. Finally, and as an ultimate catastiophe, these mendacious rogues circulated a report that we communitarians were exterminated, to the last man, by severing ourselves asunder, with the sweep of our own scythes!—and that the world had lost nothing by this little accident.

But this was pure envy and malice on the part of the neighboring farmers. The peril of our new way of life was not lest we should fail in becoming practical agriculturists, but that we should probably cease to be anything else. While our enterprise lay all in theory, we had pleased ourselves with delectable visions of the spiritualization of labor. It was to be our form of prayer and ceremonial of worship. Each stroke of the hoe was to uncover some aromatic root of wisdom, heretofore hidden from the sun. Pausing in the field, to let the wind exhale the moisture from our foreheads, we were to look upward, and catch glimpses into the far-off soul of truth. In this point of view, matters did not turn out quite so well as we anticipated. It is very true that, sometimes, gazing casually around me, out of the midst of my toil, I used to discern a richer picturesqueness in the visible scene of earth and sky. There was, at such moments, a novelty, an unwonted aspect, on the face of Nature, as if she had been taken by surprise and seen at unawares, with no opportunity to put off her real look, and assume the mask with which she mysteriously hides herself from mortals. But this was all. The clods of earth, which we so constantly belabored and turned over and over, were never etherealized into thought. Our thoughts, on the contrary, were fast becoming cloddish. Our labor symbolized nothing, and left us mentally sluggish in the dusk of the evening. Intellectual activity is incompatible with any large amount of bodily exercise. The yeoman and the scholar— the yeoman and the man of finest moral culture, though not the man of sturdiest sense and integrity—are two distinct individuals, and can never be melted or welded into one substance.

—Nathaniel Hawthorne, *The Blithedale Romance*, 1852

6. "WE MEET IN THE MIDST OF A NATION BROUGHT TO THE VERGE OF RUIN"

The reform crusade of the forties and fifties petered out with the Civil War; the postwar years were marked, on the whole, by indifference toward questions of social and political morality. The next great wave of reform came with the hard times of the nineties. It differed in interesting respects from its predecessor. Where the earlier reform crusade was philosophical, religious in inspiration, concerned largely with social and cultural rights, and concentrated in New England, the latter reform movement was opportunistic, secular, directed chiefly to economic and political changes, and stronger in the Middle West and the South than in the East. The chief vehicle for the reform movement in its early years was the Populist party, in many respects the most interesting of all American "third" parties. We give here the essential part of the platform of the party in 1892—a platform whose preamble was written by the remarkable Ignatius Donnelly of Minnesota. Though regarded as wildly socialistic at the time, almost every plank in this platform was later incorporated into law in one form or another.

PREAMBLE

THE conditions which surround us best justify our co-operation; we meet in the midst of a nation brought to the verge of moral, political, and material ruin. Corruption dominates the ballot-box, the Legislatures, the Congress, and touches even the ermine of the bench. The people are demoralized; most of the States have been compelled to isolate the voters at the polling places to prevent universal intimidation and bribery. The newspapers are largely subsidized or muzzled, public opinion silenced, business prostrated, homes covered with mortgages, labor impoverished, and the land concentrating in the hands of capitalists. The urban workmen are denied the right to organize for self-protection, imported pauperized labor beats down their wages, a hireling standing army, unrecognized by our laws, is established to shoot them down, and they are rapidly degenerating into European conditions. The fruits of the toil of millions are boldly stolen to build up colossal fortunes for a few, unprecedented in the history of mankind; and the possessors of these, in turn, despise the Republic and endanger liberty. From the same prolific womb of governmental injustice we breed the two great classes—tramps and millionaires. . . .

We have witnessed for more than a quarter of a century the struggles of the two great political parties for power and plunder, while grievous wrongs have been inflicted upon the suffering people. We charge that the controlling influences dominating both these parties have permitted the existing dreadful conditions to develop without serious effort to prevent or restrain them. Neither do they now promise us any substantial reform. They have agreed together to ignore, in the coming campaign, every issue but one. They propose to drown the outcries of a plundered people with the uproar of a sham battle over the tariff, so that capitalists, corporations, national banks, rings, trusts, watered stock, the demonetization of silver and the oppressions of the usurers may all be lost sight of. They propose to sacrifice our homes, lives, and children on the altar of mammon; to destroy the multitude in order to secure corruption funds from the millionaires.

Assembled on the anniversary of the birthday of the nation, and filled with the spirit of the grand general and chief who established our independence, we seek to restore the government of the Republic to the hands of the "plain people," with which class it originated. We assert our purposes to be identical with the purposes of the National Constitution; to form a more perfect union and establish justice, insure domestic tranquillity, provide for the common defence, promote the general welfare, and secure the blessings of liberty for ourselves and our posterity.

We declare that this Republic can only endure as a free government while built upon the love of the people for each other and for the nation; that it cannot be pinned together by bayonets; that the Civil War is over, and that every passion and resentment which grew out of it must die with it, and that we must be in fact, as we are in name, one united brotherhood of free men. . . .

PLATFORM

We declare, therefore—

First.—That the union of the labor forces of the United States this day consummated shall be permanent and perpetual; may its spirits enter into all hearts for the salvation of the Republic and the uplifting of mankind.

Second.—Wealth belongs to him who creates it, and every dollar taken from industry without an equivalent is robbery. "If any will not work, neither shall he eat." The interests of rural and civil labor are the same; their enemies are identical.

Third.—We believe that the time has come when the railroad corporations will either own the people or the people must own the railroads; and should the government enter upon the work of owning and managing all railroads, we should favor an amendment to the constitution by which all persons engaged in the government service shall be placed under a civil-service regulation of the most rigid character, so as to prevent the increase of the power of the national administration by the use of such additional government employes.

FINANCE.—We demand a national currency, safe, sound, and flexible issued by the general government only, a full legal tender for all debts, public and private, and that without the use of banking corporations; a just, equitable, and efficient means of distribution direct to the people, at a tax not to exceed 2 per cent, per annum, to be provided as set forth in the sub-treasury plan of the Farmers' Alliance, or a better system; also by payments in discharge of its obligations for public improvements.

1. We demand free and unlimited coinage of silver and gold at the present legal ratio of 16 to 1.
2. We demand that the amount of circulating medium be speedily increased to not less than $50 per capita.
3. We demand a graduated income tax.
4. We believe that the money of the country should be kept as much as possible in the hands of the people, and hence we demand that all State and national revenues shall be limited to the necessary expenses of the government, economically and honestly administered.
5. We demand that postal savings banks be established by the government for the safe deposit of the earnings of the people and to facilitate exchange.

TRANSPORTATION.—Transportation being a means of exchange and a public necessity, the government should own and operate the railroads in the interest of the people. The telegraph and telephone, like the post-office system, being a necessity for the transmission of news, should be owned and operated by the government in the interest of the people.

LAND.—The land, including all the natural sources of wealth, is the heritage of the people, and should not be monopolized for speculative purposes, and alien ownership of land should be prohibited. All land now held by railroads and other corporations in excess of their actual needs, and all lands now owned by aliens should be reclaimed by the government and held for actual settlers only.

EXPRESSION OF SENTIMENTS

Your Committee on Platform and Resolutions beg leave unanimously to report the following:

Whereas, Other questions have been presented for our consideration, we hereby submit the following, not as a part of the Platform of the People's Party, but as resolutions expressive of the sentiment of the Convention.

1. RESOLVED, That we demand a free ballot and a fair count in all elections, and pledge ourselves to secure it to every legal voter

without Federal intervention, through the adoption by the States of the unperverted Australian or secret ballot system.

2. RESOLVED, That the revenue derived from a graduated income tax should be applied to the reduction of the burden of taxation now levied upon the domestic industries of this country.

3. RESOLVED, That we pledge our support to fair and liberal pensions to ex-Union soldiers and sailors.

4. RESOLVED, That we condemn the fallacy of protecting American labor under the present system, which opens our ports to the pauper and criminal classes of the world and crowds out our wage-earners; and we denounce the present ineffective laws against contract labor, and demand the further restriction of undesirable emigration.

5. RESOLVED, That we cordially sympathize with the efforts of organized workingmen to shorten the hours of labor, and demand a rigid enforcement of the existing eight-hour law on Government work, and ask that a penalty clause be added to the said law.

6. RESOLVED, That we regard the maintenance of a large standing army of mercenaries, known as the Pinkerton system, as a menace to our liberties, and we demand its abolition; and we condemn the recent invasion of the Territory of Wyoming by the hired assassins of plutocracy, assisted by Federal officers.

7. RESOLVED, That we commend to the favorable consideration of the people and the reform press the legislative system known as the initiative and referendum.

8. RESOLVED, That we favor a constitutional provision limiting the office of President and Vice-President to one term, and providing for the election of Senators of the United States by a direct vote of the people.

9. RESOLVED, That we oppose any subsidy or national aid to any private corporation for any purpose.

10. RESOLVED, That this convention sympathizes with the Knights of Labor and their righteous contest with the tyrannical combine of clothing manufacturers of Rochester, and declare it to be a duty of all who hate tyranny and oppression to refuse to purchase the goods made by the said manufacturers, or to patronize any merchants who sell such goods.

—The Populist Party Platform, 1892

7. "WE NEED AN ANNUAL SUPPLEMENT TO THE DECALOGUE"

The sweeping reform movement of the nineties and the early years of the new century was inspired by the emergence of a series of major problems unfamiliar to an earlier and more pastoral day. These were— among others—the confusion of ethics which resulted from the attempt to apply the moral code of an individualistic, agrarian society to the practices of a corporate and industrialized society; the rise of big business and of trusts and monopolies; the grossly unequal distribution of wealth and the creation of class divisions along economic lines; the rise of the city with all its problems of policing, housing, sanitation, morals, and corruption; and the breakdown of the political and administrative system when confronted by new and heavy demands for social service.

Of all these problems perhaps the first was the most perplexing. It was to the illumination of this problem that the Wisconsin sociologist, E. A. Ross, devoted his little book on Sin and Society. *Published in 1907, the book had an immediate and widespread influence and has held its place for almost forty years as the best analysis of the problem of the ethics of corporate business.*

THE stealings and slayings that lurk in the complexities of our social relations are not deeds of the dive, the dark alley, the lonely road, and the midnight hour. They require no nocturnal prowling with muffled step and bated breath, no weapon or offer of violence. Unlike the old-time villain, the latter-day malefactor does not wear a slouch hat and a comforter, breathe forth curses and an odor of gin, go about his nefarious work with clenched teeth and an evil scowl. In the supreme moment his lineaments are not distorted with rage, or lust, or malevolence. One misses the dramatic setting, the time-honored insignia of turpitude. Fagin and Bill Sykes and Simon Legree are vanishing types. Gamester, murderer, body-snatcher, and kidnapper may appeal to a Hogarth, but what challenge finds his pencil in the countenance of the boodler, the savings-bank wrecker, or the ballot-box stuffer? Among our criminals of greed, one begins to meet the "grand style" of the great criminals of ambition, Macbeth or Richard III. The modern high-power dealer of woe wears immaculate linen, carries a silk hat and a lighted cigar, sins with a calm countenance and a serene soul, leagues or months from the evil he causes. Upon his gentlemanly presence the eventual blood and tears do not obtrude themselves.

This is why good, kindly men let the wheels of commerce and of industry redden and redden, rather than pare or lose their dividend. This is why our railroads yearly injure one employee in twenty-six, and we look in vain for that promised "day of the Lord" that "will make a man more precious than fine gold." . . .

The covenant breaker, the suborned witness, the corrupt judge, the oppressor of the fatherless,—the old-fashioned sinner, in short,—knows his victim, must hearken, perhaps to bitter upbraidings. But the tropical belt of sin we are sweeping into is largely impersonal. Our iniquity is wireless, and we know not whose withers are wrung by it. The hurt passes into that vague mass, the "public," and is there lost to view. Hence it does not take a Borgia to knead "chalk and alum and plaster" into the loaf, seeing one cannot know just who will eat that loaf, or what gripe it will give him. The purveyor or spurious life-preservers need not be a Cain. The owner of rotten tenement houses, whose "pull" enables him to ignore the orders of the health department, foredooms babies, it is true, but for all that he is no Herod.

Often there are no victims. If the crazy hulk sent out for "just one more trip" meets with fair weather, all is well. If no fire breaks out in the theatre, the sham "emergency exits" are blameless. The corrupt inspector who O.K.'s low-grade kerosene is chancing it, that is all. Many sins, in fact, simply augment risk. Evil does not dog their footsteps with relentless and heart-shaking certainty. When the catastrophe does come, the sinner salves his conscience by blasphemously calling it an "accident" or an "act of God."

Still more impersonal is sin when the immediate harm touches beneficent institutions rather than individuals. . . . The blackguarding editor is really undermining the freedom of the press. The policy kings and saloon keepers, who get out to the polls the last vote of the vicious and criminal classes, are sapping manhood suffrage. Striking engineers who spitefully desert passenger trains in mid-career are jeopardizing the right of man to work only when he pleases. The real victim of a lynching mob is not the malefactor, but the law-abiding spirit. School-board grafters who blackmail applicants for a teacher's position are stabbing the free public school. The corrupt bosses and "combines" are murdering representative government. The perpetrators of election frauds unwittingly assail the institution of the ballot. Rarely, however, are such transgressions abominated as are offenses against persons.

Because of the special qualities of the Newer Unrighteousness, because these devastating latter-day wrongs, being comely of look, do not advertise their vileness, . . . it is possible for iniquity to flourish greatly, even while men are getting better. Briber and boodler and grafter are often "good men," judged by the old tests, and would have passed for virtuous in the American community of seventy years ago. Among the chiefest sinners are now enrolled men who are pure and kindhearted, loving in their families, faithful to their friends, and generous to the needy. . . .

The conclusion of the whole matter is this:—

Our social organization has developed to a stage where the old righteousness is not enough. We need an annual supplement to the Decalogue. The growth of credit institutions, the spread of fiduciary relations, the enmeshing of industry in law, the interlacing of government and business, the multiplication of boards and inspectors,—beneficent as they all are, they invite to sin. What gateways they open to greed! What fresh parasites they let in on us! How idle in our new situation to intone the old litanies! The reality of this close-knit life is not to be *seen* and *touched*; it must be *thought*. The sins it opens the door to are to be discerned by knitting the brows rather than by opening the eyes. It takes imagination to see that bogus medical diploma, lying advertisement, and fake testimonial are death-dealing instruments. It takes imagination to see that savings-bank wrecker, loan shark, and investment swindler, in taking livelihoods take lives. It takes imagination to see that the business of debauching voters, fixing juries, seducing law-makers, and corrupting public servants is like sawing through the props of a crowded grand-stand. Whether we like it or not, we are in the organic phase, and the thickening perils that beset our path can be beheld only by the mind's eye.

The problem of security is therefore being silently transformed. Blind, instinctive reactions are no longer to be trusted. Social defense is coming to be a matter for the expert. The rearing of dikes against faithlessness and fraud calls for intelligent social engineering. If in this strait the public does not speedily become far shrewder in the grading and grilling of sinners, there is nothing for it but to turn over the defense of society to professionals.

—Edward A. Ross, *Sin and Society*, 1907

8. PORTRAIT OF THE AMERICAN AS REFORMER

The Emersonian query, "What is a man born for but to be a reformer?" might well have been the slogan of the generation that came to maturity in the 1890's. As problems crowded in on the American people, a mighty host of reformers rose up to meet them. There were Easterners like E. L. Godkin, who were inclined to think that honesty in politics would solve all problems; there were the urban reformers like Jacob Riis and Jane Addams, who worked for slum clearance and the improvement of the condition of the poor. There were agrarian reformers like Tom Watson of Georgia and Jerry Simpson of Kansas, who wanted government aid for the farmers; there were Single-Taxers like Tom Johnson and Socialists like Eugene Debs or Marxists like Daniel De Leon. There were "muckrakers" like Henry Demarest Lloyd who wrote on trusts and monopolies, and Ida Tarbell who attacked the Standard Oil, and Lincoln Steffens who exposed the "Shame of the Cities." There were Christian Socialists like Washington Gladden and Walter Rauschenbusch. There were political progressives like Bryan and T.R. and Wilson and "Fighting Bob" LaFollette. All of them were working, in their different ways, to realize the "promise of American life."

We give here partial portraits of four of these reformers. Here is a brief account of Jane Addams' work at the world-famous Hull House in Chicago; Brand Whitlock's affectionate recollection of Toledo's Mayor, "Golden Rule" Jones; Lincoln Steffens' portrait of Bob LaFollette; and Vachel Lindsay's elegy over the great Illinois Governor, John P. Altgeld.

A. JANE ADDAMS AT HULL HOUSE

I REMEMBER one family in which the father had been out of work for this same winter, most of the furniture had been pawned, and as the worn-out shoes could not be replaced the children could not go to school. The mother was ill and barely able to come for the supplies and medicines. Two years later she invited me to supper one Sunday evening in the little home which had been completely restored, and she gave as a reason for the invitation that she couldn't bear to have me remember them as they had been during that one winter, which she insisted had been unique in her twelve years of married life. She said that it was as if she had met me, not as I am ordinarily, but as I should appear misshapen with rheumatism or with a face distorted by neuralgic pain; that it was not fair to judge poor people that way. She perhaps unconsciously illustrated the difference between the relief station's relation to the poor and the Settlement's relation to its neighbors, the latter wishing to know them through all the varying conditions of life, to stand by when they are in distress, but by no means to drop intercourse with them when normal prosperity has returned, enabling the relation to become more social and free from economic disturbance.

Possibly something of the same effort has to be made within the Settlement itself to keep its own sense of proportion in regard to the relation of the crowded city quarter to the rest of the country. It was in the spring following this terrible winter, during a journey to meet lecture engagements in California, that I found myself amazed at the large stretches of open country and prosperous towns through which we passed day by day, whose existence I had quite forgotten.

In the latter part of the summer of 1895 I served as a member on a commission appointed by the mayor of Chicago to investigate conditions in the county poorhouse, public attention having become centered on it through one of those distressing stories which exaggerates the wrong in a public institution while at the same time it reveals conditions which need to be rectified. However necessary publicity is for securing reformed administration, however useful such exposures may be for political purposes, the whole is attended by such a waste of the most precious human emotions, by such a tearing of live tissue, that it can scarcely be endured. Every time I entered Hull House during the days of the investigation I would find waiting for me from twenty to thirty people whose friends and relatives were in the suspected institution, all in such acute distress of mind that to see them was to look upon the victims of deliberate torture. In most cases my visitor would state that it seemed impossible to put their invalids in any other place, but if these stories were true, something must be done. Many of the patients were taken out, only to be returned after a few days or weeks to meet the sullen hostility of their attendants and with their own attitude changed from confidence to timidity and alarm. . . .

We early found ourselves spending many hours in efforts to secure support for deserted women, insurance for bewildered widows, damages for injured operators, furniture from the clutches of the installment store. The Settlement is valuable as an information and interpretation bureau. It constantly acts between the various institutions of the city and the people for whose benefit these institutions were erected. The hospitals, the county agencies, and state asylums are often but vague rumors to the people who need them most. Another function of the Settlement to its neighborhood resembles that of the big brother whose mere presence on the playground protects the little ones from bullies.

We early learned to know the children of hard-driven mothers who went out to work all day, sometimes leaving the little things in the casual care of a neighbor, but often locking them into their tenement rooms. The first three crippled children we encountered in the neighborhood had all been injured while their mothers were at work; one had fallen out of a third-story window, another had been burned, and the third had a curved spine due to the fact that for three years he had been tied all day long to the leg of the kitchen table.

—JANE ADDAMS, *Twenty Years at Hull House*

B. MAYOR JONES PREACHES THE GOLDEN RULE

There was in Toledo one man who could sympathize with my attitude, and that was a man whose determination to accept literally and to try to practise the fundamental philosophy of Christianity had so startled and confounded the Christians everywhere that he at once became famous throughout Christendom as Golden Rule Jones. I had known of him only as the eccentric mayor of our city, and nearly every one whom I had met since my advent in Toledo spoke of him only to say something disparaging of him. The most charitable thing they said was that he was crazy. All the newspapers were against him and all the preachers. My own opinion, of course, could have been of no consequence, but I had learned in the case of Altgeld that almost universal condemnation of a man is to be examined before it is given entire credit. I do not mean to say that there was universal condemnation of Golden Rule Jones in Toledo in those days; it was simply that the institutional voices of society, the press and the pulpit, were thundering in condemnation of him. When the people came to vote for his re-election, his majorities were overwhelming, so that he used to say that everybody was against him but the people. But that is another story.

In those days I had not met him. I might have called at his office, to be sure, but I did not care to add to his burdens.

One day suddenly, as I was working on a story in my office, in he stepped with a startling, abrupt manner, wheeled a chair up to my desk, and sat down. He was a big Welshman with a sandy complexion and great hands that had worked hard in their time, and he had an eye that looked right into the center of your skull. He wore, and all the time he was in the room continued to wear, a large cream-colored slouch hat, and he had on the flowing cravat which for some inexplicable reason artists and social reformers wear, their affinity being due, no doubt, to the fact that the reformer must be an artist, of a sort; else he could not dream his dreams. I was relieved, however, to find that Jones wore his hair clipped short, and there was still about him that practical air of the very practical businessman he had been before he became mayor. He had been such a practical business man that he was worth half a million, a fairly good fortune for our town; but he had not been in office very long before all the business men were down on him and saying that what the town needed was a business man for mayor, a statement that was destined to ring in my ears for a good many years.

They disliked him, of course, because he would not do just what they told him to—that being the meaning and purpose of a business man for mayor—but insisted that there were certain other people in the city who were entitled to some of his service and consideration; namely, the working people and the poor. The politicians and the preachers objected to him on the same grounds: the unpardonable sin being to express in any but a purely ideal and sentimental form sympathy for the workers or the poor. It seemed to be particularly exasperating that he was doing all this in the name of the Golden Rule, which was for the Sunday school; and they even went so far as to bring to town another Sam Jones, the Reverend Sam Jones, to conduct a revival and to defeat the Honorable Sam Jones. The Reverend Sam Jones had big meetings and said many clever things and many true ones, the truest among them being his epigram, "I am for the Golden Rule myself, up to a certain point, and then I want to take the shotgun and the club." I think that expression marked the difference between him and our Sam Jones, in whose philosophy there was no place at all for the shotgun or the club. The preachers were complaining that Mayor Jones was not using shotguns or at least clubs on the bad people in the town; I suppose that since their own persuasions had in a measure failed, they felt that the mayor with such instruments might have made the bad people look as if they had been converted, anyway. . . .

I regard it as Jones's supreme contribution to the thought of his time that by the mere force of his own original character and personality he compelled a discussion of fundamental principles of government. Toledo today is a community which has a wider acquaintance with all the abstract principles of social relations than any other city in the land —or in the world, since when one ventures into generalities one might as well make them as sweeping as one can.

Jones's other great contribution to the science of municipal government was that of nonpartisanship in local affairs. That is the way he used to express it; what he meant was that the issues of national politics must not be permitted to obtrude themselves into municipal campaigns and that what divisions there are should be confined to local issues. There is, of course, in our cities, as in our land or any land, only one issue, that which is presented by the conflict of the aristocratic or plutocratic spirit and the spirit of democracy.

Jones used to herald himself as a man without a party, but he was a great democrat, the most fundamental I ever knew or imagined; he summed up in himself, as no other figure in our time since Lincoln, all that the democratic spirit is and hopes to be. Perhaps in this characterization I seem to behold his figure larger than it was in relation to the whole mass, but while his work may appear at first glance local, it was really general and universal. No one can estimate the peculiar and lively forces of such a personality; certainly no one can presume to limit his influence, for such a spirit is illimitable and irresistible.

—Brand Whitlock, *Forty Years of It*

C. Lincoln Steffens Is Won over by Bob LaFollette

Bob LaFollette was called the little giant. Rather short in stature, but broad and strong, he had the gift of muscled, nervous power, and he kept himself in training all his life. Every speech he made was an exercise in calisthenics. His hands and his face were expressive; they had to be to make his balled fighting fists appeal for peace and his proud, defiant countenance ask for the reasonableness he always looked for even *in* an audience he was attacking. His sincerity, his integrity, his complete devotion to his ideal, were undubitable; no one who heard could suspect his singleness of purpose or his courage. The strange contradictions in him were that he was a fighter—for peace; he battered his fist so terribly in one great speech for peace during the World War that he had to have it treated and then carried it in bandages for weeks. Art Young drew a caricature of it as a pacifist's hand across the seas. He was dictator dictating democracy, a proud man begging for the blessing of justice upon the meek, whom he organized and inspired to take it—any way. Impatient, he was slow and thorough. He prepared for a speech like a man writing a book. . . The open book of an ambitious young man who, fitted in the schools and University of Wisconsin with the common, patriotic conception of his country and his government, discovered bit by bit what the facts were, and, shocked, set out to fight for democracy, justice, honesty. He set out ambitiously on a public career, encountered a local boss in a Federal office, and appealed over his head to the people of his home county to be nominated and elected district attorney. This was his first offense; he was irregular; he defied the machine of his (Republican) party. The politicians said that Bob LaFollette worked on the delegates and the voters at night, under cover of darkness. True. And when he felt the power and suffered the methods and the lying attacks of the party and its backing higher up, he continued to work under cover and constantly, like the politicians; but also he worked in the open, day and night. His method, in brief, was to go around to towns and cross-roads, make long, carefully stated speeches of fact, and appealing to the idealism of patriotism, watch the audience for faces, mostly young faces which he thought showed inspiration. These he invited to come to him afterward; he showed them what the job was, asked them if they would do their part in their district; and so he built up an organized following so responsive to him that it was called a machine. As it was —a powerful political machine which came to control the Republican Party in Wisconsin. The Stalwarts, as the old machine men and their business backers were called, became irregulars; they voted against and fought their party. They united with the old machine Democrats to beat their party. But LaFollette drew into it democratic Democrats and independents enough to make a majority for the Republicans, who came thus in Wisconsin to represent the people.

That was Bob LaFollette's crime. When Governor LaFollette returned to his State one way and I by another route, I called on the Stalwarts for facts, provable charges, and on LaFollette only for his specific answers or admissions. As in Milwaukee, so in Madison, the indictments withered. They fell back to his one real sin: that he had taken the Republican Party away from the corrupters of it and led it to stand for—what? I said above that it represented the people, but it did that only in the sense that it labored for and gradually achieved the very moderate aims of LaFollette, a liberal, and the liberals. . . .

Bob LaFollette was restoring representative government in Wisconsin, and by his oratory and his fierce dictatorship and his relentless conspicuous persistence he was making his people understand—all of them apparently, not only the common people whom he preferred, but the best people too; they also knew. They might denounce him, they might lie to the stranger, but in their heart of hearts they knew. It was a great experiment, LaFollette's: State reform that began in the capital of the State and spread out close to the soil. It was opposed by the cities, just as city reform was opposed by the States, but the startling thing—even though I expected it—was how this State reform encountered also the resistance of the Federal government. And just as Folk and the Chicago reformers had been forced to carry their fight up out of the cities into the States whence the trail of the serpent led, so Governor LaFollette, having carried his State several times, found that he had to go on up to the Senate. The trail of corruption is the road to success for the reformer as well as for other men. He won the next election for governor and then ran for and was elected to the U. S. Senate. He did not rush off to the Senate right away. It was characteristic of him that he remained as governor months after he was promoted to the Senate. He stuck to his post till he finished and forced the Legislature to pass all his pending measures. Then and not till then did he go on . . . to the head of the system of the American government in Washington. His career there, as in his own State, is the story of the heroism it takes to fight in America for American ideals.

—The Autobiography of Lincoln Steffens

D. "To Live in Mankind Is Far More Than to Live in a Name"
(John P. Altgeld. Born December 30, 1847;
Died March 12, 1902)

Sleep softly . . . eagle forgotten . . . under the stone.
Time has its way with you there, and the clay has its own.

'We have buried him now,' thought your foes, and in secret rejoiced.
They made a brave show of their mourning, their hatred unvoiced.
They have snarled at you, barked at you, foamed at you day after day.
Now you were ended. They praised you . . . and laid you away.

The others that mourned you in silence and terror and truth,
The widow bereft of her crust, and the boy without youth,
The mocked and the scorned and the wounded, the lame and the poor
That should have remembered forever . . . remember no more.

Where are those lovers of yours, on what name do they call,
The lost, that in armies wept over your funeral pall?
They call on the names of a hundred high-valiant ones,
A hundred white eagles have risen the sons of your sons,
The zeal in their wings is a zeal that your dreaming began
The valor that wore out your soul in the service of man.

Sleep softly . . . eagle forgotten . . . under the stone,
Time has its way with you there and the clay has its own.
Sleep on, O brave-hearted, O wise man, that kindled the flame—
To live in mankind is far more than to live in a name,
To live in mankind, far, far more. . . . than to live in a name.
     —Vachel Lindsay, "The Eagle That Is Forgotten," 1912

9. "THE OLD FORMULAS DO NOT FIT PRESENT PROBLEMS"

We have already drawn upon Wilson's speeches in the 1912 campaign, and they need no further explanation. What is important is to understand the significance of the 1912 election. The mildly progressive Roosevelt administration had been followed by the more conservative administration of William Howard Taft. Failure to push through badly needed legislation regulating trusts, banks, labor, and other economic interests and activities had made Americans restless and eager for reform. The campaign of 1912 was a three-cornered race: two progressives against one conservative. The progressives, Wilson and Roosevelt, polled between them over ten million votes; the conservative, Taft, polled about three and a half million—and only eight electoral votes. Here was as unmistakable a mandate for reform as that rendered in 1932. Like F.D.R., Wilson carried out the promises of his campaign speeches.

THERE is one great basic fact which underlies all the questions that are discussed on the political platform at the present moment. That singular fact is that nothing is done in this country as it was done twenty years ago.

We are in the presence of a new organization of society. Our life has broken away from the past. The life of America is not the life that it was twenty years ago; it is not the life that it was ten years ago. We have changed our economic conditions, absolutely, from top to bottom; and, with our economic society, the organization of our life. The old political formulas do not fit the present problems; they read now like documents taken out of a forgotten age. The older cries sound as if they belonged to a past age which men have almost forgotten. Things which used to be put into the party platforms of ten years ago would sound antiquated if put into a platform now. We are facing the necessity of fitting a new social organization, as we did once fit the old organization, to the happiness and prosperity of the great body of citizens; for we are conscious that the new order of society has not been made to fit and provide the convenience or prosperity of the average man. The life of the nation has grown infinitely varied. It does not centre now upon questions of governmental structure or of the distribution of governmental powers. It centres upon questions of the very structure and operation of society itself, of which government is only the instrument. Our development has run so fast and so far along the lines sketched in the earlier day of constitutional definition, has so crossed and interlaced those lines, has piled upon them such novel structures of trust and combination, has elaborated within them a life so manifold, so full of forces which transcend the boundaries of the country itself and fill the eyes of the world, that a new nation seems to have been created which the old formulas do not fit or afford a vital interpretation of.

We have come upon a very different age from any that preceded us. We have come upon an age when we do not do business in the way in which we used to do business—when we do not carry on any of the operations of manufacture, sale, transportation, or communication as men used to carry them on. There is a sense in which in our day the individual has been submerged. In most parts of our country men work, not for themselves, not as partners in the old way in which they used to work, but generally as employees—in a higher or lower grade —of great corporations. There was a time when corporations played a very minor part in our business affairs, but now they play the chief part, and most men are the servants of corporations. . . .

Now this is nothing short of a new social age, a new era of human relationships, a new stage-setting for the drama of life.

In this new age we find, for instance, that our laws with regard to the relations of employer and employee are in many respects wholly antiquated and impossible. They were framed for another age, which nobody now living remembers, which is, indeed, so remote from our life that it would be difficult for many of us to understand it if it were described to us. The employer is now generally a corporation or a huge company of some kind; the employee is one of hundreds or of thousands brought together, not by individual masters whom they know and with whom they have personal relations, but by agents of one sort or another. Workingmen are marshaled in great numbers for the performance of a multitude of particular tasks under a common discipline. They generally use dangerous and powerful machinery, over whose repair and renewal they have no control. New rules must be devised with regard to their obligations and their rights, their obligations to their employers and their responsibilities to one another. Rules must be devised for their protection, for their compensation when injured, for their support when disabled.

There is something very new and very big and very complex about these new relations of capital and labor. A new economic society has sprung up, and we must effect a new set of adjustments. We must not pit power against weakness. The employer is generally, in our day, as I have said, not an individual, but a powerful group; and yet the workingman when dealing with his employer is still, under our existing law, an individual.

Why is it that we have a labor question at all? It is for the simple and very sufficient reason that the laboring man and the employer are not intimate associates now as they used to be in time past. Most of our laws were formed in the age when employer and employees knew each other, knew each other's characters, were associated with each other, dealt with each other as man with man. That is no longer the case. You not only do not come into personal contact with the men who have the supreme command in those corporations, but it would be out of the question for you to do it. Our modern corporations employ thousands, and in some instances hundreds of thousands, of men. The only persons whom you see or deal with are local superintendents or local representatives of a vast organization, which is not like anything that the workingmen of the time in which our laws were framed knew anything about. A little group of workingmen, seeing their employer every day, dealing with him in a personal way, is one thing, and the modern body of labor engaged as employees of the huge enterprises that spread all over the country, dealing with men of whom they can form no personal conception, is another thing. A very different thing. You never saw a corporation, any more than you ever saw a government. Many a workingman to-day never saw the body of men who are conducting the industry in which he is employed. And they never saw him. What they know about him is written in ledgers and books and letters, in the correspondence of the office, in the reports of the superintendents. He is a long way off from them.

So what we have to discuss is, not wrongs which individuals intentionally do—I do not believe there are a great many of those—but the wrongs of a system. I want to record my protest against any discussion of this matter which would seem to indicate that there are bodies of our fellow-citizens who are trying to grind us down and do us injustice. There are some men of that sort. I don't know how they sleep o'nights, but there are men of that kind. Thank God, they are not numerous. The truth is, we are all caught in a great economic system which is heartless. The modern corporation is not engaged in business as an individual. When we deal with it, we deal with an impersonal element, an immaterial piece of society. A modern corporation is a means of co-operation in the conduct of an enterprise which is so big that no one man can conduct it, and which the resources of no one man are sufficient to finance. A company is formed; that company puts out a prospectus; the promoters expect to raise a certain fund as capital stock. Well, how are they going to raise it? They are going to raise it from the public in general, some of whom will buy their stock. The moment that begins, there is formed—what? A joint stock corporation. Men begin to pool their earnings, little piles, big piles. A certain number of men are elected by the stockholders to be directors, and these directors elect a president. This president is the head of the undertaking, and the directors are its managers.

Now, do the workingmen employed by that stock corporation deal with that president and those directors? Not at all. Does the public deal with that president and that board of directors? It does not. Can anybody bring them to account? It is next to impossible to do so. If you undertake it you will find a game of hide and seek, with the objects of your search taking refuge now behind the tree of their individual personality, now behind that of their corporate irresponsibility.

And do our laws take note of this curious state of things? Do they even attempt to distinguish between a man's act as a corporation director and as an individual? They do not. Our laws still deal with us on the basis of the old system. The law is still living in the dead past which we have left behind. This is evident, for instance, with regard to the matter of employers' liability for workingmen's injuries. Suppose that a superintendent wants a workman to use a certain piece of machinery which it is not safe for him to use, and that the workman is injured by that piece of machinery. Some of our courts have held that the superintendent is a fellow-servant, or, as the law states it, a fellow-employee, and that, therefore, the man cannot recover damages for his injury. The superintendent who probably engaged the man is not his employer. Who is his employer? And whose negligence could conceivably come in there? The board of directors did not tell the employee to use that piece of machinery; and the president of the corporation did not tell him to use that piece of machinery. And so forth. Don't you see by that theory that a man never can get redress for negligence on the part of the employer? When I hear judges reason upon the analogy of the relationships that used to exist between workmen and their employers a generation ago, I wonder if they have not opened their eyes to the modern world. You know, we have a right to expect that judges will have their eyes open, even though the law which they administer hasn't awakened.

Yet that is but a single small detail illustrative of the difficulties we are in because we have not adjusted the law to the facts of the new order. . . .

The transition we are witnessing is no equable transition of growth and normal alteration; no silent, unconscious unfolding of one age into another, its natural heir and successor. Society is looking itself over, in our day, from top to bottom; is making fresh and critical analysis of its very elements; is questioning its oldest practices as freely as its newest, scrutinizing every arrangement and motive of its life; and it stands ready to attempt nothing less than a radical reconstruction, which only frank and honest counsels and the forces of generous co-operation can hold back from becoming a revolution. We are in a temper to reconstruct economic society, as we were once in a temper to reconstruct political society, and political society may itself undergo a radical modification in the process. I doubt if any age was ever more conscious of its task or more unanimously desirous of radical and extended changes in its economic and political practice.

We stand in the presence of a revolution—not a bloody revolution; America is not given to the spilling of blood—but a silent revolution, whereby America will insist upon recovering in practice those ideals which she has always professed, upon securing a government devoted to the general interest and not to special interests.

We are upon the eve of a great reconstruction. It calls for creative statesmanship as no age has done since that great age in which we set up the government under which we live, that government which was the admiration of the world until it suffered wrongs to grow up under it which have made many of our own compatriots question the freedom of our institutions and preach revolution against them. I do not fear revolution. I have unshaken faith in the power of America to keep its self-possession. Revolution will come in peaceful guise, as it came when we put aside the crude government of the Confederation and created the great Federal Union which governs individuals, not States, and which has been these hundred and thirty years our vehicle of progress. Some radical changes we must make in our law and practice. Some reconstructions we must push forward, which a new age and new circumstances impose upon us. But we can do it all in calm and sober fashion, like statesmen and patriots.

I do not speak of these things in apprehension, because all is open and aboveboard. This is not a day in which great forces rally in secret. The whole stupendous program must be publicly planned and canvassed. Good temper, the wisdom that comes of sober counsel, the energy of thoughtful and unselfish men, the habit of co-operation and of compromise which has been bred in us by long years of free gov-

ernment, in which reason rather than passion has been made to prevail
by the sheer virtue of candid and universal debate, will enable us to
win through to still another great age without violence.

—WOODROW WILSON, *The New Freedom,* 1913

10. "WANTED: AMERICAN RADICALS"

*Protest and reform are an important part of the American tradition.
Certainly this is true in the realm of literature; almost as clearly it is true
in education, in philosophy, and in the structure of society and of economy. But it will not be denied that the tradition of radicalism has been
on the wane in the twentieth century, and that even reform is no longer
as popular as it once was, nor as respectable. The New Deal was in
reality a great conservative movement (as most reforms are), one
designed to save basic American institutions by giving everyone a larger
stake in their preservation. Yet the reaction against it was strong and
even convulsive. As one Old World nation after another turned to
Socialism, many Americans became alarmed at what they thought were
the Socialistic tendencies of the New Deal reforms. They associated reform with Socialism and, by a curious confusion, associated Socialism
with Communism. In any event the decade of the forties saw the word
reform fall into disrepute, while to be called radical was almost to be
slandered. It is against this background of reaction away from the American tradition that we should read President Conant's call for a revival of
radicalism.*

. . . I have no desire to read into the words "reactionary" and "radical"
any of the usual praise or condemnation. The overtones of such words
change with the generations; the radicals of the late 1860's were radical
not on the economic issues which now seem to us to be the primary
concern of man, but on the issue of racial equality and the political realization of this equality.

Into the debate between reactionary and radical I should like to see introduced a third voice—the voice of the American radical. I use the ad-

jective advisedly, thus distinguishing this third line of approach from that of the chief vocal groups now discussing the American future— whom I shall designate, with due apologies, "American" reactionaries and "European" radicals. The adjectives, I submit, represent the background of the hopes and aspirations of each movement. For example, numerous businessmen today are saying, "If, when the war is over, the government will move out and leave us alone, we will restore the American system of free enterprise and with it American prosperity." There can be no question of the propriety of the word "American" as applied to this side of the domestic controversy. And if some object to my use of the word "reactionary," I would remind them that those who wish openly for a restoration are by definition reactionaries.

The use of the adjective "European" for our radical friends will probably offend as many as the use of the word "reactionary" for the other group. But I think it can be shown that those who have the most clearly defined objectives in their social philosophy today are those who stand to the extreme left. For them a new world is waiting to be born. The choice before our generation, to their mind, is clear-cut. To use the words of one spokesman for their new world: "On the one side there is private ownership, spiritual vulgarity, and some independence; on the other there is communal ownership, moral dignity, and police supervision. The direction of evolution seems to be from the first to the second. . . . One may therefore hope that mankind will quickly learn the conditioned reflexes necessary to live communally, so that the amount of police supervision may not increase indefinitely, and may soon decrease."

This type of radical philosophy stems from the great Continental thinkers of the nineteenth century. The names of the predecessors of the European radicals are to be found on the lists of the Fabian Society of England of a generation back. The nearest approach to their ideals is to be seen in the miraculous Russian state. Their cultural heritage has been derived from Germany, France, and England.

I hardly need to make plain at this point that I am not pinning labels on either of our two major political parties. I am speaking rather about a general line of cleavage which is often spoken of as left and right. The points of agreement and disagreement between these two groups—this rough division by which I have oversimplified the economic and political forces of today—are not to me the significant issue. It is the lack of a third choice. For I believe that if the America of the future is to emerge from the conflict of *only* these two groups, the chances are not great that it will be the kind of America in which most of us would like to live. If the extremes of the two contending forces continue to align as they do now, I fear greatly for the cause of freedom on this continent.

Hence, my hope that a new group of thinkers and of speakers will arise: a group of modern radicals in the American tradition, who will make the conflict triangular and at the same time contribute elements which are lacking in the present picture. Not that I think this American radical, whose importance I am urging, can alone solve the nation's problem any more than the American reactionary or the European radical can, but I do think he is needed in the fight.

Now, what is this American radical to be like—this successor to the men who abolished primogeniture at the founding of the Republic, who with zest destroyed the Bank of the United States in the times of Andrew Jackson?

In the first place he will be obviously more indigenous than our friends the European radicals or even our friends the American reactionaries. He springs from the American soil, firm in the belief that every man is as good as his neighbor, if not better, and is entitled to a real chance for a decent living. Instinctively in the early days of the Republic his predecessor supported the ideas of Jefferson, as against the more aristocratic and monarchical conceptions drawn from Europe.

The American radical traces his lineage through the democratic revolution of Jackson when Emerison was sounding his famous call for the American Scholar. His political ideal will, of course, be Jefferson: his prophets will be Emerson and Thoreau; his poet, Whitman. He will be respectful but not enthusiastic about Marx, Engels, and Lenin. I believe he can make a good case that his kind were the only radicals in the United States on economic matters until the close of the nineteenth century. What would this influential native-born thinker of our past advocate were he confronted with our problems of today? Let me try your patience with an exercise in imagination. Let me attempt to describe a revised and recreated being—an American radical of the 1940's.

First of all, like all radicals and also all reactionaries, in his extreme moods he will be utterly impractical. In general, however, being rooted in the American soil he will be endowed with a considerable amount of earthly common sense and a certain willingness to apply to the changes which he effects the typical American question, "Does it work?" and to take up cheerfully another trial if the answer should be no.

No one needs to be told that the American radical will be a fanatic believer in equality. Yet it will be a peculiar North American brand of doctrine. For example, he will be quite willing in times of peace to let net salaries and earnings sail way above the $25,000 mark. He believes in equality of opportunity, not equality of rewards; but, on the other hand, he will be lusty in wielding the axe against the root of inherited privilege. To prevent the growth of a caste system, which he abhors, he will be resolute in his demand to confiscate (by constitutional methods) all property once a generation. He will demand really effective inheritance and gift taxes and the breaking up of trust funds and estates. And this point cannot be lightly pushed aside, for it is the kernel of his radical philosophy.

He will favor public education, truly universal educational opportunity at every level. He will be little concerned with the future of private education, except as he values independent competing groups in every phase of American activity. By the same token he will be forever harping on the dangers of Federal control of institutions concerned with youth.

Decentralization, local responsibility, all the old shibboleths which his European radical friends have hurled into the dustbin, he will take out, polish up, and see if by any chance they may be more applicable to the future than we suspect. Of course, like the intelligent members of the other two groups, he will recognize that we are going to live in the 1950's in a highly mechanized, industrialized age. He will know that the transition from a totalitarian war economy to the kind of utopia he envisages cannot be made with safety overnight. For the American radical above all others is in the tradition of having a job for everyone; he will rack his brains to find the equivalent of those magic lands of the old frontier.

Like Jefferson when he had to choose between his antipathy to the powers of the central government and the national need for the purchase of Louisiana, the American radical will compromise his objectives to governmental action from time to time. He will be ready to invoke even the Federal government in the interests of maintaining real freedom among the great masses of the population. But, unlike the European radical, he will never cease to hope that such remedies may be only passing sins. He will not place a higher value on property rights than on human rights, for his political forebears never did. He will recall that it was "life, liberty, and the pursuit of happiness," not "life, liberty, and property," which Jefferson wrote into the Declaration of Independence.

And, of course, he will be very sensitive on such old-fashioned subjects as individual rights as opposed to the police power of the state.

If by any chance the American radical should find his influence increasing, he might advocate drastic revisions in the Constitution, for there are a number of fundamentals in our governmental structure he might like to alter. He would realize, for instance, that in a modern industrial state, government must play a much larger role than he and his friends desire. And the only hope of preventing his hereditary enemy, the Federal power, from increasing every decade is to strengthen local government. Yet when he surveys the odd mixture of areas and population which history has bequeathed to us as sovereign states, he might feel that with new areas, fewer in number and more nearly equal in population and resources, local government might become another matter.

Of course, one brand of native American philosophy stems from the barren rocks of the chilly country of the Pilgrim fathers. It might be called individual contrariness. And the American radical would have a fair share of this. He would be on many matters independent as the proverbial hog on ice. It was one of his breed in earlier times who was stopped by a friend on his way to the town meeting: "Don't you know, Ed," said the friend, "there ain't no use in going to that there meeting? Old Doc Barnes and his crowd control enough votes to carry everything they want and more too. You can't make any headway agin 'em." "That's all right," Ed replied, "but I can worry 'em some."

Nostalgia is the sleeping sickness against which the American radical would have to fight. Large cities, modern transportation, big industries would be the things difficult for his philosophy to encompass, and yet he must take them into his pattern of thought and come out with modern answers conforming to his basic philosophy of life. Organized business groups and organized labor will regard the American radical with equal suspicion; and towards both he in turn will be equally suspicious, but rarely hostile. Pressure groups are, after all, one of the recurring features in the American scene. From their conflicts has emerged the American society of our past.

And the American radical, like the American reactionary, believes it on balance to have been a good past; only he, unlike the reactionary, thinks the road ahead leads straight to a better future, a future that can come only with the change that arises out of the smoke of constant political battle. The American radical believes in the ever recurring struggle to check and put back in place groups which have attained too much power.

The fundamental philosophy of the American radical is a threat to much of the present leadership of both capital and labor. For his equalitarian doctrine, if only partially successful, would change the complexion of the struggle between management and labor. And this is the crux of his contribution to the current scene. He would use the powers of government to reorder the "haves and have-nots" every generation to give flux to our social order. And given a high degree of social mobility in America—a degree comparable to that in a pioneer community of a century ago—labor leaders would find themselves often negotiating with their blood relations. If at the same time ownership and management of industry rarely if ever were passed on by inheritance, nepotism, or patronage, many aspects of the current industrial picture would indeed be radically altered—altered in a characteristically American way.

But I must beware of pressing this utopian picture to a logical conclusion. For even if the American radical were to arise tomorrow, we may be certain that no more than any other reformer would he ever succeed in bringing about the millennium. We should judge him by the resultant of his interaction with many pressures in a social organization which faces a retailoring job if it is to be adapted to a modern industrial civilization and still preserve the elements of freedom. We should judge him by this resultant, not by the blueprints of the future he holds before our eyes.

We may ask the American radical for at least one concrete illustration of a practical method of increasing the social mobility on which he sets so much store. He would answer that the demobilization of our armed forces is a God-given moment for reintroducing the American concept of a fluid society. If it is handled properly (meaning, of course, his way), we can ensure a healthy body politic for at least a generation. Handle it improperly and we may well sow the seeds of a civil war within a decade.

Here are eleven million men (or will be if the present plans are carried through), a cross-section of the nation. A large proportion of them are under twenty-five with their careers and lifework still in the making. If their future role in the United States is determined by their merit, their talents, their character, and their grit, they and their relatives will feel this is a good land, a land of freedom come what may. If on the other hand they feel they were replaced in civilian life on the basis of the accidents of geography and birth, there will be many who will become frustrated and embittered—particularly if the general level of prosperity should fall. Here we have a change for a grand "Paul Jones."

Do we believe in equality of opportunity or not? asks the American radical. If we do, we shall set up machinery, state machinery of course (but Federally financed), to see to it that the returning soldier is retrained and placed in the kind of employment for which his talents are suited. This has been a total war: we must still use reluctantly a bit of totalitarian power. To be practical, we can't promise white-collar jobs to all the ex-soldiers. We could fix some quotas, perhaps, and see that they are fairly distributed. We could even set up agencies to lend money to groups of competent veterans who might start small retail or manufacturing businesses. We could do all within our power to get the son of a laborer who has the capacity on the ladder of management, and with enthusiasm put a son of management who does not have the capacity for desk work in the way of earning an honest living as a manual worker.

So proclaims this fanatic equalitarian. Or else, says the American radical, we can operate our placement services through private pressure groups and see that sons of business executives get jobs through other business executives, and members of union families take up work unionized by their friends. Under such conditions the layers of society probably would become more impervious than ever, we should depart further from our American ideal. And a caste-ridden society is one of potential danger—danger of eruption, danger for the liberty of all. Not governmental employment, not pensions, but governmental guarantee of real equality of opportunity for the veteran therefore would be the plank of the American radical once the war was won!

To turn from such eminently practical matters as earning a living to the problems of nourishing the human soul, we see also a difference here between the members of my hypothetical trio. For the American radical could not indulge his taste for "Old World culture" without a twinge of conscience. Therefore he would be impelled to sponsor a most difficult undertaking: the work of redefining culture in both democratic and American terms. He would have little patience—too little patience— with antiquarians, scholars, and collectors. The idea that culture is aristocratic would find no sympathy from his kind. This is one of the few points on which the American radical joins hands with his other radical friends and the Russians of the new day; his concept of art and culture would be in terms of the present and the future, in terms of every man and woman and not a special privileged few.

The American radical would be old-fashioned in his notion of the importance of individual integrity. He would be harsh on cynics and easy optimists alike. He would be committed to a free press, to tolerance of all doctrines and the maximum of tolerance for individual action. But since he would bemoan the cynicism of our youth and the intellectual dishonesty of our age, he might well be fanatical in his desire for certain reforms in education. He would surely be both unkind and unjust to this century's methods of advertising and sales promotion. For like some others he would be inclined to see in the waves of distorted facts and beguiling half-truths with which our eyes and ears are daily saturated one of the most insidious maladies of the age. How he would cope with such a problem, I do not know. But on the subject he would be vocal if he were true to the real American radical tradition.

—JAMES BRYANT CONANT, "Wanted: American Radicals," 1943

11. NOT A REVOLUTION BUT A NEW DEAL

The election of Franklin D. Roosevelt, and the reform program that he pushed through with such speed and effectiveness, were regarded in some conservative quarters as little short of revolution. Some critics went so far as to insist that the whole New Deal was a foreign importation— as Herbert Hoover put it, "a definite attempt to replace the American system of freedom with some sort of European planned existence." Actually the New Deal was neither revolutionary nor alien. It was in the familiar tradition of change and reform, and its roots were wholly in American experience. The editor here evaluates the historical significance of Roosevelt's domestic reforms.

I.

. . . We can see now that the "Roosevelt revolution" was no revolution, but rather the culmination of half a century of historical development, and that Roosevelt himself, though indubitably a leader, was an instrument of the popular will rather than a creator of, or a dictator to, that will. Indeed, the two major issues of the Roosevelt administration—the domestic issue of the extension of government control for democratic purposes, and the international issue of the rôle of America as a world power—emerged in the 1890's, and a longer perspective will see the half-century from the 1890's to the present as an historical unit. The roots of the New Deal, the origins of our participation in this war, go deep down into our past, and neither development is comprehensible except in terms of that past.

What was really but a new deal of the old cards looked, to startled and dismayed contemporaries, like a revolution for two reasons: because it was carried through with such breathless rapidity, and because in spirit at least it contrasted so sharply with what immediately preceded. But had the comparison been made not with the Coolidge-Hoover era, but with the Wilson, the Theodore Roosevelt, even the Bryan era the contrast would have been less striking than the similarities. Actually, precedent for the major part of New Deal legislation was to be found in these earlier periods. Regulation of railroads and of business dated back to the Interstate Commerce Act of 1887 and the Sherman Act of 1890, and was continuous from that time forward. The farm relief program of the Populists, and of Wilson, anticipated much that the Roosevelt administrations enacted. The beginnings of conservation can be traced to the Carey Act of 1894 and the Reclamation Act of 1902, and the first Roosevelt did as much as the second to dramatize—though less to solve—the program of conserving natural resources.

Power regulation began with the Water Power Act of 1920; supervision over securities exchanges with grain and commodities exchange acts of the Harding and Coolidge administrations; while regulation of money is as old as the Union, and the fight which Bryan and Wilson waged against the "Money Power" and Wall Street was more bitter than anything that came during the New Deal. The policy of reciprocity can be traced to the Republicans, Blaine and McKinley. Labor legislation had its beginnings in such states as Massachusetts and New York over half a century ago, while much of the program of social security was worked out in Wisconsin and other states during the second and the third decades of the new century.

There is nothing remarkable about this, nor does it detract in any way from the significance of President Roosevelt's achievements and contributions. The pendulum of American history swings gently from right to left, but there are no sharp breaks in the rhythm of our historical development; and it is to the credit of Roosevelt that he worked within the framework of American history and tradition.

2.

What, then, are the major achievements, the lasting contributions, of the first three Roosevelt administrations? First, perhaps, comes the restoration of self-confidence, the revivification of the national spirit, the reassertion of faith in democracy. . . .

More, a strong case can be made out for the propriety of that association. "The only thing we need to fear," said Mr. Roosevelt on assuming the Presidency, "is fear itself. . . . We face the arduous days that lie before us in the warm courage of national unity; with the clear consciousness of seeking old and precious moral values; with the clean satisfaction that comes from the stern performance of duty." And during twelve years of office, Mr. Roosevelt did not abate his confidence in "the future of essential democracy" or in the capacity of the American people to rise to any challenge, to meet any crisis, domestic or foreign. Those who lived through the electric spring of 1933 will remember the change from depression and discouragement to excitement and hope; those able to compare the last decade with previous decades will agree that interest in public affairs has rarely been as widespread, as alert, or as responsive.

All this may be in the realm of the intangible. If we look to more tangible things, what does the record show? Of primary importance has been the physical rehabilitation of the country. Notwithstanding the splendid achievements of the Theodore Roosevelt administrations, it became clear, during the twenties and thirties, that the natural resources of the country—its soil, forests, water power—were being destroyed at a dangerous rate. The development of the Dust Bowl, and the migration of the Oakies to the Promised Land of California, the tragic floods on the Mississippi and the Ohio, dramatized to the American people the urgency of this problem.

Roosevelt tackled it with energy and boldness. The Civilian Conservation Corps enlisted almost three million young men who planted seventeen million acres in new forests, built over six million check dams to halt soil erosion, fought forest fires and plant and animal diseases. To check erosion the government organized a co-operative program which enlisted the help of over one-fourth the farmers of the country and embraced 270 million acres of land, provided for the construction of a series of huge dams and reservoirs, and planned the creation of a hundred-mile-wide shelter belt of trees on the high plains. The resettlement Administration moved farmers off marginal lands and undertook to restore these to usefulness. More important than all this, was the TVA, a gigantic laboratory for regional reconstruction. Though much of this program owes its inspiration to the past, the contrast between the New Deal and what immediately preceded it cannot be better illustrated than by reference to Hoover's characterization of the Muscle Shoals bill of 1931 as not "liberalism" but "degeneration."

Equally important has been the New Deal achievement in the realm of human rehabilitation. Coming into office at a time when unemployment had reached perhaps fourteen million, and when private panaceas had ostentatiously failed, it was perhaps inevitable that Roosevelt should have sponsored a broad program of government aid. More important than bare relief, was the acceptance of the principle of the responsibility of the state for the welfare and security of its people—for employment, health and general welfare.

That this principle was aggressively and bitterly opposed now seems hard to believe: its establishment must stand as one of the cardinal achievements of the New Deal. Beginning with emergency legislation for relief, the Roosevelt program in the end embraced the whole field of social security—unemployment assistance, old age pensions, aid to women and children, and public health. Nor did it stop with formal "social security" legislation. It entered the domains of agriculture and labor, embraced elaborate programs of rural rehabilitation, the establishment of maximum hours and minimum wages, the prohibition of child labor, housing reform, and, eventually, enlarged aid to education. Under the New Deal the noble term "commonwealth" was given a more realistic meaning than ever before in our history.

That to Roosevelt the preservation of democracy was closely associated with this program for social and economic security is inescapably clear. He had learned well the moral of recent continental European history: that given a choice between liberty and bread, men are sorely tempted to choose bread. The task of democracy, as he conceived it, was to assure both. In a fireside chat of 1938 he said:

Democracy has disappeared in several other great nations, not because the people of those nations disliked democracy, but because they had grown tired of unemployment and insecurity, of seeing their children hungry while they sat helpless in the face of government confusion and government weakness through lack of leadership in government. Finally, in desperation, they chose to sacrifice liberty in the hope of getting something to eat. We in America know that our democratic institutions can be preserved and made to work. But in order to preserve them we need . . . to prove that the practical operation of democratic government is equal to the task of protecting the security of the people. . . . The people of America are in agreement in defending their liberties at any cost, and the first line of that defense lies in the protection of economic security.

3.

In the political realm the achievements of the New Deal were equally notable. First we must note the steady trend towards the strengthening of government and the expansion of government activities—whether for weal or for woe only the future can tell. As yet no better method of dealing with the crowding problems of modern economy and society has revealed itself, and it can be said that though government today has, quantitatively, far greater responsibilities than it had a generation or even a decade ago, it has, qualitatively, no greater power. For our Constitutional system is intact, and all power still resides in the people and their representatives in Congress, who can at any moment deprive their government of any power.

But we seem to have solved, in this country, the ancient problem of the reconciliation of liberty and order; we seem to have overcome our traditional distrust of the state and come to a realization that a strong state could be used to benefit and advance the commonwealth. That is by no means a New Deal achievement, but it is a development which has gained much from the experience of the American people with their government during the Roosevelt administrations.

It has meant, of course, a marked acceleration of the tendency towards Federal centralization. This tendency had been under way for a long time before Roosevelt came to office: a century ago liberals were deploring the decline of the states and the growth of the power of the national government. That under the impact first of depression and then of war it has proceeded at a rapid rate since 1933 cannot be denied. It is apparent in the administrative field, with the growth of bureaus and departments and civil servants—and of the budget! It is apparent in the legislative field, with the striking extension of federal authority into the fields of labor, agriculture, banking, health, education and the arts. It is apparent in the executive field with the immense increase in the power of the President. And it has been ratified by the judiciary with the acceptance and application of a broad construction of the Constitution.

Yet it cannot be said that this Federal centralization has weakened the states or local communities. What we are witnessing is a general increase in governmental activities—an increase in which the states share—witness any state budget at present. And it can be argued, too, that political centralization strengthens rather than weakens local government and the health of local communities. For if we look below forms to realities we can see that during the last decade Federal aid to farmers, to home-owners, to labor, Federal assistance in road-building, education and public health, has actually restored many communities to financial and economic health. It is by no means certain that community sentiment is weaker today than it was a generation ago.

Along with Federal centralization has gone a great increase in the power of the executive. The charge that Roosevelt has been a dictator can be dismissed, along with those hoary charges that Jefferson, Jackson, Lincoln, Theodore Roosevelt, and Wilson were dictators. American politics simply doesn't run to dictators. But Roosevelt has been a "strong" executive—as every great democratic President has been a strong executive. There is little doubt that the growing complexity of government plays into the hands of the executive; there is little doubt that Roosevelt accepted this situation cheerfully. Today Roosevelt exercises powers far vaster than those contemplated by the Fathers of the Constitution, as vast, indeed, as those exercised by the head of any democratic state in the world. Yet it cannot fairly be asserted that any of these powers has been exercised arbitrarily, or that the liberties of Americans are not so safe today as at any other time.

Two other political developments under the New Deal should be noted. The first is the revitalization of political parties; the second the return of the Supreme Court to the great tradition of Marshall, Story, Miller and Holmes. Four observations about political parties during the last decade are in order. First, the danger that our parties might come to represent a particular class or section or interest was avoided: both major parties retained—after the election of 1936—a broad national basis. Second, minor parties all but disappeared: in the elections of 1940 and 1944 the minor parties cast less than 1 per cent of the total vote— the first time this happened since 1872. Third, legislation such as the Hatch Act diminished the possibility that any party might come to be controlled by powerful vested interests or by patronage. And finally, with the organization of the PAC in the campaign of 1944, labor for the first time in our history became an important factor in elections; and labor chose to work within the framework of existing parties rather than, as elsewhere, to organize its own party.

The New Deal, as far as can be foreseen, is here to stay: there seems no likelihood of a reversal of any of the major developments in politics in the last twelve years. This was recognized by the Republicans in 1940 and again in 1944, for both platforms endorsed all the essentials of the New Deal and confined criticism to details and administration. How far the reforms and experiments of the Roosevelt era will be carried is a hazardous question. That the program of conservation will be continued and enlarged seems obvious. A recent Congress, to be sure, cavalierly ended the life of the National Resources Planning Board, but the present Congress seems disposed to undertake a Missouri Valley development along the lines of the TVA, and doubtless other "little TVA's" are ahead. Social security, too, will be maintained and possibly enlarged: whether it will come to embrace socialized medicine or a broad rehousing program is more dubious.

There may be a reaction against some of the labor legislation of the New Deal, but labor's newly discovered political power would seem to make that unlikely. It is improbable that there will be any relaxation of governmental peacetime controls over business, banking, securities, power, though here a change in taxation policies may do much to stimulate private enterprise and create an appearance of a shift away from New Deal practices. Federal centralization, which has been under way so long, is doubtless here to stay; planning, imperatively required by war, will in all probability wear off its faintly pink tinge, and flourish as a peacetime technique. And, finally, it seems probable that the restoration of the dignity of politics and statecraft, which came with 1933, will survive.

—HENRY STEELE COMMAGER, "Twelve Years of Roosevelt," 1945

～ 10 ～

Church and State

THE two most perspicacious Old World interpreters of the New, Tocqueville and Bryce, were both profoundly impressed by the position of the church and the influence of religion in America. "There is no country in the world," wrote Tocqueville,

in which the Christian religion retains a greater influence over the souls of men than in America, and there can be no greater proof of its utility, and of its conformity to human nature, than that its influence is most powerfully felt over the most enlightened and free nation on earth. . . . In the United States religion exercises but little influence upon the laws and upon the details of public opinion, but it directs the manners of the community, and by regulating domestic life, it regulates the state.

And fifty years later Bryce observed that

Christianity is in fact understood to be, though not the legally established religion, yet the national religion. So far from thinking their commonwealth Godless, the Americans conceive that the religious character of a government consists in nothing but the religious beliefs of the individual citizens, and the conformity of their conduct to that belief. They deem the general acceptance of Christianity to be one of the main sources of their national prosperity, and their nation as a special object of the Divine favor.

America, in short, is a Christian nation. In the beginning church and state were tied together, in varying degrees of intimacy; in the South it was the Anglican Church that was established, in the New England colonies the Puritan Church enjoyed a favored position. But even in the early colonial period came something new—a separation of state and church. Two great religious statesmen of this early period stamped their philosophy indelibly on American history, Roger Williams and William Penn. They introduced the concept of a separation of church and state, the concept not only of religious toleration but of religious liberty.

The principle of separation was written into the first State Constitutions, and then into the Federal Constitution. But it was one thing to establish the general principle; another to apply it, and to carry it to its logical conclusion. Disestablishment of the Anglican Church was not too difficult, for the association of that Church with the mother country naturally exposed it to public hostility. But the Congregational Church was not completely divorced from Massachusetts until the 1830's. Complete religious liberty, too, was slower of realization than of proclamation. Discriminations against Catholics, Jews, Deists, and infidels lingered on in some states until the twentieth century.

These limitations on complete separation of church and state, and complete religious liberty, have loomed large in the public mind, from decade to decade. It is when we contrast the American experiment with Old World practices that we appreciate its boldness and its originality. And it is only when—by a stretch of the imagination—we contemplate what the situation would be if different churches were legally established in different States, or if the policy of toleration and liberty did not obtain, that we fully appreciate its value.

Indeed separation of church and state and toleration of religious beliefs or disbeliefs were not so much the product of philosophical principle as of practical necessity. If one church were to be established, which one would it be? If some standard of religious orthodoxy were to be accepted, who would fix it and who would enforce it, and what would happen to those who failed to come up to it? Given a people by nature and by instinct nonconformist, and as heterogeneous in religion as in language or race, religious freedom was the only workable policy.

It was one thing to decree liberty and toleration by law; it was quite another to enforce the decrees. While no great crimes like St. Bartholomew's Eve or the imprisonment of dissenters, or pogroms against the Jews stain the pages of American history since the eighteenth century, we would delude ourselves if we supposed that Americans practiced a religious freedom as complete as that which they preach. Again and again there have been outbreaks of anti-Catholicism; large organizations like the modern Ku Klux Klan are equally intolerant of Jews and of Catholics; anti-Semitism as a social, if not a religious, manifestation is widespread and persistent; and minor sects like the Jehovah's Witnesses suffer mild persecution in community after community. We still have to elect a Catholic to the Presidency, and when

Wilson appointed Louis Brandeis to the Supreme Court he loosed a shameful flood of anti-Semitism.

Religious persecution is almost a thing of the past, but how far may the state go in enforcing ordinary police regulations, or in imposing certain educational policies, without infringing on religious freedom? Just where is the line to be drawn between authority and conscience? May communities enforce licensing ordinances that restrict religious propaganda? May they enforce anti-noise or anti-litter ordinances that appear to restrict the right of free speech or free press or free assembly for preachers? May they require a flag salute from school children whose religion repudiates such a gesture or loyalty oaths from adults who confess a similar religious prohibition? These and similar questions arose to vex the American people in the second quarter of the twentieth century.

So, too, with state or local ordinances giving apparent support to religion generally. As Tocqueville and Bryce pointed out, the United States was a Christian nation; Justice Story went so far as to insist that Christianity was established by the common law and could be enforced through the Courts. To this day most States have laws or ordinances that distinguish Sunday from weekdays, or that penalize blasphemy, or that call for some religious form of affirmation. Do these things constitute an improper recognition of religion by the state, and thus a breach in the wall of separation between church and state? If not, how far may States or local communities go in the support of religion without violating the principle of separation? May they give aid to parochial schools—indirect aid in the form of free lunches or textbooks or bus transportation, or direct aid in the form of scholarships or grants? May they permit the use of public facilities for religious purposes? These and similar questions have perplexed and divided Americans in our own day, and they have perplexed and divided the Supreme Court as well.

1. RELIGIOUS CONFORMITY IN THE BAY COLONY

The Puritan migration to Massachusetts Bay was motivated in large part by a desire for religious freedom, but the Puritans themselves did not subscribe to the principle of religious freedom, nor did they practice it—witness the banishment of Roger Williams and Anne Hutchin-

son and the persecution of the Quakers. The insistence on religious con-
formity is illuminated by the following extract from the Journal *of*
Governor Winthrop, *which tells of the dispute that raged over the*
question of a covenant of works and a covenant of grace—a dispute that
was part of the larger dispute with the recalcitrant Anne Hutchinson.

MARCH 9, (1637) The general court began. When any matter about
these new opinions was mentioned, the court was divided; yet
the greater number far were sound. They questioned the proceeding
again Mr. Wilson, for his speech in the last court, but could not fasten
upon such as had prejudiced him, etc.; but, by the vote of the greater
party, his speech was approved, and declared to have been a seasonable
advice, and no charge or accusation.

The ministers, being called to give advice about the authority of the
court in things concerning the churches, etc., did all agree of these two
things: 1. That no member of the court ought to be publicly questioned
by a church for any speech in the court, without the license of the court.
The reason was, because the court may have sufficient reason that may
excuse the sin, which yet may not be fit to acquaint the church with,
being a secret of state. The second thing was, that, in all such heresies
or errors of any church members as are manifest and dangerous to the
state, the court may proceed without tarrying for the church; but if
the opinions be doubtful, etc., they are first to refer them to the
church, etc.

At this court, when Mr. Wheelwright was to be questioned for a
sermon, which seemed to tend to sedition, etc., near all the church of
Boston presented a petition to the court for two things: 1. That as freemen they might be present in cases of judicature. 2. That the court
would declare, if they might deal in cases of conscience before the
church, etc. This was taken as a groundless and presumptuous act,
especially at this season, and was rejected with this answer: That the
court had never used to proceed judicially but it was openly; but for
matter of consultation and preparation in causes, they might and
would be private.

One Stephen Greensmith, for saying that all the ministers, except
A. B. C., did teach a covenant of works, was censured to acknowledge
his fault in every church, and fined £40.

Mr. Wheelwright, one of the members of Boston, preaching at the last fast, inveighed against all that walked in a covenant of works, as he described it to be, viz., such as maintain sanctification as an evidence of justification, etc., and called them antichrists, and stirred up the people against them with much bitterness and vehemency. For this he was called into the court, and his sermon being produced, he justified it, and confessed he did mean all that walk in such a way. Whereupon the elders of the rest of the churches were called, and asked whether they, in their ministry, did walk in such a way. They all acknowledged they did. So, after much debate, the court adjudged him guilty of sedition, and also of contempt, for that the court had appointed the fast as a means of reconciliation of the differences, etc., and he purposely set himself to kindle and increase them.

November 1 (1637) There was great hope that the late general assembly would have had some good effect in pacifying the troubles and dissensions about matters of religion; but it fell out otherwise. For though Mr. Wheelwright and those of his party had been clearly confuted and confounded in the assembly, yet they persisted in their opinions, and were as busy in nourishing contentions (the principal of them) as before. Whereupon the general court, being assembled in the 2 of the 9th month (November), and finding, upon consultation, that two so opposite parties could not contain in the same body, without apparent hazard of ruin to the whole, agreed to send away some of the principal; and for this a fair opportunity was offered by the remonstrance or petition, which they preferred to the court the 9th of the 1st month (March), wherein they affirm Mr. Wheelwright to be innocent, and that the court had condemned the truth of Christ, with divers other scandalous and seditious speeches, (as appears at large in the proceedings of this court, which were faithfully collected and published soon after the court brake up,) subscribed by more than sixty of that faction, whereof one William Aspinwall, being one, and he that drew the said petition, being then sent as a deputy for Boston, was for the same dismissed, and after called to the court and disfranchised and banished. John Coggeshall was another deputy, who, though his hand were not to the petition, yet, professing himself to approve it, etc., was also dismissed, and after disfranchised. Then the court sent warrant to Boston to send other deputies in their room; but they intended to have sent the same men again; but Mr. Cotton, coming amongst them, dissuaded them with much ado. Then the court sent for Mr. Wheelwright, and, he persisting to justify his sermon, and his whole practice and opinions, and refusing to leave either the place or his public exercisings, he was disfranchised and banished. Upon which he appealed to the king, but neither called witnesses, nor desired any act to be made of it. The court told him, that an appeal did not lie; for by the king's grant we had power to hear and determine without any reservation, etc. So he relinquished his appeal, and the court gave him leave to go to his house, upon his promise, that, if he were not gone out of our jurisdiction within fourteen days, he would render himself to one of the magistrates.

The court also sent for Mrs. Hutchinson, and charged her with divers matters, as her keeping two public lectures every week in her house, whereto sixty or eighty persons did usually resort, and for reproaching most of the ministers (viz., all except Mr. Cotton) for not preaching a covenant of free grace, and that they had not the seal of the spirit, nor were able ministers of the New Testament; which were clearly proved against her, though she sought to shift it off. And, after many speeches to and fro, at last she was so full as she could not contain, but vented her revelations; amongst which this was one, that she had it revealed to her, that she should come into New England, and should here be persecuted, and that God would ruin us and our posterity, and the whole state, for the same. So the court proceeded and banished her; but, because it was winter, they committed her to a private house, where she was well provided, and her own friends and the elders permitted to go to her, but none else.

The court called also Capt. Underhill, and some five or six more of the principal, whose hands were to the said petition; and because they stood to justify it, they were disfranchised, and such as had public places were put from them.

The court also ordered, that the rest, who had subscribed the petition, (and would not acknowledge their fault, and which near twenty of them did,) and some others, who had been chief stirrers in these contentions, etc., should be disarmed. This troubled some of them very much, especially because they were to bring them in themselves; but at last, when they saw no remedy, they obeyed.

—JOHN WINTHROP, *Journal,* 1637

2. "GOD REQUIRETH NOT A UNIFORMITY
OF RELIGION"

One of those upon whom the Puritan requirement of orthodoxy rested most heavily was Roger Williams, a Separatist who was to be the greatest religious figure of the colonial era, and one of that small handful of men who have left a permanent impress upon history. Williams sailed for the Bay Colony in 1630, refused a call from the Boston Church because it was "unseparated," preached at Salem, and for his many heresies was found guilty and banished from the Colony. In 1636 he founded along Narragansett Bay the freest of American colonies. The Bloudy Tenent was written as an attack upon John Cotton and the Puritan theocracy while Williams was in England trying to get a charter for his colony. We give here the summary which Williams himself supplied for his dialogue between Truth and Peace. Williams carried out, in the colony over whose destinies he presided, his principles of complete religious toleration. Of Williams the Italian scholar, Francesco Ruffini, has written:

Henceforth the noble cause of religious liberty may find one who will develop it with greater vigor of reasoning and more copious erudition, but never one, however fervent a believer, who will excel Roger Williams in breadth of conception and in sincerity of advancing that cause. And therefore it has been possible to say of him that while other writers, in the limitations which they place upon liberty, resemble those poets who, after declaring their hero to be invulnerable, proceed to clothe him in the commonest armor, Roger Williams, on the contrary, allows Truth to stand alone, surrounded only by her armor of light.

FIRST, that the blood of so many hundred thousand souls of Protestants and Papists, spilt in the wars of present and former ages, for their respective consciences, is not required nor accepted by Jesus Christ the Prince of Peace.

Secondly, pregnant scriptures and arguments are throughout the work proposed against the doctrine of persecution for cause of conscience.

Thirdly, satisfactory answers are given to scriptures, and objections produced by Mr. Calvin, Beza, Mr. Cotton, and the ministers of the New English churches and others former and later, tending to prove the doctrine of persecution for cause of conscience.

Fourthly, the doctrine of persecution for cause of conscience is proved guilty of all the blood of the souls crying for vengeance under the altar.

Fifthly, all civil states with their officers of justice in their respective constitutions and administrations are proved essentially civil, and there-fore not judges, governors, or defenders of the spiritual or Christian state and worship.

Sixthly, it is the will and command of God that (since the coming of his Son the Lord Jesus) a permission of the most paganish, Jewish, Turkish, or antichristian consciences and worships, be granted to all men in all nations and countries; and they are only to be fought against with that sword which is only (in soul matters) able to conquer, to wit, the sword of God's Spirit, the Word of God.

Seventhly, the state of the Land of Israel, the kings and people thereof in peace and war, is proved figurative and ceremonial, and no pattern nor president for any kingdom or civil state in the world to follow.

Eighthly, God requireth not a uniformity of religion to be enacted and enforced in any civil state; which enforced uniformity (sooner or later) is the greatest occasion of civil war, ravishing of conscience, persecution of Christ Jesus in his servants, and of the hypocrisy and destruction of millions of souls.

Ninthly, in holding an enforced uniformity of religion in a civil state, we must necessarily disclaim our desires and hopes of the Jew's conversion to Christ.

Tenthly, an enforced uniformity of religion throughout a nation or civil state, confounds the civil and religious, denies the principles of Christianity and civility, and that Jesus Christ is come in the flesh.

Eleventhly, the permission of other consciences and worships than a state professeth only can (according to God) procure a firm and lasting peace (good assurance being taken according to the wisdom of the civil state for uniformity of civil obedience from all forts).

Twelfthly, lastly, true civility and Christianity may both flourish in a state or kingdom, notwithstanding the permission of divers and contrary consciences, either of Jew or Gentile.

—ROGER WILLIAMS, *The Bloudy Tenent of Persecution,* 1644

3. MARYLAND TOLERATION ACT

Although Maryland was designed, from the first, as a refuge for Catholics persecuted in England, comparatively few of that faith came over to the colony. It was in part to meet the threat of a Protestant majority that Cecilius Calvert, Lord Baltimore, obtained the enactment of this so-called Toleration Act of 1649. In 1654 the Puritans gained control of the province and repealed the Act, but upon the restoration of Baltimore to control, the Act of 1649 was revived. Perhaps the most interesting thing about this famous law is that it should have been regarded at the time—and since—as so enlightened. Yet here as with so many other things—the Massachusetts School Law of 1647 for example—the symbolic significance of the act was of lasting importance.

FORASMUCH as in a well governed and Christian Common Wealth matters concerning Religion and the honor of God ought in the first place to bee taken, into serious consideration and endeavoured to bee settled. Be it therefore . . . enacted. . . . That whatsoever person or persons within this Province . . . shall from henceforth blaspheme God, . . . or shall deny our Saviour Jesus Christ to bee the sonne of God, or shall deny the holy Trinity the ffather sonne and holy Ghost, or the Godhead of any of the said Three persons of the Trinity or the Unity of the Godhead . . . shall be punished with death and confiscation or forfeiture of all his or her lands. . . .

. . . And whereas the inforceing of the conscience in matters of Religion hath frequently fallen out to be of dangerous Consequence in those commonwealthes where it hath been practised, And for the more quiett and peaceable governement of this Province, and the better to preserve mutauall Love and amity amongst the Inhabitants thereof. Be it Therefore . . . enacted (except as in this present Act is before Declared and sett forth) that noe person or persons whatsoever within this Province, or the Islands, Ports, Harbors, Creekes, or havens thereunto belonging professing to believe in Jesus Christ, shall from henceforth bee any waies troubled, Molested or discountenanced for or in respect of his or her religion nor in the free exercise thereof within this Province or the Islands thereunto belonging nor any way compelled to the beleife or exercise of any other Religion against his or her consent, soe as they be not unfaithful to the Lord Proprietary, or molest or conspire against the civill Government established or to bee established in this Province under him or his heires. And that all & every person and persons that shall presume Contrary to this Act and the true intent and meaning thereof directly or indirectly either in person or estate willfully to wronge disturbe trouble or molest any person whatsoever within this Province professing to believe in Jesus Christ for or in respect of his or her religion or the free exercise thereof within this Province other than is provided for in this Act that such person or persons soe offending, shalbe compelled to pay trebble damages to the party soe wronged or molested, and for every such offence shall also forfeit 20ˢ sterling in money or the value thereof . . . , Or if the parties soe offending as aforesaid shall refuse or bee unable to recompense the party soe wronged, or to satisfy such ffyne or forfeiture, then such offender shalbe severely punished by publick whipping & imprisonment during the pleasure of the Lord proprietary, or his Leiuetenant or cheife Governor of this Province for the tyme being without baile or maineprise.

—Maryland Toleration Act, April 21, 1649

4. "THE GREAT CASE OF LIBERTY OF CONSCIENCE"

For their rejection of the principle of authority in either church or state the Friends—or Quakers as they came to be called—suffered persecution not only in England but in the colonies as well. It was no wonder, therefore, that they insisted so ardently on the great principle of liberty of conscience, and safeguarded that principle so carefully in their colony of Pennsylvania. William Penn himself, with Roger Williams the greatest champion of religious liberty in the history of the New World before Jefferson, had suffered imprisonment again and again for

his faith. The essay from which we take our excerpt was the product of
one of these imprisonments.

THE great case of Liberty of Conscience, so often debated and defended (however dissatisfactorily to such as have so little conscience as to persecute for it) is once more brought to public view, by
a late act against Dissenters, and Bill, or an additional one, that we all
hoped the wisdom of our rulers had long since laid aside, as what was
fitter to be passed into an act of perpetual oblivion. The kingdoms are
alarmed at this procedure, and thousands greatly at a stand, wondering
what should be the meaning of such hasty resolutions, that seem as
fatal as they were unexpected. Some ask what wrong they have done?
Others, what peace they have broken? and all, what plots they have
formed to prejudice the present government, or occasions given to hatch
new jealousies of them and their proceedings? being not conscious to
themselves of guilt in any such respect.

For mine own part, I publicly confess myself to be a very hearty Dissenter from the established worship of these nations, as believing Protestants to have much degenerated from their first principles, and as
owning the poor despised Quakers, in life and doctrine, to have espoused the cause of God, and to be the undoubted followers of Jesus
Christ, in his most holy, strait, and narrow way, that leads to the eternal
rest. In all which I know no treason, nor any principle that would urge
me to a thought injurious to the civil peace. If any be defective in this
particular, it is equal both individuals and whole societies should answer
for their own defaults; but we are clear. . . .

First, By Liberty of Conscience, we understand not only a mere Liberty of the Mind, in believing or disbelieving this or that principle or
doctrine; but "the exercise of ourselves in a visible way of worship,
upon our believing it to be indispensably required at our hands, that if
we neglect it for fear or favor of any mortal man, we sin, and incur
divine wrath." Yet we would be so understood to extend and justify
the lawfulness of our so meeting to worship God, as not to contrive,
or abet any contrivance destructive of the government and laws of the
land, tending to matters of an external nature, directly or indirectly; but
so far only as it may refer to religious matters, and a life to come, and

consequently wholly independent of the secular affairs of this, wherein we are supposed to transgress.

Secondly, By imposition, restraint, and persecution, we do not only mean the strict requiring of us to believe this to be true, or that to be false; and upon refusal, to incur the penalties enacted in such cases; but by those terms we mean thus much, "any coercive let or hindrance to us, from meeting together to perform those religious exercises which are according to our faith and persuasion."

The question stated.

For proof of the aforesaid terms thus given, we singly state the question thus;

Whether imposition, restraint, and persecution, upon persons for exercising such a liberty of conscience as is before expressed, and so circumstantiated, be not to impeach the honor of God, the meekness of the Christian religion, the authority of Scripture, the privilege of nature, the principles of common reason, the well being of government, and apprehensions of the greatest personages of former and latter ages?

First, Then we say, that Imposition, Restraint, and Persecution, for matters relating to conscience, directly invade the divine prerogative, and divest the Almighty of a due, proper to none besides himself. And this we prove by these five particulars:

First, If we do allow the honor of our creation due to God only, and that no other besides himself has endowed us with those excellent gifts of Understanding, Reason, Judgment, and Faith, and consequently that he only is the object, as well as the author, both of our Faith, Worship, and Service; then whosoever shall interpose their authority to enact faith and worship in a way that seems not to us congruous with what he has discovered to us to be faith and worship (whose alone property it is to do it) or to restrain us from what we are persuaded is our indispensable duty, they evidently usurp this authority, and invade his incommunicable right of government over conscience: "For the Inspiration of the Almighty gives understanding: and faith is the gift of God," says the divine writ.

Secondly, Such magisterial determinations carry an evident claim to that infallibility, which Protestants have been hitherto so jealous of owning, that, to avoid the Papists, they have denied it to all but God himself. Either they have forsook their old plea; or if not, we desire to know when, and where, they were invested with that divine excellency; and whether imposition, restraint, and persecution, were ever deemed by

God the fruits of his Spirit. However, that itself was not sufficient; for unless it appears as well to us that they have it, as to them who have it, we cannot believe it upon any convincing evidence, but by tradition only, an anti-protestant way of believing.

Thirdly, It enthrones man as king over conscience, the alone just claim and privilege of his Creator; whose thoughts are not as men's thoughts, but has reserved to himself that empire from all the Caesars on earth: For if men, in reference to souls and bodies, things appertaining to this and the other world, shall be subject to their fellow-creatures, what follows, but that Caesar (however he got it) has all, God's share, and his own too? And being Lord of both, both are Caesar's, and not God's.

Fourthly, It defeats God's work of Grace, and the invisible operation of his eternal Spirit, (which can alone beget faith, and is only to be obeyed, in and about religion and worship) and attributes men's conformity to outward force and corporal punishments. A faith subject to as many revolutions as the powers that enact it.

Fifthly and lastly, Such persons assume the judgment of the great tribunal unto themselves; for to whomsoever men are imposedly or restrictively subject and accountable in matters of faith, worship and conscience; in them alone must the power of judgment reside; but it is equally true that God shall judge all by Jesus Christ, and that no man is so accountable to his fellow-creatures, as to be imposed upon, restrained, or persecuted for any matter of conscience whatever.

Thus, and in many more particulars, are men accustomed to intrench upon Divine Property, to gratify particular interests in the world; and (at best) through a misguided apprehension to imagine "they do God good service," that where they cannot give faith, they will use force; which kind of sacrifice is nothing less unreasonable than the other is abominable: God will not give his honor to another; and to him only, that searches the heart and tries the reins, it is our duty to ascribe the gifts of understanding and faith, without which none can please God.

—WILLIAM PENN,
"The Great Case of Liberty of Conscience," 1670

5. "ALL CHRISTIANS ARE EQUALLY ENTITLED TO PROTECTION"

Only to advanced thinkers like Roger Williams and William Penn in the seventeenth century, Jefferson and Madison and Mason in the eighteenth, did freedom of conscience mean what it means to most of us today. It meant toleration rather than freedom, and even toleration was not complete. Most of the new State Constitutions of the Revolutionary era contained some discriminations against Catholics, Jews, Deists, and nonbelievers, and most of them, too, provided for support of some kind to churches. We give here the article on religion from the Constitution of Maryland of 1776.

XXXIII. That, as it is the duty of every man to worship God in such manner as he thinks most acceptable to him; all persons, professing the Christian religion, are equally entitled to protection in their religious liberty; wherefore no person ought by any law to be molested in his person or estate on account of his religious persuasion or profession, or for his religious practice; unless, under colour of religion, any man shall disturb the good order, peace or safety of the State, or shall infringe the laws of morality, or injure others, in their natural, civil, or religious rights; nor ought any person to be compelled to frequent or maintain, or contribute, unless on contract, to maintain any particular place of worship, or any particular ministry; yet the Legislature may, in their discretion, lay a general and equal tax, for the support of the Christian religion; leaving to each individual the power of appointing the payment over of the money, collected from him, to the support of any particular place of worship or minister, or for the benefit of the poor of his own denomination, or the poor in general of any particular county: but the churches, chapels, glebes, and all other property now belonging to the church of England, ought to remain to the church of England forever. And all acts of Assembly, lately passed, for collecting monies for building or repairing particular churches or chapels of ease, shall continue in force, and be executed,

506

unless the Legislature shall, by act, supersede or repeal the same: but no county court shall assess any quantity of tobacco, or sum of money, hereafter, on the application of any vestrymen or church-wardens; and every encumbent of the church of England, who hath remained in his parish, and performed his duty, shall be entitled to receive the provision and support established by the act, entitled "An act for the support of the clergy of the church of England, in this Province," till the November court of this present year, to be held for the county in which his parish shall lie, or partly lie, or for such time as he hath remained in his parish, and performed his duty.

—Constitution of Maryland, 1776

6. "IF WE CONTRACT THE BONDS OF RELIGIOUS FREEDOM, NO NAME WILL TOO SEVERELY REPROACH OUR FOLLY"

Fully to appreciate the significance of the long and heroic campaign which Jefferson and Madison waged on behalf of religious freedom, we must keep in mind the religious situation which had obtained throughout the colonial era. In every colony from Maryland south, the Anglican was the Established Church. This meant that it was supported by the government, that is, through taxation or assessments or tithes; that only its clergy could officiate at marriages or baptisms; that dissenting sects existed only by tolerance. Jefferson and Madison had both grown up in the Anglican Church, but both knew too that that Church represented only a minority in the colony, that many of its clergy—in Virginia and elsewhere—had sided with the mother country in the revolutionary controversy, and that the specially privileged position which the Church enjoyed was by no means advantageous spiritually. More, both recognized that establishment was wrong not only in practice but in principle; that indeed any connection between church and state was wrong in principle.

The Declaration of Rights of 1776—drafted by the Episcopalian George Mason—had announced the principle of religious freedom, but not until 1779 was the Anglican Church formally disestablished. Even this was not satisfactory to the liberals, and Jefferson prepared a bill for absolute religious freedom and equality. This bill was fought not only by the Anglicans, but by the "dissenting" sects as well—sects quite willing to accept the principle of state support to religion as long as they got the support. The proposal to make all Christian churches in effect state churches on an equal standing, and to support them through taxation, found favor even with Patrick Henry and George Washington. Against this proposal, however, Madison directed his famous "Remonstrance" of 1784—a state paper which was to command a good deal of attention again in the church-state controversies of the 1940's.

To THE HONORABLE THE GENERAL ASSEMBLY
OF
THE COMMONWEALTH OF VIRGINIA.
A MEMORIAL AND REMONSTRANCE.

W E, THE subscribers, citizens of the said Commonwealth, having taken into serious consideration, a Bill printed by order of the last Session of General Assembly, entitled "A Bill establishing a provision for Teachers of the Christian Religion," and conceiving that the same, if finally armed with the sanctions of a law, will be a dangerous abuse of power, are bound as faithful members of a free State, to remonstrate against it, and to declare the reasons by which we are determined. We remonstrate against the said Bill,

1. Because we hold it for a fundamental and undeniable truth, "that Religion or the duty which we owe to our Creator and the Manner of discharging it, can be directed only by reason and conviction, not by force or violence."[1] The Religion then of every man must be left to the conviction and conscience of every man; and it is the right of every man to exercise it as these may dictate. This right is in its nature an unalienable right. It is unalienable; because the opinions of men, depending only on the evidence contemplated by their own minds, cannot follow the dictates of other men: It is unalienable also; because what is here a right towards men, is a duty towards the Creator. It is the duty of every man to render to the Creator such homage, and such only, as he believes to be acceptable to him. This duty is precedent both in order of time and degree of obligation, to the claims of Civil Society. Before any man

[1] Decl. Rights, Art. 16.

can be considered as a member of Civil Society, he must be considered as a subject of the Governor of the Universe: And if a member of Civil Society, who enters into any subordinate Association, must always do it with a reservation of his duty to the general authority; much more must every man who becomes a member of any particular Civil Society, do it with a saving of his allegiance to the Universal Sovereign. We maintain therefore that in matters of Religion, no man's right is abridged by the institution of Civil Society, and that Religion is wholly exempt from its cognizance. True it is, that no other rule exists, by which any question which may divide a Society, can be ultimately determined, but the will of the majority; but it is also true, that the majority may trespass on the rights of the minority.

2. Because if religion be exempt from the authority of the Society at large, still less can it be subject to that of the Legislative Body. The latter are but the creatures and vicegerents of the former. Their jurisdiction is both derivative and limited: it is limited with regard to the co-ordinate departments, more necessarily is it limited with regard to the constituents. The preservation of a free government requires not merely, that the metes and bounds which separate each department of power may be invariably maintained; but more especially, that neither of them be suffered to overleap the great Barrier which defends the rights of the people. The Rulers who are guilty of such an encroachment, exceed the commission from which they derive their authority, and are Tyrants. The People who submit to it are governed by laws made neither by themselves, nor by an authority derived from them, and are slaves.

3. Because, it is proper to take alarm at the first experiment on our liberties. We hold this prudent jealousy to be the first duty of citizens, and one of [the] noblest characteristics of the late Revolution. The freemen of America did not wait till usurped power had strengthened itself by exercise, and entangled the question in precedents. They saw all the consequences in the principle, and they avoided the consequences by denying the principle. We revere this lesson too much, soon to forget it. Who does not see that the same authority which can establish Christianity, in exclusion of all other Religions, may establish with the same ease any particular sect of Christians, in exclusion of all other Sects? That the same authority which can force a citizen to contribute three pence only of his property for the support of any one establishment, may force him to conform to any other establishment in all cases whatsoever?

4. Because, the bill violates that equality which ought to be the basis

of every law, and which is more indispensable, in proportion as the validity or expediency of any law is more liable to be impeached. If "all men are by nature equally free and independent,"[2] all men are to be considered as entering into Society on equal conditions; as relinquishing no more, and therefore retaining no less, one than another, of their natural rights. Above all are they to be considered as retaining an "*equal* title to the free exercise of Religion according to the dictates of conscience."[3] Whilst we assert for ourselves a freedom to embrace, to profess and to observe the Religion which we believe to be of divine origin, we cannot deny an equal freedom to those whose minds have not yet yielded to the evidence which has convinced us. If this freedom be abused, it is an offense against God, not against man: To God, therefore, not to men, must an account of it be rendered. As the Bill violates equality by subjecting some to peculiar burdens; so it violates the same principle, by granting to others peculiar exemptions. Are the Quakers and Mennonists the only sects who think a compulsive support of their religions unnecessary and unwarrantable? Can their piety alone be intrusted with the care of public worship? Ought their Religions to be endowed above all others, with extraordinary privileges, by which proselytes may be enticed from all others? We think too favorably of the justice and good sense of these denominations, to believe that they either covet preeminences over their fellow citizens, or that they will be seduced by them, from the common opposition to the measure.

5. Because the bill implies either that the Civil Magistrate is a competent Judge of Religious truth; or that he may employ Religion as an engine of Civil policy. The first is an arrogant pretension falsified by the contradictory opinions of Rulers in all ages, and throughout the world: The second an unhallowed perversion of the means of salvation.

6. Because the establishment proposed by the Bill is not requisite for the support of the Christian Religion. To say that it is, is a contradiction to the Christian Religion itself; for every page of it disavows a dependence on the powers of this world: it is a contradiction to fact; for it is known that this Religion both existed and flourished, not only without the support of human laws, but in spite of every opposition from them; and not only during the period of miraculous aid, but long after it had been left to its own evidence, and the ordinary care of Providence: Nay, it is a contradiction in terms; for a Religion not invented by

[2] Decl. Rights, Art. 1.
[3] Art. 16.

human policy, must have pre-existed and been supported, before it was established by human policy. It is moreover to weaken in those who profess this Religion a pious confidence in its innate excellence, and the patronage of its Author; and to foster in those who still reject it, a suspicion that its friends are too conscious of its fallacies, to trust it to its own merits.

7. Because experience witnesseth that ecclesiastical establishments, instead of maintaining the purity and efficacy of Religion, have had a contrary operation. During almost fifteen centuries, has the legal establishment of Christianity been on trial. What have been its fruits? More or less in all places, pride and indolence in the Clergy; ignorance and servility in the laity; in both, superstition, bigotry and persecution. Enquire of the Teachers of Christianity for the ages in which it appeared in its greatest lustre; those of every sect, point to the ages prior to its incorporation with Civil policy. Propose a restoration of this primitive state in which its Teachers depended on the voluntary rewards of their flocks; many of them predict its downfall. On which side ought their testimony to have greatest weight, when for or when against their interest?

8. Because the establishment in question is not necessary for the support of Civil Government. If it be urged as necessary for the support of Civil Government only as it is a means of supporting Religion, and it be not necessary for the latter purpose, it cannot be necessary for the former. If Religion be not within [the] cognizance of Civil Government, how can its legal establishment be said to be necessary to civil Government? What influence in fact have ecclesiastical establishments had on Civil Society? In some instances they have been seen to erect a spiritual tyranny on the ruins of Civil authority; in many instances they have been seen upholding the thrones of political tyranny; in no instance have they been seen the guardians of the liberties of the people. Rulers who wished to subvert the public liberties, may have found an established clergy convenient auxiliaries. A just government, instituted to secure & perpetuate it, needs them not. Such a government will be best supported by protecting every citizen in the enjoyment of his Religion with the same equal hand which protects his person and his property; by neither invading the equal rights by any Sect, nor suffering any Sect to invade those of another.

9. Because the proposed establishment is a departure from that generous policy, which, offering an asylum to the persecuted and oppressed

of every Nation and Religion, promised a lustre to our country, and an accession to the number of its citizens. What a melancholy mark is the Bill of sudden degeneracy! Instead of holding forth an asylum to the persecuted, it is itself a signal of persecution. It degrades from the equal rank of Citizens all those whose opinions in Religion do not bend to those of the Legislative authority. Distant as it may be, in its present form, from the Inquisition it differs from it only in degree. The one is the first step, the other the last in the career of intolerance. The magnanimous sufferer under this cruel scourge in foreign Regions, must view the Bill as a Beacon on our Coast, warning him to seek some other haven, where liberty and philanthropy in their due extent may offer a more certain repose from his troubles.

10. Because it will have a like tendency to banish our Citizens. The allurements presented by other situations are every day thinning their number. To superadd a fresh motive to emigration, by revoking the liberty which they now enjoy, would be the same species of folly which has dishonoured and depopulated flourishing kingdoms.

11. Because it will destroy that moderation and harmony which the forbearance of our laws to intermeddle with Religion, has produced amongst its several sects. Torrents of blood have been spilt in the old world, by vain attempts of the secular arm to extinguish Religious discord, by proscribing all difference in Religious opinions. Time has at length revealed the true remedy. Every relaxation of narrow and rigorous policy, wherever it has been tried, has been found to assuage the disease. The American Theatre has exhibited proofs, that equal and compleat liberty, if it does not wholly eradicate it, sufficiently destroys its malignant influence on the health and prosperity of the State. If with the salutary effects of this system under our own eyes, we begin to contract the bonds of Religious freedom, we know no name that will too severely reproach our folly. At least let warning be taken at the first fruit of the threatened innovation. The very appearance of the Bill has transformed that "Christian forbearance,[4] love and charity," which of late mutually prevailed, into animosities and jealousies, which may not soon be appeased. What mischiefs may not be dreaded should this enemy to the public quiet be armed with the force of a law?

12. Because the policy of the bill is adverse to the diffusion of the light of Christianity. The first wish of those who enjoy this precious gift, ought to be that it may be imparted to the whole race of mankind.

[4] Art. 16.

Compare the number of those who have as yet received it with the number still remaining under the dominion of false Religions; and how small is the former! Does the policy of the Bill tend to lessen the disproportion? No; it at once discourages those who are strangers to the light of [revelation] from coming into the Region of it; and countenances, by example the nations who continue in darkness, in shutting out those who might convey it to them. Instead of levelling as far as possible, every obstacle to the victorious progress of truth, the Bill with an ignoble and unchristian timidity would circumscribe it, with a wall of defence, against the encroachments of error.

13. Because attempts to enforce by legal sanctions, acts obnoxious to so great a proportion of Citizens, tend to enervate the laws in general, and to slacken the bands of Society. If it be difficult to execute any law which is not generally deemed necessary or salutary, what must be the case where it is deemed invalid and dangerous? and what may be the effect of so striking an example of impotency in the Government, on its general authority?

14. Because a measure of such singular magnitude and delicacy ought not to be imposed, without the clearest evidence that it is called for by a majority of citizens: and no satisfactory method is yet proposed by which the voice of the majority in this case may be determined, or its influence secured. "The people of the respective counties are indeed requested to signify their opinion respecting the adoption of the Bill to the next Session of Assembly." But the representation must be made equal, before the voice either of the Representatives or of the Counties, will be that of the people. Our hope is that neither of the former will, after due consideration, espouse the dangerous principle of the Bill. Should the event disappoint us, it will still leave us in full confidence, that a fair appeal to the latter will reverse the sentence against our liberties.

15. Because, finally, "the equal right of every citizen to the free exercise of his Religion according to the dictates of conscience" is held by the same tenure with all our other rights. If we recur to its origin, it is equally the gift of nature; if we weigh its importance, it cannot be less dear to us; if we consult the Declaration of those rights which pertain to the good people of Virginia, as the "basis and foundation of Government,"[5] it is enumerated with equal solemnity, or rather studied emphasis. Either then, we must say, that the will of the Legislature is the only measure of their authority; and that in the plentitude of this au-

[5] Decl. Rights-title.

thority, they may sweep away all our fundamental rights; or, that they are bound to leave this particular right untouched and sacred: Either we must say, that they may control the freedom of the press, may abolish the trial by jury, may swallow up the Executive and Judiciary Powers of the State; nay that they may despoil us of our very right of suffrage, and erect themselves into an independent and hereditary assembly: or we must say, that they have no authority to enact into law the Bill under consideration. We the subscribers say, that the General Assembly of this Commonwealth have no such authority: And that no effort may be omitted on our part against so dangerous an usurpation, we oppose to it, this remonstrance; earnestly praying, as we are in duty bound, that the Supreme Lawgiver of the Universe, by illuminating those to whom it is addressed, may on the one hand, turn their councils from every act which would affront his holy prerogative, or violate the trust committed to them: and on the other, guide them into every measure which may be worthy of his [blessing, may re]dound to their own praise, and may establish more firmly the liberties, the prosperity, and the Happiness of the Commonwealth.

—JAMES MADISON, "Memorial and Remonstrance," 1784

7. VIRGINIA STATUTE OF RELIGIOUS LIBERTY

This, probably the most famous single document in the history of religious freedom in America, was drafted by Jefferson some time in 1777, and introduced into the General Assembly when Jefferson was Governor in 1779. The struggle for its enactment, and for the disestablishment of the Anglican Church, Jefferson later characterized as "the severest contest in which I have ever been engaged." By 1784 Jefferson was in France, but his friends and disciples, Madison, Mason, John Taylor and others, pushed the bill through by January of 1786. Thus, wrote Madison exultantly, "was extinguished forever the ambitious hope of making laws for the human mind." And Jefferson answered that "it is honorable for us to have produced the first legislature who has had the courage to declare that the reason of man may be trusted with the formation of his own opinions." Jefferson counted the authorship of this

*bill, along with the Declaration of Independence and the establishment
of the University of Virginia, his most important contributions to mankind.*

An Act for establishing Religious Freedom.

I. WHEREAS Almighty God hath created the mind free; that all attempts to influence it by temporal punishments or burthens, or by
civil incapacitations, tend only to beget habits of hypocrisy and meanness, and are a departure from the plan of the Holy author of our religion, who being Lord both of body and mind, yet chose not to propagate it by coercions on either, as was in his Almighty power to do; that
the impious presumption of legislators and rulers, civil as well as ecclesiastical, who being themselves but fallible and uninspired men, have
assumed dominion over the faith of others, setting up their own
opinions and modes of thinking as the only true and infallible, and
as such endeavouring to impose them on others, hath established and
maintained false religions over the greatest part of the world, and
through all time; that to compel a man to furnish contributions of
money for the propagation of opinions which he disbelieves, is sinful
and tyrannical; that even the forcing him to support this or that teacher
of his own religious persuasion, is depriving him of the comfortable
liberty of giving his contributions to the particular pastor whose morals
he would make his pattern, and whose powers he feels most persuasive
to righteousness, and is withdrawing from the ministry those temporary
rewards, which proceeding from an approbation of their personal conduct, are an additional incitement to earnest and unremitting labours
for the instruction of mankind; that our civil rights have no dependence
on our religious opinions, any more than our opinions in physics or
geometry; that therefore the proscribing any citizen as unworthy the
public confidence by laying upon him an incapacity of being called to
offices of trust and emolument, unless he profess or renounce this or that
religious opinion, is depriving him injuriously of those privileges and
advantages to which in common with his fellow-citizens he has a
natural right; that it tends only to corrupt the principles of that religion it is meant to encourage, by bribing with a monopoly of worldly
honours and emoluments, those who will externally profess and con-

form to it; that though indeed these are criminal who do not withstand such temptation, yet neither are those innocent who lay the bait in their way; that to suffer the civil magistrate to intrude his powers into the field of opinion, and to restrain the profession or propagation of principles on supposition of their ill tendency, is a dangerous fallacy, which at once destroys all religious liberty, because he being of course judge of that tendency will make his opinions the rule of judgment, and approve or condemn the sentiments of others only as they shall square with or differ from his own; that it is time enough for the rightful purposes of civil government, for its officers to interfere when principles break out into overt acts against peace and good order; and finally, that truth is great and will prevail if left to herself, that she is the proper and sufficient antagonist to error, and has nothing to fear from the conflict, unless by human interposition disarmed of her natural weapons, free argument and debate, errors ceasing to be dangerous when it is permitted freely to contradict them.

II. *Be it enacted by the General Assembly,* that no man shall be compelled to frequent or support any religious worship, place or ministry whatsoever, nor shall be enforced, restrained, molested, or burthened in his body or goods, nor shall otherwise suffer on account of his religious opinions or belief; but that all men shall be free to profess, and by argument to maintain, their opinion in matters of religion, and that the same shall in no wise diminish, enlarge or affect their civil capacities.

III. And though we well know that this assembly, elected by the people for the ordinary purposes of legislation only, have no power to restrain the acts of succeeding assemblies, constituted with powers equal to our own, and that therefore to declare this act to be irrevocable would be of no effect in law; yet as we are free to declare, and do declare, that the rights hereby asserted are of the natural rights of mankind, and that if any act shall hereafter be passed to repeal the present, or to narrow its operation, such act will be an infringement of natural right.

—THOMAS JEFFERSON, Virginia Statute of Religious Freedom, 1786

8. THE SOCIALIZATION OF CHRISTIANITY

The interest of Protestant churches in the work of social reform goes back to the pre-Civil War years when men like Channing, Emerson, Parker, and others of the Unitarian denomination were so active. The movement formally called the Socialization of Christianity developed in the closing years of the nineteenth and the early years of the twentieth century. While basically the same as the earlier movement, it was wide in scope and perhaps more realistic. The Catholic Church, traditionally a social-service as well as a spiritual agency, had concerned itself increasingly with problems of economy and society. We give here the statement of the General Conference of the Federal Council of Churches in 1932, and the statement of the National Catholic Welfare Conference —a conference which officially represents the Catholic hierarchy—of 1938. This statement, prepared by the Most Reverend Edwin O'Hara, is a resume of "the principles which may be regarded as basic to the development of a Christian Social Order in a democratic society."

A. "THE SOCIAL CREED OF THE CHURCHES"

The Churches Should Stand For:

1. Practical application of the Christian principle of social well-being to the acquisition and use of wealth, subordination of speculation and the profit motive to the creative and cooperative spirit.

2. Social planning and control of the credit and monetary systems and the economic processes for the common good.

3. The right of all to the opportunity for self-maintenance; a wider and fairer distribution of wealth; a living wage, as a minimum, and above this a just share for the worker in the product of industry and agriculture.

4. Safeguarding of all workers, urban and rural, against harmful conditions of labor and occupational injury and disease.

5. Social insurance against sickness, accident, want in old age and unemployment.

6. Reduction of hours of labor as the general productivity of industry increases; release from employment at least one day in seven, with a shorter working week in prospect.

7. Such special regulation of the conditions of work of women as shall safeguard their welfare and that of the family and the community.

8. The right of employees and employers alike to organize for collective bargaining and social action; protection of both in the exercise of this right; the obligation of both to work for the public good; encouragement of cooperatives and other organizations among farmers and other groups.

9. Abolition of child labor; adequate provision for the protection, education, spiritual nurture and wholesome recreation of every child.

10. Protection of the family by the single standard of purity; educational preparation for marriage, home-making and parenthood.

11. Economic justice for the farmer in legislation, financing, transportation and the price of farm products as compared with the cost of machinery and other commodities which he must buy.

12. Extension of the primary cultural opportunities and social services now enjoyed by urban populations to the farm family.

13. Protection of the individual and society from the social, economic and moral waste of any traffic in intoxicants and habit-forming drugs.

14. Application of the Christian principle of redemption to the treatment of offenders; reform of penal and correctional methods and institutions, and of criminal court procedure.

15. Justice, opportunity and equal rights for all; mutual goodwill and cooperation among racial, economic and religious groups.

16. Repudiation of war, drastic reduction of armaments, participation in international agencies for the peaceable settlement of all controversies; the building of a cooperative world order.

17. Recognition and maintenance of the rights and responsibilities of free speech, free assembly, and a free press; the encouragement of free communication of mind with mind as essential to the discovery of truth.

—"Social Creed of the Churches," 1932

B. "A Christian Social Order"

1. That industrial and financial power must not be divorced from social responsibility; those exercising such power must always have in view the good of the industry or business as a whole and also the common good.

2. That a prominent aim of industry should be to provide stable employment so as to eliminate the insecurity and the other social ills that arise from excessive changes of employment and residence.

3. That as machinery is introduced into industry workers thereby displaced should be guaranteed adequate protection.

4. That employment should be available for workers at not less than a family living income.

5. That a Christian Social Order in America will look forward to some participation by employes in profits, and management.

6. That a wide distribution of ownership of productive property should be encouraged by legislation.

7. That there should be limitations of hours of labor in keeping with human need for rest and relaxation. This is especially true in regard to the labor of women and young persons. The industrial employment of children outside of the family should be prohibited.

8. That monopoly should be controlled in the public interest.

9. That collective bargaining through freely chosen representatives be recognized as a basic right of labor.

10. That minimum wage standards be set up by law for labor unprotected by collective bargaining.

11. That the legitimacy of the profit motive in the development and conduct of business be frankly recognized; and its control in the interest of the common good should not aim at its extinction.

12. That there must be an increase of wealth produced, if there is to be an adequate increase of wealth distributed.

13. That a proper objective of monetary policy is to avoid rapid and violent fluctuations in commodity price levels.

14. That after a man has given his productive life to industry, he should be assured of security against illness and dependent old age.

15. That a balance must be maintained between industrial and agricultural population; and between the rewards for industrial and agricultural activity.

16. That a healthy agricultural system will encourage the family farm rather than the commercial farm.

17. That a Christian Social Order involves decent housing for all the people.

18. That the family, rather than the individual, is the social and economic unit: and its needs should be recognized both by industry and by the State.

19. That there are natural rights possessed by human persons and families which God has given and which the State cannot abrogate.

20. That a Christian Social Order, organized on the basis of self-governing industries, occupations and professions, according to the plan proposed by Pius XI in his Encyclical on "Reconstructing the Social Order" will establish Social Justice and promote industrial peace.

21. That a Christian Social Order can be maintained only on the basis of a full acceptance of the person and the teachings of Jesus Christ.

Beyond the enunciation of these principles, we are charged with the further responsibility of translating them into action.

—National Catholic Welfare Conference Statement, 1938

9. "MY CREED AS AN AMERICAN CATHOLIC"

Catholics had served as Chief Justices of the Supreme Court, as Senators and Representatives, as Governors of States. But up to 1928 no Catholic had ever been even nominated to the Presidency by a major party. Alfred E. Smith's distinguished record as Governor of New York, his progressive social and economic views, and his strategic political position made him a logical candidate of the Democracy in 1928. Smith was, however, a devout Catholic, and his membership in and devotion to that church alarmed a great many Americans who were sincerely afraid of a divided allegiance. One of these, Charles C. Marshall, wrote a public letter to Governor Smith in which he set forth some of the grounds for objection to a Catholic in the White House. Governor Smith replied to this letter the following month. We give a substantial part of the Governor's reply, together with Editor Ellery Sedgwick's introductory remarks. It is probably unnecessary to add that anti-Catholicism played an important, and perhaps a decisive, part in Smith's defeat in the election of 1928.

THIS is an historic incident, historic for the country and for the Church. Now for the first time in the republic's history, under a constitution which forever forbids religious tests as qualifications for office, a candidate for the Presidency has been subjected to public questioning as to how he can give undivided allegiance to his country when his church restricts the freedom of his choice; and the candidate has answered—answered not deviously and with indirection, but straightforwardly, bravely, with the clear ring of candor.

It is an issue of infinite possibilities. Is the principle of religious tolerance, universal and complete, which every schoolboy has repeated for one hundred and fifty years, mere platitudinous vaporing? Can men worshiping God in their differing ways believe without reservation of conscience in a common political ideal? Is the United States of America based on a delusion? Can the vast experiment of the Republic, Protestant and Catholic, churched and unchurched, succeed?

And this is the converse of the question: Will the churches suffer their members to be really free? 'Thou shalt have none other gods but me,' thundered the Jewish Jehovah from Sinai, and ever since the gods of the churches have demanded that their control be not abridged nor diminished. But as the creeds clash about us, we remember that not in political programmes only may religion have its place separate and apart from politics, from public discussion, and from the laws of society. Quite elsewhere is it written, 'Render therefore unto Cæsar the things that are Cæsar's; and unto God the things that are God's.'

The discussion has served its purpose. Not in this campaign will whispering and innuendoes, shruggings and hunchings, usurp the place of reason and of argument. The thoughts rising almost unbidden in the minds of the least bigoted of us when we watch a Roman Catholic aspire to the Presidency of the United States have become matters of high, serious, and eloquent debate.

—THE EDITOR

CHARLES C. MARSHALL, ESQ.
DEAR SIR:—

In your open letter to me in the April *Atlantic Monthly* you 'impute' to American Catholics views which, if held by them, would leave open to question the loyalty and devotion to this country and its Constitution of more than twenty million American Catholic citizens. I am grateful to you for defining this issue in the open and for your courteous expression of the satisfaction it will bring to my fellow citizens for me to give 'a disclaimer of the convictions' thus imputed. Without mental reservation I can and do make that disclaimer. These convictions are held neither by me nor by any other American Catholic, as far as I know.

Before answering the argument of your letter, however, I must dispose of one of its implications. You put your questions to me in connection with my candidacy for the office of President of the United States. . . .

I should be a poor American and a poor Catholic alike if I injected religious discussion into a political campaign. Therefore I would ask you to accept this answer from me not as a candidate for any public office but as an American citizen, honored with high elective office, meeting a challenge to his patriotism and his intellectual integrity. Moreover, I call your attention to the fact that I am only a layman. The *Atlantic Monthly* describes you as 'an experienced attorney' who 'has made himself an authority upon canon law.' I am neither a lawyer nor a theologian. What knowledge of law I have was gained in the course of my long experience in the Legislature and as Chief Executive of New York State. I had no such opportunity to study theology.

My first thought was to answer you with just the faith that is in me. But I knew instinctively that your conclusions could be logically proved false. It seemed right, therefore, to take counsel with someone schooled in the Church law, from whom I learned whatever is hereafter set forth in definite answer to the theological questions you raise. . . .

Taking your letter as a whole and reducing it to commonplace English, you imply that there is conflict between religious loyalty to the Catholic faith and patriotic loyalty to the United States. Everything that has actually happened to me during my long public career leads me to know that no such thing as that is true. I have taken an oath of office in this State nineteen times. Each time I swore to defend and maintain the Constitution of the United States. All of this represents a period of public service in elective office almost continuous since 1903. I have never known any conflict between my official duties and my religious belief. No such conflict could exist. Certainly the people of this State recognize no such conflict. They have testified to my devotion to public duty by electing me to the highest office within their gift four times. You yourself do me the honor, in addressing me, to refer to 'your fidelity to the morality you have advocated in public and private life and to the religion you have revered; your great record of public trusts successfully and honestly discharged.' During the years I have discharged these trusts I have been a communicant of the Roman Catholic Church. If there were conflict, I, of all men, could not have escaped it, because I have not been a silent man, but a battler for social and political reform. These battles would in their very nature disclose this conflict if there were any.

I regard public education as one of the foremost functions of government and I have supported to the last degree the State Department of Education in every effort to promote our public-school system. The largest single item of increased appropriations under my administration appears in the educational group for the support of common schools. Since 1919, when I first became Governor, this item has grown from $9,000,000 to $82,500,000. My aim—and I may say I have succeeded in achieving it—has been legislation for child welfare, the protection of working men, women, and children, the modernization of the State's institutions for the care of helpless or unfortunate wards, the preservation of freedom of speech and opinion against the attack of war-time hysteria, and the complete reorganization of the structure of the government of the State.

I did not struggle for these things for any single element, but in the interest of all of the eleven million people who make up the State. In all of this work I had the support of churches of all denominations. I probably know as many ecclesiastics of my Church as any other layman. During my long and active public career I never received from any of them anything except co-operation and encouragement in the full and complete discharge of my duty to the State. Moreover, I am unable to understand how anything that I was taught to believe as a Catholic could possibly be in conflict with what is good citizenship. The essence of my faith is built upon the Commandments of God. The law of the land is built upon the Commandments of God. There can be no conflict between them.

Instead of quarreling among ourselves over dogmatic principles, it would be infinitely better if we joined together in inculcating obedience to these Commandments in the hearts and minds of the youth of the country as the surest and best road to happiness on this earth and to peace in the world to come. This is the common ideal of all religions. What we need is more religion for our young people, not less; and the way to get more religion is to stop the bickering among our sects which can only have for its effect the creation of doubt in the minds of our youth as to whether or not it is necessary to pay attention to religion at all.

Then I know your imputations are false when I recall the long list of other public servants of my faith who have loyally served the State. . . .

And I know your imputations are false when I recall the tens of thousands of young Catholics who have risked and sacrificed their lives in defense of our country. These fundamentals of life could not be true unless your imputations were false.

But, wishing to meet you on your own ground, I address myself to your definite questions, against which I have thus far made only general statements. I must first call attention to the fact that you often divorce sentences from their context in such a way as to give them something other than their real meaning. I will specify. . . .

You quote from the *Catholic Encyclopedia* that my Church 'regards dogmatic intolerance, not alone as her incontestable right, but as her sacred duty.' And you say that these words show that Catholics are taught to be politically, socially, and intellectually intolerant of all other people. If you had read the whole of that article in the *Catholic Encyclopedia*, you would know that the real meaning of these words is that for Catholics alone the Church recognizes no deviation from complete acceptance of its dogma. These words are used in a chapter dealing with that subject only. The very same article in another chapter dealing with toleration toward non-Catholics contains these words: 'The intolerant man is avoided as much as possible by every high-minded person. . . . The man who is tolerant in every emergency is alone lovable.' The phrase 'dogmatic intolerance' does not mean that Catholics are to be dogmatically intolerant of other people, but merely that inside the Catholic Church they are to be intolerant of any variance from the dogma of the Church. . . .

But I go further to demonstrate that the true construction of your quotations by the leaders of Catholic thought is diametrically the opposite of what you suggest it to be.

I

Your first proposition is that Catholics believe that other religions should, in the United States, be tolerated only as a matter of favor and that there should be an established church. You may find some dream of an ideal of a Catholic State, having no relation whatever to actuality, somewhere described. But, voicing the best Catholic thought on this subject, Dr. John A. Ryan, Professor of Moral Theology at the Catholic University of America, writes in *The State and the Church* of the encyclical of Pope Leo XIII, quoted by you:—

'In practice, however, the foregoing propositions have full application only to the completely Catholic State. . . . The propositions of Pope Pius IX condemning the toleration of non-Catholic sects do not now, says

Father Pohle, "apply even to Spain or the South American republics, to say nothing of countries possessing a greatly mixed population." He lays down the following general rule: "When several religions have firmly established themselves and taken root in the same territory, nothing else remains for the State than to exercise tolerance towards them all, or, as conditions exist to-day, to make complete religious liberty for individual and religious bodies a principle of government." '

That is good Americanism and good Catholicism. . . .

The American prelates of our Church stoutly defend our constitutional declaration of equality of all religions before the law. . . .

With these great Catholics I stand squarely in support of the provisions of the Constitution which guarantee religious freedom and equality.

II

I come now to the speculation with which theorists have played for generations as to the respective functions of Church and State. You claim that the Roman Catholic Church holds that, if conflict arises, the Church must prevail over the State. You write as though there were some Catholic authority or tribunal to decide with respect to such conflict. Of course there is no such thing. As Dr. Ryan writes: 'The Catholic doctrine concedes, nay, maintains, that the State is coördinate with the Church and equally independent and supreme in its own distinct sphere.'

What is the Protestant position? The Articles of Religion of your Protestant Episcopal Church (XXXVII) declare: 'The Power of the Civil Magistrate extendeth to all men, as well Clergy as Laity, in all things temporal; but hath no authority in things purely spiritual.'

Your Church, just as mine, is voicing the injunction of our common Saviour to render unto Cæsar the things that are Cæsar's, and unto God the things that are God's.

What is this conflict about which you talk? It may exist in some lands which do not guarantee religious freedom. But in the wildest dreams of your imagination you cannot conjure up a possible conflict between religious principle and political duty in the United States, except on the unthinkable hypothesis that some law were to be passed which violated the common morality of all God-fearing men. And if you can conjure up such a conflict, how would a Protestant resolve it? Obviously by the dictates of his conscience. That is exactly what a Catholic would do. . . .

It is a well-known fact that I have made all of my appointments to public office on the basis of merit and have never asked any man about his religious belief. In the first month of this year there gathered in the Capitol at Albany the first Governor's cabinet that ever sat in this State. It was composed, under my appointment, of two Catholics, thirteen Protestants, and one Jew. The man closest to me in the administration of the government of the State of New York is he who bears the title of Assistant to the Governor. He had been connected with the Governor's office for thirty years, in subordinate capacities, until I promoted him to the position which makes him the sharer with me of my every thought and hope and ambition in the administration of the State. He is a Protestant, a Republican, and a thirty-second-degree Mason. In my public life I have exemplified that complete separation of Church from State which is the faith of American Catholics to-day.

III

I next come to education. You admit that the Supreme Court guaranteed to Catholics the right to maintain their parochial schools; and you ask me whether they would have so ruled if it had been shown that children in parochial schools were taught that the State should show discrimination between religions, that Protestants should be recognized only as a matter of favor, that they should be intolerant to non-Catholics, and that the laws of the State could be flouted on the ground of the imaginary conflict. My summary answer is: I and all my children went to a parochial school. I never heard of any such stuff being taught or of anybody who claimed that it was. That any group of Catholics would teach it is unthinkable. . . .

VI

I summarize my creed as an American Catholic. I believe in the worship of God according to the faith and practice of the Roman Catholic Church. I recognize no power in the institutions of my Church to interfere with the operations of the Constitution of the United States or the enforcement of the law of the land. I believe in absolute freedom of conscience for all men and in equality of all churches, all sects, and all beliefs before the law as a matter of right and not as a matter of favor. I believe in the absolute separation of Church and State and in the strict enforcement of the provisions of the Constitution that Congress shall make no law respecting an establishment of religion or prohibiting the free exercise thereof. I believe that no tribunal of any church has any power to make any decree of any force in the law of the land, other than to establish the status of its own communicants within its own church. I believe in the support of the public school as one of the corner stones of American liberty. I believe in the right of every parent to choose whether his child shall be educated in the public school or in a religious school supported by those of his own faith. I believe in the principle of noninterference by this country in the internal affairs of other nations and that we should stand steadfastly against any such interference by whomsoever it may be urged. And I believe in the common brotherhood of man under the common fatherhood of God.

In this spirit I join with fellow Americans of all creeds in a fervent prayer that never again in this land will any public servant be challenged because of the faith in which he has tried to walk humbly with his God.

Very truly yours,
ALFRED E. SMITH
—ALFRED E. SMITH, Reply to Charles C. Marshall, 1927

10. "A WALL BETWEEN CHURCH AND STATE . . . HIGH AND IMPREGNABLE"

No one, Protestant or Catholic, denied the desirability of a separation of church and state in America, but there was no general agreement on what constituted separation. Was state aid to religion, of any kind, a violation of the principle of separation? If so, what of tax exemption for church property? Was state aid to church schools in the form of subsidized lunches, or of free bus transportation, a violation of the principle? In a famous case, Everson versus Board of Education, in 1947, the Supreme Court held that such indirect aid was not a contribution to religion, but to school children and not, therefore, a violation of the principle of separation. There was, however, a strong dissenting opinion. The issue came up in somewhat different form in the case of McCollum versus Board of Education in the following year. The question here

*was that of using the facilities of the public schools for "released time"
religious instruction—a widespread practice affecting some two million
children throughout the country.*

ACTION for mandamus by the People of the State of Illinois, on the
relation of Vashti McCollum, against the Board of Education of
School District No. 71, Champaign County, Ill., and others, to require
the Board of Education to adopt and enforce rules and regulations prohibiting all instruction in and teaching of all religious education in all
public schools in the district and in all public school houses and buildings in the district when occupied by public schools.

BLACK, J. This case relates to the power of a state to utilize its tax-
supported public school system in aid of religious instruction insofar as
that power may be restricted by the First and Fourteenth Amendments
to the Federal Constitution.

The appellant, Vashti McCollum, began this action for mandamus
against the Champaign Board of Education in the Circuit Court of
Champaign County, Illinois. Her asserted interest was that of a resident
and taxpayer of Champaign and of a parent whose child was then enrolled in the Champaign public schools. Illinois has a compulsory education law which, with exceptions, requires parents to send their children, aged seven to sixteen, to its tax-supported public schools where
the children are to remain in attendance during the hours when the
schools are regularly in session. Parents who violate this law commit a
misdemeanor punishable by fine unless the children attend private or
parochial schools which meet educational standards fixed by the State.
District boards of education are given general supervisory powers over
the use of the public school buildings within the school districts.

Appellant's petition for mandamus alleged that religious teachers, employed by private religious groups, were permitted to come weekly into
the school buildings during the regular hours set apart for secular teaching, and then and there for a period of thirty minutes substitute their
religious teaching for the secular education provided under the compulsory education law. The petitioner charged that this joint public-
school religious-group program violated the First and Fourteenth
Amendments to the United States Constitution. . . .

Although there are disputes between the parties as to various inferences that may or may not properly be drawn from the evidence concerning the religious program, the following facts are shown by the record without dispute. In 1940 interested members of the Jewish, Roman Catholic, and a few of the Protestant faiths formed a voluntary association called the Champaign Council on Religious Education. They obtained permission from the Board of Education to offer classes in religious instruction to public school pupils in grades four to nine inclusive. Classes were made up of pupils whose parents signed printed cards requesting that their children be permitted to attend; they were held weekly, thirty minutes for the lower grades, forty-five minutes for the higher. The council employed the religious teachers at no expense to the school authorities, but the instructors were subject to the approval and supervision of the superintendent of schools. The classes were taught in three separate religious groups by Protestant teachers, Catholic priests, and a Jewish rabbi, although for the past several years there have apparently been no classes instructed in the Jewish religion. Classes were conducted in the regular classrooms of the school building. Students who did not choose to take the religious instruction were not released from public school duties; they were required to leave their classrooms and go to some other place in the school building for pursuit of their secular studies. On the other hand, students who were released from secular study for the religious instructions were required to be present at the religious classes. Reports of their presence or absence were to be made to their secular teachers.

The foregoing facts, without reference to others that appear in the record, show the use of tax-supported property for religious instruction and the close cooperation between the school authorities and the religious council in promoting religious education. The operation of the state's compulsory education system thus assists and is integrated with the program of religious instruction carried on by separate religious sects. Pupils compelled by law to go to school for secular education are released in part from their legal duty upon the condition that they attend the religious classes. This is beyond all question a utilization of the tax-established and tax-supported public school system to aid religious groups to spread their faith. And it falls squarely under the ban of the First Amendment (made applicable to the States by the Fourteenth) as we interpreted it in Everson v. Board of Education. There we said: "Neither a state nor the Federal Government can set up a church. Neither can pass laws which aid one religion, aid all religions, or prefer one religion over another. Neither can force nor influence a person to go to or to remain away from church against his will or force him to profess a belief or disbelief in any religion. No person can be punished for entertaining or professing religious beliefs or disbeliefs, for church attendance or nonattendance. No tax in any amount, large or small, can be levied to support any religious activities or institutions, whatever they may be called, or whatever form they may adopt to teach or practice religion. Neither a state nor the Federal Government can, openly or secretly, participate in the affairs of any religious organizations or groups, and vice versa. In the words of Jefferson, the clause against establishment of religion by law was intended to erect 'a wall of separation between Church and State.' " The majority in the Everson case, and the minority as shown by quotations from the dissenting views agreed that the First Amendment's language, properly interpreted, had erected a wall of separation between Church and State. They disagreed as to the facts shown by the record and as to the proper application of the First Amendment's language to those facts.

Recognizing that the Illinois program is barred by the First and Fourteenth Amendments if we adhere to the views expressed both by the majority and the minority in the Everson case, counsel for the respondents challenge those views as dicta and urge that we reconsider and repudiate them. They argue that historically the First Amendment was intended to forbid only government preference of one religion over another, not an impartial governmental assistance of all religions. In addition they ask that we distinguish or overrule our holding in the Everson case that the Fourteenth Amendment made the "establishment of religion" clause of the First Amendment applicable as a prohibition against the States. After giving full consideration to the arguments presented we are unable to accept either of these contentions.

To hold that a state cannot consistently with the First and Fourteenth Amendments utilize its public school system to aid any or all religious faiths or sects in the dissemination of their doctrines and ideals does not, as counsel urge, manifest a governmental hostility to religion or religious teachings. A manifestation of such hostility would be at war with our national tradition as embodied in the First Amendment's guaranty of the free exercise of religion. For the First Amendment rests upon the premise that both religion and government can best work to achieve their lofty aims if each is left free from the other within its respective sphere. Or, as we said in the Everson case, the First Amendment has erected a wall between Church and State which must be kept high and impregnable.

Here not only are the state's tax-supported public school buildings used for the dissemination of religious doctrines. The State also affords sectarian groups an invaluable aid in that it helps to provide pupils for their religious classes through use of the state's compulsory public school machinery. This is not separation of Church and State.

The cause is reversed and remanded to the State Supreme Court for proceedings not inconsistent with this opinion.

—Justice Black,
Opinion in McCollum *v*. Board of Education, 1948

11. RELIGIOUS FREEDOM AND THE FLAG SALUTE

"A grave responsibility confronts this Court," said Mr. Justice Frankfurter in the majority opinion in the first flag salute case, "whenever in the course of litigation it must reconcile the conflicting claims of liberty and authority." We have dealt elsewhere, and at length, with this great issue of liberty and authority, an issue that affects almost every aspect of government and society. Certainly it profoundly affects the question of the relations of church and state. How perplexing that question could be was made clear in the two flag salute cases—the Gobitis and the Barnette cases. The conflicting claims here were dramatic and even extreme. On the one hand there was the requirement of the state of compulsory flag salute from all school children (with penalties for the parents who withdrew children from school), and on the other hand the religious principle of the Jehovah's Witnesses that such action was contrary to the Scriptures. Which was to prevail: the state's requirement of a gesture designed to further national unity, or the individual's claim that such a gesture violated his conscience?

In the first of these cases the Court, speaking through Mr. Justice Frankfurter, gave priority to the claims of national unity—or, more properly, to the state's claim that a flag salute would strengthen such unity. There was, however, a powerful dissenting opinion from Chief Justice Stone. This encouraged those who thought the compulsory flag salute a violation of the First Amendment to press for a reconsideration of the whole issue, and in the second flag salute case—West Virginia versus Barnette—the Court dramatically reversed its earlier position and struck down the offending flag salute laws. It would be a grievous error to suppose that Justice Frankfurter and those who agreed with him in the first case approved of compulsory flag salutes or disparaged the importance of religious liberty. The issue was far more complex than that. It had to do with the right of a state to select its own means for furthering a valid end, national unity. What Frankfurter held, essentially, was that the flag salute was a foolish and shortsighted means to this end, but that it was not for the Court to deny the state the right to be foolish and shortsighted. What Justice Jackson held, in the West Virginia case, was that the requirement of a compulsory flag salute was more than foolish; it was a violation of the First Amendment. Where wise and good men differ on a question of this complexity and delicacy we should be slow to take sides. What we should note and keep ever in mind is the area of agreement. Thus Justice Frankfurter said, "For ourselves, we might be tempted to say that the deepest patriotism is best engendered by giving unfettered scope to the most crotchety beliefs." Thus Justice Jackson said, "Compulsory unification of opinion achieves only the unanimity of the graveyard."

A. "The Flag Is the Symbol of Our National Unity"

FRANKFURTER, J. A grave responsibility confronts this Court whenever in course of litigation it must reconcile the conflicting claims of liberty and authority. But when the liberty invoked is liberty of conscience, and the authority is authority to safeguard the nation's fellowship, judicial conscience is put to its severest test. Of such a nature is the present controversy.

Lillian Gobitis, aged twelve, and her brother William, aged ten, were expelled from the public schools of Minersville, Pennsylvania, for refusing to salute the national flag as part of a daily school exercise. The local Board of Education required both teachers and pupils to participate in this ceremony. The ceremony is a familiar one. The right hand is placed on the breast and the following pledge recited in unison: "I pledge allegiance to my flag, and to the Republic for which it stands; one nation indivisible, with liberty and justice for all." While the words are spoken, teachers and pupils extend their right hands in salute to the flag. The Gobitis family are affiliated with "Jehovah's Witnesses," for whom the Bible as the Word of God is the supreme authority. The children had been brought up conscientiously to believe that such a gesture of respect for the flag was forbidden by command of scripture.

The Gobitis children were of an age for which Pennsylvania makes school attendance compulsory. Thus they were denied a free education and their parents had to put them into private schools. To be relieved of the financial burden thereby entailed, their father, on behalf of the children and in his own behalf, brought this suit. He sought to enjoin the authorities from continuing to exact participation in the flag-salute ceremony as a condition of his children's attendance at the Minersville school. . . .

We must decide whether the requirement of participation in such a ceremony, exacted from a child who refuses upon sincere religious grounds, infringes without due process of law the liberty guaranteed by the Fourteenth Amendment.

Centuries of strife over the erection of particular dogmas as exclusive or all-comprehending faiths led to the inclusion of a guarantee for religious freedom in the Bill of Rights. The First Amendment, and the Fourteenth through its absorption of the First, sought to guard against repetition of those bitter religious struggles by prohibiting the establishment of a state religion and by securing to every sect the free exercise of its faith. So pervasive is the acceptance of this precious right that its scope is brought into question, as here, only when the conscience of individuals collides with the felt necessities of society.

Certainly the affirmative pursuit of one's convictions about the ultimate mystery of the universe and man's relation to it is placed beyond the reach of law. Government may not interfere with organized or individual expression of belief or disbelief. Propagation of belief—or even of disbelief in the supernatural—is protected, whether in church or chapel, mosque or synagogue, tabernacle or meetinghouse. Likewise the Constitution assures generous immunity to the individual from imposition of penalties for offending, in the course of his own religious activities, the religious views of others, be they a minority or those who are dominant in government.

But the manifold character of man's relations may bring his conception of religious duty into conflict with the secular interests of his fellow-men. When does the constitutional guarantee compel exemption from doing what society thinks necessary for the promotion of some great common end, or from a penalty for conduct which appears dangerous to the general good? To state the problem is to recall the truth that no single principle can answer all of life's complexities. The right to freedom of religious belief, however dissident and however obnoxious to the cherished beliefs of others—even of a majority—is itself the denial of an absolute. But to affirm that the freedom to follow conscience has itself no limits in the life of a society would deny that very plurality of principles which, as a matter of history, underlies protection of religious toleration. Compare Mr. Justice Holmes in Hudson County Water Co. v. McCarter. Our present task then, as so often the case with courts, is to reconcile two rights in order to prevent either from destroying the other. But, because in safeguarding conscience we are dealing with interests so subtle and so dear, every possible leeway should be given to the claims of religious faith.

In the judicial enforcement of religious freedom we are concerned with a historic concept. See Mr. Justice Cardozo in Hamilton v. Regents. The religious liberty which the Constitution protects has never excluded legislation of general scope not directed against doctrinal loyalties of particular sects. Judicial nullification of legislation cannot be justified by attributing to the framers of the Bill of Rights views for which there is no historic warrant. Conscientious scruples have not, in the course of the long struggle for religious toleration, relieved the individual from obedience to a general law not aimed at the promotion or restriction of religious beliefs. The mere possession of religious convictions which contradict the relevant concerns of a political society does not relieve the citizen from the discharge of political responsibilities. The necessity for this adjustment has again and again been recognized. In a number of situations the exertion of political authority has been sustained, while basic considerations of religious freedom have been left inviolate. Reynolds v. United States, Davis v. Beason, Selective Draft Law Cases, Hamilton v. Regents. In all these cases the general laws in question, upheld in their application to those who refused obedience from religious conviction, were manifestations of specific powers of government deemed by the legislature essential to secure and maintain that orderly, tranquil, and free society without which religious toleration itself is unattainable. Nor does the freedom of speech assured by Due Process move in a more absolute circle of immunity than that enjoyed by religious freedom. Even if it were assumed that freedom of speech goes beyond the historic concept of full opportunity to utter and to disseminate views, however heretical or offensive to dominant opinion, and includes freedom from conveying what may be deemed an implied but rejected affirmation, the question remains whether school children, like the Gobitis children, must be excused from conduct required of all the other children in the promotion of national cohesion. We are dealing with an interest inferior to none in the hierarchy of legal values. National unity is the basis of national security. To deny the legislature the right to select appropriate means for its attainment presents a totally different order of problem from that of the propriety of subordinating the possible ugliness of littered streets to the free expression of opinion through distribution of handbills.

Situations like the present are phases of the profoundest problem confronting a democracy—the problem which Lincoln cast in memorable dilemma: "Must a government of necessity be too strong for the liberties of its people, or too weak to maintain its own existence?" No mere textual reading or logical talisman can solve the dilemma. And when the issue demands judicial determination, it is not the personal notion of judges of what wise adjustment requires which must prevail.

Unlike the instances we have cited, the case before us is not concerned with an exertion of legislative power for the promotion of some specific need or interest of secular society—the protection of the family, the promotion of health, the common defense, the raising of public revenues to defray the cost of government. But all these specific activities of government presuppose the existence of an organized political society. The ultimate foundation of a free society is the binding tie of cohesive sentiment. Such a sentiment is fostered by all those agencies of the mind and spirit which may serve to gather up the traditions of a people, transmit them from generation to generation, and thereby create that continuity of a treasured common life which constitutes a civilization. "We live by symbols." The flag is the symbol of our national unity, transcending all internal differences, however large, within the framework of the Constitution. This Court has had occasion to say that ". . . the flag is the symbol of the nation's power,—the emblem of freedom in its truest, best sense. . . . it signifies government resting on the consent of the governed; liberty regulated by law; the protection of the weak against the strong; security against the exercise of arbitrary power; and absolute safety for free institutions against foreign aggression." Halter v. Nebraska.

The case before us must be viewed as though the legislature of Pennsylvania had itself formally directed the flag-salute for the children of Minersville; had made no exemption for children whose parents were possessed of conscientious scruples like those of the Gobitis family; and had indicated its belief in the desirable ends to be secured by having its public school children share a common experience at those periods of development when their minds are supposedly receptive to its assimilation, by an exercise appropriate in time and place and setting, and one designed to evoke in them appreciation of the nation's hopes and dreams, its sufferings and sacrifices. The precise issue, then, for us to decide is whether the legislatures of the various states and the authorities in a thousand counties and school districts of this country are barred from determining the appropriateness of various means to evoke that unifying sentiment without which there can ultimately be no liberties, civil or religious. To stigmatize legislative judgment in providing for this universal gesture of respect for the symbol of our national life in the setting of the common school as a lawless inroad on that freedom of conscience which the Constitution protects, would amount to no less than the pronouncement of pedagogical and psychological dogma in a field where courts possess no marked and certainly no controlling competence. The influences which help toward a common feeling for the common country are manifold. Some may seem harsh and others no doubt are foolish. Surely, however, the end is legitimate. And the effective means for its attainment are still so uncertain and so unauthenticated by science as to preclude us from putting the widely prevalent belief in flag-saluting beyond the pale of legislative power. It mocks reason and denies our whole history to find in the allowance of a requirement to salute our flag on fitting occasions the seeds of sanction for obeisance to a leader.

The wisdom of training children in patriotic impulses by those compulsions which necessarily pervade so much of the educational process is not for our independent judgment. Even were we convinced of the folly of such a measure, such belief would be no proof of its unconstitutionality. For ourselves, we might be tempted to say that the deepest patriotism is best engendered by giving unfettered scope to the most crotchety beliefs. Perhaps it is best, even from the standpoint of those interests which ordinances like the one under review seek to promote, to give to the least popular sect leave from conformities like those here in issue. But the court-room is not the arena for debating issues of educational policy. It is not our province to choose among competing considerations in the subtle process of securing effective loyalty to the traditional ideals of democracy, while respecting at the same time individual idiosyncracies among a people so diversified in racial origins and religious allegiances. So to hold would in effect make us the school board for the country. That authority has not been given to this Court, nor should we assume it.

We are dealing here with the formative period in the development of citizenship. Great diversity of psychological and ethical opinion exists among us concerning the best way to train children for their place in society. Because of these differences and because of reluctance to permit a single, iron-cast system of education to be imposed upon a nation compounded of so many strains, we have held that, even though public education is one of our most cherished democratic institutions, the Bill of Rights bars a state from compelling all children to attend the public schools. Pierce v. Society of the Sisters of the Holy Names of Jesus and Mary. But it is a very different thing for this Court to exercise censorship over the conviction of legislatures that a particular program or exercise will best promote in the minds of children who attend the common schools an attachment to the institutions of their country.

What the school authorities are really asserting is the right to awaken in the child's mind considerations as to the significance of the flag contrary to those implanted by the parent. In such an attempt the state is normally at a disadvantage in competing with the parent's authority, so long—and this is the vital aspect of religious toleration—as parents are unmolested in their right to counteract by their own persuasiveness the wisdom and rightness of those loyalties which the state's educational system is seeking to promote. Except where the transgression of constitutional liberty is too plain for argument, personal freedom is best maintained—so long as the remedial channels of the democratic process remain open and unobstructed—when it is ingrained in a people's habits and not enforced against popular policy by the coercion of adjudicated law. That the flag-salute is an allowable portion of a school program for those who do not invoke conscientious scruples is surely not debatable. But for us to insist that, though the ceremony may be required, exceptional immunity must be given to dissidents, is to maintain that there is no basis for a legislative judgment that such an exemption might introduce elements of difficulty into the school discipline, might cast doubts in the minds of the other children which would themselves weaken the effect of the exercise.

The preciousness of the family relation, the authority and independence which give dignity to parenthood, indeed the enjoyment of all freedom, presuppose the kind of ordered society which is summarized by our flag. A society which is dedicated to the preservation of these ultimate values of civilization may in self-protection utilize the educational process for inculcating those almost unconscious feelings which bind men together in a comprehending loyalty, whatever may be their lesser differences and difficulties. That is to say, the process may be utilized so long as men's right to believe as they please, to win others to their way of belief, and their right to assemble in their chosen places of worship for the devotional ceremonies of their faith, are all fully respected.

Judicial review, itself a limitation on popular government, is a fundamental part of our constitutional scheme. But to the legislature no less than to courts is committed the guardianship of deeply-cherished liberties. Where all the effective means of inducing political changes are left free from interference, education in the abandonment of foolish legislation is itself a training in liberty. To fight out the wise use of legislative authority in the forum of public opinion and before legislative assemblies rather than to transfer such a contest to the judicial arena, serves to vindicate the self-confidence of a free people.

Reversed.

—JUSTICE FRANKFURTER, Opinion in Gobitis Case, 1940

B. "No Official, High or Petty, Can Prescribe What Shall Be Orthodox In . . . Matters of Opinion"

JACKSON, J. This case calls upon us to reconsider a precedent decision, as the Court throughout its history often has been required to do. Before turning to the Gobitis case, however, it is desirable to notice certain characteristics by which this controversy is distinguished.

The freedom asserted by these respondents does not bring them into collision with rights asserted by any other individual. It is such conflicts which most frequently require intervention of the State to determine where the rights of one end and those of another begin. But the refusal of these persons to participate in the ceremony does not interfere with or deny rights of others to do so. Nor is there any question in this case that their behavior is peaceable and orderly. The sole conflict is between authority and rights of the individuals. The State asserts power to condition access to public education on making a prescribed sign and profession and at the same time to coerce attendance by punishing both parent and child. The latter stand on a right of self-determination in matters that touch individual opinion and personal attitude.

As the present Chief Justice said in dissent in the Gobitis case, the State may "require teaching by instruction and study of all in our history and in the structure and organization of our government, including the guaranties of civil liberty which tend to inspire patriotism and love of country." Here, however, we are dealing with a compulsion of students to declare a belief. They are not merely made acquainted with the flag salute so that they may be informed as to what it is or even what it means. The issue here is whether this slow and easily neglected route to aroused loyalties constitutionally may be short-cut by substituting a compulsory salute and slogan. This issue is not prejudiced by the Court's previous holding that where a State, without compelling attendance, extends college facilities to pupils who voluntarily enroll, it may prescribe military training as part of the course without offense to the Constitution. It was held that those who take advantage of its opportunities may not on ground of conscience refuse compliance with such conditions. In the present case attendance is not optional. That case is also to be distinguished from the present one because, independently of college privileges or requirements, the State has power to raise militia and impose the duties of service therein upon its citizens.

There is no doubt that, in connection with the pledges, the flag salute is a form of utterance. Symbolism is a primitive but effective way of communicating ideas. The use of an emblem or flag to symbolize some system, idea, institution, or personality, is a short cut from mind to mind. Causes and nations, political parties, lodges and ecclesiastical groups seek to knit the loyalty of their followings to a flag or banner, a color or design. The State announces rank, function, and authority through crowns and maces, uniforms and black robes; the church speaks through the Cross, the Crucifix, the altar and shrine, and clerical raiment. Symbols of State often convey political ideas just as religious symbols come to convey theological ones. Associated with many of these symbols are appropriate gestures of acceptance of respect: a salute, a bowed or bared head, a bended knee. A person gets from a symbol the meaning he puts into it, and what is one man's comfort and inspiration is another's jest and scorn....

It is also to be noted that the compulsory flag salute and pledge requires affirmation of a belief and an attitude of mind. It is not clear whether the regulation contemplates that pupils forego any contrary convictions of their own and become unwilling converts to the prescribed ceremony or whether it will be acceptable if they simulate assent by words without belief and by a gesture barren of meaning. It is now a commonplace that censorship or suppression of expression of opinion is tolerated by our Constitution only when the expression presents a clear and present danger of action of a kind the State is empowered to prevent and punish. It would seem that involuntary affirmation could be commanded only on even more immediate and urgent grounds than silence. But here the power of compulsion is invoked without any allegation that remaining passive during a flag salute ritual creates a clear and present danger that would justify an effort even to muffle expression. To sustain the compulsory flag salute we are required to say that a Bill of Rights which guards the individual's right to speak his own mind, left it open to public authorities to compel him to utter what is not in his mind.

Whether the First Amendment to the Constitution will permit officials to order observance of ritual of this nature does not depend upon whether as a voluntary exercise we would think it to be good, bad or merely innocuous. Any credo of nationalism is likely to include what some disapprove or to omit what others think essential, and to give off different overtones as it takes on different accents or interpretations. If official power exists to coerce acceptance of any patriotic creed, what it shall contain cannot be decided by courts, but must be largely discretionary with the ordaining authority, whose power to prescribe would no doubt include power to amend. Hence validity of the asserted power to force an American citizen publicly to profess any statement of belief or to engage in any ceremony of assent to one presents questions of power that must be considered independently of any idea we may have as to the utility of the ceremony in question.

Nor does the issue as we see it turn on one's possession of particular religious views or the sincerity with which they are held. While religion supplies respondents' motive for enduring the discomforts of making the issue in this case, many citizens who do not share these religious views hold such a compulsory rite to infringe constitutional liberty of the individual. It is not necessary to inquire whether non-conformist beliefs will exempt from the duty to salute unless we first find power to make the salute a legal duty.

The Gobitis decision, however, *assumed*, as did the argument in that case and in this, that power exists in the State to impose the flag salute discipline upon school children in general. The Court only examined and rejected a claim based on religious beliefs of immunity from an unquestioned general rule. The question which underlies the flag salute controversy is whether such a ceremony so touching matters of opinion and political attitude may be imposed upon the individual by official authority under powers committed to any political organization under our Constitution. We examine rather than assume existence of this power and, against this broader definition of issues in this case, re-examine specific grounds assigned for the Gobitis decision.

1. It was said that the flag-salute controversy confronted the Court with "the problem which Lincoln cast in memorable dilemma: 'Must a government of necessity be too *strong* for the liberties of its people, or too *weak* to maintain its own existence?' " and that the answer must be in favor of strength. . . . Such oversimplification, so handy in political debate, often lacks the precision necessary to postulates of judicial reasoning. If validly applied to this problem, the utterance cited would resolve every issue of power in favor of those in authority and would require us to override every liberty thought to weaken or delay execution of their policies.

Government of limited power need not be anemic government. Assurance that rights are secure tends to diminish fear and jealousy of strong government, and by making us feel safe to live under it makes for its better support. Without promise of a limiting Bill of Rights it is doubtful if our Constitution could have mustered enough strength to enable its ratification. To enforce those rights today is not to choose weak government over strong government. It is only to adhere as a means of strength to individual freedom of mind in preference to officially disciplined uniformity for which history indicates a disappointing and disastrous end.

The subject now before us exemplifies this principle. Free public education, if faithful to the ideal of secular instruction and political neutrality, will not be partisan or enemy of any class, creed, party, or faction. If it is to impose any ideological discipline, however, each party or denomination must seek to control, or failing that, to weaken the influence of the educational system. Observance of the limitations of the Constitution will not weaken government in the field appropriate for its exercise.

2. It was also considered in the Gobitis case that functions of educa-

tional officers in states, counties and school districts were such that to interfere with their authority "would in effect make us the school board for the country."

The Fourteenth Amendment, as now applied to the States, protects the citizen against the State itself and all of its creatures—Boards of Education not excepted. These have, of course, important, delicate, and highly discretionary functions, but none that they may not perform within the limits of the Bill of Rights. . . .

3. The Gobitis opinion reasoned that this is a field "where courts possess no marked and certainly no controlling competence," that it is committed to the legislatures as well as the courts to guard cherished liberties and that it is constitutionally appropriate to "fight out the wise use of legislative authority in the forum of public opinion and before legislative assemblies rather than to transfer such a contest to the judicial arena," since all the "effective means of inducing political changes are left free."

The very purpose of a Bill of Rights was to withdraw certain subjects from the vicissitudes of political controversy, to place them beyond the reach of majorities and officials and to establish them as legal principles to be applied by the courts. One's right to life, liberty, and property, to free speech, a free press, freedom of worship and assembly, and other fundamental rights may not be submitted to vote; they depend on the outcome of no elections.

In weighing arguments of the parties it is important to distinguish between the due process clause of the Fourteenth Amendment as an instrument for transmitting the principles of the First Amendment and those cases in which it is applied for its own sake. The test of legislation which collides with the Fourteenth Amendment, because it also collides with the principles of the First, is much more definite than the test when only the Fourteenth is involved. Much of the vagueness of the due process clause disappears when the specific prohibitions of the First become its standard. The right of a State to regulate, for example, a public utility may well include, so far as the due process test is concerned, power to impose all of the restrictions which a legislature may have a "rational basis" for adopting. But freedoms of speech and of press, of assembly, and of worship may not be infringed on such slender grounds. They are susceptible of restriction only to prevent grave and immediate danger to interests which the state may lawfully protect. It is important to note that while it is the Fourteenth Amendment which bears directly upon the State it is the more specific limiting principles of the First Amendment that finally govern this case.

Nor does our duty to apply the Bill of Rights to assertions of official authority depend upon our possession of marked competence in the field where the invasion of rights occurs. True, the task of translating the majestic generalities of the Bill of Rights, conceived as part of the pattern of liberal government in the eighteenth century, into concrete restraints on officials dealing with the problems of the twentieth century, is one to disturb self-confidence. These principles grew in soil which also produced a philosophy that the individual was the center of society, that his liberty was attainable through mere absence of governmental restraints, and that government should be entrusted with few controls and only the mildest supervision over men's affairs. We must transplant these rights to a soil in which the *laissez-faire* concept or principle of non-interference has withered at least as to economic affairs, and social advancements are increasingly sought through closer integration of society and through expanded and strengthened governmental controls. These changed conditions often deprive precedents of reliability and cast us more than we would choose upon our own judgment. But we act in these matters not by authority of our competence but by force of our commissions. We cannot, because of modest estimates of our competence in such specialties as public education, withhold the judgment that history authenticates as the function of this Court when liberty is infringed.

4. Lastly, and this is the very heart of the Gobitis opinion, it reasons that "National unity is the basis of national security," that the authorities have "the right to select appropriate means for its attainment," and hence reaches the conclusion that such compulsory measures toward "national unity" are constitutional. Upon the verity of this assumption depends our answer in this case.

National unity as an end which officials may foster by persuasion and example is not in question. The problem is whether under our Constitution compulsion as here employed is a permissible means for its achievement.

Struggles to coerce uniformity of sentiment in support of some end thought essential to their time and country have been waged by many good as well as by evil men. Nationalism is a relatively recent phenomenon but at other times and places the ends have been racial or territorial security, support of a dynasty or regime, and particular plans for saving souls. As first and moderate methods to attain unity have failed, those bent on its accomplishment must resort to an ever-increasing severity. As governmental pressure toward unity becomes greater, so strife becomes more bitter as to whose unity it shall be. Probably no deeper division of our people could proceed from any provocation than from finding it necessary to choose what doctrine and whose program public educational officials shall compel youth to unite in embracing. Ultimate futility of such attempts to compel coherence is the lesson of every such effort from the Roman drive to stamp out Christianity as a disturber of its pagan unity, the Inquisition, as a means to religious and dynastic unity, the Siberian exiles as a means to Russian unity, down to the fast failing efforts of our present totalitarian enemies. Those who begin coercive elimination of dissent soon find themselves exterminating dissenters. Compulsory unification of opinion achieves only the unanimity of the graveyard.

It seems trite but necessary to say that the First Amendment to our Constitution was designed to avoid these ends by avoiding these beginnings. There is no mysticism in the American concept of the State or of the nature or origin of its authority. We set up government by consent of the governed, and the Bill of Rights denies those in power any legal opportunity to coerce that consent. Authority here is to be controlled by public opinion, not public opinion by authority.

The case is made difficult not because the principles of its decision are obscure but because the flag involved is our own. Nevertheless, we apply the limitations of the Constitution with no fear that freedom to be intellectually and spiritually diverse or even contrary will disintegrate the social organization. To believe that patriotism will not flourish if patriotic ceremonies are voluntary and spontaneous instead of a compulsory routine is to make an unflattering estimate of the appeal of our institutions to free minds. We can have intellectual individualism and the rich cultural diversities that we owe to exceptional minds only at the price of occasional eccentricity and abnormal attitudes. When they are so harmless to others or to the State as those we deal with here, the price is not too great. But freedom to differ is not limited to things that do not matter much. That would be a mere shadow of freedom. The test of its substance is the right to differ as to things that touch the heart of the existing order.

If there is any fixed star in our constitutional constellation, it is that no official, high or petty, can prescribe what shall be orthodox in politics, nationalism, religion, or other matters of opinion or force citizens to confess by word or act their faith therein. If there are any circumstances which permit an exception, they do not now occur to us.

We think the action of the local authorities in compelling the flag salute and pledge transcends constitutional limitations on their power and invades the sphere of intellect and spirit which it is the purpose of the First Amendment to our Constitution to reserve from all official control.

The decision of this Court in Minersville School District v. Gobitis and the holdings of those few per curiam decisions which preceded and foreshadowed it are overruled, and the judgment enjoining enforcement of the West Virginia Regulation is affirmed.

—JUSTICE JACKSON, Opinion in Barnette Case, 1943

11

School and Society

No OTHER people ever demanded so much of schools and of education as have the American. None other was ever so well served by its schools and its educators.

From the very beginning of our national existence, education has had very special tasks to perform in America. Democracy could not work without an enlightened electorate. The States and sections could not achieve unity without a sentiment of nationalism. The nation could not absorb tens of millions of immigrants from all parts of the globe without rapid and effective Americanization. Economic and social distinctions and privileges, severe enough to corrode democracy itself, had to be overcome. To schools went the momentous responsibility of doing these tasks—of inculcating democracy, nationalism, and equalitarianism.

The passion for education goes back to the beginnings of the Massachusetts Bay Colony; the Law of 1647, for all its inadequacy, set up the first even partially successful system of public education anywhere in the world. Only three universities in Britain antedate those of America, and by the time of independence America boasted more colleges than did the mother country, while the State Universities of the early national period represented something new under the sun.

From the first, then, education was the American religion. It was— and is—in education that we put our faith; it is our schools and colleges that are the peculiar objects of public largess and private benefaction; even in architecture we proclaim our devotion, building schools like cathedrals.

Has this faith been justified? A case might be made out for justification on purely scholarly grounds, for after all the highest of our schools of higher learning are as high as any in the world. But this is a somewhat narrow test. Let us look rather to the specific historical tasks which were imposed upon our schools and which they have fulfilled. The first

546

and most urgent task was to provide an enlightened citizenry in order that self-government might work. It is well to remember that democracy, which we take for granted, was an experiment—and largely an American experiment. It could not succeed with a people either corrupt or uninformed. People everywhere—as Jefferson and the spokesmen of the Age of Reason believed—were naturally good, but they were not naturally enlightened. To enlighten the people was the first duty of a democracy, and an enlightened people, in turn, saw to it that "schools and the means of education" were forever encouraged.

The second great task imposed upon education and on the schools was the creation of national unity. In 1789 no one could take for granted that the new nation, spread as it was over a continental domain, would hold together. Yet Americans did manage to create unity out of diversity. Powerful material forces sped this achievement: the westward movement, canals and railroads, a liberal land policy, immigration, and so forth. No less important were intellectual and emotional factors—what Lincoln called those "mystic chords of memory stretching from every battlefield and patriot grave to every living heart and hearthstone." These—the contributions of poets and novelists, naturalists and explorers, orators and painters—were transmitted to each generation anew through the schools.

The third task imposed on schools was that which we call Americanization. Each decade after 1840 saw from two to eight million immigrants pour into America. No other people had ever absorbed such large and varied racial stocks so rapidly or so successfully. It was the public school which proved itself the most efficacious of all agencies of Americanization—Americanization not only of the children but, through them, of the parents as well.

A fourth major service that the schools have rendered democracy is that of overcoming divisive forces in society and advancing understanding and equality. The most heterogeneous of modern societies—heterogeneous in race, language, color, religion, background—America might well have been a prey to ruinous class and religious divisions. The divisive forces did not, however, prevail, and one reason that they did not prevail is that the public school overcame them. In the classroom the nation's children learned and lived equality. On the playground and the athletic field the same code obtained, with rewards and applause going to achievements to which all could aspire equally, without regard to name, race, or wealth.

In spite of all the monumental services which schools have rendered American society, they have been, and are, under continuous pressure and attack. They are under pressure and attack from those who want to make them facile instruments to advance particular causes. They are attacked because they are too conservative and because they are not conservative enough; because they emphasize overmuch the old-fashioned disciplines and because they are overly progressive and fail to teach such things as spelling and geography; because they are too secular, and because they are not secular enough but permit some religious teachings. They are under attack because they cost too much money, or because they teach children to think for themselves, or because their teams do not win games, or because they do not maintain sufficiently high standards; or for a hundred and one other reasons. In one sense the controversy over education is a healthy thing—especially if we remember that men have been disputing about the nature and contents of education since the days of Plato and Aristotle. In another sense, however, it is a dangerous and even a sinister thing. It is a dangerous thing if it leads to demands that schools adapt themselves to a single pattern, if it crushes initiative and experimentalism in teachers and administrators. And it is a very dangerous thing indeed if it takes the form of pressure and intimidation—of pressure for the inculcation of some special form of Americanism or for the teaching of some special kind of economics or of history.

The sources and documents we give here are designed to illustrate the continuous concern of Americans for education, the nature of the American experiment with public schools, and the contributions of those schools, the controversy over classical and progressive education that embraces schools from the elementary to the university level, and the significance of threats to academic freedom in our own day.

1. "TO ADVANCE LEARNING AND PERPETUATE IT TO POSTERITY"

From the very nature of their faith the Puritans depended upon learning, and prized it, and it was no accident that Puritanism was strong in the universities, particularly in the University of Cambridge. An astonishing number of the Puritans who came to the New World were university graduates. S. E. Morison counts no less than one hundred and thirty-five graduates of Cambridge, Oxford and Dublin who migrated to New England before 1645. About one hundred of these came from Cambridge, and of these, thirty-five from Emmanuel College; some thirty-two came from Oxford. It is probably safe to say that no other community in the world had so large a proportion of university grad-uates, or of learned men, as did the Bay and Plymouth Colonies in the first half of the seventeenth century. As this famous account of New Englands First Fruits *tells us, one of the first things that the Puritans did was to arrange for a college. From the small seed planted in 1636 has grown, in three centuries, the greatest institution of learning in the modern world.*

AFTER God had carried us safe to *New-England,* and wee had builded our houses, provided necessaries for our liveli-hood, rear'd convenient places for Gods worship, and setled the Civill Government: One of the next things we longed for, and looked after was to advance *Learning* and perpetuate it to Posterity; dreading to leave an illiterate Ministery to the Churches, when our present Ministers shall lie in the Dust. And as wee were thinking and consulting how to effect this great Work; it pleased God to stir up the heart of one Mr. *Harvard* (a godly Gentleman, and a lover of Learning, there living amongst us) to give the one halfe of his Estate (it being in all about 1700. l.) towards the erecting of a Colledge, and all his Library: after him another gave 300. l. others after them cast in more, and the publique hand of the State added the rest: the Colledge was, by common consent, appointed to be at *Cambridge,* (a place very pleasant and accommodate) and is called (according to the name of the first founder) *Harvard Colledge.*

The Edifice is very faire and comely within and without, having in it a spacious Hall; (where they daily meet at Common Lectures) Exercises, and a large Library with some Bookes to it, the gifts of diverse of our friends, their Chambers and studies also fitted for, and possessed by the Students, and all other roomes of Office necessary and convenient, with all needfull Offices thereto belonging: And by the side of the Colledge a faire *Grammar* Schoole, for the training up of young Schollars, and fitting of them for *Academicall Learning,* that still as they are judged ripe, they may be received into the Colledge of this Schoole: Master *Corlet* is the Mr., who hath very well approved himselfe for his abilities, dexterity and painfulnesse, in teaching and education of the youth under him.

Over the Colledge is master *Dunster* placed, as President, a learned conscionable and industrious man, who hath so trained up, his Pupills in the tongues and Arts, and so seasoned them with the principles of Divinity and Christianity, that we have to our great comfort, (and in truth) beyond our hopes, beheld their progresse in Learning and god-linesse also; the former of these hath appeared in their publique declamations in *Latine* and *Greeke*, and Disputations Logicall and Philo-sophicall, which they have beene wonted (besides their ordinary Exer-cises in the Colledge-Hall) in the audience of the Magistrates, Ministers, and other Schollars, for the probation of their growth in Learning, upon set dayes, constantly once every moneth to make and uphold: The latter hath been manifested in sundry of them by the savoury breathings of their Spirits in their godly conversation. Insomuch that we are confident, if these early blossomes may be cherished and warmed with the in-fluence of the friends of Learning and lovers of this pious worke, they will by the help of God, come to happy maturity in a short time.

Over the Colledge are twelve Overseers chosen by the generall Court, six of them are of the Magistrates, the other six of the Ministers, who are to promote the best good of it, and (having a power of influence into all persons in it) are to see that every one be diligent and proficient in his proper place.

—*New Englands First Fruits*, 1643

2. "THAT LEARNING MAY NOT BE BURIED IN THE GRAVE OF OUR FATHERS"

It was not only higher learning that concerned the Puritans, but popu-lar education as well. Because that "ould deluder, Satan" lay constantly in wait for the souls of men, it was essential that men and women be able to read the Scriptures and thus come to know God and His word at first hand. So as early as 1642 the Bay Colony "ordered and decreed" that every town be responsible for the instruction of the young. The famous Act of 1647 formally provided for schools in every town of the colony; similar provision was shortly made by other New England colonies. We give here the famous law of 1647, and the tribute which the great educator Horace Mann paid to it two centuries later.

A. "Ye Ould Deluder, Satan"

IT BEING one chiefe proiect of ye ould deluder, Satan to keepe men from the knowledge of ye Scriptures, as in form^r times by keeping y^m in an unknowne tongue, so in these latt^r times by perswading from ye use of tongues, y^t so at least ye true sence & meaning of ye originall might be clouded by false glosses of saint seeming deceivers, y^t learning may not be buried in ye grave of o^r fath^{rs} in ye church and commonwealth, the Lord assisting o^r endeavo^{r}s,—

It is therefore ord^{r}ed, y^t ev^{r}y towneship in this iurisdiction, aft^r ye Lord hath increased y^m number to 50 houshold^{rs}, shall then forthwth appoint one wth in their towne to teach all such children as shall resort to him to write & reade, whose wages shall be paid eith^r by ye parents or mast^{rs} of such children, or by ye inhabitants in gen^{r}all, by way of supply, as ye maior part of those y^t ord^r ye prudentials ye towne shall appoint; provided, those y^t send their children be not oppressed by paying much more y^m they can have y^m taught for in oth^r townes; & it is furth^r ordered, y^t where any towne shall increase to ye numb^r of 100 families or househould^{rs}, they shall set up a grammer schoole, ye m^r thereof being able to instruct youth so farr as they shall be fitted for ye university, provided, y^t if any towne neglect ye performance hereof above one yeare, y^t every such towne shall pay 5 pounds to ye next schoole till they shall performe this order.

—Massachusetts School Law of 1647

B. "A Grand Mental and Moral Experiment"

It is common to say that the act of 1647 *laid the foundation* of our present system of free schools; but the truth is, it not only laid the foundation of the present system, but, in some particulars, it laid a far broader foundation than has since been built upon, and reared a far higher superstructure than has since been sustained. Modern times have witnessed great improvements in the methods of instruction, and in the motives of discipline; but, in some respects, the ancient foundation has been narrowed, and the ancient superstructure lowered. The term "grammar school," in the old laws, always meant a school where the ancient languages were taught, and where youth could be "fitted for the university." Every town containing one hundred families or householders was required to keep such a school. Were such a law in force at the present time, there are not more than twelve towns in the Commonwealth which would be exempt from its requisitions. But the term "grammar school" has wholly lost its original meaning; and the number of towns and cities which are now required by law to maintain a school where the Greek and Latin languages are taught, and where youth can be fitted for college, does not exceed thirty. The contrast between our ancestors and ourselves in this respect is most humiliating. Their meanness in wealth was more than compensated by their grandeur of soul.

The institution of a free-school system on so broad a basis, and of such ample proportions, appears still more remarkable when we consider the period in the world's history at which it was originated, and the fewness and poverty of the people by whom it was maintained. In 1647, the entire population of the colony of Massachusetts Bay is supposed to have amounted only to twenty-one thousand souls. The scattered and feeble settlements were almost buried in the depths of the forest. The external resources of the people were small, their dwellings humble, and their raiment and subsistence scanty and homely. They had no enriching commerce; and the wonderful forces of Nature had not then, as now, become gratuitous producers of every human comfort and luxury. The whole valuation of all the colonial estates, both public and private, would hardly have been equal to the inventory of many a private citizen of the present day. The fierce eye of the savage was nightly seen glaring from the edge of the surrounding wilderness; and no defence or succor, save in their own brave natures, was at hand. Yet it was then, amid all these privations and dangers, that the Pilgrim Fathers conceived the magnificent idea, not only of a universal, but of a free education, for the whole people. To find the time and the means to reduce this grand conception to practice, they stinted themselves, amid all their poverty, to a still scantier pittance; amid all their toils, they imposed upon themselves still more burdensome labors; and, amid all their perils, they braved still greater dangers. Two divine ideas filled their great hearts,—their duty to God and to posterity. For the one, they built the church; for the other, they opened the school. Religion and knowledge,—two attributes of the same glorious and eternal truth, and that truth the only one on which immortal or mortal happiness can be securely founded!

It is impossible for us adequately to conceive the boldness of the measure which aimed at universal education through the establishment of free schools. As a fact, it had no precedent in the world's history; and, as a theory, it could have been refuted and silenced by a more formidable array of argument and experience than was ever marshalled against any other institution of human origin. But time has ratified its soundness. Two centuries of successful operation now proclaim it to be as wise as it was courageous, and as beneficent as it was disinterested. Every community in the civilized world awards it the meed of praise; and states at home, and nations abroad, in the order of their intelligence, are copying the bright example. What we call the enlightened nations of Christendom are approaching, by slow degrees, to the moral elevation which our ancestors reached at a single bound; and the tardy convictions of the one have been assimilating, through a period of two centuries, to the intuitions of the other.

The establishment of free schools was one of those grand mental and moral experiments whose effects could not be developed and made manifest in a single generation.

—Horace Mann, Annual Report for 1846

3. "TO RENDER THE PEOPLE SAFE, THEIR MINDS MUST BE IMPROVED"

It is impossible to exaggerate the importance of the place that education held in Jefferson's philosophy. His faith in democracy was profound, but it was not uncritical. He believed the people naturally virtuous, but knew that they were not naturally enlightened. Democracy, he realized, could work only with a people both virtuous and enlightened. Education would provide the enlightenment. All his mature life Jefferson worked for the more general diffusion of learning among the people. He planned an elaborate system of elementary schools and academies; he worked ceaselessly for the improvement of his own college, William and Mary College; he saw to it that the ordinances for Western lands carried provision for education; he was alive to the importance of public libraries, drew a bill for their establishment, and twice turned over his own private library—one of the best in America—as a foundation for the Library of Congress. The last years of his life he gave to his favorite project, the University of Virginia. No other institution of learning is so completely the creation of a single mind and spirit. Jefferson planned it in every detail: he was the architect, drawing every window and door and fire-place; he was the landscape gardener, arranging every shrub and tree; he selected the faculty, he drew up the curriculum, he chose the books for the library, he hand-picked the student body; he carried the whole vast project through the State Legislature, and lived to see it open its doors, in 1825. He directed that on his tombstone should be engraved:

Thomas Jefferson
Author
Of the Declaration of
American Independence
Of
The Statute of Virginia
For Religious Freedom, and
Father of the University
Of Virginia

THE first stage of this education being the schools of the hundreds, wherein the great mass of the people will receive their instruction, the principal foundations of future order will be laid here. Instead, therefore, of putting the Bible and Testament into the hands of the children at an age when their judgments are not sufficiently matured for religious inquiries, their memories may here be stored with the most useful facts from Grecian, Roman, European, and American history. The first elements of morality too may be instilled into their minds; such as, when further developed as their judgments advance in strength, may teach them how to work out their own greatest happiness, by shewing them that it does not depend on the condition of life in which chance has placed them, but is always the result of a good conscience, good health, occupation, and freedom in all just pursuits.—Those whom either the wealth of their parents or the adoption of the state shall destine to higher degrees of learning, will go on to the grammar schools, which constitute the next stage, there to be instructed in the languages. The learning Greek and Latin, I am told, is going into disuse in Europe. I know not what their manners and occupations may call for: but it would be very ill-judged in us to follow their example in this instance. There is a certain period of life, say from eight to fifteen or sixteen years of age, when the mind like the body is not yet firm enough for laborious and close operations. If applied to such, it falls an early victim to premature exertion; exhibiting, indeed, at first, in these young and tender subjects, the flattering appearance of their being men while they are yet children, but ending in reducing them to be children when they should be men. The memory is then most susceptible and tenacious of impressions; and the learning of languages being chiefly a work of memory, it seems precisely fitted to the powers of this period, which is long enough too for acquiring the most useful languages, antient and modern. I do not pretend that language is science. It is only an instrument for the attainment of science. But that time is not lost which is employed in providing tools for future operation: more especially as in this case the books put into the hands of the youth for this purpose may be such as will at the same time impress their minds with useful facts and good principles. If this period be suffered to pass in idleness, the mind becomes lethargic and impotent, as would the body it inhabits if unexercised during the same time. The sympathy between body and mind during their rise, progress and decline, is too strict and obvious to endanger our being misled while we reason from the one to the other.—As soon as they are of sufficient age, it is supposed they will be sent on from the grammar schools to the university, which constitutes our third and last stage, there to study those sciences which may be adapted to their views.—By that part of our plan which prescribes the selection of the youths of genius from among the classes of the poor, we hope to avail the state of those talents which nature has sown as liberally among the poor as the rich, but which perish without use, if not sought for and cultivated.—But of all the views of this law none is more important, none more legitimate, than that of rendering the people the safe, as they are the ultimate, guardians of their own liberty. For this purpose the reading in the first stage, where *they* will receive their whole education, is proposed, as has been said, to be chiefly historical. History, by apprising them of the past, will enable them to judge of the future; it will avail them of the experience of other times and other nations; it will qualify them as judges of the actions and designs of men; it will enable them to know ambition under every disguise it may assume; and knowing it, to defeat its views. In every government on earth is some trace of human weakness, some germ of corruption and degeneracy, which cunning will discover, and wickedness insensibly open, cultivate and improve. Every government degenerates when trusted to the rulers of the people alone. The people themselves therefore are its only safe depositories. And to render even them safe, their minds must be improved to a certain degree. This indeed is not all that is necessary, though it be essentially necessary. An amendment of our constitution must here come in aid of the public education. The influence over government must be shared among all the people. If every individual which composes their mass participates of the ultimate authority, the government will be safe; because the corrupting the whole mass will exceed any private resources of wealth; and public ones cannot be provided but by levies on the people. In this case every man would have to pay his own price. The government of Great Britain has been corrupted, because but one man in ten has a right to vote for members of parliament. The sellers of the government, therefore, get nine-tenths of their price clear. It has been thought that corruption is restrained by confining the right of suffrage to a few of the wealthier of the people: but it would be more effectually restrained by an extension of that right to such numbers as would bid defiance to the means of corruption.

Lastly, it is proposed, by a bill in this revisal, to begin a public library and gallery, by laying out a certain sum annually in books, paintings, and statues.

—Thomas Jefferson, *Notes on Virginia*, 1782

4. "WHY SEND AN AMERICAN YOUTH TO EUROPE FOR EDUCATION?"

This letter, written by Jefferson from Paris while he was Minister to France, is interesting rather than important, but it expresses an attitude that was to be of considerable importance. That is the attitude that Jefferson expressed fifteen years later in his First Inaugural Address, where he spoke of his own country as "kindly separated by nature and a wide ocean from one quarter of the globe, too high-minded to endure the degradations of others." Jefferson was cosmopolitan, versatile, and sophisticated even in a century distinguished for those qualities, but notwithstanding his adoration of France and his passion for much of Old World culture—art, music, architecture, science, the salons—he never lost his feeling that the Old World was decadent and depraved and the New World youthful and virtuous, and that in all essentials the New World was better than the Old. To a generation which takes Europe and foreign study in its stride this attitude may seem curiously provincial, but it was one that deeply colored the American outlook on world affairs for many decades of the nineteenth century.

DEAR SIR,—I should sooner have answered the paragraph in your letter, of September the 19th, respecting the best seminary for the education of youth in Europe, but that it was necessary for me to make inquiries on the subject. The result of these has been, to consider the competition as resting between Geneva and Rome. . . . But why send an American youth to Europe for education? What are the objects of an useful American education? Classical knowledge, modern languages, chiefly French, Spanish, and Italian; Mathematics, Natural philosophy, Natural history, Civil history, and Ethics. In Natural philosophy, I mean to include Chemistry and Agriculture, and in Natural history, to include Botany, as well as the other branches of those departments. It is true that the habit of speaking the modern languages cannot be so well acquired in America; but every other article can be as well acquired at William and Mary college, as at any place in Europe. When college education is done with, and a young man is to prepare himself for public life, he must cast his eyes (for America) either on Law or Physics. For the former, where can he apply so advantageously as to Mr. Wythe? For the latter, he must come to Europe: the medical class of students, therefore, is the only one which need come to Europe. Let us view the disadvantages of sending a youth to Europe. To enumerate them all, would require a volume. I will select a few. If he goes to England, he learns drinking, horse racing, and boxing. These are the peculiarities of English education. The following circumstances are common to education in that, and the other countries of Europe. He acquires a fondness for European luxury and dissipation, and a contempt for the simplicity of his own country; he is fascinated with the privileges of the European aristocrats, and sees, with abhorrence, the lovely equality which the poor enjoy with the rich, in his own country; he contracts a partiality for aristocracy or monarchy; he forms foreign friendships which will never be useful to him, and loses the seasons of life for forming, in his own country, those friendships which, of all others, are the most faithful and permanent; he is led, by the strongest of all the human passions, into a spirit for female intrigue, destructive of his own and others' happiness, or a passion for whores, destructive of his health, and, in both cases, learns to consider fidelity to the marriage bed as an ungentlemanly practice, and inconsistent with happiness; he recollects the voluptuary dress and arts of the European women, and pities and despises the chaste affections and simplicity of those of his own country; he retains, through life, a fond recollection, and a hankering after those places, which were the scenes of his first pleasures and of his first connections; he returns to his own country, a foreigner, unacquainted with the practices of domestic economy, necessary to preserve him from ruin, speaking and writing his native tongue as a foreigner, and therefore unqualified to obtain those distinctions, which eloquence of the pen and tongue ensures in a free country; for I would observe to you, that what is called style in writing or speaking is formed very early in life, while the imagination is warm, and impressions are permanent. I am of opinion, that there never was an instance of a man's writing or speaking his native tongue with elegance, who passed from fifteen to twenty years of age out of the country where it was spoken. Thus, no instance exists of a person's writing two languages perfectly. That will always appear to be his native language, which was most familiar to him in his youth. It appears to me, then, that an American, coming to Europe for education, loses in his knowledge, in his morals, in his health, in his habits, and in his happiness. I had entertained only doubts on this head before I came to Europe: what I see and hear, since I came here, proves more than I had even suspected. Cast your eye over America: who are the men of most learning, of most eloquence, most beloved by their countrymen and most trusted and promoted by them? They are those who have been educated among them, and whose manners, morals, and habits, are perfectly homogeneous with those of the country.

Did you expect by so short a question, to draw such a sermon on yourself? I dare say you did not. But the consequences of foreign education are alarming to me, as an American. I sin, therefore, through zeal, whenever I enter on the subject. You are sufficiently American to pardon me for it. Let me hear of your health, and be assured of the esteem with which I am, dear Sir, your friend and servant.

—Thomas Jefferson, Letter to J. Bannister, October 15, 1785

5. THE EDUCATION PROPER IN A REPUBLIC

In versatility of interests if not in depth of thought, Benjamin Rush of Philadelphia belongs with such eighteenth-century Americans as Franklin, Jefferson, William Bentley, or Benjamin Thompson (Count Rumford). In his day the most influential and probably the most distinguished American physician, Rush was also politician, statesman, signer of the Declaration, Surgeon-General to the Army, humanitarian reformer, and educator. He had studied in Edinburgh and London, and was as familiar with schools abroad as Jefferson himself. In many ways Rush's educational ideas paralleled those of Jefferson, for like Jefferson he was deeply concerned that a democracy develop an enlightened citizenry. In other ways his ideas were more advanced and more original than those of the Sage of Monticello. Particularly interesting are Rush's observations on the education of girls.

. . . While we inculcate these republican duties upon our pupil, we must not neglect, at the same time, to inspire him with republican principles. He must be taught that there can be no durable liberty but in a republic, and that government, like all other sciences, is of a progressive nature. The chains which have bound this science in Europe are happily unloosed in America. Here it is open to investigation and improvement. While philosophy has protected us by its discoveries from a thousand natural evils, government has unhappily followed with an unequal pace. It would be to dishonor human genius, only to name the many defects which still exist in the best systems of legislation. We daily see matter of a perishable nature rendered durable by certain chemical operations. In like manner, I conceive, that it is possible to combine power in such a way as not only to encrease the happiness, but to promote the duration of republican forms of government far beyond the terms limited for them by history, or the common opinions of mankind.

To assist in rendering religious, moral and political instruction more effectual upon the minds of our youth, it will be necessary to subject their bodies to physical discipline. To obviate the inconveniences of their

559

studious and sedentary mode of life, they should live upon a temperate diet, consisting chiefly of broths, milk and vegetables. The black broth of Sparta, and the barley broth of Scotland, have been alike celebrated for their beneficial effects upon the minds of young people. They should avoid tasting spirituous liquors. They should also be accustomed occasionally to work with their hands, in the intervals of study, and in the busy seasons of the year in the country. Moderate sleep, silence, occasional solitude and cleanliness, should be inculcated upon them, and the utmost advantage should be taken of a proper direction of those great principles in human conduct,—sensibility, habit, imitations and association.

The influence of these physical causes will be powerful upon the intellects, as well as upon the principles and morals of young people. . . .

From the observations that have been made it is plain, that I consider it is possible to convert men into republican machines. This must be done, if we expect them to perform their parts properly, in the great machine of the government of the state. That republic is sophisticated with monarchy or aristocracy that does not revolve upon the wills of the people, and these must be fitted to each other by means of education before they can be made to produce regularity and unison in government.

Having pointed out those general principles, which should be inculcated alike in all the schools of the state, I proceed now to make a few remarks upon the method of conducting, what is commonly called, a liberal or learned education in a republic. . . .

Too much pains cannot be taken to teach our youth to read and write our American language with propriety and elegance. The study of the Greek language constituted a material part of the literature of the Athenians, hence the sublimity, purity and immortality of so many of their writings. The advantages of a perfect knowledge of our language to young men intended for the professions of law, physic, or divinity are too obvious to be mentioned, but in a state which boasts of the first commercial city in America, I wish to see it cultivated by young men, who are intended for the compting house, for many such, I hope, will be educated in our colleges. The time is past when an academical education was thought to be unnecessary to qualify a young man for merchandize. I conceive no profession is capable of receiving more embellishments from it. The French and German languages should likewise be carefully taught in all our colleges. They abound with useful books upon all subjects. So important and necessary are those languages, that a degree should never be conferred upon a young man who cannot speak or translate them. . . .

With the usual arts and sciences that are taught in our American colleges, I wish to see a regular course of lectures given upon History and Chronology. The science of government, whether it relates to constitutions or laws, can only be advanced by a careful selection of facts, and these are to be found chiefly in history. Above all, let our youth be instructed in the history of the ancient republics, and the progress of liberty and tyranny in the different states of Europe. I wish likewise to see the numerous facts that relate to the origin and present state of commerce, together with the nature and principles of money, reduced to such a system, as to be intelligible and agreeable to a young man. If we consider the commerce of our metropolis only as the avenue of the wealth of the state, the study of it merits a place in a young man's education; but, I consider commerce in a much higher light when I recommend the study of it in republican seminaries. I view it as the best security against the influence of hereditary monopolies of land, and, therefore, the surest protection against aristocracy. I consider its effects as next to those of religion in humanizing mankind, and lastly, I view it as the means of uniting the different nations of the world together by the ties of mutual wants and obligations. . . .

Again, let your youth be instructed in all the means of promoting national prosperity and independence, whether they relate to improvements in agriculture, manufactures, or inland navigation. Let him be instructed further in the general principles of legislation, whether they relate to revenue, or to the preservation of life, liberty or property. Let him be directed frequently to attend the courts of justice, where he will have the best opportunities of acquiring habits of comparing, and arranging his ideas by observing the discovery of truth, in the examination of witnesses, and where he will hear the laws of the state explained, with all the advantages of that species of eloquence which belongs to the bar. Of so much importance do I conceive it to be, to a young man, to attend occasionally to the decisions of our courts of law, that I wish to see our colleges established, only in county towns.

But further, considering the nature of our connection with the United States, it will be necessary to make our pupil acquainted with all the prerogatives of the national government. He must be instructed in the nature and variety of treaties. He must know the difference in the powers and duties of the several species of ambassadors. He must be taught wherein the obligations of individuals and of states are the same, and wherein they differ. In short, he must acquire a general knowledge of all those laws and forms, which unite the sovereigns of the earth, or separate them from each other.

I beg pardon for having delayed so long to say any thing of the separate and peculiar mode of education proper for women in a republic. I am sensible that they must concur in all our plans of education for young men, or no laws will ever render them effectual. To qualify our women for this purpose, they should not only be instructed in the usual branches of female education, but they should be taught the principles of liberty and government; and the obligations of patriotism should be inculcated upon them. The opinions and conduct of men are often regulated by the women in the most arduous enterprizes of life; and their approbation is frequently the principal reward of the hero's dangers, and the patriot's toils. Besides, the first impression upon the minds of children are generally derived from the women. Of how much consequence, therefore, is it in a republic, that they should think justly upon the great subject of liberty and government! . . .

Let there be free schools established in every township, or in the districts consisting of one hundred families. In these schools let children be taught to read and write the English and German languages, and the use of figures. Such of them as have parents that can afford to send them from home, and are disposed to extend their educations, may remove their children from the free school to one of the colleges.

By this plan the whole state will be tied together by one system of education. The university will in time furnish masters for the colleges, and the colleges will furnish masters for the free schools, while the free schools, in their turns, will supply the colleges and the university with scholars, students and pupils. The same systems of grammar, oratory and philosophy, will be taught in every part of the state, and the literary features of Pennsylvania will thus designate one great, and equally enlightened family.

But, how shall we bear the expense of these literary institutions?— I answer—These institutions will *lessen* our taxes. They will enlighten us in the great business of finance—they will teach us to increase the ability of the state to support government, by increasing the profits of agriculture, and by promoting manufactures. They will teach us all the modern improvements and advantages of inland navigation. They will defend us from hasty and expensive experiments in government, by unfolding to us the experience and folly of past ages, and thus, instead of adding to our taxes and debts, they will furnish us with the true secret of lessening and discharging both of them.

But, shall the estates of orphans, bachelors and persons who have no children, be taxed to pay for the support of schools from which they can derive no benefit? I answer in the affirmative, to the first part of the objection, and I deny the truth of the latter part of it. Every member of the community is interested in the propagation of virtue and knowledge in the state. But I will go further, and add, it will be true economy in individuals to support public schools. The bachelor will in time save his tax for this purpose, by being able to sleep with fewer bolts and locks to his doors—the estates of orphans will in time be benefited, by being protected from the ravages of unprincipled and idle boys, and the children of wealthy parents will be less tempted, by bad company, to extravagance. Fewer pillories and whipping posts, and smaller gaols, with their usual expenses and taxes, will be necessary when our youth are properly educated, than at present; I believe it could be proved, that the expenses of confining, trying and executing criminals, amount every year, in most of the counties, to more money than would be sufficient to maintain all the schools that would be necessary in each county. The confessions of these criminals generally show us, that their vices and punishments are the fatal consequences of the want of a proper education in early life.

—BENJAMIN RUSH,

A Plan for the Establishment of Public Schools, 1786

6. THE EDUCATION OF WOMEN

The earliest Massachusetts Bay school laws did not distinguish between boys and girls, but on the whole the colonials made little provision even for the elementary training of girls and none at all for advanced learning. In 1684 the Hopkins School of New Haven decided that "all girls be excluded as improper and inconsistent with such a grammar school as ye law injoines and as is the Designe of this settlement." The eighteenth century saw the establishment of several "female academies," and Jefferson's education bill of 1779 called for the training of girls as well as boys by the state. By the early years of the nineteenth

*century, elementary education for girls was taken for granted every-
where and secondary education was available to some. Nowhere, however, was there provision for higher education for women. In 1818 Mrs.
Emma Willard, wife of a Middlebury, Vermont, physician and head-
mistress of the Middlebury Female Seminary, proposed to Governor
Clinton of New York the establishment of a college for women. The
enlightened Clinton favored the measure; the Senate appropriated two
thousand dollars toward its consummation; but it failed in the House.
The citizens of Troy, however, came forward with money for the Troy
Female Seminary—now the Emma Willard School. The second pioneer
in this field was another Connecticut lady, Catherine Beecher, daughter
of the formidable Lyman Beecher, and sister to Henry Ward Beecher
and Harriet Beecher Stowe. In 1824 Catherine Beecher founded the
Hartford Female Seminary, which shortly became a model school of
its kind. Miss Beecher later helped found a series of seminaries and
colleges for women throughout the West. We give here a brief excerpt
from Catherine Beecher's "Suggestions Respecting Improvements in
Education."*

IT IS to *mothers,* and to *teachers,* that the world is to look for the character which is to be enstamped on each succeeding generation, for
it is to them that the great business of education is almost exclusively
committed. And will it not appear by examination that neither mothers
nor teachers have ever been properly educated for their profession. What
is *the profession* of a *Woman?* Is it not to form immortal minds, and
to watch, to nurse, and to rear the bodily system, so fearfully and
wonderfully made, and upon the order and regulation of which, the
health and well-being of the mind so greatly depends?

But let most of our sex upon whom these arduous duties devolve,
be asked; have you ever devoted any time and study, in the course of
your education, to any preparation for these duties? Have you been
taught any thing of the structure, the nature, and the laws of the body,
which you inhabit? Were you ever taught to understand the operation
of diet, air, exercise and modes of dress upon the human frame? Have
the causes which are continually operating to prevent good health, and
the modes by which it might be perfected and preserved ever been
made the subject of any *instruction?* Perhaps almost every voice would
respond, no; we have attended to almost every thing more than to

this; we have been taught more concerning the structure of the earth; the laws of the heavenly bodies; the habits and formation of plants; the philosophy of languages; more of *almost any thing*, than the structure of the human frame and the laws of health and reason. But is it not the business, the *profession* of a woman to guard the health and form the physical habits of the young? And is not the cradle of infancy and the chamber of sickness sacred to woman alone? And ought she not to know at least some of the *general principles* of that perfect and wonderful piece of mechanism committed to her preservation and care?

The *restoration* of health is the physician's profession, but the *preservation* of it falls to other hands, and it is believed that the time will come, when woman will be taught to understand something respecting the construction of the human frame; the physiological results which will naturally follow from restricted exercise, unhealthy modes of dress, improper diet, and many other causes, which are continually operating to destroy the health and life of the young.

Again let our sex be asked respecting the instruction they have received in the course of their education, on that still more arduous and difficult department of their profession, which relates to the *intellect* and the *moral susceptibilities*. Have you been taught the powers and faculties of the human mind, and the laws by which it is regulated? Have you studied how to direct its several faculties; how to restore those that are overgrown, and strengthen and mature those that are deficient? Have you been taught the best modes of *communicating* knowledge as well as of *acquiring* it? Have you learned the best mode of correcting bad *moral* habits and forming good ones? Have you made it an object to find how a selfish disposition may be made generous; how a reserved temper may be made open and frank; how pettishness and ill humor may be changed to cheerfulness and kindness? Has any woman studied her profession in this respect? It is feared the same answer must be returned, if not from all, at least from most of our sex. No; we have acquired wisdom from the observation and experience of others, on almost *all other* subjects, but the philosophy of the direction and control of the human mind has not been an object of thought or study. And thus it appears that tho' it is woman's *express business* to rear the body, and form the mind, there is scarcely anything to which her attention has been less directed. . . .

If all females were not only well educated themselves, but were prepared to communicate in an easy manner their stores of knowledge to others; if they not only knew how to regulate their own minds, tempers and habits, but how to effect improvements in those around them, the face of society would speedily be changed. The time *may* come when the world will look back with wonder to behold how much time and effort have been given to the mere cultivation of the memory, and how little mankind have been aware of what every teacher, parent, and friend could accomplish in forming the social, intellectual and moral character of those by whom they are surrounded.

—CATHERINE BEECHER,
"Suggestions Respecting Improvements in Education," 1829

7. "EDUCATION IS THE BALANCE WHEEL OF THE SOCIAL MACHINERY"

If a single name had to be chosen to represent American education, it would be, of necessity, Horace Mann. President of the Massachusetts State Senate in 1837, Mann resigned that post—as well as a promising career in politics—to take the ill-paid post of Secretary to the newly established Board of Education. Within twelve years he not only re-organized and reconstructed education throughout the State but gave an impetus to the reconstruction of public education everywhere in the land, and in other lands as well. He established the Common School Journal, *set up three Normal Schools—the first in the country—built new schools, vastly increased high school enrollment, doubled school appropriations, and reformed the curriculum. But above and beyond all this was the influence of his tremendous Annual Reports, each one a philosophical treatise on the place of education in a republic. In 1848 Mann resigned to go to Congress; four years later, defeated as anti-slavery candidate for governorship, he accepted the Presidency of the newly founded Antioch College in Ohio, and there he died. We give here an extract from his famous final report.*

NOW two or three things will doubtless be admitted to be true, be-yond all controversy, in regard to Massachusetts. By its industrial condition, and its business operations, it is exposed, far beyond any other State in the Union, to the fatal extremes of overgrown wealth and desperate poverty. Its population is far more dense than that of any other State. It is four or five times more dense than the average of all the other States taken together; and density of population has always been one of the proximate causes of social inequality. According to population and territorial extent there is far more capital in Massachusetts—capital which is movable, and instantaneously available—than in any other State in the Union; and probably both these qualifications respecting population and territory could be omitted without endangering the truth of the assertion. . . .

Now surely nothing but universal education can counterwork this tendency to the domination of capital and the servility of labor. If one class possesses all the wealth and the education, while the residue of society is ignorant and poor, it matters not by what name the relation between them may be called: the latter, in fact and in truth, will be the servile dependents and subjects of the former. But, if education be equally diffused, it will draw property after it by the strongest of all attractions; for such a thing never did happen, and never can happen, as that an intelligent and practical body of men should be permanently poor. Property and labor in different classes are essentially antagonistic; but property and labor in the same class are essentially fraternal. The people of Massachusetts have, in some degree, appreciated the truth that the unexampled prosperity of the State—its comfort, its competence, its general intelligence and virtue—is attributable to the education, more or less perfect, which all its people have received; but are they sensible of a fact equally important,—namely, that it is to this same education that two-thirds of the people are indebted for not being to-day the vassals of as severe a tyranny, in the form of capital, as the lower classes of Europe are bound to in any form of brute force?

Education then, beyond all other devices of human origin, is a great equalizer of the conditions of men,—the balance wheel of the social machinery. I do not here mean that it so elevates the moral nature as to make men disdain and abhor the oppression of their fellow men. This idea pertains to another of its attributes. But I mean that it gives each man the independence and the means by which he can resist the selfishness of other men. It does better than to disarm the poor of their hostility toward the rich: it prevents being poor. Agrarianism is the revenge of poverty against wealth. The wanton destruction of the property of others—the burning of hay-ricks, and corn-ricks, the demolition of machinery because it supersedes hand-labor, the sprinkling of vitriol on rich dresses—is only agrarianism run mad. Education prevents both the revenge and the madness. On the other hand, a fellow-feeling for one's class or caste is the common instinct of hearts not wholly sunk in selfish regard for a person or for a family. The spread of education, by enlarging the cultivated class or caste, will open a wider area over which the social feelings will expand; and, if this education should be universal and complete, it would do more than all things else to obliterate factitious distinctions in society. . . .

For the creation of wealth, then,—for the existence of a wealthy people and a wealthy nation,—intelligence is the grand condition. The number of improvers will increase as the intellectual constituency, if I may so call it, increases. In former times, and in most parts of the world even at the present day, not one man in a million has ever had such a development of mind as made it possible for him to become a contributor to art or science. . . . Let this development proceed, and contributions . . . of inestimable value, will be sure to follow. That political economy, therefore, which busies itself about capital and labor, supply and demand, interests and rents, favorable and unfavorable balances of trade, but leaves out of account the elements of a wide-spread mental development, is naught but stupendous folly. The greatest of all the arts in political economy is to change a consumer into a pro-ducer; and the next greatest is to increase the producing power,—and this to be directly obtained by increasing his intelligence. For mere delv-ing, an ignorant man is but little better than a swine, whom he so much resembles in his appetites, and surpasses in his power of mischief.

—HORACE MANN, Twelfth Annual Report, 1848

8. "THE SCHOLAR IS TO THINK WITH THE SAGE BUT TALK WITH COMMON MEN"

Theodore Parker was Horace Mann's minister, as he was minister to Louisa May Alcott and Elizabeth Peabody and Samuel Gridley Howe and so many others concerned with various aspects of education. One reason why men and women of this kind were attracted to him can be read in this extract from Parker's sermon on the "Duties of the Ameri-

can Scholar." The sermon was in part autobiographical. Parker himself was one of the most learned men of his generation, but he spoke always the language of the farm and the forum rather than that of the study.

HOW shall the scholar pay for his education? He is to give a service for the service received. Thus the miller and the farmer pay one another, each paying with service in his own kind. The scholar cannot pay back bread for bread, and cloth for cloth. He must pay in the scholar's kind, not the woodman's or the weaver's. He is to represent the higher modes of human consciousness; his culture and opportunities of position fit him for that. So he is not merely to go through the routine of his profession, as minister, doctor, lawyer, merchant, schoolmaster, politician, or maker of almanacks, and for his own advantage; he is also to represent truth, justice, beauty, philanthropy, and religion—the highest facts of human experience; he must be common, but not vulgar, and, as a star, must dwell apart from the vulgarity of the selfish and the low. He may win money without doing this, get fame and power, and thereby seem to pay mankind for their advance to him, while he rides upon their neck; but as he has not paid back the scholar's cost, and in the scholar's way, he is a debtor still, and owes for his past culture and present position.

Such is the position of the scholar everywhere, and such his consequent obligation. But in America there are some circumstances which make the position and the duty still more important. Beside the natural aristocracy of genius, talent, and educated skill, in most countries there is also a conventional and permanent nobility based on royal or patrician descent and immoveable aristocracy. Its members monopolize the high places of society, and if not strong by nature are so by position. Those men check the natural power of the class of scholars. The descendant of some famous chief of old time takes rank before the Bacons, the Shakespeares, and the Miltons of new families,—born yesterday, to-day gladdened and gladdening with the joy of their genius,—usurps their place, and for a time "shoves away the worthy bidden guest" from the honours of the public board. Here there is no such class: a man born at all is well born; with a great nature, nobly born; the career opens to all that can run, to all men that wish to try; our aristocracy is moveable, and the scholar has scope and verge enough. . . .

In America there are no royal or patrician patrons, no plebeian clients in literature, no immoveable aristocracy to withstand or even retard the new genius, talent, or skill of the scholar. There is no class organized, accredited, and confided in, to resist a new idea; only the unorganized inertia of mankind retards the circulation of thought and the march of men. Our historical men do not found historical families; our famous names of to-day are all new names in the State. American aristocracy is bottomed on money which no unnatural laws make steadfast and immoveable. To exclude a scholar from the company of rich men, is not to exclude him from an audience that will welcome and appreciate.

Then the government does not interfere to prohibit the free exercise of thought. Speaking is free, preaching free, printing free. No administration in America could put down a newspaper or suppress the discussion of an unwelcome theme. The attempt would be folly and madness. There is no "tonnage and poundage" on thought. It is seldom that lawless violence usurps the place of despotic government. The chief opponent of the new philosophy is the old philosophy. The old has only the advantage of a few years; the advantage of possession of the ground. It has no weapons of defence which the new has not for attack. What hinders the growth of the new democracy of to-day?—only the old democracy of yesterday, once green, and then full-blown, but now going to seed. Everywhere else walled gardens have been built for it to go quietly to seed in, and men appointed, in God's name or the State's, to exterminate as a weed every new plant of democratic thought which may spring up and suck the soil or keep off the sun, so that the old may quietly occupy the ground, and undisturbed continue to decay, and contaminate the air. Here it has nothing but its own stalk to hold up its head, and is armed with only such spines as it has grown out of its own substance. . . .

This peculiar relation of the man of genius to the people comes from American institutions. Here the greatest man stands nearest to the people, and without a mediator speaks to them face to face. This is a new thing: in the classic nations oratory was for the people, so was the drama, and the ballad; that was all their literature. But this came to the people only in cities: the tongue travels slow and addresses only the ear, while swiftly hurries on the printed word and speaks at once to a million eyes. . . .

Here all is changed, everything that is written is for the hands of the million. In three months Mr. Macaulay has more readers in America than Thucydides and Tacitus in twelve centuries. Literature, which was once the sacrament of the few, only a shew-bread to the people, is now the daily meat of the multitude. The best works get reprinted with great speed; the highest poetry is soon in all the newspapers. Authors know this, and write accordingly. It is only scientific works which ask for a special public. But even science, the proudest of the day, must come down from the clouds of the academy, lay off its scholastic garb, and appear before the eyes of the multitude in common work-day clothes. To large and mainly unlearned audiences Agassiz and Walker set forth the highest teachings of physics and metaphysics, not sparing difficult things, but putting them in plain speech. Emerson takes his majestic intuitions of truth and justice, which transcend the experience of the ages, and expounds them to the mechanics' apprentices, to the factory girls at Lowell and Chicopee, and to the merchants' clerks at Boston. The more original the speaker, and the more profound, the better is he relished; the beauty of the form is not appreciated, but the original substance welcomed into new life over the bench, the loom, and even the desk of the counting-house. Of a deep man the people ask clearness also, thinking he does not see a thing wholly till he sees it plain.

From this new relation of the scholar to the people, and the direct intimacy of his intercourse with men, there comes a new modification of his duty; he is to represent the higher facts of human consciousness to the people, and express them in the speech of the people; to think with the sage and saint, but talk with common men.

—THEODORE PARKER,
"Position and Duties of the American Scholar," 1849

9. THE FIRST GREAT PUBLIC LIBRARY

The public library is as characteristically American as the public school, and as important a part of the educational system. Although there were semipublic libraries even in the colonial period, and some small public libraries in various New England towns in the early na-

*tional era, the real history of the public library begins with the founda-
tion of the Boston Public Library in the early 1850's. Whether we
ascribe its origins to that remarkable Parisian, Nicolas Vattemare, who
tried to turn the Boston Athenaeum into a public library, or to the
devoted scholars who drew up the report from which we here quote,
one thing is clear: the same soil that produced Horace Mann and school
reform produced George Ticknor and the public library movement.
It was all part of that faith in democracy and the perfectibility of man
that was associated with the great reform movement of the 1840's and
the 1850's. From these small beginnings—the Massachusetts and New
Hampshire laws permitting towns to establish public libraries, and the
foundation of the Boston Public—came the library movement which
is one of the glories of American civilization: more and larger public
libraries than any other nation can count, the combination of private
philanthropy and public largess to make possible libraries in towns
throughout the country, the development of a library science which
has contributed much to making American libraries more useful than
any others on the globe. We give here first the proposed Massachusetts
Act of 1851; which was passed that same year, without the eloquent
preamble; and extracts from the Report of the Trustees of the proposed
Boston Public Library in 1852.*

A. "The Increase and Perpetuation of Public Libraries"

WHEREAS, a universal diffusion of knowledge among the people
must be highly conducive to the preservation of their freedom, a
greater equalization of their social advantages, their industrial success,
and their physical, intellectual and moral advancement and elevation;
and

Whereas, It is requisite to such a diffusion of knowledge, that while
sufficient means of good early education shall be furnished to all the
children in the Common Schools, ample and increasing sources of
useful and interesting information should be provided for the whole
people in the subsequent and much more capable and valuable periods
of life; and

Whereas, There is no way in which this can be done so effectually,

conveniently, and economically as by the formation, increase and perpetuation of Public Libraries, in the several cities and towns of this
Commonwealth, for the use and benefit of all their respective inhabitants:—

Be it enacted by the Senate and House . . . as follows:

Section 1. Any city or two of this Commonwealth is hereby authorized
to establish and maintain a public library within the same, for the use
of the inhabitants thereof, and to provide a suitable room or rooms
therefor, under such regulations for the government of said library as
may, from time to time, be prescribed by the city council of such city,
or the inhabitants of such town.

—Proposed Massachusetts Library Act,
Massachusetts House Document 124, 1851

B. "If It Can Be Done Anywhere, It Can Be Done Here, in Boston"

. . . Boston schools . . . give a first rate school education, at the public
expense, to the entire rising generation.

But when this object is attained, and it is certainly one of the highest
importance, our system of public instruction stops. Although the school
and even the college and university are, as all thoughtful persons are
well aware, but the first stages in education, the public makes no provision for carrying on the great work. It imparts, with a noble equality
of privilege, a knowledge of the elements of learning to all its children,
but it affords them no aid in going beyond the elements. It awakens
a taste for reading, but it furnishes to the public nothing to be read.
It conducts our young men and women to that point, where they are
qualified to acquire from books the various knowledge in the arts and
sciences which books contain; but it does nothing to put those books
within their reach. As matters now stand, and speaking with general
reference to the mass of the community, the public makes no provision
whatever, by which the hundreds of young persons annually educated,
as far as the elements of learning are concerned, at the public expense,
can carry on their education and bring it to practical results by private
study. . . .

We are far from intimating that a school education is not important
because it is elementary; it is, on the contrary, of the utmost value.
Neither do we say, on the other hand, because there are no libraries

which in the strict sense of the word are public, that therefore there is absolutely no way by which persons of limited means can get access to books. There are several libraries of the kind usually called public, belonging however to private corporations; and there are numerous private libraries from which books are liberally loaned to those wishing to borrow them.

It will however be readily conceded that this falls far short of the aid and encouragement which would be afforded to the reading com-munity . . . by a well supplied public library. If we had no free schooll we should not be a community without education. . . .

It needs no arguments to prove that, in a republican government, these are features of the system, quite as valuable as the direct benefit of the instruction which it imparts. But it is plain that the same princi-ples apply to the farther progress of education, in which each one must be mainly his own teacher. Why should not this prosperous and liberal city extend some reasonable amount of aid to the foundation and sup-port of a noble public library, to which the young people of both sexes, when they leave the schools, can resort for those works which pertain to general culture, or which are needful for research into any branch of useful knowledge? At present, if the young machinist, engineer, architect, chemist, engraver, painter, instrument-maker, musician (or student of any branch of science or literature) wishes to consult a valuable and especially a rare and costly work, he must buy it, often import it at an expense he can ill afford, or he must be indebted for its use to the liberality of private corporations or individuals. The trustees submit, that all the reasons which exist for furnishing the means of elementary education, at the public expense, apply in an equal degree to a reasonable provision to aid and encourage the acquisition of the knowledge required to complete a preparation for active life or to perform its duties. . . .

There is another point of view in which the subject may be re-garded,—a point of view, we mean, in which a free public library is not only seen to be demanded by the wants of the city at this time, but also seen to be the next natural step to be taken for the intellectual advancement of this whole community and for which this whole com-munity is peculiarly fitted and prepared.

Libraries were originally intended for only a very small proportion of the community in which they were established, because few persons could read, and fewer still desired to make inquiries that involved the consultation of many books. . . . (But) strong intimations . . . are already given, that ampler means and means better adapted to our peculiar condition and wants, are demanded, in order to diffuse through our society that knowledge without which we have no right to hope, that the condition of those who are to come after us will be as happy and prosperous as our own. The old roads, so to speak, are admitted to be no longer sufficient. Even the more modern turnpikes do not satisfy our wants. We ask for rail-cars and steamboats, in which many more persons—even multitudes—may advance together to the great end of life, and go faster, farther and better, by the means thus furnished to them, than they have ever been able to do before.

Nowhere are the intimations of this demand more decisive than in our own city, nor, it is believed, is there any city of equal size in the world, where added means for general popular instruction and self-culture . . . will be so promptly seized upon and so effectually used, as they will be here. One plain proof of this is, the large number of good libraries, we already possess. . . . But it is admitted . . . that these valuable libraries do not, either individually or in the aggregate, reach the great want of this city, considered as a body politic bound to train up its members in the knowledge which will best fit them for the positions in life to which they may have been born, or any others to which they may justly aspire through increased intelligence and personal worthiness. For multitudes among us have no right of access to any one of the more considerable and important of these libraries; and, except in rare instances, no library among us seeks to keep more than a single copy of any book on its shelves. . . .

And yet there can be no doubt that such reading ought to be furnished to all, as a matter of public policy and duty, on the same principle that we furnish free education, and in fact, as a part and a most important part, of the education of all. For it has been rightly judged that—under political, social and religious institutions like ours,—it is of paramount importance that the means of general information should be so diffused that the largest possible number of persons should be induced to read and understand questions going down to the very foundations of social order, which are constantly presenting themselves, and which we, as a people, are constantly required to decide, and to decide either ignorantly or wisely. That this *can* be done,—that is, that such libraries can be collected, and that they will be used to a much wider extent than libraries have ever been used before, and with much more important results, there can be no doubt; and if it can be done anywhere, it can be done here, in Boston. . . .

EDWARD EVERETT
GEORGE TICKNOR
SAMPSON REED
NATHANIEL SHURTLEFF
—Report of the Trustees of the Public Library
of the City of Boston, July, 1852

10. THE LABORATORY OF DEMOCRACY

It would be easy to compile a volume, nay a whole library, of personal narratives of schools, teaching, lyceums, libraries, and other educational activities. We must content ourselves here with a meager representation, one that tries to catch the spirit of the public school rather than to encompass its history or interpret its significance. The three excerpts given here need no explanation and little introduction. The first, describing school life in eastern Iowa in the seventies of the last century, comes from the disinguished novelist, Hamlin Garland. The second, which tells the heroic story of the founding of Tuskegee Institute in 1881, is written by the greatest leader of the Negro race in the last quarter of that century, Booker T. Washington. The third gives us still another kind of school, and a different school experience. It is written by the Russian-born Mary Antin, and tells the touching story of her introduction to the American public school in Boston. Different as they are, they all have a common theme: the role of the school as a democratizing agency.

A. SCHOOL LIFE ON THE PRAIRIE

THE school-house which was to be the center of our social life stood on the bare prairie . . . and like thousands of other similar buildings in the west, had not a leaf to shade it in summer nor a branch to break the winds of savage winter. . . . It was merely a square pine box painted a glaring white on the outside and a desolate drab within; at least drab was the original color, but the benches were mainly so greasy and hacked that original intentions were obscured. It had two doors on the eastern end and three windows on each side.

A long square stove (standing on slender legs in a puddle of bricks), a wooden chair, and a rude table in one corner, for the use of the teacher, completed the moveable furniture. The walls were roughly plastered and the windows had no curtains.

It was a barren temple of the arts even to the residents of Dry Run, and Harriet and I, stealing across the prairie one Sunday morning to look in, came away vaguely depressed. We were fond of the school and never missed a day if we could help it, but this neighborhood center seemed small and bleak and poor. . . .

The school-house which stood at the corner of our new farm was less than half a mile away, and yet on many of the winter days . . . we found it quite far enough. Hattie was now thirteen, Frank nine and I a little past eleven but nothing, except a blizzard such as I have described, could keep us away from school. Facing the cutting wind, wallowing through the drifts, battling like small intrepid animals, we often arrived at the door moaning with pain yet unsubdued, our ears frosted, our toes numb in our boots, to meet others in similar case around the roaring hot stove.

Often after we reached the school-house another form of suffering overtook us in the "thawing out" process. Our fingers and toes, swollen with blood, ached and itched, and our ears burned. Nearly all of us carried sloughing ears and scaling noses. Some of the pupils came two miles against these winds.

The natural result of all this exposure was of course, chilblains! Every foot in the school was more or less touched with this disease to which our elders alluded as if it were an amusing trifle, but to us it was no joke.

After getting thoroughly warmed up, along about the middle of the forenoon, there came into our feet a most intense itching and burning and aching, a sensation so acute that keeping still was impossible, and all over the room an uneasy shuffling and drumming arose as we pounded our throbbing heels against the floor or scraped our itching toes against the edge of our benches. The teacher understood and was kind enough to overlook this disorder. . . .

It was always too hot or too cold in our schoolroom and on certain days when a savage wind beat and clamored at the loose windows, the girls, humped and shivering, sat upon their feet to keep them warm, and the younger children with shawls over their shoulders sought permission to gather close about the stove.

Our dinner pails (stored in the entry way) were often frozen solid and it was necessary to thaw out our mince pie as well as our bread and butter by putting it on the stove. I recall, vividly, gnawing, dog-like, at the mollified outside of a doughnut while still its frosty heart made my teeth ache.

Happily all days were not like this. There were afternoons when the sun streamed warmly into the room, when long icicles formed on the eaves, adding a touch of grace to the desolate building, moments when the jingling bells of passing wood-sleighs expressed the natural cheer and buoyancy of our youthful hearts.

　　　　　　—HAMLIN GARLAND, *A Son of the Middle Border*

B. THE BEGINNINGS OF TUSKEGEE

On the morning that the school opened [1881] thirty students reported for admission. I was the only teacher. The students were about equally divided between the sexes. Most of them lived in Macon County, the county in which Tuskegee is situated and of which it is the county seat. A great many more students wanted to enter the school, but it had been decided to receive only those who were above fifteen years of age and who had previously received some education. The greater part of the thirty were public school teachers, and some of them were nearly forty years of age. With the teachers came some of their former pupils, and when they were examined it was amusing to note that in several cases the pupil entered a higher class than did his former teacher. It was also interesting to note how many big books some of them had studied and how many high-sounding subjects some of them claimed to have mastered. The bigger the book and the longer the name of the subject, the prouder they felt of their accomplishment. Some had studied Latin and one or two Greek. This they thought entitled them to special distinction.

The students who came first seemed to be fond of memorizing long and complicated rules in grammar and mathematics but had little thought or knowledge of applying these rules to the everyday affairs of their life. One subject which they liked to talk about and tell me that they had mastered in arithmetic was "banking and discount," but I soon found out that neither they nor almost any one in the neighborhood in which they lived had ever had a banking account. In registering the names of the students I found that almost every one of them had one or more initials. When I asked what the J. stood for in the name of John J. Jones, it was explained to me that this was a part of his "entitles." Most of the students wanted to get an education because they thought it would enable them to earn more money as schoolteachers. . . .

We found that the most of our students came from the country districts, where agriculture in some form or other was the main dependence of the people. We learned that about eighty-five per cent of the colored people in the Gulf states depended upon agriculture for their living. Since this was true, we wanted to be careful not to educate our students out of sympathy with agricultural life, so that they would be attracted from the country to the cities and yield to the temptation of trying to live by their wits. We wanted to give them such an education as would fit a large proportion of them to be teachers and at the same time cause them to return to the plantation districts and show the people there how to put new energy and new ideas into farming as well as into the intellectual and moral and religious life of the people. . . .

I recall one morning, when I told an old colored man who lived near and who sometimes helped me that our school had grown so large that it would be necessary for us to use the henhouse for school purposes and that I wanted him to help me give it a thorough cleaning out the next day, he replied in the most earnest manner: "What you mean, boss? You sholy ain't gwine clean out de henhouse in de *daytime?*"

A canvass was also made among the people of both races for direct gifts of money, and most of those applied to gave small sums. It was often pathetic to note the gifts of the older colored people, most of whom had spent their best days in slavery. Sometimes they would give five cents, sometimes twenty-five cents. Sometimes the contribution was a quilt or a quantity of sugar cane. I recall one old colored woman, who was about seventy years of age, who came to see me when we were raising money to pay for the farm. She hobbled into the room where I was, leaning on a cane. She was clad in rags, but they were clean. She said: "Mr. Washin'ton, God knows I spent de bes' days of my life in slavery. God knows I's ignorant an' poor, but," she added, "I knows what you an' Miss Davidson is tryin' to do. I knows you is tryin' to make better men an' better women for de colored race. I ain't got no money, but I wants you to take dese six eggs what I's been savin' up, an' I wants you to put dese six eggs into de eddication of dese boys an' gals."

Since the work at Tuskegee started, it has been my privilege to receive many gifts for the benefit of the institution, but never any, I think, that touched me so deeply as this one.

—Booker T. Washington, *Up From Slavery*

C. The Promised Land Fulfills Its Promise

In America . . . everything was free, as we had heard in Russia. Light was free; the streets were as bright as a synagogue on a holy day. Music was free; we had been serenaded, to our gaping delight, by a brass band of many pieces, soon after our installation on Union Place.

Education was free. That subject my father had written about repeatedly, as comprising his chief hope for us children, the essence of American opportunity, the treasure that no thief could touch, not even misfortune or poverty. It was the one thing that he was able to promise us when he sent for us; surer, safer than bread or shelter. On our second day I was thrilled with the realization of what this freedom of education meant. A little girl from across the alley came and offered to conduct us to school. My father was out, but we five between us had a few words of English by this time. We knew the word school. We understood. This child, who had never seen us till yesterday, who could not pronounce our names, who was not much better dressed than we, was able to offer us the freedom of the schools of Boston! No application made, no questions asked, no examinations, rulings, exclusions; no machinations, no fees. The doors stood open for every one of us. The smallest child could show us the way.

This incident impressed me more than anything I had heard in advance of the freedom of education in America. It was a concrete proof—almost the thing itself. One had to experience it to understand it. . . .

The apex of my civic pride and personal contentment was reached on the bright September morning when I entered the public school. That day I must always remember, even if I live to be so old that I cannot tell my name. To most people their first day at school is a memorable occasion. In my case the importance of the day was a hundred times magnified, on account of the years I had waited, the road I had come, and the conscious ambitions I entertained. . . .

Father himself conducted us to school. He would not have delegated that mission to the President of the United States. He had awaited the day with impatience equal to mine, and the visions he saw as he hurried us over the sun-flecked pavements transcended all my dreams. Almost his first act on landing on American soil, three years before, had been his application for naturalization. He had taken the remaining steps in the process with eager promptness, and at the earliest moment allowed by the law, he became a citizen of the United States. It is true that he had left home in search of bread for his hungry family, but he went blessing the necessity that drove him to America. The boasted freedom of the New World meant to him far more than the right to reside, travel, and work wherever he pleased; it meant the freedom to speak his thoughts, to throw off the shackles of superstition, to test his own fate, unhindered by political or religious tyranny. He was only a young man when he landed—thirty-two; and most of his life he had been held in leading-strings. He was hungry for his untasted manhood. . . .

So it was with a heart full of longing and hope that my father led us to school on that first day. He took long strides in his eagerness, the rest of us running and hopping to keep up.

At last the four of us stood around the teacher's desk; and my father, in his impossible English, gave us over in her charge, with some broken word of his hopes for us that his swelling heart could no longer contain. I venture to say that Miss Nixon was struck by something uncommon in the group we made, something outside of Semitic features and the abashed manner of the alien. My little sister was as pretty as a doll, with her clear pink-and-white face, short golden curls, and eyes like blue violets when you caught them looking up. My brother might have been a girl, too, with his cherubic contours of face, rich red color, glossy black hair, and fine eyebrows. Whatever secret fears were in his heart, remembering his former teachers, who had taught with the rod, he stood up straight and uncringing before the American teacher, his cap respectfully doffed. Next to him stood a starved-looking girl with eyes ready to pop out, and short dark curls that would not have made much of a wig for a Jewish bride.

All three children carried themselves rather better than the common run of "green" pupils that were brought to Miss Nixon. But the figure that challenged attention to the group was the tall, straight father, with his earnest face and fine forehead, nervous hands eloquent in gesture, and a voice full of feeling. This foreigner, who brought his children to school as if it were an act of consecration, who regarded the teacher of the primer class with reverence, who spoke of visions, like a man inspired, in a common schoolroom, was not like other aliens, who brought their children in dull obedience to the law; was not like the native fathers, who brought their unmanageable boys, glad to be relieved of their care. I think Miss Nixon guessed what my father's best English could not convey. I think she divined that by the simple act of delivering our school certificates to her he took possession of America.

—MARY ANTIN, *The Promised Land*

11. "TO PROMOTE THE LIBERAL EDUCATION OF THE INDUSTRIAL CLASSES"

The question of Federal aid to education is often discussed as if it were a wholly new idea. Actually Federal aid—chiefly to elementary education—goes back to 1787, and Federal aid to higher education began, in substantial fashion, with the Morrill Act of 1862. This famous Act, which appropriated some thirteen million acres of public lands to the States, gave a tremendous impetus to the establishment and development of State Universities. We give here the Morrill Act itself.

BE IT enacted by the Senate and House of Representatives of the United States of America in Congress assembled, That there be granted to the several States, for the purposes hereinafter mentioned, an amount of public land, to be apportioned to each State a quantity equal to thirty thousand acres for each senator and representative in Congress to which the States are respectively entitled by the apportionment under the census of eighteen hundred and sixty: Provided, That no mineral lands shall be selected or purchased under the provisions of this act.

SEC. 2. And be it further enacted, That the land aforesaid, after being surveyed, shall be apportioned to the several States in sections or subdivisions of sections, not less than one quarter of a section; and whenever there are public lands in a State subject to sale at private entry at one dollar and twenty-five cents per acre, the quantity to which said State shall be entitled shall be selected from such lands within the limits of such State, and the Secretary of the Interior is hereby directed to issue to each of the States in which there is not the quantity of public lands subject to sale at private entry at one dollar and twenty-five cents per acre, to which said State may be entitled under the provisions of this act, land scrip to the amount in acres for the deficiency of its distributive share: said scrip to be sold by said States and the proceeds thereof applied to the uses and purposes prescribed in this act, and for no other use or purpose whatsoever. . . .

SEC. 4. And be it further enacted, That all moneys derived from the sale of the lands aforesaid by the States to which the lands are apportioned, and from the sale of land scrip hereinbefore provided for, shall be invested in stocks of the United States, or of the States, or some other safe stocks, yielding not less than five per centum upon the par value of said stocks; and that the moneys so invested shall constitute a perpetual fund, the capital of which shall remain forever undiminished, (except so far as may be provided in section fifth of this act,) and the interest of which shall be inviolably appropriated, by each State which may take and claim the benefit of this act, to the endowment, support, and maintenance of at least one college where the leading object shall be, without excluding other scientific and classical studies, and including military tactics, to teach such branches of learning as are related to agriculture and mechanic arts, in such manner as the legislatures of the State may respectively prescribe, in order to promote the liberal and practical education of the industrial classes in the several pursuits and professions in life.

—The Morrill Act, July 2, 1862

12. "THE WORTHY FRUIT OF ACADEMIC CULTURE IS AN OPEN MIND"

A new era in higher education in America came with the election of Charles W. Eliot to the Presidency of Harvard University in 1869. Although Eliot inaugurated many sweeping reforms, he is best remembered, perhaps, for his championship of the elective system. That system is in disrepute now in some circles; we must keep in mind, when we judge it, conditions that obtained in American colleges generally when Eliot first proposed his new system. We give here an excerpt from Eliot's memorable Inaugural Address.

PHILOSOPHICAL subjects should never be taught with authority. They are not established sciences; they are full of disputed matters, open questions, and bottomless speculations. It is not the function of the teacher to settle philosophical and political controversies for the pupil, or even to recommend to him any one set of opinions as better than another. Exposition, not imposition, of opinions is the professor's part. The student should be made acquainted with all sides of these controversies, with the salient points of each system; he should be shown what is still in force of institutions or philosophies mainly outgrown, and what is new in those now in vogue. The very word "education" is a standing protest against dogmatic teaching. The notion that education consists in the authoritative inculcation of what the teacher deems true may be logical and appropriate in a convent, or a seminary for priests, but it is intolerable in universities and public schools, from primary to professional. The worthy fruit of academic culture is an open mind, trained to careful thinking, instructed in the methods of philosophic investigation, acquainted in a general way with the accumulated thought of past generations, and penetrated with humility. It is thus that the university in our day serves Christ and the church. . . .

Only a few years ago, all students who graduated at this College passed through one uniform curriculum. Every man studied the same subjects in the same proportions, without regard to his natural bent or preference. The individual student had no choice of either subjects or teachers. This system is still the prevailing system among American colleges, and finds vigorous defenders. It has the merit of simplicity. So had the school methods of our grandfathers—one primer, one catechism, one rod for all children. On the whole, a single common course of studies, tolerably well selected to meet the average needs, seems to most Americans a very proper and natural thing, even for grown men. . . .

In education, the individual traits of different minds have not been sufficiently attended to. Through all the period of boyhood the school studies should be representative; all the main fields of knowledge should be entered upon. But the young man of nineteen or twenty ought to know what he likes best and is most fit for. If his previous training has been sufficiently wide, he will know by that time whether he is most apt at language or philosophy or natural science or mathematics. If he feels no loves, he will at least have his hates. At that age the teacher may wisely abandon the schooldame's practice of giving a copy of nothing but zeros to the child who alleges that he cannot make that figure. When the revelation of his own peculiar taste and capacity comes to a young man, let him reverently give it welcome, thank God, and take courage. Thereafter he knows his way to happy, enthusiastic work, and, God willing, to usefulness and success. The civilization of a people may be inferred from the variety of its tools. There are thousands of years between the stone hatchet and the machine-shop. As tools multiply, each is more ingeniously adapted to its own exclusive purpose. So with the men that make the State. For the individual, concentration, and the highest development of his own peculiar faculty, is the only prudence. But for the State, it is variety, not uniformity, of intellectual product, which is needful. . . .

It has been alleged that the elective system must weaken the bond which unites members of the same class. This is true; but in view of another much more efficient cause of the diminution of class intimacy, the point is not very significant. The increased size of the college classes inevitably works a great change in this respect. One hundred and fifty young men cannot be so intimate with each other as fifty used to be. This increase is progressive. Taken in connection with the rising average age of the students, it would compel the adoption of methods of instruction different from the old, if there were no better motive for such change. The elective system fosters scholarship, because it gives free play to natural preferences and inborn aptitudes, makes possible enthusiasm for a chosen work, relieves the professor and the ardent disciple of the presence of a body of students who are compelled to an unwelcome task, and enlarges instruction by substituting many and various lessons given to small, lively classes, for a few lessons many times repeated to different sections of a numerous class. The College therefore proposes to persevere in its efforts to establish, improve, and extend the elective system. Its administrative difficulties, which seem formidable at first, vanish before a brief experience.

—CHARLES W. ELIOT, Inaugural Address, October 19, 1869

13. "MAKE EACH ONE OF OUR SCHOOLS AN EMBRYONIC COMMUNITY LIFE"

It is entirely appropriate that the greatest of our democratic statesmen should found a university, and that the most distinguished of our philosophers should make his primary contribution to education and should make education the basis of much of his philosophical thought. In a personal statement, written in 1930, John Dewey said philosophy should "focus about education as the supreme human interest in which, moreover, other problems, cosmological, moral, logical, come to a head." A professor at the Universities of Michigan and Chicago, Dewey had already emerged as one of America's most original and profound thinkers when, in 1899, he produced the most influential of all his many books: School and Society. In a sense this book, and Dewey's teachings and writings, may be said to have furnished the philosophical foundations for what is known as "progressive education." Perhaps the most characteristic single principle of progressive education is the principle that education is not "a preparation for life," it is life itself.

OUR school methods, and to a very considerable extent our curriculum, are inherited from the period when learning and command of certain symbols, affording as they did the only access to learning, were all-important. The ideals of this period are still largely in control, even where the outward methods and studies have been changed. We sometimes hear the introduction of manual training, art, and science into the elementary, and even the secondary, schools deprecated on the ground that they tend toward the production of specialists —that they detract from our present scheme of generous, liberal culture. The point of this objection would be ludicrous if it were not often so effective as to make it tragic. It is our present education which is highly specialized, one-sided, and narrow. It is an education dominated almost entirely by the mediaeval conception of learning. It is something which appeals for the most part simply to the intellectual aspect of our natures, our desire to learn, to accumulate information, and to get control of the

586

symbols of learning; not to our impulses and tendencies to make, to do, to create, to produce, whether in the form of utility or of art. The very fact that manual training, art, and science are objected to as technical, as tending toward mere specialism, is of itself as good testimony as could be offered to the specialized aim which controls current education. Unless education had been virtually identified with the exclusively intellectual pursuits, with learning as such, all these materials and methods would be welcome, would be greeted with the utmost hospitality.

While training for the profession of learning is regarded as the type of culture, or a liberal education, the training of a mechanic, a musician, a lawyer, a doctor, a farmer, a merchant, or a railroad manager is regarded as purely technical and professional. The result is that which we see about us everywhere—the division into "cultured" people and "workers," the separation of theory and practice. . . . While our educational leaders are talking of culture, the development of personality, etc., as the end and aim of education, the great majority of those who pass under the tuition of the school regard it only as a narrowly practical tool with which to get bread and butter enough to eke out a restricted life. If we were to conceive our educational end and aim in a less exclusive way, if we were to introduce into educational processes the activities which appeal to those whose dominant interest is to do and to make, we should find the hold of the school upon its members to be more vital, more prolonged, containing more of culture.

But why should I make this labored presentation? The obvious fact is that our social life has undergone a thorough and radical change. If our education is to have any meaning for life, it must pass through an equally complete transformation. This transformation is not something to appear suddenly, to be executed in a day by conscious purpose. It is already in progress. Those modifications of our school system which often appear (even to those most actively concerned with them, to say nothing of their spectators) to be mere changes of detail, mere improvement within the school mechanism, are in reality signs and evidences of evolution. The introduction of active occupations, of nature-study, of elementary science, of art, of history; the relegation of the merely symbolic and formal to a secondary position; the change in the moral school atmosphere, in the relation of pupils and teachers—of discipline; the introduction of more active, expressive, and self-directing factors—all these are not mere accidents, they are necessities of the larger social evolution. It remains but to organize all these factors, to appreciate them in their fulness of meaning, and to put the ideas and ideals involved into complete, uncompromising possession of our school system. To do this means to make each one of our schools an embryonic community life, active with types of occupations that reflect the life of the larger society and permeated throughout with the spirit of art, history, and science. When the school introduces and trains each child of society into membership within such a little community, saturating him with the spirit of service, and providing him with the instruments of effective self-direction, we shall have the deepest and best guaranty of a larger society which is worthy, lovely, and harmonious. . . .

From the standpoint of the child, the great waste in the school comes from his inability to utilize the experiences he gets outside the school in any complete and free way within the school itself; while, on the other hand, he is unable to apply in daily life what he is learning at school. That is the isolation of the school—its isolation from life. When the child gets into the schoolroom he has to put out of his mind a large part of the ideas, interests, and activities that predominate in his home and neighborhood. So the school, being unable to utilize this everyday experience, sets painfully to work, on another tack and by a variety of means, to arouse in the child an interest in school studies. While I was visiting in the city of Moline a few years ago, the superintendent told me that they found many children every year who were surprised to learn that the Mississippi river in the textbook had anything to do with the stream of water flowing past their homes. The geography being simply a matter of the schoolroom, it is more or less of an awakening to many children to find that the whole thing is nothing but a more formal and definite statement of the facts which they see, feel, and touch every day. When we think that we all live on the earth, that we live in an atmosphere, that our lives are touched at every point by the influences of the soil, flora, and fauna, by considerations of light and heat, and then think of what the school study of geography has been, we have a typical idea of the gap existing between the everyday experiences of the child and the isolated material supplied in such large measure in the school. This is but an instance, and one upon which most of us may reflect long before we take the present artificiality of the school as other than a matter of course or necessity. . . .

The child can carry over what he learns in the home and utilize it in the school; and the things learned in the school he applies at home. These are the two great things in breaking down isolation, in getting connection—to have the child come to school with all the experience he has got outside the school, and to leave it with something to be immediately used in his everyday life. The child comes to the traditional school with a healthy body and a more or less unwilling mind, though, in fact, he does not bring both his body and mind with him; he has to leave his mind behind, because there is no way to use it in the school. If he had a purely abstract mind, he could bring it to school with him, but his is a concrete one, interested in concrete things, and unless these things get over into school life he cannot take his mind with him. What we want is to have the child come to school with a whole mind and a whole body, and leave school with a fuller mind and an even healthier body. And speaking of the body suggests that, while there is no gymnasium in these diagrams, the active life carried on in its four corners brings with it constant physical exercise, while our gymnasium proper will deal with the particular weaknesses of children and their correction, and will attempt more consciously to build up the thoroughly sound body as the abode of the sound mind.

—JOHN DEWEY, *School and Society*, 1899

14. "THE CHIEF CHARACTERISTIC OF THE HIGHER LEARNING IS DISORDER"

The elective system, and the extension of the principles of progressive education into higher education, almost inevitably led to a reaction against what appeared to be miscellaneous and even anarchic practices. In no institution had the elective system been carried to greater extremes than at the University of Chicago. There was a certain justice, therefore, in the appointment to the Presidency of that institution of Robert M. Hutchins, chief critic of the elective system and champion of what might be called the classical education. Although subscribing to an educational philosophy very different from that which Eliot taught, Hutchins, like Eliot, has been a reformer and innovator. He had the courage, for example, to do away with intercollegiate football at the University of Chicago, to admit students after two years of high school, to abolish compulsory courses and conventional systems of grading, to introduce the

great books program, and to challenge many concepts and activities that
seemed to him to interfere with the proper business of the university—
the search for truth.

UNDER an intelligible program of general education, the student
would come to the end of the sophomore year with a solid knowledge of the foundations of the intellectual disciplines. He would be
able to distinguish and think about subject matters. He would be able
to use language and reason. He would have some understanding of
man and of what connects man with man. He would have acquired
some degree of wisdom.

On his emergence from general education what would he find? He
would find a vast number of departments and professional schools al!
anxious to give him the latest information about a tremendous variety
of subjects, some important, some trivial, some indifferent. He would
find that democracy, liberalism, and academic freedom meant that all
these subjects and fractions of subjects must be regarded as equally
valuable. It would not be democratic to hint that Scandinavian was not
as significant as law or that methods of lumbering was not as fundamental as astronomy. He would find a complete and thoroughgoing
disorder.

He would find, too, that we were proud of this disorder and resisted
attempts to correct it by calling them undemocratic and authoritarian.
As the free elective system denies that there is content to education, so
the organization of the modern university denies that there is rationality
in the higher learning. The free elective system as applied to professors
means that they can follow their own bents, gratify their own curiosity,
and offer courses in the results. The accumulation of credits in these
courses must lead, like those in any other courses, to the highest academic degrees. Discrimination among courses would be undemocratic.
The student would, then, confront an enormous miscellany, composed
principally of current or historical investigations in a terrifying multi-
plicity of fields. . . .

He would find an especially strange mixture in the field of what
might be called the productive arts. He would discover in the natural
sciences that making a highly refined gadget to make highly refined
measurements was as important as the development of a new theory of
the cosmos. He would find that making music, sculpture, or painting
was as much a university discipline as theology. But he would discover

that the Fine Arts, under the influence of the empirical sciences and the popular notion of pursuing the truth for its own sake, had become an empirical, historical, and "scientific" discipline, too. The microscopic study of Byzantine mosaics to determine their age and lineage by looking at their teeth, as it were, is as important as understanding them; in fact it is more so, because such investigation is "scientific research," and understanding is not.

This is what the young man would see as he stood gazing across the threshold of the higher learning. It may be briefly described as chaos. Who would blame him if, after one look, he decided to go into the comparative order and sanity of the business world?

How can these things be? Why is it that the chief characteristic of the higher learning is disorder? It is because there is no ordering principle in it. Certainly the principle of freedom in the current sense of that word will not unify it. In the current use of freedom it is an end in itself. But it must be clear that if each person has the right to make and achieve his own choices the result is anarchy and the dissolution of the whole. Nor can we look to the pursuit of truth for its own sake to unify the higher learning. Philistines still ask, what is truth? And all truths cannot be equally important. It is true that a finite whole is greater than any of its parts. It is also true, in the common-sense use of the word, that the New Haven telephone book is smaller than that of Chicago. The first truth is infinitely more fertile and significant than the second. The common aim of all parts of a university may and should be the pursuit of truth for its own sake. But this common aim is not sufficiently precise to hold the university together while it is moving toward it. Real unity can be achieved only by a hierarchy of truths which shows us which are fundamental and which subsidiary, which significant and which not.

The modern university may be compared with an encyclopedia. The encyclopedia contains many truths. It may consist of nothing else. But its unity can be found only in its alphabetical arrangement. The university is in much the same case. It has departments running from art to zoology; but neither the students nor the professors know what is the relation of one departmental truth to another, or what the relation of departmental truths to those in the domain of another department may be. . . .

The study of man and nature and of man and man has thus sunk under waves of empiricism and vocationalism.

—Robert Maynard Hutchins,
The Higher Learning in America, 1936

15. THE NATURE AND FUNCTION OF
ACADEMIC FREEDOM

The struggle against Communism and disloyalty, in the decade of the forties, inevitably affected education. As in the twenties, many States exacted loyalty oaths from teachers; some went so far as to single out teachers for this purpose, as if as a class they were peculiarly suspect. State-supported colleges and universities came in for investigations and purges, while superpatriotic alumni demanded that their universities rid themselves of teachers whose political and economic views did not harmonize with those of the American Legion or the Daughters of the American Revolution. There was a flare-up at Harvard when one Mr. Ober had the presumption to demand that that University dismiss men like Harlow Shapley and that it censor the public appearances and statements of members of its faculty. President Conant's response to this is a classic statement of the principle and necessity of academic freedom.

The Board of Regents' attack upon the great University of California is a familiar story and does not need elaboration here. That attack took the form of requiring special non-Communist loyalty oaths. A group of professors, outraged at this slur on their patriotism and convinced that the demand was illegal, refused to subscribe. The case was carried to the Court, which unanimously sustained the Professors and held the action of the Regents a violation of the Constitution. Here, as so often, those vocally most zealous for "Americanism" and "loyalty" were the first to violate the true principles of American democracy and to flout the Constitution.

A. "The Fortress of Our Liberties"

ONE condition is essential: freedom of discussion, unmolested inquiry. As in the early days of this century, we must have a spirit of tolerance which allows the expression of a great variety of opinions. On this point there can be no compromise even in days of an armed truce. But we should be completely unrealistic if we failed to recognize the difficulties which arise from the ideological conflict which according to the premise of this book will be with us for years to come. Excited citizens are going to be increasingly alarmed about alleged "communist infiltration" into our schools and colleges. Reactionaries are going to use the tensions inherent in our armed truce as an excuse for attacking a wide group of radical ideas and even some which are in the middle of the road.

How are we to answer the thoughtful and troubled citizen who wonders if our universities are being used as centers for fifth column activities? By emphasizing again the central position in this country of tolerance of diversity of opinion and by expressing confidence that *our* philosophy is superior to all alien importations. After all, this is but one version of the far wider problem which we encounter at the outset: how are we to win the ideological conflict if it continues on a non-shooting basis? Clearly not by destroying our basic ideas but by strengthening them; clearly not by retreating in fear from the Communist doctrine but by going out vigorously to meet it. Studying a philosophy does not mean endorsing it, much less proclaiming it. We study cancer in order to learn how to defeat it. We must study the Soviet philosophy in our universities for exactly the same reason. No one must be afraid to tackle that explosive subject before a class. If an avowed supporter of the Marx-Lenin-Stalin line can be found, force him into the open and tear his arguments to pieces with counter-arguments. Some of the success of the Communist propaganda in this country before the war was due to the fact that it was like pornographic literature purveyed through an academic black market, so to speak. For a certain type of youth this undercover kind of knowledge has a special attraction. And doctrines that are not combated in the classroom but treated merely with silence or contempt may be appealing to the immature.

The first requirement for maintaining a healthy attitude in our universities in these days, therefore, is to get the discussion of modern Marxism out into the open. The second is to recognize that we are not at peace but in a period of an armed truce. That means that the activities which go with war, such as vigorous secret intelligence, sabotage, and even planned disruption of the basic philosophy of a nation may well proceed. We must be on our guard. We must be realistic about the activities of agents of foreign powers, but at the same time be courageous in our support of the basis of our own creed, the maximum of individual freedom. We should be certain that any steps we take to counteract the work of foreign agents within our borders do not damage irreparably the very fabric we seek to save. The government, of course, must see to it that those who are employed in positions of responsibility and trust are persons of intelligence, discretion, and unswerving loyalty to the national interest. But in disqualifying others we should proceed with the greatest caution. Certain men and women who temperamentally are unsuited for employment by a Federal agency none the less can serve the nation in other ways. They may be entitled to our full respect as citizens though we may disagree with their opinions. For example, a person whose religious beliefs make him a conscientious objector is automatically disqualified from employment by the nation in matters pertaining to the use of force or preparation for the use of force. On the other hand, such a man may be an intellectual and moral leader of the greatest importance for the welfare of our society.

These obvious considerations have bearing on the problems of staffing a university. Universities, however they may be financed or controlled, are neither government bureaus nor private corporations; the professors are not hired employees. The criteria for joining a community of scholars are in some ways unique. They are not to be confused with the requirements of a Federal bureau. For example, I can imagine a naïve scientist or a philosopher with strong loyalties to the advancement of civilization and the unity of the world who would be a questionable asset to a government department charged with negotiations with other nations; the same man because of his professional competence might be extremely valuable to a university. Such conclusions are obvious to anyone who takes the trouble to think carefully about the degrees of prudence and sophistication met with in human beings. Such considerations will be self-evident to all who analyze the complex problem of loyalty.

The third condition necessary for maintaining free inquiry within our universities is to ask the scholars themselves to declare their own basic social philosophy. We must then be prepared in our universities to be sure that we have a variety of views represented and that in the classroom our teachers be careful scholars rather than propagandists. But the unpopular view must be protected for we would be quite naïve to imagine that there are no reactionaries who would like to drive all liberals from the halls of learning. . . .

Those who worry about radicalism in our schools and colleges are often either reactionaries who themselves do not bear allegiance to the traditional American principles or defeatists who despair of the success of our own philosophy in an open competition. The first group are consciously or unconsciously aiming at a transformation of this society, perhaps initially not as revolutionary or violent as that which the Soviet agents envisage, but one eventually equally divergent from our historic goals. The others are unduly timid about the outcome of a battle of *ideas*; they lack confidence in our own intellectual armament. (I mean literally the battle of ideas, not espionage or sabotage by secret agents.) They often fail to recognize that diversity of opinion within the framework of loyalty to our free society is not only basic to a university but to the entire nation. For in a democracy with our traditions only those reasoned convictions which emerge from diversity of opinion can lead to that unity and national solidarity so essential for the welfare of our country—essential not only for our own security but even more a requisite for intelligent action toward the end we all desire, namely, the conversion of the present armed truce into a firm and lasting peace.

Like all other democratic institutions based on the principles of toleration, individual freedom, and the efficacy of rational methods, the universities are certain to meet with many difficulties as they seek to preserve their integrity during this period of warring ideologies. But we would do well to remember this is not the first time that communities of scholars have been disturbed by doctrinal quarrels so deep-seated as to be in the nature of smoldering wars. The history of Oxford and Cambridge during the Civil Wars of the seventeenth century is interesting reading on this point. At that time the "true friends of learning" rallied to the support of those ancient institutions and protected them against the excesses of both sides. Today, likewise, the friends of learning must recognize the dangers which might threaten the universities if tempers rise as the armed truce lengthens. They must seek to increase the number of citizens who understand the true nature of universities, the vital importance of the tradition of free inquiry, the significance of life tenure for the older members of each faculty, the fact that violent differences of opinion are essential for education. They must be realistic about the fanatic followers of the Soviet philosophy who seek to infiltrate, control, and disrupt democratic organizations including student clubs. But they must also recognize the threat that comes from those reactionaries who are ready if a wave of hysteria should mount to purge the institutions of all doctrines contrary to their views. In short, our citadels of learning must be guarded by devoted laymen in all walks of life who realize the relation between education and American democracy. So protected, the universities need not worry unduly about infiltration of Marxist subversive elements or intimidation from without. They will remain secure fortresses of our liberties.

—JAMES BRYANT CONANT, *Education in a Divided World*, 1948

B. "SUBVERSION FROM WITHIN BY THE WHITTLING AWAY OF THE VERY PILLARS OF OUR FREEDOM"

The record ... discloses that for approximately a year and a half prior to April 21, 1950, the Regents, the faculty and the Alumni Association had considered the question of ways and means to implement the stated policy of the Regents of barring members of the Communist Party from employment at the University by means of a "Loyalty Oath." These discussions culminated in a meeting held on April 21, 1950, at which the Regents passed a resolution providing that after July 1, 1950, the beginning date of the new academic year, conditions precedent to employment or renewal of employment at the University would be (1) execution of the constitutional oath required of public officials of the State of California, and (2) acceptance of appointment by a letter which contained the following provision:

"Having taken the constitutional oath of office required of public officials of the State of California, I hereby formally acknowledge my acceptance of the position and salary named, and also state that I am not a member of the Communist Party or any other organization which advocates the overthrow of the government by force or violence, and that I have no commitments in conflict with my responsibilities with respect to impartial scholarship and free pursuit of truth. I understand that the foregoing statement is a condition of my employment and a consideration of payment of my salary."

The resolution further provided that,

"In the event that a member of the faculty fails to comply with any foregoing requirement applicable to him he shall have the right to petition the President of the University for a review of his case by the Committee on Privilege and Tenure of the Academic Senate, including an investigation of and full hearing on the reasons for his failure so to do. Final action shall not be taken by the Board of Regents until the Committee on Privilege and Tenure, after such investigation and hearing, shall have had an opportunity to submit to the Board, through the President of the University, its findings and recommendations. It is recognized that final determination in each case is the prerogative of the Regents."

Some thirty-nine professors at the University who refused to sign the affirmation set forth in the Regents' resolution accepted what they apparently believed to be the alternative to the signing of the oath as set forth in the resolution and petitioned the President of the University for a hearing before the Committee on Privilege and Tenure of the Academic Senate. The hearing resulted in favorable findings and recommendations by that committee as to each of the professors. On July 21, 1950, the Regents met and by a vote of 10 to 9 accepted those recommendations and appointed the non-signing professors to the faculty for the coming academic year. Following the passage of the resolution one of the Regents gave notice that he would change his vote from "No" to "Aye" and move to reconsider at the next meeting. At the next meeting of the Regents, on August 25, 1950, a motion to reconsider the matter of the appointments was passed by a vote of twelve to ten (one absent member stated by telegram that he would vote "no" if he were present), and the resolution adopting the recommendations of the Committee on Privilege and Tenure and appointing the professors to the faculty was defeated by a like vote of twelve to ten. Following this a motion was unanimously carried granting the non-signing professors ten days in which to comply by signing the statement prescribed in the resolution of April 21. . . .

The validity of the action taken by the Regents on August 25, 1950, is first challenged by petitioners on the ground that the affirmative statement demanded as a condition to their continued employment is a violation of Section 3 of Article XX of the Constitution which prescribes the form of oath for all officers, executive and judicial, and concludes with the prohibition that "no other oath, declaration or test, shall be required as a qualification for any office or public trust.". . .

At this late date it is hardly open to question but that the people of California in adopting Section 3 of Article XX also meant to include in our state Constitution that fundamental concept of what Mr. Chief Justice Hughes referred to as "freedom of conscience" and Mr. Justice Holmes called the "principle of free thought." Paraphrasing their words we conclude that the people of California intended, at least, that no one could be subjected, as a condition to holding office, to any test of political or religious belief other than his pledge to support the Constitutions of this state and of the United States; that that pledge is the highest loyalty that can be demonstrated by any citizen, and that the exacting of any other test of loyalty would be antithetical to our fundamental concept of freedom. Any other conclusion would be to approve that which from the beginning of our government has been denounced as the most effective means by which one special brand of political or economic philosophy can entrench and perpetuate itself to the eventual exclusion of all others; the imposition of any more inclusive test would be the forerunner of tyranny and oppression.

It is a well established principle of constitutional interpretation that the meaning of any particular provision is to be ascertained by considering the Constitution as a whole and that the duty of the court in interpreting the Constitution is to harmonize all its provisions. . . .

In the problem of interpretation with which we are presently confronted, we find in the specific mandate of Section 9 of Article IX of our Constitution, providing that the University shall be entirely independent of all political or sectarian influence, a standard by which to decide the question of whether or not the petitioners herein are to be included within the term "office or public trust" as used in Section 3 of Article XX. It goes without saying that in the practical conduct of the affairs of the University the burden of so preserving it free from sectarian and political influence must be borne by the faculty as well as by the Regents. Hence, if the faculty of the University can be subjected to any more narrow test of loyalty than the constitutional oath, the constitutional mandate in Section 9 of Article IX would be effectively frustrated, and our great institution now dedicated to learning and the search for truth reduced to an organ for the propagation of the ephemeral political, religious, social and economic philosophies, whatever they may be, of the majority of the Board of Regents of that moment.

It must be concluded that the members of the faculty of the University, in carrying out this most important task, fall within the class of persons to whom the framers of the Constitution intended to extend the protection of Section 3 of Article XX.

While this court is mindful of the fact that the action of the Regents was at the outset undoubtedly motivated by a desire to protect the University from the influences of subversive elements dedicated to the overthrow of our constitutional government and the abolition of our civil liberties, we are also keenly aware that equal to the danger of subversion from without by means of force and violence is the danger of subversion from within by the gradual whittling away and the resulting disintegration of the very pillars of our freedom.

It necessarily follows that the requirement that petitioners sign the form of contract prescribed in the Regents' resolution of April 21, 1950, was and is invalid, being in violation both of Section 3 of Article XX and Section 9 of Article IX of the Constitution of the State of California, and that petitioners cannot be denied reappointment to their posts solely because of their failure to comply with the invalid condition therein set forth.

—JUDGE PEEK.

Opinion in Tolman *v*. Regents of University of California, 1951

16. "LIBRARIES ARE THE VESSELS IN WHICH THE SEED CORN FOR THE FUTURE IS STORED"

Dorothy Canfield Fisher needs no introduction; the pioneer father to whom she here refers was President of the Universities of Nebraska and Ohio State and Librarian of Columbia University.

THE one true library pioneer whom I knew intimately was my father. He was an educator who preached a crusade for universal free public education long before that principle was taken for granted. When the movement was well started and would obviously go forward of its own impetus, he began another crusade—for universal free public libraries. These he saw as the needed rung in the educational ladder before the American citizenry could step off into that permanent intellectual maturity without which the hopes of the country's founders would come to nothing. What was the use of teaching Americans to read intelligently if they did not find around them an adequate supply of intelligently selected books to read?

My father and other generous-spirited library pioneers of his generation never doubted that with books and readers brought together the trick was done. But there have been times when I have been glad that they were in their graves and not with me as I have looked, shocked, at the echoing emptiness of certain well-stocked but neglected libraries. My father's wholehearted drive towards providing books might have lost some of the power of his ardor and courage had he guessed what nobody then knew—that there are mysterious, shut doors inside human heads which must be opened before the right books are taken from those open shelves and read. How could the pioneers of the library movement dream of the invisible barrier which rears itself inexplicably between the busy, happy reading-public of childhood, clustering in well-conducted children's rooms reading children's classics with delight, and those children grown up to be the general public, who read no classics, none, nothing but an occasional best seller, and the magazines? . . .

They thought—or no, they did not think, they took for granted—that an educated citizenry . . . would spontaneously and eagerly throng into the public library in knowledge-hungry crowds, if the doors could be opened to them, using books as tools to advance themselves steadily year by year in good taste, cultivation, good judgment, sound information. There is no doubt that they would be aghast to see that this is not exactly what happens—to put it mildly. They would be horrified by the statistics showing the large percentage of our population which cannot read with ease, and will not of its own accord read any book beyond the comprehension of an eighth grade child. They would be staggered by the small proportion of the population of any community which uses the books so freely offered by the public libraries. . . . Yes, I think the forefathers of the free public library would have turned rather pale at some of the things we know, and they did not, about the relationship between books and human beings.

But, remembering their ardor, their willingness to give their lives to the cause, I do not for a moment believe that they would be disheartened. I am sure that after they had had time just to catch their breath they would have turned from their crusade for a wider public recognition of the vital need for books in a democracy, to an impassioned attack on the mystery of why a democracy doesn't use its books as it should. They were determined . . . to open to their countrymen those doors to knowledge, understanding and joy called books. . . .

Rising with a strong wingbeat of the imagination, they may catch a glimpse of libraries of the future circulating not only those sheets of paper marked with printed symbols of words which so large a part of our race translate with difficulty into ideas, but paintings, music (why not?), records of poems read by the poets themselves, motion-picture films of far places, of mechanical processes hard to put into these word symbols, of the stars in their courses, of instruction in sports and dancing, in hygiene, in homemaking, in the care of children, in gardening, in all the arts.

Yet there is an aspect of the library movement now, in our troubled times, rising melodramatically into view, undreamed of, I think, by its founders, with all their greatness of vision. They took for granted some forms of freedom, assumed that liberty to think was as pervasive in modern life as the air we breathe. And we have been tragically taught that this freedom is the first object of attack whenever democracy is threatened. Highly as the founders valued the institution of public libraries . . . it did not occur to them, I think, that public libraries play a vital part in preserving that intellectual freedom without which any form of government is a blighting tyranny. It was only in the lurid light from the book-burning auto-da-fé in Germany, that the library took on its true shape of protecting fortress, that we saw it as the very stronghold of freedom. Since then few of our generation can pass a public library—from the humblest village collection of books to the grandest white marble urban palace—without a lift of the heart, both in thankfulness that it is there and in determination to do our share in preserving the shelter that it gives to the living seeds of intellectual life.

—DOROTHY CANFIELD FISHER, "The Stronghold of Freedom," 1939

Part III

America as a World Power

12

Peace and War

It is sobering to reflect how much of U.S. history has been taken up, in one way or another, with war, preparation for war, or solution of the problems left by war. During the century and three-quarters since Independence, the United States has been engaged in major wars for twenty-five years—one year out of every seven of national existence. If the periods of preparation and of reconstruction were added, the proportion would be much larger. During the last decade war has become the normal and peace the abnormal situation. Nor is there any compelling reason to believe that the next few decades will usher in the reign of peace. Even if the United States does not become involved in a major war—and with it the rest of the Western world—there is every reason to believe that she will have to continue on a war basis, and that her economy, her politics, her diplomacy, and her psychology will be closer to that of war than to that of peace.

Let us then look at some of the qualities the people of the United States have revealed when, in the past, they have been confronted by the issues of war. We can discern both principles and policies that are consistent over several generations; we can detect, too, some modifications that have come under the pressure of total war.

There is first the principle that the civil is superior to the military—a principle inherited from the British and flourishing in all English-speaking countries. This principle, which Americans take pretty much for granted, is the exception, however, rather than the rule. Yet Americans have fairly consistently maintained it. It is recognized in the constitutional system, which makes the President commander-in-chief of the armed forces of the nation: a position far more than merely titular. It has always been recognized by the army itself, by leading generals, and by the public, and is an important part of the American tradition.

Some observers fear that this Anglo-Saxon principle of the superiority of the civil to the military is in serious danger today. Never before in our history has the military exerted so much influence or exercised so much power. Yet, so far, there is no reason to doubt that the American people are still loyal to the principle of ultimate civilian control.

Not unconnected with this basic principle is a consideration that cannot but command interest abroad. It is this: that heretofore there has existed no military class or caste in the United States and that no special distinction has ever attached to the officer's uniform. The military is respected, like any other profession. But the military does not have a preferred position in society, as it had in Germany, in France, in Russia, even in democratic Britain.

As American society is democratic, democracy characterizes the military. The democratic and even equalitarian character of armies was most prominent in the nineteenth century, but even in the two World Wars it is probable that the American armies were the most democratic in the world. In the Civil War companies elected their own officers, while higher-ranking officers were customarily selected by state governors from civilian ranks—and often for any but military reasons. That situation was not conducive to military discipline, but it did emphasize the extent to which the war was a people's war. Even in the Second World War, relations between officers and privates were customarily more intimate in the American than in the British or French or even the Russian armies.

A third characteristic is that Americans have always, heretofore, been unprepared for war. In a sense every war has taken the United States by surprise, even when—as in 1941, for example—there has been ample warning. From the point of view of a people eager to win a war, this is a very distressing situation. But from the point of view of a democratic and peaceable people, it is not so much distressing as natural and almost inevitable. For what, after all, is the alternative to unpreparedness? It is, of course, preparedness. And preparedness is no simple matter of universal military training or the stock-piling of arms and ordnance. It goes far deeper than that. It is primarily psychological. It requires a military-mindedness, a war-mindedness, or it will not work at all. The kind of people who are prepared for war are those who are thoroughly military-minded. They are the people who accept war as the normal thing, who give priority to the military, who maintain and cherish a military class, who subordinate their politics, their economy, their educational system, their culture, to the demands of the military.

This, too, may be in process of change. In a world swept by confused alarms of struggle and flight, readiness for war is imposed on almost every nation and imposed implacably on that nation which has become the leader of one of the camps. To be unready, now, is to be criminally negligent. We have probably entered an era of peacetime conscription, universal military service, continuous officer training, immense annual appropriations for the military, and the concentration of a substantial part of production and of scientific research on military needs. If we have, and if this situation persists for some time, we may expect profound changes in our economy and our government.

Because Americans have almost always been unprepared for war, and because they regard war as abnormal, they have fought wars as amateurs. This was distinctly less true of the Second World War than of any of its predecessors, to be sure, and the era of the amateur spirit in warfare may have passed. Yet from the Revolution to the eve of World War II, the amateur spirit prevailed. We raised armies any old way, officered them by chance, permitted business as usual. Even during the Second World War there was no such total mobilization of man and woman power in the United States as in Britain, for example, no such rigorous controls of the economy, no such heavy burden of taxation.

We pay a high price for unpreparedness and for carelessness and for the amateur spirit, but it is important to remember that we would pay a high price, too, for the alternatives. As the opposite of unpreparedness is constant preparedness, so the opposite of the amateur spirit is the professional spirit. The professional spirit in the military is not something that can be adopted at a moment's notice, and then disposed of; it is something deeply ingrained in character, habit, and conduct. It requires a large officer class, a military-minded people, a government that concentrates on military concerns, the mobilization of all national resources for the purpose of war. If we get depressed over the spectacle of the amateur spirit in war, it is consoling to remember that in the great conflicts of the twentieth century it was the amateurs, like Britain and the United States, who won, and the professionals, like Germany and Japan, who lost.

A fifth principle is that Americans must be convinced that the war they are fighting is just, that the cause they champion is good, and that they are not the aggressors. They have ever been reluctant to start wars, and they have never fought well in wars whose motives or character they distrusted. The themes of the just cause and of nonaggression run all through American history. The Declaration of Independence appealed to "a decent respect to the opinions of mankind," and was probably the first document in modern history that did so. Even the national anthem sounds this note: "Then conquer we must, for our cause it is just, and this be our motto, in God is our trust." What other national anthem, after all, pays respect to this principle? As many people in the United States doubted the righteousness of the War of 1812 and the Mexican War, both were badly managed and feebly supported. And both Wilson and Franklin Roosevelt devoted an immense amount of thought and energy to making clear the moral issues of the wars into which they led the U.S. people.

A sixth generalization has to do with the manner in which Americans wage war and can be expected to wage war in the future. It cannot be surprising that the American people fight wars pretty much as they do other things—in industry, in farming, in government, for example. They like large-scale organization; they prefer to fight with machinery, with the best and the most arms and equipment; they reveal in war as in peace an immeasurable inventiveness and ingenuity. This was true all through the nineteenth century, and it is true today. Yet it is important to remember that though Americans prefer to fight with the best equipment—and who does not?—they can fight without it. The Confederates, after all, lacked both men and equipment but fought as well as the Federals.

Two observations about our character and habits in peace-making—or in reconstruction—are relevant. Americans are not a vindictive people, nor are they cankered by that sense of insecurity and inferiority that requires the ostentatious display of power or signs of triumph. They have never, therefore, imposed harsh terms on defeated enemies, nor have they nursed grievances against the defeated. The wars with England may be alleged as exceptions to this generalization, but actually they are not. The Civil War in the United States was as bitter a conflict as any of its kind in modern history, but no leader of the rebellion lost his life as a penalty for his conduct.

1. LEXINGTON AND CONCORD

The battles of Lexington and Concord are ever memorable as the first blows for independence, the shots "heard round the world." To the student of the American character they are of further significance. For two things about these battles at once command our attention. The first is that they were fought by civilians, by amateurs, by men who rallied to the defense of their own, fought courageously, and then went home again. The second is that those who fought, fought a defensive battle. "If they mean to have a war, let it begin here," Captain Parker is supposed to have said, on Lexington Common, and that historic defiance might be taken as the American maxim for all wars in which they have been engaged. The "official" account of the Battle of Lexington is by no means objective; what is important about it is that it should have been issued at all—that the Congress should have thought it so important to establish the fact that the British fired the first shots. We give the essential part of that official account, and Emerson's commemorative poem, "Concord Hymn."

A. AMERICAN ACCOUNT OF THE BATTLE OF LEXINGTON

WATERTOWN, April 26th, 1775.
In provincial congress of Massachusetts, to the inhabitants
of Great Britain.

FRIENDS: and fellow subjects—Hostilities are at length commenced in this colony by the troops under the command of general Gage, and it being of the greatest importance, that an early, true, and authentic account of this inhuman proceeding should be known to you, the congress of this colony have transmitted the same, and from want of a session of the hon. continental congress, think it proper to address you on the alarming occasion.

By the clearest depositions relative to this transaction, it will appear that on the night preceding the nineteenth of April instant, a body of the king's troops, under the command of colonel Smith, were secretly landed at Cambridge, with an apparent design to take or destroy the military and other stores, provided for the defence of this colony, and deposited at Concord—that some inhabitants of the colony, on the night aforesaid, whilst travelling peaceably on the road, between Boston and Concord, were seized and greatly abused by armed men, who appeared to be officers of general Gage's army; that the town of Lexington, by these means, was alarmed, and a company of the inhabitants mustered on the occasion—that the regular troops on their way to Concord, marched into the said town of Lexington, and the said company, on their approach, began to disperse—that, notwithstanding this, the regulars rushed on with great violence and first began hostilities, by firing on said Lexington company, whereby they killed eight, and wounded several others—that the regulars continued their fire, until those of said company, who were neither killed nor wounded, had made their escape—that colonel Smith, with the detachment then marched to Concord, where a number of provincials were again fired on by the troops, two of them killed and several wounded, before the provincials fired on them, and provincials were again fired on by the troops, produced an engagement that lasted through the day, in which many of the provincials and more of the regular troops were killed and wounded.

To give a particular account of the ravages of the troops, as they retreated from Concord to Charlestown, would be very difficult, if not impracticable; let it suffice to say, that a great number of the houses on the road were plundered and rendered unfit for use, several were burnt, women in child-bed were driven by the soldiery naked into the streets, old men peaceably in their houses were shot dead, and such scenes exhibited as would disgrace the annals of the most uncivilized nation.

These, brethren, are marks of ministerial vengeance against this colony, for refusing with her sister colonies, a submission to slavery; but they have not yet detached us from our royal sovereign. We profess to be his loyal and dutiful subjects, and so hardly dealt with as we have been, are still ready with our lives and fortunes, to defend his person, family, crown and dignity. Nevertheless, to the persecution and tyranny of his cruel ministry we will not tamely submit—appealing to Heaven for the justice of our cause, we determine to die or be free. . . .

By order,
Joseph Warren, President.
—Account by the Provincial Congress at Watertown, April 26, 1775

B. "Concord Hymn"

By the rude bridge that arched the flood,
Their flag to April's breeze unfurled,
Here once the embattled farmers stood
And fired the shot heard round the world.

The foe long since in silence slept;
Alike the conqueror silent sleeps;
And Time the ruined bridge has swept
Down the dark stream which seaward creeps.

On this green bank, by this soft stream,
We set to-day a votive stone;
That memory may their deed redeem,
When, like our sires, our sons are gone.

Spirit, that made those heroes dare
To die, and leave their children free,
Bid Time and Nature gently spare
The shaft we raise to them and thee.
—Ralph Waldo Emerson, "Concord Hymn," 1837

2. "HAD THIS DAY BEEN WANTING, THE WORLD HAD NEVER SEEN THE LAST STAGE OF PERFECTION"

The story of the failure of the Congress to pay the soldiers who had fought heroically for years against the British is familiar enough. Neglect, and the betrayal of obligations, led to mutinies; led to a proposal that Washington overthrow the supine Congress and make himself king; and led to the "Newburgh Address" calling on the officers of the Continental Army to take by force what they were entitled to, or to abandon the government that had shown itself incapable of gratitude. It was this latter suggestion that Washington met and defeated by his famous address to the officers of the Army. The preliminaries of Wash-

*ington's reply belong to American folklore. "When the General," wrote
Colonel David Cobb of the 5th Massachusetts,*

*took his station in the desk of the pulpit . . . he took out his written address
from his coat pocket, and his spectacles, with his other hand, from his waistcoat pocket, and then addressed the officers in the following manner:
"Gentlemen, you will permit me to put on my spectacles, for I have not only
grown gray, but almost blind, in the service of my country." This little address, with the mode and manner of delivering it, drew tears from many of
the officers.*

*The significance of Washington's reply lies not only in this memorable
episode, but in the devastating rebuke to all those who would use the
military to coerce the civilian authority.*

To the Officers of the Army

Head Quarters, Newburgh, March 15, 1783.

GENTLEMEN: By an anonymous summons, an attempt has been
made to convene you together; how inconsistent with the rules of
propriety! how unmilitary! and how subversive of all order and discipline, let the good sense of the Army decide.

In the moment of this Summons, another anonymous production
was sent into circulation, addressed more to the feelings and passions,
than to the reason and judgment of the Army. The author of the piece,
is entitled to much credit for the goodness of his Pen and I could wish
he had as much credit for the rectitude of his Heart, for, as Men see
thro' different Optics, and are induced by the reflecting faculties of the
Mind, to use different means, to attain the same end, the Author of
the Address, should have had more charity, than to mark for Suspicion,
the Man who should recommend moderation and longer forbearance,
or, in other words, who should not think as he thinks, and acts as he
advises. But he had another plan in view, in which candor and liberality
of Sentiment, regard to justice, and love of Country, have no part;
and he was right, to insinuate the darkest suspicion, to effect the black-
est designs.

That the Address is drawn with great Art, and is designed to answer
the most insidious purposes. That it is calculated to impress the Mind,

with an idea of premeditated injustice in the Sovereign power of the United States, and rouse all those resentments which must unavoidably flow from such a belief. That the secret mover of this Scheme (whoever he may be) intended to take advantage of the passions, while they were warmed by the recollection of past distresses, without giving time for cool, deliberative thinking, and that composure of Mind which is so necessary to give dignity and stability to measures is rendered too obvious, by the mode of conducting the business, to need other proof than a reference to the proceeding.

Thus much, Gentlemen, I have thought it incumbent on me to observe to you, to shew upon what principles I opposed the irregular and hasty meeting which was proposed to have been held on Tuesday last: and not because I wanted a disposition to give you every oppertunity consistent with your own honor, and the dignity of the Army, to make known your grievances. If my conduct heretofore, has not evinced to you, that I have been a faithful friend to the Army, my declaration of it at this time wd. be equally unavailing and improper. But as I was among the first who embarked in the cause of our common Country. As I have never left your side one moment, but when called from you on public duty. As I have been the constant companion and witness of your Distresses, and not among the last to feel, and acknowledge your Merits. As I have ever considered my own Military reputation as inseperably connected with that of the Army. As my Heart has ever expanded with joy, when I have heard its praises, and my indignation has arisen, when the mouth of detraction has been opened against it, it can *scarcely be supposed*, at this late stage of the War, that I am indifferent to its interests. But, how are they to be promoted? The way is plain, says the anonymous Addresser. If War continues, remove into the unsettled Country; there establish yourselves, and leave an ungrateful Country to defend itself. But who are they to defend? Our Wives, our Children, our Farms, and other property which we leave behind us, or, in this state af hostile seperation, are we to take the two first (the latter cannot be removed), to perish in a Wilderness, with hunger, cold and nakedness? If Peace takes place, never sheath your Swords Says he untill you have obtained full and ample justice; this dreadful alternative, of either deserting our Country in the extremest hour of her distress, or turning our Arms against it, (which is the apparent object, unless Congress can be compelled into instant compliance) has something so shocking in it, that humanity revolts at the idea. My God!

what can this writer have in view, by recommending such measures?
Can he be a friend to the Army? Can he be a friend to this Country?
Rather, is he not an insidious Foe? Some Emissary, perhaps, from New
York, plotting the ruin of both, by sowing the seeds of discord and
seperation between the Civil and Military powers of the Continent?
And what a Compliment does he pay to our Understandings, when
he recommends measures in either alternative, impracticable in their
Nature?

But here, Gentlemen, I will drop the curtain, because it wd. be as
imprudent in me to assign my reasons for this opinion, as it would be
insulting to your conception, to suppose you stood in need of them. A
moment's reflection will convince every dispassionate Mind of the
physical impossibility of carrying either proposal into execution.

There might, Gentlemen, be an impropriety in my taking notice,
in this Address to you, of an anonymous production, but the manner
in which that performance has been introduced to the Army, the effect
it was intended to have, together with some other circumstances, will
amply justify my observations on the tendency of that Writing. With
respect to the advice given by the Author, to suspect the Man, who
shall recommend moderate measures and longer forbearance, I spurn
it, as every Man, who regards that liberty, and reveres that justice for
which we contend, undoubtedly must; for if Men are to be precluded
from offering their Sentiments on a matter, which may involve the
most serious and alarming consequences, that can invite the consideration of Mankind, reason is of no use to us; the freedom of Speech may
be taken away, and, dumb and silent we may be led, like sheep, to the
Slaughter.

I cannot, in justice to my own belief, and what I have great reason
to conceive is the intention of Congress, conclude this Address, without
giving it as my decided opinion, that that Honble Body, entertain
exalted sentiments of the Services of the Army; and, from a full conviction of its merits and sufferings, will do it compleat justice. That their
endeavors, to discover and establish funds for this purpose, have been
unwearied, and will not cease, till they have succeeded, I have not a
doubt. But, like all other large Bodies, where there is a variety of
different Interests to reconcile, their deliberations are slow. Why then
should we distrust them? and, in consequence of that distrust, adopt
measures, which may cast a shade over that glory which, has been so
justly acquired; and tarnish the reputation of an Army which is cele-

brated thro' all Europe, for its fortitude and Patriotism? and for what is this done? to bring the object we seek nearer? No! most certainly, in my opinion, it will cast it at a greater distance.

For myself (and I take no merit in giving the assurance, being induced to it from principles of gratitude, veracity and justice), a grateful sence of the confidence you have ever placed in me, a recollection of the chearful assistance, and prompt obedience I have experienced from you, under every vicissitude of Fortune, and the sincere affection I feel for an Army, I have so long had the honor to Command, will oblige me to declare, in this public and solemn manner, that, in the attainment of compleat justice for all your toils and dangers, and in the gratification of every wish, so far as may be done consistently with the great duty I owe my Country, and those powers we are bound to respect, you may freely command my Services to the utmost of my abilities.

While I give you these assurances, and pledge myself in the most unequivocal manner, to exert whatever ability I am possessed of, in your favor, let me entreat you, Gentlemen, on your part, not to take any measures, which, viewed in the calm light of reason, will lessen the dignity, and sully the glory you have hitherto maintained; let me request you to rely on the plighted faith of your Country, and place a full confidence in the purity of the intentions of Congress; that, previous to your dissolution as an Army they will cause all your Accts. to be fairly liquidated, as directed in their resolutions, which were published to you two days ago, and that they will adopt the most effectual measures in their power, to render ample justice to you, for your faithful and meritorious Services. And let me conjure you, in the name of our common Country, as you value your own sacred honor, as you respect the rights of humanity, and as you regard the Military and National character of America, to express your utmost horror and detestation of the Man who wishes, under any specious pretences, to overturn the liberties of our Country, and who wickedly attempts to open the flood Gates of Civil discord, and deluge our rising Empire in Blood. By thus determining, and thus acting, you will pursue the plain and direct road to the attainment of your wishes. You will defeat the insidious designs of our Enemies, who are compelled to resort from open force to secret Artifice. You will give one more distinguished proof of unexampled patriotism and patient virtue, rising superior to the pressure of the most complicated sufferings; And you will, by the dignity of your Conduct, afford occasion for Posterity to say, when speaking of the glorious example you have exhibited to Mankind, "had this day been wanting, the World had never seen the last stage of perfection to which human nature is capable of attaining."

—GEORGE WASHINGTON,
Address to the Officers of the Army, March 15, 1783

3. "I SHALL NEVER SURRENDER NOR RETREAT"

We take for granted that Americans do not know when they are licked and so keep on fighting, and we take for granted, too, that they fight as well when they are the underdog as when they have superiority in arms or men. This was true at Bunker Hill and Princeton; it was true again and again of both Union and Confederate soldiers; it was true at Midway and Bastogne. It is not that Americans have a monopoly on courage, or that they are even more courageous than other people; it is rather that democratic armies who know what they are fighting for customarily fight better than professional armies who do not care about either issues or countries. And there is another factor that we must not overlook: that habits and necessities of frontier life and, later, of the playing field ingrained in Americans the instinctive feeling that the greater the odds the greater the necessity for courage, and that it is always wrong to quit. This is a long introduction to a short but memorable document. In 1835 the American settlers in Texas organized for independence. The Mexicans not unnaturally refused to acquiesce in the breakup of their nation and early in 1836 General Santa Anna moved into Texas with a large army. The Texans took their stand in the Alamo, outside San Antonio, and it was from that now historic spot that the Commandant, William Travis, sent his famous message.

COMMANDANCY of the Alamo, Bexar, February 24, 1836.— To the people of Texas and all Americans in the world.

Fellow citizens and compatriots: I am besieged by a thousand or more of the Mexicans under Santa Anna. I have sustained a continual bombardment and cannonade for twenty-four hours and have not lost a man. The enemy has demanded a surrender at discretion; other-

wise the garrison are to be put to the sword if the fort is taken.
I have answered the demand with a cannon shot, and our flag still
waves proudly from the walls. *I shall never surrender nor retreat.*
Then, I call on you in the name of liberty, of patriotism, and everything dear to the American character, to come to our aid with all dis-
patch. The enemy is receiving reinforcements daily and will no doubt
increase to three or four thousand in four or five days. If this call is
neglected, I am determined to sustain myself as long as possible and
die like a soldier who never forgets what is due to his own honor
and that of his country. VICTORY OR DEATH.

WILLIAM BARRET TRAVIS
Lieutenant Colonel Commandant

P.S. The Lord is on our side. When the enemy appeared in sight
we had not three bushels of corn. We have since found in deserted
houses eighty or ninety bushels and got into the walls twenty or thirty
head of beeves.

—HENDERSON YOAKUM, *History of Texas*

4. THE CHARACTER OF THE AMERICAN
SOLDIER

*We have already suggested that democratic, voluntary, and amateur
armies differ in marked respects from professional armies. That difference was dramatized in the Battles of Bunker Hill and of New Orleans,
which brought Old World and New World armies together. Because
the Civil War was entirely an American affair, Americans themselves
failed to realize how remarkable the Civil War soldier was—remarkable
for his dislike of discipline, his cavalier attitude toward officers, his
insistence on knowing what he was fighting about, his tenacity, courage,
and good behavior. We give here a brief comment on the character
of the American soldier by an American journalist, William Shanks.*

GENERALLY speaking, any two European powers at war are
represented each by a single army, which are brought together
upon a field of battle to decide at a blow the question in dispute,
and thus the European generals are afforded better chances for the

display of tactical abilities. In Europe, cavalry plays an important part on every battle-field, while in this country its assistance has seldom been asked in actual battle, though a no less effective application has been made of it in destroying communications. Except in the battle of General Sheridan, and in some instances where accident has brought cavalry into battle, our troopers were never legitimately employed. The art of marching as practiced in Europe was also varied here, and the European system of supplying an army is very different from our own. Their lines of march are decided by the necessities for providing cantonments in the numerous villages of the country, while on this continent marches are retarded, if not controlled, by the necessity of carrying tents for camps. The parallel which is here merely outlined might be pursued by one better fitted for the task to a highly suggestive and interesting conclusion.

In the same sense, and in still better defined contrast, the armies of America and of Europe have differed in their *personnel*. The armies of the principal powers of Europe are composed of men forced to arms by necessity in time of peace, and conscriptions in time of war; not, like the people of our own country, volunteering when the crisis demanded, with a clear sense of the danger before them, and for the stern purpose of vindicating the flag, and forcing obedience to the laws of the country. The European soldiers are conscripted for life, become confirmed in the habits of the camp, and are subjected to a system of discipline which tends to the ultimate purpose of rendering them mere pliant tools in the hands of a leader; while those of the United States, separated from the outer world only by the lax discipline necessary to the government of a camp, are open to every influence that books, that letters, and, to a certain extent, that society can lend. The highest aim of the European system is to sink individuality, and to teach the recruit that he is but the fraction of a great machine, to the proper working of which his perfectness in drill and discipline is absolutely necessary. In the United States volunteer army this same system was only partially enforced, and individuality was lost only on the battle-field, and then only so far as was necessary to *morale* did the man sink into the soldier. The private who in camp disagreed and disputed with his captain on questions of politics or science was not necessarily disobedient and demoralized on the battle-field. No late opportunity for a comparison between the prowess of our own and any European army has been presented, though the reader will have very little difficulty in convincing himself that the discipline of our troops in the South was better than that of the English in the Crimea or the French in Italy; while the "outrages of the Northern soldiers," at which England murmured in her partiality for the rebels, were not certainly as horrible as those committed by her own troops in India.

—WILLIAM SHANKS,
Personal Recollections of Distinguished Generals, 1866

5. GENERAL McCLELLAN TRIES TO TAKE CHARGE OF THE WAR

There is no more firmly established principle in Anglo-American constitutionalism than that of the supremacy of the civil over the military authority, in time of war as of peace. From Washington to Eisenhower American generals have been alert to observe and to reaffirm this principle. Yet from time to time it is challenged—challenged not in any crude attempt to seize power by force, but indirectly in the effort to impose policy upon the civil authority. The most spectacular attempt of this kind in our history—certainly up to our own day—came during the Civil War when General George McClellan tried to take the direction of the war out of the hands of President Lincoln. A prewar Democrat, McClellan disapproved of turning the war for union into a war to end slavery, and wanted to conduct it with a nice regard to that "peculiar institution." For Lincoln McClellan had nothing but contempt; on one occasion he allowed Lincoln to wait for him for over an hour, and then came in and went up to bed without a word to the President. Popular with the soldiers, and with certain elements of the public who wanted to use him as a foil for Lincoln, McClellan thought of himself as the savior of the country both on the battlefield and in councils of state. Unfortunately for the country he was unable to win victories on the battlefield, and fortunately for the country he was not allowed to play any part in the formulation of nonmilitary policy. Removed by Lincoln after the failure of the Peninsular Campaign, he was reinstated, fought the Battle of Antietam, failed to crush Lee, and was once again removed—

this time for good. In 1864 the Democrats nominated him on a platform that characterized the war as a failure. His defeat marked the end of the attempt to destroy Lincoln through a military hero, and the last time for eighty-seven years that a major party has tried to exploit a military reputation for the purpose of substituting military direction of policy for civil.

We give here McClellan's letter to Lincoln in which the general argued the necessity of avoiding any attack upon slavery. It is interesting to note that this letter was written while McClellan was still Commander of the Army of the Potomac.

HEADQUARTERS ARMY OF THE POTOMAC
July 7, 1862

MR. PRESIDENT: You have been fully informed that the rebel army is in the front, with the purpose of overwhelming us by attacking our positions or reducing us by blocking our river communications. I cannot but regard our condition as critical, and I earnestly desire, in view of possible contingencies, to lay before your excellency, for your private consideration, my general views concerning the existing state of rebellion, although they do not strictly relate to the situation of this army, or strictly come within the scope of my official duties. . . .

The time has come when the government must determine upon a civil and military policy, covering the whole ground of our national trouble.

The responsibility of determining, declaring, and supporting such civil and military policy, and of directing the whole course of national affairs in regard to the rebellion, must now be assumed and exercised by you, or our cause will be lost. The Constitution gives you power, even for the present terrible exigency.

This rebellion has assumed the character of a war; as such it should be regarded, and it should be conducted upon the highest principles known to Christian civilization. It should not be a war looking to the subjugation of the people of any State, in any event. It should not be at all a war upon a population, but against armed forces and political organizations. Neither confiscation of property, political execution of persons, territorial organization of States, or forcible abolition of slavery, should be contemplated for a moment.

In prosecuting the war, all private property and unarmed persons should be strictly protected, subject only to the necessity of military operation; all private property taken for military use should be paid or receipted for; pillage and waste should be treated as high crimes; all unnecessary trespass sternly prohibited, and offensive demeanor by the military towards citizens promptly rebuked. Military arrests should not be tolerated, except in places where active hostilities exist; and oaths, not required by enactments, constitutionally made, should be neither demanded nor received.

Military government should be confined to the preservation of public order and the protection of political right. Military power should not be allowed to interfere with the relations of servitude either by supporting or impairing the authority of the master, except for repressing disorder, as in other cases. Slaves, contraband under the act of Congress, seeking military protection, should receive it. The right of the government to appropriate permanently to its own service claims to slave labor should be asserted and the right of the owner to compensation therefor should be recognized. This principle might be extended, upon grounds of military necessity and security, to all the slaves of a particular State, thus working manumission in such State; and in Missouri, perhaps in Western Virginia also, and possibly even in Maryland, the expediency of such a measure is only a question of time. A system of policy thus constitutional, and pervaded by the influences of Christianity and freedom, would receive the support of almost all truly loyal men, would deeply impress the rebel masses and all foreign nations, and it might humbly be hoped that it would commend itself to the favor of the Almighty.

Unless the principles governing the future conduct of our struggle shall be made known and approved, the effort to obtain requisite forces will be almost hopeless. A declaration of radical views, especially upon slavery, will rapidly disintegate our present armies. . . .

In carrying out any system of policy which you may form, you will require a commander-in-chief of the army, one who possesses your confidence, understands your views, and who is competent to execute your orders, by directing the military forces of the nation to the accomplishment of the objects by you proposed. I do not seek that place for myself. I am willing to serve you in such position as you may assign to me, and I will do so as faithfully as ever subordinate served superior.

I may be on the brink of eternity; and as I hope forgiveness from my Maker, I have written this letter with sincerity towards you and from love for my country.

George B. McClellan
Major General Commanding
—GEORGE B. McCLELLAN, Letter to President Lincoln, July, 1862

6. "IN VICTORY MAGNANIMITY, IN PEACE GOOD WILL"

The greatest war leader of the English peoples since Washington, Winston Churchill, himself half-English, half-American, has formulated for us the maxim by which we conduct war:

> *In War: Resolution*
> *In Defeat: Defiance*
> *In Victory: Magnanimity*
> *In Peace: Good Will*

Magnanimity and good will characterized the two greatest leaders of the American people during the Civil War, Lincoln and Lee. Tragically, Lincoln was killed and his policy of magnanimity and good will repudiated by those who took over control of the government, with consequences which are with us even yet. Lee's influence persisted, in defeat as in victory, and his advice to his countrymen, that they should accept the verdict of Appomattox and turn their energies to reconstructing their own society, was generally accepted. We give here three historic documents: Lincoln's profound and moving Second Inaugural Address; Lee's noble farewell to the Army of Northern Virginia; and Lee's advice to his countrymen to bury contention with the war.

A. "WITH MALICE TOWARD NONE, WITH CHARITY FOR ALL"

FELLOW-COUNTRYMEN:—At this second appearing to take the oath of the presidential office there is less occasion for an extended address than there was at the first. Then a statement somewhat in detail of a course to be pursued seemed fitting and proper. Now, at the expiration of four years, during which public declarations have been constantly called forth on every point and phase of the great contest which still absorbs the attention and engrosses the energies of the nation, little that is new could be presented. The progress of our arms, upon which all else chiefly depends, is as well known to the public as to myself, and it is, I trust, reasonably satisfactory and encouraging to all. With high hope for the future, no prediction in regard to it is ventured.

On the occasion corresponding to this four years ago all thoughts were anxiously directed to an impending civil war. All dreaded it, all sought to avert it. While the inaugural address was being delivered from this place, devoted altogether to *saving* the Union without war, insurgent agents were in the city seeking to *destroy* it without war—seeking to dissolve the Union and divide effects by negotiation. Both parties deprecated war, but one of them would *make* war rather than let the nation survive, and the other would *accept* war rather than let it perish, and the war came.

One eighth of the whole population was colored slaves, not distributed generally over the Union, but localized in the southern part of it. These slaves constituted a peculiar and powerful interest. All knew that this interest was somehow the cause of the war. To strengthen, perpetuate, and extend this interest was the object for which the insurgents would rend the Union even by war, while the Government claimed no right to do more than to restrict the territorial enlargement of it. Neither party expected for the war the magnitude or the duration which it has already attained. Neither anticipated that the *cause* of the conflict might cease with or even before the conflict itself should cease. Each looked for an easier triumph, and a result less fundamental and astounding. Both read the same Bible and pray to the same God, and each invokes His aid against the other. It may seem strange that any men should dare to ask a just God's assistance in wringing their bread from the sweat of other men's faces, but let us judge not, that we be not judged. The prayers of both could not be answered. That of neither has been answered fully. The Almighty has His own purposes. "Woe unto the world because of offenses; for it must needs be that offenses come, but woe to that man by whom the offense cometh." If we shall suppose that American slavery is one of those offenses which, in the providence of God, must needs come, but which, having continued through His appointed time, He now wills to remove, and that He gives to both North and South this terrible war as the woe due to those by whom the offense came, shall we discern therein any departure from those divine attributes which the believers in a living God always ascribe to Him? Fondly do we hope, fervently do we pray, that this mighty scourge of war may speedily pass away. Yet, if God wills that it continue until all the wealth piled by the bondsman's two hundred and fifty years of unrequited toil shall be sunk, and until every drop of blood drawn with the lash shall be paid by another drawn with the sword, as was said three thousand years ago, so still it must be said, "The judgments of the Lord are true and righteous altogether."

With malice toward none, with charity for all, with firmness in the right as God gives us to see the right, let us strive on to finish the work we are in, to bind up the nation's wounds, to care for him who shall have borne the battle and for his widow and his orphan, to do all which may achieve and cherish a just and lasting peace among ourselves and with all nations.

—ABRAHAM LINCOLN, Second Inaugural Address, March 4, 1865

B. "AVOID THE USELESS SACRIFICE"

Headquarters, Army of Northern Virginia,

April 10, 1865.

After four years of arduous service, marked by unsurpassed courage and fortitude, the Army of Northern Virginia has been compelled to yield to overwhelming numbers and resources. I need not tell the survivors of so many hard-fought battles, who have remained steadfast to the last, that I have consented to this result from no distrust of them; but, feeling that valour and devotion could accomplish nothing that could compensate for the loss that would have attended the continuation of the contest, I have determined to avoid the useless sacrifice of those whose past services have endeared them to their countrymen. By the terms of the agreement, officers and men can return to their homes and remain there until exchanged. You will take with you the satisfaction that proceeds from the consciousness of duty faithfully performed; and I earnestly pray that a merciful God will extend to you His blessing and protection. With an increasing admiration of your constancy and devotion to your country, and a grateful remembrance of your kind and generous consideration of myself, I bid you an affectionate farewell.

—ROBERT E. LEE, Farewell to His Army, April 10, 1865

C. "BURY CONTENTION WITH THE WAR"

I have received your letter of [August 23, 1865] and in reply will state the course I have pursued under circumstances similar to your own and will leave you to judge of its propriety. Like yourself, I have since the cessation of hostilities advised all with whom I have conversed on the subject, who come within the terms of the President's proclamations, to take the oath of allegiance and accept in good faith the amnesty offered. But I have gone further and have recommended to those who were excluded from their benefits to make application, under the *proviso* of the proclamation of the 29th of May, to be embraced in its provisions. Both classes, in order to be restored to their former rights and privileges, were required to perform a certain act, and I do not see that an acknowledgment of fault is expressed in one more than the other. The war being at an end, the Southern states having laid down their arms, and the questions at issue between them and the Northern states having been decided, I believe it to be the duty of every one to unite in the restoration of the country and the re-establishment of peace and harmony. These considerations governed me in the counsels I gave to others and induced me on the 13th of June to make application to be included in the terms of the amnesty proclamation. I have not received an answer and cannot inform you what has been the decision of the President. But whatever that may be, I do not see how the course I have recommended and practised can prove detrimental to the former President of the Confederate States. It appears to me that the allayment of passion, the dissipation of prejudice, and the restoration of reason will alone enable the people of the country to acquire a true knowledge and form a correct judgment of the events of the past four years. It will, I think, be admitted that Mr. Davis has done nothing more than all the citizens of the Southern states and should not be held accountable for acts performed by them in the exercise of what had been considered by them unquestionable right. I have too exalted an opinion of the American people to believe that they will consent to injustice, and it is only necessary, in my opinion, that truth should be known for the rights of every one to be secured. I know of no surer way of eliciting the truth than by burying contention with the war.

ROBERT E. LEE

—J. WILLIAM JONES, *Personal Reminiscences of General Robert E. Lee*

7. "THE MOST FEARFUL ATROCITIES ...
THAT WAS EVER HEARD OF"

It would be seriously misleading to leave the impression that Americans always fought honorably and treated their enemies magnanimously. From colonial days on through the nineteenth century the pages of American history are stained with atrocities toward the Indians—and sometimes toward others as well, the Filipinos, for example. Perhaps the worst example of this in our history was the massacre of the peaceful Cheyenne Indians in southeastern Colorado—a massacre which came just at the time that Grant and Lee were locked in battle along the iron lines of Petersburg. We give here an excerpt from the testimony of Major Wynkoop to the Congressional Committee investigating the outrage.

FROM evidence of officers at this post I understand that on the 28th day of November, 1864, Colonel J. M. Chivington, with the 3d regiment of Colorado cavalry (one hundred-days men) and a battalion of the 1st Colorado cavalry arrived at this post, ordered a portion of the garrison to join him, under the command of Major Scott J. Anthony, against the remonstrances of the officers of the post, who stated circumstances of which he was well aware, attacked the camp of friendly Indians, the major portion of which were composed of women and children. The affidavits which become a portion of this report will show more particulars of that massacre; any one whom I have spoken to, whether officers or soldiers, agree in the relation that the most fearful atrocities were committed that was ever heard of; women and children were killed and scalped, children shot at their mother's breast, and all the bodies mutilated in the most horrible manner. Numerous eye-witnesses have described scenes to me, coming under the notice of Colonel Chivington, of the most disgusting and horrible character, the dead bodies of females profaned in such a manner that the recital is sickening. Colonel J. M. Chivington all the time inciting his troops to these diabolical outrages previous to the slaughter; commencing, he addressed his command, arousing in them, by his language, all their worst passions, urging them

626

on to the work of committing all these diabolical outrages, knowing himself all the circumstances of these Indians resting on the assurances of protection from the government given them by myself and Major S. J. Anthony; he kept his command in entire ignorance of the same, and when it was suggested that such might be the case, he denied it positively, stating that they were still continuing their depredations and lay there threatening the fort. I beg leave to draw the attention of the colonel commanding to the fact, established by the enclosed affidavits, that two-thirds or more of that Indian village were women and children. I desire also to state that Colonel J. M. Chivington is not my superior officer, but is a citizen mustered out of the United States service, and also to the time this inhuman monster committed this unprecedented atrocity he was a citizen by reason of his term of service having expired, he having lost his regulation command some months previous. Colonel Chivington reports officially that between five and six hundred Indians were left dead upon the field. I have been informed by Captain Booth, district inspector, that he visited the field and counted but sixty-nine bodies, and by others who were present, but that few, if any, over that number were killed, and that two-thirds of them were women and children. I beg leave to further state, for the information of the colonel commanding, that I talked to every officer in Fort Lyon, and many enlisted men, and that they unanimously agree that all the statements I have made in this report are correct. In conclusion, allow me to say that from the time I held the consultation with the Indian chiefs, on the headwaters of Smoky Hill, up to the date of the massacre by Colonel Chivington, not one single depredation had been committed by the Cheyenne and Arapaho Indians; the settlers of the Arkansas valley had returned to their camps and had been resting in perfect security, under assurances from myself that they would be in no danger for the present, by that means saving the country from what must inevitably become a famine were they to lose their crops; the lines of communication to the States were opened, and travel across the plains rendered perfectly safe through the Cheyenne and Arapaho country. Since this last horrible murder by Chivington the country presents a scene of desolation; all communication is cut off with the States, except by sending large bodies of troops, and already over a hundred whites have fallen as victims to the fearful vengeance of these betrayed Indians. All this country is ruined; there can be no such thing as peace in the future but by the total annihilation of all these Indians on the plains. I have most reliable information to the effect that the Cheyennes and Arapahoes have allied themselves with the Kiowas, Comanches and Sioux, and are congregated to the number of ——— thousand on the Smoky Hill. Let me also draw the attention of the colonel commanding to the fact stated by the affidavits, that John Smith, United States interpreter, a soldier and citizen were presented in the Indian camp by permission of the commanding officer of this camp, another evidence to the fact of these same Indians being regarded as friendly Indians; also, that Colonel Chivington states in his official report that he fought from nine hundred to one thousand Indians, and left from five to six hundred dead upon the field, the sworn evidence being that there were but five hundred souls in the village, two thirds of them being women and children, and that there were but from sixty to seventy killed, the major portion of whom were women and children. It will take many more troops to give security to the travellers and settlers in this country and to make any kind of successful warfare against the Indians. I am at work placing Fort Lyon in a state of defence, having all, both citizens and soldiers located here, employed upon the works, and expect to have them soon completed and of such a nature that a comparatively small garrison can hold the fort against any attack by Indians. Hoping that my report may receive the particular attention of the colonel commanding, I respectfully submit the same.

Your obedient servant,

E. W. Wynkoop,
Major, Com'dg 1st Veteran Cavalry and Fort Lyon, C. T.
Lieutenant J. E. Tappan,
A. A. A. General, District of Upper Arkansas.

—Major E. W. Wynkoop,
Testimony before Congressional Committee, 1865

8. "THE HAY FLEET"

John Hay called the Spanish American-War "a splendid little war." That was not, perhaps, the way the Cubans looked at it, or the Spaniards, or even those many Americans who fell victim to yellow fever or malaria. Yet the term is understandable enough. No other major war—perhaps no other war of modern times—had brought such speedy and complete victory at so little cost. Dewey destroyed the Spanish fleet in Manila Bay without losing a man; Sampson and Schley destroyed Cervera's fleet in Santiago Harbor with the loss of a single sailor; the military expedition through Puerto Rico was described by Finley Peter Dunne as "Gin'ral Miles' Gran' Picnic and Moonlight Excursion." The tradition of a humorous commentary on war—as on public affairs generally—is very old in our history. The ablest of all such commentators was doubtless the gifted journalist, creator of the immortal Dooley and Hennessy, Finley Peter Dunne, from whom we take this description of the "Hay Fleet."

MR. DOOLEY had been reading about General Shafter's unfortunately abandoned enterprise for capturing Santiago by means of a load of hay, and it filled him with great enthusiasm. Laying down his paper, he said: "By dad, I always said they give me frind Shafter th' worst iv it. If they'd left him do th' job th' way he wanted to do it, he'd 've taken Sandago without losin' an ounce."

"How was it he wanted to do it?" Mr. Hennessy asked.

"Well," said Mr. Dooley, " 'twas this way. This is th' way it was. Ol' Cervera's fleet was in th' harbor an' bottled up, as th' man says. Shafter he says to Sampson: 'Look here, me bucko, what th' divvle ar-re ye loafin' ar-round out there f'r,' he says, 'like a dep'ty sheriff at a prize fight?' he says. 'Why don't ye go in, an' smash th' Castiles?' he says. 'I'm doin' well where I am,' says Sampson. 'Th' navy iv th' United States,' he says, 'which is wan iv th' best, if not th' best, in th' wurruld,' he says, 'was not,' he says, 'intinded f'r sthreet fightin',' he says. 'We'll stay here,' he says, 'where we ar-re,' he says, 'until,' he says, 'we can equip th' ships with noomatic tire wheels,' he says, 'an' ball bearin's,' he says.

" 'Well,' says Shafter, 'if ye won't go in,' he says, 'we'll show ye th' way,' he says. An' he calls on Cap Brice, that was wan iv th' youngest an' tastiest dhressers in th' whole crool an' devastatin' war. 'Cap,' he says, 'is they anny hay in th' camp?' he says. 'Slathers iv it,' says th' cap. 'Onless,' he says, 'th' sojers et it,' he says. 'Th' las' load iv beef that come down fr'm th' undhertakers,' he says, 'was not good,' he says. 'Ayether,' he says, ' 'twas improperly waked,' he says, 'or,' he says, 'th' pall-bearers was careless,' he says. 'Annyhow,' he says, 'th' sojers won't eat it; an', whin I left, they was lookin' greedily at th' hay,' he says. 'Cap,' says

Gin'ral Shafter, 'if anny man ates a wisp, shoot him on th' spot,' he says. 'Those hungry sojers may desthroy me hopes iv victhry,' he says. 'What d'ye mane?' says Cap Brice. 'I mane this,' says Gin'ral Shafter. 'I mane to take yon fortress,' he says. 'I'll sind ye in, Cap,' he says, 'in a ship protected be hay,' he says. 'Her turrets 'll be alfalfa, she'll have three inches iv solid timithy to th' water line, an' wan inch iv th' best clover below th' wather line,' he says. 'Did ye iver see an eight-inch shell pinithrate a bale iv hay?' he says. 'I niver did," says Cap Brice. 'Maybe that was because I niver see it thried,' he says. 'Be that as it may,' says Gin'ral Shafter, 'ye niver see it done. No more did I,' he says. 'Onless,' he says, 'they shoot pitchforks,' he says, 'they'll niver hur-rt ye,' he says. 'Ye'll be onvincible,' he says. 'Ye'll pro-ceed into th' harbor,' he says, 'behind th' sturdy armor iv projuce,' he says. 'Let ye'er watchword be "Stay on th' far-rm," an' go on to victhry,' he says. 'Gin'ral,' says Cap Brice, 'how can I thank ye f'r th' honor?' he says. ' 'Tis no wondher th' men call ye their fodder,' he says. 'Twas a joke Cap Brice med at th' time. 'I'll do th' best I can,' he says; 'an', if I die in th' attempt,' he says, 'bury me where the bran-mash'll wave over me grave,' he says.

"An' Gin'ral Shafter he got together his fleet, an' put th' armor on it. 'Twas a formidable sight. They was th' cruiser 'Box Stall,' full armored with sixty-eight bales iv th' finest grade iv chopped feed; th' 'R-red Barn,' a modhern hay battleship, protected be a whole mow iv timothy; an' th' gallant little 'Haycock,' a torpedo boat shootin' deadly missiles iv explosive oats. Th' expedition was delayed be wan iv th' mules sthrollin' down to th' shore an' atin' up th' afther batthry an' par-rt iv th' ram iv th' 'R-red Barn' an', befure repairs was made, Admiral Cervera heerd iv what was goin' on. 'Glory be to the saints,' he says, 'what an injaynious thribe these Yankees is!' says he. 'On'y a few weeks ago they thried to desthroy me be dumpin' a load iv coal on me,' he says; 'an' now,' he says, 'they're goin' to smother me in feed,' he says. 'They'll be rollin' bar'ls iv flour on me fr'm th' heights next,' he says. 'I'd betther get out,' he says. ' 'Tis far nobler,' he says, 'to purrish on th' ragin' main,' he says, 'thin to die with ye'er lungs full iv hayseed an' ye'er eyes full iv dust,' he says. 'I was born in a large city,' he says; 'an' I don't know th' rules iv th' barn,' he says. An' he wint out, an' took his lickin'.

" 'Twas too bad Shafter didn't get a chanst at him, but he's give th' tip to th' la-ads that makes th' boats. No more ixpinsive steel an' ir'n, but good ol' grass fr'm th' twinty-acre meadow. Th' ship-yards'll be moved fr'm th' say, an' laid down in th' neighborhood iv Polo, Illinye, an' all th' Mississippi Valley'll ring with th' sound iv th' scythe an' th' pitchfork buildin' th' definse iv our counthry's honor. Thank th' Lord, we've winrows an' winrows iv Shafter's armor plate between here an' Dubuque."

Mr. Hennessy said good-night. "As me cousin used to say," he remarked, "we're through with wan hell iv a bad year, an' here goes f'r another like it."

"Well," said Mr. Dooley, "may th' Lord niver sind us a foolisher wan than this!"

—FINLEY PETER DUNNE, "The Hay Fleet," 1898

9. "TURN NOT THEIR NEW-WORLD VICTORIES TO GAIN!"

Protest against a war that seemed unjustified found memorable literary expression in Lowell's Biglow Papers *and Thoreau's "Civil Disobedience." It found no less eloquent expression again at the end of the century when, fresh from an easy conquest of Spain, American armies turned to the subjugation of the Filipinos. The reaction to this Far Eastern venture took two forms: a protest against political and economic imperialism, and a protest against an unanticipated, undeclared, and—seemingly—unnecessary war against a people who appeared to be fighting only for their liberty. With extraordinary unanimity poets, novelists, historians, and philosophers championed "anti-imperialism" and denounced the "unjust war." Of all the literary documents of that time two are particularly memorable: William Vaughn Moody's great "Ode in Time of Hesitation" and Mark Twain's "To a Person Sitting in Darkness." We give here some of the verses of the "Ode."*

v

Lies! lies! It cannot be! The wars we wage
Are noble, and our battles still are won
By justice for us, ere we lift the gage.

We have not sold our loftiest heritage.
The proud republic hath not stooped to cheat
And scramble in the market-place of war;
Her forehead weareth yet its solemn star.
Here is her witness: this, her perfect son,
This delicate and proud New England soul
Who leads despisèd men, with just-unshackled feet,
Up the large ways where death and glory meet,
To show all peoples that our shame is done,
That once more we are clean and spirit-whole.

.   .   .   .   .

VIII

Was it for this our fathers kept the law?
This crown shall crown their struggle and their ruth?
Are we the eagle nation Milton saw
Mewing its mighty youth,
Soon to possess the mountain winds of truth,
And be a swift familiar of the sun
Where aye before God's face his trumpets run?
Or have we but the talons and the maw,
And for the abject likeness of our heart
Shall some less lordly bird be set apart?—
Some gross-billed wader where the swamps are fat?
Some gorger in the sun? Some prowler with the bat?

IX

Ah no!
We have not fallen so.
We are our fathers' sons: let those who lead us know!
'Twas only yesterday sick Cuba's cry
Came up the tropic wind, Now help us, for we die!"
Then Alabama heard,
And rising, pale, to Maine and Idaho
Shouted a burning word.
Proud state with proud impassioned state conferred,
And at the lifting of a hand sprang forth,
East, west, and south, and north,
Beautiful armies. Oh, by the sweet blood and young

Shed on the awful hill slope at San Juan,
By the unforgotten names of eager boys
Who might have tasted girls' love and been stung
With the old mystic joys
And starry griefs, now the spring nights come on,
But that the heart of youth is generous,—
We charge you, ye who lead us,
Breathe on their chivalry no hint of stain!
Turn not their new-world victories to gain!
One least leaf plucked for chaffer from the bays
Of their dear praise,
One jot of their pure conquest put to hire,
The implacable republic will require;
With clamor, in the glare and gaze of noon,
Or subtly, coming as a thief at night,
But surely, very surely, slow or soon
That insult deep we deeply will requite.
Tempt not our weakness, our cupidity!
For save we let the island men go free,
Those baffled and dislaureled ghosts
Will curse us from the lamentable coasts
Where walk the frustrate dead.
The cup of trembling shall be drainèd quite,
Eaten the sour bread of astonishment,
With ashes of the hearth shall be made white
Our hair, and wailing shall be in the tent;
Then on your guiltier head
Shall our intolerable self-disdain
Wreak suddenly its anger and its pain;
For manifest in that disastrous light
We shall discern the right
And do it, tardily.—O ye who lead,
Take heed!
Blindness we may forgive, but baseness we will smite.
—WILLIAM VAUGHN MOODY, "An Ode in Time of Hesitation," 1901

10. "PROPER LANGUAGE FOR A SUBORDINATE TO USE TO A SUPERIOR"

Here we are back with the old question of the relations of the civil and the military in a democracy. As we have indicated, the question rarely arises in any gross or direct form: never since the days of Burr and Wilkinson have there been even gestures toward military ventures of a treasonable nature. Here the distinguished elder statesman, Henry L. Stimson, tells how he met the challenge of insubordination from an officer who thought that he was strong enough to defy the War Department.

THE basic instrument for the modernization of the Army, in 1911, was the General Staff, and it was therefore natural that Stimson's first and most important battle should have been for the protection of this body and its authority. The General Staff of the American Army was the creation of Elihu Root, and Stimson always ranked this achievement as one of the two or three most important in all the long and brilliant career of the ablest man he ever knew. The General Staff was a German invention, but Mr. Root's adaptation of it was designed to meet the peculiar problems of the American Army. His General Staff, organized under a Chief of Staff responsible to the Secretary of War and the President, was designed to meet three requirements: civilian control in the executive branch, sound general planning, and constant cross-fertilization between the line of the Army and its high command in Washington. Failure to meet any one of these basic requirements after the Civil War had made the Army a stultified plaything of ambitious generals and their political friends in Congress. By changing the title of the Army's ranking officer from "Commanding General" to "Chief of Staff," Root emphasized the principle of civilian control by the President as Commander in Chief—the "Chief of Staff" held his power as the President's agent, not as an independent commander. By establishing his General Staff free of routine administrative duties Root emphasized its basic function of policy making. By providing for limited terms of service for its members, he insured a constant movement of officers from the Staff to the line and back. He thus struck the first blow in a campaign to end forever the authority of armchair officers who had never commanded troops, but who knew their way around Capitol Hill. Ten years later it fell to Stimson to finish this particular job.

The Chief of Staff of the Army when Stimson became Secretary on May 22, 1911, was Major General Leonard Wood. This remarkable officer Stimson held as the finest soldier of his acquaintance until he met another Chief of Staff thirty years later. Wood had started as an Army surgeon, but his energy and driving zest for command had brought him into the line of the Army. He had commanded the Rough Riders of Theodore Roosevelt, and in Cuba he had won a great reputation as a colonial adminstrator. Wood was imaginative, relatively young, and as yet unhardened by the bitter disappointments which marked his later career. He and Stimson at once became warm personal friends; they shared an enthusiasm for horses and for hunting; together they inspected Army camps in the West and combined business with pleasure. In Washington they fought together in defense of the General Staff.

Their principal adversary was Major General Fred C. Ainsworth, the Adjutant General. Ainsworth, another doctor, had risen to high office in Washington by reason of his great administrative skill and his even greater skill in dealing with Congressmen. He was a master of paper work and politics, but unfortunately he was greedy for power, and he hated the whole concept of the General Staff, just as he disapproved of all the ideas for Army reform which attracted the sympathetic support of Stimson and Wood. The Adjutant General in law and principle was subordinate to the Chief of Staff, but in practice Ainsworth had been able to preserve his authority under Wood's predecessors; in some respects, because of his influence with Congressmen, he had been the most powerful officer in the War Department. Wood, taking office in 1910, set out to become master in his own house.

When Stimson arrived in Washington, Wood and Ainsworth were already at loggerheads; as an incident of their conflict, there was in session a board of officers (headed by Ainsworth himself) to study the administrative procedures of the War Department. This apparently harmless subject was full of explosive possibilities, for Ainsworth regarded himself as the high priest of Army administration, and any opinion contrary to his own would not be well received. Late in 1911, the board of officers reported; the minority report recommended the abolition of the bimonthly muster roll. This was a radical recommendation, for the muster roll was the Army's basic administrative record. But the minority report was approved by Wood and then by Stimson; they believed that the new methods would give fully satisfactory results and save much time. Ainsworth did not agree, and on February 9, 1912, after a six-week delay, he submitted his views to Wood in a memorandum so grossly insubordinate that as soon as he read it Stimson realized that the time for drastic action had come. Once before he had been forced to warn Ainsworth against insubordination. Now in a bitter outburst against "incompetent amateurs" Ainsworth laid down a challenge which could not be ignored. The memorandum went so far as to impugn the honor and good faith of any who would tamper with the muster roll.

"I glanced at it [Ainsworth's memorandum] and at once seeing its character directed Wood to turn it over to me and to pay no further attention to it. I told him I would attend to it myself and for him to keep his mouth shut.

"The only member of the Department whom I consulted was Crowder, Judge Advocate General. I asked him to read the memorandum and advise me what disciplinary measures the law allowed. He came to my house and we discussed it. He suggested two ways of treating it, one by administrative punishment and the other by court-martial. He himself started to recommend the administrative punishment. I told him no, that I intended to court-martial him. . . . I told him I proposed to find out whether the Army was ready to stand for the kind of language that General Ainsworth had used as proper language for a subordinate to use to a superior. I intended to put it up to the general officers of the Army to say whether that was proper or not. I told him also that I preferred to use a big gun rather than a little gun. When I had to deal a blow, I believed in striking hard. He loyally acquiesced in my decision and under my direction at once commenced the formulation of charges and selection of a court. I also consulted the President and Mr. Root. Both concurred with me in thinking that a court-martial should be ordered. The President said to me: 'Stimson, it has fallen to you to do a dirty job which your predecessors ought to have done before you.'

"Root said that when a man pulls your nose there is nothing to be done but to hit him. . . .

"I concluded . . . that a measure of discipline must be taken at once if at all and I therefore relieved Ainsworth as soon as the paper could be prepared."

—HENRY L. STIMSON and MCGEORGE BUNDY, *On Active Service*

11. "A GREAT PRINCIPLE WAS NEVER LOST SO CASUALLY"

"Our worst wartime mistake," Eugene Rostow has called the Japanese relocation program, and Professor Corwin has characterized it as "the most drastic invasion of the rights of citizens of the United States by their own government that has thus far occurred in the history of our nation." Alarmed by the possibility of sabotage from Japanese-Americans along the Pacific Coast, and under the apprehension that all persons of Japanese ancestry were potentially disloyal, the War Department persuaded President Roosevelt to authorize the "relocation" of some 112,000 West Coast Japanese. A majority of these were American citizens. Subsequent events indicated that the fear of sabotage or disloyalty from the Japanese in America was unfounded. Twice the Supreme Court passed on the constitutionality of this wartime relocation program; both times it sustained the President but on diverse and shifting grounds. A third case, toward the close of the war, granted a writ of habeas corpus to a loyal Japanese-American.

THE conception of the war power under the American Constitution rests on the experience of the Revolution and the Civil War. It rests on basic political principles which men who had endured those times of trouble had fully discussed and carefully set forth. The chief architects of the conception were men of affairs who had participated in war, and had definite and well-founded ideas about the role of the professional military mind in the conduct of war.

The first and dominating principle of the war power under the Constitution is that the Commander-in-Chief of the armed forces must be a civilian, elected and not promoted to his office. In no other way can the subordination of the military to the civil power be assured. And in every democracy, the relationship between civil and military power is the crucial issue—the issue on which its capacity to survive in time of crisis ultimately depends.

The second principle governing the war power in a democracy is that of responsibility. Like every other officer of government, soldiers must answer for their decisions to the nation's system of law, and not to the Chief of Staff alone. Where military decisions lead to conflicts between individuals and authority—as in the Japanese exclusion program—the courts must adjudicate them. It is essential to every democratic value in society that official action, taken in the name of the war power, should be held to standards of responsibility under such circumstances. The courts have not in the past, and should not now, declare such problems to be beyond the reach of judicial review. The present Supreme Court is dominated by the conviction that in the past judicial review has unduly limited the freedom of administrative action. But surely the right answer to bad law is good law, rather than no law at all. The court must review the exercise of military power in a way which permits ample freedom to the executive, yet assures society as a whole that appropriate standards of responsibility have been met.

The issue for judicial decision in these cases is not lessened or changed by saying that the war power includes any steps required to win the war. The problem is still one of judgment as to what helps win a war. Who is to decide whether there was a sensible reason for doing what was done? Is it enough for the general to say that when he acted, he honestly thought it was a good idea to do what he did?

Unless the courts require a showing, in cases like these, of an intelligible relationship between means and ends, society has lost its basic protection against the abuse of military power. The general's good intentions must be irrelevant. There should be evidence in court that his military judgment had a suitable basis in fact.

The history of this question in the Supreme Court is unmistakable. The earlier decisions of the court had vigorously asserted that "what are the allowable limits of military discretion, and whether or not they have been overstepped in a particular case, are judicial questions"; and that there must be evidence enough to satisfy the court as to the need for the action taken. They had made it clear that the law is not neutral in such issues, but has a positive preference for protecting civil rights where possible, and a long-standing suspicion of the military mind when acting outside its own sphere.

Yet in the Japanese-American cases there was literally no evidence whatever by which the court might test the responsibility of General DeWitt's action. Dozens of Supreme Court decisions had said that the court would not pass on serious constitutional questions without a record before it, establishing the essential facts. Those cases were all ignored. One hundred thousand persons were sent to concentration camps on a record which wouldn't support a conviction for stealing a dog.

The earlier cases not only established the rule that there must be an independent judicial examination of the justification for a military act. They went much further. They declared a simple rule-of-thumb as a guide in handling cases involving military discretion, in which the military undertook to arrest, hold, or try people. So long as the civil courts were open and functioning, the Supreme Court had previously held, there could be no military necessity for allowing generals to hold, try, or punish people. The safety of the country could be thoroughly protected against treason, sabotage, and like crimes by ordinary arrest and trial in the civil courts, unless the courts were shut by riot, invasion, or insurrection.

That was the moral of the great case of *Ex Parte Milligan,* decided in 1866. *Ex Parte Milligan* is a monument in the democratic tradition, and until now it has been the animating force in this branch of our law. To be sure, there is a tendency nowadays to treat *Ex Parte Milligan* as outmoded, as if new methods of "total" warfare made the case an anachronism; but those who take this view have forgotten the circumstances of the Civil War, when fifth columns, propaganda, sabotage, and espionage were rife.

Ex Parte Milligan illustrates the point. Milligan was convincingly charged with active participation in a fifth column plot worthy of Hitler. A group of armed and determined men planned to seize federal arsenals at Columbus, Indianapolis, and at three points in Illinois, and then to release Confederate prisoners of war held in those states. Thus they would create a Confederate army behind the Union lines in Tennessee. Milligan and his alleged co-conspirators acted in Indiana, Missouri, Illinois, and in other border states. Their strategy had a political arm. The Union was to be split politically, and a Northwest Confederation was to be declared, friendly to the South, and embracing six states. This was not an idle dream. It was sponsored by a well-financed society, the Sons of Liberty, thought to have 300,000 members, many of them rich and respectable, and the planned uprising would coincide with the Chicago convention of the Democratic Party, which was then sympathetic to abandoning the war and recognizing the Confederacy.

The unanimous court which freed Milligan for civil trial was a court of fire-eating Unionists. Mr. Justice Davis, who wrote for the majority, was one of President Lincoln's closest friends. The Chief Justice, who wrote for the concurring minority, was a valiant supporter of the war, whatever his shortcomings in other respects. Yet the court had no difficulty in freeing Milligan, and facing down the outcry provoked by the decision.

The court held in Milligan's case that it was unconstitutional to try him before a military commission, rather than a court of law. There was little doubt of his guilt. But it was beyond the powers of the military to measure or punish it. . . .

Yet in the cases of the Japanese-Americans the Supreme Court held the precedent of *Ex Parte Milligan* inapplicable. The reasoning is extraordinarily dangerous. The Japanese-Americans, the court said, were detained by a civilian agency, not by the Army. The program was not exclusively a matter for military administration, and it was enforceable under a statute by ordinary criminal remedies. Therefore, it did not present the question of the power of military tribunals to conduct trials under the laws of war.

But the Japanese-Americans were ordered detained by a general, purporting to act on military grounds. The military order was enforceable, on pain of imprisonment. While a United States marshal, rather than a military policeman, assured abedience to the order, the ultimate sanction behind the marshal's writ is the same as that of the military police: the bayonets of United States troops. It is hardly a ground for distinction that the general's command was backed by the penalty of civil imprisonment, or that he obtained civilian aid in running the relocation camps. The starting point for the entire program was a military order, which had to be obeyed.

In *Ex Parte Milligan* the Supreme Court had said that the military could not constitutionally arrest, nor could a military tribunal constitutionally try, civilians charged with treason and conspiracy to destroy the state by force, at a time when the civil courts were open and functioning. Yet under the plan considered in the Japanese-American cases, people not charged with crime are imprisoned without even a military trial, on the ground that they have the taint of Japanese blood. It would seem clear that if it is illegal to arrest and confine people after an unwarranted military trial, it is surely even more illegal to arrest and confine them without any trial at all. But the Supreme Court says that the issues of the *Milligan* case were not involved in this case because the evacuees were committed to camps by military orders, not by military tribunals, and because their jailers did not wear uniforms!

There are, then, two basic constitutional problems concealed in the court's easy dismissal of *Ex Parte Milligan*: the arrest, removal, and confinement of persons without trial, pending examination of their loyalty; and the indefinite confinement of persons found to be disloyal. On both counts, at least as to citizens, the moral of *Ex Parte Milligan* is plain.

As for the Japanese *aliens* involved in the evacuation program, the constitutional problem is different. In time of war, the government possesses great powers over enemy aliens, which are to be exercised, the courts say, for the "single purpose" of preventing enemy aliens from aiding the enemy. They may be interned if dangerous and their property in the United States may be taken into custody. Yet they are entitled to our general constitutional protections and individual liberty—to trial by jury, the writ of habeas corpus, and the other basic rights of the person. Is it permissible to intern all the Japanese who live on the West Coast, but to allow German and Italian aliens, and Japanese who live elsewhere, general freedom? Surely the control and custody of enemy aliens in wartime should be reasonably equal and even-handed.

The Japanese exclusion program rests on five propositions of the utmost potential menace:

1. Protective custody, extending over three or four years, is a permitted form of imprisonment in the United States.

2. Political opinions, not criminal acts, may contain enough danger to justify such imprisonment.

3. Men, women, and children of a given racial group, both Americans and resident aliens, can be presumed to possess the kind of dangerous ideas which require their imprisonment.

4. In time of war or emergency the military—perhaps without even the concurrence of the legislature—can decide what political opinions require imprisonment, and which groups are infected with them.

5. The decision of the military can be carried out without indictment, trial, examination, jury, the confrontation of witnesses, counsel for the

defense, the privilege against self-incrimination, or any of the other safeguards of the Bill of Rights.

The idea of punishment only for individual criminal behavior is basic to all systems of civilized law. A great principle was never lost so casually. Mr. Justice Black's comment was weak to the point of impotence: "Hardships are a part of war, and war is an aggregation of hardships." It was an answer in the spirit of cliché: "Don't you know there's a war going on?" It ignores the rights of citizenship, and the safeguards of trial practice which have been the historical attributes of liberty.

—EUGENE V. ROSTOW, "Our Worst War Time Mistake," 1945

12. "THE MORAL EQUIVALENT OF WAR"

The American tradition of interest in peace is very old—as old, certainly, as William Penn's Essay towards the Present and Future Peace of Europe of 1693. And it is at least suggestive that Americans have won the Nobel Prize for Peace more frequently than for literature or the sciences, and that the award has gone more frequently to Americans than to people of any other nation. William James never received the Nobel award—either for peace or for philosophy, though he might well have honored either—but his essay on the "Moral Equivalent of War," published the month of his death—August, 1910—has long been an inspiration to those seeking some alternative to war. It belongs not so much with practical schemes for peace—like William Ladd's proposal for a Congress of nations—as with such philosophical and inspirational arguments as Charles Sumner's "True Grandeur of Nations" of 1845.

THE war against war is going to be no holiday excursion or camping party. The military feelings are too deeply grounded to abdicate their place among our ideals until better substitutes are offered than the glory and shame that come to nations as well as to individuals from the ups and downs of politics and the vicissitudes of trade. There is something highly paradoxical in the modern man's relation to war. Ask all our millions, north and south, whether they would vote now (were such a thing possible) to have our war for the Union expunged from history, and the record of a peaceful transition to the present time substituted for that of its marches and battles, and probably hardly a handful of eccentrics would say yes. Those ancestors, those efforts, those memories and legends, are the most ideal part of what we now own together, a sacred spiritual possession worth more than all the blood poured out. Yet ask those same people whether they would be willing in cold blood to start another civil war now to gain another similar possession, and not one man or woman would vote for the proposition. In modern eyes, precious though wars may be, they must not be waged solely for the sake of the ideal harvest. Only when forced upon one, only when an enemy's injustice leaves us no alternative, is a war now thought permissible. . . .

It is plain that on this subject civilized man has developed a sort of double personality. If we take European nations, no legitimate interest of any one of them would seem to justify the tremendous destructions which a war to compass it would necessarily entail. It would seem as though common sense and reason ought to find a way to reach agreement in every conflict of honest interests. I myself think it our bounden duty to believe in such international rationality as possible. But, as things stand, I see how desperately hard it is to bring the peace-party and the war-party together, and I believe that the difficulty is due to certain deficiencies in the program of pacificism which set the militarist imagination strongly, and to a certain extent justifiably, against it. In the whole discussion both sides are on imaginative and sentimental ground. . . .

Militarism is the great preserver of our ideals of hardihood, and human life with no use for hardihood would be contemptible. Without risks of prizes for the darer, history would be insipid indeed; and there is a type of military character which every one feels that the race should never cease to breed, for every one is sensitive to its superiority. The duty is incumbent on mankind, of keeping military characters in stock—of keeping them, if not for use, then as ends in themselves and as pure pieces of perfection,—so that Roosevelt's weaklings and mollycoddles may not end by making everything else disappear from the face of nature.

This natural sort of feeling forms, I think, the innermost soul of army-writings. Without any exception known to me, militarist authors take a highly mystical view of their subject, and regard war as a biological or sociological necessity, uncontrolled by ordinary psychological checks and motives. When the time of development is ripe the war must come, reason or no reason, for the justifications pleaded are invariably fictitious. War is, in short, a permanent human *obligation*. . . .

Having said thus much in preparation, I will now confess my own utopia. I devoutly believe in the reign of peace and in the gradual advent of some sort of a socialistic equilibrium. The fatalistic view of the war-function is to me nonsense, for I know that war-making is due to definite motives and subject to prudential checks and reasonable criticisms, just like any other form of enterprise. And when whole nations are the armies, and the science of destruction vies in intellectual refinement with the sciences of production, I see that war becomes absurd and impossible from its own monstrosity. Extravagant ambitions will have to be replaced by reasonable claims, and nations must make common cause against them. I see no reason why all this should not apply to yellow as well as to white countries, and I look forward to a future when acts of war shall be formally outlawed as between civilized peoples.

All these beliefs of mine put me squarely into the anti-militarist party. But I do not believe that peace either ought to be or will be permanent on this globe, unless the states pacifically organized preserve some of the old elements of army-discipline. . . . We must make new energies and hardihoods continue the manliness to which the military mind so faithfully clings. Martial virtues must be the enduring cement; intrepidity, contempt of softness, surrender of private interest, obedience to command, must still remain the rock upon which states are built—unless, indeed, we wish for dangerous reactions against commonwealths fit only for contempt, and liable to invite attack whenever a centre of crystallization for military-minded enterprise gets formed anywhere in their neighborhood.

The war-party is assuredly right in affirming and reaffirming that the martial virtues, although originally gained by the race through war, are absolute and permanent human goods. Patriotic pride and ambition in their military form are, after all, only specifications of a more general competitive passion. They are its first form, but that is no reason for supposing them to be its last form. Men now are proud of belonging to a conquering nation, and without a murmur they lay down their persons and their wealth, if by so doing they may fend off subjection. But who can be sure that *other aspects of one's country* may not, with time and education and suggestion enough, come to be regarded with similarly effective feelings of pride and shame? Why should men not some day feel that it is worth a blood-tax to belong to a collectivity superior in *any* ideal respect? Why should they not blush with indignant shame if the community that owns them is vile in any way whatsoever? Individuals, daily more numerous, now feel this civic passion. It is only a question of blowing on the spark till the whole population gets incandescent, and on the ruins of the old morals of military honor, a stable system of morals of civic honor builds itself up. What the whole community comes to believe in grasps the individual as in a vise. The war-function has grasped us so far; but constructive interests may some day seem no less imperative, and impose on the individual a hardly lighter burden.

Let me illustrate my idea more concretely. There is nothing to make one indignant in the mere fact that life is hard, that men should toil and suffer pain. The planetary conditions once for all are such, and we can stand it. But that so many men, by mere accidents of birth and opportunity, should have a life of *nothing else* but toil and pain and hardness and inferiority imposed upon them, should have *no* vacation, while others natively no more deserving never get any taste of this campaigning life at all,—*this* is capable of arousing indignation in reflective minds. It may end by seeming shameful to all of us that some of us have nothing but campaigning, and others nothing but unmanly ease. If now—and this is my idea—there were, instead of military conscription a conscription of the whole youthful population to form for a certain number of years a part of the army enlisted against *Nature*, the injustice would tend to be evened out, and numerous other goods to the commonwealth would follow. The military ideals of hardihood and discipline would be wrought into the growing fibre of the people; no one would remain blind as the luxurious classes now are blind, to man's relations to the globe he lives on, and to the permanently sour and hard foundations of his higher life. To coal and iron mines, to freight trains, to fishing fleets in December, to dishwashing, clothes-washing, and window-washing, to road-building and tunnel-making, to foundries and stoke-holes, and to the frames of skyscrapers, would our gilded youths be drafted off, according to their choice, to get the childishness knocked out of them, and to come back into society with healthier sympathies and soberer ideas. They would have paid their blood-tax, done their own part in the immemorial human warfare against nature; they would tread the earth more proudly, the women would value them more highly, they would be better fathers and teachers of the following generation.

Such a conscription, with the state of public opinion that would have required it, and the many moral fruits it would bear, would preserve in the midst of a pacific civilization the manly virtues which the military party is so afraid of seeing disappear in peace. We should get toughness without callousness, authority with as little criminal cruelty as possible, and painful work done cheerily because the duty is temporary, and threatens not, as now, to degrade the whole remainder of one's life. I spoke of the 'moral equivalent' of war. So far, war has been the only force that can discipline a whole community, and until an equivalent discipline is organized, I believe that war must have its way. But I have no serious doubt that the ordinary prides and shames of social man, once developed to a certain intensity, are capable of organizing such a moral equivalent as I have sketched, or some other just as effective for preserving manliness of type. It is but a question of time, of skilful propagandism, and of opinion-making men seizing historic opportunities.

The martial type of character can be bred without war. Strenuous honor and disinterestedness abound elsewhere. Priests and medical men are in a fashion educated to it, and we should all feel some degree of it imperative if we were conscious of our work as an obligatory service to the state. We should be *owned*, as soldiers are by the army, and our pride would rise accordingly. We could be poor, then, without humiliation, as army officers now are. The only thing needed henceforward is to inflame the civic temper as past history has inflamed the military temper. H. G. Wells, as usual, sees the centre of the situation. "In many ways," he says "military organization is the most peaceful of activities. When the contemporary man steps from the street, of clamorous insincere advertisement, push, adulteration, underselling and intermittent employment into the barrack-yard, he steps on to a higher social plane, into an atmosphere of service and coöperation and of infinitely more honorable emulations. Here at least men are not flung out of employment to degenerate because there is no immediate work for them to do. They are fed and drilled and trained for better services. Here at least a man is supposed to win promotion by self-forgetfulness and not by self-seeking. And beside the feeble and irregular endowment of research by commercialism, its little shortsighted snatches at profit by innovation and scientific economy, see how remarkable is the steady and rapid development of method and appliances in naval and military affairs!" . . .

Wells adds that he thinks that the conceptions of order and discipline, the tradition of service and devotion, of physical fitness, unstinted exertion, and universal responsibility, which universal military duty is now teaching European nations, will remain a permanent acquisition, when the last ammunition has been used in the fireworks that celebrate the final peace. I believe as he does. It would be simply preposterous if the only force that could work ideals of honor and standards of efficiency into English or American natures should be the fear of being killed by the Germans or Japanese. Great indeed is Fear, but it is not, as our military enthusiasts believe and try to make us believe, the only stimulus known for awakening the higher ranges of men's spiritual energy. The amount of alteration in public opinion which my utopia postulates is vastly less than the difference between the mentality of those black warriors who pursued Stanley's party on the Congo with their cannibal war-cry of "Meat! Meat!" and that of the 'general staff' of any civilized nation. History has seen the latter interval bridged over: the former one can be bridged over much more easily.

—William James, "The Moral Equivalent of War," 1910

~ 13 ~

Isolation, Intervention, and World Power

IF WE could somehow get the same perspective on American history that we have on the history of Greece or Rome or even of England and France, we might see that the most remarkable thing about America was not the achievement of democracy or of equality, or the solution of the problem of Federalism or the achievement of a high standard of living or of those other things embraced in the phrase, "American way of life"—not any of these, but the rise out of obscurity to world power. That a people who were late-comers on the stage of history, and whose fierce energies were long devoted to the elementary tasks of conquering a wilderness, should within a century and a half emerge as the dominant power on the globe, was nothing less than marvelous.

In this process of emergence into world power a few persistent themes are particularly interesting and significant. Let us enumerate some of them.

First, America was, from the beginning, part of what we have come to call the Atlantic Community. Americans have too long, and too devoutly, dwelt on what is American about America and they sometimes lose sight of what is, after all, elementary: that in language, in faith, in moral and ethical values, in all that goes to make up civilization, America is part of Western Christendom. For generations, after Independence, Americans turned deliberately and almost convulsively inward, cultivating their own interests as they cultivated their own soil. But in the late nineteenth and through the whole of the twentieth century, the interdependence of America and Europe has become once again clear, and there has come a revival of interest in, and appreciation of, the Atlantic Community.

Second, during a good part of the nineteenth century Americans tried, rather self-consciously, to divorce themselves from the Old World. Isolationism was rooted in geography and in history, but it was cultivated by romanticism. There was the obvious geographical separation—and, notwithstanding miracles of rapid transportation and communication, that still exists. There was the equally obvious heritage of a generation of quarreling and of warfare. There was the inescapable lure—or pressure—of the West, of the frontier, of undeveloped resources directing the interests and energies of men westward across mountains and prairies and plains rather than eastward across oceans. But besides and beyond all these was an intellectual—we would now call it a psychological—impulse toward isolation. "Kindly separated by Nature and a wide ocean from one-quarter of the globe," said Jefferson in his First Inaugural Address, and the most interesting word is "kindly." For reasons not hard to understand or even to sympathize with, Americans of the late eighteenth and early nineteenth century convinced themselves that the New World was morally superior to the Old, that where the Old World was decadent and depraved, ridden by priests and war lords and kings, sunk in superstition and poverty and vice, the New World was brave and innocent and free. This was not merely an early manifestation of what we later learned to call Babbitry; it was an attitude that so wise and sophisticated a man as Jefferson subscribed to and expressed. It is an attitude that, in a curious way, still lingers on in some quarters.

A third theme, and one closely connected with the second, is the principle of American hegemony in the Western Hemisphere. This principle first found formal expression in the Monroe Doctrine. Various corollaries—of various degrees of legitimacy—elaborated upon it, while from time to time Presidents and Secretaries of State provided variations on the central theme. There was the variation of the Ostend Manifesto, of 1854, for example, and the later variation of the reaction against the French venture under Maximilian, and the subsequent variation of Cleveland's Venezuelan policy, Secretary Olney stating flatly that the word of America was "fiat" throughout the Hemisphere. Later on what was a unilateral policy was transformed into a multilateral policy; Wilson enlisted the ABC powers in the solution of the Mexican question; Franklin Roosevelt inaugurated a Good Neighbor policy which was—supposedly—an affair of mutual aid and co-operation. Whatever the fortunes or misfortunes of American relations with

the states south of the Rio Grande, one principle was clear and steady—
that as against the rest of the world the American states stood together,
rejecting alike interference or territorial aggrandizement.

A fourth theme of American history has been a persistent interest
in the West and—after the mid-nineteenth century—in the Pacific.
American ships led the way to Oriental waters even in the eighteenth
century; Admiral Perry opened Japan to the West; America early
took a friendly interest in China; American missionaries and traders
made Hawaii a New England outpost. The acquisition of Oregon
and of California and, later, of Alaska, made sure that the United
States would be a Pacific power, and for a century thereafter American
interest in the Pacific and the Far East mounted. Even before the
Spanish War we had taken over Samoa and Hawaii, and if the nation
as a whole was not prepared for the Philippine adventure the Navy
was. Nothing fosters sympathy like benevolence and American benevolence toward the Chinese at the turn of the century—a benevolence
dubiously expressed in the Open Door policy and the application of
Boxer indemnity funds to educate Chinese students—made a profound
impression on the American character.

What is perhaps most interesting about American interest in the
Pacific and the Far East is that it has been, historically, connected with
isolationism. Those who believe we should turn our backs on Europe
have ever been ready to turn toward Asia, and in the 1950's the most
ardent isolationists are eager to plunge into Asiatic affairs, even into
Asiatic wars.

A fifth theme is one that can be discerned at a very early stage: the
sense of mission toward the rest of the world, of mission and of
responsibility for liberty and democracy everywhere on the globe. It
was prophetic that the Continental Congress sent both a mission and
an army to liberate Canada, and equally prophetic that the Canadians
showed no interest in either group of emissaries. "The world is my
country, All mankind are my brethren," wrote Tom Paine, and half a
century later Garrison echoed his words: "My country is the world, my
countrymen are mankind." Other peoples do not have this sense of
responsibility, or if they do it takes a different form—the form of
expansion and conquest. To the average American "Manifest Destiny"
meant not only the manifest destiny of the United States to rule over
most of North America, but the no less manifest destiny of the American
idea to rule the world. Thus in a sense Americans have always been

busybodies, concerning themselves with the affairs of other peoples. They have sympathized with the Greeks, the Poles, the Hungarians, the Latin Americans, the Jews, the Chinese, the Irish; they are always passing resolutions designed to influence conditions in distant lands. Congressmen who fiercely resent a whisper of criticism of American domestic affairs think nothing of passing sweeping resolutions telling the English to give Ireland Home Rule. While this sense of mission and of responsibility has its embarrassing side, it has, too, its beneficent side. If it makes for the passing of overmany resolutions, it makes, too, for a policy of assistance to those who struggle for freedom everywhere. Thus the Truman Doctrine, while it was in one way a new departure, had its roots deep in American experience and American philosophy.

Not unconnected with this sense of mission and of responsibility, has been a sixth theme—a persistent concern for arbitration and conciliation, for international law, and for international organizations designed to preserve peace. The first provisions for the arbitration of a boundary dispute were those written into Jay's Treaty; the first use of an economic boycott to preserve peace came with Jefferson's Embargo; the first agreement for an unfortified boundary was that concluded by Rush and Bagot in 1818; the first serious proposal for an international court came from the pen of the New Englander, William Ladd; probably the first successful arbitration of a *casus belli* was the Washington arbitration of the Alabama Claims, in 1871. Volumes have been written on the origin of the League of Nations, but the name that will be longest remembered is that of Woodrow Wilson, and whatever may be the ultimate verdict on the United Nations, the paternity of F. D. Roosevelt will not be challenged. The Bryan "cooling-off" treaties, the Kellogg Pact, the various agreements with Latin-American nations, all confess American readiness to renounce war as an instrument of national policy, and to resort to arbitration.

Yet there is another side to all this. Americans have not in fact either renounced war or eschewed it. A good part of American energy has been devoted to the waging of war. For all the American interest in arbitration and conciliation, Americans have not been willing to submit their differences with Mexico or with Spain to arbitration. And for all their interest in international organizations, Americans walked out on the League of Nations. There is nothing remarkable in all this; it merely means that with Americans as with others weekday performance does not always come up to Sunday profession.

Behind all these particular themes lies one basic principle, not unique to America but shared by all major powers: the search for national security. In America this search was conducted in special circumstances and for special purposes. It was conducted, during most of our history, within the framework of geographical isolation. In other words the United States was, for long, in effect an island, and was able to take full advantage of that good fortune. The United States was not vulnerable to European enemies; she encountered no serious rivals or enemies in the Western Hemisphere. She was able, therefore, to dispense with standing army and large navy, and to allow nature to take its course as far as foreign relations were concerned. All this was convenient, but it provided a poor education for the future, and when America did become a world power, inextricably involved in world affairs and world wars, she had lots to learn and lots to unlearn.

The task of illustrating America's emergence out of isolation into world power in a single chapter is insuperable. We have given here the most fragmentary representation of some of the basic themes of American foreign policy; to have done more would have required not another chapter but another volume. The emphasis is, quite deliberately, on the twentieth century and, especially, on the last decade. For it was in the twentieth century that the great issues of the past came to a head, that the great controversies about the place of America in the world were agitated and, in part, settled. And it was, particularly, in the decade of the forties that the United States finally assumed that dominant station among the powers of the earth that even the most enraptured of the Fathers had not anticipated. Not ambitious for power, America had achieved power. Rejecting responsibility, she had been unable to escape it. Inclined to parochialism, she had been thrust into the center of internationalism. Fundamentally peaceful, she had been led by circumstances to become the Arsenal of Democracy and then the Arsenal of the West. The only great nation to emerge from the war unscathed, she elected to assume responsibility for relief and reconstruction, and to put her skills and her wealth at the disposal of less fortunate peoples. The only democratic power able to resist Communism, she was required to commit herself to that perilous task throughout the globe.

1. THE BASES OF ISOLATIONISM

One of the major principles of American foreign policy emerged at the very beginning of our national history—the principle of holding aloof from Old World politics and wars. This principle grew out of a variety of considerations, geographical, political, military, and sentimental or psychological. It grew out of the obvious factor of geographical isolation. It grew out of a perfectly logical fear of embroilment in Old World wars. It grew out of the notion, or hope, that America was about to create something new under the sun and that contact with or involvement with the Old World would endanger the experiment. It grew out of the romantic assumption that the New World was innocent and virtuous, the Old World decadent and depraved, and that the less the two had to do with each other the better.

Isolation found formal expression at the very beginning of our national history, in the rejection of the alleged obligations of the Treaty of Alliance with France, and the Proclamation of Neutrality. It found informal expression in the even more influential Farewell Address which Washington left as a testament to his countrymen, in Jefferson's First Inaugural Address, and in innumerable statements from leaders in American public life. To assemble even a small representation of these is a thankless task, for they are all variations on a theme—and in course of time Americans kept the variations, and forgot the theme. The theme was not one of complete isolation. It was—as Washington and Jefferson both put it—that America has a set of primary interests that differ from those of the Old World. It was not one of complete avoidance of association with the Old World, but of avoidance of permanent alliances. It is appropriate to remember that Washington warned his countrymen against inveterate antipathies as well as against passionate attachments. It is equally appropriate to recall that that ardent American, Jefferson, was prepared to "marry the British fleet and nation" rather than see France in control of the Mississippi. Washington and Jefferson represented different political attitudes, if not philosophies, but on foreign policy they agreed.

A. "THE INSIDIOUS WILES OF FOREIGN INFLUENCE"

. . . Observe good faith and justice toward all nations. In the execution of such a plan nothing is more essential than that permanent, inveterate antipathies against particular nations and passionate attachments for others should be excluded, and that in place of them just and amicable feelings toward all should be cultivated. The nation which indulges toward another an habitual hatred or an habitual fondness is in some degree a slave. It is a slave to its animosity or to its affection, either of which is sufficient to lead it astray from its duty and its interest. Antipathy in one nation against another disposes each more readily to offer insult and injury, to lay hold of slight causes of umbrage, and to be haughty and intractable when accidental or trifling occasions of dispute occur. . . .

So, likewise, a passionate attachment of one nation for another produces a variety of evils. Sympathy for the favorite nation, facilitating the illusion of an imaginary common interest in cases where no real common interest exists, and infusing into one the enmities of the other, betrays the former into a participation in the quarrels and wars of the latter without adequate inducement or justification. . . .

Against the insidious wiles of foreign influence (I conjure you to believe me, fellow-citizens) the jealousy of a free people ought to be *constantly* awake, since history and experience prove that foreign influence is one of the most baneful foes of republican government. But that jealousy, to be useful, must be impartial, else it becomes the instrument of the very influence to be avoided, instead of a defense against it. Excessive partiality for one foreign nation and excessive dislike of another cause those whom they actuate to see danger only on one side, and serve to veil and even second the arts of influence on the other. Real patriots who may resist the intrigues of the favorite are liable to become suspected and odious, while its tools and dupes usurp the applause and confidence of the people to surrender their interests.

The great rule of conduct for us in regard to foreign nations is, in extending our commercial relations to have with them as little *political* connection as possible. So far as we have already formed engagements let them be fulfilled with perfect good faith. Here let us stop.

Europe has a set of primary interests which to us have none or a very remote relation. Hence she must be engaged in frequent controversies, the causes of which are essentially foreign to our concerns. Hence, therefore, it must be unwise in us to implicate ourselves by artificial ties in the ordinary vicissitudes of her politics or the ordinary combinations and collisions of her friendships or enmities. . . .

It is our true policy to steer clear of permanent alliances with any portion of the foreign world, so far, I mean, as we are now at liberty to do it; for let me not be understood as capable of patronizing infidelity to existing engagements. I hold the maxim no less applicable to public than to private affairs that honesty is always the best policy. I repeat, therefore, let those engagements be observed in their genuine sense. But in my opinion it is unnecessary and would be unwise to extend them.

—GEORGE WASHINGTON, Farewell Address, September 17, 1796

B. "AMERICA HAS A HEMISPHERE TO ITSELF"

. . . In whatever governments they end they will be *American* governments, no longer to be involved in the never-ceasing broils of Europe. The European nations constitute a separate division of the globe; their localities make them part of a distinct system; they have a set of interests of their own in which it is our business never to engage ourselves. America has a hemisphere to itself. It must have its separate system of interests, which must not be subordinated to those of Europe. The insulated state in which nature has placed the American continent, should so far avail it that no spark of war kindled in the other quarters of the globe should be wafted across the wide oceans which separate us from them. And it will be so. In fifty years more the United States alone will contain fifty millions of inhabitants, and fifty years are soon gone over. The peace of 1763 is within that period. I was then twenty years old, and of course remember well all the transactions of the war preceding it. And you will live to see the epoch now equally ahead of us; and the numbers which will then be spread over the other parts of the American hemisphere, catching long before that the principles of our portion of it, and concurring with us in the maintenance of the same system. You see how readily we run into ages beyond the grave; and even those of us to whom that grave is already opening its quiet bosom. I am anticipating events of which you will be the bearer to me in the Elysian fields fifty years hence.

—THOMAS JEFFERSON,
Letter to Baron von Humboldt, December 6, 1813

2. THE MONROE DOCTRINE

The Monroe Doctrine is too familiar to justify any elaborate explanation. In a remarkable fashion it caught up various strands of American foreign policy and wove them into a whole as important symbolically as practically. It said, or implied, that the Old World must keep out of the New, and that the New World would hold aloof from the Old; it implied that European expansion even along the Pacific Coast threatened American interests; it foreshadowed our subsequent Latin-American policy.

It should be remembered that the immediate occasion for Monroe's statement—not a formal declaration but part of the annual message of 1823—was the proposal from the English Prime Minister, George Canning, for a joint Anglo-American declaration on Latin America. President Monroe made the statement of policy a purely American one. We give here excerpts from Monroe's annual message and Polk's restatement of the Doctrine at the time of the Texas and Oregon crisis, in 1845.

A. The Monroe Doctrine

. . . At the proposal of the Russian Imperial Government, made through the minister of the Emperor residing here, a full power and instructions have been transmitted to the minister of the United States at St. Petersburg to arrange by amicable negotiation the respective rights and interests of the two nations on the northwest coast of this continent. A similar proposal had been made by His Imperial Majesty to the Government of Great Britain, which has likewise been acceded to. The Government of the United States has been desirous by this friendly proceeding of manifesting the great value which they have invariably attached to the friendship of the Emperor and their solicitude to cultivate the best understanding with his Government. In the discussions to which this interest has given rise and in the arrangements by which they may terminate the occasion has been judged proper for asserting, as a principle in which the rights and interests of the United States are involved, that the American continents, by the free and independent condition which

656

they have assumed and maintain, are henceforth not to be considered as subjects for future colonization by any European powers. . . .

It was stated at the commencement of the last session that a great effort was then making in Spain and Portugal to improve the condition of the people of those countries, and that it appeared to be conducted with extraordinary moderation. It need scarcely be remarked that the result has been so far very different from what was then anticipated. Of events in that quarter of the globe, with which we have so much intercourse and from which we derive our origin, we have always been anxious and interested spectators. The citizens of the United States cherish sentiments the most friendly in favor of the liberty and happiness of their fellow-men on that side of the Atlantic. In the wars of the European powers in matters relating to themselves we have never taken any part, nor does it comport with our policy so to do. It is only when our rights are invaded or seriously menaced that we resent injuries or make preparation for our defense. With the movements in this hemisphere we are of necessity more immediately connected, and by causes which must be obvious to all enlightened and impartial observers. The political system of the allied powers is essentially different in this respect from that of America. This difference proceeds from that which exists in their respective Governments; and to the defense of our own, which has been achieved by the loss of so much blood and treasure, and matured by the wisdom of their most enlightened citizens, and under which we have enjoyed unexampled felicity, this whole nation is devoted. We owe it, therefore, to candor and to the amicable relations existing between the United States and those powers to declare that we should consider any attempt on their part to extend their system to any portion of this hemisphere as dangerous to our peace and safety. With the existing colonies or dependencies of any European power we have not interfered and shall not interfere. But with the Governments who have declared their independence and maintained it, and whose independence we have, on great consideration and on just principles, acknowledged, we could not view any interposition for the purpose of oppressing them, or controlling in any other manner their destiny, by any European power in any other light than as the manifestation of an unfriendly disposition toward the United States. In the war between those new Governments and Spain we declared our neutrality at the time of their recognition, and to this we have adhered. and shall continue to adhere, provided no change shall occur which, in the judgment of the competent authorities of this Government, shall make a corresponding change on the part of the United States indispensable to their security.

The late events in Spain and Portugal shew that Europe is still unsettled. Of this important fact no stronger proof can be adduced than that the allied powers should have thought it proper, on any principle satisfactory to themselves, to have interposed by force in the internal concerns of Spain. To what extent such interposition may be carried, on the same principle, is a question in which all independent powers whose governments differ from theirs are interested, even those most remote, and surely none more so than the United States. Our policy in regard to Europe, which was adopted at an early stage of the wars which have so long agitated that quarter of the globe, nevertheless remains the same, which is, not to interfere in the internal concerns of any of its powers; to consider the government *de facto* as the legitimate government for us; to cultivate friendly relations with it, and to preserve those relations by a frank, firm, and manly policy, meeting in all instances the just claims of every power, submitting to injuries from none. But in regard to those continents circumstances are eminently and conspicuously different. It is impossible that the allied powers should extend their political system to any portion of either continent without endangering our peace and happiness; nor can anyone believe that our southern brethren, if left to themselves, would adopt it of their own accord. It is equally impossible, therefore, that we should behold such interposition in any form with indifference. If we look to the comparative strength and resources of Spain and those new Governments, and their distance from each other, it must be obvious that she can never subdue them. It is still the true policy of the United States to leave the parties to themselves, in the hope that other powers will pursue the same course.

—JAMES MONROE, Seventh Annual Message to Congress, 1823

B. "THE AMERICAN SYSTEM OF GOVERNMENT IS ENTIRELY DIFFERENT FROM THAT OF EUROPE"

... The rapid extension of our settlements over our territories heretofore unoccupied, the addition of new States to our Confederacy, the expansion of free principles, and our rising greatness as a nation are attracting the attention of the powers of Europe, and lately the doctrine has been broached in some of them of a "balance of power" on this continent to check our advancement. The United States, sincerely desirous of preserving relations of good understanding with all nations, can not in silence permit any European interference on the North American continent, and should any such interference be attempted will be ready to resist it at any and all hazards.

It is well known to the American people and to all nations that this Government has never interfered with the relations subsisting between other governments. We have never made ourselves parties to their wars or their alliances; we have not sought their territories by conquest; we have not mingled with parties in their domestic struggles; and believing our own form of government to be the best, we have never attempted to propagate it by intrigues, by diplomacy, or by force. We may claim on this continent a like exemption from European interference. The nations of America are equally sovereign and independent with those of Europe. They possess the same rights, independent of all foreign interposition, to make war, to conclude peace, and to regulate their internal affairs. The people of the United States can not, therefore, view with indifference attempts of European powers to interfere with the independent action of the nations on this continent. The American system of government is entirely different from that of Europe. Jealousy among the different sovereigns of Europe, lest any one of them might become too powerful for the rest, has caused them anxiously to desire the establishment of what they term the "balance of power." It can not be permitted to have any application on the North American continent, and especially to the United States. We must ever maintain the principle that the people of this continent alone have the right to decide their own destiny. Should any portion of them, constituting an independent state, propose to unite themselves with our Confederacy, this will be a question for them and us to determine without any foreign interposition. We can never consent that European powers shall interfere to prevent such a union because it might disturb the "balance of power" which they may desire to maintain upon this continent. Near a quarter of a century ago the principle was distinctly announced to the world, in the annual message of one of my predecessors, that—

The American continents, by the free and independent condition which they have assumed and maintain, are henceforth not to be considered as subjects for future colonization by any European powers.

This principle will apply with greatly increased force should any European power attempt to establish any new colony in North America. In the existing circumstances of the world the present is deemed a proper occasion to reiterate and reaffirm the principle avowed by Mr. Monroe and to state my cordial concurrence in its wisdom and sound policy. The reassertion of this principle, especially in reference to North America, is at this day but the promulgation of a policy which no European power should cherish the disposition to resist. Existing rights of every European nation should be respected, but it is due alike to our safety and our interests that the efficient protection of our laws should be extended over our whole territorial limits, and that it should be distinctly announced to the world as our settled policy that no future European colony or dominion shall with our consent be planted or established on any part of the North American continent.

—JAMES K. POLK, First Annual Message to Congress, 1845

3. "TURNING THE EYES OUTWARD INSTEAD OF INWARD"

At no time in its history was the United States really isolated—witness its involvement in the Napoleonic Wars, for example, or its persistent interest in revolutionary movements in Greece or Hungary or the Latin-American states, or its profound concern for the European reaction at the time of the Civil War. But active participation in world affairs did not come until after the Civil War, and the emergence of the United States as a world power cannot be dated earlier than the decade of the 1890's. By that time the frontier was, in effect, gone; the continent had been settled; American industry was looking for overseas markets; American interests were global rather than merely hemispheric. American interest in—and participation in—world affairs, once aroused, developed with great rapidity. The Spanish War, the acquisition of Hawaii and the Philippines, the construction of the Panama Canal, the Open Door policy, active participation in the suppression of the Boxer uprising, the peace-making between Japan and Russia, the relations of Germany, France and Britain on the Continent and in Africa—all these things combined to dramatize the American rise to world power. Few Americans were psychologically prepared for the obligations and responsibilities that went along with this new, and unavoidable, position. Among those who ceaselessly worked to educate the American people to an understanding of what was involved in world power, none was more influential than Captain, later Admiral, Mahan. Author of a series of epoch-making books on the influence of sea power in history, Mahan was likewise a publicist of note, deeply concerned with the role of America in world affairs and the obligations of that role. We quote here from an article, "The Interest of America in Sea Power."

. . . The interesting and significant feature of this changing attitude is the turning of the eyes outward, instead of inward only, to seek the welfare of the country. To affirm the importance of distant markets, and the relation to them of our own immense powers of production, implies logically the recognition of the link that joins the products and the markets,—that is, the carrying trade; the three together constituting that chain of maritime power to which Great Britain owes her wealth and greatness. Further, is it too much to say that, as two of these links, the shipping and the markets, are exterior to our own borders, the acknowledgment of them carries with it a view of the relations of the United States to the world radically distinct from the simple idea of self-sufficingness? We shall not follow far this line of thought before there will dawn the realization of America's unique position, facing the older worlds of the East and West, her shores washed by the oceans which touch the one or the other, but which are common to her alone.

Coincident with these signs of change in our own policy there is restlessness in the world at large which is deeply significant, if not ominous. It is beside our purpose to dwell upon the internal state of Europe, whence, if disturbances arise, the effect upon us may be but partial and indirect. But the great seaboard powers there do not stand on guard against their continental rivals only; they cherish also aspirations for commercial extension, for colonies, and for influence in distant regions, which may bring, and, even under our present contracted policy, already have brought them into collision with ourselves. The incident of the Samoa Islands, trivial apparently, was nevertheless eminently suggestive of European ambitions. America then roused from sleep as to interests closely concerning her future. At this moment internal troubles are imminent in the Sandwich Islands, where it should be our fixed determination to allow no foreign influence to equal our own. All over the world German commercial and colonial push is coming into collision with other nations: witness the affair of the Caroline Islands with Spain; the parti-

tion of New Guinea with England; the yet more recent negotiation between these two powers concerning their share in Africa viewed with
deep distrust and jealousy by France; the Samoa affair; the conflict between German control and American interests in the islands of the
western Pacific; and the alleged Progress of German influence in Central
and South America. It is noteworthy that, while these various contentions are sustained with the aggressive military spirit characteristic of the
German Empire, they are credibly said to arise from the national temper
more than from the deliberate policy of the government, which in this
matter does not lead, but follows, the feeling of the people,—a condition
much more formidable.

There is no sound reason for believing that the world has passed into
a period of assured peace outside the limits of Europe. Unsettled political
conditions, such as exist in Haiti, Central America, and many of the
Pacific Islands, especially the Hawaiian group, when combined with
great military or commercial importance as is the case with most of these
positions, involve, now as always, dangerous germs of quarrel, against
which it is prudent at least to be prepared. Undoubtedly, the general
temper of nations is more averse from war than it was of old. If no less
selfish and grasping than our predecessors, we feel more dislike to the
discomforts and sufferings attendant upon a breach of peace; but to retain that highly valued repose and the undisturbed enjoyment of the returns of commerce, it is necessary to argue upon somewhat equal terms
of strength with an adversary. It is the preparedness of the enemy, and
not acquiescence in the existing state of things, that now holds back the
armies of Europe.

On the other hand, neither the sanctions of international law nor the
justice of a cause can be depended upon for a fair settlement of differences, when they come into conflict with a strong political necessity on
the one side opposed to comparative weakness on the other. In our still-
pending dispute over the seal-fishing of Bering Sea, whatever may be
thought of the strength of our argument, in view of generally admitted
principles of international law, it is beyond doubt that our contention is
reasonable, just, and in the interest of the world at large. But in the attempt to enforce it we have come into collision not only with national
susceptibilities as to the honor of the flag, which we ourselves very
strongly share, but also with a state governed by a powerful necessity, and
exceedingly strong where we are particularly weak and exposed. Not
only has Great Britain a mighty navy and we a long defenceless seacoast,

but it is a great commercial and political advantage to her that her larger colonies, and above all Canada, should feel that the power of the mother country is something which they need, and upon which they can count. . . . These feelings of attachment and mutual dependence supply the living spirit, without which the nascent schemes for Imperial Federation are but dead mechanical contrivances; nor are they without influence upon such generally unsentimental considerations as those of buying and selling, and the course of trade.

This dispute, seemingly paltry yet really serious, sudden in its appearance and dependent for its issue upon other considerations than its own merits, may serve to convince us of many latent and yet unforeseen dangers to the peace of the western hemisphere, attendant upon the opening of a canal through the Central American Isthmus. In a general way, it is evident enough that this canal, by modifying the direction of trade routes, will induce a great increase of commercial activity and carrying trade throughout the Caribbean Sea; and that this now comparatively deserted nook of the ocean will become, like the Red Sea, a great thoroughfare of shipping, and will attract, as never before in our day, the interest and ambition of maritime nations. Every position in that sea will have enhanced commercial and military value, and the canal itself will become a strategic centre of the most vital importance. Like the Canadian Pacific Railroad, it will be a link between the two oceans; but, unlike it, the use, unless most carefully guarded by treaties, will belong wholly to the belligerent which controls the sea by its naval power. In case of war, the United States will unquestionably command the Canadian Railroad, despite the deterrent force of operations by the hostile navy upon our seaboard; but no less unquestionably will she be impotent, as against any of the great maritime powers, to control the Central American canal. Militarily speaking, and having reference to European complications only, the piercing of the Isthmus is nothing but a disaster to the United States, in the present state of her military and naval preparation. It is especially dangerous to the Pacific coast; but the increased exposure of one part of our seaboard reacts unfavorably upon the whole military situation.

Despite a certain great original superiority conferred by our geographical nearness and immense resources,—due, in other words, to our natural advantages, and not to our intelligent preparations,—the United States is woefully unready, not only in fact but in purpose to assert in the Caribbean and Central America a weight of influence proportioned to the extent of her interests. We have not the navy, and, what is worse, we are not willing to have the navy, that will weigh seriously in any disputes with those nations whose interests will conflict there with our own. We have not, and we are not anxious to provide, the defence of the seaboard which will leave the navy free for its work at sea. We have not, but many other powers have, positions, either within or on the borders of the Caribbean which not only possess great natural advantages for the control of that sea, but have received and are receiving that artificial strength of fortification and armament which will make them practically inexpugnable. That which I deplore, and which is a sober, just, and reasonable cause of deep national concern is that the nation neither has nor cares to have its sea frontier so defended, and its navy of such power, as shall suffice, with the advantages of our position, to weigh seriously when inevitable discussions arise,—such as we have recently had about Samoa and Bering Sea, and which may at any moment come up about the Caribbean Sea or the canal. . . .

It is perfectly reasonable and legitimate, in estimating our needs of military preparation, to take into account the remoteness of the chief naval and military nations from our shores, and the consequent difficulty of maintaining operations at such a distance. It is equally proper, in framing our policy, to consider the jealousies of the European family of states, and their consequent unwillingness to incur the enmity of a people so strong as ourselves; their dread of our revenge in the future, as well as their inability to detach more than a certain part of their forces to our shores without losing much of their own weight in the councils of Europe. In truth, a careful determination of the force that Great Britain or France could probably spare for operations against our coasts, if the latter were suitably defended, without weakening their European position or unduly exposing their colonies and commerce, is the starting-point from which to calculate the strength of our own navy. If the latter be superior to the force that can thus be sent against it, and the coast be so defended as to leave the navy free to strike where it will we can maintain our rights; not merely the rights which international law concedes, and which the moral sense of nations now supports, but also those equally real rights which, though not supported by law, depend upon a clear preponderance of interest, upon obviously necessary policy, upon self-preservation, either total or partial.

—CAPTAIN ALFRED MAHAN,
"The Interest of America in Sea Power," 1897

4. THE ACQUISITION OF THE PHILIPPINES

"The march of events," President McKinley wrote in these instructions to the American Peace Commissioners at Paris, "rules and overrules human action." Certainly when America went to the rescue of the Cubans, few anticipated that the first major battle would come in Manila Bay, and that we would feel compelled to take over the Philippines. McKinley himself was long in doubt about the right policy toward these Islands; in the end he instructed the American Commissioners to insist upon their cession because he could not see any practical alternative. The question of the acquisition of the Philippines precipitated one of the great debates of American politics. Those opposed to this venture in "Old World imperialism" rallied to Bryan, who fought the campaign of 1900 on the issue of anti-imperialism. His defeat settled the question temporarily rather than permanently. The Filipinos themselves put up a long and stout resistance to the American conquerors; not until 1902 could it be said that the Islands were pacified. The Democratic party, meantime, stood committed to ultimate Philippine independence. The Jones Act of 1916 promised independence at the earliest practicable time, and under Franklin Roosevelt the party made good that promise.

IT IS my earnest wish that the United States in making peace should follow the same high rule of conduct which guided it in facing war. It should be as scrupulous and magnanimous in the concluding settlement as it was just and humane in its original action. The luster and the moral strength attaching to a cause which can be confidently rested upon the considerate judgment of the world should not under any illusion of the hour be dimmed by ulterior designs which might tempt us into excessive demands or into an adventurous departure on untried paths. It is believed that the true glory and the enduring interests of the country will most surely be served if an unselfish duty conscientiously accepted and a signal triumph honorably achieved shall be crowned by such an example of moderation, restraint, and reason in victory as best comports with the traditions and character of our enlightened Republic.

Our aim in the adjustment of peace should be directed to lasting results and to the achievement of the common good under the demands of civilization, rather than to ambitious designs. The terms of the protocol were framed upon this consideration. The abandonment of the Western Hemisphere by Spain was an imperative necessity. . . .

The Philippines stand upon a different basis. It is none the less true, however, that, without any original thought of complete or even partial acquisition, the presence and success of our arms at Manila imposes upon us obligations which we can not disregard. The march of events rules and overrules human action. Avowing unreservedly the purpose which has animated all our effort, and still solicitous to adhere to it, we can not be unmindful that, without any desire or design on our part, the war has brought us new duties and responsibilities which we must meet and discharge as becomes a great nation on whose growth and career from the beginning the Ruler of Nations has plainly written the high command and pledge of civilization.

Incidental to our tenure in the Philippines is the commercial opportunity to which American statesmanship can not be indifferent. It is just to use every legitimate means for the enlargement of American trade; but we seek no advantages in the Orient which are not common to all. Asking only the open door for ourselves, we are ready to accord the open door to others. The commercial opportunity which is naturally and inevitably associated with this new opening depends less on large territorial possession than upon an adequate commercial basis and upon broad and equal privileges. . . .

In view of what has been stated, the United States can not accept less than the cession in full right and sovereignty of the island of Luzon. It is desirable, however, that the United States shall acquire the right of entry for vessels and merchandise belonging to citizens of the United States into such ports of the Philippines as are not ceded to the United States upon terms of equal favor with Spanish ships and merchandise, both in relation to port and customs charges and rates of trade accorded to citizens of one country within the territory of another. You are therefore instructed to demand such concession, agreeing on your part that Spain shall have similar rights as to her subjects and vessels in the ports of any territory in the Philippines ceded to the United States.

—President McKinley,
Instructions to American Peace Commissioners, September, 1898

5. THE OPEN DOOR IN CHINA

Almost every American knows about the Open Door policy for China, but almost every one, too, would be hard put to it to tell what the phrase means. As Tyler Dennett said of the Hay circular notes, "It would have taken more than a lawyer to define what new rights had been recognized, or required, or even what had actually been said." But, he added, "Such comment is beside the point. These notes had not been put forward by a lawyer as a contribution to the law of nations, but by a publicist to crystallize public opinion."

The immediate occasion for the Hay notes was the danger of a partition of China which might have excluded the United States and harmed American interests. The historical background was a long tradition of interest in, and sympathy with, the Chinese in their struggle against foreign exploitation. For it has long been one of the paradoxes of American policy and public opinion, that American isolationism has been directed to Europe alone, and that the most ardent isolationists have customarily been those most eager to intervene in Far Eastern affairs. This pattern has persisted into the middle of the twentieth century.

We give here the first of Secretary Hay's notes attempting to commit the great powers to a policy of hands-off in China. Although the replies to Hay's first note were, for the most part, evasive, Hay promptly announced that the powers had accepted the policy he laid down. Subsequent events were to make clear that this was an expression of faith rather than of fact.

DEPARTMENT OF STATE
WASHINGTON, September 6, 1899.

SIR: At the time when the Government of the United States was informed by that of Germany that it had leased from His Majesty the Emperor of China the port of Kiao-chao and the adjacent territory in the province of Shantung, assurances were given to the ambassador of the United States at Berlin by the Imperial German minister for foreign affairs that the rights and privileges insured by treaties with China to citizens of the United States would not thereby suffer or be in any-wise impaired within the area over which Germany had thus obtained control.

More recently, however, the British Government recognized by a formal agreement with Germany the exclusive right of the latter country to enjoy in said leased area and the contiguous "sphere of influence or interest" certain privileges, more especially those relating to railroads and mining enterprises; but, as the exact nature and extent of the rights thus recognized have not been clearly defined, it is possible that serious conflicts of interest may at any time arise, not only between British and German subjects within said area, but that the interests of our citizens may also be jeopardized thereby.

Earnestly desirous to remove any cause of irritation and to insure at the same time to the commerce of all nations in China the undoubted benefits which should accrue from a formal recognition by the various powers claiming "spheres of interest" that they shall enjoy perfect equality of treatment for their commerce and navigation within such "spheres," the Government of the United States would be pleased to see His German Majesty's Government give formal assurances and lend its coöperation in securing like assurances from the other interested powers that each within its respective sphere of whatever influence—

First. Will in no way interfere with any treaty port or any vested interest within any so-called "sphere of interest" or leased territory it may have in China.

Second. That the Chinese treaty tariff of the time being shall apply to all merchandise landed or shipped to all such ports as are within said "sphere of interest" (unless they be "free ports"), no matter to what nationality it may belong, and that duties so leviable shall be collected by the Chinese Government.

Third. That it will levy no higher harbor dues on vessels of another nationality frequenting any port in such "sphere" than shall be levied on vessels of its own nationality, and no higher railroad charges over lines built, controlled, or operated within its "sphere" on merchandise belonging to citizens or subjects of other nationalities transported through such "sphere" than shall be levied on similar merchandise belonging to its own nationals transported over equal distances.

The liberal policy pursued by His Imperial German Majesty in declaring Kiao-chao a free port and in aiding the Chinese Government in the establishment there of a custom-house are so clearly in line with the proposition which this Government is anxious to see recognized that it entertains the strongest hope that Germany will give its acceptance and hearty support.

The recent ukase of His Majesty the Emperor of Russia declaring the port of Talien-wan open during the whole of the lease under which it is held from China, to the merchant ships of all nations, coupled with the categorical assurances made to this Government by His Imperial Majesty's representative at this capital at the time, and since repeated to me by the present Russian ambassador, seem to insure the support of the Emperor to the proposed measure. Our ambassador at the Court of St. Petersburg has, in consequence, been instructed to submit it to the Russian Government and to request their early consideration of it. A copy of my instruction on the subject to Mr. Tower is herewith inclosed for your confidential information.

The commercial interests of Great Britain and Japan will be so clearly served by the desired declaration of intentions, and the views of the Governments of these countries as to the desirability of the adoption of measures insuring the benefits of equality of treatment of all foreign trade throughout China are so similar to those entertained by the United States, that their acceptance of the propositions herein outlined and their cooperation in advocating their adoption by the other powers can be confidently expected. I enclose herewith copy of the instruction which I have sent to Mr. Choate on the subject.

In view of the present favorable conditions, you are instructed to submit the above considerations to His Imperial German Majesty's minister for foreign affairs, and to request his early consideration of the subject.

Copy of this instruction is sent to our ambassadors at London and at St. Petersburg for their information.

I have, etc., JOHN HAY

—JOHN HAY, Letter to Henry White, September 6, 1899

6. "GOD . . . HAS MADE US THE MASTER ORGANIZERS OF THE WORLD"

The argument for the acquisition of the Philippines, as put forth by President McKinley, was one thing; the argument for their retention another. Although the United States had no imperialist tradition, in the sense that Britain and France had such a tradition, imperialism came naturally to a good many Americans. The arguments in favor of imperialism were a hodgepodge of considerations, commercial, military, political, and moral. All of these were blended in the speeches of Senator Beveridge of Indiana, one of the most eloquent and effective of the champions of imperialism. What is particularly interesting in this speech is the combination of shrewd practical considerations with the mystical sense of racial destiny.

MR. PRESIDENT, the times call for candor. The Philippines are ours forever, "territory belonging to the United States," as the Constitution calls them. And just beyond the Philippines are China's illimitable markets. We will not retreat from either. We will not repudiate our duty in the archipelago. We will not abandon our opportunity in the Orient. We will not renounce our part in the mission of our race, trustee, under God, of the civilization of the world. And we will move forward to our work, not howling out regrets like slaves whipped to their burdens, but with gratitude for a task worthy of our strength, and thanksgiving to Almighty God that He has marked us as His chosen people, henceforth to lead in the regeneration of the world.

This island empire is the last land left in all the oceans. If it should prove a mistake to abandon it, the blunder once made would be irretrievable. If it proves a mistake to hold it, the error can be corrected when we will. Every other progressive nation stands ready to relieve us.

But to hold it will be no mistake. Our largest trade henceforth must be with Asia. The Pacific is our ocean. More and more Europe will

670

manufacture the most it needs, secure from its colonies the most it consumes. Where shall we turn for consumers of our surplus? Geography answers the question. China is our natural customer. She is nearer to us than to England, Germany, or Russia, the commercial powers of the present and the future. They have moved nearer to China by securing permanent bases on her borders. The Philippines give us a base at the door of all the East.

Lines of navigation from our ports to the Orient and Australia; from the Isthmian Canal to Asia; from all Oriental ports to Australia, converge at and separate from the Philippines. They are a self-supporting, dividend-paying fleet, permanently anchored at a spot selected by the strategy of Providence, commanding the Pacific. And the Pacific is the ocean of the commerce of the future. Most future wars will be conflicts for commerce. The power that rules the Pacific, therefore, is the power that rules the world. And, with the Philippines, that power is and will forever be the American Republic. . . .

Here, then, Senators, is the situation. Two years ago there was no land in all the world which we could occupy for any purpose. Our commerce was daily turning toward the Orient, and geography and trade developments made necessary our commercial empire over the Pacific. And in that ocean we had no commercial, naval, or military base. To-day we have one of the three great ocean possessions of the globe, located at the most commanding commercial, naval, and military points in the eastern seas, within hail of India, shoulder to shoulder with China, richer in its own resources than any equal body of land on the entire globe, and peopled by a race which civilization demands shall be improved. Shall we abandon it? That man little knows the common people of the Republic, little understands the instincts of our race, who thinks we will not hold it fast and hold it forever, administering just government by simplest methods. We may trick up devices to shift our burden and lessen our opportunity; they will avail us nothing but delay. We may tangle conditions by applying academic arrangements of self-government to a crude situation; their failure will drive us to our duty in the end. . . .

But, Senators, it would be better to abandon this combined garden and Gibraltar of the Pacific, and count our blood and treasure already spent a profitable loss, than to apply any academic arrangement of self-government to these children. They are not capable of self-government. How could they be? They are not a self-governing race. They are Orientals, Malays, instructed by Spaniards in the latter's worst estate. . . .

The Declaration of Independence does not forbid us to do our part in the regeneration of the world. If it did, the Declaration would be wrong, just as the Articles of Confederation, drafted by the very same men who signed the Declaration, was found to be wrong. The Declaration has no application to the present situation. It was written by self-governing men for self-governing men. . . .

Mr. President, this question is deeper than any question of party politics; deeper than any question of the isolated policy of our country even; deeper even than any question of constitutional power. It is elemental. It is racial. God has not been preparing the English-speaking and Teutonic peoples for a thousand years for nothing but vain and idle self-contemplation and self-admiration. No! He has made us the master organizers of the world to establish system where chaos reigns. He has given us the spirit of progress to overwhelm the forces of reaction throughout the earth. He has made us adepts in government that we may administer government among savage and senile peoples. Were it not for such a force as this the world would relapse into barbarism and night. And of all our race He has marked the American people as His chosen nation to finally lead in the regeneration of the world. This is the divine mission of America, and it holds for us all the profit, all the glory, all the happiness possible to man. We are trustees of the world's progress, guardians of its righteous peace. The judgment of the Master is upon us: "Ye have been faithful over a few things; I will make you ruler over many things."

What shall history say of us? Shall it say that we renounced that holy trust, left the savage to his base condition, the wilderness to the reign of waste, deserted duty, abandoned glory, forget our sordid profit even, because we feared our strength and read the charter of our powers with the doubter's eye and the quibbler's mind? Shall it say that, called by events to captain and command the proudest, ablest, purest race of history in history's noblest work, we declined that great commission? Our fathers would not have had it so. No! They founded no paralytic government, incapable of the simplest acts of administration. They planted no sluggard people, passive while the world's work calls them. They established no reactionary nation. They unfurled no retreating flag. . . .

Blind indeed is he who sees not the hand of God in events so vast, so harmonious, so benign. Reactionary indeed is the mind that perceives not that this vital people is the strongest of the saving forces of the world;

that our place, therefore, is at the head of the constructing and redeem-
ing nations of the earth; and that to stand aside while events march on is
a surrender of our interests, a betrayal of our duty as blind as it is base.
Craven indeed is the heart that fears to perform a work so golden and
so noble; that dares not win a glory so immortal.
     —ALBERT J. BEVERIDGE, Speech in the Senate, January 9, 1900

7. THE PLATT AMENDMENT

*By the Teller Amendment of April, 1898, the United States disclaimed
in advance any intention of annexing Cuba, promising to leave the
government of the island in the hands of its people. On the conclusion
of the war the Cubans drew up a constitution, modeled on that of the
United States, but without any special provision for future relations
with the United States. The American government, unwilling to acquiesce in a complete break between the two countries, insisted on adding a series of provisions known collectively as the Platt Amendment—
an amendment which seriously limited Cuban control over foreign relations and gave the United States the right to intervene in its domestic
affairs in certain circumstances. The United States acted under these
provisions on a number of occasions. Both American and Cuban opinion,
however, became increasingly critical of the philosophy behind the Platt
Amendment, and in 1934 the United States took the lead in abrogating
it entirely. While the abrogation of the Platt Amendment, which we give
here, presumably returned to Cuba control over her own external as well
as internal affairs, it would be folly to suppose that in the realm of
foreign relations Cuba is a free agent.*

A. TREATY WITH CUBA EMBODYING THE PLATT
AMENDMENT

ART. I. The Government of Cuba shall never enter into any treaty or
other compact with any foreign power or powers which will impair or
tend to impair the independence of Cuba, nor in any manner authorize
or permit any foreign power or powers to obtain by colonization or for

military or naval purposes, or otherwise, lodgement in or control over any portion of said island.

ART. II. The Government of Cuba shall not assume or contract any public debt to pay the interest upon which, and to make reasonable sinking-fund provision for the ultimate discharge of which, the ordinary revenues of the Island of Cuba, after defraying the current expenses of the Government shall be inadequate.

ART. III. The Government of Cuba consents that the United States may exercise the right to intervene for the preservation of Cuban independence, the maintenance of a government adequate for the protection of life, property, and individual liberty, and for discharging the obligations with respect to Cuba imposed by the treaty of Paris on the United States, now to be assumed and undertaken by the government of Cuba.

ART. IV. All Acts of the United States in Cuba during its military occupancy thereof are ratified and validated, and all lawful rights acquired thereunder shall be maintained and protected.

ART. V. The Government of Cuba will execute, and as far as necessary extend, the plans already devised or other plans to be mutually agreed upon, for the sanitation of the cities of the island, to the end that a recurrence of epidemics and infectious diseases may be prevented thereby assuring protection to the people and commerce of Cuba, as well as to the commerce of the southern ports of the United States and the people residing therein.

ART. VI. The Isle of Pines shall be omitted from the boundaries of Cuba, specified in the Constitution, the title thereto being left to future adjustment by treaty.

ART. VII. To enable the United States to maintain the independence of Cuba, and to protect the people thereof, as well as for its own defense, the government of Cuba will sell or lease to the United States lands necessary for coaling or naval stations at certain specified points to be agreed upon with the President of the United States.

—Treaty with Cuba, May 22, 1903

B. Abrogation of the Platt Amendment

The United States of America and the Republic of Cuba, being animated by the desire to fortify the relations of friendship between the two countries, and to modify, with this purpose, the relations established between them by the Treaty of Relations signed at Havana,

May 22, 1903, have appointed, with this intention, as their pleni-
potentiaries: . . .

Who, after having communicated to each other their full powers,
which were found to be in good and due form, have agreed upon the
following articles:

Art. I. The Treaty of Relations which was concluded between the
two contracting parties on May 22, 1903, shall cease to be in force, and
is abrogated, from the date on which the present treaty goes into effect.

Art. II. All the acts effected in Cuba by the United States of America
during its military occupation of the island, up to May 20, 1902, the
date on which the Republic of Cuba was established, have been ratified
and held as valid; and all rights legally acquired by virtue of those acts
shall be maintained and protected.

Art. III. Until the two contracting parties agree to the modification
or abrogation of the stipulations of the agreement in regard to the lease
to the United States of America of lands in Cuba for coaling and naval
stations signed by the President of the Republic of Cuba on February
16, 1903, and by the President of the United States of America on the
23rd day of the same month and year, the stipulations of that agreement
with regard to the naval station of Guantanamo shall continue in effect.
The supplementary agreement in regard to naval or coaling stations
signed between the two governments on July 2, 1903, shall continue in
effect in the same form and on the same conditions with respect to
the naval station at Guantanamo. So long as the United States of
America shall not abandon the said naval station of Guantanamo or
the two governments shall not agree to a modification of its present
limits, the station shall continue to have the territorial area that it
now has, with the limits that it has on the date of the signature of the
present treaty.

Art. IV. If at any time in the future a situation should arise that
appears to point to an outbreak of contagious disease in the territory of
either of the contracting parties, either of the two governments shall,
for its own protection, and without its act being considered unfriendly,
exercise freely and at its discretion the right to suspend communications
between those of its ports that it may designate and all or part of the
territory of the other party, and for the period that it may consider to
be advisable.

Art. V. The present Treaty shall be ratified by the contracting parties

in accordance with their respective Constitutional methods; and shall
go into effect on the date of the exchange of their ratifications, which
shall take place in the city of Washington as soon as possible.

—*U.S. Statutes at Large*, May 29, 1934

8. "WE MUST PROVE OURSELVES . . . FRIENDS . . . UPON TERMS OF EQUALITY AND HONOR"

*In theory and in principle President Wilson was against every form
and manifestation of imperialism or of what it was popular to call
"dollar diplomacy." Very early in his administration he attempted to
reverse or modify some of the policies upon which his predecessors had
embarked. He withdrew administrative support from a proposed bankers'
loan to China. He announced that "one of the chief objects of my
administration will be to cultivate the friendship and deserve the confidence of our sister Republics of Central and South America." He
worked constantly for the liberation of the Philippines and, in the Jones
Act of 1916, gave the Islands a very large measure of self-government.
Although under heavy pressure to intervene with force in troubled
Mexico, he limited intervention as much as he thought possible, and
encouraged the independent and liberal forces in that stricken country.
Perhaps the most important pronouncement of Latin-American policy
came in his Mobile Address of October, 1913—an address which was
welcomed throughout Latin America as the herald of a new day in Pan-
American relations.*

. . . The future, ladies and gentlemen, is going to be very different
for this hemisphere from the past. These States lying to the south of us,
which have always been our neighbors, will now be drawn closer to us
by innumerable ties, and, I hope, chief of all, by the tie of a common
understanding of each other. Interest does not tie nations together; it
sometimes separates them. But sympathy and understanding does unite
them, and I believe that by the new route that is just about to be opened,
while we physically cut two continents asunder, we spiritually unite
them. It is a spiritual union which we seek. . . .

There is one peculiarity about the history of the Latin American

States which I am sure they are keenly aware of. You hear of "concessions" to foreign capitalists in Latin America. You do not hear of concessions to foreign capitalists in the United States. They are not granted concessions. They are invited to make investments. The work is ours, though they are welcome to invest in it. We do not ask them to supply the capital and do the work. It is an invitation, not a privilege; and States that are obliged, because their territory does not lie within the main field of modern enterprise and action, to grant concessions are in this condition, that foreign interests are apt to dominate their domestic affairs, a condition of affairs always dangerous and apt to become intolerable. What these States are going to see, therefore, is an emancipation from the subordination, which has been inevitable, to foreign enterprise and an assertion of the splendid character which, in spite of these difficulties, they have again and again been able to demonstrate. The dignity, the courage, the self-possession, the self-respect of the Latin American States, their achievements in the face of all these adverse circumstances, deserve nothing but the admiration and applause of the world. They have had harder bargains driven with them in the matter of loans than any other peoples in the world. Interest has been exacted of them that was not exacted of anybody else, because the risk was said to be greater; and then securities were taken that destroyed the risk—an admirable arrangement for those who were forcing the terms! I rejoice in nothing so much as in the prospect that they will now be emancipated from these conditions, and we ought to be the first to take part in assisting in that emancipation. I think some of these gentlemen have already had occasion to bear witness that the Department of State in recent months has tried to serve them in that wise. In the future they will draw closer and closer to us because of circumstances of which I wish to speak with moderation and, I hope, without indiscretion.

We must prove ourselves their friends, and champions upon terms of equality and honor. You cannot be friends upon any other terms than upon the terms of equality. You cannot be friends at all except upon the terms of honor. We must show ourselves friends by comprehending their interest whether it squares with our own interest or not. It is a very perilous thing to determine the foreign policy of a nation in the terms of material interest. It not only is unfair to those with whom you are dealing, but it is degrading as regards your own actions.

Comprehension must be the soil in which shall grow all the fruits of friendship, and there is a reason and a compulsion lying behind all this which is dearer than anything else to the thoughtful men of America.

I mean the development of constitutional liberty in the world. Human rights, national integrity, and opportunity as against material interests— that, ladies and gentlemen, is the issue which we now have to face. I want to take this occasion to say that the United States will never again seek one additional foot of territory by conquest. She will devote herself to showing that she knows how to make honorable and fruitful use of the territory she has, and she must regard it as one of the duties of friendship to see that from no quarter are material interests made superior to human liberty and national opportunity. I say this, not with a single thought that anyone will gainsay it, but merely to fix in our consciousness what our real relationship with the rest of America is. It is the relationship of a family of mankind devoted to the development of true constitutional liberty. We know that that is the soil out of which the best enterprise springs. We know that this is a cause which we are making in common with our neighbors, because we have had to make it for ourselves.

—WOODROW WILSON, Address at Mobile, Alabama, October 27, 1913

9. THE POLICY OF THE GOOD NEIGHBOR

What Wilson formulated in principle, Franklin D. Roosevelt applied in practice. In his Inaugural Address Roosevelt had called for the policy of the Good Neighbor, and by such gestures as the abrogation of the Platt Amendment, the withdrawal of American marines from Caribbean countries, and the transformation of the Monroe Doctrine from a uni-lateral to a multilateral policy, he did more to encourage understanding and co-operation among the nations of the Americas than had any of his predecessors. We give here an excerpt from an address on the Good Neighbor policy.

. . . Long before I returned to Washington as President of the United States, I had made up my mind that, pending what might be called a more opportune moment on other continents, the United States could best serve the cause of peaceful humanity by setting an example. That was why on the 4th of March, 1933, I made the following declaration:

In the field of world policy I would dedicate this nation to the policy of the good neighbor—the neighbor who resolutely respects himself and because he does so, respects the rights of others—the neighbor who respects his obligations and respects the sanctity of his agreements in and with a world of neighbors.

This declaration represents my purpose; but it represents more than a purpose, for it stands for a practice. To a measurable degree it has succeeded; the whole world now knows that the United States cherishes no predatory ambitions. We are strong; but less powerful nations know that they need not fear our strength. We seek no conquest; we stand for peace.

In the whole of the Western Hemisphere our good neighbor policy has produced results that are especially heartening.

The noblest monument to peace and to neighborly economic and social friendship in all the world is not a monument in bronze or stone but the boundary which unites the United States and Canada—3,000 miles of friendship with no barbed wire, no gun or soldier, and no passport on the whole frontier.

Mutual trust made that frontier—to extend the same sort of mutual trust throughout the Americas was our aim.

The American republics to the south of us have been ready always to cooperate with the United States on a basis of equality and mutual respect, but before we inaugurated the good neighbor policy there was among them resentment and fear, because certain administrations in Washington had slighted their national pride and their sovereign rights.

In pursuance of the good neighbor policy, and because in my younger days I had learned many lessons in the hard school of experience, I stated that the United States was opposed definitely to armed intervention.

We have negotiated a Pan-American convention embodying the principle of non-intervention. We have abandoned the Platt amendment which gave us the right to intervene in the internal affairs of the Republic of Cuba. We have withdrawn American marines from Haiti. We have signed a new treaty which places our relations with Panama on a mutually satisfactory basis. We have undertaken a series of trade agreements with other American countries to our mutual commercial profit. At the request of two neighboring republics, I hope to give assistance in the final settlement of the last serious boundary dispute between any of the American nations.

Throughout the Americas the spirit of the good neighbor is a practical and living fact. The twenty-one American republics are not only living together in friendship and in peace; they are united in the determination so to remain. . . .

Of all the nations of the world today we are in many ways most singularly blessed. Our closest neighbors are good neighbors. If there are remoter nations that wish us not good but ill, they know that we are strong; they know that we can and will defend ourselves and defend our neighborhood.

We seek to dominate no other nation. We ask no territorial expansion. We oppose imperialism. We desire reduction in world armaments.

We believe in democracy; we believe in freedom; we believe in peace. We offer to every nation of the world the handclasp of the good neighbor. Let those who wish our friendship look us in the eye and take our hand.

—FRANKLIN D. ROOSEVELT,
Address at Chautauqua, New York, August 14, 1936

10. "THE WORLD MUST BE MADE SAFE FOR DEMOCRACY"

By any standards this is one of the great addresses of American history, one to rank alongside Washington's Farewell Address, Jefferson's First Inaugural, Lincoln's Second Inaugural, and Wilson's First Inaugural Address. Wilson had been successful in avoiding entry into the war during his first administration, and he was re-elected on the slogan, "He kept us out of war." But, as he observed in a series of speeches in 1916, the time might come when he could not maintain both peace and honor. That time came, so he thought, when Germany announced unrestricted submarine warfare and when German U-boats sank American ships. On April 2, 1917, Wilson appeared before a special session of Congress and made this appeal for a declaration of war; four days later Congress declared war.

In the years of disillusionment that followed the defeat of the Treaty of Versailles, it was fashionable to be either cynical or derisive about the phrase, "The world must be made safe for democracy." It should be obvious that these memorable words were not a call to democratize the world, but a simple statement of fact—that there could be no peace in a world where democracy was not safe. It took another world war to bring that principle home to us; it is, today, the elementary and basic principle of our foreign policy.

. . . With a profound sense of the solemn and even tragical character of the step I am taking and of the grave responsibilities which it involves, but in unhesitating obedience to what I deem my constitutional duty, I advise that the Congress declare the recent course of the Imperial German Government to be in fact nothing less than war against the government and people of the United States; that it formally accept the status of belligerent which has thus been thrust upon it; and that it take immediate steps not only to put the country in a more thorough state of defense but also to exert all its power and employ all its resources to bring the Government of the German Empire to terms and end the war.

What this will involve is clear. It will involve the utmost practicable coöperation in counsel and action with the governments now at war with Germany, and, as incident to that, the extension to those governments of the most liberal financial credits, in order that our resources may so far as possible be added to theirs. It will involve the organization and mobilization of all the material resources of the country to supply the materials of war and serve the incidental needs of the Nation in the most abundant and yet the most economical and efficient way possible. It will involve the immediate full equipment of the navy in all respects but particularly in supplying it with the best means of dealing with the enemy's submarines. It will involve the immediate addition to the armed forces of the United States already provided for by law in case of war at least five hundred thousand men, who should, in my opinion, be chosen upon the principle of universal liability to service, and also the authorization of subsequent additional increments of equal force so soon as they may be needed and can be handled in training. It will involve also, of course, the granting of adequate credits to the Government, sustained, I hope, so far as they can equitably be sustained by the present generation, by well conceived taxation. . . .

While we do these things, these deeply momentous things, let us be very clear, and make very clear to all the world what our motives and our objects are. My own thought has not been driven from its habitual and normal course by the unhappy events of the last two months, and I do not believe that the thought of the Nation has been altered or clouded by them. I have exactly the same things in mind now that I had in mind when I addressed the Senate on the twenty-second of January last; the same that I had in mind when I addressed the Congress on the third of February and on the twenty-sixth of February. Our object now, as then, is to vindicate the principles of peace and justice in the life of the world as against selfish and autocratic power and to set up amongst the really free and self-governed peoples of the world such a concert of purpose and of action as will henceforth insure the observance of those principles. Neutrality is no longer feasible or desirable where the peace of the world is involved and the freedom of its peoples, and the menace to that peace and freedom lies in the existence of autocratic governments backed by organized force which is controlled wholly by their will, not by the will of their people. We have seen the last of neutrality in such circumstances. We are at the beginning of an age in which it will be insisted that the same standards of conduct and of responsibility for wrong done shall be observed among nations and their governments that are observed among the individual citizens of civilized states.

We have no quarrel with the German people. We have no feeling towards them but one of sympathy and friendship. It was not upon their impulse that their government acted in entering this war. It was not with their previous knowledge or approval. It was a war determined upon as wars used to be determined upon in the old, unhappy days when peoples were nowhere consulted by their rulers and wars were provoked and waged in the interest of dynasties or of little groups of ambitious men who were accustomed to use their fellow men as pawns and tools. . . .

We are accepting this challenge of hostile purpose because we know that in such a Government, following such methods, we can never have a friend; and that in the presence of its organized power, always lying in wait to accomplish we know not what purpose, there can be no assured security for the democratic Governments of the world. We are now about to accept gauge of battle with this natural foe to liberty and shall, if necessary, spend the whole force of the nation to check and nullify its pretensions and its power. We are glad, now that we see the facts with no veil of false pretense about them, to fight thus for the ultimate peace of the world and for the liberation of its peoples, the German peoples included: for the rights of nations great and small and the privilege of men everywhere to choose their way of life and of obedience. The world must be made safe for democracy. Its peace must be planted upon the tested foundations of political liberty. We have no selfish needs to serve. We desire no conquest, no dominion. We seek no indemnities for ourselves, no material compensation for the sacrifices we shall freely make. We are but one of the champions of the rights of mankind. We shall be satisfied when those rights have been made as secure as the faith and the freedom of nations can make them. . . .

It is a distressing and oppressive duty, Gentlemen of the Congress, which I have performed in thus addressing you. There are, it may be, many months of fiery trial and sacrifice ahead of us. It is a fearful thing to lead this great peaceful people into war, into the most terrible and disastrous of all wars, civilization itself seeming to be in the balance. But the right is more precious than peace, and we shall fight for the things which we have always carried nearest our hearts,—for democracy, for the right of those who submit to authority to have a voice in their own Governments, for the rights and liberties of small nations, for a universal dominion of right by such a concert of free peoples as shall bring peace and safety to all nations and make the world itself at last free. To such a task we can dedicate our lives and our fortunes, everything that we are and everything that we have, with the pride of those who know that the day has come when America is privileged to spend her blood and her might for the principles that gave her birth and happiness and the peace which she has treasured. God helping her, she can do no other.

—WOODROW WILSON, Address to Congress, April 2, 1917

11. THE FOURTEEN POINTS

In his address calling for war on Germany, President Wilson reminded Congress and the American people that he was primarily concerned with vindicating "the principles of peace and justice in the life of the world," and called for a "concert of purpose and of action." That concert was to create an international order which should abolish war as an instrument of national policy. More and more, as the war went on, Wilson addressed himself to the two great problems of the future: making a just peace, and establishing an international organization to maintain that peace. We give here the famous Fourteen Points—what Wilson hoped would be the basis of a lasting peace. It is popular, now, to regard this program as excessively naïve and even misguided, yet it cannot be said that our own generation has gone much beyond it, and many of the principles of the Fourteen Points are as valid and as vital today as when Wilson first announced them.

Gentlemen of the Congress:

. . . It will be our wish and purpose that the processes of peace, when they are begun, shall be absolutely open and that they shall involve and permit henceforth no secret understandings of any kind. The day of conquest and aggrandizement is gone by; so is also the day of secret covenants entered into in the interest of particular governments and likely at some unlooked-for moment to upset the peace of the world. It is this happy fact, now clear to the view of every public man whose thoughts do not still linger in an age that is dead and gone, which makes it possible for every nation whose purposes are consistent with justice and the peace of the world to avow now or at any other time the objects it has in view.

We entered this war because violations of right had occurred which touched us to the quick and made the life of our own people impossible unless they were corrected and the world secured once for all against their recurrence. What we demand in this war, therefore, is nothing peculiar to ourselves. It is that the world be made fit and safe to live in; and particularly that it be made safe for every peace-loving nation which, like our own, wishes to live its own life, determine its own institutions, be assured of justice and fair dealing by the other peoples of the world as against force and selfish aggression. All the peoples of the world are in effect partners in this interest, and for our own part we see very clearly that unless justice be done to others it will not be done to us. The program of the world's peace, therefore, is our program: and that program, the only possible program, as we see it, is this:

I. Open covenants of peace, openly arrived at, after which there shall be no private international understandings of any kind but diplomacy shall proceed always frankly and in the public view.

II. Absolute freedom of navigation upon the seas, outside territorial waters, alike in peace and in war, except as the seas may be closed in whole or in part by international action for the enforcement of international covenants.

III. The removal, so far as possible, of all economic barriers and the establishment of an equality of trade conditions among all the nations consenting to the peace and associating themselves for its maintenance.

IV. Adequate guarantees given and taken that national armaments will be reduced to the lowest point consistent with domestic safety.

V. A free, open-minded, and absolutely impartial adjustment of all colonial claims, based upon a strict observance of the principle that in determining all such questions of sovereignty the interests of the populations concerned must have equal weight with the equitable claims of the government whose title is to be determined.

VI. The evacuation of all Russian territory and such a settlement of all questions affecting Russia as will secure the best and freest coöperation of the other nations of the world in obtaining for her an unhampered and unembarrassed opportunity for the independent determination of her own political development and national policy and assure her of a sincere welcome into the society of free nations under institutions of her own choosing; and, more than a welcome, assistance also of every kind that she may need and may herself desire. The treatment accorded Russia by her sister nations in the months to come will be the acid test of their good will, of their comprehension of her needs as distinguished from their own interests, and of their intelligent and unselfish sympathy.

VII. Belgium, the whole world will agree, must be evacuated and restored, without any attempt to limit the sovereignty which she enjoys in common with all other free nations. No other single act will serve as this will serve to restore confidence among the nations in the laws which they have themselves set and determined for the government of their relations with one another. Without this healing act the whole structure and validity of international law is forever impaired.

VIII. All French territory should be freed and the invaded portions restored, and the wrong done to France by Prussia in 1871 in the matter of Alsace-Lorraine, which has unsettled the peace of the world for nearly fifty years, should be righted, in order that peace may once more be made secure in the interest of all.

IX. A readjustment of the frontiers of Italy shall be effected along clearly recognizable lines of nationality.

X. The peoples of Austria-Hungary, whose place among the nations we wish to see safeguarded and assured, should be accorded the freest opportunity of autonomous development.

XI. Rumania, Serbia, and Montenegro should be evacuated; occupied territories restored; Serbia accorded free and secure access to the sea; and the relations of the several Balkan states to one another determined by friendly counsel along historically established lines of allegiance and nationality; and international guarantees of the political and economic independence and territorial integrity of the several Balkan states should be entered into.

XII. The Turkish portions of the present Ottoman Empire should be assured a secure sovereignty, but the other nationalities which are now under Turkish rule should be assured an undoubted security of life and an absolutely unmolested opportunity of autonomous development, and the Dardanelles should be permanently opened as a free passage to the ships and commerce of all nations under international guarantees.

XIII. An independent Polish state should be erected which should include the territories inhabited by indisputably Polish populations, which should be assured a free and secure access to the sea, and whose political and economic independence and territorial integrity should be guaranteed by international covenant.

XIV. A general association of nations must be formed under specific covenants for the purpose of affording mutual guarantees of political independence and territorial integrity to great and small states alike.

In regard to these essential rectifications of wrong and assertions of right we feel ourselves to be intimate partners of all the governments and peoples associated together against the Imperialists. We cannot be separated in interest or divided in purpose. We stand together until the end.

For such arrangements and covenants we are willing to fight and to continue to fight until they are achieved; but only because we wish the right to prevail and desire a just and stable peace such as can be secured only by removing the chief provocations to war, which this program does not remove. We have no jealousy of German greatness, and there is nothing in this program that impairs it. We grudge her no achievement or distinction of learning or of pacific enterprise such as have made her record very bright and very enviable. We do not wish to injure her or to block in any way her legitimate influence or power. We do not wish to fight her either with arms or with hostile arrangements of trade if she is willing to associate herself with us and the other peace-loving nations of the world in covenants of justice and law and fair dealing. We wish her only to accept a place of equality among the peoples of the world,—the new world in which we now live,—instead of a place of mastery.

Neither do we presume to suggest to her any alteration or modification of her institutions. But it is necessary, we must frankly say, and necessary as a preliminary to any intelligent dealings with her on our part, that we should know whom her spokesmen speak for when they speak to us, whether for the Reichstag majority or for the military party and the men whose creed is imperial domination.

We have spoken now, surely, in terms too concrete to admit of any further doubt or question. An evident principle runs through the whole program I have outlined. It is the principle of justice to all peoples and nationalities, and their right to live on equal terms of liberty and safety with one another, whether they be strong or weak. Unless this principle be made its foundation no part of the structure of international justice can stand. The people of the United States could act upon no other principle; and to the vindication of this principle they are ready to devote their lives, their honor, and everything that they possess. The moral climax of this the culminating and final war for human liberty has come, and they are ready to put their own strength, their own highest purpose, their own integrity and devotion to the test.

—Woodrow Wilson, Address to Congress, January 8, 1918

12. "WE DO NOT PROFESS TO BE CHAMPIONS OF LIBERTY AND THEN CONSENT TO SEE LIBERTY DESTROYED"

As in the past, and again in the future, making the peace proved to be harder than winning the war. Wisely or unwisely, Wilson decided to incorporate the Covenant of the League of Nations into the Treaty of Peace. Largely for partisan reasons the Republicans, under the leadership of Henry Cabot Lodge, waged war on the League. The form their warfare took was a demand for a long series of reservations—reservations which, so Wilson thought, emasculated the League itself. The crucial fight came over Article Ten of the League Covenant. We give here Wilson's defense of that article in the course of his last campaign—a campaign which ended in his breakdown and collapse at Pueblo, Colo-

rado, on September 25, 1919. Now that the dust has settled after this great controversy, it can be seen that while Wilson was excessively stubborn in his refusal to countenance reservations to the League Covenant, the opposition was responsible for a betrayal of American obligations toward the maintenance of world order. As so often in the past, history has vindicated those who were bold, generous, and magnanimous rather than those who were timid, suspicious and self-centered.

. . . You have heard a great deal about Article X of the Covenant of the League of Nations.[1] Article X speaks the conscience of the world. Article X is the article which goes to the heart of this whole bad business, for that article says that the members of this League (that is intended to be all the great nations of the world) engage to respect and to preserve against all external aggression the territorial integrity and political independence of the nations concerned. That promise is necessary in order to prevent this sort of war from recurring, and we are absolutely discredited if we fought this war and then neglect the essential safeguard against it. You have heard it said, my fellow citizens, that we are robbed of some degree of our sovereign, independent choice by articles of that sort. Every man who makes a choice to respect the rights of his neighbors deprives himself of absolute sovereignty, but he does it by promising never to do wrong, and I cannot for one see anything that robs me of any inherent right that I ought to retain when I promise that I will do right, when I promise that I will respect the thing which, being disregarded and violated, brought on a war in which millions of men lost their lives, in which the civilization of mankind was in the balance, in which there was the most outrageous exhibition ever witnessed in the history of mankind of the rapacity and disregard for right of a great armed people.

We engage in the first sentence of Article X to respect and preserve from external aggression the territorial integrity and the existing political independence not only of the other member States, but of all States,

[1] Article 10. The Members of the League undertake to respect and preserve as against external aggression the territorial integrity and existing political independence of all Members of the League. In case of any such aggression or in case of any threat or danger of such aggression the Council shall advise upon the means by which this obligation shall be fulfilled.

and if any member of the League of Nations disregards that promise, then what happens? The council of the League advises what should be done to enforce the respect for that Covenant on the part of the nation attempting to violate it, and there is no compulsion upon us to take that advice except the compulsion of our good conscience and judgment. It is perfectly evident that if, in the judgment of the people of the United States the council adjudged wrong and that this was not a case for the use of force, there would be no necessity on the part of the Congress of the United States to vote the use of force. But there could be no advice of the council on any such subject without a unanimous vote, and the unanimous vote includes our own, and if we accepted the advice we would be accepting our own advice. For I need not tell you that the representatives of the Government of the United States would not vote without instructions from their Government at home, and that what we united in advising we could be certain that the American people would desire to do. There is in that Covenant not only not a surrender of the independent judgment of the Government of the United States, but an expression of it, because that independent judgment would have to join with the judgment of the rest.

But when is that judgment going to be expressed, my fellow citizens? Only after it is evident that every other resource has failed, and I want to call your attention to the central machinery of the League of Nations. If any member of that League, or any nation not a member, refuses to submit the question at issue either to arbitration or to discussion by the council, there ensues automatically by the engagements of this Covenant an absolute economic boycott. There will be no trade with that nation by any member of the League. There will be no interchange of communication by post or telegraph. There will be no travel to or from that nation. Its borders will be closed. No citizen of any other State will be allowed to enter it, and no one of its citizens will be allowed to leave it. It will be hermetically sealed by the united action of the most powerful nations in the world. And if this economic boycott bears with unequal weight, the members of the League agree to support one another and to relieve one another in any exceptional disadvantages that may arise out of it.

I want you to realize that this war was won not only by the armies of the world. It was won by economic means as well. Without the economic means the war would have been much longer continued. What happened was that Germany was shut off from the economic resources of the rest of the globe and she could not stand it. A nation that is boycotted is a nation that is in sight of surrender. Apply this economic, peaceful, silent, deadly remedy and there will be no need for force. It is a terrible remedy. It does not cost a life outside the nation boycotted, but it brings a pressure upon that nation which, in my judgment, no modern nation could resist. . . .

This is the first treaty in the history of civilization in which great powers have associated themselves together in order to protect the weak. I need not tell you that I speak with knowledge in this matter, knowledge of the purpose of the men with whom the American delegates were associated at the peace table. They came there, every one that I consulted with, with the same idea, that wars had arisen in the past because the strong took advantage of the weak, and that the only way to stop wars was to bind ourselves together to protect the weak; that the example of this war was the example which gave us the finger to point the way of escape: That as Austria and Germany had tried to put upon Serbia, so we must see to it that Serbia and the Slavic peoples associated with her, and the peoples of Rumania, and the people of Bohemia, and the peoples of Hungary and Austria for that matter, should feel assured in the future that the strength of the great powers was behind their liberty and their independence and was not intended to be used, and never should be used for aggression against them. . . .

Now, when you have that picture in your mind, that this treaty was meant to protect those who could not protect themselves, turn the picture and look at it this way:

Those very weak nations are situated through the very tract of country —between Germany and Persia—which Germany had meant to conquer and dominate, and if the nations of the world do not maintain their concert to sustain the independence and freedom of those peoples, Germany will yet have her will upon them, and we shall witness the very interesting spectacle of having spent millions upon millions of American treasure and, what is much more precious, hundreds of thousands of American lives, to do a futile thing, to do a thing which we will then leave to be undone at the leisure of those who are masters of intrigue, at the leisure of those who are masters in combining wrong influences to overcome right influences, of those who are the masters of the very things that we hate and mean always to fight. For, my fellow citizens, if Germany should ever attempt that again, whether we are in the League of Nations or not, we will join to prevent it. We do not stand off and see murder done. We do not profess to be the champions of liberty and then consent to see liberty destroyed. We are not the friends and advocates of free government and then willing to stand by and see free government die before our eyes. If a power such as Germany was, but thank God no longer is, were to do this thing upon the fields of Europe, then America would have to look to it that she did not do it also upon the fields of the Western Hemisphere, and we should at last be face to face with a power which at the outset we could have crushed, and which now it is within our choice to keep within the harness of civilization. . . .

I want to call your attention . . . to Article XI, following Article X, of the Covenant of the League of Nations. That article, let me say, is the favorite article in the treaty, so far as I am concerned. It says that every matter which is likely to affect the peace of the world is everybody's business; that it shall be the friendly right of any nation to call attention in the League to anything that is likely to affect the peace of the world or the good understanding between nations, upon which the peace of the world depends, whether that matter immediately concerns the nation drawing attention to it or not. In other words, at present we have to mind our own business. Under the Covenant of the League of Nations we can mind other peoples' business, and anything that affects the peace of the world, whether we are parties to it or not, can by our delegates be brought to the attention of mankind. We can force a nation on the other side of the globe to bring to that bar of mankind any wrong that is afoot in that part of the world which is likely to affect good understanding between nations, and we can oblige them to show cause why it should not be remedied. There is not an oppressed people in the world which cannot henceforth get a hearing at that forum, and you know, my fellow citizens, what a hearing will mean if the cause of those people is just. The one thing that those who are doing injustice have most reason to dread is publicity and discussion, because if you are challenged to give a reason why you are doing a wrong thing it has to be an exceedingly good reason, and if you give a bad reason you confess judgment and the opinion of mankind goes against you.

—Woodrow Wilson, Address at Indianapolis, September 4, 1919

13. A QUARANTINE AGAINST AGGRESSOR NATIONS

The rise of totalitarianism in Europe and in Asia, and the failure of the League to enforce peace, led to a renewal of large-scale aggression and warfare in the decade of the thirties. Japan led the way with an invasion of Manchuria in 1931; Italy followed with an attack upon unoffending Ethiopia; Germany embarked upon a policy of aggression and aggrandizement that in the end exploded into World War II. First by its failure to join the League of Nations or the World Court, then by a series of so-called neutrality acts whose folly was matched only by their futility, the United States pretty much eliminated itself as a force in international affairs. Deeply concerned for the maintenance of peace, and profoundly convinced that democracy and freedom could not survive in a world dominated by totalitarian nations, President Roosevelt tried time and again to rally American opinion to a more positive program on behalf of peace and freedom. Public opinion, however, remained apathetic. We give here extracts from Roosevelt's famous Quarantine speech of October, 1937—a speech which accurately forecast what was to happen, but which brought down upon the President an avalanche of criticism.

. . . The political situation in the world, which of late has been growing progressively worse, is such as to cause grave concern and anxiety to all the peoples and nations who wish to live in peace and amity with their neighbors.

Some fifteen years ago the hopes of mankind for a continuing era of international peace were raised to great heights when more than sixty nations solemnly pledged themselves not to resort to arms in furtherance of their national aims and policies. The high aspirations expressed in the Briand-Kellogg Peace Pact and the hopes for peace thus raised have of late given away to a haunting fear of calamity. The present reign of terror and international lawlessness began a few years ago.

692

It began through unjustified interference in the internal affairs of other nations or the invasion of alien territory in violation of treaties and has now reached a stage where the very foundations of civilization are seriously threatened. The landmarks and traditions which have marked the progress of civilization toward a condition of law, order, and justice are being wiped away.

Without a declaration of war and without warning or justification of any kind, civilians, including women and children, are being ruthlessly murdered with bombs from the air. In times of so-called peace ships are being attacked and sunk by submarines without cause or notice. Nations are fomenting and taking sides in civil warfare in nations that have never done them any harm. Nations claiming freedom for themselves deny it to others. . . .

The situation is definitely of universal concern. The questions involved relate not merely to violations of specific provisions of particular treaties; they are questions of war and of peace, of international law, and especially of principles of humanity. It is true that they involve definite violations of agreements, and especially of the Covenant of the League of Nations, the Briand-Kellogg Pact, and the Nine Power Treaty. But they also involve problems of world economy, world security, and world humanity.

It is true that the moral consciousness of the world must recognize the importance of removing injustices and well-founded grievances; but at the same time it must be aroused to the cardinal necessity of honoring sanctity of treaties, of respecting the rights and liberties of others, and of putting an end to acts of international aggression.

It seems to be unfortunately true that the epidemic of world lawlessness is spreading.

When an epidemic of physical disease starts to spread, the community approves and joins in a quarantine of the patients in order to protect the health of the community against the spread of the disease.

It is my determination to pursue a policy of peace and to adopt every practicable measure to avoid involvement in war. It ought to be inconceivable that in this modern era, and in the face of experience, any nation could be so foolish and ruthless as to run the risk of plunging the whole world into war by invading and violating in contravention of solemn treaties the territory of other nations that have done them no real harm and which are too weak to protect themselves adequately.

Yet the peace of the world and the welfare and security of every nation is today being threatened by that very thing.

No nation which refuses to exercise forbearance and to respect the freedom and rights of others can long remain strong and retain the confidence and respect of other nations. No nation ever loses its dignity or good standing by conciliating its differences and by exercising great patience with and consideration for the rights of other nations.

War is a contagion, whether it be declared or undeclared. It can engulf states and peoples remote from the original scene of hostilities. We are determined to keep out of war, yet we cannot insure ourselves against the disastrous effects of war and the dangers of involvement. We are adopting such measures as will minimize our risk of involvement, but we cannot have complete protection in a world of disorder in which confidence and security have broken down.

If civilization is to survive the principles of the Prince of Peace must be restored. Shattered trust between nations must be revived.

Most important of all, the will for peace on the part of peace-loving nations must express itself to the end that nations that may be tempted to violate their agreements and the rights of others will desist from such a cause. There must be positive endeavors to preserve peace.

America hates war. America hopes for peace. Therefore, America actively engages in the search for peace.

—FRANKLIN D. ROOSEVELT, Speech at Chicago, October 5, 1937

14. THE FOUR FREEDOMS

The story of the gradual American involvement in the Second World War—an involvement made inevitable by the policies pursued by the totalitarian aggressors—is too familiar to relate here. By the time Roosevelt delivered his Four Freedoms speech, the United States was already committed to Allied victory. Congress had, reluctantly, modified the shortsighted neutrality legislation, inaugurated a modest rearmament program, and provided for peacetime conscription, while the President, on his own authority, had exchanged fifty "over-age destroyers" for air and naval bases from Newfoundland to British Guiana—the best bargain since the Louisiana Purchase. Roosevelt seized the occasion of his annual message to Congress of 1941 to formulate a program for America and for the free world.

TO THE CONGRESS OF THE UNITED STATES:

I ADDRESS you, the Members of the Seventy-Seventh Congress, at a moment unprecedented in the history of the Union. I use the word "unprecedented," because at no previous time has American security been as seriously threatened from without as it is today. . . .

Every realist knows that the democratic way of life is at this moment being directly assailed in every part of the world—assailed either by arms, or by secret spreading of poisonous propaganda by those who seek to destroy unity and promote discord in nations still at peace. During sixteen months this assault has blotted out the whole pattern of democratic life in an appalling number of independent nations, great and small. The assailants are still on the march, threatening other nations, great and small.

Therefore, as your President, performing my constitutional duty to "give to the Congress information of the state of the Union," I find it necessary to report that the future and the safety of our country and of our democracy are overwhelmingly involved in events far beyond our borders. . . .

Our national policy is this.

First, by an impressive expression of the public will and without regard to partisanship, we are committed to all-inclusive national defense.

Second, by an impressive expression of the public will and without regard to partisanship, we are committed to full support of all those resolute peoples, everywhere, who are resisting aggression and are thereby keeping war away from our Hemisphere. By this support, we express our determination that the democratic cause shall prevail; and we strengthen the defense and security of our own nation.

Third, by an impressive expression of the public will and without regard to partisanship we are committed to the proposition that principles of morality and considerations for our own security will never permit us to acquiesce in a peace dictated by aggressors and sponsored by appeasers. We know that enduring peace cannot be bought at the cost of other people's freedom. . . .

Our most useful and immediate role is to act as an arsenal for them as well as for ourselves. They do not need man power. They do need billions of dollars worth of the weapons of defense. . . .

Let us say to the democracies: "We Americans are vitally concerned in your defense of freedom. We are putting forth our energies, our resources and our organizing powers to give you the strength to regain and maintain a free world. We shall send you, in ever-increasing numbers, ships, planes, tanks, guns. This is our purpose and our pledge." In fulfillment of this purpose we will not be intimidated by the threats of dictators that they will regard as a breach of international law and as an act of war our aid to the democracies which dare to resist their aggression. Such aid is not an act of war, even if a dictator should unilaterally proclaim it so to be. When the dictators are ready to make war upon us, they will not wait for an act of war on our part. They did not wait for Norway or Belgium or the Netherlands to commit an act of war. Their only interest is in a new one-way international law, which lacks mutuality in its observance, and, therefore, becomes an instrument of oppression.

The happiness of future generations of Americans may well depend upon how effective and how immediate we can make our aid felt. No one can tell the exact character of the emergency situations that we may be called upon to meet. The Nation's hands must not be tied when the Nation's life is in danger. We must all prepare to make the sacrifices that the emergency—as serious as war itself—demands. Whatever stands in the way of speed and efficiency in defense preparations must give way to the national need.

A free nation has the right to expect full cooperation from all groups. A free nation has the right to look to the leaders of business, of labor, and of agriculture to take the lead in stimulating effort, not among other groups but within their own groups. The best way of dealing with the few slackers or trouble makers in our midst is, first, to shame them by patriotic example, and, if that fails, to use the sovereignty of government to save government.

As men do not live by bread alone, they do not fight by armaments alone. Those who man our defenses, and those behind them who build our defenses, must have the stamina and courage which come from an unshakable belief in the manner of life which they are defending. The mighty action which we are calling for cannot be based on a disregard of all things worth fighting for.

The Nation takes great satisfaction and much strength from the things which have been done to make its people conscious of their individual stake in the preservation of democratic life in America. Those things have toughened the fibre of our people, have renewed their faith and strengthened their devotion to the institutions we make ready to protect. Certainly this is no time to stop thinking about the social and economic problems which are the root cause of the social revolution which is today a supreme factor in the world.

There is nothing mysterious about the foundations of a healthy and strong democracy. The basic things expected by our people of their political and economic systems are simple. They are: equality of opportunity for youth and for others; jobs for those who can work; security for those who need it; the ending of special privilege for the few; the preservation of civil liberties for all; the enjoyment of the fruits of scientific progress in a wider and constantly rising standard of living.

These are the simple and basic things that must never be lost sight of in the turmoil and unbelievable complexity of our modern world. The inner and abiding strength of our economic and political systems is dependent upon the degree to which they fulfill these expectations.

Many subjects connected with our social economy call for immediate improvement. As examples: We should bring more citizens under the coverage of old age pensions and unemployment insurance. We should widen the opportunities for adequate medical care. We should plan a better system by which persons deserving or needing gainful employment may obtain it.

I have called for personal sacrifice. I am assured of the willingness of almost all Americans to respond to that call. . . .

In the future days, which we seek to make secure, we look forward to a world founded upon four essential human freedoms.

The first is freedom of speech and expression—everywhere in the world.

The second is freedom of every person to worship God in his own way—everywhere in the world.

The third is freedom from want—which, translated into world terms, means economic understandings which will secure to every nation a healthy peace time life for its inhabitants—everywhere in the world.

The fourth is freedom from fear—which, translated into world terms, means a world-wide reduction of armaments to such a point and in such a thorough fashion that no nation will be in a position to commit an act of physical aggression against any neighbor—anywhere in the world.

That is no vision of a distant millennium. It is a definite basis for a kind of world attainable in our own time and generation. That kind of world is the very antithesis of the so-called new order of tyranny which the dictators seek to create with the crash of a bomb.

To that new order we oppose the greater conception—the moral order. A good society is able to face schemes of world domination and foreign revolutions alike without fear.

Since the beginning of our American history we have been engaged in change—in a perpetual peaceful revolution—a revolution which goes on steadily, quietly adjusting itself to changing conditions—without the concentration camp or the quick-lime in the ditch. The world order which we seek is the cooperation of free countries, working together in a friendly, civilized society.

This nation has placed its destiny in the hands and heads and hearts of its millions of free men and women; and its faith in freedom under the guidance of God. Freedom means the supremacy of human rights everywhere. Our support goes to those who struggle to gain those rights or keep them. Our strength is in our unity of purpose.

To that high concept there can be no end save victory.

—FRANKLIN D. ROOSEVELT,
Annual Message to Congress, January 6, 1941

15. THE ATLANTIC CHARTER

Like Wilson, Roosevelt was continually and deeply concerned with "war aims," that is, with creating a postwar order of peace and freedom. In a sense the Atlantic Charter was a Second World War equivalent to the Fourteen Points. It will be noted, however, that it is much simpler and more general—thus avoiding the danger of prior commitment to specific policies—and that it is a joint rather than a unilateral statement. Roosevelt and Churchill worked it out together while at sea off Newfoundland.

THE President of the United States of America and the Prime Minister, Mr. Churchill, representing His Majesty's Government in the United Kingdom, being met together, deem it right to make known certain common principles in the national policies of their respective countries on which they base their hopes for a better future for the world.

First, their countries seek no aggrandizement, territorial or other;

Second, they desire to see no territorial changes that do not accord with the freely expressed wishes of the peoples concerned;

Third, they respect the right of all peoples to choose the form of government under which they will live; and they wish to see sovereign rights and self government restored to those who have been forcibly deprived of them;

Fourth, they will endeavor, with due respect for their existing obligations, to further the enjoyment by all States, great or small, victor or vanquished, of access, on equal terms, to the trade and to the raw materials of the world which are needed for their economic prosperity;

Fifth, they desire to bring about the fullest collaboration between all nations in the economic field with the object of securing, for all, improved labor standards, economic advancement and social security;

Sixth, after the final destruction of the Nazi tyranny, they hope to see established a peace which will afford to all nations the means of dwelling in safety within their own boundaries, and which will afford assurance that all the men in all the lands may live out their lives in freedom from fear and want;

Seventh, such a peace should enable all men to traverse the high seas and oceans without hindrance;

Eighth, they believe that all of the nations of the world, for realistic as well as spiritual reasons must come to the abandonment of the use of force. Since no future peace can be maintained if land, sea or air armaments continue to be employed by nations which threaten, or may threaten, aggression outside of their frontiers, they believe, pending the establishment of a wider and permanent system of general security, that the disarmament of such nations is essential. They will likewise aid and encourage all other practicable measures which will lighten for peace-loving peoples the crushing burden of armaments.

FRANKLIN D. ROOSEVELT
WINSTON S. CHURCHILL
—The Atlantic Charter, August 14, 1941

16. "THE TRUE GOAL WE SEEK IS . . . ABOVE AND BEYOND THE UGLY FIELD OF BATTLE"

The attack on Pearl Harbor brought a prompt declaration of war against both Japan and Germany; two days later President Roosevelt reviewed the history of American efforts for peace, and reminded the American people that the war involved not only the survival of the nation but the survival of all those spiritual values which Americans had always cherished. We give here the closing paragraphs of this eloquent war address.

THERE is no such thing as security for any Nation—or any individual—in a world ruled by the principles of gangsterism.

There is no such thing as impregnable defense against powerful aggressors who sneak up in the dark and strike without warning.

We have learned that our ocean-girt hemisphere is not immune from severe attack—that we cannot measure our safety in terms of miles on any map any more.

We may acknowledge that our enemies have performed a brilliant feat of deception, perfectly timed and executed with great skill. It was a thoroughly dishonorable deed, but we must face the fact that modern warfare as conducted in the Nazi manner is a dirty business. We don't like it—we didn't want to get in it—but we are in it and we're going to fight it with everything we've got.

I do not think any American has any doubt of our ability to administer proper punishment to the perpetrators of these crimes.

Your Government knows that for weeks Germany has been telling Japan that if Japan did not attack the United States, Japan would not share in dividing the spoils with Germany when peace came. She was promised by Germany that if she came in she would receive the complete perpetual control of the whole of the Pacific area—and that means not only the Far East, but also all of the islands in the Pacific, and also a stranglehold on the west coast of North, Central, and South America.

We know also that Germany and Japan are conducting their military

700

and naval operations in accordance with a joint plan. That plan considers all peoples and Nations which are not helping the Axis powers as common enemies of each and every one of the Axis powers.

That is their simple and obvious grand strategy. And that is why the American people must realize that it can be matched only with similar grand strategy. We must realize for example that Japanese successes against the United States in the Pacific are helpful to German operations in Libya; that any German success against the Caucasus is inevitably an assistance to Japan in her operations against the Dutch East Indies; that a German attack against Algiers or Morocco opens the way to a German attack against South America, and the Canal.

On the other side of the picture, we must learn also to know that guerrilla warfare against the Germans in, let us say, Serbia or Norway helps us; that a successful Russian offensive against the Germans helps us; and that British successes on land or sea in any part of the world strengthen our hands.

Remember always that Germany and Italy, regardless of any formal declaration of war, consider themselves at war with the United States at this moment just as much as they consider themselves at war with Britain or Russia. And Germany puts all the other Republics of the Americas into the same category of enemies. The people of our sister Republics of this hemisphere can be honored by that fact.

The true goal we seek is far above and beyond the ugly field of battle. When we resort to force, as now we must, we are determined that this force shall be directed toward ultimate good as well as against immediate evil. We Americans are not destroyers—we are builders.

We are now in the midst of a war, not for conquest, not for vengeance, but for a world in which this Nation, and all that this Nation represents, will be safe for our children. We expect to eliminate the danger from Japan, but it would serve us ill if we accomplished that and found that the rest of the world was dominated by Hitler and Mussolini.

We are going to win the war and we are going to win the peace that follows.

And in the difficult hours of this day—through dark days that may be yet to come—we will know that the vast majority of the members of the human race are on our side. Many of them are fighting with us. All of them are praying for us. For in representing our cause, we represent theirs as well—our hope and their hope for liberty under God.

—Franklin D. Roosevelt, Address of December 9, 1941

17. "POWER MUST BE LINKED WITH RESPONSIBILITY"

By the beginning of 1945 it was clear that victory over Germany was a matter of months, and that ultimate victory over Japan was certain. More and more, therefore, the President's thoughts turned to the vexatious problems of peace-making, and of the establishment of an international order. To this end the President had already held a series of conferences with leaders of the Allied powers—at Casablanca, at Quebec, at Moscow, at Teheran, while the momentous Yalta Conference was just a month ahead. Already, too, representatives of the United Nations had met at Dumbarton Oaks, outside Washington, to draw up the agenda for the ultimate meeting that was to create a permanent United Nations organization. In what was to be his last annual message to Congress—broadcast that same day to the nation at large—Roosevelt pleaded for patience, tolerance, and understanding in the difficult days ahead.

. . . It is not only a common danger which unites us, but a common hope. Ours is an association not of governments but of peoples—and the peoples' hope is peace. Here, as in England; in England, as in Russia; in Russia, as in China; in France, and through the continent of Europe, and throughout the world; wherever men love freedom, the hope and purpose of the people are for peace—a peace that is durable and secure.

It will not be easy to create this peoples' peace. We have seen already, in areas liberated from the Nazi and the Fascist tyranny, what problems peace will bring. And we delude ourselves if we attempt to believe wishfully that all these problems can be solved overnight.

The firm foundation can be built—and it will be built. But the continuance and assurance of a living peace must, in the long run, be the work of the people themselves.

We ourselves, like all peoples who have gone through the difficult processes of liberation and adjustment, know of our own experience how great the difficulties can be. We know that they are not difficulties peculiar to any continent or any Nation. Our own Revolutionary War left behind it, in the words of one American historian, "an eddy of lawlessness and disregard of human life." There were separatist movements of one kind or another in Vermont, Pennsylvania, Virginia, Tennessee, Kentucky, and Maine. There were insurrections, open or threatened, in Massachusetts and New Hampshire. We worked out for ourselves these difficulties—as the peoples of the liberated areas of Europe, faced with complex problems of adjustment, will work out their difficulties for themselves.

Peace can be made and kept only by the united determination of free and peace-loving peoples who are willing to work together—willing to help one another—willing to respect and tolerate and try to understand one another's opinions and feelings.

In the future world the misuse of power, as implied in the term "power politics," must not be a controlling factor in international relations. That is the heart of the principles to which we have subscribed. In a democratic world, as in a democratic Nation, power must be linked with responsibility, and obliged to defend and justify itself within the framework of the general good.

In our disillusionment after the last war we gave up the hope of achieving a better peace because we had not the courage to fulfill our responsibilities in an admittedly imperfect world.

We must not let that happen again, or we shall follow the same tragic road again—the road to a third world war.

We can fulfill our responsibilities for maintaining the security of our own country only by exercising our power and our influence to achieve the principles in which we believe, and for which we have fought.

It is true that the statement of principles in the Atlantic Charter does not provide rules of easy application to each and every one of the tangled situations in this war-torn world. But it is a good and a useful thing—it is an essential thing—to have principles toward which we can aim.

And we shall not hesitate to use our influence—and to use it now—to secure so far as is humanly possible the fulfillment of the principles of the Atlantic Charter. We have not shrunk from the military responsibilities brought on by this war. We cannot and will not shrink from the political responsibilities which follow in the wake of battle.

To do this we must be on our guard not to exploit and exaggerate the differences between us and our Allies, particularly with reference to the peoples who have been liberated from Fascist tyranny. That is not the way to secure a better settlement of those differences, or to secure international machinery which can rectify mistakes which may be made.

I must admit concern about many situations—the Greek and Polish for example. But those situations are not as easy or as simple to deal with as some spokesmen, whose sincerity I do not question, would have us believe. We have obligations, not necessarily legal, to the exiled governments, to the underground leaders, and to our major Allies who came much nearer the shadows than we did.

We and our Allies have declared that it is our purpose to respect the right of all peoples to choose the form of government under which they will live and to see sovereign rights and self-government restored to those who have been forcibly deprived of them. But with internal dissension, with many citizens of liberated countries still prisoners of war or forced to labor in Germany, it is difficult to guess the kind of self-government the people really want. . . .

It is our purpose to help the peace-loving peoples of Europe to live together as good neighbors, to recognize their common interests, and not to nurse their traditional grievances against one another.

But we must not permit the many specific and immediate problems of adjustment connected with the liberation of Europe to delay the establishment of permanent machinery for the maintenance of peace. Under the threat of a common danger, the United Nations joined together in war to preserve their independence and their freedom. They must now join together to make secure the independence and freedom of all peace-loving states, so that never again shall tyranny be able to divide and conquer.

International peace and well-being, like national peace and well-being, require constant alertness, continuing cooperation, and organized effort.

International peace and well-being, like national peace and well-being, can be secured only through institutions capable of life and growth.

—Franklin D. Roosevelt,
Address on the State of the Union, January 6, 1945

18. THE ABIDING PRINCIPLES OF AMERICAN
FOREIGN POLICY

The problems that confronted Harry S. Truman when he succeeded to the Presidency on the death of Roosevelt were as grave and as complex as those that confronted Andrew Johnson when he succeeded the martyred Lincoln. Like Johnson, Truman tried faithfully to carry out the policies of his predecessor, and like Johnson, too, he encountered not only bitter partisan hostility but—what was more serious—apathy and disillusionment. Nevertheless, in the realm of foreign policy Truman was largely successful in carrying on where Roosevelt left off. We give here his succinct statement of the fundamentals of American foreign policy in an address in New York in October, 1945.

1. We seek no territorial expansion or selfish advantage. We have no plans for aggression against any other state, large or small. We have no objective which need clash with the peaceful aims of any other nation.
2. We believe in the eventual return of sovereign rights and self-government to all peoples who have been deprived of them by force.
3. We shall approve no territorial changes in any friendly part of the world unless they accord with the freely expressed wishes of the people concerned.
4. We believe that all peoples who are prepared for self-government should be permitted to choose their own form of government by their own freely expressed choice, without interference from any foreign source. That is true in Europe, in Asia, in Africa, as well as in the Western Hemisphere.
5. By the combined and cooperative action of our war Allies, we shall help the defeated enemy states establish peaceful, democratic governments of their own free choice. And we shall try to attain a world in which Nazism, Fascism, and military aggression cannot exist.
6. We shall refuse to recognize any government imposed upon any nation by the force of any foreign power. In some cases it may be im-

possible to prevent forceful imposition of such a government. But the United States will not recognize any such government.

7. We believe that all nations should have the freedom of the seas and equal rights to the navigation of boundary rivers and waterways and of rivers and waterways which pass through more than one country.

8. We believe that all states which are accepted in the society of nations should have access on equal terms to the trade and the raw materials of the world.

9. We believe that the sovereign states of the Western Hemisphere, without interference from outside the Western Hemisphere, must work together as good neighbors in the solution of their common problems.

10. We believe that full economic collaboration between all nations, great and small, is essential to the improvement of living conditions all over the world, and to the establishment of freedom from fear and freedom from want.

11. We shall continue to strive to promote freedom of expression and freedom of religion throughout the peace-loving areas of the world.

12. We are convinced that the preservation of peace between nations requires a United Nations Organization composed of all the peace-loving nations of the world who are willing jointly to use force if necessary to insure peace.

That is the foreign policy which guides the United States now. That is the foreign policy with which it confidently faces the future.

It may not be put into effect tomorrow or the next day. But none the less, it is our policy; and we shall seek to achieve it. It may take a long time, but it is worth waiting for, and it is worth striving to attain. . . .

—HARRY S. TRUMAN, Address at New York, October 27, 1945

19. "THE GREATEST OPPORTUNITY EVER OFFERED A SINGLE NATION"

With victory, the One World that Wendell Willkie and Franklin Roosevelt had hoped to create broke into two, and the democratic peoples, under the leadership of the United States, prepared to renew the contest with totalitarianism. Simple old-fashioned isolationism, the isolationism of the America Firsters, seemed dead beyond recall, but isolationism takes many forms, some of them strange, and there was a real danger that America might turn her back on Europe and concentrate her interests on the Pacific area, or that America might try to control the affairs of the West without bothering to consult her wartime associates and allies. Henry Stimson—Secretary of War under Taft, Secretary of State under Hoover, and Secretary of War again under F. D. Roosevelt, and the most distinguished of our "elder statesmen"—here explains the challenge to Americans in the second half of the twentieth century.

WE AMERICANS today face a challenging opportunity, perhaps the greatest ever offered to a single nation. It is nothing less than a chance to use our full strength for the peace and freedom of the world. This opportunity comes when many of us are confused and unready. Only two years ago we triumphantly ended the greatest war in history. Most of us then looked forward eagerly to the relative relaxation of peace. Reluctantly we have now come to understand that victory and peace are not synonymous. Over large areas of the world we have nothing better than armed truce; in some places there is open fighting; everywhere men know that there is yet no stable settlement. Close on the heels of victory has loomed a new world crisis.

Particularly to Americans the appearance of disquieting facts and possibilities has been upsetting. We are having our first experience of constant, full-scale activity in world politics. Other nations have lived for years as principals in the give-and-take of diplomacy. Until now we have been, except in wartime, on the fringe. It is no wonder that, when suddenly placed in the center of the alarms and excursions of international affairs, we are abnormally sensitive. And, of course, it does not help to find ourselves selected as chief target for the abuse and opposition of a very bad-mannered group of men who take their orders from the Kremlin. It is not surprising, then, that many of us are confused and unhappy about our foreign relations, and that some are tempted to seek refuge from their confusion either in retreat to isolationism or in suggested solutions whose simplicity is only matched by their folly. In the main, our difficulties arise from unwillingness to face reality.

It must be admitted that the elements of the new unrest appear to be unusually complex and trying. The war-shattered world must be rebuilt; the problem of atomic energy insistently demands solution; the present policy of Russia must be frustrated. But it is my belief that the American people have it well within their power to meet and resolve all of these problems. The essential test is one of will and understanding. We require a skilful foreign policy, of course, but we may have confidence that the farsighted and experienced men now in charge of our State Department know how to frame a policy. In outline the President and the Secretary of State have already set their course. They can develop their policy with success, however, only if they have the understanding support, on basic principles, of the American people.

First, and most important, Americans must now understand that the United States has become, for better or worse, a wholly committed member of the world community. This has not happened by conscious choice; but it is a plain fact, and our only choice is whether or not to face it. For more than a generation the increasing interrelation of American life with the life of the world has out-paced our thinking and our policy; our refusal to catch up with reality during these years was the major source of our considerable share of the responsibility for the catastrophe of World War II.

It is the first condition of effective foreign policy that this nation put away forever any thought that America can again be an island to herself. . . .

As a corollary to this first great principle, it follows that we shall be wholly wrong if we attempt to set a maximum or margin to our activity as members of the world. The only question we can safely ask today is whether in any of our actions on the world stage we are doing enough. In American policy toward the world there is no place for grudging or limited participation, and any attempt to cut our losses by setting bounds to our policy can only turn us backward onto the deadly road toward self-defeating isolation.

Our stake in the peace and freedom of the world is not a limited liability. Time after time in other years we have tried to solve our foreign problems with half-way measures, acting under the illusion that we could be partly in the world and partly irresponsible. Time after time our Presidents and Secretaries of State have been restrained, by their own fears or by public opinion, from effective action. It should by now be wholly clear that only failure, and its follower, war, can result from such efforts at a cheap solution. . . .

It is altogether fitting and proper, of course, that we should not waste our substance in activity without result. It is also evident that we cannot do everything we would like to do. But it would be shriveling timidity for America to refuse to play to the full her present necessary part in the world. And the certain penalty for such timidity would be failure.

The troubles of Europe and Asia are not "other people's troubles"; they are ours. The world is full of friends and enemies; it is full of warring ideas; but there are no mere "foreigners," no merely "foreign" ideologies, no merely "foreign" dangers, any more. Foreign affairs are now our most intimate domestic concern. All men, good or bad, are now our neighbors. All ideas dwell among us.

A second principle, and one which requires emphasis as a necessary complement to any policy of full participation, is that we are forced to act in the world as it is, and not in the world as we wish it were, or as we would like it to become. It is a world in which we are only one of many peoples and in which our basic principles of life are not shared by all our neighbors. It has been one of the more dangerous aspects of our internationalism in past years that too often it was accompanied by the curious assumption that the world would overnight become good and clean and peaceful everywhere if only America would lead the way. The most elementary experience of human affairs should show us all how naive and dangerous a view that is. . . .

We have been very patient with the Soviet Government, and very hopeful of its good intentions. I have been among those who shared in these hopes and counseled this patience. The magnificent and loyal war effort of the Russian people, and the great successful efforts at friendliness made during the war by President Roosevelt, gave us good reason for hope. I have believed—and I still believe—that we must show good faith in all our dealings with the Russians, and that only by so doing can we leave the door open for Russian good faith toward us. I cannot too strongly express my regret that since the early spring of 1945—even before the death of Mr. Roosevelt—the Soviet Government has steadily pursued an obstructive and unfriendly course. It has been our hope that the Russians would choose to be our friends; it was and is our conviction that such a choice would be to their advantage. But, for the time being, at least, those who determine Russian policy have chosen otherwise, and their choice has been slavishly followed by Communists everywhere.

No sensible American can now ignore this fact, and those who now choose to travel in company with American Communists are very clearly either knaves or fools. . . .

An equal and opposite error is made by those who argue that Americans by strong-arm methods, perhaps even by a "preventive war," can and should rid the world of the Communist menace. I cannot believe that this view is widely held. For it is worse than nonsense; it results from a hopeless misunderstanding of the geographical and military situation, and a cynical incomprehension of what the people of the world will tolerate from *any* nation. Worst of all, this theory indicates a totally wrong assessment of the basic attitudes and motives of the American people. Even if it were true that the United States now had the opportunity to establish forceful hegemony throughout the world, we could not possibly take that opportunity without deserting our true inheritance. Americans as conquerors would be tragically miscast.

The world's affairs cannot be simplified by eager words. We cannot take refuge from reality in the folly of black-and-white solutions. . . .

But our main answer to the Russians is not negative, nor is it in any sense anti-Russian. Our central task in dealing with the Kremlin is to demonstrate beyond the possibility of misunderstanding that freedom and prosperity, hand in hand, can be stably sustained in the western democratic world. This would be our greatest task even if no Soviet problem existed, and to the Soviet threat it is our best response.

Soviet intransigence is based in very large part on the hope and belief that all non-Communist systems are doomed. Soviet policy aims to help them die. We must hope that time and the success of freedom and democracy in the western world will convince both the Soviet leaders and the Russian people now behind them that our system is here to stay. This may not be possible; dictators do not easily change their hearts, and the modern armaments they possess may make it hard for their people to force such a change. Rather than be persuaded of their error, the Soviet leaders might in desperation resort to war, and against that possibility we have to guard by maintaining our present military advantages. We must never forget that while peace is a joint responsibility, the decision for war can be made by a single Power; our military strength must be maintained as a standing discouragement to aggression.

I do not, however, expect the Russians to make war. I do not share the gloomy fear of some that we are now engaged in the preliminaries of an inevitable conflict. Even the most repressive dictatorship is not perfectly unassailable from within, and the most frenzied fanaticism is never unopposed. Whatever the ideological bases of Soviet policy, it seems clear that some at least of the leaders of Russia are men who have a marked respect for facts. We must make it wholly evident that a non-aggressive Russia will have nothing to fear from us. We must make it clear, too, that the western non-Communist world is going to survive in growing economic and political stability. If we can do this, then slowly— but perhaps less slowly than we now believe—the Russian leaders may either change their minds or lose their jobs.

The problem of Russia is thus reduced to a question of our own fitness to survive. I do not mean to belittle the Communist challenge. I only mean that the essential question is one which we should have to answer if there were not a Communist alive. Can we make freedom and prosperity real in the present world? If we can, Communism is no threat. If not, with or without Communism, our own civilization would ultimately fail.

The immediate and pressing challenge to our belief in freedom and prosperity is in western Europe. Here are people who have traditionally shared our faith in human dignity. These are the nations by whose citizens our land was settled and in whose tradition our civilization is rooted. They are threatened by Communism—but only because of the dark shadows cast by the hopelessness, hunger and fear that have been the aftermath of the Nazi war. Communism or no Communism, menace or no menace, it is our simple duty as neighbors to take a generous part in helping these great peoples to help themselves.

The reconstruction of western Europe is a task from which Americans can decide to stand apart only if they wish to desert every principle by which they claim to live. And, as a decision of policy, it would be the most tragic mistake in our history. We must take part in this work; we must take our full part; we must be sure that we do enough. . . .

As we take part in the rebuilding of Europe, we must remember that we are building world peace, not an American peace. Freedom demands tolerance, and many Americans have much to learn about the variety of forms which free societies may take. There are Europeans, just as there are Americans, who do not believe in freedom, but they are in a minority, and—as the Editor of this review so clearly explained in its last issue—we shall not be able to separate the sheep from the goats merely by asking whether they believe in our particular economic and political system. Our cooperation with the free men of Europe must be founded on the basic principles of human dignity, and not on any theory that their way to freedom must be exactly the same as ours. We cannot ask that Europe be rebuilt in the American image. If we join in the task of reconstruction with courage, confidence and goodwill, we shall learn— and teach—a lot. But we must start with a willingness to understand.

The reconstruction of western Europe is the immediate task. With it we have, of course, a job at home. We must maintain freedom and prosperity here. This is a demanding task in itself, and its success or failure will largely determine all our other efforts. If it is true that our prosperity depends on that of the world, it is true also that the whole world's economic future hangs on our success at home. We must go forward to new levels of peacetime production, and to do this we must all of us avoid the pitfalls of laziness, fear and irresponsibility. Neither real profits nor real wages can be permanently sustained—and still less increased—by anything but rising production.

But I see no reason for any man to face the American future with any other feeling than one of confident hope. However grave our problems, and however difficult their solution, I do not believe that this country is ready to acknowledge that failure is foreordained. It is our task to disprove and render laughable that utterly insulting theory. Our future does not depend on the tattered forecasts of Karl Marx. It depends on us.

In counseling against policies which ignore the facts of the world as it is, I do not, of course, mean to argue that we can for a moment forget the nature of our final goal.

Lasting peace and freedom cannot be achieved until the world finds a way toward the necessary government of the whole. It is important that this should be widely understood, and efforts to spread such understanding are commendable. The riven atom, uncontrolled, can be only a growing menace to us all, and there can be no final safety, short of full control throughout the world. Nor can we hope to realize the vast potential wealth of atomic energy until it is disarmed and rendered harmless. Upon us, as the people who first harnessed and made use of this force, there rests a grave and continuing responsibility for leadership in turning it toward life, not death. . . .

It is clear, then, that in this country we are still free to maintain our freedom. We are called to an unprecedented effort of cooperation with our friends in every country. Immediately, we are called to act in the rebuilding of civilization in that part of the world which is closest to us in history, politics and economics. We are required to think of our prosperity, our policy and our first principles as indivisibly connected with the facts of life everywhere. We must put away forever the childishness of parochial hopes and un-American fears.

We need not suppose that the task we face is easy, or that all our undertakings will be quickly successful. The construction of a stable peace is a longer, more complex and greater task than the relatively simple work of war-making. But the nature of the challenge is the same. The issue before us today is at least as significant as the one which we finally faced in 1941. By a long series of mistakes and failures, dating back over a span of more than 20 years, we had in 1941 let it become too late to save ourselves by peaceful methods; in the end we had to fight. This is not true today. If we act now, with vigor and understanding, with steadiness and without fear, we can peacefully safeguard our freedom. It is only if we turn our backs, in mistaken complacence or mistrusting timidity, that war may again become inevitable.

How soon this nation will fully understand the size and nature of its present mission, I do not dare to say. But I venture to assert that in very large degree the future of mankind depends on the answers to this question. And I am confident that if the issues are clearly presented, the American people will give the right answer. Surely there is here a fair and tempting challenge to all Americans, and especially to the nation's leaders, in and out of office.

—HENRY L. STIMSON, "The Challenge to Americans," 1947

20. THE CONTROL OF ATOMIC ENERGY

The atomic bomb had been created by the scientists of the United Nations working with the engineers and technicians of the United States. Hiroshima and Nagasaki, and the development of the cold war, raised in critical form the question of the control of the new weapon. Americans, alarmed by the danger from possible Russian possession of the bomb, insisted upon keeping the processes of manufacture a "secret"; as every scientist predicted, this was impossible, and in September, 1949, the Russians detonated an atomic bomb. The first session of the United Nations General Assembly created an atomic energy commission to try to work out some policy that would prevent the use of atomic energy for destructive purposes and develop its potentialities for creative purposes. In June, 1946, the sage Bernard Baruch presented the American plan—a plan built in large part upon proposals already formulated by Dean Acheson and David Lilienthal. The United Nations Commission accepted the American plan by a vote of ten to nothing, with Russia and Poland abstaining, but Russia prevented the plan from being accepted by the Security Council. The essential difference between the American and the Russian plans was this: The American plan would not make the bomb available to other nations until adequate provisions for security and inspection had been agreed upon; the Russian plan called for outlawing the manufacture of the bomb and destroying all existing stock piles. Meantime the United States, Britain and Canada agreed on a provisional program for research in atomic energy, while the United States itself set up a five-man civilian Atomic Energy Commission which was given a monopoly on all fissionable materials, processes, facilities, patents, technical and scientific information. David Lilienthal, long-time head of the TVA, was appointed first chairman of the Atomic Energy Commission.

We give here extracts from Baruch's speech on the control of atomic energy, and a brief observation from Lilienthal himself on the potential value of atomic energy.

A. "A Choice Between the Quick and the Dead"

WE ARE here to make a choice between the quick and the dead. That is our business.

Behind the black portent of the new atomic age lies a hope which, seized upon with faith, can work our salvation. If we fail, then we have damned every man to be the slave of Fear. Let us not deceive ourselves: We must elect World Peace or World Destruction.

Science has torn from nature a secret so vast in its potentialities that our minds cower from the terror it creates. Yet terror is not enough to inhibit the use of the atomic bomb. The terror created by weapons has never stopped man from employing them. For each new weapon a defense has been produced, in time. But now we face a condition in which adequate defense does not exist.

Science, which gave us this dread power, shows that it *can* be made a giant help to humanity, but science does *not* show us how to prevent its baleful use. So we have been appointed to obviate that peril by finding a meeting of the minds and the hearts of our peoples. Only in the will of mankind lies the answer. . . .

In this crisis, we represent not only our governments but, in a larger way, we represent the peoples of the world. We must remember that the people do not belong to the governments but that the governments belong to the peoples. We must answer their demands; we must answer the world's longing for peace and security. . . .

The United States proposes the creation of an International Atomic Development Authority, to which should be entrusted all phases of the development and use of atomic energy, starting with the raw material and including—

1. Managerial control or ownership of all atomic-energy activities potentially dangerous to world security.

2. Power to control, inspect, and license all other atomic activities.

3. The duty of fostering the beneficial uses of atomic energy.

4. Research and development responsibilities of an affirmative character intended to put the Authority in the forefront of atomic knowledge and thus to enable it to comprehend, and therefore to detect, misuse of atomic energy. To be effective, the Authority must itself be the world's leader in the field of atomic knowledge and development and thus supplement its legal authority with the great power inherent in possession of leadership in knowledge.

I offer this as a basis for beginning our discussion. . . .

When an adequate system for control of atomic energy, including the renunciation of the bomb as a weapon, has been agreed upon and put into effective operation and condign punishments set up for violations of the rules of control which are to be stigmatized as international crimes, we propose that—

1. Manufacture of atomic bombs shall stop;

2. Existing bombs shall be disposed of pursuant to the terms of the treaty; and

3. The Authority shall be in possession of full information as to the know-how for the production of atomic energy.

Let me repeat, so as to avoid misunderstanding: My country is ready to make its full contribution toward the end we seek, subject of course to our constitutional processes and to an adequate system of control becoming fully effective, as we finally work it out.

Now as to violations: In the agreement, penalties of as serious a nature as the nations may wish and as immediate and certain in their execution as possible should be fixed for—

1. Illegal possession or use of an atomic bomb;

2. Illegal possession, or separation, of atomic material suitable for use in an atomic bomb;

3. Seizure of any plant or other property belonging to or licensed by the Authority;

4. Willful interference with the activities of the Authority;

5. Creation or operation of dangerous projects in a manner contrary to, or in the absence of, a license granted by the international control body.

It would be a deception, to which I am unwilling to lend myself, were I not to say to you and to our peoples that the matter of punishment lies at the very heart of our present security system. It might as well be admitted, here and now, that the subject goes straight to the veto power contained in the Charter of the United Nations so far as it relates to the field of atomic energy. The Charter permits penalization only by concurrence of each of the five great powers—the Union of Soviet Socialist Republics, the United Kingdom, China, France, and the United States.

I want to make very plain that I am concerned here with the veto power only as it affects this particular problem. There must be no veto to protect those who violate their solemn agreements not to develop or use atomic energy for destructive purposes. . . .

I now submit the following measures as representing the fundamental features of a plan which would give effect to certain of the conclusions which I have epitomized.

1. *General.* The Authority should set up a thorough plan for control of the field of atomic energy, through various forms of ownership, dominion, licenses, operation, inspection, research, and management by competent personnel. After this is provided for, there should be as little interference as may be with the economic plans and the present private, corporate, and state relationships in the several countries involved.

2. *Raw Materials.* The Authority should have as one of its earliest purposes to obtain and maintain complete and accurate information on world supplies of uranium and thorium and to bring them under its dominion. The precise pattern of control for various types of deposits of such materials will have to depend upon the geological, mining, refining, and economic facts involved in different situations.

The Authority should conduct continuous surveys so that it will have the most complete knowledge of the world geology of uranium and thorium. Only after all current information on world sources of uranium and thorium is known to us all can equitable plans be made for their production, refining, and distribution.

3. *Primary Production Plants.* The Authority should exercise complete managerial control of the production of fissionable materials. This means that it should control and operate all plants producing fissionable materials in dangerous quantities and must own and control the product of these plants.

4. *Atomic Explosives.* The Authority should be given sole and exclusive right to conduct research in the field of atomic explosives. Research activities in the field of atomic explosives are essential in order that the Authority may keep in the forefront of knowledge in the field of atomic energy and fulfill the objective of preventing illicit manufacture of bombs. Only by maintaining its position as the best-informed agency will the Authority be able to determine the line between intrinsically dangerous and non-dangerous activities.

5. *Strategic Distribution of Activities and Materials.* The activities entrusted exclusively to the Authority because they are intrinsically dangerous to security should be distributed throughout the world. Similarly, stockpiles of raw materials and fissionable materials should not be centralized.

6. *Non-Dangerous Activities.* A function of the Authority should be promotion of the peacetime benefits of atomic energy.

Atomic research (except in explosives), the use of research reactors, the production of radio-active tracers by means of non-dangerous reactors, the use of such tracers, and to some extent the production of power should be open to nations and their citizens under reasonable licensing arrangements from the Authority. Denatured materials, whose use we know also requires suitable safeguards, should be furnished for such purposes by the Authority under lease or other arrangement. Denaturing seems to have been overestimated by the public as a safety measure.

7. *Definition of Dangerous and Non-Dangerous Activities.* Although a reasonable dividing line can be drawn between dangerous and non-dangerous activities, it is not hard and fast. Provision should, therefore, be made to assure constant reexamination of the questions and to permit revision of the dividing line as changing conditions and new discoveries may require.

8. *Operations of Dangerous Activities.* Any plant dealing with uranium or thorium after it once reaches the potential of dangerous use

must be not only subject to the most rigorous and competent inspection by the Authority, but its actual operation shall be under the management, supervision, and control of the Authority.

9. *Inspection.* By assigning intrinsically dangerous activities exclusively to the Authority, the difficulties of inspection are reduced. If the Authority is the only agency which may lawfully conduct dangerous activities, then visible operation by others than the Authority will constitute an unambiguous danger signal. Inspection will also occur in connection with the licensing functions of the Authority.

10. *Freedom of Access.* Adequate ingress and egress for all qualified representatives of the Authority must be assured. Many of the inspection activities of the Authority should grow out of, and be incidental to, its other functions. Important measures of inspection will be associated with the tight control of raw materials, for this is a keystone of the plan. The continuing activities of prospecting, survey, and research in relation to raw materials will be designed not only to serve the affirmative development functions of the Authority but also to assure that no surreptitious operations are conducted in the raw-materials field by nations or their citizens.

11. *Personnel.* The personnel of the Authority should be recruited on a basis of proven competence but also so far as possible on an international basis.

12. *Progress by Stages.* A primary step in the creation of the system of control is the setting forth, in comprehensive terms, of the functions, responsibilities, powers, and limitations of the Authority. Once a charter for the Authority has been adopted, the Authority and the system of control for which it will be responsible will require time to become fully organized and effective. The plan of control will, therefore, have to come into effect in successive stages. These should be specifically fixed in the Charter or means should be otherwise set forth in the Charter for transitions from one stage to another, as contemplated in the resolution of the United Nations Assembly which created this Commission.

13. *Disclosures.* In the deliberations of the United Nations Commission on Atomic Energy, the United States is prepared to make available the information essential to a reasonable understanding of the proposals which it advocates. Further disclosures must be dependent, in the interests of all, upon the effective ratification of the treaty. When the Authority is actually created, the United States will join the other nations in making available the further information essential to that organization

for the performance of its functions. As the successive stages of international control are reached, the United States will be prepared to yield, to the extent required by each stage, national control of activities in this field to the Authority.

14. *International Control.* There will be questions about the extent of control to be allowed to national bodies, when the Authority is established. Purely national authorities for control and development of atomic energy should to the extent necessary for the effective operation of the Authority be subordinate to it. This is neither an endorsement nor a disapproval of the creation of national authorities. The Commission should evolve a clear demarcation of the scope of duties and responsibilities of such national authorities. . . .

—BERNARD BARUCH,
Address before U.N. Atomic Energy Commission, June 14, 1946

B. "ONE OF THOSE GREAT MOUNTAIN PEAKS OF HISTORY"

We are still afflicted by the Myth of the Atom Bomb. The prospects for the future of democracy, in the sense in which I have been discussing that matter, seems to me adversely affected by this Myth.

The Myth is simply this: Atomic energy is useful only as a bomb, a weapon, and is actually nothing else.

If the Myth that atomic energy is simply a military weapon becomes a fixed thing in our minds, if we accept the error that it can never be anything else, we will never make it anything but a weapon. If we will drift into the belief, which so many appear already to hold, that all we need for our nation to be secure in a troubled world is this powerful weapon, we will tend to relax, when we should be eternally vigilant and alert.

The Myth will cause us to fall into an even deeper pit of error. We will grow forgetful of the true sources of a democracy's vitality and the true sources of our nation's strength. We will be misled into believing that America is strong because of military force alone, when in truth the foundation of our strength and amazing vitality is not in material things but rather in the spirit of this nation, in the faiths we cherish.

We are a people with a faith in each other, and when we lose that faith we are weak, however heavily armed. We are a people with a faith in reason, and the unending pursuit of new knowledge; and when we lose that faith we are insecure, though we be ever so heavily armed. We are a people with a faith in God, with a deep sense of stewardship to our Creator, the Father of us all; and when that is no longer strong within us we are weak and we are lost, however heavily armed with weapons—even with atomic weapons—we may be.

Nothing good ever comes from running away from reality; I am not urging that we put on a set of blinders so we will not see the dark and somber facts. But we must not become so preoccupied solely with the destructiveness of atomic energy that we think of its majestic discovery as a force of destruction and nothing else.

Our physical safety, our peace of mind, our clarity of thinking, and the conservation and strengthening of our faith in individual freedom require that all of us try to develop, rather promptly, a greater sense of balance about atomic energy. An important element in that better perspective we must seek is a fuller understanding that atomic energy discoveries, like life itself, have their dark and somber side, and also have their bright and hopeful side. Atomic energy bears that same duality that has faced man from time immemorial, a duality expressed in the Book of Books thousands of years ago: "See, I have set before thee this day life and good and death and evil . . . therefore choose life . . ."

Tens of thousands of men and women are today engaged upon pioneering forays into the atomic unknown. They work with strange elements, new to man, as well as with the commonplaces of concrete and lead. Some work with no other equipment than their trained imagination and a blackboard, others with some of the most complex and ponderous mechanisms of all time. It is the brighter, the more hopeful and beneficial actualities and promises of our unfolding knowledge that occupy the time and effort of a large segment of these thousands of men and women who make up the atomic energy enterprise of this country.

Atomic energy is a force as fundamental to life as the force of the sun, the force of gravity, the forces of magnetism. It is an unfolding of new knowledge that goes to the very heart of all physical things. Perhaps the greatest single opportunity for new fundamental knowledge about the nature of the physical world lies in the development of atomic energy. Within the atomic nucleus are those deep forces, so terribly destructive if used for warfare, so beneficent if used to search out the cause and cure of disease, so almost magical in their ability to pierce the veil of life's secrets.

In the widening knowledge of the atom we have the means for making our time one of the two or three most vital, most intense and stimulating periods of all history. In the atomic adventure we sight one of those great mountain peaks of history, a towering symbol of one of the faiths that makes man civilized, the faith in knowledge. I look forward to atomic development not simply as a search for new energy, but more significantly as a beginning of a period of human history in which this faith in knowledge can vitalize man's whole life.

Developments in the nucleus of the atom can by their force and example and stimulus spread to advances in all fields of knowledge. Indeed, by the contagion of achievement these advances may appear quite outside the physical sciences, in skills of statesmanship and human relations, and in the development of imagination and the spirit. In times like this, men rise above the plains of history.

Our chance for great adventure can however be lost to us. If this feeling of living in a very fruitful and special period is not sensed by people generally, and by our representatives and civic leaders, the atomic adventure may be stifled in the throes of politics, of routine, of sluggishness and apathy. The daring and style that pushed back other American frontiers will be missing.

—DAVID E. LILIENTHAL, *This I Do Believe*

21. "TO THE RESCUE AND LIBERATION OF THE OLD"

The phrase we use here comes not from a chapter of postwar history, but from the dark days of 1940 and—needless to say—from the intrepid warrior who rallied the English-speaking nations of the world to resist tyranny and destruction. Britain, Churchill promised, would fight on to the end, fight on "until in God's good time the new world, with all its power and might, steps forth to the rescue and liberation of the old." That time came, with Pearl Harbor, and the New World fulfilled that mission and that destiny. But it was soon clear that military victory was not, in itself, enough; that a great work of rescue and liberation remained. Many ancient nations had been ravaged and all but destroyed; others, like England, had weakened and all but beggared themselves in the heroic fight for freedom. And the end of the war did not bring either peace or order; it brought, instead, a new threat from the East. In response to the desperate need of the stricken nations of Western

Europe and of the Mediterranean area, and to the imminent danger of attack by Russia or of subversion from within, the United States moved with energy and wisdom to the task of rescue. Much had already been accomplished by Lend-Lease, by the UNRRA, and by direct loans to Britain and indirect loans from world banks to other nations. But a new and vastly significant chapter in the history of the United States as a world power opened with the announcement of the Truman Doctrine in March, 1947. This was followed, shortly after, by the proposal of what has come to be known as the Marshall Plan. The Truman Doctrine— the doctrine of containing Communism wherever it threatened free nations—was formally adopted by Congress with aid to Greece and Turkey. The Marshall Plan, too, was adopted after prolonged and heated debates, and eventually the United States poured over ten billion dollars into European recovery, with gratifying results. To these two policies Truman added, in 1949, a third—known as Point Four—to afford scientific and technological aid to the backward peoples of the world. Although Point Four offered almost limitless possibilities for economic, social, and humanitarian progress, Congress was niggardly in its support, and little was actually accomplished.

We give here the Truman proposal, Secretary Marshall's outline for European recovery, and those paragraphs from Truman's Inaugural Address that outlined Point Four.

A. THE TRUMAN DOCTRINE

. . . I believe that it must be the policy of the United States to support free peoples who are resisting attempted subjugation by armed minorities or by outside pressures.

I believe that we must assist free peoples to work out their own destinies in their own way.

I believe that our help should be primarily through economic and financial aid which is essential to economic stability and orderly political processes.

The world is not static, and the status quo is not sacred. But we cannot allow changes in the status quo in violation of the charter of the United Nations by such methods as coercion, or by such subterfuges as political infiltration. In helping free and independent nations to maintain their freedom, the United States will be giving effect to the principles of the charter of the United Nations.

It is necessary only to glance at a map to realize that the survival and integrity of the Greek nation are of grave importance in a much wider situation. If Greece should fall under the control of an armed minority, the effect upon its neighbor, Turkey, would be immediate and serious. Confusion and disorder might well spread throughout the entire Middle East. . . .

Should we fail to aid Greece and Turkey in this fateful hour, the effect will be far reaching to the west as well as to the east. We must take immediate and resolute action. . . .

The seeds of totalitarian regimes are nurtured by misery and want. They spread and grow in the evil soil of poverty and strife. They reach their full growth when the hope of a people for a better life has died. We must keep that hope alive. The free peoples of the world look to us for support in maintaining their freedoms.

If we falter in our leadership, we may endanger the peace of the world—and we shall surely endanger the welfare of this nation.

Great responsibilities have been placed upon us by the swift movement of events. I am confident that the Congress will face these responsibilities squarely.

—President Truman, Message to Congress, March 12, 1947

B. The Marshall Plan

In considering the requirements for the rehabilitation of Europe the physical loss of life, the visible destruction of cities, factories, mines, and railroads was correctly estimated, but it has become obvious during recent months that this visible destruction was probably less serious than the dislocation of the entire fabric of European economy. . . .

The truth of the matter is that Europe's requirements for the next 3 or 4 years of foreign food and other essential products—principally from America—are so much greater than her present ability to pay that she must have substantial additional help, or face economic, social, and political deterioration of a very grave character.

The remedy lies in breaking the vicious circle and restoring the confidence of the European people in the economic future of their own countries and of Europe as a whole. The manufacturer and the farmer throughout wide areas must be able and willing to exchange their products for currencies the continuing value of which is not open to question.

Aside from the demoralizing effect on the world at large and the possibilities of disturbances arising as a result of the desperation of the people concerned, the consequences to the economy of the United States should be apparent to all. It is logical that the United States should do whatever it is able to do to assist in the return of normal economic health in the world, without which there can be no political stability and no assured peace. Our policy is directed not against any country or doctrine but against hunger, poverty, desperation, and chaos. Its purpose should be the revival of a working economy in the world so as to permit the emergence of political and social conditions in which free institutions can exist. Such assistance, I am convinced, must not be on a piecemeal basis as various crises develop. Any assistance that this Government may render in the future should provide a cure rather than a mere palliative. Any government that is willing to assist in the task of recovery will find full cooperation, I am sure, on the part of the United States Government. Any government which maneuvers to block the recovery of other countries cannot expect help from us. Furthermore, governments, political parties, or groups which seek to perpetuate human misery in order to profit therefrom politically or otherwise will encounter the opposition of the United States.

It is already evident that, before the United States Government can proceed much further in its efforts to alleviate the situation and help start the European world on its way to recovery, there must be some agreement among the countries of Europe as to the requirements of the situation and the part those countries themselves will take in order to give proper effect to whatever action might be undertaken by this Government. It would be neither fitting nor efficacious for this Government to undertake to draw up unilaterally a program designed to place Europe on its feet economically. This is the business of the Europeans. The initiative, I think, must come from Europe. The role of this country should consist of friendly aid in the drafting of a European program and of later support of such a program so far as it may be practical for us to do so. The program should be a joint one, agreed to by a number, if not all European nations.

An essential part of any successful action on the part of the United States is an understanding on the part of the people of America of the character of the problem and the remedies to be applied. Political passion and prejudice should have no part. With foresight, and a willingness on the part of our people to face up to the vast responsi-

bility which history has clearly placed upon our country, the difficulties I have outlined can and will be overcome.
—GEORGE C. MARSHALL, Address at Harvard University, June 5, 1947

C. POINT FOUR

... *Fourth,* we must embark on a bold new program for making the benefits of our scientific advances and industrial progress available for the improvement and growth of under-developed areas.

More than half the people of the world are living in conditions approaching misery. Their food is inadequate. They are victims of disease. Their economic life is primitive and stagnant. Their poverty is a handicap and a threat both to them and to more prosperous areas.

For the first time in history, humanity possesses the knowledge and the skill to relieve the suffering of these people.

The United States is pre-eminent among nations in the development of industrial and scientific techniques. The material resources which we can afford to use for the assistance of other peoples are limited. But our imponderable resources in technical knowledge are constantly growing and are inexhaustible.

I believe that we should make available to peace-loving peoples the benefits of our store of technical knowledge in order to help them realize their aspirations for a better life. And, in cooperation with other nations, we should foster capital investment in areas needing development.

Our aim should be to help the free peoples of the world, through their own efforts, to produce more food, more clothing, more materials for housing, and more mechanical power to lighten their burdens.

We invite other countries to pool their technological resources in this undertaking. Their contributions will be warmly welcomed. This should be a cooperative enterprise in which all nations work together through the United Nations and its specialized agencies wherever practicable. It must be a world wide effort for the achievement of peace, plenty, and freedom.

With the cooperation of business, private capital, agriculture, and labor in this country, this program can greatly increase the industrial activity in other nations and can raise substantially their standards of living.

Such new economic developments must be devised and controlled to benefit the peoples of the areas in which they are established. Guarantees to the investor must be balanced by guarantees in the interest of the people whose resources and whose labor go into these developments.

The old imperialism—exploitation for foreign profit—has no place in our plans. What we envisage is a program of development based on the concepts of democratic fair-dealing.

All countries, including our own, will greatly benefit from a constructive program for the better use of the world's human and natural resources. Experience shows that our commerce with other countries expands as they progress industrially and economically.

Greater production is the key to prosperity and peace. And the key to greater production is a wider and more vigorous application of modern scientific and technical knowledge.

Only by helping the least fortunate of its members to help themselves can the human family achieve the decent, satisfying life that is the right of all people.

Democracy alone can supply the vitalizing force to stir the peoples of the world into triumphant action, not only against their human oppressors, but also against their ancient enemies—hunger, misery, and despair.

—PRESIDENT TRUMAN, Inaugural Address, January 19, 1949

22. THE ATLANTIC COMMUNITY

In one sense all the great events of the decade of the forties—the War, the Truman Doctrine, the Marshall Plan, the Atlantic Pact—may be interpreted as a defense of the Atlantic Community. A very real thing in the eighteenth century, that community was lost sight of or taken for granted in the nineteenth. But in the twentieth century the United States twice went to war against central Europe to save the Atlantic states—Britain, France and Belgium in the first war, those nations plus Holland and the Scandinavian states in the second. And as the fighting war gave way to the cold war, as the hoped-for One World divided implacably into two, it became clearer than ever before that the states on both sides of the North Atlantic had a common body of interests, a common sense of traditions and values.

At mid-century came a "great debate" over foreign policy, a debate which is not yet wholly ended. Though it assumed, almost from day to day, different forms, it was actually a continuation of the earlier debate over the historical function and the destiny of the United States—a debate that had flourished in the late thirties and been silenced only by war itself. Was it the destiny of the United States to turn its back upon Old World Europe and its face toward still older Asia, to abandon Western Christendom to its fate and make the Pacific a new Mediterranean of a new empire? Or was it the destiny of the United States rather to maintain, strengthen, and prosper its historical ties with those nations that had founded and peopled the New World, had transmitted to it religion and law and literature, and that shared with it a common civilization? As the clamor of controversy died down, in mid-summer of 1951, it appeared that the American people still understood their historical function and their destiny, and that they would continue to pledge their lives, their fortunes, and their honor to the salvation of the West.

More than any other public figure, Walter Lippmann is responsible for dramatizing for us the historical significance of the Atlantic Community and for making clear just what is involved in the great decisions that the American people are taking. We give here two brief excerpts from his books on war aims and foreign policy.

A. "A Great Community . . . From Which No Member
Can Be Excluded and None Can Resign"

THE special characteristic of British-American relations is that the British Commonwealth is both inside and outside the area of America's defensive commitments. Canada lies in the midst of it; Australia and New Zealand within it. Thus the overthrow of the American position in the world would mean the break-up of the British Commonwealth. At the same time the citadel of British power is the United Kingdom and the outlying strong points from Gibraltar to Singapore are at the strategic frontiers of the Americas. Thus the overthrow of the British position in the world would mean a revolutionary change in the system of defense within which the American republics have lived for more than a century.

There are twenty American republics and there are, counting Eire and South Africa, six British nations within this community. All of these twenty-six states are self-governing. Though some are much more powerful than others, the sovereignty of their independence is attested by the fact that Eire within the British Commonwealth and the Argentine and Chile within the Pan-American system have been free to remain neutral. They have been free to stay out of the war, even though the war is fought to preserve the system of security which enables them to make this sovereign choice. This is the proof that in fact the British Commonwealth is a commonwealth and not an empire, that the association of American republics is not the façade of United States imperialism. . . .

It is the demonstrated fact that London cannot and does not dominate so small, so near, so weak, and so strategically important a dominion as Eire, but must treat with it as a sovereign independent state. It has been demonstrated that the United States cannot and does not dominate on the crucial issue of war and peace American republics like the Argentine and Chile. How insubstantial then is the fear that Britain could dominate a powerful nation like the United States, or be dominated by the United States. Can it then be denied that the British-American connection is, through the facts of geography and the results of historic experience, a community of interest and not a plan of domination or a scheme of empire?

Nor is it, nor can it be, a plan for the combined domination of the world by the English-speaking nations. . . . We can see this when we fix our attention upon the other nations which, like Britain, have their vital interests both within and outside the New World. The first of these is France. For a hundred years the only enemy of France has been Germany, and the one frontier France had to defend was her frontier facing Germany. But when France is unable to defend that frontier, as seemed possible in 1917 and was the fact in 1940, it is immediately evident in the New World that the security of France is indispensable to the security of the New World.

The fall of France in 1940 was a conclusive demonstration that France is a member of the great defensive system in which the American republics live. The fall of France laid Spain and Portugal open to the possibility of invasion and domination. This in turn opened up the question of the security of the Spanish and Portuguese island stepping-stones in the Atlantic. The fall of France gave Germany the sea and air bases from which Britain was besieged and American shipping along our Eastern shore and in the Caribbean subjected to a devastating raid.

The fall of France uncovered the West Coast of Africa from above Casablanca to Dakar, and opened up the threat, in the event of a German victory in Europe, of a sea-borne and air-borne invasion of South America. The fall of France had equally momentous consequences in the Pacific. The surrender of French Indo-China to Japan completed the envelopment of the Philippines, and provided the base from which Japan conquered Burma and closed the Burma Road and thus cut off China from her allies.

It follows that France, though a state in continental Europe, is primarily a member of the same community to which the United States belongs. The security of France is an American interest, and the security of the American position is a French interest. The same holds true, and for the same reasons, of Spain and Portugal. The vital interests of the British nations, the American nations, and of the Latin nations on both sides of the Atlantic, and across the Pacific, are so enmeshed by geography, by the strategic necessity, and by historic formation that their paramount interests are, when tested in the fires of total war, inseparable. They can fall separately. None of them, not the most powerful, not the two most powerful among them combined—namely the United Kingdom and the United States—can stand comfortably and securely without the others. The proof that clinches the demonstration is that the British nations and the American nations are compelled for their own survival to liberate France and to foster the restoration of the power of France.

Other nations are vitally involved in the system of security to which we belong. The Netherlands is a small state in Europe with a great empire overseas in the Pacific and with important colonies in the New World. The Netherlands is also one of the outer bastions of both France and Britain. The same is true of Belgium, which has an empire on the Atlantic and is also an outer bastion. Another member of the Atlantic Community is Denmark, which only very recently retired from her colonial possessions in the West Indies, which on the northern approaches to the American continent holds Greenland as a colony and, until recently, was related to Iceland because both had the same king. Norway, too, is a member. For Norway is a country which in relation to Europe is strategically an island lying on the outer limits of the Atlantic world.

Thus the violation of Denmark and Norway, as of the Netherlands and Belgium, was instantly recognized in the Americas and in

Britain as a breach in their defenses, and in Norway and in Denmark, as in the Netherlands and Belgium, it was instantly recognized that liberation and restoration depended upon the victory of the British and American nations. Thus when we say that they are members of the same community of interest, we are making an avowal which has been put to the acid test and is no mere amiable generalization. . . .

At the end of the eighteenth and the beginning of the nineteenth century most of the nations of the New World won their sovereign independence from the parent nations in the Old World. But the separation, though it is absolute in the realm of self-government, has never existed in the realm of strategic security. The original geographic and historic connections across the Atlantic have persisted. The Atlantic Ocean is not the frontier between Europe and the Americas. It is the inland sea of a community of nations allied with one another by geography, history, and vital necessity.

The members of this community may not all love one another, and they have many conflicting interests. But that is true of any community except perhaps the community of the saints. The test of whether a community exists is not whether we have learned to love our neighbors but whether, when put to the test, we find that we do act as neighbors. By that test all the centuries of experience since the discovery of the Americas have shown that there is peace and order on this side of the Atlantic only when there is peace and order among our neighbors on the other side of the Atlantic. Whenever they have been involved in great wars, the New World has been involved. When they have had peace from great wars, as they did have from Waterloo to the first invasion of Belgium, there have been no great international wars that concerned the Americas.

Not what men say, not what they think they feel, but what in fact when they have to act they actually do—that is the test of community. By that test there is a great community on this earth from which no member can be excluded and none can resign. This community has its geographical center in the great basin of the Atlantic.

The security of this community turns upon the relations of the two great powers—Britain and the United States. In this area and at this phase of historic time, they have the arsenals and the military formations necessary to the waging of war. And therefore their alliance is the nucleus of force around which the security of the whole region must

necessarily be organized, to which, when their alliance is firm, the other members of the community will in their own interest freely adhere.
—WALTER LIPPMANN, *U.S. Foreign Policy*, 1943

B. THE AMERICAN DESTINY

The great debates of our generation have, in the last analysis, been between those who denied and those who affirmed the need for positive measures to defend the Republic, to maintain foreign intercourse, and to conserve and promote internal order and well-being.

The details of the debates have been confusing. But in retrospect we can now see that the underlying issue in foreign affairs was whether we could still take for granted our long immunity and effortless security. Those who thought we could appeared as pacifists or as isolationists: they did not like armaments, or they did not believe in strategic defenses, or they opposed alliances, or they would not enter an organized association with other nations. Those who thought our immunity was over advocated military preparedness, or the League of Nations, or partnerships and alliances with friendly powers. Among them, as among their pacifist or isolationist opponents, there was much disagreement.

This basic issue has now been settled; there are no responsible voices left to say, as there were a few years ago, that no positive measures of any kind, not even fortifying our outposts, are necessary or desirable. Instead of debating the need for any positive policy, we have now to deliberate upon what kind of positive policy we need.

It is certain that isolationism and laissez-faire belong to the past, and the debate, which has consumed so large a part of our best intellectual energies for more than forty years, is nearly concluded. In the end the verdict is sure to be that the security and prosperity and welfare of the United States cannot be left to chance, that the fundamental issues of national existence have now to be dealt with consciously and positively. . . .

Fate has brought it about that America is at the center, no longer on the edges, of Western civilization. In this fact resides the American destiny. We can deny the fact and refuse our destiny. If we do, Western civilization, which is the glory of our world, will become a disorganized and decaying fringe around the Soviet Union and the emergent people of Asia. But if we comprehend our destiny we shall become equal to it. The vision is there, and our people need not perish.

For America is now called to do what the founders and the pioneers always believed was the American task: to make the New World a place where the ancient faith can flourish anew, and its eternal promise at last be redeemed. To ask whether the American nation will rise to this occasion and be equal to its destiny is to ask whether Americans have the will to live. We need have no morbid doubts about that.

The American idea is not an eccentricity in the history of mankind. It is a hope and a pledge of fulfillment. The American idea is founded upon an image of man and of his place in the universe, of his reason and his will, his knowledge of good and evil, his hope of a higher and a natural law which is above all governments, and indeed of all particular laws: this tradition descends to Americans, as to all the Westerners, from the Mediterranean world of the ancient Greeks, Hebrews, and Romans. The Atlantic is now the mediterranean sea of this culture and this faith.

It is no accident—it is indeed historic and providential—that the formation of the first universal order since classical times should begin with the binding together of the dismembered parts of Western Christendom. From this beginning a great prospect offers itself: that the schism between East and West, which opened up in the Dark Ages from the fifth to the eleventh centuries of our era, may at last be healed.

This, I believe, is the prophecy which events announce. Whether we now hear it gladly or shrink away from it suspiciously, it will yet come to pass.

—WALTER LIPPMANN, *U.S. War Aims,* 1944

Part IV

Old Problems in a New Age

14

The Struggle for Racial Equality

IN HIS Peoria speech of 1854 Abraham Lincoln asserted that "slavery deprives our republican example of its just influence in the world; enables the enemies of free institutions with plausibility to taunt us as hypocrites; causes the real friends of freedom to doubt our sincerity; and forces so many good men among ourselves into an open war with the very fundamental principles of civil liberty." The denial of equal rights to Negroes during the Second World War, and the world-wide revolution which ensued, had much the same effect. It enabled our enemies once again to taunt us with hypocrisy, and to assert that though we proclaimed equality we practiced racism. A time when the colored peoples of Africa and Asia were bursting their century-old bonds, and when some two score African and Asian nations moved resolutely onto the historical stage, was not an auspicious one for the maintenance of racial discrimination in a nation which was making a bid for political and moral leadership of the free world.

As the centenary of the Civil War, emancipation, and the Reconstruction Amendments approached, Negroes in the South, and in many parts of the North as well, were still second-class citizens. Negro children were fobbed off with schools that were not only segregated but materially and academically inferior, and Negro youths were denied entrance to State universities for whose support they were taxed. When Negroes traveled they were forced to sit in segregated waiting rooms, ride in segregated sections of buses and trains, to eat in segregated dining rooms. They were condemned to segregation in most public places as well—playgrounds, swimming pools, theaters, and even churches. And half a century after Booker T. Washington's Atlanta Speech calling for economic partnership between Negroes and whites, Southern Negroes were still tenant farmers and Northern Negroes still largely unskilled workers. North

735

and South alike, urban Negroes—and by 1960 that meant most of them—
lived in slums that would have been called ghettos had they been in
Warsaw or Prague. Their right to vote and to hold office—guaranteed
them by the Constitution itself—was flouted and even their most elementary rights were denied, rights presumably sacred: freedom of speech,
freedom of assembly, freedom of association, and a fair trial.

The great Swedish sociologist, Gunnar Myrdal, called all this the
American Dilemma, and it was. The Dilemma, wrote Myrdal, "is the
ever-raging conflict between, on the one hand, the valuations preserved
on the general plane which we . . . call 'the American creed,' where the
American thinks, talks, and acts under the influence of high national and
Christian precepts, and, on the other hand, the valuation on specific
planes of individual and group living, where personal and local interests,
economic, social, and sectional jealousies; considerations of community
prestige and conformity; group prejudice against particular persons or
types of people; and all sorts of miscellaneous wants, impulses, and
habits, dominate his outlook" (*An American Dilemma,* I, xliii). That
dilemma weighed heavily on the conscience of most Northerners, and
of many Southerners as well, though most Southerners had learned to
live with it and even to ignore it. They contrasted the position of the
free Negro not with their own but with that of the slave, and concluded
that the Negro was, after all, making great progress, and should be content with that progress. They knew that there was a "Negro problem,"
just as their grandfathers had known that there was a slavery problem,
but they persuaded themselves that the problem would somehow work
itself out, all in good time, and concluded that nothing was to be gained
and much was to be lost by rushing things. They knew that evolution was
better than revolution, and they knew too that evolution was a slow
process, and they did not understand why Negroes should not take the
same satisfaction in gradual evolution as they did. Basic to their attitude
was one explicit and one implicit assumption. The explicit assumption
was that Southerners knew best—the Southern white, that is—and that
race relations would take care of themselves if only outsiders, e.g.,
Northerners, would leave the South alone. The implicit assumption—
which was explicit enough under pressure—was that the Negro was
after all inferior to the white, and that he should not therefore expect
genuine equality, political, economic, or social. The Southern solution
to the Negro problem was, then, at its best merely ameliorative.

It was the New Deal, and the Second World War, which made the first real dent in this façade of complacency and intransigence; the New Deal by leveling up the economic condition of the Negro and by some rather ineffectual gestures toward desegregation, and the war by ending segregation in some elements of the armed forces and in defense industries, and by giving to Negroes themselves a new experience and a new dimension of hope and expectation. With the coming of peace many Negroes who had seen and even experienced equality in Europe were unwilling to go back to their old position of inferiority in their own country. Many, too, returned not to their old homes in the South, but to Northern cities, and the movement of Negroes from South to North accelerated sharply in the decades until 1964, when the majority of Negroes lived in the North; New York had the largest Negro population of any State, and New York City, Washington, Philadelphia, and Detroit were the largest Negro cities. This meant new economic and educational opportunities for hundreds of thousands of Negroes. It meant, too, that the Negroes were now a power to be reckoned with politically, for though they could not vote in the South, they could and did vote in the North. As it was not practicable to deny economic and social rights to those who held political power, the contrast between the condition of Negroes North and South sharpened with every year.

The new attitude toward the Negro was dramatized by a series of State and Federal laws, and Executive Orders, forbidding racial discrimination in employment and in the civil service—orders often dishonored or evaded by local authorities. It was dramatized even more effectively by a series of Supreme Court decisions chipping away at the walls of discrimination which had been erected by the South. One series of decisions looked to the implementation of the requirements of due process of law. Another required political parties to act as public, not private, organizations, and to admit Negroes to primaries. A third series announced the beginning of the end of discrimination in public facilities such as housing and transportation. The climax of this judicial assault on the doctrine and practice of white supremacy came with the historic school desegregation case of 1954—Brown *versus* Board of Education of Topeka—which reversed the fifty-year-old Plessy *versus* Ferguson decision, vindicated Justice Harlan's dissenting opinion in that memorable case, and overthrew the "separate but equal" doctrine with the simple proposition that what was separate was not equal.

Brown *versus* Topeka called for desegregation of public schools "with all deliberate speed," and thus inaugurated more than a decade of turmoil and struggle. For Southerners saw clearly enough the implications of this doctrine: what today applied to schools would apply tomorrow to all other public facilities and accommodations. They resisted therefore with a kind of desperation, resisted at first by subterfuge and evasion and delay, and then by outright violence. In the border States—except in parts of Virginia and Tennessee—there was reluctant acquiescence, but the "Deep" South was intransigent, and ten years after the judicial fiat there were no Negro children in the schools of South Carolina, Alabama, or Mississippi and only token desegregation in other States.

As so often in the past—and not in the South alone—defiance took on a cloak of legality. After the first shock, Southerners gathered their intellectual as well as their physical resources for resistance. While White Citizens Councils—a kind of respectable Ku Klux Klan—were resorting to force and intimidation, over ninety Southern Congressmen issued a statement denouncing the Supreme Court decision as a usurpation of power, and calling on the South for resistance.

Perhaps the most important development in the long struggle for Negro rights was not in the Courts or in the Congress, but in the ranks of the Negroes themselves. Under Booker T. Washington Negro leadership had been cooperative and acquiescent; under W. E. B. Du Bois it was defiant but highly intellectual. Now under men like Philip Randolph and Thurgood Marshall and the Reverend Martin Luther King, Jr., the Negroes took affairs pretty much into their own hands. They embarked upon vigorous programs of publicity, political campaigns, sit-in demonstrations, orderly marches to city halls and to schools, and eventually a grand march on the city of Washington itself. Along with all this, Negroes employed the tactic of the economic boycott—as in the campaign for desegregated buses in Montgomery—and in this they had the support of important segments of Northern consumers, white and Negro alike. Southern authorities responded to these measures— the demonstration, the sit-in, the boycott—with wholesale arrests, but with almost monotonous regularity Federal Courts voided these arrests and asserted the constitutional right of Negroes to agitate peacefully for their constitutional rights.

Meantime the issue of civil rights moved back into the halls of Congress, where it had troubled the surface of the political waters during the Reconstruction years, and occasionally thereafter. Every President after Franklin Roosevelt insisted on the necessity of Federal action, but little action materialized. A civil rights bill was passed early in Eisenhower's second administration, but it proved curiously ineffective. President Kennedy insisted on the enactment of a broad civil rights program embracing political, economic, and social rights. The Congress did not reject his arguments or his importunities, but ignored them. His tragic death, however, did not end the matter; President Johnson was as determined as President Kennedy to achieve that equality so long promised and so long denied, and in midsummer of 1964, after prolonged parliamentary maneuvers and filibusters, Congress did finally enact a civil rights bill. Although it was not the beginning of the end of inequality, it was assuredly the end of the beginning.

1. THE CIVIL WAR AMENDMENTS, 1868-70

The so-called Civil War Amendments—numbers Thirteen, Fourteen, and Fifteen—were designed to guarantee not only freedom but civil rights to the Negro. The Thirteenth needs no explanation. The Fourteenth was originally formulated to assure validity to the civil rights bill of 1866, whose constitutionality was in question. In the course of its Congressional career, new and somewhat irrelevant sections were added; we give here only those sections addressed to the position of the freedman. The Fifteenth Amendment, designed to assure the vote to freedmen, was couched in language so ambiguous that it invited evasion. Though both Amendments provided for Congressional enforcement the Congress failed until very recently to implement the provisions of these Amendments by appropriate legislation.

S EC. 1. Neither slavery nor involuntary servitude, except as a punishment for crime whereof the party shall have been dully convicted, shall exist within the United States, or any place subject to their jurisdiction.

Sec. 2. Congress shall have power to enforce this article by appropriate legislation.

—The Thirteenth Amendment, December 18, 1865

Sec. 1. All persons born or naturalized in the United States, and subject to the jurisdiction thereof, are citizens of the United States and of the State wherein they reside. No State shall make or enforce any law which shall abridge the privileges or immunities of citizens of the United States; nor shall any State deprive any person of life, liberty, or property, without due process of law; nor deny to any person within its jurisdiction the equal protection of the laws.

Sec. 2. Representatives shall be apportioned among the several States according to their respective numbers, counting the whole number of persons in each State, excluding Indians not taxed. But when the right to vote at any election for the choice of electors for President and Vice President of the United States, Representatives in Congress, the Executive and Judicial officers of a State, or the members of the Legislature thereof, is denied to any of the male inhabitants of such State, being twenty-one years of age, and citizens of the United States, or in any way abridged, except for participation in rebellion, or other crime, the basis of representation therein shall be reduced in the proportion which the number of such male citizens shall bear to the whole number of male citizens twenty-one years of age in such State. . . .

—The Fourteenth Amendment, July 28, 1868

Sec. 1. The right of citizens of the United States to vote shall not be denied or abridged by the United States or by any State on account of race, color, or previous condition of servitude—

Sec. 2. The Congress shall have power to enforce this article by appropriate legislation—

—The Fifteenth Amendment, March 30, 1870

2. THE FREEDMAN'S CASE

George Washington Cable was the most distinguished Southern writer during the Reconstruction era. Though he fought in the Confederate Army he did not share the Southern view of the war, Reconstruction, or the Negro. He first achieved literary fame with The Great South, *a series of essays on the postwar South, published in* Scribner's

Magazine. *A few years later came his most famous book,* Old Creole Days, *a group of stories which rejected the romantic view of the Creoles. With* The Silent South, *from which this essay is drawn, Cable broke sharply with the Southern view of the freedman. His book earned him such hostility in his own section that in 1885 he moved to Northampton, Massachusetts. For the rest of his life he devoted himself to writing and lecturing about the South and the Negro.*

THE NATION'S ATTITUDE

THE GREATEST social problem before the American people today is, as it has been for a hundred years, the presence among us of the Negro.

No comparable entanglement was ever drawn round itself by any other modern nation with so serene a disregard of its ultimate issue, or with a more distinct national responsibility. The African slave was brought here by cruel force, and with everybody's consent except his own. Everywhere the practice was favored as a measure of common aggrandizement. When a few men and women protested, they were mobbed in the public interest, with the public consent. There rests, therefore, a moral responsibility on the whole nation never to lose sight of the results of African-American slavery until they cease to work mischief and injustice. . . .

WHAT THE WAR LEFT

The old alien relation might have given way if we could only, while letting that pass, have held fast by the other old ideas. But they were all bound together. See our embarrassment. For more than a hundred years we had made these sentiments the absolute essentials to our self-respect. And yet if we clung to them, how could we meet the Freedman on equal terms in the political field? Even to lead would not compensate us; for the fundamental profession of American politics is that the leader is servant to his followers. It was too much. The ex-master and ex-slave— the quarterdeck and the forecastle, as it were—could not come together. But neither could the American mind tolerate a continuance of martial law. The agonies of Reconstruction followed.

The vote, after all, was a secondary point, and the robbery and bribery on one side, and whipping and killing on the other were but huge accidents of the situation. The two main questions were really these: on the Freedman's side, how to establish republican state government under the same recognition of his rights that the rest of Christendom accorded him; and on the former master's side, how to get back to the old semblance of republican state government, and—allowing that the Freedman was *de facto* a voter—still to maintain a purely arbitrary superiority of all whites over all blacks, and a purely arbitrary equality of all blacks among themselves as an alien, menial, and dangerous class.

Exceptionally here and there some one in the master caste did throw off the old and accept the new ideas, and, if he would allow it, was instantly claimed as a leader by the newly liberated thousands around him. But just as promptly the old master race branded him also an alien reprobate, and in ninety-nine cases out of a hundred, if he had not already done so, he soon began to confirm by his actions the brand on his cheek. However, we need give no history here of the dreadful episode of Reconstruction. Under an experimentative truce its issues rest today upon the pledge of the wiser leaders of the master class: Let us but remove the hireling demagogue, and we will see to it that the Freedman is accorded a practical, complete, and cordial recognition of his equality with the white man before the law. As far as there has been any understanding at all, it is not that the originally desired ends of Reconstruction have been abandoned, but that the men of North and South have agreed upon a new, gentle, and peaceable method for reaching them; that, without change as to the ends in view, compulsory Reconstruction has been set aside and a voluntary Reconstruction is on trial.

It is the fashion to say we paused to let the "feelings engendered by the war" pass away, and that they are passing. But let not these truths lead us into error. The sentiments we have been analyzing, and upon which we saw the old compulsory Reconstruction go hard aground— these are not the "feelings engendered by the war." We must disentangle them from the "feelings engendered by the war," and by Reconstruction. They are older than either. But for them slavery would have perished of itself, and emancipation and Reconstruction been peaceful revolutions.

Indeed, as between master and slave, the "feelings engendered by the war" are too trivial, or at least were too short-lived, to demand our present notice. One relation and feeling the war destroyed: the patriarchal tie and its often really tender and benevolent sentiment of dependence and protection. When the slave became a Freedman, the sentiment of alienism became for the first time complete. The abandonment of this relation was not one-sided; the slave, even before the master, renounced it. Countless times, since Reconstruction began, the master has tried, in what he believed to be everybody's interest, to play on that old sentiment. But he found it a harp without strings. The Freedman could not formulate, but he could see, all our old ideas of autocracy and subserviency, of master and menial, of an arbitrarily fixed class to guide and rule, and another to be guided and ruled. He rejected the overture. The old master, his well-meant condescensions slighted, turned away estranged, and justified himself in passively withholding that simpler protection without patronage which any one American citizen, however exalted, owes to any other, however humble. Could the Freedman in the bitterest of those days have consented to throw himself upon just that one old relation, he could have found a physical security for himself and his house such as could not, after years of effort, be given him by constitutional amendments, Congress, United States marshals, regiments of regulars, and ships of war. But he could not; the very nobility of the civilization that had held him in slavery had made him too much a man to go back to that shelter; and by his manly neglect to do so he has proved to us who once ruled over him that, be his relative standing among the races of men what it may, he is worthy to be free.

FREED—NOT FREE

To be a free man is his [the Negro's] still distant goal. Twice he has been a Freedman. In the days of compulsory Reconstruction he was freed in the presence of his master by that master's victorious foe. In these days of voluntary Reconstruction he is virtually freed by the consent of his master, but the master retaining the exclusive right to define the bounds of his freedom. Many everywhere have taken up the idea that this state of affairs is the end to be desired and the end actually sought in Reconstruction as handed over to the state. I do not charge such folly to the best intelligence of any American community; but I cannot ignore my own knowledge that the average thought of some regions rises to no better idea of the issue. The belief is all too common that the nation, having aimed at a wrong result and missed, has left us of the Southern states to get now such other result as we think best. I say this belief is not universal. There are those among us who see that America has no room for a state of society which makes its lower classes harmless by abridging their liberties, or, as one of the favored class lately said to me, has "got 'em so they don't give no trouble." There is a growing number who see that the one thing we cannot afford to tolerate at large is a class of people less than citizens; and that every interest in the land demands that the Freedman be free to become in all things, as far as his own personal gifts will lift and sustain him, the same sort of American citizen he would be if, with the same intellectual and moral caliber, he were white.

Thus we reach the ultimate question of fact. Are the Freedman's liberties suffering any real abridgment? The answer is easy. The letter of the laws, with a few exceptions, recognizes him as entitled to every right of an American citizen; and to some it may seem unimportant that there is scarcely one public relation of life in the South where he is not arbitrarily and unlawfully compelled to hold toward the white man the attitude of an alien, a menial, and a probable reprobate, by reason of his race and color. One of the marvels of future history will be that it was counted a small matter, by a majority of our nation, for six millions of people within it, made by its own decree a component part of it, to be subjected to a system of oppression so rank that nothing could make it seem small except the fact that they had already been ground under it for a century and a half.

Examine it. It proffers to the Freedman a certain security of life and property, and then holds the respect of the community, that dearest of earthly boons, beyond his attainment. It gives him certain guarantees against thieves and robbers, and then holds him under the unearned contumely of the mass of good men and women. It acknowledges in constitutions and statutes his title to an American's freedom and aspirations, and then in daily practice heaps upon him in every public place the most odious distinctions, without giving ear to the humblest plea concerning mental or moral character. It spurns his ambition, tramples upon his languishing self-respect, and indignantly refuses to let him either buy with money, or earn by any excellence of inner life or outward behavior, the most momentary immunity from these public indignities even for his wife and daughters. Need we cram these pages with facts in evidence, as if these were charges denied and requiring to be proven? They are simply the present avowed and defended state of affairs peeled of its exteriors.

Nothing but the habit, generations old, of enduring it could make it endurable by men not in actual slavery. Were we whites of the South to remain every way as we are, and our six million blacks to give place to any sort of whites exactly their equals, man for man, in mind, morals, and wealth, provided only that they had tasted two years of American freedom, and were this same system of tyrannies attempted upon them, there would be as bloody an uprising as this continent has ever seen. We can say this quietly. There is not a scruple's weight of present danger. These six million Freedmen are dominated by nine million whites immeasurably stronger than they, backed by the virtual consent of thirty-odd millions more. Indeed, nothing but the habit of oppression could make such oppression possible to a people of the intelligence and virtue of our Southern whites, and the invitation to practice it on millions of any other than the children of their former slaves would be spurned with a noble indignation.

Suppose, for a moment, the tables turned. Suppose the courts of our Southern states, while changing no laws requiring the impaneling of jurymen without distinction as to race, etc., should suddenly begin to draw their thousands of jurymen all black, and well-nigh every one of them counting, not only himself, but all his race, better than any white man. Assuming that their average of intelligence and morals should be not below that of jurymen as now drawn, would a white man, for all that, choose to be tried in one of those courts? Would he suspect nothing? Could one persuade him that his chances of even justice were all they should be, or all they would be were the court not evading the law in order to sustain an outrageous distinction against him because of the accidents of his birth? Yet only read white man for black man, and black man for white man, and that—I speak as an eyewitness—has been the practice for years, and is still so today; an actual emasculation, in the case of six million people both as plaintiff and defendant, of the right of trial by jury.

In this and other practices the outrage falls upon the Freedman. Does it stop there? Far from it. It is the first premise of American principles that whatever elevates the lower stratum of the people lifts all the rest, and whatever holds it down holds all down. For twenty years, therefore, the nation has been working to elevate the Freedman. It counts this one of the great necessities of the hour. It has poured out its wealth publicly and privately for this purpose. It is confidently hoped that it will soon bestow a royal gift of millions for the reduction of the illiteracy so largely shared by the blacks. Our Southern states are, and for twenty years have been, taxing themselves for the same end. The private charities alone of the other states have given twenty millions in the same good cause. Their colored seminaries, colleges, and normal schools dot our whole Southern country, and furnish our public colored schools with a large part of their teachers. All this and much more has been or is being done in order that, for the good of himself and everybody else in the land, the colored man may be elevated as quickly as possible from all the debasements of slavery and semi-slavery to the full stature and integrity of citizenship. And it is in the face of all this that the adherent of the old regime stands in the way to every public privilege and place—steamer landing, railway platform, theater, concert hall, art display, public library, public school, courthouse, church, everything—flourishing the hot branding iron of ignominious distinctions. He forbids the Freedman to go into the water until *he* is satisfied that he knows how to swim and, for fear he should learn, hangs millstones about his neck. This is what we are told is a small matter that will settle itself. Yes, like a roosting curse, until the outraged intelligence of the South lifts its indignant protest against this stupid firing into our own ranks.

—George Washington Cable, "The Freedman's Case in Equity," 1885

3. FREDERICK DOUGLASS CALLS ON THE FREEDMAN TO ORGANIZE FOR SELF-PROTECTION

Frederick Douglass, the greatest Negro leader of the Civil War generation, was born in slavery, but escaped to freedom as early as 1838. Almost at once he attached himself to the Abolitionist cause and for twenty years worked ceaselessly with Garrison, Phillips, and other leaders of the Abolitionist cause. During the Civil War he helped recruit Negro soldiers for the Union Army and advised Lincoln on problems of race relationships and the future of the Negro. He early saw what Booker T. Washington was to insist upon, the importance of economic equality for the Negro. By the 1880's—when young Booker T. Washington emerged on the scene—Douglass was the patriarch of the Negro race, speaking with an authority that no other Negro could command. This speech was delivered at a Negro convention in Louisville, Kentucky, in 1883.

IT IS OUR lot to live among a people whose laws, traditions, and prejudices have been against us for centuries, and from these they are not yet free. To assume that they are free from these evils simply because they have changed their laws is to assume what is utterly unreasonable and contrary to facts. Large bodies move slowly. Individuals may be converted on the instant and change their whole course of life. Nations never. Time and events are required for the conversion of nations. Not even the character of a great political organization can be changed by a new platform. It will be the same old snake though in a new skin. Though we have had war, reconstruction and abolition as a nation, we still linger in the shadow and blight of an extinct institution. Though the colored man is no longer subject to be bought and sold, he is still surrounded by an adverse sentiment which fetters all his movements. In his downward course he meets with no resistance, but his course upward is resented and resisted at every step of his progress. If he comes in ignorance, rags and wretchedness, he conforms to the popular belief of his character, and in that character he is welcome. But if he shall come as a gentleman, a scholar, and a statesman, he is hailed as a contradiction to the national faith concerning his race, and his coming is resented as impudence. In the one case he may provoke contempt and derision, but in the other he is an affront to pride, and provokes malice. Let him do what he will, there is at present, therefore, no escape for him. The color line meets him everywhere, and in a measure shuts him out from all respectable and profitable trades and callings. In spite of all your religion and laws he is a rejected man.

He is rejected by trade unions, of every trade, and refused work while he lives, and burial when he dies, and yet he is asked to forget his color, and forget that which everybody else remembers. If he offers himself to a builder as a mechanic, to a client as a lawyer, to a patient as a physician, to a college as a professor, to a firm as a clerk; to a Government Department as an agent, or an officer, he is sternly met on the color line, and his claim to consideration in some way is disputed on the ground of color.

Not even our churches, whose members profess to follow the despised Nazarene, whose home, when on earth, was among the lowly and despised, have yet conquered this feeling of color madness, and what is true of our churches is also true of our courts of law. Neither is free from this all-pervading atmosphere of color hate. The one describes the Deity as impartial, no respecter of persons, and the other the Goddess of Justice as blindfolded, with sword by her side and scales in her hand held evenly between high and low, rich and poor, white and black, but both are the images of American imagination, rather than American practices.

Taking advantage of the general disposition in this country to impute crime to color, white men *color* their faces to commit crime and wash off the hated color to escape punishment. In many places where the commission of crime is alleged against one of our color, the ordinary processes of the law are set aside as too slow for the impetuous justice of the infuriated populace. They take the law into their own bloody hands and proceed to whip, stab, shoot, hang, or burn the alleged culprit, without the intervention of courts, counsel, judges, juries, and witnesses. In such cases it is not the business of the accusers to prove guilt, but it is for the accused to prove his innocence, a thing hard for any man to do, even in a court of law, and utterly impossible for him to do in these infernal Lynch courts. A man accused, surprised, frightened and captured by a motley crowd, dragged with a rope around his neck in midnight-darkness to the nearest tree, and told in the coarsest terms of profanity to prepare for death, would be more than human if he did not, in his terror-stricken appearance, more confirm suspicion of guilt than the contrary. Worse still, in the presence of such hell-black outrages, the pulpit is usually dumb, and the press in the neighborhood is silent or openly takes sides with the mob. There are occasional cases in which white men are lynched, but one sparrow does not make a summer. Every one knows that what is called Lynch law is peculiarly the law for colored people and for nobody else. If there were no other grievance than this horrible and barbarous Lynch law custom, we should be justified in assembling, as we have now done, to expose and denounce it. But this is not all. Even now, after twenty years of so-called emancipation, we are subject to lawless raids of midnight riders, who, with blackened faces, invade our homes and perpetrate the foulest of crimes upon us and our families. This condition of things is too flagrant and notorious to require specifications or proof. Thus in all the relations of life and death we are met by the color line. We cannot ignore it if we would, and ought not if we could. It hunts us at midnight, it denies us accommodation in hotels and justice in the courts; excludes our children from schools, refuses our sons the chance to learn trades, and compels us to pursue only such labor as will bring the least reward. While we recognize the color line as a hurtful force, a mountain barrier to our progress, wounding our bleeding feet with its flinty rocks at every step, we do not despair. We are a hopeful people. This convention is a proof of our faith in you, in reason, in truth, and justice—our belief that prejudice, with all its malign accompaniments, may yet be removed by peaceful means; that, assisted by time and events and the growing enlightenment of both races, the color line will ultimately become harmless. When this shall come it will then only be used, as it should be, to distinguish one variety of the human family from another. It will cease to have any civil, political, or moral significance, and colored conventions will then be dispensed with as anachronisms, wholly out of place, but not till then. . . .

If the six millions of colored people of this country, armed with the Constitution of the United States, with a million votes of their own to lean upon, and millions of white men at their back, whose hearts are responsive to the claims of humanity, have not sufficient spirit and wisdom to organize and combine to defend themselves from outrage, discrimination, and oppression, it will be idle for them to expect that the Republican party or any other political party will organize and combine for them or care what becomes of them. Men may combine to prevent cruelty to animals, for they are dumb and cannot speak for themselves; but we are men and must speak for ourselves, or we shall not be spoken for at all. We have conventions in America for Ireland, but we should have none if Ireland did not speak for herself. It is because she makes a noise and keeps her cause before the people that other people go to her help. It was the sword of Washington and of Lafayette that gave us Independence. In conclusion upon this color objection, we have to say that we meet here in open daylight. There is nothing sinister about us. The eyes of the nation are upon us. Ten thousand newspapers may tell if they choose of whatever is said and done here. They may commend our wisdom or condemn our folly, precisely as we shall be wise or foolish.

We put ourselves before them as honest men, and ask their judgment upon our work. . . .

—Frederick Douglass,
"Why a Colored Convention?," September 24, 1883

4. "THE AGITATION OF QUESTIONS OF SOCIAL EQUALITY IS THE EXTREMEST FOLLY"

By the 1890's Washington was widely recognized as the spokesman for his race. It was as such that he was invited to deliver the address at the Cotton States' Exposition in Atlanta, Georgia, in September, 1895. In this address, which aroused greater enthusiasm among whites than among Negroes, he proclaimed that the two races could be as separate as the fingers in all things purely social, yet one as the hand in all things essential to progress. This acquiescence—strategic rather than fundamental—in social inequality aroused widespread exasperation among Northern Negro leaders.

ONE-THIRD of the population of the South is of the Negro race. No enterprise seeking the material, civil, or moral welfare of this section can disregard this element of our population and reach the highest success. I but convey to you, Mr. President and Directors, the sentiment of the masses of my race when I say that in no way have the value and manhood of the American Negro been more fittingly and generously recognized than by the managers of this magnificent Exposition at every stage of its progress. It is a recognition that will do more to cement the friendship of the two races than any occurrence since the dawn of freedom.

Not only this, but the opportunity here afforded will awaken among us a new era of industrial progress. Ignorant and inexperienced, it is not strange that in the first years of our new life we began at the top instead of at the bottom; that a seat in Congress or the State Legislature was more sought than real estate or industrial skill; that the political convention or stump speaking had more attractions than starting a dairy farm or truck garden.

A ship lost at sea for many days suddenly sighted a friendly vessel. From the mast of the unfortunate vessel was seen a signal: "Water, water; we die of thirst!" The answer from the friendly vessel at once came back: "Cast down your bucket where you are." A second time the signal, "Water, water; send us water!" ran up from the distressed vessel, and was answered: "Cast down your bucket where you are." The captain of the distressed vessel, at last heeding the injunction, cast down his bucket, and it came up full of fresh, sparkling water from the mouth of the Amazon River. To those of my race who depend upon bettering their condition in a foreign land, or who underestimate the importance of cultivating friendly relations with the Southern white man, who is his next door neighbor, I would say: "Cast down your bucket where you are"—cast it down in making friends in every manly way of the people of all races by whom we are surrounded.

Cast it down in agriculture, mechanics, in commerce, in domestic service, and in the professions. And in this connection it is well to bear in mind that whatever other sins the South may be called to bear, when it comes to business, pure and simple, it is in the South that the Negro is given a man's chance in the commercial world, and in nothing is this Exposition more eloquent than in emphasizing this chance. Our greatest danger is that in the great leap from slavery to freedom we may overlook the fact that the masses of us are to live by the productions of our hands, and fail to keep in mind that we shall prosper in proportion as we learn to dignify and glorify common labor, and put brains and skill into the common occupations of life; shall prosper in proportion as we learn to draw the line between the superficial and the substantial, the ornamental gewgaws of life and the useful. No race can prosper till it learns that there is as much dignity in tilling a field as in writing a poem. It is at the bottom of life we must begin, and not at the top. Nor should we permit our grievances to overshadow our opportunities.

To those of the white race who look to the incoming of those of foreign birth and strange tongue and habits for the prosperity of the South, were I permitted I would repeat what I say to my own race, "Cast down your bucket where you are." Cast it down among the 8,000,000 Negroes whose habits you know, whose fidelity and love you have tested in days when to have proved treacherous meant the ruin of your firesides. Cast down your bucket among these people who have, without strikes and labor wars, tilled your fields, cleared your forests, builded your railroads and cities, and brought forth treasures from the bowels of the earth, and helped make possible this magnificent representation of the progress of the South. Casting down your bucket among my people, helping and encouraging them as you are doing on these grounds, and, with education of head, hand and heart, you will find that they will buy your surplus land, make blossom the waste places in your fields, and run your factories. While doing this, you can be sure in the future, as in the past, that you and your families will be surrounded by the most patient, faithful, law-abiding, and unresentful people that the world has seen. As we have proved our loyalty to you in the past, in nursing your children, watching by the sick bed of your mothers and fathers, and often following them with tear-dimmed eyes to their graves, so in the future, in our humble way, we shall stand by you with a devotion that no foreigner can approach, ready to lay down our lives, if need be, in defense of yours, interlacing our industrial, commercial, civil, and religious life with yours in a way that shall make the interests of both races one. In all things that are purely social we can be as separate as the fingers, yet one as the hand in all things essential to mutual progress.

There is no defense or security for any of us except in the highest intelligence and development of all. If anywhere there are efforts tending to curtail the fullest growth of the Negro, let these efforts be turned into stimulating, encouraging, and making him the most useful and intelligent citizen. Effort or means so invested will pay a thousand per cent interest. These efforts will be twice blessed—blessing him that gives and him that takes.

There is no escape through law of man or God from the inevitable:

> The laws of changeless justice bind
> Oppressor with oppressed;
> And close as sin and suffering joined
> We march to fate abreast.

Nearly sixteen millions of hands will aid you in pulling the load upwards, or they will pull against you the load downwards. We shall constitute one-third and more of the ignorance and crime of the South, or one-third its intelligence and progress; we shall contribute one-third to the business and industrial prosperity of the South, or we shall prove a veritable body of death, stagnating, depressing, retarding every effort to advance the body politic.

Gentlemen of the Exposition, as we present to you our humble effort at an exhibition of our progress, you must not expect overmuch. Starting thirty years ago with ownership here and there in a few quilts and pumpkins and chickens (gathered from miscellaneous sources), remember the path that has led from these to the invention and production of agricultural implements, buggies, steam engines, newspapers, books, statuary, carving, paintings, the management of drug stores and banks has not been trodden without contact with thorns and thistles. While we take pride in what we exhibit as a result of our independent efforts, we do not for a moment forget that our part in this exhibition would fall short of your expectations but for the constant help that has come to our educational life, not only from the Southern States, but especially from Northern philanthropists, who have made their gifts a constant stream of blessing and encouragement.

The wisest among my race understand that the agitation of questions of social equality is the extremest folly, and that progress in the enjoyment of all the privileges that will come to us must be the result of severe and constant struggle rather than of artificial forcing. No race that has anything to contribute to the markets of the world is long in any degree ostracized. It is important and right that all privileges of the law be ours, but it is vastly more important that we be prepared for the exercise of those privileges. The opportunity to earn a dollar in a factory just now is worth infinitely more than the opportunity to spend a dollar in an opera house.

In conclusion, may I repeat that nothing in thirty years has given us more hope and encouragement, and drawn us so near to you of the white race, as this opportunity offered by the Exposition; and here bending, as it were, over the altar that represents the results of the struggles of your race and mine, both starting practically empty-handed three decades ago, I pledge that, in your effort to work out the great and intricate problem which God has laid at the doors of the South, you shall have at all times the patient, sympathetic help of my race; only let this be constantly in mind that, while from representations in these buildings of the products of field, of forest, of mine, of factory, letters, and art, much good will come, yet far above and beyond material benefits will be the higher good, that let us pray God will come, in a blotting out of sectional differences and racial animosities and suspicions, in a determination to administer absolute justice, in a willing obedience among all classes to the mandates of law. This, coupled with our material prosperity, will bring into our beloved South a new heaven and a new earth.

—BOOKER T. WASHINGTON, "The Atlanta Address," 1895

5. "MR. WASHINGTON REPRESENTS THE OLD ATTITUDE OF SUBMISSION"

At the beginning of the century the young W. E. B. Du Bois, trained at Harvard and Berlin, challenged the Washingtonian program of compromise and concession. It was folly, said Du Bois, to suppose that Negroes could ever win either economic security or social equality or achieve self-respect. Du Bois first attacked Washington openly in his essay which appeared in The Souls of Black Folk *in 1903. Two years later Du Bois and his followers met at Niagara Falls to inaugurate what came to be called the Niagara Movement. "We want the Constitution of the country enforced," said the Niagara platform. "We want the Fourteenth Amendment carried out to the letter." Four years later the Niagara group with the aid of many liberals like John Dewey and Jane Addams founded the National Association for the Advancement of Colored People.*

Of Mr. Booker T. Washington

EASILY the most striking thing in the history of the American Negro since 1876 is the ascendancy of Mr. Booker T. Washington. It began at the time when war memories and ideals were rapidly passing; a day of astonishing commercial development was dawning; a sense of doubt and hesitation overtook the freedmen's sons,—then it was that his leading began. Mr. Washington came, with a single definite programme, at the psychological moment when the nation was a little ashamed of having bestowed so much sentiment on Negroes, and was concentrating its energies on Dollars. His programme of industrial education, conciliation of the South, and submission and silence as to civil and political rights, was not wholly original; the Free Negroes from 1830 up to war-time had striven to build industrial schools, and the American Missionary Association had from the first taught various trades; and Price and others had sought a way of honorable alliance with the best of the Southerners. But Mr. Washington first indissolubly linked these things; he put enthusiasm, unlimited energy, and perfect

754

faith into this programme, and changed it from a by-path into a veritable Way of Life. And the tale of the methods by which he did this is a fascinating study of human life.

It startled the nation to hear a Negro advocating such a programme after many decades of bitter complaint; it startled and won the applause of the South, it interested and won the admiration of the North; and after a confused murmur of protest, it silenced if it did not convert the Negroes themselves.

To gain the sympathy and cooperation of the various elements comprising the white South was Mr. Washington's first task; and this, at the time Tuskegee was founded, seemed, for a black man, well-nigh impossible. And yet ten years later it was done in the word spoken at Atlanta: "In all things purely social we can be as separate as the five fingers, and yet one as the hand in all things essential to mutual progress." This "Atlanta Compromise" is by all odds the most notable thing in Mr. Washington's career. The South interpreted it in different ways: the radicals received it as a complete surrender of the demand for civil and political equality; the conservatives, as a generously conceived working basis for mutual understanding. So both approved it, and to-day its author is certainly the most distinguished Southerner since Jefferson Davis, and the one with the largest personal following.

Next to this achievement comes Mr. Washington's work in gaining place and consideration in the North. Others less shrewd and tactful had formerly essayed to sit on these two stools and had fallen between them; but as Mr. Washington knew the heart of the South from birth and training, so by singular insight he intuitively grasped the spirit of the age which was dominating the North. And so thoroughly did he learn the speech and thought of triumphant commercialism, and the ideals of material prosperity, that the picture of a lone black boy poring over a French grammar amid the weeds and dirt of a neglected home soon seemed to him the acme of absurdities. One wonders what Socrates and St. Francis of Assisi would say to this.

And yet this very singleness of vision and thorough oneness with his age is a mark of the successful man. It is as though Nature must needs make men narrow in order to give them force. So Mr. Washington's cult has gained unquestioning followers, his work has wonderfully prospered, his friends are legion, and his enemies are confounded. To-day he stands as the one recognized spokesman of his ten million fellows, and one of the most notable figures in a nation of seventy millions.

One hesitates, therefore, to criticise a life which, beginning with so little, has done so much. And yet the time is come when one may speak in all sincerity and utter courtesy of the mistakes and shortcomings of Mr. Washington's career, as well as of his triumphs, without being thought captious or envious, and without forgetting that it is easier to do ill than well in the world.

The criticism that has hitherto met Mr. Washington has not always been of this broad character. In the South especially has he had to walk warily to avoid the harshest judgments,—and naturally so, for he is dealing with the one subject of deepest sensitiveness to that section. Twice—once when at the Chicago celebration of the Spanish-American War he alluded to the color-prejudice that is "eating away the vitals of the South," and once when he dined with President Roosevelt—has the resulting Southern criticism been violent enough to threaten seriously his popularity. In the North the feeling has several times forced itself into words, that Mr. Washington's counsels of submission overlooked certain elements of true manhood, and that his educational programme was unnecessarily narrow. Usually, however, such criticism has not found open expression, although, too, the spiritual sons of the Abolitionists have not been prepared to acknowledge that the schools founded before Tuskegee, by men of broad ideals and self-sacrificing spirit, were wholly failures or worthy of ridicule. While, then, criticism has not failed to follow Mr. Washington, yet the prevailing public opinion of the land has been but too willing to deliver the solution of a wearisome problem into his hands, and say, "If that is all you and your race ask, take it."

Among his own people, however, Mr. Washington has encountered the strongest and most lasting opposition, amounting at times to bitterness, and even to-day continuing strong and insistent even though largely silenced in outward expression by the public opinion of the nation. Some of this opposition is, of course, mere envy; the disappointment of displaced demagogues and the spite of narrow minds. But aside from this, there is among educated and thoughtful colored men in all parts of the land a feeling of deep regret, sorrow, and apprehension at the wide currency and ascendancy which some of Mr. Washington's theories have gained. These same men admire his sincerity of purpose, and are willing to forgive much to honest endeavor which is doing something worth the doing. They cooperate with Mr. Washington as far as they conscientiously can; and, indeed, it is no ordinary tribute to this man's tact and power that, steering as he must between so many diverse interests and opinions, he so largely retains the respect of all.

But the hushing of the criticism of honest opponents is a dangerous thing. It leads some of the best of the critics to unfortunate silence and paralysis of effort, and others to burst into speech so passionately and intemperately as to lose listeners. Honest and earnest criticism from those whose interests are most nearly touched,—criticism of writers by readers, of government by those governed, of leaders by those led,—this is the soul of democracy and the safeguard of modern society. If the best of the American Negroes receive by outer pressure a leader whom they had not recognized before, manifestly there is here a certain palpable gain. Yet there is also irreparable loss,—a loss of that peculiarly valuable education which a group receives when by search and criticism it finds and commissions its own leaders. The way in which this is done is at once the most elementary and the nicest problem of social growth. History is but the record of such group-leadership; and yet how infinitely changeful is its type and character! And of all types and kinds, what can be more instructive than the leadership of a group within a group?— that curious double movement where real progress may be negative and actual advance be relative retrogression. All this is the social student's inspiration and despair.

Now in the past the American Negro has had instructive experience in the choosing of group leaders, founding thus a peculiar dynasty which in the light of present conditions is worth while studying. When sticks and stones and beasts form the sole environment of a people, their attitude is largely one of determined opposition to and conquest of natural forces. But when to earth and brute is added an environment of men and ideas, then the attitude of the imprisoned group may take three main forms,—a feeling of revolt and revenge; an attempt to adjust all thought and action to the will of the greater group; or, finally, a determined effort at self-realization and self-development despite environing opinion. The influence of all of these attitudes at various times can be traced in the history of the American Negro, and in the evolution of his successive leaders. . . .

Then came the Revolution of 1876, the suppression of the Negro votes, the changing and shifting of ideals, and the seeking of new lights in the great night. Douglass, in his old age, still bravely stood for the ideals of his early manhood,—ultimate assimilation *through* self-assertion, and on no other terms. For a time Price arose as a new leader, destined, it seemed, not to give up, but to re-state the old ideals in a form less repugnant to the white South. But he passed away in his prime. Then came the new leader. Nearly all the former ones had become leaders by the silent suffrage of their fellows, had sought to lead their own people alone, and were usually, save Douglass, little known outside their race. But Booker T. Washington arose as essentially the leader not of one race but of two,—a compromiser between the South, the North, and the Negro. Naturally the Negroes resented, at first bitterly, signs of compromise which surrendered their civil and political rights, even though this was to be exchanged for larger chances of economic development. The rich and dominating North, however, was not only weary of the race problem, but was investing largely in Southern enterprises, and welcomed any method of peaceful cooperation. Thus, by national opinion, the Negroes began to recognize Mr. Washington's leadership; and the voice of criticism was hushed.

Mr. Washington represents in Negro thought the old attitude of adjustment and submission; but adjustment at such a peculiar time as to make his programme unique. This is an age of unusual economic development, and Mr. Washington's programme naturally takes an economic cast, becoming a gospel of Work and Money to such an extent as apparently almost completely to overshadow the higher aims of life. Moreover, this is an age when the more advanced races are coming in closer contact with the less developed races, and the race-feeling is therefore intensified; and Mr. Washington's programme practically accepts the alleged inferiority of the Negro races. Again, in our own land, the reaction from the sentiment of war time has given impetus to race-prejudice against Negroes, and Mr. Washington withdraws many of the high demands of Negroes as men and American citizens. In other periods of intensified prejudice all the Negro's tendency to self-assertion has been called forth; at this period a policy of submission is advocated. In the history of nearly all other races and peoples the doctrine preached at such crises has been that manly self-respect is worth more than lands and houses, and that a people who voluntarily surrender such respect, or cease striving for it, are not worth civilizing.

In answer to this, it has been claimed that the Negro can survive only through submission. Mr. Washington distinctly asks that black people give up, at least for the present, three things,—

First, political power,

Second, insistence on civil rights,

Third, higher education of Negro youth,—

and concentrate all their energies on industrial education, the accumulation of wealth, and the conciliation of the South. This policy has been courageously and insistently advocated for over fifteen years, and has been triumphant for perhaps ten years. As a result of this tender of the palm-branch, what has been the return? In these years there have occurred:

1. The disfranchisement of the Negro.

2. The legal creation of a distinct status of civil inferiority for the Negro.

3. The steady withdrawal of aid from institutions for the higher training of the Negro.

These movements are not, to be sure, direct results of Mr. Washington's teachings; but his propaganda has, without a shadow of doubt, helped their speedier accomplishment. The question then comes: Is it possible, and probable, that nine millions of men can make effective progress in economic lines if they are deprived of political rights, made a servile caste, and allowed only the most meagre chance for developing their exceptional men? If history and reason give any distinct answer to these questions, it is an emphatic *No.* And Mr. Washington thus faces the triple paradox of his career:

1. He is striving nobly to make Negro artisans business men and property-owners; but it is utterly impossible, under modern competitive methods, for workingmen and property-owners to defend their rights and exist without the right of suffrage.

2. He insists on thrift and self-respect, but at the same time counsels a silent submission to civic inferiority such as is bound to sap the manhood of any race in the long run.

3. He advocates common-school and industrial training, and depreciates institutions of higher learning; but neither the Negro commonschools, nor Tuskegee itself, could remain open a day were it not for teachers trained in Negro colleges, or trained by their graduates.

—W. E. B. Du Bois, *The Souls of Black Folk*, 1903

6. "SEPARATE BUT EQUAL"

The case of Plessy versus Ferguson in 1896 wrote finis to the judicial nullification of the Congressional program designed to guarantee equal rights to Negroes. By accepting—or inventing—the doctrine of separate

*but equal accommodations, it threw the mantle of judicial approval over
segregation. Almost sixty years later it was to be reversed in the famous
case of Brown versus Topeka. We give here not only the decision of
Justice Brown but the historic dissenting opinion by Justice Harlan.*

BROWN, J. This case turns upon the constitutionality of an act of
the general assembly of the state of Louisiana, passed in 1890, providing for separate railway carriages for the white and colored races. . . .

The constitutionality of this act is attacked upon the ground that it
conflicts both with the 13th Amendment of the Constitution, abolishing
slavery, and the 14th Amendment, which prohibits certain restrictive
legislation on the part of the states.

1. That it does not conflict with the 13th Amendment, which abolished
slavery and involuntary servitude, except as a punishment for crime,
is too clear for argument. . . .

A statute which implies merely a legal distinction between the white
and colored races—a distinction which is founded in the color of the
two races, and which must always exist so long as white men are distinguished from the other race by color—has no tendency to destroy the
legal equality of the two races, or re-establish a state of involuntary
servitude. Indeed, we do not understand that the 13th Amendment is
strenuously relied upon by the plaintiff in error in this connection. . . .

The object of the amendment was undoubtedly to enforce the absolute
equality of the two races before the law, but in the nature of things
it could not have been intended to abolish distinctions based upon
color, or to enforce social, as distinguished from political, equality, or a
commingling of the two races upon terms unsatisfactory to either. Laws
permitting, and even requiring, their separation in places where they
are liable to be brought into contact do not necessarily imply the inferiority of either race to the other, and have been generally, if not
universally, recognized as within the competency of the state legislatures
in the exercise of their police power. The most common instance of this
is connected with the establishment of separate schools for white and
colored children, which have been held to be a valid exercise of the
legislative power even by courts of states where the political rights of
the colored race have been longest and most earnestly enforced. . . .

It is claimed by the plaintiff in error that, in any mixed community, the reputation of belonging to the dominant race, in this instance the white race, is *property,* in the same sense that a right of action, or of inheritance, is property. Conceding this to be so, for the purposes of this case, we are unable to see how this statute deprives him of, or in any way affects his right to, such property. If he be a white man and assigned to a colored coach, he may have his action for damages against the company for being deprived of his so-called property. Upon the other hand, if he be a colored man and be so assigned, he has been deprived of no property, since he is not lawfully entitled to the reputation of being a white man. . . .

So far, then, as a conflict with the 14th Amendment is concerned, the case reduces itself to the question whether the statute of Louisiana is a reasonable regulation, and with respect to this there must necessarily be a large discretion on the part of the legislature. In determining the question of reasonableness it is at liberty to act with reference to the established usages, customs, and traditions of the people, and with a view to the promotion of their comfort, and the preservation of the public peace and good order. Gauged by this standard, we cannot say that a law which authorizes or even requires the separation of the two races in public conveyances is unreasonable or more obnoxious to the 14th Amendment than the acts of Congress requiring separate schools for colored children in the District of Columbia, the constitutionality of which does not seem to have been questioned, or the corresponding acts of state legislatures.

We consider the underlying fallacy of the plaintiff's argument to consist in the assumption that the enforced separation of the two races stamps the colored race with a badge of inferiority. If this be so, it is not by reason of anything found in the act, but solely because the colored race chooses to put that construction upon it. The argument necessarily assumes that if, as has been more than once the case, and is not unlikely to be so again, the colored race should become the dominant power in the state legislature, and should enact a law in precisely similar terms, it would thereby relegate the white race to an inferior position. We imagine that the white race, at least, would not acquiesce in this assumption. The argument also assumes that social prejudice may be overcome by legislation, and that equal rights cannot be secured to the Negro except by an enforced commingling of the two races. We cannot accept this proposition. If the two races are to meet on terms of social equality, it must be the result of natural affinities, a mutual appreciation of each other's merits and a voluntary consent of individuals. . . . Legislation is powerless to eradicate racial instincts or to abolish distinctions based upon physical differences, and the attempt to do so can only result in accentuating the difficulties of the present situation. If the civil and political rights of both races be equal, one cannot be inferior to the other civilly or politically. If one race be inferior to the other socially, the Constitution of the United States cannot put them upon the same plane.

HARLAN, J., dissenting. . . . In respect of civil rights, common to all citizens, the Constitution of the United States does not, I think, permit any public authority to know the race of those entitled to be protected in the enjoyment of such rights. Every true man has pride of race, and under appropriate circumstances, when the rights of others, his equals before the law, are not to be affected, it is his privilege to express such pride and to take such action based upon it as to him seems proper. But I deny that any legislative body or judicial tribunal may have regard to the race of citizens when the civil rights of those citizens are involved. Indeed such legislation as that here in question is inconsistent, not only with that equality of rights which pertains to citizenship, national and state, but with the personal liberty enjoyed by everyone within the United States. . . .

In my opinion, the judgment this day rendered will, in time, prove to be quite as pernicious as the decision made by this tribunal in the Dred Scott Case. It was adjudged in that case that the descendants of Africans who were imported into this country and sold as slaves were not included nor intended to be included under the word "citizens" in the Constitution, and could not claim any of the rights and privileges which that instrument provided for and secured to citizens of the United States; that at the time of the adoption of the Constitution they were "considered as a subordinate and inferior class of beings, who had been subjugated by the dominant race, and, whether emancipated or not, yet remained subject to their authority, and had no rights or privileges but such as those who held the power and the government might choose to grant them." The recent amendments of the Constitution, it was supposed, had eradicated these principles from our institutions. But it seems that we have yet, in some of the states, a dominant race, a superior class of citizens, which assumes to regulate the enjoyment of civil rights, common to all citizens, upon the basis of race. The present decision, it may well be apprehended, will not only stimulate aggressions, more or less brutal and irritating, upon the admitted rights of colored citizens, but will encourage the belief that it is possible, by means of state enactments, to defeat the beneficent purposes which the people of the United States had in view when they adopted the recent amendments of the Constitution, by one of which the blacks of this country were made citizens of the United States and of the states in which they respectively reside and whose privileges and immunities, as citizens, the states are forbidden to abridge. Sixty millions of whites are in no danger from the presence here of eight millions of blacks. The destinies of the two races in this country are indissolubly linked together, and the interests of both require that the common government of all shall not permit the seeds of race hate to be planted under the sanction of law. What can more certainly arouse race hate, what more certainly create and perpetuate a feeling of distrust between these races, than state enactments which in fact proceed on the ground that colored citizens are so inferior and degraded that they cannot be allowed to sit in public coaches occupied by white citizens? That, as all will admit, is the real meaning of such legislation as was enacted in Louisiana. . . .

If evils will result from the commingling of the two races upon public highways established for the benefit of all, they will be infinitely less than those that will surely come from state legislation regulating the enjoyment of civil rights upon the basis of race. We boast of the freedom enjoyed by our people above all other peoples. But it is difficult to reconcile that boast with a state of the law which, practically, puts the brand of servitude and degradation upon a large class of our fellow citizens, our equals before the law. The thin disguise of "equal" accommodations for passengers in railroad coaches will not mislead anyone, or atone for the wrong this day done. . . .

I am of opinion that the statute of Louisiana is inconsistent with the personal liberty of citizens, white and black, in that state, and hostile to both the spirit and letter of the Constitution of the United States. If laws of like character should be enacted in the several states of the Union, the effect would be in the highest degree mischievous. Slavery as an institution tolerated by law would, it is true, have disappeared from our country, but there would remain a power in the states, by sinister legislation, to interfere with the full enjoyment of the blessings of freedom; to regulate civil rights, common to all citizens, upon the basis of race; and to place in a condition of legal inferiority a large body of American citizens, now constituting a part of the political community, called the people of the United States, for whom and by whom, through representatives, our government is administered. Such a system is inconsistent with the guarantee given by the Constitution to each state of a republican form of government, and may be stricken down by Congressional action, or by the courts in the discharge of their solemn duty to maintain the supreme law of the land, anything in the Constitution or laws of any state to the contrary notwithstanding.

For the reasons stated, I am constrained to withhold my assent from the opinion and judgment of the majority.

—Opinions of HENRY BILLINGS BROWN and JOHN MARSHALL HARLAN, Plessy *v*. Ferguson, 1896.

7. "TO SECURE THESE RIGHTS"

Although born and raised in a border State, President Truman showed himself more concerned with the problem of civil rights for Negroes than any of his predecessors. In 1946 he established a committee on civil rights with a mandate to undertake a full-scale investigation of the civil rights situation and report its findings and recommendations to the President and Congress. We give here the Executive Order and an excerpt from the general introduction describing vividly the persistent denial of Negro rights.

A. EXECUTIVE ORDER 9980
DECEMBER 5, 1956

W HEREAS the preservation of civil rights guaranteed by the Constitution is essential to domestic tranquility, national security, the general welfare, and the continued existence of our free institutions, and

WHEREAS the action of individuals who take the law into their own hands and inflict summary punishment and wreak personal vengeance is subversive of our democratic system of law enforcement and public criminal justice, and gravely threatens our form of government; and

WHEREAS it is essential that all possible steps be taken to safeguard our civil rights:

Now, Therefore, by virtue of the authority vested in me as President of the United States by the Constitution and the statutes of the United States, it is hereby ordered as follows:

1. There is hereby created a committee to be known as the President's Committee on Civil Rights, which shall be composed of the following-named members, who shall serve without compensation. . . .

2. The Committee is authorized on behalf of the President to inquire into and to determine whether and in what respect current law-enforcement measures and the authority and means possessed by Federal, State, and local governments may be strengthened and improved to safeguard the civil rights of the people.

3. All executive departments and agencies of the Federal Government are authorized and directed to cooperate with the Committee in its work, and to furnish the Committee such information or the services of such persons as the Committee may require in the performance of its duties.

4. When requested by the Committee to do so, persons employed in any of the executive departments and agencies of the Federal Government shall testify before the Committee and shall make available for the use of the Committee such documents and other information as the Committee may require.

5. The Committee shall make a report of its studies to the President in writing, and shall in particular make recommendations with respect to the adoption or establishment, by legislation or otherwise, of more adequate and effective means and procedures for the protection of the civil rights of the people of the United States.

6. Upon rendition of its report to the President, the Committee shall cease to exist, unless otherwise determined by further Executive Order.

—HARRY S. TRUMAN, "To Secure These Rights," 1947

B. THE REPORT OF THE PRESIDENT'S COMMITTEE ON CIVIL RIGHTS

The United States has made remarkable progress toward the goal of universal education for its people. The number and variety of its schools and colleges are greater than ever before. Student bodies have become increasingly representative of all the different peoples who make up our population. Yet we have not finally eliminated prejudice and discrimination from the operation of either our public or our private schools and colleges. Two inadequacies are extremely serious. We have failed to provide Negroes and, to a lesser extent, other minority group members with equality of educational opportunities in our public institutions, particularly at the elementary and secondary school levels. We have allowed discrimination in the operation of many of our private institutions of higher education, particularly in the North with respect to Jewish students.

Discrimination in public schools.—The failure to give Negroes equal educational opportunities is naturally most acute in the South, where approximately 10 million Negroes live. The South is one of the poorer sections of the country and has at best only limited funds to spend on its schools. With 34.5 percent of the country's population, 17 southern states and the District of Columbia have 39.4 percent of our school children. Yet the South has only one-fifth of the taxpaying wealth of the nation. Actually, on a percentage basis, the South spends a greater share of its income on education than do the wealthier states in other parts of the country. For example, Mississippi, which has the lowest expenditure per school child of any state, is ninth in percentage of income devoted to education. A recent study showed Mississippi spending 3.41 percent of its income for education as against New York's figure of only 2.61 percent. But this meant $400 per classroom unit in Mississippi, and $4,100 in New York. Negro and white school children both suffer because of the South's basic inability to match the level of educational opportunity provided in other sections of the nation.

But it is the South's segregated school system which most directly discriminates against the Negro. This segregation is found today in 17 southern states and the District of Columbia. Poverty-stricken though it was after the close of the Civil War, the South chose to maintain two sets of public schools, one for whites and one for Negroes. With respect to education, as well as to other public services, the Committee believes that the "separate but equal" rule has not been obeyed in practice. There is a marked difference in quality between the educational opportunities offered white children and Negro children in the separate schools. Whatever test is used—expenditure per pupil, teachers' salaries, the number of pupils per teacher, transportation of students, adequacy of school buildings and educational equipment, length of school term, extent of curriculum—Negro students are invariably at a disadvantage. Opportunities for Negroes in public institutions of higher education in the South—particularly at the professional graduate school level—are severely limited.

Statistics in support of these conclusions are available. Figures provided by the United States Office of Education for the school year, 1943-44, show that the average length of the school term in the areas having separate schools was 173.5 days for whites and 164 for Negroes; the number of pupils per teacher was 28 for white and 34 for Negroes; and the average annual salary for Negro teachers was lower than that for white teachers in all but three of the 18 areas. Salary figures are as follows:

State or District of Columbia	Average annual salary of principals, supervisors, and teachers in schools for—	
	Whites	Negroes
Alabama	$1,158	$ 661
Arkansas	924	555
Delaware	1,953	1,814
Florida	3,530	970
Georgia	1,123	515
Louisiana	1,683	828
Maryland	2,085	2,002
Mississippi	1,107	342
Missouri	1,397	[1]1,590
North Carolina	1,380	1,249
Oklahoma	1,428	1,438
South Carolina	1,203	615
Tennessee	1,071	1,010
Texas	1,395	946
Virginia	1,364	1,129
District of Columbia	2,610	2,610

[1] Higher salaries due to the fact that most Negro schools are located in cities where all salaries are higher.

The South has made considerable progress in the last decade in narrowing the gap between educational opportunities afforded the white children and that afforded Negro children. For example, the gap between the length of the school year for whites and the shorter one for Negroes has been narrowed from 14.8 days in 1939-40 to 9.5 days in 1943-44. Similarly, the gap in student load per teacher in white and Negro schools has dropped from 8.5 students in 1939-40 to six students in 1943-44.

In spite of the improvement which is undoubtedly taking place, the Committee is convinced that the gap between white and Negro schools can never be completely eliminated by means of state funds alone. The cost of maintaining separate, but truly equal, school systems would seem to be utterly prohibitive in many of the southern states. It seems probable that the only means by which such a goal can finally be won will be through federal financial assistance. The extension of the federal grant-in-aid for educational purposes, already available to the land-grant colleges and, for vocational education, to the secondary school field, seems both imminent and desirable.

Whether the federal grant-in-aid should be used to support the maintenance of separate schools is an issue that the country must soon face.

In the North, segregation in education is not formal, and in some states is prohibited. Nevertheless, the existence of residential restrictions in many northern cities has had discriminatory effects on Negro education. In Chicago, for example, the schools which are most crowded and employ double shift schedules are practically all in Negro neighborhoods.

Other minorities encounter discrimination. Occasionally Indian children attending public schools in the western states are assigned to separate classrooms. Many Texas schools segregate Mexican American children in separate schools. In California segregation of Mexican American children was also practiced until recently. The combined effect of a federal court ruling, and legislative action repealing the statute under which school boards claimed authority to segregate, seems to have ended this pattern of discrimination in California schools.

Discrimination in private schools.—The second inadequacy in our present educational practices in America is the religious and racial discrimination that exists in the operation of some private educational institutions, both with respect to the admission of students and the treatment of them after admission.

The Committee is absolutely convinced of the importance of the private educational institution in a free society. It does not question the right of groups of private citizens to establish such institutions, determine their character and policies, and operate them. But it does believe that such schools immediately acquire a public character and importance. Invariably they enjoy government support, if only in the form of exemption from taxation and in the privilege of income-tax deduction extended to their benefactors. Inevitably, they render public service by training our young people for life in a democratic society. Consequently, they are possessed of a public responsibility from which there is no escape.

Leading educators assert that a careful selection in admissions practices may be necessary to insure a representative and diversified student body. Liberal arts colleges, in particular, have used this reasoning to limit the number of students enrolled from any one race or religion, as well as from any geographical section, preparatory school, or socio-economic background.

Nevertheless it is clear that there is much discrimination, based on prejudice, in admission of students to private colleges, vocational schools, and graduate schools. Since accurate statistical data is almost impossible to obtain this is difficult to prove. But competent observers are agreed that existence of this condition is widespread. Application blanks of many American colleges and universities include questions pertaining to the candidate's racial origin, religious preference, parents' birthplace, etc. In many of our northern educational institutions enrollment of Jewish students seems never to exceed certain fixed points and there is never more than a token enrollment of Negroes.

The impact of discriminatory practices in private education is illustrated by the situation in New York City. The students of the city colleges of New York are predominantly Jewish, resulting in part from the discrimination practiced by some local private institutions. These colleges have high academic standards, but graduates from them with excellent records have been repeatedly denied admission to private and nonsectarian professional schools. A Special Investigating Committee of the Council of the City of New York, recently established to examine this situation, found convincing evidence of discrimination against graduates of the city colleges by the medical schools in the city in violation of the Civil Rights Act of New York. The Investigating Committee, after questioning witnesses and examining application blanks, concluded that various professional schools tried to get information about applicants which would indicate their race, religion, or national origin for "a purpose other than judging their qualifications for admission." Jews are not alone in being affected by these practices. One witness, a member of a medical school's admission committee, admitted to a prejudice against Irish Catholics which affected his judgment. The number of Negroes attending these medical schools has been extremely low; less than 50 have been graduated from them in 25 years.

Certainly the public cannot long tolerate practices by private educational institutions which are in serious conflict with patterns of democratic life, sanctioned by the overwhelming majority of our people. By the closing of the door through bigotry and prejudice to equality of educational opportunity, the public is denied the manifold social and economic benefits that the talented individual might otherwise contribute to our society.

"To Secure These Rights," 1947

8. EQUALITY IN THE ARMED SERVICES, 1948

In 1941 President Roosevelt had banned racial discrimination in defense industries. Discrimination and segregation, however, persisted in the armed services except on bases and in small units and ships. The heroic participation of many Negroes in the war and their experience with equality in European countries made this situation intolerable. In 1948, under pressure from A. Philip Randolph, who threatened a mass civil disobedience campaign against the draft, President Truman launched a new attack on discrimination in the armed services. This proved only partially successful.

WHEREAS it is essential that there be maintained in the armed services of the United States the highest standards of democracy, with equality of treatment and opportunity for all those who serve in our country's defense:

Now, therefore, by virtue of the authority vested in me as President of the United States, by the Constitution and the statutes of the United States, and as Commander in Chief of the armed services, it is hereby ordered as follows:

1. It is hereby declared to be the policy of the President that there shall be equality of treatment and opportunity for all persons in the armed services without regard to race, color, religion or national origin. This policy shall be put into effect as rapidly as possible, having due regard to the time required to effectuate any necessary changes without impairing efficiency or morale.

2. There shall be created in the National Military Establishment an advisory committee to be known as the President's Comittee on Equality of Treatment and Opportunity in the Armed Services, which shall be composed of seven members to be designated by the President.

3. The Committee is authorized on behalf of the President to examine into the rules, procedures and practices of the armed services in order to determine in what respect such rules, procedures and practices may be altered or improved with a view to carrying out the policy of this order. The Committee shall confer and advise with the Secretary of Defense, the Secretary of the Army, the Secretary of the Navy, and the Secretary of the Air Force, and shall make such recommendations to the President and to said Secretaries as in the judgment of the Committee will effectuate the policy hereof.

4. All executive departments and agencies of the Federal Government are authorized and directed to cooperate with the Committee in its work, and to furnish the Committee such information or the services of such persons as the Committee may require in the performance of its duties. . . .

—Harry S. Truman, Executive Order 9981, 1948

9. EQUAL OPPORTUNITIES FOR ALL: TRUMAN'S CIVIL RIGHTS PROGRAM

In this notable message on February 2, 1948, President Truman called on Congress to implement the program recommended by his committee on civil rights. Although the message produced next to nothing in the way of legislation, it dramatized existing inequalities. Together with "To Secure These Rights," it helped prepare the way for public acceptance of the Supreme Court decision of 1954.

TO THE CONGRESS OF THE UNITED STATES:

IN THE state of the Union message on January 7, 1948, I spoke of five great goals toward which we should strive in our constant effort to strengthen our democracy and improve the welfare of our people. The first of these is to secure fully our essential human rights. I am now presenting to the Congress my recommendations for legislation to carry us forward toward that goal.

This Nation was founded by men and women who sought these shores that they might enjoy greater freedom and greater opportunity than they had known before. The founders of the United States proclaimed to the world the American belief that all men are created equal, and that governments are instituted to secure the inalienable rights with which all men are endowed. In the Declaration of Independence and the Constitution of the United States they eloquently expressed the aspirations of all mankind for equality and freedom.

These ideals inspired the peoples of other lands, and their practical fulfillment made the United States the hope of the oppressed everywhere. Throughout our history men and women of all colors and creeds, of all races and religions, have come to this country to escape tyranny and discrimination. Millions strong, they have helped build this democratic Nation and have constantly reinforced our devotion to the great ideals of liberty and equality. With those who preceded them, they have helped to fashion and strengthen our American faith—a faith that can be simply stated:

We believe that all men are created equal and that they have the right to equal justice under law.

We believe that all men have the right to freedom of thought and of expression and the right to worship as they please.

We believe that all men are entitled to equal opportunities for jobs, for homes, for good health, and for education.

We believe that all men should have a voice in their government, and that government should protect, not usurp, the rights of the people.

These are the basic civil rights which are the source and the support of our democracy.

Today the American people enjoy more freedom and opportunity than ever before. Never in our history has there been better reason to hope for the complete realization of the ideals of liberty and equality.

We shall not, however, finally achieve the ideals for which this Nation was founded so long as any American suffers discrimination as a result of his race, or religion, or color, or the land of origin of his forefathers.

Unfortunately there still are examples—flagrant examples—of discrimination which are utterly contrary to our ideals. Not all groups of our population are free from the fear of violence. Not all groups are free to live and work where they please or to improve their conditions of life by their own efforts. Not all groups enjoy the full privileges of citizenship and participation in the Government under which they live.

We cannot be satisfied until all our people have equal opportunities for jobs, for homes, for education, for health, and for political expression, and until all our people have equal protection under the law. . . .

The protection of civil rights is the duty of every government which derives its powers from the consent of the people. This is equally true of local, State, and National Governments. There is much that the States can and should do at this time to extend their protection of civil rights. Wherever the law-enforcement measures of State and local governments are inadequate to discharge this primary function of government, these measures should be strengthened and improved.

The Federal Government has a clear duty to see that constitutional guaranties of individual liberties and of equal protection under the laws are not denied or abridged anywhere in our Union. That duty is shared by all three branches of the Government, but it can be fulfilled only if the Congress enacts modern, comprehensive civil-rights laws, adequate to the needs of the day, and demonstrating our continuing faith in the free way of life.

I recommend, therefore, that the Congress enact legislation at this session directed toward the following specific objectives:

1. Establishing a permanent Commission on Civil Rights, a Joint Congressional Committee on Civil Rights, and a Civil Rights Division in the Department of Justice.

2. Strengthening existing civil-rights statutes.

3. Providing Federal protection against lynching.

4. Protecting more adequately the right to vote.

5. Establishing a Fair Employment Practice Commission to prevent unfair discrimination in employment.

6. Prohibiting discrimination in interstate transportation facilities.

7. Providing home rule and suffrage in Presidential elections for the residents of the District of Columbia.

8. Providing statehood for Hawaii and Alaska and a greater measure of self-government for our island possessions.

9. Equalizing the opportunities for residents of the United States to become naturalized citizens.

10. Settling the evacuation claims of Japanese-Americans. . . .

The legislation I have recommended for enactment by the Congress at the present session is a minimum program if the Federal Government is to fulfill its obligation of insuring the Constitutional guaranties of individual liberties and of equal protection under the law.

Under the authority of existing law the executive branch is taking every possible action to improve the enforcement of the civil-rights statutes and to eliminate discrimination in Federal employment, in providing Federal services and facilities, and in the armed forces.

I have already referred to the establishment of the Civil Rights Division of the Department of Justice. The Federal Bureau of Investigation will work closely with this new Division in the investigation of Federal civil-rights cases. Specialized training is being given to the Bureau's agents so that they may render more effective service in this difficult field of law enforcement.

It is the settled policy of the United States Government that there shall be no discrimination in Federal employment or in providing Federal services and facilities. Steady progress has been made toward this objective in recent years. I shall shortly issue an Executive order containing a comprehensive restatement of the Federal nondiscrimination policy, together with apropriate measures to ensure compliance.

During the recent war and in the years since its close we have made much progress toward equality of opportunity in our armed services without regard to race, color, religion, or national origin. I have instructed the Secretary of Defense to take steps to have the remaining instances of discrimination in the armed services eliminated as rapidly as possible. The personnel policies and practices of all the services in this regard will be made consistent.

I have instructed the Secretary of the Army to investigate the status of civil rights in the Panama Canal Zone with a view to eliminating such discrimination as may exist there. If legislation is necessary, I shall make appropriate recommendations to the Congress. . . .

The position of the United States in the world today makes it especially urgent that we adopt these measures to secure for all our people their essential rights.

The peoples of the world are faced with the choice of freedom or enslavement, a choice between a form of government which harnesses the state in the service of the individual and a form of government which chains the individual to the needs of the state.

We in the United States are working in company with other nations who share our desire for enduring world peace and who believe with us that, above all else, men must be free. We are striving to build a world family of nations—a world where men may live under governments of their own choosing and under laws of their own making.

As part of that endeavor, the Commission on Human Rights of the United Nations is now engaged in preparing an international bill of human rights by which the nations of the world may bind themselves by international covenant to give effect to basic human rights and fundamental freedoms. We have played a leading role in this undertaking designed to create a world order of law and justice fully protective of the rights and the dignity of the individual.

To be effective in these efforts, we must protect our civil rights so that by providing all our people with the maximum enjoyment of personal freedom and personal opportunity we shall be a stronger nation— stronger in our leadership, stronger in our moral position, stronger in the deeper satisfactions of a united citizenry.

We know that our democracy is not perfect. But we do know that it offers a fuller, freer, happier life to our people than any totalitarian nation has ever offered.

If we wish to inspire the peoples of the world whose freedom is in jeopardy, if we wish to restore hope to those who have already lost their civil liberties, if we wish to fulfill the promise that is ours, we must correct the remaining imperfections in our practice of democracy.

We know the way. We need only the will.

—HARRY S. TRUMAN, Civil Rights Message, 1948

10. "SEPARATE EDUCATIONAL FACILITIES ARE INHERENTLY UNEQUAL"

The famous case of Brown v. Board of Education, one of the landmarks of American law, tested the validity of State laws providing for racial segregation in the public schools. In it the Court reversed the doctrine of Plessy versus Ferguson, that the Fourteenth Amendment does not outlaw segregation so long as equal facilities are provided for each race. The Court here ruled that "Separate educational facilities are inherently unequal." The Court followed this ruling with another on May 31, 1955, which established the principle that desegregation must proceed with "all deliberate speed" and assigned to the lower courts the responsibility for applying this principle. These rulings inaugurated a sub-

stantial revolution in the legal status of Negroes not only in the field of education but in other areas as well. We give here the first and historic opinion.

WARREN, C. J. These cases come to us from the States of Kansas, South Carolina, Virginia, and Delaware. They are premised on different facts and different local conditions, but a common legal question justifies their consideration together in this consolidated opinion.

In each of the cases, minors of the Negro race, through their legal representatives, seek the aid of the courts in obtaining admission to the public schools of their community on a nonsegregated basis. In each instance, they have been denied admission to schools attended by white children under laws requiring or permitting segregation according to race. This segregation was alleged to deprive the plaintiffs of the equal protection of the laws under the Fourteenth Amendment. In each of the cases other than the Delaware case, a three-judge federal district court denied relief to the plaintiffs on the so-called "separate but equal" doctrine announced by this Court in Plessy v. Ferguson. Under that doctrine, equality of treatment is accorded when the races are provided substantially equal facilities, even though these facilities be separate. In the Delaware case, the Supreme Court of Delaware adhered to that doctrine, but ordered that the plaintiffs be admitted to the white schools because of their superiority to the Negro schools.

The plaintiffs contend that segregated public schools are not "equal" and cannot be made "equal," and that hence they are deprived of the equal protection of the laws. Because of the obvious importance of the question presented, the Court took jurisdiction. Argument was heard in the 1952 term, and re-argument was heard this term on certain questions propounded by the Court.

Re-argument was largely devoted to the circumstances surrounding the adoption of the Fourteenth Amendment in 1868. It covered exhaustively consideration of the Amendment in Congress, ratification by the states, then existing practices in racial segregation, and the views of proponents and opponents of the Amendment. This discussion and our own investigation convince us that, although these sources cast some light, it is not enough to resolve the problem with which we are faced. At best, they are inconclusive. The most avid proponents of the post-War Amendments undoubtedly intended them to remove all legal distinctions among "all persons born or naturalized in the United States." Their opponents, just as certainly, were antagonistic to both the letter and the spirit of the Amendments and wished them to have the most limited effect. What others in Congress and the state legislatures had in mind cannot be determined with any degree of certainty.

An additional reason for the inconclusive nature of the Amendment's history, with respect to segregated schools, is the status of public education at that time. In the South, the movement toward free common schools, supported by general taxation, had not yet taken hold. Education of white children was largely in the hands of private groups. Education of Negroes was almost nonexistent, and practically all of the race were illiterate. In fact, any education of Negroes was forbidden by law in some states. Today, in contrast, many Negroes have achieved outstanding success in the arts and sciences as well as in the business and professional world. It is true that public education had already advanced further in the North, but the effect of the Amendment on Northern States was generally ignored in the congressional debates. Even in the North, the conditions of public education did not approximate those existing today. The curriculum was usually rudimentary; ungraded schools were common in rural areas; the school term was but three months a year in many states; and compulsory school attendance was virtually unknown. As a consequence, it is not surprising that there should be so little in the history of the Fourteenth Amendment relating to its intended effect on public education.

In the first cases in this Court construing the Fourteenth Amendment, decided shortly after its adoption, the Court interpreted it as proscribing all state-imposed discriminations against the Negro race. The doctrine of "separate but equal" did not make its appearance in this Court until 1896 in the case of Plessy v. Ferguson, supra, involving not education but transportation. American courts have since labored with the doctrine for over half a century. In this Court, there have been six cases involving the "separate but equal" doctrine in the field of public education. In Cumming v. Board of Education and Gong Lum v. Rice, the validity of the doctrine itself was not challenged. In more recent cases, all on the graduate school level, inequality was found in that specific benefits enjoyed by white students were denied to Negro students of the same educational qualifications. In none of these cases was it necessary to re-examine the doctrine to grant relief to the Negro plaintiff. And in

Sweatt v. Painter, the Court expressly reserved decision on the question whether Plessy v. Ferguson should be held inapplicable to public education.

In the instant cases, that question is directly presented. Here, unlike Sweatt v. Painter, there are findings below that the Negro and white schools involved have been equalized, or are being equalized, with respect to buildings, curricula, qualifications and salaries of teachers, and other "tangible" factors. Our decision, therefore, cannot turn on merely a comparison of these tangible factors in the Negro and white schools involved in each of the cases. We must look instead to the effect of segregation itself on public education.

In approaching this problem, we cannot turn the clock back to 1868 when the Amendment was adopted, or even to 1896 when Plessy v. Ferguson was written. We must consider public education in the light of its full development and its present place in American life throughout the Nation. Only in this way can it be determined if segregation in public schools deprives these plaintiffs of the equal protection of the laws.

Today, education is perhaps the most important function of state and local governments. Compulsory school attendance laws and the great expenditures for education both demonstrate our recognition of the importance of education to our democratic society. It is required in the performance of our most basic public responsibilities, even service in the armed forces. It is the very foundation of good citizenship. Today it is a principal instrument in awakening the child to cultural values, in preparing him for later professional training, and in helping him to adjust normally to his environment. In these days, it is doubtful that any child may reasonably be expected to succeed in life if he is denied the opportunity of an education. Such an opportunity, where the state has undertaken to provide it, is a right which must be made available to all on equal terms.

We come then to the question presented: Does segregation of children in public schools solely on the basis of race, even though the physical facilities and other "tangible" factors may be equal, deprive the children of the minority group of equal educational opportunities? We believe that it does.

In Sweatt v. Painter, in finding that a segregated law school for Negroes could not provide them equal educational opportunities, this Court relied in large part on "those qualities which are incapable of objective measurement but which make for greatness in a law school."

In McLaurin v. Oklahoma State Regents, the Court, in requiring that a Negro admitted to a white graduate school be treated like all other students, again resorted to intangible considerations: ". . . his ability to study, to engage in discussions and exchange views with other students, and, in general, to learn his profession." Such considerations apply with added force to children in grade and high schools. To separate them from others of similar age and qualifications solely because of their race generates a feeling of inferiority as to their status in the community that may affect their hearts and minds in a way unlikely ever to be undone. The effect of this separation on their educational opportunities was well stated by a finding in the Kansas case by a court which nevertheless felt compelled to rule against the Negro plaintiffs:

Segregation of white and colored children in public schools has a detrimental effect upon the colored children. The impact is greater when it has the sanction of the law; for the policy of separating the races is usually interpreted as denoting the inferiority of the Negro group. A sense of inferiority affects the motivation of a child to learn. Segregation with the sanction of law, therefore, has a tendency to retard the educational and mental development of Negro children and to deprive them of some of the benefits they would receive in a racially integrated school system.

Whatever may have been the extent of psychological knowledge at the time of Plessy v. Ferguson, this finding is amply supported by modern authority. Any language in Plessy v. Ferguson contrary to this finding is rejected.

We conclude that in the field of public education the doctrine of "separate but equal" has no place. Separate educational facilities are inherently unequal. Therefore, we hold that the plaintiffs and others similarly situated for whom the actions have been brought are, by reason of the segregation complained of, deprived of the equal protection of the laws guaranteed by the Fourteenth Amendment. This disposition makes unnecessary any discussion whether such segregation also violates the Due Process Clause of the Fourteenth Amendment.

Because these are class actions, because of the wide applicability of this decision, and because of the great variety of local conditions, the formulation of decrees in these cases presents problems of considerable complexity. On re-argument, the consideration of appropriate relief was necessarily subordinated to the primary question—the constitutionality of segregation in public education. We have now announced that such segregation is a denial of the equal protection of the laws. In order that

we may have the full assistance of the parties in formulating decrees, the cases will be restored to the docket, and the parties are requested to present further argument. . . . The Attorney General of the United States is again invited to participate. The Attorneys General of the states requiring or permitting segregation in public education will also be permitted to appear as *amici curiae* upon request to do so by September 15, 1954, and submission of briefs by October 1, 1954.
It is so ordered.

—CHIEF JUSTICE EARL WARREN

11. "BROWN *v.* TOPEKA IS A NAKED EXERCISE
OF JUDICIAL POWER"

Though the Supreme Court directed that integration proceed "with all deliberate speed," the deliberateness was far more conspicuous than the speed. There was at first some disposition to acquiesce in the judicial mandate, but opposition grew and hardened, and hastily organized White Citizens Councils conspired to frustrate the operation of the Brown Decision. On March 12, 1956, ninety-six Southern Congressmen —it was practically unanimous—issued a Declaration denouncing the Supreme Court decision as a violation of the Constitution, calling on their States to refuse obedience to it, and pledging themselves to resist it "by all lawful means."

W E REGARD the decision of the Supreme Court in the school cases as clear abuse of judicial power. It climaxes a trend in the Federal judiciary undertaking to legislate, in derogation of the authority of Congress, and to encroach upon the reserved rights of the states and the people.

The original Constitution does not mention education. Neither does the Fourteenth Amendment nor any other amendment. The debates preceding the submission of the Fourteenth Amendment clearly show that there was no intent that it should affect the systems of education maintained by the states.

The very Congress which proposed the amendment subsequently provided for segregated schools in the District of Columbia.

When the amendment was adopted in 1868, there were thirty-seven states in the Union. Every one of the twenty-six states that had any substantial racial differences among its people either approved the operation of segregated schools already in existence or subsequently established such schools by action of the same law-making body which considered the Fourteenth Amendment.

As admitted by the Supreme Court in the public school case (Brown v. Board of Education), the doctrine of separate but equal schools "apparently originated in Roberts v. City of Boston (1849), upholding school segregation against attack as being violative of a state constitutional guarantee of equality." This constitutional doctrine began in the North —not in the South—and it was followed not only in Massachusetts but in Connecticut, New York, Illinois, Indiana, Michigan, Minnesota, New Jersey, Ohio, Pennsylvania and other northern states until they, exercising their rights as states through the constitutional processes of local self-government, changed their school systems.

In the case of Plessy v. Ferguson in 1896 the Supreme Court expressly declared that under the Fourteenth Amendment no person was denied any of his rights if the states provided separate but equal public facilities. This decision has been followed in many other cases. It is notable that the Supreme Court, speaking through Chief Justice Taft, a former President of the United States, unanimously declared in 1927 in Lum v. Rice that the "separate but equal" principle is ". . . within the discretion of the state in regulating its public schools and does not conflict with the Fourteenth Amendment."

This interpretation, restated time and again, became a part of the life of the people of many of the states and confirmed their habits, customs, traditions and way of life. It is founded on elemental humanity and common sense, for parents should not be deprived by Government of the right to direct the lives and education of their own children.

Though there has been no constitutional amendment or act of Congress changing this established legal principle almost a century old, the Supreme Court of the United States, with no legal basis for such action, undertook to exercise their naked judicial power and substituted their personal political and social ideas for the established law of the land.

This unwarranted exercise of power by the court, contrary to the Constitution, is creating chaos and confusion in the states principally affected. It is destroying the amicable relations between the white and Negro races that have been created through ninety years of patient effort by the good people of both races. It has planted hatred and suspicion where there has been heretofore friendship and understanding.

Without regard to the consent of the governed, outside agitators are threatening immediate and revolutionary changes in our public school systems. If done, this is certain to destroy the system of public education in some of the states.

With the gravest concern for the explosive and dangerous condition created by this decision and inflamed by outside meddlers:

We reaffirm our reliance on the Constitution as the fundamental law of the land.

We decry the Supreme Court's encroachments on rights reserved to the states and to the people, contrary to established law and to the Constitution.

We commend the motives of those states which have declared the intention to resist forced integration by any lawful means.

We appeal to the states and people who are not directly affected by these decisions to consider the constitutional principles involved against the time when they too, on issues vital to them, may be the victims of judicial encroachment.

Even though we constitute a minority in the present Congress, we have full faith that a majority of the American people believe in the dual system of government which has enabled us to achieve our greatness and will in time demand that the reserved rights of the states and of the people be made secure against judicial usurpation.

We pledge ourselves to use all lawful means to bring about a reversal of this decision which is contrary to the Constitution and to prevent the use of force in its implementation.

In this trying period, as we all seek to right this wrong, we appeal to our people not to be provoked by the agitators and troublemakers invading our states and to scrupulously refrain from disorder and lawless acts.

—"Southern Declaration on Integration," March 12, 1956

12. THE CIVIL RIGHTS ACT OF 1957

Eisenhower, as well as Truman, had requested legislation to provide Federal enforcement of the guarantees of civil rights written into the Constitution and expounded by the Supreme Court. This hotly contested act—the first of its kind since Reconstruction—went part way toward meeting these Presidential requests. It created a Federal Civil Rights Commission, established a Civil Rights Division in the office of the Attorney General, empowered Federal prosecutors to obtain injunctions against those who denied any citizen his rights under the Constitution, and permitted trial of offenders in contempt of these injunctions without jury in civil cases, but with jury in criminal cases.

A N ACT to provide means of further securing and protecting the civil rights of persons within the jurisdiction of the United States.

PART I—ESTABLISHMENT OF THE COMMISSION ON CIVIL RIGHTS

SEC. 101. (a) There is created in the executive branch of the Government a Commission on Civil Rights (hereinafter called the "commission").

(b) The commission shall be composed of six members who shall be appointed by the President by and with the advice and consent of the Senate. Not more than three of the members shall at any one time be of the same political party.

(c) The President shall designate one of the members of the commission as chairman and one as vice chairman. The vice chairman shall act as chairman in the absence or disability of the chairman, or in the event of a vacancy in that office.

(d) Any vacancy in the commission shall not affect its powers and shall be filled in the same manner, and subject to the same limitation with respect to party affiliations as the original appointment was made.

(e) Four members of the commission shall constitute a quorum.

RULES OF PROCEDURE OF THE COMMISSION

SEC. 102. (e) If the commission determines that evidence or testimony at any hearing may tend to defame, degrade or incriminate any person, it shall (1) receive such evidence or testimony in executive session; (2) afford such person an opportunity voluntarily to appear as a witness; and (3) receive and dispose of requests from such person to subpoena additional witnesses.

(g) No evidence or testimony taken in executive session may be released or used in public sessions without the consent of the commission. Whoever releases or uses in public without the consent of the commission evidence or testimony taken in executive session shall be fined not more than $1,000, or imprisoned for not more than one year.

(h) In the discretion of the commission, witnesses may submit brief and pertinent sworn statements in writing for inclusion in the record. The commission is the sole judge of the pertinency of testimony and evidence adduced at its hearings.

(i) Upon payment of the cost thereof, a witness may obtain a transcript copy of his testimony given at a public session or, if given at an executive session, when authorized by the commission.

DUTIES OF THE COMMISSION

SEC. 104 (a). The commission shall—

(1) Investigate allegations in writing under oath or affirmation that certain citizens of the United States are being deprived of their right to vote and have that vote counted by reason of their color, race, religion or national origin; which writing, under oath or affirmation, shall set forth the facts upon which such belief or beliefs are based.

(2) Study and collect information concerning legal developments constituting a denial of equal protection of the laws under the Constitution; and

(3) Appraise the laws and policies of the Federal Government with respect to equal protection of the laws under the Constitution.

(b) The commission shall submit interim reports to the President (3) and to the congress at such times as either the commission or the President shall deem desirable and shall submit to the President (4) and to the Congress a final and comprehensive report of its activities, findings, and recommendations not later than two years from the date of the enactment of this act.

(c) Sixty days after the submission of its final report and recommendations the commission shall cease to exist.

POWERS OF THE COMMISSION

SEC. 105 (a) (5). There shall be a full-time staff director for the commission who shall be appointed by the President by and with the advice and consent of the Senate and who shall receive compensation at a rate, to be fixed by the President, not in excess of $22,500 a year. The President shall consult with the commission before submitting the nomination of any person for appointment to the position of staff director. Within the limitations of its appropriations, the commission may appoint (6) such other personnel as it deems advisable, in accordance with the civil service and classification laws . . .

(b) The commission shall not accept or utilize services of voluntary or uncompensated personnel . . .

(c) The commission may constitute such advisory committees (i) within states composed of citizens of that state and may consult with governors, attorneys general and other representatives of state and local governments, and private organizations, as it deems advisable.

(e) All Federal agencies shall cooperate fully with the commission to the end that it may effectively carry out its functions and duties.

(f) The commission, or on the authorization of the commission any subcommittee of two or more members, at least one of whom shall be of each major political party, may, for the purpose of carrying out the provisions of this act, hold such hearings and act at such times and places as the commission or such authorized subcommittee may deem advisable. Subpoenas for the attendance and testimony of witnesses or the production of written or other matter may be issued in accordance with the rules of the commission as contained in Section 102 (j) and (k) of this act, over the signature of the chairman of the commission or of such subcommittee, and may be served by any person designated by such chairman.

(g) In case of contumacy or refusal to obey a subpoena, any District Court of the United States or the United States Court of any territory or possession, or the District Court of the United States for the District of Columbia, within the jurisdiction of which the inquiry is carried on or within the jurisdiction of which said person guilty of contumacy or refusal to obey is found or resides or transacts business, upon application by the Attorney General of the United States shall have jurisdiction to issue to such person an order requiring such person to appear before the commission or a subcommittee thereof, there to produce evidence if so ordered, or there to give testimony touching the matter under investigation; and any failure to obey such order of the court may be punished by said court as a contempt thereof.

Part II—To Provide for an Additional Assistant Attorney General

Sec. III. There shall be in the Department of Justice one additional assistant attorney general, who shall be appointed by the President, by and with the advice and consent of the Senate, who shall assist the Attorney General in the performance of his duties, and who shall receive compensation at the rate prescribed by law for other assistant attorneys general.

Part IV—To Provide Means of Further Securing and Protecting the Right to Vote

Sec. 131. (c) Add, immediately following the present text, (13) four new subsections to read as follows:

(b) No person, whether acting under color of law or otherwise, shall intimidate, threaten, coerce or attempt to intimidate, threaten or coerce any other person for the purpose of interfering with the right of such other person to vote or to vote as he may choose, or of causing such other person to vote for, or not to vote for, any candidate for the office of President, Vice President, Presidential elector, member of the Senate or member of the House of Representatives, delegates or commissioners from the territories or possessions, at any general, special, or primary election held solely or in part for the purpose of selecting or electing any such candidate.

(c) Whenever any person has engaged or there are reasonable grounds to believe that any person is about to engage in any act or practice which would deprive any other person of any right or privilege secured by subjection (a) or (b), the Attorney General may institute for the United States, or in the name of the United States, a civil action or other proper proceeding for preventive relief, including an application for a permanent or temporary injunction, restraining order, or other order. In any proceeding hereunder the United States shall be liable for costs the same as a private person.

(d) The district courts of the United States shall have jurisdiction of proceedings instituted pursuant to this section and shall exercise the same without regard to whether the party aggrieved shall have exhausted any administrative or other remedies that may be provided by law.

(e) (14) Any person cited for an alleged contempt under this act shall be allowed to make his full defense by counsel learned in the law; and the court before which he is cited or tried, or some judge thereof, shall immediately, upon his request, assign to him such counsel, not exceeding two, as he may desire, who shall have free access to him at all reasonable hours. He shall be allowed, in his defense, to make any proof that he can produce by lawful witnesses, and shall have the like process of the court to compel his witnesses to appear at his trial or hearing, as is usually granted to compel witnesses to appear on behalf of the prosecution. If such person shall be found by the court to be financially unable to provide for such counsel, it shall be the duty of the court to provide such counsel.

Part V—To Provide Trial by Jury for Proceedings to Punish Criminal Contempts of Court Growing Out of Civil Rights Cases and to Amend the Judicial Code Relating to Federal Jury Qualifications

Sec. 151. In all cases of criminal contempt arising under the provisions of this act, the accused, upon conviction, shall be punished by fine or imprisonment or both; Provided however, that in case the accused is a natural person the fine to be paid shall not exceed the sum of $1,000, nor shall imprisonment exceed the term of six months; Provided further, That in any such proceeding for criminal contempt, at the discretion of the judge, the accused may be tried with or without a jury; Provided further, however, That in the event such proceeding for criminal contempt be tried before a judge without a jury and the sentence of the court on conviction is a fine in excess of the sum of $300 or imprisonment in excess of forty-five days, the accused in said proceeding, upon demand therefor, shall be entitled to a trial de novo before a jury, which shall conform as near as may be to the practice in other criminal cases.

This section shall not apply to contempts committed in the presence of the court or so near thereto as to interfere directly with the administration of justice nor to the misbehavior, misconduct or disobedience, of any officer of the court in respect to the writs, orders, or process of the court.

Nor shall anything herein or in any other provision of law be construed to deprive courts of their power, by civil contempt proceedings, without a jury, to secure compliance with or to prevent obstruction of, as distinguished from punishment for violations of, any lawful writ, process, order, rule, decree, or command of the court in accordance with the prevailing usages of law and equity, including the power of detention. . . .

—Civil Rights Act of 1957, September 9, 1957

13. CRISIS IN LITTLE ROCK

A. The Eisenhower Address on Little Rock. September 24, 1957

With the passing of time, Southern resistance to desegregation grew and became "massive." Within a few months, in 1956, five Southern States adopted forty-two segregation measures. Georgia made it a felony for any school official to spend tax money for public schools in which the races were mixed; Mississippi made it a crime for any organization to institute desegregation proceedings in the State courts; Virginia went to the extreme of closing some of her public schools altogether. State resistance came to a head in Arkansas. In the late summer of 1957, Governor Orville Faubus called out the State National Guard under orders, not to protect Negro children in their right to attend school, but to prevent them from exercising that right. When these troops were withdrawn on order of the Federal district judge, mobs aided by the local authorities prevented Negroes from entering the local high school. On September 24, President Eisenhower ordered Federal troops to Little Rock to preserve order; at the same time he addressed the nation on the subject. The people of Arkansas responded by re-electing Faubus to the governorship, and Faubus persisted in his tactics of obstruction until the following year. Eventually order was restored, the troops withdrawn, and token desegregation took place.

MY FELLOW Citizens . . . I must speak to you about the serious situation that has arisen in Little Rock. . . . In that city, under the leadership of demagogic extremists, disorderly mobs have deliberately prevented the carrying out of proper orders from a federal court. Local authorities have not eliminated that violent opposition and, under the law, I yesterday issued a proclamation calling upon the mob to disperse.

This morning the mob again gathered in front of the Central High

School of Little Rock, obviously for the purpose of again preventing the carrying out of the court's order relating to the admission of Negro children to that school.

Whenever normal agencies prove inadequate to the task and it becomes necessary for the executive branch of the federal government to use its powers and authority to uphold federal courts, the President's responsibility is inescapable.

In accordance with that responsibility, I have today issued an Executive Order directing the use of troops under federal authority to aid in the execution of federal law at Little Rock, Arkansas. This became necessary when my Proclamation of yesterday was not observed, and the obstruction of justice still continues.

It is important that the reasons for my action be understood by all our citizens.

As you know, the Supreme Court of the United States has decided that separate public educational facilities for the races are inherently unequal and therefore compulsory school segregation laws are unconstitutional. . . .

During the past several years, many communities in our southern states have instituted public school plans for gradual progress in the enrollment and attendance of school children of all races in order to bring themselves into compliance with the law of the land.

They thus demonstrated to the world that we are a nation in which laws, not men, are supreme.

I regret to say that this truth—the cornerstone of our liberties—was not observed in this instance. . . .

Here is the sequence of events in the development of the Little Rock school case.

In May of 1955, the Little Rock School Board approved a moderate plan for the gradual desegregation of the public schools in that city. It provided that a start toward integration would be made at the present term in the high school, and that the plan would be in full operation by 1963. . . . Now this Little Rock plan was challenged in the courts by some who believed that the period of time as proposed in the plan was too long.

The United States Court at Little Rock, which has supervisory responsibility under the law for the plan of desegregation in the public schools, dismissed the challenge, thus approving a gradual rather than an abrupt change from the existing system. The court found that the school board had acted in good faith in planning for a public school system free from racial discrimination.

Since that time, the court has on three separate occasions issued orders directing that the plan be carried out. All persons were instructed to refrain from interfering with the efforts of the school board to comply with the law.

Proper and sensible observance of the law then demanded the respectful obedience which the nation has a right to expect from all its people. This, unfortunately, has not been the case at Little Rock. Certain misguided persons, many of them imported into Little Rock by agitators, have insisted upon defying the law and have sought to bring it into disrepute. The orders of the court have thus been frustrated.

The very basis of our individual rights and freedoms rests upon the certainty that the President and the Executive Branch of Government will support and insure the carrying out of the decisions of the federal courts, even, when necessary with all the means at the President's command. . . .

Mob rule cannot be allowed to override the decisions of our courts.

Now, let me make it very clear that federal troops are not being used to relieve local and state authorities of their primary duty to preserve the peace and order of the community. . . .

The proper use of the powers of the Executive Branch to enforce the orders of a federal court is limited to extraordinary and compelling circumstances. Manifestly, such an extreme situation has been created in Little Rock. This challenge must be met and with such measures as will preserve to the people as a whole their lawfully protected rights in a climate permitting their free and fair exercise.

The overwhelming majority of our people in every section of the country are united in their respect for observance of the law—even in those cases where they may disagree with that law. . . .

A foundation of our American way of life is our national respect for law.

In the South, as elsewhere, citizens are keenly aware of the tremendous disservice that has been done to the people of Arkansas in the eyes of the nation, and that has been done to the nation in the eyes of the world.

At a time when we face grave situations abroad because of the hatred that communism bears toward a system of government based on human rights, it would be difficult to exaggerate the harm that is being done to the prestige and influence, and indeed to the safety, of our nation and the world.

Our enemies are gloating over this incident and using it everywhere to misrepresent our whole nation. We are portrayed as a violator of those standards of conduct which the peoples of the world united to proclaim in the Charter of the United Nations. There they affirmed "faith in fundamental human rights" and "in the dignity and worth of the human person" and they did so "without distinction as to race, sex, language or religion."

And so, with deep confidence, I call upon the citizens of the State of Arkansas to assist in bringing to an immediate end all interference with the law and its processes. If resistance to the federal court orders ceases at once, the further presence of federal troops will be unnecessary and the City of Little Rock will return to its normal habits of peace and order and a blot upon the fair name and high honor of our nation in the world will be removed.

Thus will be restored the image of America and of all its parts as one nation, indivisible, with liberty and justice for all.

—Eisenhower's Address on Little Rock, 1957

Arkansas undertook to nullify the decision of the Supreme Court as Georgia had nullified the decision of the Court in 1832. In this opinion, notable because in it each judge concurred by name, the Court resoundingly rejected a doctrine which, if permitted to stand, would have made the Constitution, in the words of Marshall, "a magnificent structure to look at but totally unfit for use."

B. COOPER *v.* AARON, 1958

OPINION of the Court by the CHIEF JUSTICE, Mr. Justice BLACK, Mr. Justice FRANKFURTER, Mr. Justice DOUGLAS, Mr. Justice BURTON, Mr. Justice CLARK, Mr. Justice HARLAN, Mr. Justice BRENNAN, and Mr. Justice WHITTAKER.

As this case reaches us it raises questions of the highest importance to the maintenance of our federal system of government. It necessarily involves a claim by the governor and legislature of a state that there is no duty on state officials to obey federal court orders resting on this Court's considered interpretation of the United States Constitution. Specifically it involves actions by the governor and legislature of Arkansas upon the premise that they are not bound by our holding in Brown v. Board of Education. . . .

On May 17, 1954, this Court decided that enforced racial segregation in the public schools of a state is a denial of the equal protection of the laws enjoined by the Fourteenth Amendment. Brown v. Board of Education.

The Court postponed, pending further argument, formulations of a decree to effectuate this decision. That decree was rendered May 31, 1955. Brown v. Board of Education, . . . [under which] the district courts were directed to require "a prompt and reasonable start toward full compliance," and to take such action as was necessary to bring about the end of racial segregation in the schools "with all deliberate speed." . . .

On May 20, 1954, three days after the first Brown opinion, the Little Rock District School Board adopted, and on May 23, 1954, made public, a statement of policy entitled "Supreme Court Decision—Segregation in the Public Schools." In this statement the Board recognized that "It is our responsibility to comply with Federal Constitutional Requirements and we intend to do so when the Supreme Court of the United States outlines the method to be followed."

Thereafter the Board undertook studies of the administrative problems confronting the transition to a desegregated public school system in Little Rock. It instructed the Superintendent of Schools to prepare a plan . . . The plan provided for desegregation at the senior high school level (grades 10 through 12) as the first stage. Desegregation at the junior high and elementary levels was to follow. It was contemplated that desegregation at the high school level would commence in the fall of 1957, and the expectation was that complete desegregation of the school system would be accomplished by 1963. . . .

While the School Board was thus going forward with its preparation for desegregating the Little Rock school system, other state authorities, in contrast, were actively pursuing a program designed to perpetuate in Arkansas, the system of racial segregation which this Court had held violated the Fourteenth Amendment. First came, in November 1956, an amendment to the State Constitution flatly commanding the Arkansas General Assembly to oppose "in every Constitutional manner the Un-Constitutional desegregation decisions of May 17, 1954 and May 31, 1955 of the United States Supreme Court," Ark. Const. Amend. 44, and, through the initiative, a pupil assignment law. Pursuant to this state constitutional command, a law relieving school children from compulsory attendance at racially mixed schools, was enacted by the General Assembly in February, 1957. . . .

On September 2, 1957, the day before these Negro students were to enter Central High, the school authorities were met with drastic opposing action on the part of the Governor of Arkansas who dispatched units of the Akansas National Guard to the Central High School grounds, and placed the school "off limits" to colored students.

The next school day was Monday, September 23, 1957. The Negro children entered the high school . . . under the protection of the Little Rock Police Department and members of the Arkansas State Police. But the officers caused the children to be removed from the school during the morning because they had difficulty controlling a large and demonstrating crowd which had gathered at the high school. On September 25, however, the President of the United States dispatched federal troops to Central High School and admission of the Negro students to the school was thereby effected. Regular army troops continued at the high school until November 27, 1957. They were then replaced by federalized National Guardsmen who remained throughout the balance of the school year. Eight of the Negro students remained in attendance at the school throughout the school year.

We come now to the aspect of the proceedings presently before us. On February 20, 1958, the School Board and the Superintendent of Schools filed a petition in the District Court seeking a postponement of their program of desegregation. Their position in essence was that because of extreme hostility, which they stated had been engendered largely by the official attitudes and actions of the Governor and Legislature, the maintenance of a sound educational program at Central High School, with the Negro students in attendance, would be impossible. The Board therefore proposed that the Negro students already admitted to the school be withdrawn and sent to segregated schools, and that all further steps to carry out the Board's desegregation program be postponed for a period later suggested by the Board to be two and one-half years. . . .

One may well sympathize with the position of the Board in the face of the frustrating conditions which have confronted it, but regardless of the Board's good faith, the actions of the other state agencies responsible for those conditions compel us to reject the Board's legal position. . . .

The constitutional rights of respondents are not to be sacrificed or yielded to the violence and disorder which have followed upon the actions of the Governor and Legislature. . . .

. . . the constitutional rights of children not to be discriminated against in school admission on grounds of race or color declared by this Court in the Brown case can neither be nullified openly and directly by state

legislators or state executive or judicial officers, nor nullified indirectly
by them through evasive schemes for segregation whether attempted
"ingeniously or ingenuously." . . .

What has been said, in the light of the facts developed, is enough to
dispose of the case. However, we should answer the premise of the actions
of the Governor and Legislature that they are not bound by our holding
in the Brown case. It is necessary only to recall some basic constitutional
propositions which are settled doctrine.

Article VI of the Constitution makes the Constitution the "supreme
Law of the Land." In 1803, Chief Justice Marshall, speaking for a unanimous Court, referring to the Constitution as "the fundamental and paramount law of the nation," declared in the notable case of Marbury v.
Madison that "It is emphatically the province and duty of the judicial
department to say what the law is." This decision declared the basic
principle that the federal judiciary is supreme in the exposition of the
law of the Constitution, and that principle has ever since been respected
by this Court and the country as a permanent and indispensable feature
of our constitutional system. It follows that the interpretation of the
Fourteenth Amendment enunciated by this Court in the Brown case is
the supreme law of the land . . .

No state legislator or executive or judicial officer can war against
the Constitution without violating his undertaking to support it . . .

It is, of course, quite true that the responsibility for public education
is primarily the concern of the states, but it is equally true that such
responsibilities, like all other state activity, must be exercised consistently
with federal constitutional requirements as they apply to state action.
The Constitution created a government dedicated to equal justice under
law. The Fourteenth Amendment embodied and emphasized that ideal.
State support of segregated schools through any arrangement, management, funds, or property cannot be squared with the Amendment's
command that no state shall deny to any person within its jurisdiction
the equal protection of the laws. The right of a student not to be segregated on racial grounds in schools so maintained is indeed so fundamental and pervasive that it is embraced in the concept of due process of
law. . . . The basic decision in Brown was unanimously reached by this
Court only after the case had been briefed and twice argued and the
issue had been given the most serious consideration. Since the first Brown
opinion three new Justices have come to the Court. They are at one
with the Justices still on the Court who participated in that basic decision

as to its correctness, and that decision is now unanimously reaffirmed. The principles announced in that decision and the obedience of the states to them, according to the command of the Constitution, are indispensable for the protection of the freedoms guaranteed by our fundamental charter for all of us. Our constitutional idea of equal justice under law is thus made a living truth.

—Cooper *v.* Aaron, 1958

14. THE COURT VINDICATES THE NAACP, 1958

The NAACP had long spearheaded the struggle for Negro rights in the South. One method whereby Southern whites fought back, against the Brown and other decisions and the new program for civil rights, was a rash of laws harassing the NAACP. On the surface, these laws merely required of the NAACP—and of other organizations—full disclosure: membership lists, records, finances, and so forth. Clearly membership lists gave State and local authorities an opportunity to bring social or economic pressure on members of unpopular organizations. Though the task of weighing the interest of society in full disclosure and the interest of society in voluntary association was a difficult one, the court rightly held that the legislation was a violation of the freedom of association and therefore void.

HARLAN, J. We review from the standpoint of its validity under the Federal Constitution a judgment of civil contempt entered against the National Association for the Advancement of Colored People, in the courts of Alabama. The question presented is whether Alabama, consistently with the Due Process Clause of the Fourteenth Amendment, can compel petitioner to reveal to the State's Attorney General the names and addresses of all its Alabama members and agents, without regard to their positions or functions in the Association. The judgment of contempt was based upon petitioner's refusal to comply fully with a court order requiring in part the production of membership lists. Petitioner's claim is that the order, in the circumstances shown by this record, violated rights assured to petitioner and its members under the Constitution. . . .

Petitioner produced substantially all the data called for . . . except its membership lists, as to which it contended that Alabama could not constitutionally compel disclosure. . . .

The Association both urges that it is constitutionally entitled to resist official inquiry into its membership lists, and that it may assert, on behalf of its members, a right personal to them to be protected from compelled disclosure by the State of their affiliation with the Association as revealed by the membership lists. We think that petitioner argues more appropriately the rights of its members, and that its nexus with them is sufficient to permit that it act as their representative before this Court. In so concluding, we reject respondent's argument that the Association lacks standing to assert here constitutional rights pertaining to the members, who are not of course parties to the litigation. . . .

If petitioner's rank-and-file members are constitutionally entitled to withhold their connection with the Association despite the production order, it is manifest that this right is properly assertable by the Association. To require that it be claimed by the members themselves would result in nullification of the right at the very moment of its assertion. . . .

We thus reach petitioner's claim that the production order in the state litigation trespasses upon fundamental freedoms protected by the Due Process Clause of the Fourteenth Amendment. Petitioner argues that in view of the facts and circumstances shown in the record, the effect of compelled disclosure of the membership lists will be to abridge the rights of its rank-and-file members to engage in lawful association in support of their common beliefs. It contends that governmental action which, although not directly suppressing association, nevertheless carries this consequence, can be justified only upon some overriding valid interest of the State.

Effective advocacy of both public and private points of view, particularly controversial ones, is undeniably enhanced by group association, as this Court has more than once recognized by remarking upon the close nexus between the freedoms of speech and assembly.

It is beyond debate that freedom to engage in association for the advancement of beliefs and ideas is an inseparable aspect of the "liberty" assured by the Due Process Clause of the Fourteenth Amendment, which embraces freedom of speech. [Cites cases] Of course, it is immaterial whether the beliefs sought to be advanced by association pertain to political, economic, religious or cultural matters, and state action which may have the effect of curtailing the freedom to associate is subject to the closest scrutiny.

The fact that Alabama, so far as is relevant to the validity of the contempt judgment presently under review, has taken no direct action to restrict the right of petitioner's members to associate freely, does not end inquiry into the effect of the production order. In the domain of these indispensable liberties, whether of speech, press, or association, the decisions of this Court recognize that abridgement of such rights, even though unintended, may inevitably follow from varied forms of governmental action. . . .

It is hardly a novel perception that compelled disclosure of affiliation with groups engaged in advocacy may constitute as effective a restraint on freedom of association as the forms of governmental action in the cases above were thought likely to produce upon the particular constitutional rights there involved. This Court has recognized the vital relationship between freedom to associate and privacy in one's associations. When referring to the varied forms of governmental action which might interfere with freedom of assembly, it said in American Communications Ass'n v. Douds, "A requirement that adherents of particular religious faiths or political parties wear identifying arm-bands, for example, is obviously of this nature." Compelled disclosure of membership in an organization engaged in advocacy of particular beliefs is of the same order. Inviolability of privacy in group association may in many circumstances be indispensable to preservation of freedom of association, particularly where a group espouses dissident beliefs.

We think that the production order, in the respects here drawn in question, must be regarded as entailing the likelihood of a substantial restraint upon the exercise by petitioner's members of their right to freedom of association. Petitioner has made an uncontroverted showing that on past occasions revelation of the identity of its rank-and-file members has exposed these members to economic reprisals, loss of employment, threat of physical coercion, and other manifestations of public hostility. . . .

It is not sufficient to answer, as the State does here, that whatever repressive effect compulsory disclosure of names of petitioner's members may have upon participation by Alabama citizens in petitioner's activities follows not from *state* action but from *private* community pressures. The crucial factor is the interplay of governmental and private action, for it is only after the initial exertion of state power represented by the production order that private action takes hold. . . .

—JUSTICE JOHN MARSHALL HARLAN,
Opinion in NAACP *v.* Alabama, 1958

15. CRISIS IN MONTGOMERY: THE NEGRO TAKES OVER

During the decade of the fifties a new, more vigorous, and more resourceful group of young Negroes seized the leadership of the movement for Negro rights. Chief among these was the Reverend Martin Luther King, Jr., a graduate of Morehouse College, Crozier Theological Seminary, with a doctor's degree from Boston University. The Reverend King early came under the influence of the great Indian leader Mahatma Gandhi, and saw the possibilities of combining Gandhi's program of civil disobedience with the Christian doctrines of nonviolence. The first major test of his philosophy and of this new leadership came in Montgomery, Alabama, in the mid-1950's. The new philosophy proved effective, and, as the Reverend King tells us, "integrated buses now roll daily through the city . . . a meaning-crowded symbolism."

THE LAST half century has seen crucial changes in the life of the American Negro. The social upheavals of the two world wars, the great depression, and the spread of the automobile have made it both possible and necessary for the Negro to move away from his former isolation on the rural plantation. The decline of agriculture and the parallel growth of industry have drawn large numbers of Negroes to urban centers and brought about a gradual improvement in their economic status. New contacts have led to a broadened outlook and new possibilities for educational advance. All of these factors have conjoined to cause the Negro to take a fresh look at himself. His expanding life experiences have created within him a consciousness that he is an equal element in a larger social compound and accordingly should be given rights and privileges commensurate with his new responsibilities. Once plagued with a tragic sense of inferiority resulting from the crippling effects of slavery and segregation, the Negro has now been driven to re-evaluate himself. He has come to feel that he is somebody. His religion reveals to him that God loves all His children and that the important thing about a man is not "his specificity but his fundamentum"—not the texture of his hair or the color of his skin but his eternal worth to God. . . .

Along with the Negro's changing image of himself has come an awakening moral consciousness on the part of millions of white Americans concerning segregation. Ever since the signing of the Declaration of Independence, America has manifested a schizophrenic personality on the question of race. She has been torn between selves—a self in which she proudly professed democracy and a self in which she has sadly practiced the antithesis of democracy. The reality of segregation, like slavery, has always had to confront the ideals of democracy and Christianity. Indeed, segregation and discrimination are strange paradoxes in a nation founded on the principle that all men are created equal. This contradiction has disturbed the consciences of whites both North and South, and has caused many of them to see that segregation is basically evil.

Climaxing this process was the Supreme Court's decision outlawing segregation in the public schools. For all men of good will May 17, 1954, marked a joyous end to the long night of enforced segregation. In unequivocal language the Court affirmed that "separate but equal" facilities are inherently unequal, and that to segregate a child on the basis of his race is to deny that child equal protection of the law. This decision brought hope to millions of disinherited Negroes who had formerly dared only to dream of freedom. It further enhanced the Negro's sense of dignity and gave him even greater determination to achieve justice.

This determination of Negro Americans to win freedom from all forms of oppression springs from the same deep longing that motivates oppressed peoples all over the world. The rumblings of discontent in Asia and Africa are expressions of a quest for freedom and human dignity by people who have long been the victims of colonialism and imperialism. So in a real sense the racial crisis in America is a part of the larger world crisis.

But the numerous changes which have culminated in a new sense of dignity on the part of the Negro are not of themselves responsible for the present crisis. If all men accepted these historical changes in good faith there would be no crisis. The crisis developed when the collective pressures to achieve fair goals for the Negro met with tenacious and determined resistance. Then the emerging new order, based on the principle of democratic equalitarianism, came face to face with the older order, based on the principles of paternalism and subordination. The crisis was not produced by outside agitators, NAACP'ers, Montgomery Protesters, or even the Supreme Court. The crisis developed, paradoxically, when the most sublime principles of American democracy—imperfectly realized for almost two centuries—began fulfilling themselves and met with the brutal resistance of forces seeking to contract and repress freedom's growth.

The resistance has risen at times to ominous proportions. Many states have reacted in open defiance. The legislative halls of the South still ring loud with such words as "interposition" and "nullification." Many public officials are using the power of their offices to defy the law of the land. Through their irresponsible actions, their inflammatory statements, and their dissemination of distortions and half-truths, they have succeeded in arousing abnormal fears and morbid antipathies within the minds of underprivileged and uneducated whites, leaving them in such a state of excitement and confusion that they are led to acts of meanness and violence that no normal person would commit.

This resistance to the emergence of the new order expresses itself in the resurgence of the Ku Klux Klan. Determined to preserve segregation at any cost, this organization employs methods that are crude and primitive. It draws its members from underprivileged groups who see in the Negro's rising status a political and economic threat. Although the Klan is impotent politically and openly denounced from all sides, it remains a dangerous force which thrives on racial and religious bigotry. Because of its past history, whenever the Klan moves there is fear of violence.

Then there are the White Citizens Councils. Since they occasionally recruit members from a higher social and economic level than the Klan, a halo of partial respectability hovers over them. But like the Klan they are determined to preserve segregation despite the law. Their weapons of threat, intimidation, and boycott are directed both against Negroes and against any whites who stand for justice. They demand absolute conformity from whites and abject submission from Negroes. The Citizens Councils often argue piously that they abhor violence, but their defiance of the law, their unethical methods, and their vitriolic public pronouncements inevitably create the atmosphere in which violence thrives. . . .

As in other social crises the defenders of the status quo in the South argue that they were gradually solving their own problems until external pressure was brought to bear upon them. The familiar complaint in the South today is that the Supreme Court's decision on education has set us back a generation in race relations, that people of different races who had long lived at peace have now been turned against one another. But this is a misinterpretation of what is taking place. When a subject people moves toward freedom, they are not creating a cleavage, but are revealing the cleavage which apologists of the old order have sought to conceal. It is not the movement for integration which is creating a cleavage in the United States today. The depth of the cleavage that existed, the true nature of which the moderates failed to see and make clear, is being revealed by the resistance to integration.

During a crisis period, a desperate attempt is made by the extremists to influence the minds of the liberal forces in the ruling majority. So, for example, in the present transition white Southerners attempt to convince Northern whites that the Negroes are inherently criminal. They seek instances of Negro crime and juvenile delinquency in Northern communities and then say: "You see, the Negroes are problems to you. They create problems wherever they go." The accusation is made without reference to the true nature of the situation. Environmental problems of delinquency are interpreted as evidence of racial criminality. Crises arising in Northern schools are interpreted as proofs that Negroes are inherently delinquent. The extremists do not recognize that these school problems are symptoms of urban dislocation, rather than expressions of racial deficiency. Criminality and delinquency are not racial; poverty and ignorance breed crime whatever the racial group may be.

In the attempt to influence the minds of Northern and Southern liberals, the segregationists are often subtle and skillful. Those who are too smart to argue for the validity of segregation and racial inferiority on the basis of the Bible set forth their arguments on cultural and sociological grounds. The Negro is not ready for integration, they say; because of academic and cultural lags on the part of the Negro, the integration of schools will pull the white race down. They are never honest enough to admit that the academic and cultural lags in the Negro community are themselves the result of segregation and discrimination. The best way to solve any problem is to remove its cause. It is both rationally unsound and sociologically untenable to use the tragic effects of segregation as an argument for its continuation.

All of these calculated patterns—the defiance of Southern legislative bodies, the activities of White Supremacy organizations, and the distortions and rationalizations of the segregationists—have mounted up to massive resistance. This resistance grows out of the desperate attempt of the white South to perpetuate a system of human values that came into being under a feudalistic plantation system and which cannot survive in a day of growing urbanization and industrial expansion. These are the rock-bottom elements of the present crisis. . . .

History has thrust upon our generation an indescribably important destiny—to complete a process of democratization which our nation has too long developed too slowly, but which is our most powerful weapon for world respect and emulation. How we deal with this crucial situation will determine our moral health as individuals, our cultural health as a region, our political health as a nation, and our prestige as a leader of the free world. The future of America is bound up with the solution of the present crisis. The shape of the world today does not permit us the luxury of a faltering democracy. The United States cannot hope to attain the respect of the vital and growing colored nations of the world unless it remedies its racial problems at home. If America is to remain a first-class nation, it cannot have a second-class citizenship.

The Negro himself has a decisive role to play if integration is to become a reality. Indeed, if first-class citizenship is to become a reality for the Negro he must assume the primary responsibility for making it so. Integration is not some lavish dish that the federal government or the white liberal will pass out on a silver platter while the Negro merely furnishes the appetite. One of the most damaging effects of past segregation on the personality of the Negro may well be that he has been victimized with the delusion that others should be more concerned than himself about his citizenship rights. . . .

Oppressed people deal with their oppression in three characteristic ways. One way is acquiescence: the oppressed resign themselves to their doom. They tacitly adjust themselves to oppression, and thereby become conditioned to it. In every movement toward freedom some of the oppressed prefer to remain oppressed. . . .

A second way that oppressed people sometimes deal with oppression is to resort to physical violence and corroding hatred. Violence often brings about momentary results. Nations have frequently won their independence in battle. But in spite of temporary victories, violence never brings permanent peace. It solves no social problem; it merely creates new and more complicated ones. . . .

If the American Negro and other victims of oppression succumb to the temptation of using violence in the struggle for freedom, future generations will be the recipients of a desolate night of bitterness, and our chief legacy to them will be an endless reign of meaningless chaos. Violence is not the way.

The third way open to oppressed people in their quest for freedom is the way of nonviolent resistance. Like the synthesis in Hegelian philosophy, the principle of nonviolent resistance seeks to reconcile the truths of two opposites—acquiescence and violence—while avoiding the extremes and immoralities of both. The nonviolent resister agrees with the person who acquiesces that one should not be physically aggressive toward his opponent; but he balances the equation by agreeing with the person of violence that evil must be resisted. He avoids the nonresistance of the former and the violent resistance of the latter. With nonviolent resistance, no individual or group need submit to any wrong, nor need anyone resort to violence in order to right a wrong.

It seems to me that this is the method that must guide the actions of the Negro in the present crisis in race relations. Through nonviolent resistance the Negro will be able to rise to the noble height of opposing the unjust system while loving the perpetrators of the system. The Negro must work passionately and unrelentingly for full stature as a citizen, but he must not use inferior methods to gain it. He must never come to terms with falsehood, malice, hate, or destruction.

Nonviolent resistance makes it possible for the Negro to remain in the South and struggle for his rights. The Negro's problem will not be solved by running away. He cannot listen to the glib suggestion of those who would urge him to migrate en masse to other sections of the country. By grasping his great opportunity in the South he can make a lasting contribution to the moral strength of the nation and set a sublime example of courage for generations yet unborn.

By nonviolent resistance, the Negro can also enlist all men of good will in his struggle for equality. The problem is not a purely racial one, with Negroes set against whites. In the end, it is not a struggle between people at all, but a tension between justice and injustice. Nonviolent resistance is not aimed against oppressors but against oppression. Under its banner consciences, not racial groups, are enlisted.

If the Negro is to achieve the goal of integration, he must organize himself into a militant and nonviolent mass movement. All three elements are indispensable. The movement for equality and justice can only be a success if it has both a mass and militant character; the barriers to be overcome require both. Nonviolence is an imperative in order to bring about ultimate community. . . .

Nonviolence can touch men where the law cannot reach them. When the law regulates behavior it plays an indirect part in molding public sentiment. The enforcement of the law is itself a form of peaceful persuasion. But the law needs help. The courts can order desegregation of the public schools. But what can be done to mitigate the fears, to disperse the hatred, violence and irrationality gathered around school integration, to take the initiative out of the hands of racial demagogues, to release respect for the law? In the end, for laws to be obeyed, men must believe they are right.

Here nonviolence comes in as the ultimate form of persuasion. It is the method which seeks to implement the just law by appealing to the conscience of the great decent majority who through blindness, fear, pride, or irrationality have allowed their consciences to sleep.

The nonviolent resisters can summarize their message in the following simple terms: We will take direct action against injustice without waiting for other agencies to act. We will not obey unjust laws or submit to unjust practices. We will do this peacefully, openly, cheerfully because our aim is to persuade. We adopt the means of nonviolence because our end is a community at peace with itself. We will try to persuade with our words, but if our words fail, we will try to persuade with our acts. We will always be willing to talk and seek fair compromise, but we are ready to suffer when necessary and even to risk our lives to become witnesses to the truth as we see it.

—Martin Luther King, Jr.,
"Where Do We Go from Here?," 1958

16. THE PROBLEM OF THE SIT-INS

Most of the pressure for vindicating the rights of Negroes had traditionally come from the North—and from the white community, though always with the inspiration and guidance of Negro leaders like Frederick Douglass, Booker T. Washington, W. E. B. Du Bois, and Thurgood Marshall. In the 1950's, Southern Negroes began to take matters into their own hands. In a number of cities they staged successful demonstra-

tions against segregation in streetcars and buses. In the spring of 1960, Negro students, inspired by Gandhi's passive resistance movement, began to "sit in" at lunch counters in drugstores and at shopping centers, and within a short time this "sit-in" movement had swept across the whole South. Southern authorities responded with wholesale arrests. Garner versus Louisiana, the first of these cases to reach the Supreme Court, upheld the "sit-ins" on somewhat narrow grounds, but Justice Douglas' concurring opinion, which we give here, took much broader ground. In subsequent decisions the Court tended to adopt the Douglas position on the rights of access to public facilities of all kinds.

DOUGLAS, J., concurring: If these cases had arisen in the Pacific northwest—the area I know best—I could agree with the opinion of the Court. For while many communities north and south, east and west, at times have racial problems, those areas which have never known segregation would not be inflamed or aroused by the presence of a member of a minority race in a restaurant. But in Louisiana racial problems have agitated the people since the days of slavery. The landmark case of Plessy v. Ferguson—the decision that announced in 1896 the now-repudiated doctrine of "separate but equal" facilities for whites and blacks— came from Louisiana which had enacted in 1890 a statute requiring segregation of the races on railroad trains. In the environment of a segregated community I can understand how the mere presence of a Negro at a white lunch counter might inflame some people as much as fisticuffs would in other places. For the reasons stated by Mr. Justice Harlan in these cases, I read the Louisiana opinions as meaning that this law includes "peaceful conduct of a kind that foreseeably may lead to public disturbance"— a kind of "generally known condition" that may be "judicially noticed" even in a criminal case.

It is my view that a state may not constitutionally enforce a policy of segregation in restaurant facilities. Some of the arguments assumed that restaurants are "private" property in the sense that one's home is "private" property. They are, of course, "private" property for many purposes of the Constitution. Yet so are street railways, power plants, warehouses, and other types of enterprises which have long been held to be affected with a public interest. Where constitutional rights are involved, the proprietary interests of individuals must give way. Towns, though wholly owned by private interests, perform municipal functions and are held to the same constitutional requirements as ordinary municipalities. Marsh v. State of Alabama. State regulation of private enterprise falls when it discriminates against interstate commerce. Port Richmond Ferry v. Board of Chosen Freeholders of Hudson County. State regulation of private enterprise that results in impairment of other constitutional rights should stand on no firmer footing, at least in the area where facilities of a public nature are involved.

Long before Chief Justice Waite wrote the opinion in Munn v. State of Illinois, holding that the prices charged by grain warehouses could be regulated by the state, a long list of businesses had been held to be "affected with a public interest." Among these were ferries, common carriers, hackmen, bakers, millers, wharfingers, and innkeepers. The test used in Munn v. State of Illinois was stated as follows: "Property does become clothed with a public interest when used in a manner to make it of public consequence, and affect the community at large." In reply to the charge that price regulation deprived the warehouses of property, Chief Justice Waite stated, "There is no attempt to compel these owners to grant the public an interest in their property, but to declare their obligations, if they use it in this particular manner."

There was a long span between Munn v. Illinois and Nebbia v. People of State of New York, which upheld the power of a state to fix the price of milk. A business may have a "public interest" even though it is not a "public utility" in the accepted sense, even though it enjoys no franchise from the state, and even though it enjoys no monopoly. The examples cover a wide range from price control to prohibition of certain types of business. Various systems or devices designed by states or municipalities to protect the wholesomeness of food in the interests of health are deep-seated as any exercise of the police power. Adams v. City of Milwaukee. . . .

Under Louisiana law, restaurants are a form of private property affected with a public interest. Local Boards of Health are given broad powers. The city of Baton Rouge in its City Code requires all restaurants to have a permit. The Director of Public Health is given broad powers of inspection and permits issued can be suspended. Permits are not transferable. One who operates without a permit commits a separate offense each day a violation occurs. Moreover, detailed provisions are made concerning the equipment that restaurants must have, the protection of ready-to-eat foods and drink, and the storage of food.

Restaurants, though a species of private property, are in the public domain. Or to paraphrase the opinion in Nebbia v. New York, restaurants in Louisiana have a "public consequence" and "affect the community at large."

While the concept of a business "affected with a public interest" normally is used as a measure of a state's police power over it, it also has other consequences. A state may not require segregation of the races on conventional public utilities any more than it can segregate them in ordinary public facilities. . . . It was this idea that the first Mr. Justice Harlan, dissenting in Plessy v. Ferguson, advanced. Though a common carrier is private enterprise, "its work" he maintained is public. And there can be no difference, in my view, between one kind of business that is regulated in the public interest and another kind so far as the problem of racial segregation is concerned. I do not believe that a state that licenses a business can license it to serve only whites or only blacks or only yellows or only browns. Race is an impermissible classification when it comes to parks or other municipal facilities by reason of the Equal Protection Clause of the Fourteenth Amendment. By the same token, I do not see how a state can constitutionally exercise its licensing power over business either in terms or in effect to segregate the races in the licensed premises. The authority to license a business for public use is derived from the public. Negroes are as much a part of that public as are whites. A municipality granting a license to operate a business for the public represents Negroes as well as all other races who live there. A license to establish a restaurant is a license to establish a public facility and necessarily imports, in law, equality of use for all members of the public. I see no way whereby licenses issued by a state to serve the public can be distinguished from leases of public facilities for that end.

One can close the doors of his home to anyone he desires. But one who operates an enterprise under a license from the government enjoys a privilege that derives from the people. Whether retail stores, not licensed by the municipality, stand on a different footing is not presented here. But the necessity of a license shows that the public has rights in respect to those premises. The business is not a matter of mere private concern. Those who license enterprises for public use should not have under our Constitution the power to license it for the use of only one race. For there is the overriding constitutional requirement that all state power be exercised so as not to deny equal protection to any group. As the first Mr. Justice Harlan stated in dissent in Plessy v. Ferguson, "in view of the constitution, in the eye of the law, there is in this country no superior, dominant, ruling class of citizens. There is no caste here. Our constitution is color-blind. . . ."

JUSTICE WILLIAM DOUGLAS,
Opinion in Garner *v.* Louisiana, 1961

17. POLICY AND REALITY IN NEGRO EMPLOYMENT

Back in the 1880's Frederick Douglass had made clear that without economic security the Negro would be helpless. Without economic security, Booker T. Washington added, the Negro could not hope to win political rights. Increasingly even the sharpest critics of the Douglass-Washington school of thought came to see the validity of this position. For notwithstanding the most persistent efforts to insure fair treatment in employment practices, the Negro was still almost everywhere fobbed off with the lowest paid jobs; he was the last to be hired and the first to be fired. William Peters, a Northern journalist, here describes for us how even the Federal Government lent itself to this conspiracy.

TO SEE the situation in detail, let us look first at the question of federal government employment. In principle at least, equal opportunity for federal employment has existed since the Civil Service Act of 1883, which provided for open competitive examinations, with vacancies to be filled from the three highest scorers, "with sole reference to merit and fitness." It was not, however, until 1940 that the use of photographs in applications was discontinued and the word "race" added to a general prohibition of discrimination for "political or religious opinions."

In 1941, when President Roosevelt set up his Committee on Fair Employment Practice, its duties were primarily to halt discrimination in work on defense contracts, though it also received reports from the Civil Service Commission on all complaints of discrimination in federal employment. The effectiveness of the Commission's anti-discrimination program under this arrangement can be surmised from its 1946 report to President Truman that with more than eight million placements, not to mention thousands of other personnel actions in the federal service since 1941, only 1,871 complaints of discrimination had been received. Of these a finding of discrimination had been made in exactly fifty-eight cases, an average of less than twelve per year.

In 1948, President Truman, re-emphasizing the government's policy, created a Fair Employment Practice Board within the Civil Service Commission. In 1955, President Eisenhower replaced it with his Committee on Government Employment Policy. A significant difference between the two groups is that the Truman Board, while it had, like the Eisenhower Committee, power only to recommend action to the heads of departments, was specifically ordered to report to the President any instance in which its recommendation was not "promptly and fully carried out." The present Committee is under no such stricture.

There appears to be no question today of what the government's policy is. In his order creating the Committee on Government Employment Policy, President Eisenhower stated in unmistakable language that "it is the policy of the United States Government that equal opportunity be afforded all qualified persons, consistent with law, for employment in the Federal Government," and that "this policy necessarily excludes and prohibits discrimination against any employee or applicant for employment in the Federal Government because of race, color, religion, or national origin."

Under such a policy, rigidly adhered to, it would be reasonable to expect that Negroes, widely excluded from skilled, semi-skilled, clerical, and supervisory jobs in private business and industry in the South, would turn in large numbers to the federal government, where "merit and fitness" are the only tests. This is particularly true when the wide discrepancy between white and Negro incomes in the South is considered—a discrepancy which widens sharply as educational level increases. It stands to reason that well-educated Negroes with equal access to federal government jobs in the South would be found perhaps even in disproportionately large numbers among the upper echelons of Southern federal employees.

To determine the actual situation, a number of independent studies of federal agencies in several Southern cities were made during 1958 at the instance of this writer. The results indicate with remarkable consistency that, with rare exceptions, Negroes are not employed above the level of janitorial and labor services by federal agencies in the South.

Consider, for example, Greensboro, North Carolina, a city which houses more than twenty federal agencies. Of them only two currently employ Negroes in other than menial jobs. Here, as in most places in the South, the Post Office Department is the outstanding exception. Greensboro's post office employs approximately twenty-five Negro clerks and carriers, while the Postal Transportation Service hires about a hundred Negroes as mail handlers and even has two in supervisory capacities, both as foremen on the highway post offices. The other exception is the Internal Revenue Service, where six of the approximately four hundred employees are Negroes: three working as clerks, three more as tax agents or examiners.

But the other federal agencies in Greensboro, including the Departments of Agriculture, the Air Force, the Army, Commerce, the Interior, Labor, the Navy, State, and the Treasury, as well as the offices of the U. S. Attorney, District Court, FBI, Marine Corps, U. S. Marshal, Bureau of Narcotics, Probation Office, Selective Service and Social Security Boards, Veterans Employment Service, and Weather Bureau have among them *not a single Negro employee* above the level of janitor or laborer.

In Charleston, South Carolina, where the U. S. Naval Yard provides employment for about seven thousand people and the activities and spending of the Navy Department and naval personnel constitute a major factor in the economy, the picture is not much better. For while it is true that about 40 per cent of the Naval Yard employees are Negroes, only a half dozen at most hold supervisory jobs, and some of these are supervisors in name only, since they have few, if any, employees working under them. In the entire clerical department of the Naval Yard there are exactly three Negro women typists; the civilian police department guarding this vast establishment includes a single Negro, with the rank of private.

With this kind of record, it is ironic that Charleston's Naval Yard has sometimes been cited as an example of successful integration, though it is true that some years ago eating and toilet facilities at the installation were desegregated. Yet Eli Ginzberg, in his recent book, *The Negro Potential,* records as fact the testimony of a senior naval officer in the spring of 1954. "At a regional conference on the problem of skill called by the National Manpower Council," he writes, "he reported that at the Charleston Naval Shipyard there was no longer any discrimination whatever against the Negro." The recent appraisal of an informant in a position to know is probably nearer the mark: that a token representation of Negroes in jobs other than menial ones is all that the local administrators of the Naval Yard are granting or are willing to grant.

Elsewhere in Charleston the picture is even bleaker. At Headquarters, Sixth Naval District, there is one Negro mimeograph operator and a Negro janitor. In the U. S. Customs House there are no Negroes. Above the level of janitorial and labor services there are no Negroes in Charleston's Internal Revenue Service, none in the Justice Department, none in the federal court, and none in any of the other branches of the federal judiciary. Here again the Post Office is the outstanding exception, with three or four Negro clerks, a majority of Negro carriers, but no Negroes in supervisory jobs.

The Post Office is also a major exception to the general picture in Birmingham, Alabama, with fifty-six Negro mail handlers, forty Negro clerks, and eighty-five Negro carriers. Once again, though, while intelligent, well-trained, experienced, and well-educated Negroes have frequently taken examinations for promotions above the clerk and carrier level, these promotions in Birmingham have gone only to whites. Early in 1958 a Negro clerk was assigned to the post office at Ensley, a suburb of Birmingham. When objections were raised, Post Office officials capitulated, and the man was transferred. He resigned in disgust and moved to California.

In connection with Veterans Hospitals, it should be noted that several years ago, under orders from Washington, patients in all V. A. Hospitals were integrated. The results, as in the case of the armed forces, were a vivid illustration of what could be done where there was a firm determination to apply non-discrimination policies. Overnight, for example, in the V. A. Hospital at Jackson, Mississippi, patients were moved into newly painted wards on a completely integrated basis. Within the hospital there was no difficulty. And when a bill was introduced in the 1957 special session of the Mississippi State Legislature to cancel the state's authority to donate land for a new eleven-million-dollar V. A. Hospital in Jackson, Governor J. P. Coleman warned the legislators, "There's a great movement now to build a new V. A. Hospital in Memphis, and it would be an easy thing for them to switch this hospital to Memphis if we made what they considered unreasonable restrictions." The threat of loss to the state of eleven million dollars of federal money was sufficient to stem the tide, and the Veterans Hospital in which Negroes and whites will share wards equally will remain in Jackson.

In Knoxville, Tennessee, the Departments of Agriculture, Commerce, Health, Education and Welfare, Labor, and the Treasury, as well as the FBI, Federal Housing Authority, Geological Survey, Small Business Administration, Referee in Bankruptcy, and Veterans Administration have no Negroes employed *in any capacity,* while the federal judiciary has only a single Negro court crier. Here the exceptions are the Post Office, with twenty-four Negro carriers, clerks, and custodial employees out of a work force of more than five hundred, and the Tennessee Valley Authority, with some twenty Negroes, including an assistant to the general manager, an electrical engineer, an economic statistician, and clerks, a typist, a receptionist, and a guard in addition to some forty Negroes employed as janitors, laborers, and tradesmen. Total employment with the TVA is more than fourteen hundred. With a federal payroll of more than twenty-two hundred in Knoxville, fewer than a hundred jobs are held by Negroes, even if janitorial and labor services are included.

But of all the Southern cities in which information was gathered, the most shocking results came from Atlanta, the South's largest city. They were the more shocking in view of Atlanta's record of good race relations and the fact that, where desegregation of public facilities has been accomplished—as in Atlanta's golf courses—there has been no difficulty. It is also worth noting that under Mayor William B. Hartsfield's enlightened guidance Atlanta has hired Negro policemen, two of whom were promoted to the rank of detective in 1955. In 1956, Atlanta's railroad station waiting rooms for interstate passengers were desegregated, and a year earlier the first Atlanta Arts Festival open to Negro exhibitors and spectators was held in Piedmont Park marking the park's first use for an integrated event.

Atlanta is one of the Southern cities which has elected a Negro to its school board and in which a Negro has served on the policy board of the Community Chest. Here, too, the traditional excuse that Negroes are unqualified for semi-skilled, skilled, and white collar jobs is belied by the presence of six Negro colleges which in 1958 alone handed out 573 graduate and undergraduate degrees. Here, then, is one Southern city in which the city administration and business and civic leaders have demonstrated the possibilities for progress and in which trained and educated Negroes are readily available.

Yet of more than thirty major federal agencies in Atlanta, many with numerous important subdivisions, only five have permanent Negro employees above the level of janitorial and labor services. Of these three qualify only as technical execptions: one—the Army—has a single Negro clerical worker, another—the housing agencies—has Negro race relations advisers and their secretaries (where, by definition, the jobs must be filled by Negroes), and a third—the U. S. Penitentiary—has a Negro chaplain, and Negro guards and parole officers all for work primarily with Negroes. In all Atlanta there are only two federal agencies in which Negroes can honestly be said to have been hired or promoted above menial employment on an unsegregated basis. One is the Health, Education and Welfare Department's Communicable Disease Center, where two Negro technicians and two or three Negro biologic aides are employed. The other, not surprisingly, is the Post Office, where Negroes are working as carriers, clerks, truck drivers, and mail handlers. In addition two Negroes supervise segregated departments, and two Negro sub-station superintendents serve in segregated sub-stations.

The list of federal agencies in Atlanta in which no Negroes are employed in clerical, administrative, or supervisory capacities—or, indeed, in any capacity other than janitorial and labor services—is too long to include here. . . .

This, then, is the true state of federal government employment in the South today: non-discriminatory policies are flagrantly violated and Negroes, even in the Post Office Department, are systematically excluded from higher paying, more responsible jobs for which many are qualified. How is it done? To answer that question, it is necessary to look briefly into the system of federal hiring and the complaint procedures of the President's Committee on Government Employment Policy. . . .

These failures of the federal government to give more than lip service to its own policies with regard to discrimination in employment unfortunately fit snugly into the basic strategy of Southern segregationists, making the federal executive the unwitting accomplice of the general plot on the part of segregationists to deny jobs to Southern Negroes. With this as their announced policy, Southern segregationists can hardly fail to appreciate the federal government's obvious reluctance to make its employment policies work. And if there were any doubt in the South about where the federal government stood, it would most surely be dispelled by the knowledge that segregation itself is being perpetuated by agencies of the federal government.

Throughout the South, for example, the U. S. Department of Agriculture has employed Negro county agents to advise Negro farmers on better farming practices. Not only is this county agent program segregated in the sense that Negro agents work only with Negro farmers, but with perhaps fifty exceptions, the nine hundred Negro county agents in the South have segregated officers in other parts of town from their white counterparts. Even the lines of supervision of Negro and white county agents have traditionally been separate, and where this pattern has recently begun to change, the Negro agent has invariably become the assistant to the white agent, thus effectively holding his income below that of his white colleague.

Much the same situation prevails in the case of the Agriculture Department's home demonstration agents in the South, and when one turns to soil conservation technicians the picture is even worse. Of the nearly three thousand government soil conservation technicians in the U. S., fewer than thirty are Negroes, and the proof that these few jobs are allocated on a segregated basis lies in the fact that in all the Northern states not a single Negro is employed in such a job. The same is true of the farmers' home supervisors, who in each agricultural county supervise farm loans. Of the nearly five thousand such individuals employed by the Department of Agriculture, either as supervisors or as assistants, and with a case load of nearly sixty thousand Negro farmers, there are few Negroes in these jobs—one or two in each of several Southern states at most. It is a sad corollary that most of the farm loans made to Negroes in the South are made in those few counties where there is a Negro supervisor or assistant.

This means, in plain language, that white employees of the federal government are using their offices to discriminate against Negroes in such things as the granting of government loans. And there are clear indications throughout the South today that this kind of discrimination is increasingly being aimed at Negroes outspoken in their insistence on public school desegregation, the right to vote, and other causes unpopular with the segregationists.

—WILLIAM PETERS, *The Southern Temper,* 1959

18. EQUAL RIGHTS: THE UNENDING STRUGGLE

The Deep South resisted desegregation with almost fanatical stubborn-ness, and the struggle for desegregation and for civil rights had to be fought out city by city and State by State. Negroes—and their white supporters—called for desegregation not only in schools and buses, but in public parks, swimming pools, athletic fields, in stores, restaurants, theaters. Almost every contest followed a familiar pattern. Negroes would exercise their right to equal access of public facilities; local or State authorities would arrest them on the charge of creating public disorder; then the case would go on appeal to the higher courts. In almost every instance the right of the Negro to exercise—or to agitate for the exercise of—his constitutional right, was vindicated, though often in vain, for few Southern communities were prepared to accept the judicial verdict. We give here two notable judicial decisions—the first, Wright versus Georgia, sustained the right of Negroes to use municipal parks; the second, Peterson versus Greenville, sustained the right of Negroes to service at lunch counters and struck down state ordinances requiring segregation in these and similar facilities.

A. WRIGHT *v.* GEORGIA, 1963

WARREN, C. J. Petitioners, six young Negroes, were convicted of breach of the peace for peacefully playing basketball in a public park in Savannah, Georgia, on the early afternoon of Monday, January 23, 1961. The record is devoid of evidence of any activity which a breach of the peace statute might be thought to punish. Finding that there is no adequate state ground to bar review by this Court and that the convictions are violative of due process of law secured by the Fourteenth Amendment, we hold that the judgments below must be reversed.

Only four witnesses testified at petitioners' trial: the two arresting officers, the city recreational superintendent and a sergeant of police. All were prosecution witnesses. No witness contradicted any testimony given by any other witnesses. On the day in question the petitioners were playing in a basketball court at Daffin Park, Savannah, Georgia. The park is owned and operated by the city for recreational purposes, is about 50 acres in area, and is customarily used only by whites. A white woman notified the two police officer witnesses of the presence of petitioners in the park. They investigated, according to one officer, "because some colored people were playing in the park. I did not ask this white lady how old these people were. As soon as I found out these were colored people I immediately went there." The officer also conceded that "I have never made previous arrests in Daffin Park because people played basketball there. . . . I arrested these people for playing basketball in Daffin Park. One reason was because they were negroes. I observed the conduct of these people, when they were on the basketball Court and they were doing nothing besides playing basketball, they were just normally playing basketball, and none of the children from the schools were there at that particular time." The other officer admitted that petitioners "were not necessarily creating any disorder, they were just 'shooting at the goal,' that's all they were doing, they wasn't disturbing anything." Petitioners were neat and well dressed. Nevertheless, the officers ordered the petitioners to leave the park. One petitioner asked one of the officers "by what authority" he asked them to leave; the officer responded that he "didn't need any orders to come out there. . . ." But he admitted that "it is [not] unusual for one to inquire 'why' they are being arrested. When arrested the petitioners obeyed the police orders and without disturbance entered the cruiser to be transported to police headquarters. No crowd assembled.

The recreational superintendent's testimony was confused and contradictory. In essence he testified that school children had preference in the use of the park's playground facilities but that there was no objection to use by older persons if children were not there at the time. No children were present at this time. The arrests were made at about 2 P.M. The schools released their students at 2:30 and, according to one officer, it would have been at least 30 minutes before any children could have reached the playground. The officer also stated that he did not know whether the basketball court was reserved for a particular age group and did not know the rules of the City Recreational Department. It was conceded at the trial that no signs were posted in the park indicating what areas, if any, were reserved for younger children at particular hours. In oral argument before this Court it was conceded that the regulations of the park were not printed.

The accusation charged petitioners with assembling "for the purpose of disturbing the public peace . . ." and not dispersing at the command of the officers. The jury was charged, with respect to the offense itself, only in terms of the accusation and the statute. Upon conviction five petitioners were sentenced to pay a fine of $100 or to serve five months in prison. Petitioner Wright was sentenced to pay a fine of $125 or to serve six months in prison.

Petitioners' principal contention in this Court is that the breach of the peace statute did not give adequate warning that their conduct violated that enactment in derogation of their rights under the Due Process Clause of the Fourteenth Amendment of the Constitution of the United States. . . .

Since there is some question as to whether the Georgia Supreme Court considered petitioners' claim of vagueness to have been properly raised in the demurrer we prefer to rest our jurisdiction upon a firmer foundation. We hold, for the reason set forth hereinafter, that there was no adequate state ground for the Georgia court's refusal to consider error in the denial of petitioners' motions for a new trial. . . .

Three possible bases for petitioners' convictions are suggested. First, it is said that failure to obey the command of a police officer constitutes a traditional form of breach of the peace. Obviously, however, one cannot be punished for failing to obey the command of an officer if that command is itself violative of the Constitution. The command of the officers in this case was doubly a violation of petitioners' constitutional rights. It was obviously based, according to the testimony of the arresting officers themselves, upon their intention to enforce racial discrimination in the park. For this reason the order violated the Equal Protection Clause of the Fourteenth Amendment. See New Orleans City Park Improvement Ass'n v. Detiege. . . . The command was also violative of petitioners' rights because, as will be seen, the other asserted basis for the order—the possibility of disorder by others—could not justify exclusion of the petitioners from the park. Thus petitioners could not constitutionally be convicted for refusing to obey the officers. If petitioners were held guilty of violating the Georgia statute because they disobeyed the officers, this case falls within the rule that a generally worded statute which is construed to punish conduct which cannot constitutionally be punished is unconstitutionally vague to the extent that it fails to give adequate warning of the boundary between the constitutionally permissible and constitutionally impermissible applications of the statute. . . .

Second, it is argued that petitioners were guilty of a breach of the peace because their activity was likely to cause a breach of the peace by others. The only evidence to support this contention is testimony of one of the police officers that "The purpose of asking them to leave was to keep down trouble, which looked like to me might start—there were five or six cars driving around the park at the time, white people." But that officer also stated that this "was [not] unusual traffic for that time of day." And the park was 50 acres in area. Respondent contends the petitioners were forewarned that their conduct would be held to violate the statute. . . . But it is sufficient to say again that a generally worded statute, when construed to punish conduct which cannot be constitutionally punished, is unconstitutionally vague. And the possibility of disorder by others cannot justify exclusion of persons from a place if they otherwise have a constitutional right (founded upon the Equal Protection Clause) to be present. . . .

Third, it is said that the petitioners were guilty of a breach of the peace because a park rule reserved the playground for the use of younger people at the time. However, neither the existence nor the posting of any such rule has been proved. . . . The police officers did not inform them of it because they had no knowledge of any such rule themselves. Furthermore, it is conceded that there was no sign or printed regulation which would give notice of any such rule.

Under any view of the facts alleged to constitute the violation it cannot be maintained that petitioners had adequate notice that their conduct was prohibited by the breach of the peace statute. It is well established that a conviction under a criminal enactment which does not give adequate notice that the conduct charged is prohibited is violative of due process. . . .

B. Peterson v. Greenville, 1963

WARREN, C. J. The petitioners were convicted in the Recorder's Court of the City of Greenville, South Carolina, for violating the trespass statute of that State. Each was sentenced to pay a fine of $100 or in lieu thereof to serve 30 days in jail. An appeal to the Greenville County Court was dismissed, and the Supreme Court of South Carolina affirmed. . . . We granted certiorari to consider the substantial federal questions presented by the record. . . .

The 10 petitioners are Negro boys and girls who, on August 9, 1960, entered the S. H. Kress store in Greenville and seated themselves at the lunch counter for the purpose, as they testified, of being served. When the Kress manager observed the petitioners sitting at the counter, he "had one of [his] . . . employees call the Police Department and turn off the lights and state the lunch counter closed." A captain of police and two other officers responded by proceeding to the store in a patrol car where they were met by other policemen and two state agents who had preceded them there. In the presence of the police and the state agents, the manager "announced that the lunch counter was being closed and would everyone leave" the area. The petitioners, who had been sitting at the counter for five minutes, remained seated and were promptly arrested. The boys were searched, and both boys and girls were taken to police headquarters.

The manager of the store did not request the police to arrest petitioners; he asked them to leave because integrated service was "contrary to local customs" of segregation at lunch counters and in violation of the following Greenville City ordinance requiring separation of the races in restaurants:

It shall be unlawful for any person owning, managing or controlling any hotel, restaurant, cafe, eating house, boarding-house or similar establishment to furnish meals to white persons and colored persons in the same room, or at the same table, or at the same counter; . . .

The manager and the police conceded that the petitioners were clean, well dressed, unoffensive in conduct, and that they sat quietly at the counter which was designed to accommodate 59 persons. The manager described his establishment as a national chain store of 15 or 20 departments, selling over 10,000 items. He stated that the general public was invited to do business at the store and that the patronage of Negroes was solicited in all departments of the store other than the lunch counter.

Petitioners maintain that South Carolina has denied them right of free speech, both because their activity was protected by the First and Fourteenth Amendments and because the trespass statute did not require a showing that the Kress manager gave them notice of his authority when he asked them to leave. Petitioners also assert that they have been deprived of the equal protection of the laws secured to them against state action by the Fourteenth Amendment. We need decide only the last of the questions thus raised.

The evidence in this case establishes beyond doubt that the Kress management's decision to exclude petitioners from the lunch counter was made because they were Negroes. It cannot be disputed that under our decisions "private conduct abridging individual rights does no violence to the Equal Protection Clause unless to some significant extent the State in any of its manifestations has been found to have become involved in it. . . ."

It cannot be denied that here the City of Greenville, an agency of the State, has provided by its ordinance that the decision as to whether a restaurant facility is to be operated on a desegregated basis is to be reserved to it. When the State has commanded a particular result, it has saved to itself the power to determine that result and thereby "to a significant extent" has "become involved" in it, and, in fact, has removed that decision from the sphere of private choice. It has thus effectively determined that a person owning, managing or controlling an eating place is left with no choice of his own but must segregate his white and Negro patrons. The Kress management in deciding to exclude Negroes, did precisely what the city law required.

Consequently, these convictions cannot stand, even assuming, as respondent contends, that the manager would have acted as he did independently of the existence of the ordinance. The State will not be heard to make this contention in support of the convictions. For the convictions had the effect, which the State cannot deny, of enforcing the ordinance passed by the City of Greenville, the agency of the State. When a state agency passes a law compelling persons to discriminate against other persons because of race, and the State's criminal processes are employed in a way which enforces the discrimination mandated by that law, such a palpable violation of the Fourteenth Amendment cannot be saved by attempting to separate the mental urges of the discriminators.

Reversed.

19. THE RIGHT TO VOTE: THE UNENDING STRUGGLE

With grandfather clauses and all-white party primaries outlawed, and poll taxes prohibited by constitutional amendment, Southern States resorted to new techniques to frustrate Negro voters. One of the most overt was the Louisiana requirement that in all elections the race of

*the candidate be designated on the ballot. A unanimous court held this
a violation of the Equal Protection Clause of the Fourteenth Amendment.*

CLARK, J. Appelants, residents of East Baton Rouge, Louisiana, are
Negroes. Each sought election to the School Board of that parish
in the 1962 Democratic Party primary election. Prior to the election
they filed this suit against the Secretary of State of Louisiana seeking
to enjoin the enforcement of Act 538 of the 1960 Louisiana Legislature . . . which requires the Secretary to print, in parentheses, the race
of each candidate opposite his name on all ballots. Asserting that the
statute violated, *inter alia,* the Fourteenth and Fifteenth Amendments,
appellants sought both preliminary and permanent injunctions and a
temporary restraining order. A United States district judge denied the
motion for a temporary restraining order and a three-judge court was
convened. After a hearing on the merits, the preliminary injunction was
denied with one judge dissenting. Thereafter the appellants sought to
amend their complaint so as to show that the primary election had been
held and that both appellants had been defeated because of the operation
and enforcement of the statute here under attack. They further alleged
that they "intend to be candidates in the next duly constituted democratic
primary election for nomination as members of the East Baton Rouge
Parish School Board. . . ." Leave to amend was denied by the district
judge and the three-judge court thereafter denied the request for a permanent injunction. We have concluded that the compulsory designation
by Louisiana of the race of the candidate on the ballot operates as a
discrimination against appellants and is therefore violative of the
Fourteenth Amendment's Equal Protection Clause. In view of this we
do not reach appellants' other contentions.

At the outset it is well that we point out what this case does not
involve. It has nothing whatever to do with the right of a citizen to cast
his vote for whomever he chooses and for whatever reason he pleases
or to receive all information concerning a candidate which is necessary
to a proper exercise of his franchise. It has to do only with the right of
a State to require or encourage its voters to discriminate upon the grounds
of race. In the abstract, Louisiana imposes no restriction upon anyone's
candidacy nor upon an elector's choice in the casting of his ballot. But

by placing a racial label on a candidate at the most crucial stage in the electoral process—the instant before the vote is cast—the State furnishes a vehicle by which racial prejudice may be so aroused as to operate against one group because of race and for another. This is true because by directing the citizen's attention to the single consideration of race or color, the State indicates that a candidate's race or color is an important —perhaps paramount—consideration in the citizen's choice, which may decisively influence the citizen to cast his ballot along racial lines. Hence in a State or voting district where Negroes predominate, that race is likely to be favored by a racial designation on the ballot, while in those communities where other races are in the majority, they may be preferred. The vice lies not in the resulting injury but in the placing of the power of the State behind a racial classification that induces racial prejudice at the polls.

As we said in NAACP v. Alabama . . . : "The crucial factor is the interplay of governmental and private action. . . ." Here the statute under attack prescribes the form and content of the official ballot used in all elections in Louisiana. The requirement that "[e]very application for or notification or declaration of candidacy, and every certificate of nomination and every nomination paper filed . . . shall show for each candidate named therein, whether such candidate is of the Caucasian race, the Negro race or other specified race" was not placed in the statute until 1960. Prior to that time the primary election ballot contained no information on the candidates other than their names; nor did the general election ballot, which only grouped the named candidates according to their respective political party. The 1960 amendment added "race" as the single item of information other than the name of the candidate. This addition to the statute in the light of "private attitudes and pressures" towards Negroes at the time of its enactment could only result in that "repressive effect" which "was brought to bear only after the exercise of governmental power." . . .

Nor can the attacked provision be deemed to be reasonably designed to meet legitimate governmental interests in informing the electorate as to candidates. We see no relevance in the State pointing up the race of the candidate as bearing upon his qualifications for office. Indeed, this factor in itself "underscores the purely racial character and purpose" of the statute. . . .

The State contends that its Act is nondiscriminatory because the labeling provision applies equally to Negro and white. Obviously,

Louisiana may not bar Negro citizens from offering themselves as candidates for public office, nor can it encourage its citizens to vote for a candidate solely on account of race. . . . And that which cannot be done by express statutory prohibition cannot be done by indirection. Therefore, we view the alleged equality as superficial. Race is the factor upon which the statute operates and its involvement promotes the ultimate discrimination which is sufficient to make it invalid. . . . The judgment is therefore reversed.

Reversed.

—Justice Tom Clark,
Opinion in Anderson *v.* Martin, 1964

20. THE END OF THE POLL TAX: THE TWENTY-FOURTH AMENDMENT, 1964

With the ratification of the thirty-eighth State—South Dakota—the Twenty-fourth Amendment went into effect January 23, 1964.

THE RIGHT of citizens of the United States to vote in any primary or other election for President or Vice President, or for Senator or Representative in Congress, shall not be denied or abridged by the United States or any other state by reason of failure to pay any poll tax or other tax.

—The Constitution of the United States

21. "MY DUNGEON SHOOK"

By the 1960's James Baldwin had come to be generally recognized as America's foremost Negro novelist. Long resident in Paris, where he wrote his first notable success, Giovanni's Room, *he returned to the United States in 1957 and has taken an active part in the struggle for civil rights. His most notable contribution to this crusade was "The Fire Next Time," which appeared in* The New Yorker *magazine in 1963.*

We give here a letter inspired by the centennial of the Emancipation Proclamation, which was published first in The Progressive.

DEAR JAMES:

I have begun this letter five times and torn it up five times. I keep seeing your face, which is also the face of your father and my brother. Like him, you are tough, dark, vulnerable, moody—with a very definite tendency to sound truculent because you want no one to think you are soft. You may be like your grandfather in this, I don't know, but certainly both you and your father resemble him very much physically. Well, he is dead, he never saw you, and he had a terrible life; he was defeated long before he died because, at the bottom of his heart, he really believed what white people said about him. This is one of the reasons that he became so holy. I am sure that your father has told you something about all that. Neither you nor your father exhibit any tendency towards holiness: you really *are* of another era, part of what happened when the Negro left the land and came into what the late E. Franklin Frazier called "the cities of destruction." You can only be destroyed by believing that you really are what the white world calls a *nigger*. I tell you this because I love you, and please don't you ever forget it.

I have known both of you all your lives, have carried your Daddy in my arms and on my shoulders, kissed and spanked him and watched him learn to walk. I don't know if you've known anybody from that far back; if you've loved anybody that long, first as an infant, then as a child, then as a man, you gain a strange perspective on time and human pain and effort. Other people cannot see what I see whenever I look into your father's face, for behind your father's face as it is today are all those other faces which were his. Let him laugh and I see a cellar your father does not remember and a house he does not remember and I hear in his present laughter his laughter as a child. Let him curse and I remember him falling down the cellar steps, and howling, and I remember, with pain, his tears, which my hand or your grandmother's so easily wiped away. But no one's hand can wipe away those tears he sheds invisibly today, which one hears in his laughter and in his speech and in his songs. I know what the world has done to my brother and how narrowly he has survived it. And I know, which is much worse, and this is the crime of which I accuse my country and my countrymen, and for which neither I nor time nor history will ever forgive them, that they have destroyed and are destroying hundreds of thousands of lives and do not know it and do not want to know it. One can be, indeed one must strive to become, tough and philosophical concerning destruction and death, for this is what most of mankind has been best at since we have heard of man. (But remember: *most* of mankind is not *all* of mankind.) But is it not permissible that the authors of devastation should also be innocent. It is the innocence which constitutes the crime.

Now, my dear namesake, these innocent and well-meaning people, your countrymen, have caused you to be born under conditions not very far removed from those described for us by Charles Dickens in the London of more than a hundred years ago. (I hear the chorus of the innocents screaming, "No! This is not true! How *bitter* you are!"—but I am writing this letter to *you,* to try to tell you something about how to handle *them,* for most of them do not yet really know that you exist. I *know* the conditions under which you were born, for I was there. Your countrymen were *not* there, and haven't made it yet. Your grandmother was also there, and no one has ever accused her of being bitter. I suggest that the innocents check with her. She isn't hard to find. Your countrymen don't know that *she* exists, either, though she has been working for them all their lives.)

Well, you were born, here you came, something like fifteen years ago; and though your father and mother and grandmother, looking about the streets through which they were carrying you, staring at the walls into which they brought you, had every reason to be heavyhearted, yet they were not. For here you were, Big James, named for me—you were a big baby, I was not—here you were: to be loved. To be loved, baby, hard, at once, and forever, to strengthen you against the loveless world. Remember that: I know how black it looks today, for you. It looked bad that day, too, yes, we were trembling. We have not stopped trembling yet, but if we had not loved each other none of us would have survived. And now you must survive because we love you, and for the sake of your children and your children's children.

This innocent country set you down in a ghetto in which, in fact, it intended that you should perish. Let me spell out precisely what I mean by that, for the heart of the matter is here, and the root of my dispute with my country. You were born where you were born and faced the future that you faced because you were black and *for no other reason.*

The limits of your ambition were, thus, expected to be set forever. You were born into a society which spelled out with brutal clarity, and in as many ways as possible, that you were a worthless human being. You were not expected to aspire to excellence: you were expected to make peace with mediocrity. Wherever you have turned, James, in your short time on this earth, you have been told where you could go and what you could do (and *how* you could do it) and where you could live and whom you could marry. I know your countrymen do not agree with me about this, and I hear them saying, "You exaggerate." They do not know Harlem, and I do. So do you. Take no one's word for anything, including mine—but trust your experience. Know whence you came. If you know whence you came, there is really no limit to where you can go. The details and symbols of your life have been deliberately constructed to make you believe what white people say about you. Please try to remember that what they believe, as well as what they do and cause you to endure, does not testify to your inferiority but to their inhumanity and fear. Please try to be clear, dear James, through the storm which rages about your youthful head today, about the reality which lies behind the words *acceptance* and *integration*. There is no reason for you to try to become like white people and there is no basis whatever for their impertinent assumption that *they* must accept *you*. The really terrible thing, old buddy, is that *you* must accept *them*. And I mean that very seriously. You must accept them and accept them with love. For these innocent people have no other hope. They are, in effect, still trapped in a history which they do not understand; and until they understand it, they cannot be released from it. They have had to believe for many years, and for innumerable reasons, that black men are inferior to white men. Many of them, indeed, know better, but, as you will discover, people find it very difficult to act on what they know. To act is to be committed, and to be committed is to be in danger. In this case, the danger, in the minds of most white Americans, is the loss of their identity. Try to imagine how you would feel if you woke up one morning to find the sun shining and all the stars aflame. You would be frightened because it is out of the order of nature. Any upheaval in the universe is terrifying because it so profoundly attacks one's sense of one's own reality. Well, the black man has functioned in the white man's world as a fixed star, as an immovable pillar: and as he moves out of his place, heaven and earth are shaken to their foundations. You, don't be afraid. I said that it was intended that you should perish in the ghetto, perish by never being allowed to go behind the white man's definitions, by never being allowed to spell your proper name. You have, and many of us have, defeated this intention; and, by a terrible law, a terrible paradox, those innocents who believed that your imprisonment made them safe are losing their grasp of reality. But these men are your brothers—your lost, younger brothers. And if the word *integration* means anything, this is what it means: that we, with love, shall force our brothers to see themselves as they are, to cease fleeing from reality and begin to change it. For this is your home, my friend, do not be driven from it; great men have done great things here, and will again, we can make America what America must become. It will be hard, James, but you come from sturdy, peasant stock, men who picked cotton and dammed rivers and built railroads, and, in the teeth of the most terrifying odds, achieved an unassailable and monumental dignity. You come from a long line of great poets, some of the greatest poets since Homer. One of them said, *The very time I thought I was lost, My dungeon shook and my chains fell off.*

You know, and I know, that the country is celebrating one hundred years of freedom one hundred years too soon. We cannot be free until they are free. God bless you, James, and Godspeed.

Your uncle,

James

—James Baldwin, "My Dungeon Shook: A Letter to My Nephew" from *The Fire Next Time,* 1963

22. "WE FACE A MORAL CRISIS"

No President was ever more deeply committed to the principle of equality than John F. Kennedy. This commitment, which had deep moral roots, was strengthened by the President's sense of history. He knew that the United States was in danger of forfeiting her moral— and with it her political—leadership in the free world by her policies of racism, and he was very concerned for that position. And just as Lincoln had realized that the day of slavery was over, and that world opinion would no longer tolerate it, so Kennedy realized that the day of racism was over, and that the world would no longer tolerate it. None of

Kennedy's addresses was marked by greater eloquence or passion than this plea for the enactment of a fair and just civil rights bill, delivered only a few months before his assassination.

THIS AFTERNOON, following a series of threats and defiant statements, the presence of Alabama National Guardsmen was required at the University of Alabama to carry out the final and unequivocal order of the United States District Court of the Northern District of Alabama.

That order called for the admission of two clearly qualified young Alabama residents who happened to have been born Negro.

That they were admitted peacefully on the campus is due in a good measure to the conduct of the students of the University of Alabama who met their responsibilities in a constructive way.

I hope that every American, regardless of where he lives, will stop and examine his conscience about this and other related incidents.

This nation was founded by men of many nations and backgrounds. It was founded on the principle that all men are created equal, and that the rights of every man are diminished when the rights of one man are threatened.

Today we are committed to a worldwide struggle to promote and protect the rights of all who wish to be free. And when Americans are sent to Vietnam or West Berlin we do not ask for whites only.

It ought to be possible, therefore, for American students of any color to attend any public institution they select without having to be backed up by troops. It ought to be possible for American consumers of any color to receive equal service in places of public accommodation, such as hotels and restaurants, and theaters and retail stores without being forced to resort to demonstrations in the street.

And it ought to be possible for American citizens of any color to register and to vote in a free election without interference or fear of reprisal.

It ought to be possible, in short, for every American to enjoy the privileges of being American without regard to his race or his color.

In short, every American ought to have the right to be treated as he would wish to be treated, as one would wish his children to be treated. But this is not the case.

The Negro baby born in America today, regardless of the section or the state in which he is born, has about one-half as much chance of completing high school as a white baby, born in the same place, on the same day; one-third as much chance of completing college; one-third as much chance of becoming a professional man; twice as much chance of becoming unemployed; about one-seventh as much chance of earning $10,000 a year; a life expectancy which is seven years shorter and the prospects of earning only half as much.

This is not a sectional issue. Difficulties over segregation and discrimination exist in every city, in every state of the Union, producing in many cities a rising tide of discontent that threatens the public safety.

Nor is this a partisan issue. In a time of domestic crisis, men of good will and generosity should be able to unite regardless of party or politics.

This is not even a legal or legislative issue alone. It is better to settle these matters in the courts than on the streets, and new laws are needed at every level. But law alone cannot make men see right.

We are confronted primarily with a moral issue. It is as old as the Scriptures and is as clear as the American Constitution. The heart of the question is whether all Americans are to be afforded equal rights and equal opportunities; whether we are going to treat our fellow Americans as we want to be treated.

If an American, because his skin is dark, cannot eat lunch in a restaurant open to the public; if he cannot send his children to the best public school available; if he cannot vote for the public officials who represent him; if, in short, he cannot enjoy the full and free life which all of us want, then who among us would be content to have the color of his skin changed and stand in his place?

Who among us would then be content with the counsels of patience and delay? One hundred years of delay have passed since President Lincoln freed the slaves, yet their heirs, their grandsons, are not fully free. They are not yet freed from the bonds of injustice; they are not yet freed from social and economic oppression.

And this nation, for all its hopes and all its boasts, will not be fully free until all its citizens are free.

We preach freedom around the world, and we mean it. And we cherish our freedom here at home. But are we to say to the world— and much more importantly to each other—that this is the land of the free, except for the Negroes; that we have no second-class citizens, except Negroes; that we have no class or caste system, no ghettos, no master race, except with respect to Negroes.

Now the time has come for this nation to fulfill its promise. The events in Birmingham and elsewhere have so increased the cries for equality that no city or state or legislative body can prudently choose to ignore them.

The fires of frustration and discord are burning in every city, North and South. Where legal remedies are not at hand, redress is sought in the streets in demonstrations, parades and protests, which create tensions and threaten violence—and threaten lives.

We face, therefore, a moral crisis as a country and a people. It cannot be met by repressive police action. It cannot be left to increased demonstrations in the streets. It cannot be quieted by token moves or talk. It is time to act in the Congress, in your state and local legislative body, and above all, in all of our daily lives.

It is not enough to pin the blame on others, to say this is a problem of one section of the country or another, or deplore the facts that we face. A great change is at hand, and our task, our obligation is to make that revolution, that change peaceful and constructive for all.

Those who do nothing are inviting shame as well as violence. Those who act boldly are recognizing right as well as reality.

Next week I shall ask the Congress of the United States to act, to make a commitment it has not fully made in this century to the proposition that race has no place in American life or law.

The Federal judiciary has upheld that proposition in a series of forthright cases. The Executive Branch has adopted that proposition in the conduct of its affairs, including the employment of Federal personnel, and the use of Federal facilities, and the sale of Federally financed housing.

But there are other necessary measures which only the Congress can provide, and they must be provided at this session.

The old code of equity law under which we live commands for every wrong a remedy. But in too many communities, in too many parts of the country wrongs are inflicted on Negro citizens and there are no remedies in law.

Unless the Congress acts their only remedy is the street.

I am, therefore, asking the Congress to enact legislation giving all Americans the right to be served in facilities which are open to the public—hotels, restaurants and theaters, retail stores and similar establishments. This seems to me to be an elementary right.

Its denial is an arbitrary indignity that no American in 1963 should have to endure, but many do.

I have recently met with scores of business leaders, urging them to take voluntary action to end this discrimination. And I've been encouraged by their response. And in the last two weeks over 75 cities have seen progress made in desegregating these kinds of facilities.

But many are unwilling to act alone. And for this reason nationwide legislation is needed, if we are to move this problem from the streets to the courts.

I'm also asking Congress to authorize the Federal Government to participate more fully in lawsuits designed to end segregation in public education. We have succeeded in persuading many districts to desegregate voluntarily. Dozens have admitted Negroes without violence.

Today a Negro is attending a state-supported institution in every one of our 50 states. But the pace is very slow.

Too many Negro children entering segregated grade schools at the time of the Supreme Court's decision nine years ago will enter segregated high schools this fall, having suffered a loss which can never be restored.

The lack of an adequate education denies the Negro a chance to get a decent job. The orderly implementation of the Supreme Court decision therefore, cannot be left solely to those who may not have the economic resources to carry their legal action or who may be subject to harassment.

Other features will also be requested, including greater protection for the right to vote.

But legislation, I repeat, cannot solve this problem alone. It must be solved in the homes of every American in every community across our country.

In this respect, I want to pay tribute to those citizens, North and South, who've been working in their communities to make life better for all. They are acting not out of a sense of legal duty but out of a sense of human decency. Like our soldiers and sailors in all parts of the world, they are meeting freedom's challenge on the firing line and I salute them for their honor—their courage.

My fellow Americans, this is a problem which faces us all, in every city of the North as well as the South.

Today there are Negroes unemployed, two or three times as many compared to whites, inadequate in education, moving into the large cities, unable to find work, young people particularly out of work, without hope, denied equal rights, denied the opportunity to eat at a restaurant or a lunch counter, or go to a movie theater, denied the right to a decent education, denied the right to attend a state university even though qualified.

It seems to me that these are matters which concern us all—not merely Presidents, or Congressmen, or Governors, but every citizen of the United States.

This is one country. It has become one country because all of us and all the people who came here had an equal chance to develop their talents.

We cannot say to 10 percent of the population that "you can't have that right. Your children can't have the chance to develop whatever talents they have, that the only way that they're going to get their rights is to go in the street and demonstrate."

I think we owe them and we owe ourselves a better country than that.

Therefore, I'm asking for your help in making it easier for us to move ahead and provide the kind of equality of treatment which we would want ourselves—to give a chance for every child to be educated to the limit of his talent.

As I've said before, not every child has an equal talent or an equal ability or equal motivation. But they should have the equal right to develop their talent and their ability and their motivation to make something of themselves.

We have a right to expect that the Negro community will be responsible, will uphold the law. But they have a right to expect that the law will be fair, that the Constitution will be color blind, as Justice Harlan said at the turn of the century.

This is what we're talking about. This is a matter which concerns this country and what it stands for, and in meeting it I ask the support of all of our citizens.

Thank you very much.

—John F. Kennedy, radio and television address, June, 1963

23. THE CIVIL RIGHTS ACT OF 1964

The Civil Rights Act of 1964, passed with the dynamic support of President Lyndon B. Johnson, will probably prove to have been the most far-reaching piece of legislation since the Wagner Act, and certainly the most controversial since Taft-Hartley. In addition to the provisions given below, the law contains sections prohibiting discrimination in employment, together with lengthy provisions for its own enforcement.

A N ACT to enforce the constitutional right to vote, to confer jurisdiction upon the district courts of the United States to provide injunctive relief against discrimination in public accommodations, to authorize the Attorney General to institute suits to protect constitutional rights in public facilities and public education, to extend the Commission on Civil Rights, to prevent discrimination in federally assisted programs, to establish a Commission on Equal Employment Opportunity, and for other purposes. . . .

TITLE I—VOTING RIGHTS

SEC. 101 (2). No person acting under color of law shall—

(a) in determining whether any individual is qualified under State law or laws to vote in any Federal election, apply any standard, practice, or procedure different from the standards, practices, or procedures applied under such law or laws to other individuals within the same county, parish, or similar political subdivision who have been found by State officials to be qualified to vote; . . .

(c) employ any literacy test as a qualification for voting in any Federal election unless (i) such test is administered to each individual wholly in writing; and (ii) a certified copy of the test and of the answers given by the individuals is furnished to him within twenty-five days of the submission of his request made within the period of time during which records and papers are required to be retained and preserved pursuant to title III of the Civil Rights Act of 1960. . . .

TITLE II—INJUNCTIVE RELIEF AGAINST DISCRIMINATION IN PLACES OF PUBLIC ACCOMMODATION

SEC. 201. (a) All persons shall be entitled to the full and equal enjoyment of the goods, services, facilities, privileges, advantages, and accommodations of any place of public accommodation, as defined in this section, without discrimination or segregation on the ground of race, color, religion, or national origin.

(b) Each of the following establishments which serves the public is a place of public accommodation within the meaning of this title if its operations affect commerce, or if discrimination or segregation by it is supported by State action:

(1) any inn, motel, or other establishment which provides lodging to transient guests, other than an establishment located within a building which contains not more than five rooms for rent or hire and which is actually occupied by the proprietor of such establishment as his residence;

(2) any restaurant, cafeteria, lunch room, lunch counter, soda fountain, or other facility principally enaged in selling food for consumption on the premises . . . ;

(3) any motion picture house, theater, concert hall, sports arena, stadium or other place of exhibition or entertainment. . . .

(d) Discrimination or segregation by an establishment is supported by State action within the meaning of this title if such discrimination or segregation (1) is carried on under color of any law, statute, ordinance, or regulation; or (2) is carried on under color of any custom or usage required or enforced by officials of the State or political subdivision thereof. . . .

Sec. 202. All persons shall be entitled to be free, at any establishment or place, from discrimination or segregation of any kind on the ground of race, color, religion, or national origin, if such discrimination or segregation is or purports to be required by any law, statute, ordinance, regulation, rule, or order of a State or any agency or political subdivision thereof. . . .

Sec. 206. (a) Whenever the Attorney General has reasonable cause to believe that any person or group of persons is engaged in a pattern or practice of resistance to the full enjoyment of any of the rights secured by this title, the Attorney General may bring a civil action in the appropriate district court of the United States by filing with it a complaint . . . requesting such preventive relief, including an application for a permanent or temporary injunction, restraining order or other order against the person or persons responsible for such pattern or practice, as he deems necessary to insure the full enjoyment of the rights herein described.

Title VI—Nondiscrimination in Federally Assisted Programs

Sec. 601. No person in the United States shall, on the ground of race, color, or national origin, be excluded from participation in, be denied the benefits of, or be subjected to discrimination under any program or activity receiving Federal financial assistance.

Bibliography

Chapter 1. The People

1. THE INFLUENCE OF THE NEW WORLD ON THE OLD
JOHN R. SEELEY, *The Expansion of England*. London, 1883, 87-92.

2. "THE DISINHERITED, THE DISPOSSESSED"
STEPHEN VINCENT BENÉT, *Western Star*. New York: Rinehart & Company, Inc., 1943, 20-21, 116.

3. THE INHABITANTS OF COLONIAL VIRGINIA
ROBERT BEVERLEY, *The History and Present State of Virginia* (1705), ed. by Louis B. Wright. Chapel Hill, N. C.: University of North Carolina Press, 1947, 286-88.

4. THE COMING OF THE PILGRIMS
WILLIAM BRADFORD, *Bradford's History "Of Plimoth Plantation"* (1630). Boston: Commonwealth of Massachusetts, 1899, 23-35, *passim*.

5. "THIS IS THE DOOR THOU HAST OPENED"
EDWARD JOHNSON, *Wonder-Working Providence of Sion's Savior . . . in New England* (1655), ed. by James F. Jameson. New York: Charles Scribner's Sons, 1910, 51-54, *passim*.

6. "WHAT IS AN AMERICAN?"
MICHEL-GUILLAUME JEAN DE CRÈVECOEUR, *Letters from an American Farmer*, Letter III. London, 1782 and var. eds. Reprinted in Henry Steele Commager, ed., *America in Perspective*. New York: Random House, 1947, 1 ff.

7. THE "DESPISED RACES"
ROBERT LOUIS STEVENSON, *Across the Plains*. New York, 1892, 62-68.

8. "THE SOULS OF BLACK FOLK"
W. E. BURGHARDT DU BOIS, *The Souls of Black Folk*. Chicago: A. C. McClurg & Company, 1903, 215-26, *passim*.

9. A MAP OF NEW YORK
JACOB RIIS, *How the Other Half Lives*. New York, 1890, 23 ff.

10. "I LIFT MY LAMP BESIDE THE GOLDEN DOOR"
EMMA LAZARUS, "The New Colossus" (1886), *The Poems of Emma Lazarus*. New York, 1889.

11. A TEST OF OPPORTUNITY, NOT OF CHARACTER
WOODROW WILSON, Veto of Literacy Test for Immigrants, January 28, 1915,

in Henry Steele Commager, ed., *Documents of American History*. New York: Appleton-Century-Crofts, Inc., 1950, Doc. No. 404.

12. PUTTING UP THE BARS
United States Bureau of Immigration, *Annual Report of the Commissioner-General*. Washington, 1923, in Commager, ed., *Documents of American History*, Doc. No. 422.

13. THE AMERICAN LANGUAGE
HENRY L. MENCKEN, "The American Language," *Yale Review* (Spring 1936), XXV, 538-49, *passim*.

14. "THE THREE SOUTHWESTERN PEOPLES"
PAUL HORGAN, "The Three Southwestern Peoples," in Maurice Garland Fulton and Paul Horgan, eds., *New Mexico's Own Chronicle*. Dallas: Banks Upshaw Company, 1937, 345-49.

15. THE TWENTIETH-CENTURY AMERICAN
HENRY STEELE COMMAGER, *The American Mind*. New Haven, Conn.: Yale University Press, 1950, 411-25, *passim*.

Chapter 2. The Land

1. THE SPACIOUSNESS AND DIVERSITY OF THE AMERICAN SCENE
FRANK ERNEST HILL, *What Is American?* New York: The John Day Company, Inc., 1933, 4-10, *passim*.

2. THE RHYTHM OF FLOWING WATERS
CONSTANCE LINDSAY SKINNER, "Rivers and American Folk," in Appendix to the volumes of the *Rivers of America* series. New York: Rinehart & Company, Inc., var. eds.

3. "THE EXTREME FRUITFULNESS OF THAT COUNTRY"
ROBERT BEVERLEY, *The History and Present State of Virginia* (1705), ed. by Louis B. Wright. Chapel Hill, N. C.: University of North Carolina Press, 1947, 314-19.

4. "A HIDEOUS AND DESOLATE WILDERNESS"
WILLIAM BRADFORD, *Bradford's History "Of Plimoth Plantation"* (1630) Boston: Commonwealth of Massachuetts, 1899, 94-97.

5. "AMERICAN AREAS WITHOUT A TRACE OF EUROPE'S SOIL"
WALT WHITMAN, "Specimen Days and Collect," *Complete Prose Works*. Boston, 1891, 141-44.

6. THE SIGNIFICANCE OF THE FRONTIER
FREDERICK JACKSON TURNER, "The Significance of the Frontier in American History," *Report of the American Historical Association* (1893), 199-227, *passim*.

7. A DEMOCRATIC LAND SYSTEM
　A. "THE COMMON BENEFIT OF THE UNITED STATES" Resolution of Con-

gress on Public Lands, October 10, 1780, in Henry Steele Commager, ed., *Documents of American History*. New York: Appleton-Century-Crofts, Inc., 1950, Doc. No. 75.

B. THE LAND ORDINANCE OF 1785. Land Ordinance of May 20, 1785, in *Ibid.*, Doc. No. 78.

8. A BELT OF TREES FOR THE ARID WEST

FERDINAND V. HAYDEN, Letter to the Commissioner of the General Land Office, July 1, 1867, in *Report of the Commissioner of General Land Office, for the Year 1867*. Washington, 1867, 135 ff.

9. THE ARID REGIONS OF THE WEST

JOHN WESLEY POWELL, *Report on the Lands of the Arid Region of the United States* (1879), in Commager, ed., *Documents of American History*, Doc. No. 302.

10. FORESTS, PROSPERITY, AND PROGRESS

CARL SCHURZ, *The Need of a Rational Forest Policy in the United States*. Philadelphia, 1889, 3-7.

11. "FROM PLYMOUTH ROCK TO DUCKTOWN"

STUART CHASE, *Rich Land, Poor Land: A Study of Waste in the Natural Resources of America*, New York: McGraw-Hill Book Company, Inc., Whittlesey House, 1936, 34-44, *passim*.

12. A PROGRAM OF CONSERVATION

THEODORE ROOSEVELT, Seventh Annual Message to Congress, December 3, 1907, in Commager, ed., *Documents of American History*, Doc. No. 369.

13. THE TVA AND THE SEAMLESS WEB OF NATURE

DAVID E. LILIENTHAL, *TVA, Democracy on the March*. New York: Harper & Brothers, 1944, 13-14, 25-26, 48-49, 52-53.

Chapter 3. Fundamentals of the American Political System

1. THE MAYFLOWER COMPACT

The Mayflower Compact, November 11, 1620, in Henry Steele Commager, ed., *Documents of American History*. New York: Appleton-Century-Crofts, Inc., 1950, Doc. No. 11.

2. THE FUNDAMENTAL ORDERS OF CONNECTICUT

The Fundamental Orders of Connecticut, January 14, 1639, in Commager, ed., *Documents of American History*, Doc. No. 16.

3. AN EARLY ASSERTION OF COLONIAL INDEPENDENCE

Massachusetts' Declaration of Liberties, June 10, 1661, in Commager, ed., *Documents of American History*, Doc. No. 24.

4. THE ORIGIN AND NATURE OF GOVERNMENT

JOHN LOCKE, "An Essay concerning the True Original Extent and End of

Civil Government," *Two Treatises concerning Government* (1690). Reprinted in Edwin A. Burtt, ed., *The English Philosophers from Bacon to Mill*. New York: The Modern Library, 1939, 437-61, *passim*.

5. NATURAL LAW AND DEMOCRACY
JOHN WISE, *A Vindication of the Government of New-England Churches* (1717). Boston, 1862, *passim*.

6. GOVERNMENT IS LIMITED
A. "PARLIAMENT CANNOT MAKE TWO AND TWO FIVE." JAMES OTIS, "The Rights of the British Colonies" (1764), ed. by C. F. Mullett, University of Missouri, *Studies*, Columbia, Mo., 1929, IV, 49 ff.
B. "IN ALL FREE STATES THE CONSTITUTION IS FIXED." Letters of the Massachusetts House to the British Ministry, January, 1768, in Commager, ed., *Documents of American History*, Doc. No. 44.

7. THE DECLARATION OF INDEPENDENCE
The Declaration of Independence, July 4, 1776, in Commager, ed., *Documents of American History*, Doc. No. 66.

8. REVOLUTION LEGALIZED
A. "HOW CAN THE PEOPLE INSTITUTE GOVERNMENTS?" JOHN ADAMS, "Autobiography," June 7, 1775, in Charles Francis Adams, ed., *The Works of John Adams*. Boston, 1851, III, 19-20.
B. CONCORD DEMANDS A CONSTITUTIONAL MEETING. Resolutions of the Concord Town Meeting, October 22, 1776, in Commager, ed., *Documents of American History*, Doc. No. 68.

9. THE VIRGINIA BILL OF RIGHTS
THE VIRGINIA BILL OF RIGHTS. GEORGE MASON, The Virginia Bill of Rights, June 12, 1776, in Commager, ed., *Documents of American History*, Doc. No. 67.

10. THE CONSTITUTION: PREAMBLE AND BILL OF RIGHTS
Constitution of the United States, in Commager, ed., *Documents of American History*, Doc. No. 87.

11. THE NORTHWEST ORDINANCE
The Northwest Ordinance, July 13, 1787, in Commager, ed., *Documents of American History*, Doc. No. 82.

12. THE PRINCIPLES OF EQUALITY IN AMERICAN SOCIETY
Speech of Charles Pinckney of South Carolina, June 25, 1787, in Charles C. Tansill, ed., *Documents Illustrative of the Formation of the Union of the American States*. Washington: Government Printing Office, 1927, 267-73.

13. WHAT IS A REPUBLIC?
A. "A GOVERNMENT WHICH DERIVES ALL ITS POWERS FROM THE PEOPLE." JAMES MADISON, *The Federalist*, No. 39 (1788), var. eds.
B. "IT IS REPRESENTATION INGRAFTED UPON DEMOCRACY." THOMAS PAINE, *Rights of Man; Part the Second* (1792). Reprinted in Philip S. Foner,

ed., *The Complete Writings of Thomas Paine.* New York: The Citadel Press, 1945, I, 369-72, *passim.*

14. WASHINGTON'S FAREWELL ADDRESS
GEORGE WASHINGTON, Farewell Address, September 17, 1796, in Commager, ed., *Documents of American History,* Doc. No. 100.

15. "WE ARE ALL REPUBLICANS, WE ARE ALL FEDERALISTS"
THOMAS JEFFERSON, First Inaugural Address, March 4, 1801, in Commager, ed., *Documents of American History,* Doc. No. 106.

16. "A CONSTITUTION FRAMED FOR AGES TO COME"
Opinion of Chief Justice John Marshall, Cohens *v.* Virginia, 6 Wheaton 264 (1821).

17. THE GETTYSBURG ADDRESS
ABRAHAM LINCOLN, The Gettysburg Address, November 19, 1863, in Commager, ed., *Documents of American History,* Doc. No. 228.

18. LIBERTY, THE NECESSARY CONDITION OF PROGRESS
HENRY GEORGE, *Progress and Poverty.* New York, 1879, II, 543-49, *passim.*

19. "THERE IS NOTHING MYSTERIOUS ABOUT DEMOCRACY"
Donald Porter Geddes, ed., *Franklin Delano Roosevelt, A Memorial.* New York: The Dial Press, 1945, 168-74, *passim.*

20. "THIS I DEEPLY BELIEVE"
DAVID E. LILIENTHAL, *This I Do Believe.* New York: Harper & Brothers, 1949, x-xiii.

Chapter 4. The Machinery of Government

1. HOW TO BALANCE CLASSES AND FACTIONS IN A REPUBLIC
JAMES MADISON, *The Federalist,* No. 10 (1787), var. eds.

2. DAVY CROCKETT RUNS FOR THE LEGISLATURE
DAVID CROCKETT, *A Narrative of the Life of David Crockett.* Philadelphia, 1834, 138-44, *passim.*

3. ANDREW JACKSON IS INAUGURATED
MRS. SAMUEL HARRISON SMITH, *The First Forty Years of Washington Society, Portrayed by Family Letters of Mrs. Samuel Harrison Smith,* ed. by Gaillard Hunt. New York: Charles Scribner's Sons, 1908, 290-97, *passim.*

4. THE SPOILS SYSTEM
A. ROTATION IN OFFICE. ANDREW JACKSON, First Inaugural Message, December 8, 1829, in James D. Richardson, ed., *A Compilation of the Messages and Papers of the Presidents,* N.p.: Bureau of National Literature and Art, 1904, II, 448-49.
B. THE SPOILS OF VICTORY. WILLIAM MARCY, Speech of 1831, in Henry Steele Commager, ed., *Documents of American History.* New York: Appleton-Century-Crofts, Inc., 1950, Doc. No. 139.

5. "TROUBLES OF A CANDIDATE"
PETER FINLEY DUNNE, "Troubles of a Candidate," *Mr. Dooley's Philosophy.* New York: Harper & Brothers, 1906, 229-34.

6. "HONEST GRAFT AND DISHONEST GRAFT"
WILLIAM L. RIORDAN, *Plunkitt of Tammany Hall.* New York: McClure, Phillips & Company, 1905, 3-10, *passim.*

7. "BOSS PENDERGAST"
RALPH COGHLAN, "Boss Pendergast," *The Forum* (February, 1937), XCVII, 67-72, *passim.*

8. INVISIBLE GOVERNMENT
ELIHU ROOT, Speech to the New York Constitutional Convention, August 30, 1915, in Commager, ed., *Documents of American History,* Doc. No. 406.

9. "LET'S GO BACK TO THE SPOILS SYSTEM"
JOHN FISCHER, "Let's Go Back to the Spoils System," *Harper's Magazine* (October, 1945), CXCI, 362 ff.

10. POLITICAL PARTIES IN AMERICA
HENRY STEELE COMMAGER, "American Political Parties," *Parliamentary Affairs* (Winter, 1949), III, 214-25.

11. PUBLIC AND POLITICAL ASSOCIATIONS IN THE UNITED STATES
ALEXIS DE TOCQUEVILLE, *Democracy in America* (1835, 1840), ed. by H. S. Commager. New York: Oxford University Press, 1947, 109-12, 319-30, *passim.*

12. "IT IS OF THE VERY ESSENCE OF AMERICANISM"
GEORGE SANTAYANA, *Character and Opinion in the United States.* New York: Charles Scribner's Sons, 1920, 193-97.

Chapter 5. Democracy, or Majority Rule and Minority Rights

1. "CHERISH THE SPIRIT OF THE PEOPLE"
Letter of Thomas Jefferson to Edward Carrington, January 16, 1787, in Paul L. Ford, ed., *The Writings of Thomas Jefferson.* New York: G. P. Putnam's Sons, 1894, IV, 357-61.

2. "IT IS ESSENTIAL TO LIBERTY THAT THE RIGHTS OF THE RICH BE SECURED"
JOHN ADAMS, "A Defence of the Constitutions of Government of the United States of America" (1787-88), in Charles Francis Adams, ed., *The Works of John Adams.* Boston, 1851, VI, 88-90.

3. "THE COMBINATIONS OF CIVIL SOCIETY ARE NOT LIKE THOSE OF A SET OF MERCHANTS"
BENJAMIN FRANKLIN, "On the Legislative Branch" (1789), in John Bigelow, ed., *The Complete Works of Benjamin Franklin.* New York, 1888, X, 188-91, *passim.*

4. "WE ARE DESCENDING INTO A LICENTIOUS DEMOCRACY"
FISHER AMES, "The Dangers of American Liberty" (1805), in Seth Ames, ed., *The Works of Fisher Ames*. Boston, 1854, II, 392-99, *passim*.

5. "DARE WE FLATTER OURSELVES THAT WE ARE A PECULIAR PEOPLE?"
JAMES KENT, Speech at the New York Constitutional Convention, 1821, in Henry Steele Commager, ed., *Documents of American History*. New York: Appleton-Century-Crofts, Inc., 1950, Doc. No. 124.

6. THE TYRANNY OF THE MAJORITY
ALEXIS DE TOCQUEVILLE, *Democracy in America* (1835), ed. by H. S. Commager. New York: Oxford University Press, 1947, 156-69, *passim*.

7. THE NUMERICAL AND THE CONCURRENT MAJORITIES
JOHN C. CALHOUN, "A Disquisition on Government" (ca. 1848-50), in Richard K. Crallé, ed., *The Works of John Calhoun*. New York, 1854, I, 28-36, *passim*.

8. "DEMOCRACY FURNISHES ITS OWN CHECKS AND BALANCES"
HENRY STEELE COMMAGER, *Majority Rule and Minority Rights*. New York: Peter Smith, 1950, 58-61.

9. "THE PEOPLE IS FIRM AND TRANQUIL"
GEORGE BANCROFT, "The Office of the People in Art, Government, and Religion" (1835), *Literary and Historical Miscellanies*. New York, 1855, 421-426, *passim*.

10. "EVERY AMERICAN IS AN APOSTLE OF THE DEMOCRATIC CREED"
ALEXANDER MACKAY, *The Western World, or Travels in the United States in 1846 and 1847*. Philadelphia, 1849, III. Reprinted in H. S. Commager, ed., *America in Perspective*. New York: Random House, 1947, 112 ff.

11. THE REAL MEANING OF THE PRINCIPLES OF THE DECLARATION
A. "THEY MEANT TO SET UP A STANDARD FOR A FREE SOCIETY." ABRAHAM LINCOLN, Speech at Springfield, Illinois, June 26, 1857, in *Ibid.*, I, 226 ff.
B. "TO LIFT ARTIFICIAL WEIGHTS FROM ALL SHOULDERS." ABRAHAM LINCOLN, Message to Congress, July 4, 1861, in *Ibid.*, II, 55 ff.

12. "DID YOU SUPPOSE THAT DEMOCRACY WAS ONLY FOR POLITICS?"
WALT WHITMAN, "Democratic Vistas" (1871), *Collected Prose Works*. Boston, 1891, 198-205, 219-23.

13. "THE ETERNAL MOB"
H(ENRY) L. MENCKEN, *Notes on Democracy*. New York: Alfred A. Knopf, Inc., 1926, 44-65, *pasism*.

14. "DEMOCRACY IS NOT DYING"
FRANKLIN D. ROOSEVELT, Third Inaugural Address, January 20, 1941, in Samuel I. Rosenman, ed., *The Public Papers and Addresses of Franklin D. Roosevelt*. New York: Harper & Brothers, 1950, Vol. 10, 1941, 3-6.

15. THE FAULTS AND STRENGTH OF AMERICAN DEMOCRACY
A. THE TRUE FAULTS OF AMERICAN DEMOCRACY. JAMES BRYCE, *The American Commonwealth*. New York, 1888, II, 450 ff.
B. THE STRENGTH OF AMERICAN DEMOCRACY. *Ibid.*, 457 ff.

Chapter 6.   State and Nation

1. "WITH OUR FATE WILL THE DESTINY OF UNBORN MILLIONS BE INVOLVED"
GEORGE WASHINGTON, Circular to the States, June 8, 1783, in John C. Fitzpatrick, ed., *The Writings of George Washington*. Washington: Government Printing Office, 1938, XXVI, 483 ff.

2. THE CONSTITUTION PARTLY FEDERAL, PARTLY NATIONAL
JAMES MADISON, *The Federalist,* No. 39 (1788), var. eds.

3. "A RISING, NOT A SETTING SUN"
BENJAMIN FRANKLIN, *Speech at the Federal Convention,* September 17, 1787, in Charles C. Tansill, ed., *Documents Illustrative of the Formation of the Union of the American States.* Washington: Government Printing Office, 1927, 803-7.

4. STRICT OR BROAD CONSTRUCTION?
A. "LACE THEM UP STRAITLY WITHIN THE ENUMERATED POWERS"
THOMAS JEFFERSON, Opinion on the Constitutionality of the Bank, February 15, 1791, in Henry Steele Commager, ed., *Documents of American History*. New York: Appleton-Century-Crofts, Inc., 1950, Doc. No. 94.
B. "THERE ARE IMPLIED AS WELL AS EXPRESS POWERS." ALEXANDER HAMILTON, Opinion on the Constitutionality of the Bank, February 23, 1791, in *Ibid.,* Doc. No. 93.

5. THE CONSTITUTION A COMPACT
A. KENTUCKY RESOLUTIONS. THOMAS JEFFERSON, Kentucky Resolutions, November 16, 1798, in Commager, ed., *Documents of American History,* Doc. No. 102.
B. VIRGINIA RESOLUTIONS. JAMES MADISON, Virginia Resolutions, December 24, 1798, in *Ibid.,* Doc. No. 102.

6. "THE ORIGIN OF THIS GOVERNMENT AND THE SOURCE OF ITS POWER"
DANIEL WEBSTER, Second Reply to Hayne, January 26, 1830, in Edward Everett, ed., *The Works of Daniel Webster.* Boston, 1851, III, 321 ff.

7. "A COMPACT IS A BINDING OBLIGATION"
ANDREW JACKSON, Proclamation to the People of South Carolina, December 10, 1832, in Commager, ed., *Documents of American History,* Doc. No. 144.

8. "A SEPARATION OF THESE STATES IS A NORMAL IMPOSSIBILITY"
DANIEL WEBSTER, Seventh of March (1850) Speech, in J. W. McIntyre, ed., *The Writings and Speeches of Daniel Webster.* Boston: Little, Brown and Company, 1903, X, 57-58, 92-98, *passim.*

9. "THE FICTITIOUS IDEA OF ONE PEOPLE OF THE UNITED STATES"
JEFFERSON DAVIS, *The Rise and Fall of the Confederate Government.* New York, 1881, I, 157-59.

10. "THE UNION IS OLDER THAN THE CONSTITUTION"
ABRAHAM LINCOLN, First Inaugural Address, March 4, 1861, in Commager, ed., *Documents of American History*, Doc. No. 202.

11. THE FOURTEENTH AMENDMENT
The Fourteenth Amendment, July 28, 1868, in Commager, ed., *Documents of American History*, Doc. No. 272.

12. "GOVERNMENT AT THE SERVICE OF HUMANITY"
WOODROW WILSON, First Inaugural Address, March 4, 1913, in Commager, ed., *Documents of American History*, Doc. No. 389.

13. BROADENING THE COMMERCE POWER
Opinion of Chief Justice Hughes, National Labor Relations Board *v.* Jones & Laughlin Steel Corporation, 301 U.S. 1 (1937).

14. "THE OBSOLESCENCE OF FEDERALISM"
HAROLD J. LASKI, "The Obsolescence of Federalism," *The New Republic* (May 3, 1939), XCVIII, 367-69.

15. CENTRAL POLICY AND LOCAL ADMINISTRATION
DAVID E. LILIENTHAL, *This I Do Believe*. New York: Harper & Brothers, 1949, 73-82, 89-91.

Chapter 7. The Welfare State and Rugged Individualism

1. TRUE AND FALSE PRINCIPLES OF ECONOMY IN THE BAY COLONY
JOHN WINTHROP, *The History of New England from 1603 to 1649*, ed. by James Savage. Boston, 1853, I, 313-17. Entry of November 9, 1639.

2. AN EARLY PROGRAM OF SOCIAL SECURITY
THOMAS PAINE, *Rights of Man* (1791). Reprinted in Philip S. Foner, ed., *The Complete Writings of Thomas Paine*. New York: The Citadel Press, 1945, I, 425-29, *passim*.

3. "ALL COMMUNITIES ARE APT TO LOOK TO GOVERNMENT FOR TOO MUCH"
MARTIN VAN BUREN, Message to Congress, September 4, 1837, in James D. Richardson, ed., *A Compilation of the Messages and Papers of the Presidents*. N. p.: Bureau of National Literature and Art, 1896, III, 344-45.

4. AFFECTATION WITH A PUBLIC INTEREST
Opinion of Chief Justice Morrison Waite, Munn *v.* Illinois, 94 U.S. 113 (1876).

5. "LIBERTY, INEQUALITY, SURVIVAL OF THE FITTEST"
WILLIAM GRAHAM SUMNER, "The Challenge of Facts" (ca. 1880), *The Challenge of Facts and Other Essays*, ed. by Albert G. Keller. New Haven: Yale University Press, 1914, 23-34, *passim*.

6. THE COURTS AS GUARDIANS OF THE STATUS QUO
   A. "SUCH GOVERNMENTAL INTERFERENCES DISTURB THE . . . SOCIAL FABRIC"
   Opinion of Judge Robert Earl, *In Re* Jacobs, 98 New York 98 (1885).

B. "THE POLICE POWER WILL HAVE BEEN WIDENED TO A GREAT AND DANGEROUS DEGREE." Opinion of Justice George Sutherland, Adkins, *v.* Children's Hospital, 261 U.S. 525 (1923).

7. "THE DOCTRINE OF *Laissez-Faire* IS UNSAFE IN POLITICS AND UNSOUND IN MORALS"
Statement of Richard T. Ely, in "Report of the Organization of the American Economic Association," *Publications,* American Economic Association (March, 1886), I, 1 ff.

8. GOVERNMENT IS BUT ONE OF THE TOOLS OF MAN
LESTER F. WARD, *The Psychic Factors of Civilization.* New York: Ginn & Company, 1893, 258-86, *passim.*

9. THE COURTS ACCEPT GOVERNMENTAL REGULATION
A. "THE FOURTEENTH AMENDMENT DOES NOT ENACT HERBERT SPENCER'S *Social Statics.*" Dissenting Opinion of Justice Oliver Wendell Holmes, Lochner *v.* New York, 106 U.S. 45 (1905).
B. "THE LIBERTY SAFEGUARDED IS LIBERTY IN A SOCIAL ORGANIZATION WHICH REQUIRES PROTECTION." Opinion of Chief Justice Charles E. Hughes, West Coast Hotel Co. *v.* Parrish, 300 U.S. 379 (1937).

10. "THE OLD ORDER CHANGETH"
WOODROW WILSON, *The New Freedom.* New York: Doubleday & Company, Inc., 1913, 15-20.

11. THE PHILOSOPHY OF RUGGED INDIVIDUALISM
HERBERT HOOVER, Veto of the Muscle Shoals Bill, March 3, 1931, in Commager, ed., *Documents of American History,* Doc. No. 470.

12. "WHETHER MEN SERVE GOVERNMENT OF WHETHER GOVERNMENT EXISTS TO SERVE MEN"
FRANKLIN D. ROOSEVELT, Commonwealth Club Address, September 23, 1932, in Samuel I. Rosenman, ed., *The Public Papers and Addresses of Franklin D. Roosevelt.* New York: Random House, 1938, Vol. I, 1928-1932, 742 ff.

13. THE FAIR DEAL SUCCEEDS THE NEW DEAL
HARRY S. TRUMAN, "State of the Union" Message, January, 1949, *Congressional Record,* 81st Congress, 1st Session, 66-69.

14. "THE AGENDA OF LIBERALISM"
WALTER LIPPMANN, *The Good Society.* Boston: Little, Brown & Company, 1937, 205 ff.

Chapter 8. Liberty and Order

1. THE MASSACHUSETTS BODY OF LIBERTIES
(NATHANIEL WARD), Massachusetts Body of Liberties, 1641, in William H. Whitmore, ed., *A Bibliographical Sketch of the Laws of the Massachusetts Colony.* Boston, 1890, 33-53, *passim.*

2. "A TRUE PICTURE OF A COMMONWEALTH"
ROGER WILLIAMS, Letter to the Town of Providence on the Limits of Freedom, January, 1655, in *Letters of Roger Williams*. Publications of the Narragansett Club, Providence, R. I., 1874, VI, 278-79.

3. "THE PUBLIC JUDGMENT WILL CORRECT FALSE REASONING"
THOMAS JEFFERSON, Second Inaugural Address, March 4, 1805, in Paul L. Ford, ed., *The Writings of Thomas Jefferson*. New York: G. P. Putnam's Sons, 1892, VIII, 346.

4. ON THE MURDER OF ELIJAH LOVEJOY
WENDELL PHILLIPS, Speech on the Murder of the Rev. E. P. Lovejoy, December 8, 1837, in James Redpath, ed., *Speeches, Lectures, and Letters by Wendell Phillips*. Boston, 1863, First series, 2-10.

5. THE DUTY OF CIVIL DISOBEDIENCE
HENRY DAVID THOREAU, "Civil Disobedience" (1849), *The Writings of Henry David Thoreau*. Cambridge, 1893, IV, 356-87, *passim*.

6. HUCK AND JIM ON THE RAFT
MARK TWAIN, *The Adventures of Huckleberry Finn*. New York: Harper & Brothers, 1885, Chap. 16, var. eds.

7. THE CONSTITUTIONAL LIMITS OF FREE SPEECH
A. "A CLEAR AND PRESENT DANGER." Opinion of Justice Oliver Wendell Holmes, Schenck *v.* United States, 249 U.S. 47 (1919).
B. "FREE TRADE IN IDEAS." Dissenting Opinion of Justice Oliver Wendell Holmes, Abrams *v.* United States, 250 U.S. 616 (1919).

8. "IT IS THE FUNCTION OF SPEECH TO FREE MEN FROM THE BONDAGE OF IRRATIONAL FEAR"
Opinion of Justice Louis D. Brandeis, Whitney *v.* California, 274 U.S. 257 (1927).

9. "TO THE END THAT CHANGES MAY BE OBTAINED BE PEACEFUL MEANS"
Opinion of Chief Justice Hughes, De Jonge *v.* Oregon, 229 U.S. 353 (1937).

10. "TO AN ANXIOUS FRIEND"
WILLIAM ALLEN WHITE, "To An Anxious Friend," Emporia *Gazette,* July 27, 1922, in Helen Ogden Mahin, ed., *The Editor and His People: Editorials by William Allen White*. New York: The Macmillan Company, 1924, 348-49.

11. "THE INDISPENSABLE OPPOSITION"
WALTER LIPPMANN, "The Indispensable Opposition," *The Atlantic Monthly* (August, 1939), CLXIV, 186-90.

12. "YOU CANNOT CREATE LOYALTY BY COMPULSION"
ZECHARIAH CHAFEE, JR., *Free Speech in the United States*. Cambridge, Mass.: Harvard University Press, 1941, 559-65.

13. THE LOYALTY PROGRAM
HARRY S. TRUMAN, Loyalty Order, March 22, 1947. *New York Times,* March 23, 1947.

14. "WHO IS LOYAL TO AMERICA?"
HENRY STEELE COMMAGER, "Who Is Loyal to America?" *Harper's Magazine* (September, 1947), CXCV, 193-99.
15. "DUE NOTICE TO THE FBI"
BERNARD DE VOTO, "Due Notice to the FBI," *Harper's Magazine* (October, 1949), CXCIX, 65-68.
16. CIVIL RIGHTS IN THE NATION'S CAPITAL
(ROBERT CARR), *To Secure These Rights.* The Report of the President's Committee on Civil Rights. Washington: Government Printing Office, 1947, 87-95.
17. A UNIVERSAL DECLARATION OF HUMAN RIGHTS
United Nations, Universal Declaration of Human Rights, December 6, 1948, United Nations General Assembly, 2nd. Session, Doc. A/811.

Chapter 9. The Tradition of Change and Reform

1. EVERY GENERATION HAS A RIGHT TO MAKE ITS OWN CONSTITUTION
   A. "SOME MEN LOOK AT CONSTITUTIONS WITH SANCTIMONIOUS REVERENCE" Letter of Thomas Jefferson to Samuel Kercheval, July 12, 1816, in Paul L. Ford, ed., *The Writings of Thomas Jefferson.* New York: G. P. Putnam's Sons, 1899, X, 42-44.
   B. "ALL EYES ARE OPEN TO THE RIGHTS OF MAN." Letter of Thomas Jefferson to Roger C. Weightman, June 24, 1826, in *Ibid.,* X, 390-92.
2. THE DECLARATION OF INDEPENDENCE AND THE SPIRIT OF REFORM
   A. "THE STANDARD OF EMANCIPATION IS NOW UNFURLED." WILLIAM LLOYD GARRISON, *The Liberator* (Boston), Vol. I., No. I., January 1, 1831. Reprinted in *William Lloyd Garrison, 1805-1879: the Story of his Life Told by his Children.* Boston, 1885, I, 224 ff.
   B. "ALL MEN AND WOMEN ARE CREATED EQUAL." ELIZABETH C. STANTON, SUSAN B. ANTHONY, and MATILDA J. GAGE, *The History of Woman Suffrage.* New York, 1881, I, 70 ff.
3. THE FERMENT OF REFORM
THEODORE PARKER, "Theodore Parker's Experience As a Minister" (1859), *Autobiographical and Miscellaneous Pieces.* London, 1865, 277-82, 303 ff.
4. MAN THE REFORMER
RALPH WALDO EMERSON, "Man, the Reformer" (1841), *Nature, Addresses and Lectures: Emerson's Works.* Boston, 1883, I, 215 ff.
5. THE SEARCH FOR UTOPIA
   A. THE CONSTITUTION OF THE BROOK FARM ASSOCIATION. The Constitution of the Brook Farm Association, 1841, in OCTAVIUS B. FROTHINGHAM, *Transcendentalism in New England.* New York, 1876, 159 ff.
   B. BLITHEDALE. NATHANIEL HAWTHORNE, *The Blithedale Romance.* Boston, 1852, var. eds.

6. "WE MEET IN THE MIDST OF A NATION BROUGHT TO THE VERGE OF RUIN"
The Populist Party Platform, July 4, 1892, in Henry Steele Commager, ed.,
Documents of American History. New York: Appleton-Century-Crofts,
Inc., 1950, Doc. No. 325.

7. "WE NEED AN ANNUAL SUPPLEMENT TO THE DECALOGUE"
EDWARD A. ROSS, *Sin and Society.* Boston: Houghton Mifflin Company,
1907, 9-14, 40-42.

8. PORTRAIT OF THE AMERICAN AS REFORMER
A. JANE ADDAMS AT HULL HOUSE. JANE ADDAMS, *Twenty Years at Hull
House.* New York: The Macmillan Company, 1910, 66-88, *passim.*
B. MAYOR JONES PREACHES THE GOLDEN RULE. BRAND WHITLOCK, *Forty
Years of It.* New York: D. Appleton & Company, 1914, 112 ff.
C. LINCOLN STEFFENS IS WON OVER BY BOB LAFOLLETTE. LINCOLN
STEFFENS, *The Autobiography of Lincoln Steffens.* New York: Harcourt,
Brace & Company, 1931, 458 ff.
D. "TO LIVE IN MANKIND IS FAR MORE THAN TO LIVE IN A NAME."
VACHEL LINDSAY, "The Eagle That Is Forgotten" (1912), *Collected Poems.*
New York: The Macmillan Company, 1923.

9. "THE OLD FORMULAS DO NOT FIT PRESENT PROBLEMS"
WOODROW WILSON, *The New Freedom.* New York: Doubleday & Company,
Inc., 1913, 3-32, *passim.*

10. "WANTED: AMERICAN RADICALS"
JAMES B. CONANT, "Wanted: American Radicals," *The Atlantic Monthly*
(May, 1943), CLXXI, 42-45.

11. NOT A REVOLUTION BUT A NEW DEAL
HENRY STEELE COMMAGER, "Twelve Years of Roosevelt," *American Mercury* (April, 1945), LX, 391-401, *passim.*

Chapter 10. Church and State

1. RELIGIOUS CONFORMITY IN THE BAY COLONY
JOHN WINTHROP, *Winthrop's Journal "History of New England," 1630-1649,*
ed. by James Kendall Hosmer. New York: Charles Scribner's Sons, 1908, I,
210-11, 239-41.

2. "GOD REQUIRETH NOT A UNIFORMITY OF RELIGION"
ROGER WILLIAMS, *The Bloudy Tenent of Persecution for Cause of Conscience* (1644). Publications of the Narrangansett Club, Providence, R. I.,
1867, first series, III, 3-4.

3. MARYLAND TOLERATION ACT
Maryland Toleration Act, April 21, 1649, in Commager, ed., *Documents
of American History,* Doc. No. 22.

4. "THE GREAT CASE OF LIBERTY OF CONSCIENCE"
WILLIAM PENN, "The Great Case of Liberty of Conscience once more briefly debated and defended by the Authority of Reason, Scripture, and Antiquity" (1670), in *The Select Works of William Penn*. London, 1782, III, 1 ff.

5. "ALL CHRISTIANS ARE EQUALLY ENTITLED TO PROTECTION"
The Constitution of Maryland, Article 33, 1776, in Francis N. Thorpe, ed., *The Federal and State Constitutions, Colonial Charters and Other Organic Laws of the States*. Washington: Government Printing Office, 1909, III, 1689-90.

6. "IF WE CONTRACT THE BONDS OF RELIGIOUS FREEDOM, NO NAME WILL TOO SEVERELY REPROACH OUR FOLLY"
JAMES MADISON, "A Memorial and Remonstrance on the Religious Rights of Man" (1784), in Gaillard Hunt, ed., *The Writings of James Madison*. New York: G. P. Putnam's Sons, 1901, II, 183-91.

7. VIRGINIA STATUTE OF RELIGIOUS LIBERTY
Virginia Statute of Religious Liberty, January 16, 1786, in W. W. Hening, ed., *Statutes at Large of Virginia*, XII, 84 ff.

8. THE SOCIALIZATION OF CHRISTIANITY
A. "THE SOCIAL CREED OF THE CHURCHES." Federal Council of Churches, *The Social Ideals of the Churches* (1932), 18-19.
B. "A CHRISTIAN SOCIAL ORDER." MOST REVEREND EDWIN O'HARA, Statement of National Catholic Welfare Conference, in *Catholic Action, Social Action Number*, June, 1938.

9. "MY CREED AS AN AMERICAN CATHOLIC"
ALFRED E. SMITH, Reply to Charles C. Marshall, in *The Atlantic Monthly* (May, 1927), CXXXIX, 721-28, *passim*.

10. "A WALL BETWEEN CHURCH AND STATE ... HIGH AND IMPREGNABLE"
Opinion of Justice Hugo Black, McCullom *v.* Board of Education, 333 U.S. 203 (1948).

11. RELIGIOUS FREEDOM AND THE FLAG SALUTE
A. "THE FLAG IS THE SYMBOL OF OUR NATIONAL UNITY." Opinion of Justice Felix Frankfurter, The Gobitis Case, 310 U.S. 586 (1940).
B. "NO OFFICIAL, HIGH OR PETTY, CAN PRESCRIBE WHAT SHALL BE ORTHO- DOX IN ... MATTERS OF OPINION." Opinion of Justice Robert Jackson, West Virginia State Board *v.* Barnette, 319 U.S. 624 (1943).

Chapter 11. School and Society

1. "TO ADVANCE LEARNING AND PERPETUATE IT TO POSTERITY"
Author unknown, *New Englands First Fruits* (1643), 12-16, in Sabin Reprints, Quarto Series, No. VII. New York, 1865.

2. "THAT LEARNING MAY NOT BE BURIED IN THE GRAVE OF OUR FATHERS"
A. "YE OULD DELUDER, SATAN." Massachusetts School Law of 1647, in Henry Steele Commager, ed., *Documents of American History*. New York: Appleton-Century-Crofts, Inc., 1950, Doc. No. 20.
B. "A GRAND MENTAL AND MORAL EXPERIMENT." HORACE MANN, Report for 1846, *Annual Reports of the Board of Education of Massachusetts for the Years 1845-1848*. Boston, 1891, 109-12.
3. "TO RENDER THE PEOPLE SAFE, THEIR MINDS MUST BE IMPROVED"
THOMAS JEFFERSON, "Notes on the State of Virginia" (1782), in Paul L. Ford, ed., *The Writings of Thomas Jefferson*. New York: G. P. Putnam's Sons, 1894, III, 252-55.
4. "WHY SEND AN AMERICAN YOUTH TO EUROPE FOR EDUCATION?"
Letter of Thomas Jefferson to J. Bannister, Junior, October 15, 1785, in Andrew A. Lipscomb and Albert E. Bergh, eds., *The Writings of Thomas Jefferson*. Washington: Thomas Jefferson Memorial Association, 1903, V, 185-88.
5. THE EDUCATION PROPER IN A REPUBLIC
BENJAMIN RUSH, "A Plan for the Establishment of Public Schools and the Diffusion of Knowledge in Pennsylvania" (1786). Reprinted in Dagobert Runes, ed., *The Selected Writings of Benjamin Rush*. New York: Philosophical Society, 1947, 91-100, *passim*.
6. THE EDUCATION OF WOMEN
CATHERINE BEECHER, "Suggestions Respecting Improvements in Education, Presented to the Trustees of the Hartford Female Seminary," (1829). Reprinted in Willystine Goodsell, ed., *Pioneers of Women's Education in the United States*. New York: McGraw-Hill Book Company, Inc., 1931, 147-50.
7. "EDUCATION IS THE BALANCE WHEEL OF THE SOCIAL MACHINERY"
HORACE MANN, "Intellectual Education As a Means of Removing Poverty, and Securing Abundance," Twelfth Annual Report (1848), *Annual Reports of the Board of Education of Massachusetts for the Years 1845-1848*. Boston, 1891, 246 ff.
8. "THE SCHOLAR IS TO THINK WITH THE SAGE BUT TALK WITH COMMON MEN"
THEODORE PARKER, "The Position and Duties of the American Scholar" (1849), in Frances Power Cobbe, ed., *The Collected Works of Theodore Parker*. London, 1864, VII, 223-31, *passim*.
9. THE FIRST GREAT PUBLIC LIBRARY
A. "THE INCREASE AND PERPETUATION OF PUBLIC LIBRARIES." Proposed Massachusetts Library Act, Massachusetts House Document 124, 1851. Reprinted in JESSE H. SHERRA, *Foundations of the Public Library*. Chicago: University of Chicago Press, 1949, 192.
B. "IF IT CAN BE DONE ANYWHERE, IT CAN BE DONE HERE, IN BOSTON" Report of the Trustees of the Public Library of the City of Boston, July, 1852. Reprinted in *Ibid.*, Appendix.

10. THE LABORATORY OF DEMOCRACY

A. SCHOOL LIFE ON THE PRAIRIE. HAMLIN GARLAND, *A Son of the Middle Border*. New York: The Macmillan Company, 1917, 95, 111 ff.

B. THE BEGINNINGS OF TUSKEGEE. BOOKER T. WASHINGTON, *Up From Slavery*. New York: Doubleday & Company, Inc., 1901, 121 ff.

C. THE PROMISED LAND FULFILLS ITS PROMISE. MARY ANTIN, *The Promised Land*. New York: Houghton Mifflin Company, 1912, 186, 198, 202 ff.

11. "TO PROMOTE THE LIBERAL . . . EDUCATION OF THE INDUSTRIAL CLASSES" The Morrill Act, July 2, 1862, in Commager, ed., *Documents of American History,* Doc. No. 216.

12. "THE WORTHY FRUIT OF ACADEMIC CULTURE IS AN OPEN MIND" CHARLES W. ELIOT, Inaugural Address, October 19, 1869, in Samuel Eliot Morison, ed., *The Development of Harvard University Since the Inauguration of President Eliot, 1869-1929*. Cambridge, Mass.: Harvard University Press, 1930, lxi ff.

13. "MAKE EACH ONE OF OUR SCHOOLS AN EMBRYONIC COMMUNITY LIFE" JOHN DEWEY, *The School and Society* (1899). Chicago: University of Chicago Press, 1920, rev. ed., 22-28, 67-68.

14. "THE CHIEF CHARACTERISTIC OF THE HIGHER LEARNING IS DISORDER" ROBERT MAYNARD HUTCHINS, *The Higher Learning in America*. New Haven, Conn.: Yale University Press, 1936, 91-95, 101-3, *passim*.

15. THE NATURE AND FUNCTION OF ACADEMIC FREEDOM

A. "THE FORTRESS OF OUR LIBERTIES." JAMES BRYANT CONANT, *Education in A Divided World*. Cambridge, Mass.: Harvard University Press, 1948, 172-80.

B. "SUBVERSION FROM WITHIN BY THE WHITTLING AWAY OF THE VERY PILLARS OF OUR FREEDOM." Opinion of Judge Peek, Tolman *et al. v.* the Regents of the University of California, District Court of Appeals of California, April 6, 1951.

16. "LIBRARIES ARE THE VESSELS IN WHICH THE SEED CORN FOR THE FUTURE IS STORED" DOROTHY CANFIELD FISHER, "The Stronghold of Freedom," in *The Library of Tomorrow,* ed. by Emily M. Danton. Chicago: American Library Association, 1939, 22 ff.

Chapter 12. Peace and War

1. LEXINGTON AND CONCORD

A. AMERICAN ACCOUNT OF THE BATTLE OF LEXINGTON. Account by the Provincial Congress at Watertown, Massachusetts, April 26, 1775, in HEZEKIAH NILES, *Principles and Acts of the Revolution in America*. Baltimore, 1822, 434-35.

B. "Concord Hymn." Ralph Waldo Emerson, "Concord Hymn" (1837), *Poems. Var. eds.*

2. "had this day been wanting, the world had never seen the last stage of perfection"
George Washington, Address to the Officers of the Army, Headquarters, March 15, 1783, in John C. Fitzpatrick, ed., *The Writings of George Washington.* Washington: Government Printing Office, 1938, XXVI, 222-27.

3. "i shall never surrender nor retreat"
William Barret Travis, Address to the People of Texas and All Americans in the World, February 24, 1836, in Henderson K. Yoakum, *History of Texas from Its First Settlement.* New York, 1856, 767-68.

4. the character of the american soldier
William F. G. Shanks, *Personal Recollections of Distinguished Generals.* New York: Harper & Brothers, 323-26.

5. general mcclellan tries to take charge of the war
Letter of George B. McClellan to President Lincoln, July 7, 1862, in E. McPherson, ed., *Political History of the Great Rebellion.* New York, 1864, 385 ff.

6. "in victory magnanimity, in peace good will"
A. "With Malice toward None, with Charity for All." Abraham Lincoln, Second Inaugural Address, March 4, 1865, in James D. Richardson, ed., *A Compilation of the Messages and Papers of the Presidents.* N.p.: National Bureau of Literature and Art, 1904, VI, 276-77.
B. "Avoid the Useless Sacrifice." Robert E. Lee, Farewell Address to His Army, April 10, 1865, in Robert E. Lee (Jr.), *Recollections and Letters of General Robert E. Lee.* New York: Doubleday & Company, Inc., 1904, 153-54.
C. "Bury Contention with the War." Letter of Robert E. Lee, in J. Williams, *Personal Reminiscences, Anecdotes, and Letters of General Robert E. Lee.* New York, 1875.

7. "the most fearful atrocities . . . that was ever heard of"
Major E. W. Wynkoop, Testimony before Congressional Committee, 1865, in *Report,* 39th Congress, 2nd Session, Senate Doc. 156, 63-64.

8. "the hay fleet"
Finley Peter Dunne, "The Hay Fleet," *Mr. Dooley in the Hearts of His Countrymen.* Boston: Small, Maynard & Company, 1899, 210-15.

9. "turn not their new-world victories to gain!"
William Vaughn Moody, "An Ode in Time of Hesitation" (1901), in John M. Manly, ed., *The Poems and Plays of William Vaughn Moody.* Boston: Houghton Mifflin Company, 1912, I.

10. "proper language for a subordinate to use to a superior"
Henry L. Stimson and McGeorge Bundy, *On Active Service in Peace and War.* New York: Harper & Brothers, 1948, 32-35.

11. "A GREAT PRINCIPLE WAS NEVER LOST SO CASUALLY"
EUGENE V. ROSTOW, "Our Worst Wartime Mistake," *Harper's Magazine* (September, 1945, CXCI, 144-49.

12. "THE MORAL EQUIVALENT OF WAR"
WILLIAM JAMES, "The Moral Equivalent of War," Documents of the American Association of International Conciliation, No. 27, 1910, 311-28.

Chapter 13. Isolation, Intervention and World Power

1. THE BASES OF ISOLATIONISM
   A. "THE INSIDIOUS WILES OF FOREIGN INFLUENCE." GEORGE WASHINGTON, Farewell Address, in Richardson, ed., *Messages and Papers of the Presidents,* I, 213 ff.
   B. "AMERICA HAS A HEMISPHERE TO ITSELF." Thomas Jefferson to Baron von Humboldt, December 6, 1813, in Paul L. Ford, ed., *Writings of Thomas Jefferson.* New York: G. P. Putnam's Sons, 1898, IX, 431.

2. THE MONROE DOCTRINE
   A. THE MONROE DOCTRINE, in Henry Steele Commager, ed., *Documents of American History,* Doc. No. 127.
   B. "THE AMERICAN SYSTEM OF GOVERNMENT IS ENTIRELY DIFFERENT" JAMES K. POLK, Annual Message to Congress, December 2, 1845, in Commager, *Documents,* Doc. No. 167.

3. "TURNING THE EYES OUTWARD INSTEAD OF INWARD"
ALFRED T. MAHAN, *The Interest of America in Sea Power.* Boston, 1897, 10 ff.

4. THE ACQUISITION OF THE PHILIPPINES
WILLIAM MCKINLEY, Instructions to Peace Commissioners, in U. S. House Documents, 55th Congress, 2d Session, Doc. No. 1, I, 907.

5. THE OPEN DOOR IN CHINA
Hay's Circular Letter, September 6, 1899, in Commager, *Documents,* Doc. No. 350.

6. "GOD . . . HAS MADE US THE MASTER ORGANIZERS OF THE WORLD"
Albert J. Beveridge, in R. J. BARTLETT, *The Record of American Diplomacy.* New York: Alfred A. Knopf, Inc., 1947, 385 ff.

7. THE PLATT AMENDMENT
   A. TREATY WITH CUBA, May 21, 1903, in Commager, *Documents,* Doc. No. 360.
   B. ABROGATION OF THE PLATT AMENDMENT, May 29, 1934, in Commager, *Documents,* Doc. No. 491.

8. "WE MUST PROVE OURSELVES FRIENDS"
WOODROW WILSON, Address at Mobile, October 27, 1913, in Commager, *Documents,* Doc. No. 394.

9. THE POLICY OF THE GOOD NEIGHBOR
FRANKLIN D. ROOSEVELT, Address, August 14, 1936, *Peace and War, United States Foreign Policy*. Washington: Government Printing Office, 1943, 323 ff.

10. "THE WORLD MUST BE MADE SAFE FOR DEMOCRACY"
WOODROW WILSON, Address to Congress, April 2, 1917, in Commager, *Documents*, Doc. No. 418.

11. THE FOURTEEN POINTS
WOODROW WILSON, Address to Congress, January 8, 1918, in Commager, *Documents*, Doc. No. 423.

12. "WE DO NOT PROFESS TO BE CHAMPIONS OF LIBERTY"
WOODROW WILSON, Address at Indianapolis, September 4, 1919. U.S. 66th Congress, 1st Session, Sen. Doc. No. 120, 19.

13. A QUARANTINE AGAINST AGGRESSOR NATIONS
FRANKLIN D. ROOSEVELT, Address at Chicago, October 5, 1937, in *Peace and War, United States Foreign Policy*. Washington: Government Printing Office, 1943, 383.

14. THE FOUR FREEDOMS
FRANKLIN D. ROOSEVELT, Annual Message to Congress, January 6, 1941, in Commager, *Documents*, Doc. No. 537.

15. THE ATLANTIC CHARTER
FRANKLIN D. ROOSEVELT and WINSTON CHURCHILL, August 14, 1941, in *Peace and War*. Washington, 1943, 717 ff.

16. "THE TRUE GOAL WE SEEK"
FRANKLIN D. ROOSEVELT, Fireside Chat of December 9, 1941, in S. I. Rosenman, ed., *Public Papers and Addresses of Franklin D. Roosevelt*. New York: Harper & Brothers, 1950, 1941 vol., item 127.

17. "POWER MUST BE LINKED WITH RESPONSIBILITY"
FRANKLIN D. ROOSEVELT, Address on the State of the Union, January 6, 1945, in *ibid*, 1944-45 vol., item 126A.

18. THE ABIDING PRINCIPLES OF AMERICAN FOREIGN POLICY
HARRY S. TRUMAN, Address at New York, October 27, 1945. U. S. Department of State, *Bulletin*, Vol. XIII, 653 ff.

19. "THE GREATEST OPPORTUNITY EVER OFFERED A SINGLE NATION"
HENRY L. STIMSON, "The Challenge to Americans," in *Foreign Affairs* (October, 1947).

20. THE CONTROL OF ATOMIC ENERGY
A. "A CHOICE BETWEEN THE QUICK AND THE DEAD." BERNARD BARUCH, Address before U.N. Atomic Energy Commission. U.S. Department of State, *Bulletin*, Vol. XIV, 1057 ff.
B. "ONE OF THOSE GREAT MOUNTAIN PEAKS OF HISTORY." DAVID E. LILIENTHAL, *This I Do Believe*. New York: Harper & Brothers, 1950, 143 ff.

21. "TO THE RESCUE AND LIBERATION OF THE OLD"
   A. THE TRUMAN DOCTRINE. HARRY S. TRUMAN, Message to Congress,
   March 12, 1947, in Commager, *Documents,* Doc. No. 577.
   B. THE MARSHALL PLAN. Remarks by Secretary George C. Marshall at
   Harvard University, June 5, 1947, in Commager, *Documents,* Doc. No. 580.
   C. POINT FOUR. HARRY S. TRUMAN, Inaugural Address, January 19, 1949,
   in Commager, *Documents,* Doc. No. 588.
22. THE ATLANTIC COMMUNITY
   A. "A GREAT COMMUNITY." WALTER LIPPMANN, *U.S. Foreign Policy:
   Shield of the Republic.* Boston: Little, Brown & Company, 1943, 129 ff.
   B. THE AMERICAN DESTINY. WALTER LIPPMANN, *U.S. War Aims.* Boston:
   Little, Brown & Company, 1944, 199 ff.

Chapter 14. The Struggle for Racial Equality

1. THE CIVIL WAR AMENDMENTS, 1868-70
Constitution of the United States.
2. THE FREEDMAN'S CASE
GEORGE WASHINGTON CABLE, "The Freedman's Case in Equity," *Century
Magazine,* January, 1885.
3. FREDERICK DOUGLASS CALLS ON THE FREEDMAN TO ORGANIZE FOR SELF-PRO-
TECTION
FREDERICK DOUGLASS, "Why A Colored Convention?," in *Three Addresses on
the Relations Subsisting Between the White and Colored People of the United
States.* Washington, 1886, 3-23.
4. "THE AGITATION OF QUESTIONS OF SOCIAL EQUALITY IS THE EXTREMEST FOLLY"
BOOKER T. WASHINGTON, an address delivered at the Cotton States' Exposi-
tion in Atlanta, Georgia, 1895, in Carter G. Woodson, ed., *Negro Orators
and Their Orations.* Washington, 1925, 580-83.
5. "MR. WASHINGTON REPRESENTS THE OLD ATTITUDE OF SUBMISSION"
W. E. B. Du BOIS, "Of Booker T. Washington," in *The Souls of Black Folk.*
Chicago, 1903.
6. "SEPARATE BUT EQUAL"
Opinions of Henry Billings Brown and John Marshall Harlan, Plessy *v.*
Ferguson, 163 U.S. 537 (1896).
7. "TO SECURE THESE RIGHTS"
   A. EXECUTIVE ORDER 9980. In *To Secure These Rights.* Washington, 1947,
   viii-ix.
   B. THE REPORT OF THE PRESIDENT'S COMMITTEE ON CIVIL RIGHTS. Washing-
   ton, 1947, 62-67.
8. EQUALITY IN THE ARMED SERVICES
HARRY S. TRUMAN, Executive Order 9981, July 26, 1948, in *Freedom to Serve.*
Washington, 1950, xi-xii.

9. EQUAL OPPORTUNITIES FOR ALL: TRUMAN'S CIVIL RIGHTS PROGRAM
HARRY S. TRUMAN, Civil Rights Message, February 2, 1948, in U.S. House Documents, No. 516, 80th Congress, 2d Session.

10. "SEPARATE EDUCATIONAL FACILITIES ARE INHERENTLY UNEQUAL"
Opinion of Chief Justice Earl Warren, Brown *v*. Topeka, 347 U.S. 483 (1954).

11. "BROWN *v*. TOPEKA IS A NAKED EXERCISE OF JUDICIAL POWER"
"Southern Declaration on Integration," in the *New York Times,* March 12, 1956.

12. THE CIVIL RIGHTS ACT OF 1957
71 *U.S. Statutes at Large,* 634 (September 9, 1957).

13. CRISIS IN LITTLE ROCK
    A. THE EISENHOWER ADDRESS ON LITTLE ROCK. In *Public Papers of the Presidents: Dwight D. Eisenhower,* 1957, No. 198.
    B. COOPER *v*. AARON. 358 U.S. 1 (1958).

14. THE COURT VINDICATES THE NAACP
Opinion of Justice John Marshall Harlan, NAACP *v*. Alabama, 357 U.S. 449 (1958).

15. CRISIS IN MONTGOMERY: THE NEGRO TAKES OVER
MARTIN LUTHER KING, JR., "Where Do We Go from Here?," in *Stride Toward Freedom.* New York: Harper & Row, 1958.

16. THE PROBLEM OF THE SIT-INS
Opinion of Justice William Douglas, Garner *v*. Louisiana, 82 *Supreme Court Reporter,* 248, 1961.

17. POLICY AND REALITY IN NEGRO EMPLOYMENT
WILLIAM PETERS, *The Southern Temper.* Garden City, N.Y.: Doubleday & Co., 1959, 242-62.

18. EQUAL RIGHTS: THE UNENDING STRUGGLE
    A. WRIGHT *v*. GEORGIA. 373 U.S. 284 (1963).
    B. PETERSON *v*. GREENVILLE. 373 U.S. 244 (1963).

19. THE RIGHT TO VOTE: THE UNENDING STRUGGLE
Opinion of Justice Tom Clark, Anderson *v*. Martin, 84 *Supreme Court Reporter* 454, 1964.

20. THE END OF THE POLL TAX: THE TWENTY-FOURTH AMENDMENT
Constitution of the United States.

21. "MY DUNGEON SHOOK"
JAMES BALDWIN, "My Dungeon Shook: Letter to My Nephew on the One Hundredth Anniversary of the Emancipation." *The Fire Next Time.* New York: Dial Press, 1963.

22. "WE FACE A MORAL CRISIS"
JOHN F. KENNEDY, Address Given over Radio and Television, June 11, 1963. *New York Times,* June 12, 1963.

23. THE CIVIL RIGHTS ACT OF 1964
Public Law 88-352, 88th Congress, 2d session (July 2, 1964).

Index

(The index for Part Four, "Old Problems in a New Age," begins on page 870.)

INDEX FOR PART FOUR:

"Old Problems in a New Age"